OXFORD MEDICAL PUBLICATIONS

Fitness for Work

FITNESS FOR WORK
The Medical Aspects

Edited by

F. C. Edwards
Formerly Senior Employment Medical Adviser, Medical Division,
Health and Safety Executive

R. I. McCallum
Consultant in Occupational Medicine,
Institute of Occupational Medicine, Edinburgh;
Emeritus Professor of Occupational Health and Hygiene,
University of Newcastle upon Tyne

and

P. J. Taylor
International Medical Adviser, Unilever Ltd, London

OXFORD   NEW YORK   TORONTO   MELBOURNE
OXFORD UNIVERSITY PRESS

Oxford University Press, Walton Street, Oxford OX2 6DP
Oxford New York Toronto
Delhi Bombay Calcutta Madras Karachi
Petaling Jaya Singapore Hong Kong Tokyo
Nairobi Dar es Salaam Cape Town
Melbourne Auckland
and associated companies in
Berlin Ibadan

Oxford is a trade mark of Oxford University Press

Published in the United States
by Oxford University Press, New York

© Royal College of Physicians 1988

First published 1988
Reprinted (with corrections) 1989

British Library Cataloguing in Publication Data
Fitness for work: the medical aspects.—
(Oxford medical publications).
1. Industrial health
I. Edwards, F. C. II. McCallum, R. I.
III. Taylor, P. J.
363.1'1
ISBN 0-19-261774-5
ISBN 0-19-261702-8 pbk

Library of Congress Cataloging-in-Publication Data
Fitness for work: the medical aspects/edited by F.C. Edwards,
R.I. McCallum, and P.J. Taylor.
(Oxford medical publications)
Includes index.
1. Disability evaluation. 2. Chronically ill—Employment.
3. Handicapped—Employment. 4. Vocational qualifications—
Evaluation. I. Edwards, F. C. II. McCallum, R. I. III. Taylor,
P. J. (Peter J.), 1929–1987. IV. Series.
[DNLM: 1. Occupational Medicine. 2. Physical Fitness.
WA 400 F546] RC963.4.F57 1988 616.9'803—dc19 88-12431

ISBN 0-19-261774-5
ISBN 0-19-261702-8 (pbk)

Set by Graphicraft Ltd, Hong Kong
Printed in Great Britain
by Dotesios Printers Ltd, Trowbridge

Foreword

Raymond Hoffenberg, President, Royal College of Physicians, London

It is common in clinical practice to come across a patient who has suffered a myocardial infarct in the distant past and was consigned to a sedentary and undemanding job or put off work permanently, and who now presents dull, demoralized, and depressed. In contrast, we all know clinical colleagues who have shrugged off the same disability and returned speedily and cheerfully to full and productive work. The purpose of this book is to provide a more rational approach to the employment of those who have or have had any form of disability.

The Faculty of Occupational Medicine deserves full credit for its publication. The idea was first put to it by the Health and Safety Executive's Medical Division. With the Faculty's ready and enthusiastic approval a steering group was set up with the College, under the chairmanship of Dr Peter Taylor, who was then Dean of the Faculty. Dr Peter Taylor and Dr Felicity Edwards, together with the steering group, undertook the formidable task of commissioning, collating, and editing the contributions from clinical specialists and occupational physicians. From the start it was envisaged that the main readership would be medical, but the essentially practical approach ensures that it will also be a valuable source of reference to management and unions; all those, in fact, who have an interest in providing a fit and healthy workforce. As each chapter was drafted it was considered by the steering group and, in most cases, by selected experts and the appropriate specialty committee of the Royal College of Physicians. The final product thus reflects many views and carries with it their collective weight of authority.

The advice and recommendations contained in this book should make it easier to decide the type of work that can safely and properly be undertaken by those who have or have had a medical condition or health problem. We hope that patients themselves will benefit from the wider opportunities that will stem from the advice given here, so enabling them to work, wherever possible, at their maximal or optimal capacity.

The College is proud of this new production. We acknowledge gratefully the efforts that were put into it by Dr Peter Taylor and Dr Ian McCallum as Chairmen of the steering group; by the steering group members, all of the contributors and referees; and finally by Dr Felicity Edwards without whose persuasiveness, energy, and persistence this could not have been achieved.

December 1987

Preface

The stimulus for this report came originally from the Health and Safety Executive's Medical Division, who approached the Royal College of Physicians of London and its Faculty of Occupational Medicine. A steering group, under the Chairmanship of the late Dr Peter Taylor, was set up by the College and the Faculty to plan and produce the report, with the requirements of hospital specialists, general practitioners, and occupational physicians particularly in mind.

Apart from specific activities for which detailed guidelines exist, such as heavy goods vehicle drivers, airline pilots, and professional divers, the vast majority of jobs have no clear criteria of fitness and precise guidelines cannot be laid down. Thus the need for informed advice on medical aspects of fitness for work covering a wide range of medical conditions is evident. Some chronic diseases, while not excluding work altogether, can clearly limit the scope of employment, but the restrictions that may be imposed on such patients are often unnecessary and without any rational basis. While it must be accepted that there may be diverse views on employability in many medical conditions, such problems should always be the subject of informed discussion between the employer, occupational medical adviser, the patient's own doctor, and the patient. This report provides a basis for such discussions.

Occupational medicine is often thought of as being concerned only with the effects of work on health, i.e. the prevention of occupational disease and of the effects of exposure to various environmental hazards, but equally it is about the effects of health on work, the fitness for work, and the rehabilitation of the individual. Occupational medicine is essentially a clinical specialty and throughout this book authors emphasize the need for close collaboration between occupational physicians and their clinical colleagues. Each chapter has been written jointly by a clinician practising in the specialty and an occupational physician, and it is hoped that one outcome will be that clinicians and occupational physicians will be brought closer together, enabling them to see each other's point of view.

Most firms, particularly small ones, still have no occupational health service or medical advice of their own. Medical guidance on fitness for work usually comes from the patient's family or hospital doctor. Unfortunately, inappropriate advice may be given, either because not enough is known by doctors about the jobs their patients do, or because employers are unaware of the way in which advances in medical treatment have improved prognosis.

The up-to-date specialist opinion and background information given here on a number of medical conditions should improve both the relevance and consistency of advice. It should also reduce discrimination, often on irrelevant health grounds, against those who are at work or seeking work. As with any clinical judgement, the medical advice that is given on a patient remains the responsibility of the doctor concerned, and the general guidance contained in this book must always be interpreted in the light, not only of the effect of the illness or disability on the individual patient, but also of the special requirements of the job.

We hope that the report will be of use not only to doctors in occupational medicine, but also to those in general practice or hospital medicine, and of interest to occupational health nurses, managers, and personnel staff. It will provide an essential core of information and advice on the effects of health on work for doctors in training for the examination for Associate-ship of the Faculty of Occupational Medicine (AFOM).

It was decided to retain some overlapping sections in different chapters, for example those on haemophilia, cervical spondylosis, and ankylosing spondy-litis, because these reflected the different approaches and expertise of the authors. In spite of the speed with which the picture of Acquired Immune Deficiency Syndrome (AIDS) is changing as further knowledge of the disease develops, the steering group felt strongly that it should be included in the book because of its importance in relation to public concern about employ-ability and safety at work.

F.C.E.
R.I.McC.

April 1988

Note: The authors have used the male personal pronoun in the text where both genders are intended.

Acknowledgements

Our thanks go first to the authors who responded so well to the steering group's comments and suggestions, as well as to our colleagues on the steering group itself. All gave their time unstintingly. We also acknowledge the help given by the respective college committees, the Faculty of Ophthalmologists, and the many specialist referees. We owe a particular debt to Dr Andrew Raffle, editor of *Medical Aspects of Fitness to Drive*, for his encouragement and advice.

Our special thanks go to Miss Doreen Shaw of the Health and Safety Executive, for the considerable secretarial help she provided throughout the progress of this project and to Mrs Lynn Nash, Assistant Secretary of the Faculty of Occupational Medicine, who organized the Steering Group Meetings and acted as Committee Secretary from the beginning. We acknowledge with gratitude the financial contribution made by IBM United Kingdom Ltd., to the College, specifically to assist with this work.

Fig. 9.2 is reproduced with permission of Dr D. Chaffin and the Editor of the *Journal of Occupational Medicine*. Tables 16.2 and 16.3 are from Newman Taylor A.J. 'Occupational allergy' in *Allergy: an international textbook* (ed. M.H. Lessof, T.H. Lee, and D.M. Kemeny), John Wiley (1987). Fig. 21.1 is reproduced with permission of Professor J.L. Cooper and John Wiley & Sons Ltd. Tables 21.1, 21.2, and 21.3 are reproduced from *Oxford Textbook of Psychiatry* (ed. Michael Gelder, Dennis Gath, and Richard Mayou), Oxford University Press (1983). Tables 22.1, 22.2, and 22.3 are reproduced with permission of PHLS.

Peter John Taylor 1929–1987
A Tribute

Dr Peter Taylor was President of the Society of Occupational Medicine in 1975 when the formation of the Faculty was first suggested. He helped to guide the Royal College of Physicians towards the foundation of a Faculty of Occupational Medicine in 1978, became the Faculty's first Vice Dean, its second Dean, and was committed to ensuring the Faculty's success.

At the time Peter Taylor was Dean of the Faculty of Occupational Medicine, the suggestion was made that a book of this nature should be compiled. He immediately recognized the potential importance and value of such a publication and welcomed the idea with enthusiasm. He accepted the chairmanship of the steering group and played an important part in the development of the project. As was usual, Peter Taylor was unstinting of his time and energy and his personal contribution to this project was considerable.

His approach to this publication reflected his commitment to his profession and to the specialty in which he worked. He was deeply interested in all aspects of disability and its relief and was internationally recognized for his work on sickness absence and also for his wide knowledge and sound sense concerning the whole range of occupational health.

Peter Taylor's sudden and unexpected death on 6 January 1987 has meant the loss of an exceptional occupational physician and of a warm, wise, and friendly man with time for everyone. He is greatly missed by all who knew him.

John Aldridge
Dean of the Faculty of Occupational Medicine

Contents

Contributors

R. McL. Archibald
Occupational Physician, Merton and Sutton Health Authority; former Medical Director, National Coal Board.

P. J. Baylis
Group Occupational Health Physician. The Wellcome Foundation Ltd. London.

L. Beeley
Consultant Clinical Pharmacologist, Queen Elizabeth Hospital, Birmingham.

G. Bennett
Chief Medical Officer, Civil Aviation Authority, London.

R. J. Blow
Physician, BUPA Medical Centre, London; formerly Senior Medical Adviser, Standard Telephones and Cables PLC, London.

J. A. Bonnell
Medical Adviser to the Electricity Council; formerly Chief Medical Officer, Central Electricity Generating Board.

E. M. Botheroyd
Senior Employment Medical Adviser, Health and Safety Executive, Aberdeen.

I. Brown
UK Medical Adviser, Dow Chemical Co Ltd., Kings Lynn.

G. V. P. Chamberlain
Professor of Obstetrics and Gynaecology, St. George's Hospital Medical School, London.

G. M. Cochrane
Consultant Physician in Rehabilitation Medicine, Mary Marlborough Lodge, Oxford.

R. R. A. Coles
Assistant Director and Coordinator of Clinical Studies, MRC Institute of Hearing Research, University Park, Nottingham.

A. G. Cross
Consulting Ophthalmic Surgeon, St. Mary's Hospital and Moorfield's Eye Hospital, London.

P. A. M. Diamond
Head of Medical Service, London Regional Transport.

J. A. Dick
Consultant in Occupational Medicine; formerly Deputy Director of Medical Services, British Coal.

F. C. Edwards
Formerly Senior Employment Medical Adviser, Medical Division, Health and Safety Executive, Merseyside.

H. G. Egdell
Consultant Psychiatrist, Royal Liverpool Hospital.

P. M. Emerson
Consultant Haematologist, John Radcliffe Hospital, Oxford.

H. O. Engel
Formerly Senior Medical Officer, Ford Motor Company.

M. L. E. Espir
Honorary Consultant Neurologist, Charing Cross Hospital; formerly Principal Medical Officer, Civil Service Occupational Health Service.

J. M. D. Gallwey
Consultant Physician, Harrison Department of Genito-urinary Medicine, Radcliffe Infirmary, Oxford.

R. B. Godwin-Austen
Consultant Neurologist to the Nottingham and Derby Hospitals.

R. Gokal
Consultant Nephrologist, Hon. Lecturer University of Manchester.

R. H. Greenwood
Consultant Physician, United Norwich Hospitals.

A. P. Hopkins
Physician in Charge, Department of Neurological Sciences, St. Bartholomew's Hospital, London.

F. A. Horrocks
Registrar in Psychiatry, Countess of Chester Hospital; formerly Medical Officer (Occupational Health). Clwyd County Council.

M. I. V. Jayson
Professor of Rheumatology, Rheumatic Diseases Centre, University of Manchester.

W. E. O. Jones
Administrative Principal, Medical Division, Health and Safety Executive, London.

H. B. S. Kemp
Consultant Surgeon, Royal National Orthopaedic Hospital, London.

K. Lee
Formerly Medical Adviser, Occupational Health Unit, Cheshire County Council, Chester.

I. McColl
Professor of Surgery, Guy's Hospital, London.

E. B. Macdonald
Chief Medical Adviser, International Business Machines UK Ltd, Portsmouth.

D. P. Manning
Senior Medical Officer, Ford Motor Company, Halewood.

L. J. Marks
Senior Medical Officer, Artificial Limb and Appliance Centre, Royal National Orthopaedic Hospital, London.

D. M. Miller
Deputy Chief Medical Officer, Marks and Spencer PLC, London.

A. J. Newman Taylor
Consultant Physician, Brompton Hospital, London.

M. C. Petch
Consultant Cardiologist, Papworth Hospital, Cambridge.

I. Picton-Robinson
Senior Medical Officer, Austin Rover Group, Birmingham.

P. A. B. Raffle
Chairman, Medical Commission on Accident Prevention; formerly Chief Medical Officer, London Transport.

I. G. Rennie
Chief Medical Officer to Kodak Ltd, Headstone Drive, Harrow, Middlesex.

R. J. G. Rycroft
Consultant Dermatologist, St. John's Hospital for Diseases of the Skin, London; and Senior Employment Medical Adviser (Dermatology), Health and Safety Executive, London.

A. Sinclair
Chief Medical Officer, British Steel Corporation.

J. F. Taylor
Medical Adviser to Department of Transport, London.

C. A. Veys
Chief Medical Officer, Michelin Tyre PLC, Stoke-on-Trent.

J. W. Warburton
Consultant Psychiatrist, Leighton Hospital, Crewe, Cheshire.

C. White
Formerly Chief Medical Adviser of Cadbury Schweppes PLC.

R. J. Wyke
Senior Medical Registrar, Walsgrave Hospital, Coventry; formerly Research Fellow, The Liver Unit, Kings College Hospital and Dental School, Denmark Hill, London.

C. B. Wynn Parry
Director of Rehabilitation and Consultant Rheumatologist, Royal National Orthopaedic Hospital, London.

Steering group members

Sir Raymond Hoffenberg
(President, Royal College of Physicians, London).

Dr P. J. Taylor (deceased)
Late International Medical Adviser Unilever Ltd, London. (Chairman until January 1987).

Dr R. I. McCallum
Emeritus Professor of Occupational Health & Hygiene, University of Newcastle Upon Tyne. (Chairman from January 1987).

Dr J. F. L. Aldridge
Dean of the Faculty of Occupational Medicine.

Dr R. McL Archibald
Former Chief Medical Officer, National Coal Board.

Dr D. A. Chamberlain
Consultant Cardiologist, Royal Sussex County Hospital, Brighton.

Dr J. J. Daly
Consultant Physician, Sheffield District Health Authority.

Dr J. P. Horder
Visiting Professor, Department of Clinical Epidemiology and General Practice, Royal Free Hospital Medical school, London.

Dr K. H. Nickol
Senior Medical Officer, Ford Motor Company, Basildon, Essex.

Dr C. B. Wynn Parry
Director of Rehabilitation and Consultant Rheumatologist, Royal National Orthopaedic Hospital, London.

Dr F. C. Edwards
Former Senior Employment Medical Adviser, Medical Division, Health and Safety Executive. (Honorary Secretary).

Dr D. A. Pyke
(Registrar, Royal College of Physicians).

Mr D. B. Lloyd
(Secretary, Royal College of Physicians).

Mrs L. Nash
Assistant Secretary, Faculty of Occupational Medicine, (Committee Secretary).

1

Introduction

F. C. Edwards

This book on medical aspects of fitness for work gathers together specialist advice on employment aspects of a number of medical conditions, so that family practitioners, hospital consultants, occupational physicians, and other doctors can best advise on how a patient's illness might affect his work. Although decisions on return to work or on placement must depend on many factors, it is hoped that this book, which combines the best clinical and occupational health practice, will be used by doctors as a source of reference and will remind them about the occupational implications of illness.

The book is arranged in chapters according to specialty, each chapter written jointly by a clinician and an occupational health physician. For each specialty the chapter outlines the conditions covered; notes relevant statistics; discusses clinical aspects, including treatment, that may affect work capacity; notes rehabilitation requirements or special needs at the workplace; discusses problems that may arise at work and any necessary work restrictions; notes any current advisory or statutory medical standards; and makes recommendations on the employment aspects of the conditions covered. A chapter on the possible effects of medication on work performance is also included. Appendices summarizing regulations on driving, aviation, merchant shipping, and diving conclude the report.

The first two chapters cover general aspects applicable to any condition. This chapter deals mainly with the principles underlying medical assessments of fitness to work, contacts between medical practitioners and the work place; and confidentiality of medical information. Chapter 2 covers legislative and administrative aspects and outlines the services available to assist with employment.

CONTACTS BETWEEN THE PATIENT'S DOCTOR AND THE WORKPLACE

The importance of contact between the patient's own doctor and the workplace cannot be overemphasized. We suggest that consultants, as well as family practitioners, ask the patient if there is a medical adviser at the workplace and, if so, obtain written consent to contact him/her, or the occupational health nurse in the absence of an occupational physician.

Where there is no occupational health service, early contact between the patient's doctor and management (usually the personnel manager) may also be invaluable. It helps the employer to know when the patient is likely to be back at work, or whether some work adjustment will be needed, while family practitioners and consultants will be helped by knowing more about the type of work their patient does.

Employers with about 100 people or more will have some member of management designated to look after the placing of individuals within the organization. He may usefully be addressed as 'Job Placement Officer'. Organizations with more than 300 employees may well have their own occupational health nursing staff and a Personnel Officer detailed to look after job placement. The occupational health nurse may have a considerable amount of responsibility herself, a considerable knowledge of the workings of the organization, and be a useful person to address. Employers with 1000 or more employees may well have either full-time or part-time medical advisers to whom recommendations should be directed.

Confidentiality

Usually any recommendations and advice on placement or return to work are based on the functional effects of the medical condition, the diagnosis itself rarely being necessary. A simple statement that the patient is medically 'fit' or 'unfit' for a particular job often suffices, but occasionally further information may need to be disclosed. The certificated reason for any sickness absence is, of course, often known by personnel departments, who maintain their own confidential records.

The patient's consent to the passage of confidential health information to other doctors, occupational health nurses, employers, or to staff of the careers or employment services, for instance, must be obtained, usually in writing. The purposes of this should be made clear to the patient: it may be to help him with suitable work, and/or to maintain his own, and others', health and safety. If the patient is found to be medically unfit for employment of a certain kind, a full explanation should be given to him of why the disclosure of unfitness is necessary. Further advice may be found in the Faculty of Occupational Medicine's *Guidance on ethics for occupational physicians* 1986[1] (see Appendix to this chapter).

IMPAIRMENT, DISABILITY, AND HANDICAP

It is common experience that disabled workers are often highly motivated, with excellent work and attendance records. When medical fitness for work is assessed, what matters is often not the medical condition itself, but the associated loss of function, and any resulting disability or handicap, bearing in mind that a disability seen in the consulting room may be irrelevant to the performance of a particular job. The patient's condition should be interpreted in functional terms and in the context of the job requirements. Handicap may result directly from an impairment (for instance, severe facial disfigurement) or more usually from the resulting disability.

The confusion about the correct use of these terms has been clarified by several workers.[2-6] Duckworth's report *The classification and measurement of disablement* (1983) provides a comprehensive review.[7] To be consistent, the simplified scheme of the *International classification of impairments, disabilities and handicaps* (WHO 1980)[8] should be used, as follows. A disease, disorder or injury produces an *impairment* (change in normal structure or function). A *disability* is a resulting reduction or loss of an ability to perform an activity, e.g. climbing stairs, or manipulating a keyboard. A *handicap* is a social disadvantage, resulting from an impairment or disability, that limits or prevents the fulfilment of a normal role. As examples:

1. A relatively minor impairment, the loss of a finger, would be both a major disability and an occupational handicap to a pianist, although not to a labourer.

2. A relatively common impairment, defective colour vision, limits the ability to discriminate between certain hues. This may occasionally be a handicap at work, although there are, in fact, very few occupations for which colour vision defect is a significant handicap.

Prevalence of disability in populations of working age

Figures on the prevalence of disability and/or handicap in different populations vary according to the definitions and methods used and the groups sampled. Much of the uncertainty about the numbers of disabled people in the workforce or seeking work arises from these variations in definition and ascertainment and (in some surveys) from the reluctance of people to register as disabled. The major survey[9] of the handicapped and impaired in Britain in 1969 (the Harris survey) provides the basis for most recent discussions about prevalence of disability in the community. This survey suggested that there were about 1½ million people aged over 16 who were physically handicapped; of those aged 16–64, 3.9 per cent were thought to be impaired and 1.2 per cent substantially handicapped. An Office of Health Economics paper (1977) compared these data with reports from other countries[3] (Table 1.1). Other British surveys (the *General Household Survey* and the *Poverty Survey*) indicate that Harris underestimated. In the *General Household Survey* (1982), for instance, 11.9 per cent of men aged 16–64 reported a long-standing illness 'limiting' their activities.[10] Differences

Table 1.1   Prevalence of disability, handicap, limitation, or impairment in five countries (from Taylor 1977[3])

Study population	Percentage of specified population
USA, 1966 (age 18–64)	
disabled	17.2
severe	5.9
occupational	4.9
secondary	6.4
Australia, 1968 (age 15–64)	
chronic limiting condition	8.4
Denmark, 1961–62 (age 15–61)	
physically handicapped	6.5
Great Britain, 1968–69 (age 16–64)	
impaired	3.9
handicapped	1.2
Israel, 1965–66 (men aged 14–64, women aged 14–59)	
vocationally handicapped	2.9

between surveys seem mainly due to the inclusion of non-physical handicaps, and to different methods of reporting and sampling.[11] Common to all these surveys is the rise in prevalence of disability with increasing age and, to a lesser extent, with manual as opposed to non-manual social class or occupational groups.

Work forces have also been studied and Table 1.2 summarizes the findings of two British[12-14] and two Scandinavian[15,16] studies. Taylor and Fairrie[12] found that the prevalence of disability was about 10 per cent of men working in the refinery they studied (Table 1.2). A markedly increased prevalence of disability/handicap with age, particularly over 50 years, was found. Substantial proportions of the workforce were found to be sufficiently incapacitated to need 'rehabilitation measures' such as work accommodation, and/or would have been restricted in their ability to perform if their jobs had been more demanding. The commonest causes of disablement in all four studies were circulatory, respiratory, and musculoskeletal disorders. These were the main causes of ill-health retirement over a two-year period in British Steel,[17] while the main causes of ill-health retirement in coal miners (between 1981 and 1983) were musculoskeletal, psychological, cardiovascular, and respiratory conditions, in that order (R. Archibald, personal communication). The two earlier British studies[12-14] highlighted the inadequacies of the Register of Disabled Persons and the Quota Scheme: these will be discussed

Table 1.2 Prevalence of disablement affecting working capacity in two British and two Scandinavian workforces

	Working population		Chronic disability affecting employment		Comment
	Sample size	Workforce	no.	%	
Taylor and Fairrie 1968[12,13]	1995 (M)	oil refinery (Britain)	206	10.3	
Taylor *et al.* 1970[14]	11 399 (M)	7 companies (Britain)	1233	10.8	
Jarvikoski and Tuunainen 1978[16]	c.2300 (M & F) (responders)	Helsinki city employees (Finland)	not given	10–17	'Estimate of subjective need for rehabilitation'
Heijbel 1978[15]	3846 (M & F)	Volvo Skövde Works (Sweden)	527*	13.7	*physical reasons only: 'condition-ally employable'

in more detail in Chapter 2. The prevalence of different medical conditions will be indicated in the specialty chapters.

The following sections explain why medical assessments of fitness for work are needed; indicate briefly the situations where medical standards may apply; note the lack of relevance of such assessments to inclusion in pension schemes; and outline the different approaches needed according to when and for whom an assessment is indicated.

The primary purpose of a medical assessment of fitness for work is to make sure that an individual is fit to perform the task involved effectively and without risk to his own or to others' health and safety. The main areas where health advice is needed are as follows:

1.　The patient's condition may limit, reduce or prevent him performing the job effectively (e.g. musculoskeletal conditions that limit mobility, or manipulative ability).

2.　The patient's condition might be made worse by the job (e.g. excessive physical exertion in some cardio-respiratory conditions; exposure to certain allergens in asthma).

3.　The patient's condition is likely to make it unsafe for him to do the job (e.g. liability to sudden unconsciousness in a hazardous situation; risk of damage to the remaining eye or ear in a patient with monocular vision or monaural hearing in certain work environments).

4.　The patient's condition is likely to make it unsafe both for him and others, whether fellow workers and/or the community (e.g. road or railway driving in someone who is liable to sudden unconsciousness or to behave abnormally).

5.　The patient's condition might make it unsafe for the community (e.g. for consumers of the product, if a food-handler transmits infection).

There is usually a clear distinction between the first-party risks of 2 and 3 and the third-party risks of 5. In 4, first- and third-party risks may both be present.

　　Thus, when assessing a patient's fitness to work, his doctor must consider the following factors. First, the level of skill, physical and mental capacity, sensory acuity, etc. needed for effective performance of the work. Secondly, any possible adverse effects of the work itself or of the work environment on the patient's health. Thirdly, the possible 'health and safety' implications of the patient's medical condition when undertaking the work in question, for himself, fellow workers, and/or the community. For some jobs it should also be remembered that there may be an 'emergency' component in addition to the 'routine' job structure, and higher standards of fitness may thus be needed on occasion for the former.

Medical standards

Medical standards may be advisory or statutory. Standards are often laid down where work entails entering a new environment which may present some hazard to the individual, such as the increased or decreased atmospheric pressures encountered in compressed-air work, diving, high altitudes, flying. Standards are also laid down for work where there is a potential risk of a medical condition resulting in accidents, as in transport; or transmitting infection, as in food-handling. For onerous or arduous work such as the Mines Rescue Service or the Fire Service, very high standards of physical fitness are needed. Specific medical standards will need to be met in such types of work: where relevant, such advisory and/or statutory standards arc noted in each specialty chapter.

Pension schemes

Many doctors and personnel managers in industry still believe that their company pension fund requires high standards of medical fitness for new entrants. Direct enquiry to the pension fund itself usually demonstrates that this is not the case. Fortunately, most pension funds follow the general principle recommended by the Occupational Pension Board: 'Fit for employment—fit for the pension fund'.[18] It was the Board's view that 'The concern of an employer, when assessing a prospective employee, should be with ability to perform the job efficiently. There is no reason why pension scheme considerations should influence the employer's decision whether to employ him.' A survey of private sector pension schemes found similar attitudes.[19] In general, therefore, a disease or disability should not *per se* be a reason for exclusion from pension schemes, nor used as an excuse to refuse employment, unless it adversely affects job performance or health and safety. Where company schemes still operate against the disabled, attempts should be made to amend them.

When an assessment of medical fitness is needed

An assessment of medical fitness may be needed for those who are

(1) already in employment;

(2)   unemployed, but being considered for a particular job (pre-employment assessment);

(3)   unemployed, but without a specific job in mind.

For (1) and (2), the assessment will be related to a particular job, or to a defined range of alternative work in a given workplace. The assessment is to help both employer and employee, and should be clearly related to the job in question. Further advice on pre-employment screening is available from the HSE.[20] However, for (3), where there may be no specific job in view, the assessment must inevitably be more open-ended: health assessments may be required, for instance, by the employment or careers services in their attempt to find suitable work for unemployed disabled people. It is thus all the more important to avoid unnecessary medical restrictions or labels (such as 'epileptic'), as these tend to follow the individual in his search for work and may limit his future choice unduly.

Recruitment and disclosure

Employers often use health questionnaires as part of their recruitment process. Some individuals may be reluctant to disclose a medical condition to a future employer (sometimes with their own doctor's support) for fear that this may lose them the job. Although understandable, it must be pointed out that should an accident at work arise due to the concealed condition, dismissal on medical grounds may follow. An Industrial Tribunal would be likely to support the dismissal if the employee had failed to disclose the relevant condition. Patients should be discouraged from concealing a potentially hazardous medical condition, such as epilepsy, if it is relevant to the job in question.

It is noted above that for some jobs statutory medical standards exist (e.g. driving) and that for others employing organizations lay down their own advisory medical standards (e.g. food handling). For the majority of jobs, however, no agreed advisory medical standards exist, and for many jobs there need be no special health requirements. It is important to stress that health information on prospective employees should be requested only if related to the job in question. If the employer has identified fitness criteria essential for the job, then it is reasonable to ask the candidate for details of medical conditions that would be relevant. Floyd and Espir have recently made a case for *a code of practice on recruitment and disclosure*.[21] They propose that job application forms should be accompanied by an indication of any health standards or physical qualifications required and of any medical conditions that would be a bar to certain types of job, but that no questions about health or disabilities should be included on job application forms themselves. If health information were necessary, applicants should be asked to complete a separate health declaration form which should be inspected and interpreted only by health professionals, and only after the candidate had been selected, subject to satisfactory health. They emphasized that if recruits were obliged to disclose details of their health, employers should have a corresponding obligation to treat that information responsibly and sensitively.

Employees

The *stages* at which a health appraisal might be necessary for someone in employment are as follows. *Job change*, still working for the same employer, possibly for transfer or promotion. The employee should be told of any special health requirements or qualifications for the new post and the health appraisal should relate to these. Job change may include more seniority or responsibility, for instance, or include overseas posting with considerable increase in travel. All these might have to be taken into account. *Periodic review* of individual health may be undertaken in some circumstances and will relate to specific requirements (for instance, regular assessment of visual acuity in some jobs). *Return to work after illness or injury* usually merits a health assessment and is discussed further below. Employees returning to work after *prolonged absence* often have special needs that should be taken into account where possible. Finally, the question of *retirement on grounds of ill health* may need to be considered. This is also discussed below.

Young people

Medical advice on occupation or training given to a young person who has not yet started his career often has a different slant compared with that given to an adult developing the same medical condition late in an established career. The later stages of a particular vocation may involve jobs incompatible with the young person's medical condition, or its foreseeable development. Also, the adult's experience may compensate for the possible disadvantages of the disease or disability that develops late. It is particularly important that young people entering employment are given appropriate and consistent medical advice when it is needed. For instance, although a school-leaver with epilepsy might be eligible for an ordinary driving licence at the time of recruitment, it would be most inadvisable for him to take up a position where vocational driving might be an essential part of his progress in that particular career.

Severely disabled people

Where a medical condition has so reduced the individual's employment abilities or potential that he is incapable either of continuing in his existing work or of working in any open competitive employment, then sheltered work of some kind may be the only alternative to premature medical retirement, on the one hand, or to continued unemployment on the other. Further details of sheltered work are given in Chapter 2.

THE ASSESSMENT OF MEDICAL FITNESS FOR WORK

The remainder of this chapter summarizes the main points relevant to:

(1) making the assessment;

(2) recording or presenting the assessment;

(3) matching the individual with the requirements of the task;

(4) recommendations and advice following the assessment.

General framework for the assessment

From the occupational point of view, the clinician's assessment should always be in terms of functional capacity and the actual diagnosis need not be reported. Even so, an opinion on the medical fitness of an individual is being conveyed to others and the patient's consent is needed for the information to be passed on, in confidence. This has been discussed above.

To estimate the individual's level of function, general assessments of all systems should be made, with special attention both to those which are disordered and to those which may be relevant to the work. As well as physical systems, sensory and perceptual abilities may need to be noted. Frequently, psychological reactions, such as responsiveness, alertness, and other features of the general mental state may be relevant. The effects of different treatment regimes on work suitability should also be considered; the possible effects of some medication on alertness, or the optimal position of an arthrodesis, are only two of many examples. *Each of the specialty chapters which follow outlines the main points to be considered in the respective conditions, but a summary list of the main features relevant to an assessment of fitness for work for use as a general framework, is listed in the Appendix at the end of this chapter.*

Objective tests

The results of any objective tests of function relevant to the working situation should be noted. For instance, the physical work capacity of an individual may be estimated ergometrically using standard exercise tests, step tests, or different task simulations. Cardio-respiratory function may be relevant. Muscular strength and lifting ability can be assessed objectively by using either dynamic or static strength tests.

Presentation of the assessment

If a written report is needed it should be legible, clearly laid out, and should be signed and dated. The report should mention any functional limitations and outline activities that may, or may not, be undertaken. Any health or safety implications should be noted and the assessment should aim at a positive statement about the patient's abilities. Any adaptations or ergonomic alterations to the work that would be helpful should be indicated (work accommodation is discussed later in the chapter). Recommendations on restriction or limitation of employment should be unambiguous and precise, and should only be made if definitely indicated.

Many standard functional profiles of individual abilities have been used in North America and Scandinavia, and in this country, mainly in the Armed Services. These profiles, which resemble each other, are known by acronyms of the initial letter of the parts of the body assessed, e.g. PULHEEMS, GULHEMP, PULSES. In the GULHEMP profile, for instance, each division is graded from 1–7 according to standards adopted by the authors.[22] Other profiles have combined the evaluation of physical abilities with indications of the frequency with which certain activities may be undertaken.[23] Although these profiles are relatively objective and systematic, and allow for consistent recordings on the same individual over a period of time, they take time to complete and much of the information may not be needed. Many doctors in industry who have tried to introduce a PULHEEMS type of system have found that it does not always help when dealing with the practical, and often complex, problems affecting individual employees.

Other simpler classifications are often used in clinical settings, e.g. the New York Heart Association's Impairment of Cardiac Functions. Graded in terms of symptoms, such classifications are of less use in assessing occupational fitness than in recording clinical progress or deterioration. Other scales (e.g. the Barthel Index) used to grade degree of damage or recovery after stroke, for instance, are used to assess outcome after different rehabilitation procedures, and often form part of occupational therapy assessments.

Matching the individual with the job

A functional assessment of the individual's capacities will be of most use when as much is known about the job as about the individual assessed. Ideally, the requirements of the task should be categorized, so that a match can be made with the individual's capacity. Both in France and in Germany job matching of this kind is used formally in some work settings, but formal job analysis and matching is rarely used at the workplace in the UK. In industry, however, this ideal is often met in practice when personnel staff and managers, company doctors, and supervisors discuss the placement needs of their disabled employees and, as both worker abilities and task requirements are well known to them, a theoretical match is often super-fluous. Outside the workplace itself, more formal assessments may be made in medical rehabilitation or occupational therapy departments; and in the MSC's employment rehabilitation centres where occupational skills can be tested using standard equipment, as well as by work rehearsal in different settings. The types of assessment provided by the Manpower Services Commission (MSC) are discussed further in Chapter 2.

The requirements of the task

Too often, medical statements simply state 'fit for light work only'. The separation of work into 'light', 'medium', and 'heavy' often results in an individual being unduly limited in his choice of work. A refinement of this broad grading is adopted by the US Department of Labor in its *Dictionary of occupational titles*.[24] Jobs are graded according to physical demands, environmental conditions, certain levels of skill and knowledge, and specific vocational preparation (training time) required. The *physical demands* of a job are defined in six terms: strength; climbing and balance; stoop, kneel, crouch, and crawl; reach, handle, finger, and feel; talk and hear; and visual demands. The *strength demands* embrace lifting, carrying, pushing, and pulling; jobs are divided into five categories according to the maximum lift required and the frequency of such lifting or carrying. These categories are reproduced in the Appendix to this chapter.

If the energy or metabolic requirements of a particular task are known, the individual's work capacity may be estimated and, if expressed in the same units, a comparison between the energy cost of the work and the physiological work capacity of the individual may be made. This has been used in assessing work capacity of patients with heart disease. Energy requirements of tasks have been estimated using calories per square metre per hour, or using metabolic equivalents, or 'Mets'. (The 'Met' is an arbitrary unit recommended by the American Heart Association. One 'Met' is the approximate energy expended while sitting at rest, and is defined as the rate of energy expenditure requiring an oxygen consumption of 3.5 ml/kg body weight/min.)

The metabolic costs of many working activities have been published[25-28] and the equivalents for the five grades of physical demands in terms of muscular strength adopted by the US Department of Labor are included in the Appendix to this chapter. Work physiology assessments in occupational medicine provide a quantitative way of matching the patient to his work[29] and are commonly used in Scandinavia and the USA.

Recommendations following assessment

If the patient is employed, it is often possible to make a medical judgement on whether he is:

(1) capable of performing the work without any ill effects;

(2) capable of performing the work but with reduced efficiency and/or effectiveness;

(3) capable of performing the work although this may adversely affect his existing medical condition;

(4) capable of performing the work but not without unacceptable risks to the health and safety of himself, other workers, or the community;

(5) physically or mentally incapable of performing the work in question.

For the employed patient, where the judgement is (2)—(5), the options include work accommodation; alternative work on a temporary or permanent basis; sheltered work; or, in the last resort, retirement on medical grounds. These are considered later in the chapter.

If the patient is unemployed but is being given a pre-employment assessment for recruitment to a particular job, the same range of options (1) to (5) also applies. However, *if the unemployed patient is not being considered for a specific job,* then the recommendation following the assessment cannot relate to specific job requirements and must be more open-ended (see above). It is particularly important that no unnecessary medical restrictions are made.

Advice following the assessment

Following an assessment of fitness for work, the employee may be found fit for his usual work; fit for modified work with the same employer; fit for alternative work with the same employer, or fit for alternative employment; fit for sheltered work; or retirement on grounds of ill health may be the only option. These are discussed below.

The return to work

Even if the patient is assessed as medically fit for a return to his previous job without modification, medical advice may still be needed on the time of return to work. A clear indication by the consultant or family practitioner to the patient, or to the employer or occupational physician, on when work may be resumed, should be given wherever possible. Work should be resumed as soon as the individual is physically and mentally fit enough, having regard to his own and others' health and safety. Return to work at the right time can assist recovery, while undue delay can aggravate the sense of uselessness and isolation that so often accompanies incapacity due to major illness or injury.

The contact between the patient's doctor and his employer or occupational physician stressed earlier in the chapter will mean that any preparation for the patient's return to work can be put in hand. Recommendations on when work may be resumed and on the patient's functional and work capacities should be clear and specific.

Work accommodation

The patient's condition may be such that his previous work needs to be modified, either temporarily or permanently. Two aspects of the job are usually involved, place and time. Simple features such as bench height, type of chair or stool, or lighting, may need adjustment, or more sophisticated aids or adaptations may be required. The workplace environment may need adapting, for example by building a ramp or widening a doorway to improve access for wheelchairs. Financial assistance may be available from the Manpower Services Commission and further details are included in Chapter 2.

Certain time features of the work may need adjustment, for instance more flexible working hours, more frequent rest pauses, alterations to shift work or arrangements to avoid rush-hour travel. A short period of unpaced work may be necessary before resuming paced work. Sometimes the way in which the patient relates to fellow workers may need attention.

Alternative work

In many occupations, work accommodation or job restructuring is not possible and some type of suitable alternative work is recommended. This is usually judged individually by the occupational physician. Many large companies with occupational health services have formal systems for advising management of the need for employees to undertake alternative work, often on a temporary basis, with regular review of the individual if the aim is eventual return to the previous work.[30] Where there are no occupational health services, the MSC's Disablement Resettlement Officers (DROs) can visit the workplace to advise on work accommodation or alternative work; the Employment Medical Advisory Service (EMAS) can provide medical advice. Both union and management agreement to such changes may be needed and there may be difficulties. (Sheltered work is discussed in Chapter 2.)

Premature medical retirement

This may have to be considered as a last resort, if suitable alternative or sheltered work cannot be provided or if the employee will not accept it. After illness or injury the gradual recovery of fitness can be regarded as crossing the 'threshold of employability' determined by the relative task requirements. This 'threshold' may be lowered by work accommodations or by alternative work. Persistent or increasing disability may mean that the 'threshold' of fitness for a particular job is unlikely to be attained, or only after further treatment (K. H. Nickol, personal communication). It may then be necessary for the doctor to recommend retirement on medical grounds, particularly if further treatment is impossible, ineffective, or is declined. Other reasons for medical retirement include increasingly severe mobility problems, as well as the non-availability of suitable alternative work. A management decision on premature retirement on grounds of ill health should never be made without a supporting medical opinion that has taken the requirements of the job fully into account. Chapter 2 discusses other aspects of premature medical retirement in relation to the law.

Summary

Medical fitness may thus be relevant when illness or injury reduce performance, or affect health and safety at the workplace; it may also be specifically relevant to certain onerous or hazardous tasks for which medical standards exist. Medical fitness should always be judged in relation to the work, and not the pension scheme. It has little relevance in a wide range of employment: very many medical conditions, and virtually all minor health problems, have no implications for work and should not debar from employment. It is hoped that this book will help to minimize unfair employment discrimination on grounds of ill health.

Appendix

FRAMEWORK FOR ASSESSING FITNESS FOR WORK

An evaluation of general physical and mental health forms the background to more specific assessments. Guiding principles throughout will be the *patient's residual abilities* in terms of *likely requirements at the workplace*. Many of these aspects are listed below. Not all will be relevant to any one individual, while some are relevant to more than one type of condition, or to more than one system or specialty.

Assessment should include the results of relevant tests.

1. *General*: stamina; ability to cope with full working day, or shiftwork; liability to fatigue, etc.

2. *Mobility*: ability to get to work, and exit safely; to walk, climb, bend, stoop, crouch, etc.

3.   *Locomotor*: general/specific joint function and range; reach of arms; gait; back/spinal function, etc.

4.   *Posture*: ability to stand or sit for certain times; any postural restraints; work in confined spaces, etc.

5.   *Muscular*: specific palsies or weakness; tremor; ability to lift, push or pull, with weight/time abilities if known; strength tests, etc.

6.   *Manual skill*: any defects in dexterity, ability to grip, or grasp, etc.

7.   *Co-ordination*, including hand/eye co-ordination if relevant.

8.   *Balance*: ability to work at heights; vertigo.

9.   *Cardio-respiratory limitations*, including exercise tolerance, and how this was tested: respiratory function and reserve; sub-maximal exercise tests, aerobic work capacity, if relevant.

10.   *Liability to unconsciousness*, including nature of episodes, timing, any precipitating factors, etc.

11.   *Sensory aspects*: may be relevant for the actual work, or in order to get about a hazardous environment safely.

   (a)   *Vision*: ability for fine/close work, distant vision, visual standards corrected or uncorrected, any aids in use or needed. Visual fields. Colour vision defects may occasionally be relevant. Is the eyesight good enough to cope with a difficult working environment with possible hazards?

   (b)   *Hearing*: each ear; can warning signals or instructions be heard?

   For both vision and hearing it is very important that if only one eye or one ear is functioning, this should be noted so that the remaining organ can be adequately protected against possible hazards.

12.   *Communication/speech*: two-way communication: hearing or speech defects; reason for limitation.

13.   *Cerebral function* will be very relevant after head injury, cerebrovascular accident, other neurological conditions, and in those with some mental handicap: the presence of any confusion; disorientation; impairment of memory, intellect, verbal, or numerical aptitudes, etc.

14.   *Mental state*: psychiatric assessments may mention anxiety, relevant phobias, mood, withdrawal, relationships with other people, etc.

15.   *Motivation*: may well be the most important. With it, other defects may be surmounted; without it, difficulties may not be overcome. It can be

particularly difficult to assess by a doctor who has not previously known the patient.

16. *Treatment of the condition*: special effects of treatment may be relevant, e.g. drowsiness, inattention, as side-effects of some medication; implications of different types of treatment in one condition (e.g. insulin as opposed to oral treatment for diabetes).

17. *Further treatment*: if further treatment is planned, e.g. further orthopaedic or surgical procedures, these may need to be mentioned.

18. *Prognosis*: if the clinical prognosis is likely to affect work placement, e.g. likely improvements in muscle strength, or decline in exercise tolerance, these should be indicated.

19. *Special needs*: these may be dietary; need for a clean area for self-treatment, e.g. injection; or relate to time, e.g. frequent rest pauses, no paced or shift work, etc.

20. *Aids or appliances* in use or needed. Artificial aids (implanted) may be relevant (pacemakers and the working environment; artificial joints). Aids to mobility may have implications for work (e.g. wheelchair). Prostheses/orthoses should be mentioned. Artificial aids or appliances that could help at the workplace should be indicated.

21. *Special third-party risks* that could be transmitted to other workers or to the community, e.g. via the product due to infection in food-handlers, etc.

REQUIREMENTS OF THE TASK

These may relate not only to the present job but also to the future career. Some of the following aspects may be relevant:

1. *Work demands*: physical (e.g. mobility needs; strength for certain activities; lifting/carrying; climbing/balancing; stooping/bending; postural constraints; reach requirements; dexterity/manipulative ability, etc.—see next section of this appendix for further detail); *intellectual/perceptual demands*; types of skill involved in tasks.

2. *Work environment*: physical aspects (e.g. extremes of temperature, humidity, noise, vibration; changes in atmospheric pressure; fumes/dust); risk factors (e.g. chemical or biological hazards; working at heights).

3. *Organizational/social aspects*, e.g. working in small groups or alone; intermittent or regular pressure of work; need for tact in public relations, etc.

4. *Temporal aspects*, e.g. need for early start; type of shiftwork; day or night work; arrangements for rest pauses or breaks, etc.

5. *Ergonomic aspects*: workplace (e.g. need to climb stairs; distance from toilet facilities; access for wheelchairs, etc.); workstation (e.g. height of work-bench; adequate lighting; type of equipment or controls used, etc.).

6. *Travel*, e.g. need to work in areas remote from health care or where there are risks not found in the UK.

FROM 'SELECTED CHARACTERISTICS OF OCCUPATIONS DEFINED IN THE DICTIONARY OF OCCUPATIONAL TITLES', US DEPARTMENT OF LABOR (1981)[24]

Physical demands

The physical demands listed in this publication serve as a means of expressing both the physical requirements of the job and the physical capacities (specific physical traits) a worker must have to meet those required by many jobs (perceiving by the sense of vision), and also the name of a specific capacity possessed by many people (having the power of sight). The worker must possess physical capacities at least in an amount equal to the physical demands made by the job.

The factors

1. Strength

This factor is expressed in terms of sedentary, light, medium, heavy, and very heavy. It is measured by involvement of the worker with one or more of the following activities:

(a) Worker position(s):

(i) standing: remaining on one's feet in an upright position at a workstation without moving about;

(ii) walking: moving about on foot;

(iii) sitting: remaining in the normal seated position.

(b) Worker movement of objects (including extremities used):

(i) lifting: raising or lowering an object from one level to another (includes upward pulling);

(ii) carrying: transporting an object, usually holding it in the hands or arms or on the shoulder;

(iii) pushing: exerting force upon an object so that the object moves away from the force (includes slapping, striking, kicking, and treadle actions);

(iv) pulling: exerting force upon an object so that the object moves toward the force (includes jerking).

The five degrees of Physical Demands Factor No. 1 (strength), are as follows:

(estimated equivalents in Mets[28])

S Sedentary Work (under 2 Mets) Lifting 10 lbs. maximum and occasionally lifting and/or carrying such articles as dockets, ledgers, and small tools. Although a sedentary job is defined as one which involves sitting, a certain amount of walking and standing is often necessary in carrying out job duties. Jobs are sedentary if walking and standing are required only occasionally and other sedentary criteria are met.

L Light Work (2–3 Mets) Lifting 20 lbs. maximum with frequent lifting and/or carrying of objects weighing up to 10 lbs. Even though the weight lifted may be only a negligible amount, a job is in this category when it requires walking or standing to a significant degree, or when it involves sitting most of the time with a degree of pushing and pulling of arm and/or leg controls.

M Medium Work (4–5 Mets) Lifting 50 lbs. maximum with frequent lifting and/or carrying of objects weighing up to 25 lbs.

H Heavy Work (6–8 Mets) Lifting 100 lbs. maximum with frequent lifting and/or carrying of objects weighing up to 50 lbs.

V Very Heavy Work (over 8 Mets) Lifting objects in excess of 100 lbs. with frequent lifting and/or carrying of objects weighing 50 lbs. or more.

2. Climbing and/or balancing
(a) Climbing: ascending or decending ladders, stairs, scaffolding, ramps, poles, ropes, and the like, using the feet and legs and/or hands and arms.

(b) Balancing: maintaining body equilibrium to prevent falling when walking, standing, crouching, or running on narrow, slippery, or erratically moving surfaces; or maintaining body equilibrium when performing gymnastic feats.

3. Stooping, kneeling, crouching, and/or crawling
(a) Stooping: bending the body downward and forward by bending the spine at the waist.

(b) Kneeling: bending the legs at the knees to come to rest on the knee or knees.

(c) Crouching: bending the body downward and forward by bending the legs and the spine.

(d) Crawling: moving about on the hands and knees or hands and feet.

4. Reaching, handling, fingering, and/or feeling
(a) Reaching: extending the hands and arms in any direction.

(b)   Handling: seizing, holding, grasping, turning, or otherwise working with the hand or hands (fingering not involved).

(c)   Fingering: picking, pinching, or otherwise working with the fingers primarily (rather than with the whole hand or arm as in handling).

(d)   Feeling: perceiving such attributes of objects and materials as size, shape, temperature, or texture, by means of receptors in the skin, particularly those of the fingertips.

5.   *Talking and/or hearing*

(a)   Talking: expressing or exchanging ideas by means of the spoken word.

(b)   Hearing: perceiving the nature of sounds by the ear.

6.   *Seeing*

Obtaining impressions through the eyes of the shape, size, distance, motion, color or other characteristics of objects. The major visual functions are: (a) acuity, far and near, (b) depth perception, (c) field of vision, (d) accommodation, and (e) color vision. The functions are defined as follows:

(a)   Acuity, far—clarity of vision at 20 feet or more; acuity, near—clarity of vision at 20 inches or less.

(b)   Depth perception—three-dimensional vision. The ability to judge distance and space relationships so as to see objects where and as they actually are.

(c)   Field of vision—the area that can be seen up and down or to the right or left while the eyes are fixed on a given point.

(d)   Accommodation—adjustment of the lens of the eye to bring an object into sharp focus. This item is especially important when doing near-point work at varying distances from the eye.

(e)   Color vision—the ability to identify and distinguish colors.

EXTRACTS FROM THE FACULTY OF OCCUPATIONAL MEDICINE'S GUIDANCE ON ETHICS FOR OCCUPATIONAL PHYSICIANS (1986)[1]

'Fitness for work

There are many instances in medical practice, particularly in occupational medicine, where some information on the health of an individual has to be given to people outside the confines of the normal doctor–patient relationship. Although in many cases a statement as to the "fitness" or "unfitness" or limitations on the type of employment of the person will suffice, there are occasions when further information may have to be disclosed. This should be done only with the informed consent of the individual. Advice to management on fitness for work should be submitted in a formal manner not only as a matter of principle, but also because documents may at some future time have to be disclosed to a court or industrial tribunal.

Advice given to management about the results of a medical examination should generally be confined to advice on ability and limitations of function. Findings should be expressed only in general terms excluding clinical details. When the employee himself has given the information to management this restriction need not apply. Discussions with management on further courses of action consequent upon the medical examination should take account of possible alternatives, with emphasis on those which are likely to be of benefit to the individual. Statements such as "fit for light duties" should be avoided as their interpretation can cause misunderstandings and even resentment. The physician should bear in mind that it is the employer who is responsible for allocating duties even though the decision should take account of constructive professional advice wherever practicable.

In certain circumstances the occupational physician carries out routine examinations or assessments to determine the fitness of an individual for a particular job (e.g. HGV/PSV, pre-placement, food-handlers). Sometimes the examinations are statutory; sometimes they are not. It should not be inferred from his attendance that the individual necessarily agrees to the examination and to the disclosure of the result. The occupational physician should himself recognise and make it clear to the individual that he is acting as an impartial "medical examiner" and will therefore report his conclusions to those who have appointed him. The Faculty considers that the individual has the right to be informed of the findings of the clinical examination, but these should not be disclosed to a third party (including his own doctor) without the individual's informed consent.

It is the Faculty's view that detailed clinical information resulting for example from executive medical examinations, (which should of course be voluntary), should not be passed to the employer where it would be open to misinterpretation, but only to a medically qualified adviser, and even then only with the consent of the individual. The Faculty does not support the practice of informing employers about the results of individual executive medical examinations. It is for the employee to decide what information, if any, he wishes to disclose or have disclosed by the physician and to whom.

Recently, the issue of urine testing for drugs and alcohol has been the subject of intensive discussion in the USA and to a lesser extent in the UK. Occupational physicians are advised that such tests may be acceptable at pre-employment examinations provided that the subjects are informed in advance of the nature of the test and later of the results. Great care should be taken to develop a testing protocol that includes the retesting of positive specimens in order to avoid the possibility of action being taken on a false positive. The Faculty does not support the general introduction of random screening of existing employees. If exceptional circumstances require this, the very greatest care must be taken to plan such a programme and discuss its implications with management, workers' representatives, and probably also with company lawyers.

Occasionally an occupational physician, when acting in a role other than that of "independent medical examiner" (e.g. in a therapeutic or research role) may find that an individual is unfit for a job where the safety of other workers or of the public is concerned. He should then take great care to explain fully why he thinks the disclosure of unfitness is necessary. If sufficient time is taken in explanation, there is rarely difficulty in obtaining agreement. When this is not obtained the occupational physician is faced with an ethical dilemma. No firm guidance is possible, and each situation must be considered on its merits. On such occasions it may be useful for the occupational physician to discuss the issue with an experienced colleague.

The occupational physician should be aware that he may have an individual responsibility under Sections 7 and 8 of the Health and Safety at Work Act to act in good faith *vis-à-vis* his employer. Thus, if he were to discover that one of the Company vehicle drivers had developed a condition likely to cause him to be a source of danger to other employees or the public, he should do his best to persuade the employee to allow him to release relevant information to management. If no such agreement is obtained however, it is still his responsibility to tell the employee that he will advise management that he should cease to drive Company vehicles even though the physician must then give no reason other than medical unfitness. At the same time he should discuss the matter with the general practitioner, and they should both endeavour to persuade the patient to inform the Driver and Vehicle Licensing Centre, a responsibility of the individual under the Road Traffic Act.

Occupational physicians are usually involved in providing impartial professional advice to company pension schemes when an employee's state of health has deteriorated to the point when premature medical retirement due to incapacity may be necessary. The physician should normally see and examine the employee personally unless circumstances make this impracticable. He should also, with consent, communicate fully with the individual's general practitioner about the course of action he intends to take. In order to give proper advice occupational physicians should familiarise themselves with the various provisions of the company's pension scheme.'

REFERENCES

1. Royal College of Physicians, Faculty of Occupational Medicine. Guidance on ethics for occupational physicians. 3rd ed. 1986.
2. Agerholm M. Handicaps and the handicapped. A nomenclature and classification of intrinsic handicaps. Roy Soc Health J 1975;**95**:3–8.
3. Taylor DG. Physical impairment: social handicap. London: Office of Health Economics, 1977.
4. Wood PHN. Appreciating the consequences of disease; the International Classification of Impairments, Disabilities and Handicaps. WHO Chronicle 1980;**34**:376–80.
5. Wood PHN. The language of disablement: a glossary relating to disease and its consequences. International Rehabilitation Medicine 1980;**2**:86–92.
6. Tait F. Disabled or handicapped: what is the difference? Health Trends 1981; **13**:109–11.
7. Duckworth D. The classification and measurement of disablement. London: HMSO, 1983.
8. World Health Organisation. International classification of impairments, disabilities and handicaps. Geneva: WHO, 1980.
9. Harris AI. Handicapped and impaired in Great Britain. London: HMSO, 1971: (Pts I and II).
10. Office of Population Censuses & Surveys. General Household Survey—1982. London. HMSO, 1984.
11. Townsend P. Poverty in the United Kingdom. London: Penguin Books, 1979.
12. Taylor PJ, Fairrie AJ. Chronic disabilities and capacity for work. (A study of 3299 men aged 16–24 in a general practice and an oil refinery.) Br J Prev & Soc Med 1968;**22**:86–93.
13. Taylor PJ, Fairrie AJ. Chronic disability in men of middle age. A study of 165 men in a general practice and a refinery. Brit J Prev & Soc Med 1968;**22**:183–92.
14. Taylor PJ with Barrett JD, Fletcher GC, et al. A combined survey of chronic disability in industrial employees. Trans Soc Occup Med 1970;**20**:98–102.
15. Heijbel CA. Occurrence of personal handicaps in an industrial population, survey and appraisal: Physical demands and the disabled. Scand J Rehab Med 1978;(suppl 6):182–92.
16. Jarvikoski A, Tuunainen K. The need for early rehabilitation among Finnish municipal employees. Scand J Rehab Med 1978;**10**:115–20.
17. Fanning D. Ill health retirement as an indicator of morbidity. J Soc Occup Med 1981;**31**:103–11.
18. Occupational pension scheme cover for disabled people. Cmnd 6849. London: HMSO, 1977.
19. Davoud M, Kettle M. Multiple sclerosis and its effect upon employment. Multiple Sclerosis Society, 1980.
20. Health and Safety Executive. Pre-employment Health Screening. Guidance Note MS20. London: HMSO, 1982.
21. Floyd M, Espir MLE. Assessment of medical fitness for employment: the case for a code of practice. Lancet 1986;**ii**:207–9.

22. Koyl LF, Hanson PM. Age, physical ability and work potential. Washington: National Council of Aging, 1969.
23. Hanman B. The evaluation of physical ability. New Engl J Med 1958;**258**: 986–93.
24. US Department of Labor. Selected characteristics of occupations defined in the Dictionary of Occupational Titles. Washington: US Government Printing Office, 1981.
25. Karvonen MJ. Work and activity classification. In: Larson LA ed. Fitness, health and work capacity: international standards for assessment. New York: MacMillan, 1974.
26. Brammell HL. Early rehabilitation of the post infarction patient. In: Long C ed. Prevention and rehabilitation in ischemic heart disease. Baltimore: Williams & Wilkins, 1980.
27. Ellestad MH. Stress testing in ischemic heart disease. In: Long C ed. Prevention and rehabilitation in ischemic heart disease. Baltimore: Williams & Wilkins, 1980.
28. Mitchell DK. Principles of vocational rehabilitation: a contemporary view. In: Long C ed. Prevention and rehabilitation in ischemic heart disease. Baltimore: Williams & Wilkins, 1980.
29. Erb BD. Applying work physiology to occupational medicine. Occupational Health and Safety 1981;**50**:20–4.
30. Deacon SP, Congdon GJ. Rehabilitation after illness and injury—a study of temporary alternative work arrangements. J Soc Occup Med 1984;**34**:46–9.

2

Legal and administrative aspects

F. C. Edwards

INTRODUCTION

This chapter outlines some of the ways in which the law may affect the employment of people with a health problem and the services available to help patients obtain or return to work.

SOME LEGAL ASPECTS OF THE EMPLOYMENT OF 'DISABLED' PEOPLE

The common law

Common law is not enshrined in legislation, but has developed over the years mainly as a result of decisions of the courts in particular cases, based on previous precedents and case law. Under the general law of tort or civil wrongs, there is a duty of care on the employer to avoid injuring the employee, although the employer is not under an absolute duty to ensure safety and it is necessary to prove negligence. The employer's general duty is to each individual employee.

The following two cases illustrate how common law judgments may take account of disability and how disclosure of disability may affect the outcome. In 1951 Paris, who was blind in one eye and whose sound eye was injured at work as it was not protected by safety glasses, successfully brought an action against his employer, Stepney Borough Council.[1] The Council was judged negligent because, knowing that he was blind in one eye, it had not taken additional safety precautions for Paris to protect his remaining eye. In 1952 Cork sued his employer Kirby McLean Ltd following a fall from some stairs. Although the employer was held liable, damages were reduced by 50 per cent because the employee had not disclosed either that he was suffering from epilepsy or that he had been advised by his doctor not to work at heights.[2]

The Health and Safety at Work etc. Act, 1974[3]

The employer's responsibilities are more clearly defined in this Act, the culmination of over a century of legislation. The Health and Safety at Work

Act is superimposed on earlier Acts and the duties imposed by some of these (e.g. the Mines and Quarries Act, 1954; the Factories Act, 1961; and the Offices, Shops and Railway Premises Act, 1963) must still be met, although most of their enforcement provisions have been replaced in the new legislation.

The Health and Safety Commission (HSC) was set up by the Act as a tripartite body (Government, Confederation of British Industry (CBI), Trades Union Congress (TUC)) and is responsible for policy, while the Health and Safety Executive (HSE) is responsible for enforcing the Act's requirements. The Executive has several divisions, of which the largest is the Factory Inspectorate (HMFI). The Employment Medical Advisory Service (EMAS) is the field force of the medical division of HSE and will be described in the second section of this chapter.

The Act covers everyone at work, including the self-employed, but excludes domestic servants in private households. About 5 million people not covered by previous acts are now protected by legislation for the first time: these are people working mainly in services, such as primary, secondary, and further education, and in the health services.

Employers' duties

The Act imposes general duties on both employers and employees. Under Section 2, the employer has to ensure 'so far as is reasonably practicable' the health, safety, and welfare at work of all his employees, and must avoid putting at risk the health and safety of others through his work activities. The Act does not refer specifically to disabled employees, but applies equally to all employees, whatever their state of health.

The employer thus has a statutory duty under the Act to a disabled employee, assuming that the employer knows, or ought reasonably to have known, of the disability. The employer should assess any problems likely to arise from the disability and make proper arrangements to avoid risks or hazards, for example by taking certain precautions or allocating particular work. He therefore needs informed advice on an employee's health in jobs where some medical conditions might impose health and safety risks.

Employees' duties

Under Section 7, the employee, while at work, must take 'reasonable care' for the health and safety of himself and of other persons who may be affected by his acts or omissions at work. This duty could be taken to include disclosing a medical condition which he knew might have health and safety risks in the work in question although, apart from those jobs where statutory medical standards apply (see Chapter 1 and Appendices at the end of the book), there is no legal obligation to disclose matters of health to an employer or to a prospective employer. If, however, an employee failed to disclose that he had epilepsy, for instance, when working in a job where this could pose a hazard, he might be in breach of his statutory duty under Section 7 of the Health and Safety at Work Act. Although no prosecutions of this nature have apparently occurred under the Act, failure to disclose has been accepted in cases of alleged unfair dismissal under the Employment Protection Act.

Medical conditions should be disclosed if they might have health and safety implications in the work concerned; any possible risks may then be appraised by the employer so that he can make arrangements to reduce or abolish the risks. Concealment of a relevant disabling condition from the employer may also reduce the employer's responsibility in this context (see above *re* Cork and Kirby McLean).

Employment Protection Act

Existing employment protection legislation was incorporated into the Employment Protection (Consolidation) Act in 1978 and subsequent amendments.

Unfair dismissal

Every dismissal is presumed to be unfair and the onus is on the employer to justify it. Actions for unfair dismissal are heard by Industrial Tribunals. Employees have to fulfil certain requirements in order to bring such actions, the chief of which is continuous employment for two years in the job concerned.

The employer, as defendant in an action for unfair dismissal, must first show a fair reason for the dismissal and then that he acted reasonably. There are five fair reasons, the most important of which from the health point of view is capability. Ill health can be judged fair grounds for dismissal under the Act if an employee, because of his health problem, becomes incapable of carrying out his work; this could include cases where health and safety at work might be put at risk. Another fair reason is illegality, if, for example, the employee cannot continue to be employed in the work in question without contravening a statutory duty or restriction. Thus, if a patient lost his current driving licence because of a medical condition or for any other reason, he would not be able to continue driving at work and it would be illegal to continue to employ him as a driver.

Decisions of Industrial Tribunals do not have the power of the law, but judgments of the higher Employment Appeal Tribunals do have important effects on precedent. From Industrial and Employment Appeal Tribunal cases over the last few years it has become established that, to act reasonably in dismissing an employee on grounds of ill health, the employer should always discuss the problem with the employee and should obtain medical advice, usually through the patient's family practitioner, the company doctor, or a specialist, but always with the consent of the employee. If the employee refuses to let the employer approach his doctors, his subsequent dismissal is likely to be judged fair. If the employer has not discussed the case fully with the employee, the decision is likely to be judged unfair. The third step that should be taken is to offer the employee suitable alternative employment, if available. If this were not considered by management, this could make the dismissal unfair. For further discussion see Carter, 1986.[4]

Absence from work

Absence through sickness, especially if long-lasting or recurrent, may also occasionally be a fair reason for dismissal, if the employer is unable to find temporary replacement for the work and the work is vital to the business. Factors which have to be taken into account by tribunals are the nature of the illness, the likely length of the continuing absence, and the likelihood of a return to work in the near future. As in the previous paragraph, the employee should be warned, medical advice sought, and time allowed for improvement in attendance.

Many companies have a 'trigger' level of the total number of days of self-certified sickness absence, above which the employee is asked to see a doctor (usually his own doctor or the company's medical adviser) for a medical report. Continuing irregular sickness, even with medical certificates, may be judged a 'conduct' issue rather than a 'medical' issue by tribunals.

The Disabled Persons (Employment) Acts, 1944 and 1958

The main Act relating to the employment of disabled persons was introduced in 1944, amended in 1958, and is still in force. The background to the Act was mainly concern about disabled war veterans. During the 1914–18 war, Papworth Village Settlement was founded by Varrier-Jones so that disabled people could learn new work skills. Some government centres were then set up to retrain disabled veterans and these were taken over by the Ministry of Labour in 1919 as Government Training Centres. Employers were encouraged to provide work for disabled veterans by a national roll scheme introduced at about the same time. During the 1920s and 30s, blind and disabled civilians were admitted to the schemes and residential training colleges for the disabled were set up. During the 1939–45 war there was a further emphasis on retraining civilian disabled people to help the war effort. In the armed forces, particularly in the Royal Air Force, it became vital to intensify medical rehabilitation for highly skilled servicemen so that they could return to action as soon as possible after injury.

The Act was based on the report of the Tomlinson Committee (1943). The main principles which the Tomlinson Committee established were:

(1) the majority of disabled people are capable of working on their own merit in the ordinary job market given careful assessment of their capacity, matching of jobs and individuals, and the right support; and

(2) only a minority of disabled people, because of the severity of their disability, are capable only of work under special (sheltered) conditions.

The 1944 Act aimed to help disabled people to get and keep suitable jobs. It:

(1) established a register of disabled people for employment;

(2) established a framework for the provision of vocational rehabilitation, training, and resettlement services for disabled people;

(3) placed certain duties and obligations on employers concerning the employment of registered disabled people;

(4) provided for sheltered employment opportunities to be made available for severely disabled people; and

(5) established a National Advisory Council and local Disablement Advisory Committees to advise and assist the Secretary of State for Employment on matters relating to the employment and training of disabled people.

These provisions are described in the rest of this chapter.

Tomlinson recommended three main measures to help disabled people find suitable work:

1. Industrial Rehabilitation Units were to be set up to assess and overcome the individual's handicaps, to include individual assessment and a certain amount of reconditioning and restoring physical function, following the end of medical treatment or rehabilitation. Further specialist training for disabled people was to be made available and a specialized placing service was proposed.

2. Disabled people were to be integrated into the normal workforce wherever possible, with the help of a quota scheme and a voluntary register.

3. Those too severely disabled to work in open employment were to have special provision in sheltered workshops and some reserved designated occupations.

Underlying the recommendations was the proposal that rehabilitation back to work, after medical treatment, should be provided by the Ministry of Labour. The employment rehabilitation and resettlement services have subsequently developed apart from the National Health Service; this means that a positive act of referral has to made from the health to the employment services.

Definition of a disabled person

The Act provided a definition of a disabled person for employment purposes, that is someone who 'on account of injury, disease or congenital deformity, is substantially handicapped in obtaining or keeping employment . . . of a kind which, apart from the injury, disease or deformity would be suited to his age, experience and qualifications.' The disability must be likely to last at least 12 months and the person must want, and have a reasonable prospect of obtaining and keeping, some form of paid employment and have reached the statutory school-leaving age. This definition also applies to those eligible for some of the services provided and to those who choose to register as disabled with the Department of Employment, while further clauses apply to those suitable only for sheltered work.

CURRENT SERVICE FOR DISABLED PEOPLE

Although the Disabled Persons (Employment) Act, 1944 outlined above is still in force, there have been many changes both in the services provided under the Act and in the departments responsible for them. Responsibility originally lay with the Ministry of Labour until, in 1970, this became the Department of Employment (DE). The Employment and Training Act, 1973 established the Manpower Services Commission (MSC), which became responsible for the public employment and training services, including those intended for disabled people (except for the Careers Service and the Employment Medical Advisory Service). The Manpower Services Commission, like the Health and Safety Commission, is separate from government but is answerable to the Secretary of State for Employment and to the Secretaries of State for Scotland and Wales. In October 1987 responsibility for employment services (including jobcentres, restart courses, sheltered employment, and services for the disabled other than the employment rehabilitation programme) was returned to the Department of Employment. The Manpower Services Commission kept responsibility for rehabilitation and training services. Access to these services is primarily through the DE's jobcentres, which are supported by area and regional management structures and by policy branches at DE's and MSC's head offices in Sheffield and London.

Disabled people are able to benefit from the full range of MSC's employment and training services. In addition, there are a number of specialist types of assistance intended for those disabled people whose employment problems are significantly different from those of their able-bodied counterparts. The main ones are described below.

The Disablement Resettlement Officer Service

The keystone of the provisions introduced at the end of the last war is the Disablement Resettlement Officer (DRO). Based in jobcentres, the DRO places job seekers with disabilities and arranges for assessment, employment rehabilitation, and/or training if needed. Disablement Resettlement Officers are responsible for administering the Quota Scheme and maintaining the Register of Disabled Persons. There are also Blind Persons Resettlement Officers (BPRO) and a small number who work at hospitals (Hospital Resettlement Officers). In 1982 MSC reviewed its services to disabled people[5] and DROs now provide help to those disabled people who require specialist occupational counselling and advice and those who have particular difficulties in finding employment because of the effects of their disability. People with disabilities whose needs are similar to other jobseekers are helped by mainstream jobcentre staff. A Disablement Advisory Service (DAS), with teams throughout the country to advise employers on employing people with disabilities, was established in 1983.

The Disablement Resettlement Officer (DRO) obtains medical advice about clients in confidence from the Regional Medical Service, from hospital doctors if there has been recent hospital treatment, or from Employment Medical Advisers. For help with work placement, rehabilitation, or training, doctors should refer their patients direct to the DRO: contact can be made by telephoning the nearest jobcentre. Where specific medical advice is needed on health and work, patients may be referred directly to the Employment Medical Advisory Service: contact may be made by telephoning the nearest Health and Safety Executive office. The Disablement Resettlement Officer, however, is the main entry point to many of the services, schemes, and other facilities outlined below.

The Register of Disabled Persons

This voluntary register was set up under the 1944 Act, to help disabled people obtain employment. Disabled people who wish to apply to register should get in touch with their local jobcentre. Both those in employment and those seeking employment may register. Those wishing to register must fit the definition of a disabled person and the other eligibility conditions, quoted on p. 30.

There is normally no charge to the disabled person for registering and the DE pays the cost of Regional Medical Service examinations to supply supporting medical evidence if needed. Hospital medical staff do not charge for providing medical evidence but, if the patient has not had recent hospital treatment and is unable to attend the Regional Medical Service, he may prefer to obtain the medical evidence from his own family practitioner. In this case a charge is usually made by the practitioner to the patient, as this is outside his NHS duties and DE has no arrangement for paying family practitioners for this. A certificate of registration (the green card) will be issued by the DRO if the criteria are fulfilled; the certificate is valid for a minimum of one year and a maximum of 10 years.

Advantages of registration

1. All employers with 20 or more workers have a duty to employ a proportion of registered disabled people ('the Quota'—see below).

2. Vacancies for car-park attendants and passenger electric-lift attendants are reserved for registered disabled people ('designated employment').

3. Employment in sheltered workshops is generally reserved for registered disabled people who are very severely handicapped.

4. Registered disabled people may also obtain help under some special schemes as outlined below.

Despite these advantages, however, the number registering has declined from a maximum of around one million in 1950 and is now under half a million. The reluctance on the part of many disabled persons to register may imply that they do not see any advantages in registering and/or that they do not consider themselves to be disabled. Many of those eligible for registration refuse to accept a green card, feeling that this implies a degree of social stigma. Another possible reason for the fall in numbers of those choosing to register is the improvement in employment protection legislation. The changes that have occurred in the distribution and type of disabling and other medical conditions in those of working age since the Second World War must also have contributed to this decline.

The Quota Scheme

Employers with 20 or more employees have a statutory duty to employ at least 3 per cent registered disabled people (the Quota). However, as the numbers on the register have declined to under half a million, employers are expected to comply with an impracticable duty. Several rounds of discussion and consultation have taken place in the last 10 years on both the Quota Scheme and the Register. At the time of writing, both are unchanged.

Code of Good Practice on the Employment of Disabled People

This was published by the Manpower Service Commission in 1984.[6] It is a non-statutory code for employers that suggests objectives, contains examples of good practice, and gives specific and practical advice on the help and schemes available. Local Disablement Advisory Service teams are promoting the code throughout the country.

Special schemes from the Manpower Services Commission

The following special schemes are available through either the Disablement Resettlement Officer or the Disablement Advisory Service:

1. *Adaptations to premises and equipment.* Grants are available to employers to enable essential adaptations to be undertaken to help them recruit or retain a given disabled person. Widening doorways, and adding ramps, special toilet facilities, hoists or lifts, and special fitments to standard equipment are some examples. The employees do not need to be registered.

2. *Special aids to employment.* Special equipment is provided free to individual registered disabled persons on permanent loan, if it is needed by the person to obtain or to keep employment. Examples include purpose-built desks, benches or seats, electric typewriters, telephone amplifiers, and reading and writing aids. Among the aids provided under this scheme is a variety of sophisticated equipment for the blind and partially sighted.

3. *Assistance with fares to work.* This is available only to registered disabled people who are unable to use public transport and incur extra costs in getting to work as a result. Financial assistance is given towards the cost of private transport (usually taxi fares) and is obtainable through the DRO.

4. *The Job Introduction Scheme.* This is available to any disabled person. Under this scheme a weekly payment is made by MSC to employers to help contribute towards the wages of a disabled person for a trial period, usually of about six weeks. Entry to the scheme is usually through the DRO. The scheme is used when employers have reasonable reservations about the disabled person's ability to do the job but the DRO considers him to be suitable. The trial period gives the disabled person the chance to prove his suitability for the job.

5. *Personal Reader Service.* Financial aid may be available for certain visually handicapped people toward the cost of a part-time, sighted reader to help them at work.

Sheltered employment

Disabled people who seek help from the DE's jobcentres in finding work are classified as either 'Section I' or 'Section II', irrespective of whether they are registered under the 1944 Act. Section I disabled people are considered to be suitable for open employment. Those whom the Disablement Resettlement Officer considers to be so severely disabled that they are unlikely to obtain, or keep, a job other than under sheltered conditions, are classified as Section II. Only Section II registered disabled people are eligible to receive support under the Sheltered Employment Programme (Remploy factories, sheltered workshops, and Sheltered Placement Scheme). In deciding the appropriate classification, DROs take into account up-to-date medical advice on the severity of the disability, the employment record, and the results of efforts to find a job for the individual.

The Sheltered Employment Programme currently provides work under sheltered conditions for some 17 400 severely disabled people who are unable to obtain and retain jobs in open employment. Employment is available in 225 sheltered workshops and factories run by local authorities, voluntary bodies, and Remploy, and in placements under the Sheltered Placement Scheme. Financial support is provided by the DE.

Many people working in sheltered conditions are mentally handicapped or have long-standing psychiatric disabilities. Other disability groups that benefit from sheltered employment are the very severely physically handicapped, and those severely disabled by cerebal palsy, spina bifida, or epilepsy.

Sheltered Placement Scheme

The Sheltered Placement Scheme, previously known as Sheltered Industrial Groups, currently provides some 3000 places for severely disabled people to work alongside the able-bodied, either singly, or in small groups. A sponsor (either a local authority, a voluntary organization, or Remploy) employs the disabled person and pays the wages and National Insurance contributions. The host firm provides the work and any equipment necessary and pays the sponsor for the work done, this payment being based on the actual work output. DE contributes financially towards the remaining cost of the sponsorship. The Sheltered Placement Scheme is only available to registered disabled people who cannot compete for jobs in the open labour market. Enquiries should be made through the DRO.

Advisory bodies

The 1944 Act established national and local statutory bodies to advise and assist the Secretary of State for Employment on matters related to the employment of disabled people.

The National Advisory Council on Employment of Disabled People

This body advises on national policy issues and on the development of programmes to assist the employment and training of disabled people. The Chairman and members, of whom there are 24, are drawn from both sides of industry, the medical profession, and disabled people's organizations.

Committees for the Employment of Disabled People

Under the 1944 Act, about 200 Disablement Advisory Committees were set up throughout the country, to help with local problems and with individual disabled people in the district concerned. They were replaced in 1981 by a smaller number of Committees for the Employment of Disabled People and their roles were re-defined. There are now 86 of these committees that survey the employment-related needs of disabled people and local provision for them, stimulate needed developments in the services, encourage publicity and marketing, and deal with individual problems. Independent chairmen are appointed by the Department of Employment and the committees have up to 12 members drawn from employers and employees, the local authority, the medical profession, and disabled people's organizations. Each committee is encouraged to develop appropriate policies for its own area.

The Employment Rehabilitation Service

There are 27 Employment Rehabilitation Centres (ERCs) in Great Britain. The first centre was opened in 1943 and the service includes two residential centres, one in the south and one in the north of England, that can cater for people unable to attend on a daily basis for geographical or other reasons. Originally known as Industrial Rehabilitation Units, 17 of the centres are sited near skillcentres (formerly Government Training Centres) in industrial areas.

Each centre offers assessment, employment rehabilitation, and jobsearch training, depending upon each client's requirements. Assessment of needs and capabilities involves the use of psychometric and work-sampling tests as well as health assessment. If rehabilitation in the form of simulated workshop or commercial experience is required to improve confidence and capability, the client will move to an ERC section or undertake a work placement with an employer. If it is felt that the client needs more specific help, e.g. with jobsearch techniques, this element only will be provided. The staff include occupational psychologists, social workers, rehabilitation instructional officers for assessment, training, and supervision; resettlement officers, as well as medical and nursing staff; thus health advice is available in each centre.

Referral to an ERC is usually arranged through the DRO, although ways of expanding the sources of referral are being studied. A direct medical referral route was introduced in 1980; doctors in general or hospital practice may refer their patients to the doctor at the ERC, in strict medical confidence.

The length of a course at an ERC varies according to the client's needs. Assessment may last up to two weeks. If a rehabilitation course is to follow, this may extend the stay to 6–7 weeks depending on the client's rate of progress. Clients with more serious conditions may need to stay longer (up to six months). About 14 000 people attended ERCs during 1986–87, the majority of them (90 per cent) with health problems or disabilities. Most courses are full-time, although there are arrangements for patients still undergoing hospital treatment to attend part-time courses at some centres.

Recent developments in employment rehabilitation

The system has become more flexible over the last few years, particularly following a review of the service published in 1981, which made specific recommendations.[7] Following this review and a trial of the suggested developments, another MSC report in 1984 proposed further measures to improve the effectivenss of the service.[8] One of the main proposals was that, in areas of the country where no ERC existed, a community service should be set up on a pilot basis to undertake vocational assessment and jobsearch training, with practical experience for clients gained through attachments with local employers. This new approach is named Assistance towards Employment (ASSET) and, if the three pilot ASSET centres are successful, it may be adopted in other areas. Health input to these teams is at present provided by doctors and nurses from the Employment Medical Advisory Service.

A more recent internal Development Report produced in July 1987 has outlined the way forward for the Employment Rehabilitation Service. The main recommendations are that there will be more emphasis on assessment, improved geographical coverage, and a move away from the institutionalized image of ERCs. This will be achieved in various ways. Mobile assessment facilities, operating from ERCs or ASSET centres (already available in the South West and North Wales) will be encouraged throughout the network. Free-standing assessment and counselling teams will also be set up. Work placements with local employers will be expanded along the lines of those run at ASSET centres and some ERCs. Other aspects of rehabilitation will be more tailored to individual requirements.

In addition to provision of ERCs and ASSET centres, the MSC gives financial support to a small number of voluntary bodies and local authorities which act as agencies for employment rehabilitation. These agencies cater for groups of clients with specialized needs (blind, cerebral palsied, mentally ill, for example). The main bodies supported in this way are the Royal National Institute for the Blind (RNIB), the Spastics Society and some smaller bodies in the mental health field. MSC is currently considering an expansion of this form of employment rehabilitation to help clients with special needs in a wider geographical area.

Reorganization

Under the reorganization of DE and MSC, the employment rehabilitation service remains with MSC. However, instead of employment rehabilitation facilities being managed by MSC regional management, head office will take over responsibility for both policy and the operation of the service. The link between head office and ERC, ASSET, and other local staff will be through a divisional manager appointed in each region to develop and manage assessment and rehabilitation services.

Medical services at ERCs

Formerly provided by family practitioners, the medical input to employment rehabilitation is now provided almost entirely by EMAS, with part-time medical and full-time nursing services to 26 of the 27 ERCs. The Employment Medical Adviser at the centre, apart from his appraisal of the client's health and its relation to occupation, particularly from the health and safety aspect, establishes links with family practitioners, hospital staff, and occupational physicians in the area. Wherever possible, medical students and family practitioners in vocational training schemes are encouraged to visit the centres to learn more about this often neglected aspect of their medical work. In a similar way, the ERC nurse is a link with occupational health nurses and other nurses.

On the basis of medical evidence submitted with the client's application (usually one of the DP forms has been completed by a hospital doctor, the regional medical service, or the general practitioner) and following a preliminary health screening by the ERC nurse, the Employment Medical Adviser will assess the client and may contact the client's family or hospital doctor for further information and advice. All medical records are kept in strict confidence in the medical department of the centre and are not seen by lay staff. However, the client has signed a release form agreeing that advice related to his medical condition can be passed on to help his employment assessment and return to work: only occupationally relevant aspects of the medical condition need to be passed on to other ERC staff. An ERC assessment is particularly useful when a patient is unable to return to his former job because of recent illness, injury, or operation.

The Employment Medical Advisory Service (EMAS)

This service was set up as an independent medical advisory service under the EMAS Act of 1972 but since the Health and Safety Executive (HSE) was established in 1974 under the HSAW Act, EMAS has been the field force of the Medical Division of the Health and Safety Executive. EMAS has about 100 doctors and nurses in the field, backed up by specialist medical and nursing support at head office.

EMAS medical and nursing staff are based at HSE offices throughout Great Britain and provide an open access service whose main objectives are to prevent ill health related to work or the work environment, and to advise on medical suitability for work. This latter aspect (the effects of health on work) means that EMAS staff are available to give a specialist opinion on

medical suitability for work to employers and employees, to trade unions, to
the Manpower Services Commission and its clients, to any individual in or
seeking employment, to doctors and their patients, and to young people.

EMAS doctors and nurses are trained in occupational health. EMAS work
includes regular health supervision of people working on hazardous processes; special studies or investigations of suspected hazards or populations
at risk; advising on the development of occupational health services;
approving and monitoring the training of first aiders at work; advising on
medical aspects of fitness for work and training of school-leavers, clients at
rehabilitation or training centres, other clients referred by the Manpower
Services Commission, and employees in a wide variety of industries.
Altogether EMAS undertakes about 20 000 examinations each year of this
nature (medical suitability for work), either in EMAS offices or in the medical
departments of the Employment Rehabilitation Centres, Asset Centres, or
Skillcentres.

EMAS staff co-operate closely with the Disablement Resettlement Officers
of the Manpower Services Commission, and EMAS also provides medical
and nursing services to the MSC's Employment Rehabilitation Centres
(ERCs), which assess and prepare people for starting or returning to work
after injury, illness, or unemployment. Employment Medical Advisers at
ERCs can take direct referrals of patients from their doctors, if a quick
assessment is needed. Doctors working in industry may also find this direct
medical referral system useful if an employee needs an assessment for
alternative work.

Although some employers have their own occupational health services to
advise them, the majority of employers, particularly in small firms, do not
have access to such services and may need to call on EMAS for advice. Any
employer might be faced with the need to re-introduce a key employee to
work after a serious illness or accident, for example. Too few employers yet
have a systematic approach to getting specialist advice in this area and
EMAS encourages them to make arrangements for doing so.

To help employers, the Health and Safety Executive has published a
guidance note which advises on when pre-employment health screening may
be useful and examines the objectives and the principles of such screening.[9]
Disabled people and medical practitioners needing advice on any aspect of
fitness for work, and employers needing advice on any aspect of the
employment of disabled people can contact their nearest EMAS office.
Regional and area EMAS offices are listed in the telephone directory under
Health and Safety Executive.

The Careers Service

Under the Employment and Training Act, 1973, each local education
authority (LEA) is required to provide vocational guidance and a placement

service for young people in schools and in further education, apart from universities. After leaving school young people can choose whether to use the Careers Service and/or jobcentres for help to find work. Most choose the Careers Service.[10]

In exercising this responsibility, each local education authority in England and Wales and each education authority in Scotland is subject to the general guidance of the Secretaries of State for Employment, for Wales, and for Scotland respectively. Statutory guidance is issued to authorities from the respective departments. The Careers Service is funded mainly through the rate support grant, with additional 'Strengthening Scheme' funding from central government. The Department of Employment's Careers Service Branch provides guidance and advice to local education authorities and Careers Service staff, and obtains information about the performance of the Careers Service. There is, however, no direct line management from central government since Careers Service staff are employed by the local education authorities. Inspection and monitoring of performance of services in England is carried out from seven regional offices. These Careers Service Inspectors are Department of Employment staff and work in close association with the Inspectors of Schools from the Department of Education and Science. Similar arrangements apply in Wales and Scotland.

Handicapped young people

The organization of each Careers Service varies according to the local authority concerned. Some authorities offer a general service, whereby all careers officers have responsibility for disabled or handicapped youngsters, but most local education authorities have careers officers who specialize in work with young people who have special employment needs, including those caused by medical conditions. Additional training in the occupational implications of disabilities as well as in other aspects of disability is given. There are about 200 specialist careers officers in post in Great Britain. The professional training of careers officers is the responsibility of the Local Government Training Board.

Careers officers, particularly the specialist careers officers, liaise with the School Medical Service and the Employment Medical Advisory Service (EMAS). Before they leave school, children with a disability or medical condition that may affect their suitability for some jobs are notified by the school medical officer on a standard form (Y9) to the Employment Medical Adviser, the local careers officer and their general practitioner; a more detailed form (Y10) is used for young people with more severe conditions. Referral varies widely in effectiveness throughout the country and alternative arrangements have been under discussion for some time.

Under the Factories Act, 1961 employers are required to notify the careers officer within seven days of taking on a young person under the age of 18. This is done on form F2404. If the careers officer, after matching up this form with a previously issued Y9 or Y10, thinks that the young person is in an occupation that may be hazardous or unsuitable, he will contact EMAS and/or the employer and the young person. The F2404 system is also under discussion at present.

Further education

On the UCCA application form for university entrance there is a section for further information which includes: '(d) Physical or other disabilities which might necessitate special arrangements or facilities (see UCCA handbook).' The relevant paragraph of that handbook includes the following: 'If you have a physical or other disability you should write well in advance of completing the UCCA form to your preferred universities indicating the courses in which you are interested, the nature and extent of your disability and any special needs that you may have. Your application will be considered on the same academic criteria as that of any other applicant, but universities will need to know in advance the degree of any disability so that they can discuss special provision with you.' Advice concerning facilities for disabled students in universities is available from the National Bureau for Handicapped Students, 40 Brunswick Square, London WC1N 1AZ. Certain universities specialize in supplementary provision for particular types of disability and further education colleges can make special arrangements.

Handicapped students

The work of the National Bureau for Handicapped Students   The National Bureau for Handicapped Students (NBHS) was set up in 1975. It is a voluntary organization based in London, but with a regional network, and is concerned with developing opportunities in further, higher, and adult education and training for handicapped people. Its work covers the whole range of handicap, whether physical, sensory, or learning difficulty.

Its activities include: *Information and advice service to students*: enquiries on admission to college; special provision; financial assistance. *Information service to colleges*: enquiries on admission policies; curriculum development; resources. *Monitoring policy*: submission of evidence to central government on all issues affecting handicapped people in education and training, e.g. Youth Training Scheme. *Encouraging good practice*: by establishing effective links with colleges of further, higher, and adult education; collecting examples of good practice. *Education and information*: by publications and by regional and national conferences and seminars.

A number of specialist careers officers have regular contact with either national or regional offices of the NBHS. Membership of the organization is open to any institution, concern, or individual with an interest in its work.[11]

Youth Training Scheme (YTS)

Special help for young people with disabilities

The Youth Training Scheme (YTS) offers young school-leavers a planned programme of vocational training and work experience, providing an opportunity to gain—or work towards—a relevant vocational qualification. Sixteen-year-old school-leavers can receive two years of training, and 17-year-old leavers one year. By April 1988 every provider of YTS training must have achieved full status as an Approved Training Organization, according to MSC criteria.

For the purposes of YTS, young people with disabilities are defined as those who 'suffer from a physical, mental or sensory handicap, and/or have moderate or severe learning difficulties which put them at a substantial disadvantage in the labour market'. This definition includes those with moderate or severe learning difficulties and the crucial point is whether or not the young person has such difficulties, not how they are caused. This is broader than the definition of disability in the 1944 Employment Act used in adult training.

A range of special help is currently available for young people with disabilities on YTS:

(1) relaxed eligibility criteria to enable them to enter YTS up to the age of 21 without losing entitlement to two years of training;

(2) extension of training by up to six months if necessary to enhance employment prospects;

(3) pre-YTS assessment courses lasting up to 13 weeks (included in the six-month extension of training);

(4) Permanent Additional Funding for the Disabled, an extra grant paid in respect of each eligible trainee to cover the cost of specialized training programmes tailored to individual needs;

(5) Special Aids to Employment scheme, providing long-term loans of specialized tools and equipment;

(6) Adaptations to Premises and Equipment scheme, providing a contribution towards the cost of adaptations to the premises of providers of training or work-experience;

(7) Personal Reader Service for the Blind, providing funding for a sighted reader for blind or visually impaired trainees;

(8) Communication Service for the Deaf, providing funding for communicators, lip-speakers, or note-takers for deaf or hearing-impaired trainees;

(9)   Special Residential Allowance to cover the additional costs of providing specialized accommodation and medical supervision for those who need residential care while training.

The special help outlined above is intended to enable young people with disabilities to train alongside their peers in mainstream programmes wherever possible. For those who would find this difficult, however, places are provided on schemes specializing in the training of young people with disabilities.

The MSC estimates that a significant minority of YTS trainees (maybe up to 20 per cent) are in some way *disadvantaged* and/or *disabled*. In the light of this, current provision for these young people is being evaluated and a major strategy developed to allow training-providers to design flexible training programmes catering for each individual young person's special needs. The results of this initiative will be considered in the review of YTS funding, which is being undertaken by MSC's Youth Training Board. One of the five main areas on which the review is concentrating is training provision for the most disadvantaged, including young people with disabilities. It is hoped that any recommendations from the review that are accepted by government will be implemented in 1988.

Training provision for adults with disabilities

The following paragraphs outline some of the training schemes available for disabled people at the time of writing this chapter. In 1987, however, MSC started to undertake a major review of its training schemes. Furture schemes may well be different therefore, but provision for people with disabilities will always be available and doctors should remember that the best point of entry to any scheme is likely to be through the *Disablement Resettlement Officer* (DRO) at the nearest jobcentre.

MSC's job training schemes

The new scheme, started in 1987, is the MSC's major adult training initiative. Intended to help any adult who has been signing on as unemployed at an unemployment benefit office for at least six months, the scheme offers purpose-made training programmes, so that training can be linked to the individual's needs and abilities. Every programme contains practical experience in the workplace with the use of structured work-based learning and a range of other flexible training methods, such as open learning. Apart from this, the old Job Traning Scheme and other schemes still continue and are outlined below.

The majority of adults with disabilities train on MSC programmes alongside able-bodied people without any special arrangements or relaxations of eligibility rules. In addition to the new Job Training Scheme, the MSC's adult training programmes are the old Job Training Scheme, the Wider Opportunities Training Programme, and Training for Enterprise.

Within these programmes, provision ranges from preparatory courses offering help with literacy and numeracy to higher level courses such as computing and management skills. There are also courses for people wishing to become self-employed or to set up their own small business. Training can take place in skillcentres, colleges of further education, private colleges, and employers' establishments.

The old Job Training Scheme and Wider Opportunities Training Programme may relax certain of their eligibility rules for people with disabilities. Again, the Disablement Resettlement Officer in the local jobcentre will have further details.

Individual training throughout with an employer

This scheme allows individuals with disabilities to train with an employer. In this way training can be tailored to meet the needs of the trainee. The scheme aims to provide training which will equip trainees with a skill or semi-skill which is transferable from one place of employment to another. As an employer must undertake to employ a trainee for a period of at least six months after the training period, the scheme can also lead to long-term employment.

Although the training period normally lasts from four weeks to 12 months, longer periods can be considered. While training, the trainee receives either wages or a Job Training Scheme allowance. If the trainee is receiving wages, MSC can pay the employer a training fee equivalent to the basic old Job Training Scheme allowance, which will decrease as the trainee becomes more skilled and receives more wages. Similarly, if the trainee is receiving a training allowance from MSC, this will decrease over time and the employer will be expected to make up the difference.

In addition, off-the-job training costs can be negotiated. Finally, trainees may also be eligible for Special Aids to Employment.

Release for Training Scheme

Under the Release for Training Scheme, MSC support can be provided for disabled people who are already in employment but who are experiencing difficulties which can only be resolved by a period of essential training.

Two categories of disabled people are eligible for support under the scheme:

(1) an employee who becomes disabled and who requires training as part of the rehabilitation process in order to stay with an employer;

(2)   a disabled employee whose career development or further progression with the employer can only be assisted by a period of essential training.

A training fee can be paid by MSC to the employer which will be equivalent to the weekly flat rate Job Training Scheme allowance. If a training fee is paid, the employer must undertake to continue to employ the trainee for at least six months after the period of training. The cost of training outside the employer's premises (e.g. at RNIB Colleges etc.) will be met by MSC. Throughout the training period, the employer must continue to pay wages to the employee.

Professional Training Scheme

Under the Professional Training Scheme disabled people of suitable ability may receive help to meet the cost of courses of higher level study, including university degree courses, for employment at a professional level.

The scheme is meant to help people with disabilities who have been unable to get a local education authority (LEA) grant. MSC will consider part-funding of courses under this scheme, depending on the individual circumstances of the applicant.

The Professional Training Scheme differs from other MSC schemes in that it pays a grant which is based on the rate laid down by the Department of Education and Science for students. Training must be vocational and equip trainees with the skills needed to enter employment in their chosen field. Courses which have been sponsored include accountancy, law, physiotherapy (for partly sighted people), systems analysis, and for the certificate of qualification in social work.

Residential training colleges for people with disabilities

Four residential training colleges cater for all types of disability except blindness in an age range of 16–58. There is also provision for residential training for visually handicapped and hearing-impaired trainees at special residential centres. The training available at the Royal National Institute for the Blind Commercial Training Centre in London covers the skills needed for employment in the clerical and secretarial fields. For hearing-impaired trainees there are courses run by the Doncaster School for the Deaf which cover a wide range of skills from commercial to industrial, including catering. These courses are open to applicants from the age of 16 onwards.

The four residential training colleges for people with disabilities are:

- Finchale Training College, Durham DH1 5RZ (Tel. Durham (0385) 62634);

- Portland Training College for the Disabled, Nottingham Road, Mansfield, Notts NG18 4TJ (Tel. Mansfield (0623) 792141-2);

- Queen Elizabeth's Training College, Leatherhead Court, Leatherhead, Surrey KT22 OBN (Tel. Oxshott (037 284) 2204);

- St. Loye's College for Training the Disabled for Commerce and Industry, Fairfield House, Topsham Road, Exeter, Devon EX2 6EP (Tel. Exeter (0392) 55428).

These colleges are run by voluntary organizations with support from MSC. There is a wide range of courses on offer, including clerical and secretarial, engineering, electronics, and horticulture.

The following establishments also provide residential training:

- Royal National Institute for the Blind (RNIB), Commercial Training College, London;

- Royal National Institute for the Blind, North London School of Physiotherapy;

- Royal National Institute for the Deaf, Abbotskerswell, Devon;

- Occupational Training for the Visually Handicapped, at Letchworth Skillcentre;

- Royal National College for the Blind, Hereford;

- Queen Alexandra College for the Blind, Birmingham;

- Doncaster College for the Deaf (ex Yorkshire Residential School for the Deaf).

Disabled Persons Liaison Officers

A Disabled Persons Liaison Officer can be found at each of MSC's Training Division's 55 Area Offices, covering all of England, Scotland, and Wales. Apart from his other duties, for instance he may be the office manager, the officer should:

(1) be able to advise on enquiries about MSC's training provision for adults and young people in the area;

(2) act as a point of contact for other interested professional bodies and voluntary organizations on matters concerning the training provision for adults and young people within the area;

(3) monitor the numbers of young disabled people joining YTS in that area to ensure that they receive a fair share of the provision in that area— MSC is committed to a policy of equal opportunity for all young people entering the scheme, including the disabled, and is regularly monitoring the effectiveness of its policy, both locally and nationally.

The Community Programme (CP)

This is one of the principal schemes to help long-term unemployed people. It aims to provide temporary jobs of up to a year's duration usually, on projects which will make a significant contribution towards improving the employment prospects of participants and will create something of practical benefit to the community. Jobs are part-time or full-time and aim to provide unemployed people with valuable work experience and re-introduce them to the habits and disciplines of working life.

Places on the Community Programme are open to people who have been continuously unemployed for at least 12 months and are in receipt of an appropriate state benefit. In the case of disabled people, both registered and unregistered, the qualifying period of unemployment is reduced to six months.

Those employed on the CP receive a weekly wage based on the local rate for the same, or broadly similar work.

The types of project operated under CP include environmental improvement, energy efficiency, advice and information, and arts and cultural projects. Other projects provide services for particular groups of people, including the elderly, children and young people, and the disabled.

Voluntary Organizations

In addition to the extensive and complex government services described above, the role of voluntary organizations in assisting people with disabilities has always been outstanding in the United Kingdom. The links between central and local government and voluntary bodies in the provision of sheltered employment have already been noted. They also co-operate in providing residential accommodation and training. An example of this is the Queen Elizabeth's Foundation for the Disabled, one of whose main establishments, the Queen Elizabeth's Training College, offers a number of courses sponsored by the Manpower Services Commission (see p. 45).

The voluntary organizations have other important roles in a number of ways. Such organizations fall into two broad groups, those that are concerned with the welfare of people with any type of disability and those that relate to specific disabilities. There are several hundred voluntary bodies in the UK that are concerned with helping to deal with the various problems and needs of disabled people and it is impossible to mention more than a few here. The addresses of those that are mentioned are in Appendix 5.

Groups concerned with disability in general
Such groups can offer advice, information, and help on a number of aspects that can affect people with disabilities. These include education, employment,

access and safety, housing, equipment, aids to daily living and to mobility, and help with many other problems. Some of the general organizations are in close touch with government and have an important influence on many aspects of government policy relating to disablement, including benefits and welfare.

Royal Association for Disability and Rehabilitation (RADAR)   This influential organization was formed in 1977 from the merger of the British Council for the Rehabilitation of the Disabled and the Central Council for the Disabled. It acts as a co-ordinating body for many of the voluntary groups serving disabled people. RADAR is also a source of information, help and advice, publishing two journals—*The Bulletin* (published monthly for 11 months of the year with the exception of January) and *Contact* (a quarterly magazine). *The Bulletin* circulates information on legal and parliamentary developments, access, conferences and courses, sport and leisure activities, and housing, and provides information on RADAR's own campaigns. An employment committee has been examining aspects of the employment of disabled people in recent years. The *Employers' guide to disabilities* was published by RADAR in 1982 to commemorate the International Year of Disabled People. This useful guide for employers outlines the points about a number of common disabilities that employers might need to know. It was updated in 1985 and a second edition was published in 1986.[12] The *Directory for disabled people*,[11] published in association with RADAR, is a comprehensive reference book covering statutory and other services, education and employment, housing, legislation, and other subjects. It is now in its fourth edition (1985).

The Disabled Living Foundation (DLF)   A renowned information and advisory service, the Disabled Living Foundation provides a comprehensive service on many aspects of disability, particularly in respect of adaptations and aids and equipment. Although employment aspects are not primary to the Foundation, it can advise employers and others on how to help disabled people at work, and deals with a number of enquiries about employment.[13] The Foundation, a charitable trust that is concerned with both physical and mental disabilities and multiple handicaps, is particularly expert on all aspects of ordinary daily living and some of its studies have contributed towards advances in the design of equipment and housing, and to the solution of practical problems. Local authorities and others throughout the country can use the information service, and the Foundation's aids centre in London provides a continuously updated exhibition of aids of many varieties.

Opportunities for the Disabled   This organization was established in 1980 by a group of employers in the City of London to ensure that disabled jobseekers were given a fair chance of recruitment into open employment. The aim is to help people with disabilities to get appropriate jobs and also to provide a service to employers, including advice and guidance on special equipment. The organization has developed remarkably in the last few years and now has over 10 regional offices throughout England, as well as its headquarters in the City. It produces regular newsletters, and information and advice are available. One of the ways in which Opportunities has developed has been to operate with the help of people on secondment from various employers, thus creating a two-way link between the organization and employers. Special seminars and conferences are arranged from time to time and the organization is a remarkable example of the way in which goodwill, effort, and a practical approach can help in this particular field.

The National Council for Voluntary Organizations (NCVO) Wide-ranging information is available through the NCVO. Selective lists of publications are available and these cover bibliographies, central and local government, charities and voluntary organizations, education and employment, finance, health and housing, legal aspects and social welfare, and advice and transport. Information can be obtained on a number of different voluntary organizations.

Specific disability groups

Many of these exist and the number is growing. They provide a very useful source of support, help, practical advice, and influence on behalf of the patients concerned. Two of the oldest are the Royal National Institutes for the Blind and for the Deaf. Appendix 5 gives details of some of these groups.

ACKNOWLEDGEMENTS

With acknowledgement to the many colleagues in the Health and Safety Executive, the Department of Employment, and the Manpower Services Commission for their help with Chapters 1 and 2 and particularly for information about the changes in the government services outlined. These were correct in October 1987.

REFERENCES

1. *Paris* v. *Stepney Borough Council* (1951) AC 367, 1 All ER 42.
2. *Cork* v. *Kirby McLean* (1952) 2 All ER 402.
3. Health and Safety at Work etc. Act, 1974, c. 37. London: HMSO, 1974.
4. Carter T. Health and safety at work: implications of current legislation. In: Edwards FC, Espir MLE, Oxley J, eds. Epilepsy and employment. International Congress and Symposium Series no. 86. London: Royal Society of Medicine Services Ltd, 1986.

5. Manpower Services Commission. Review of assistance for disabled people. A Report to the Commission 1982, ESP 109. Sheffield: MSC, 1982.
6. Manpower Services Commission. Code of good practice on the employment of disabled people. Sheffield: MSC, 1984.
7. Manpower Services Commission. Employment rehabilitation—a review of the Manpower Services Commission's employment rehabilitation services. ESP 76. Sheffield: MSC, 1981.
8. Manpower Services Commission. Employment rehabilitation—proposals for the development of the Manpower Services Commission's Rehabilitation Service. A report to the Manpower Services Commission. Sheffield: MSC, 1984.
9. Health and Safety Executive. Pre-employment health screening. Guidance note MS 20. London: HMSO, 1982.
10. Kent A. The Careers Service. In: Kettle M, Massie B, eds. Employer's guide to disabilities. 2nd ed. Cambridge: Woodhead-Faulkner Ltd, 1986.
11. Darnbrough A, Kinrade E. Directory for disabled people. A handbook of information and opportunities for disabled and handicapped people. 4th ed. Cambridge: Woodhead-Faulkner Ltd, in association with the Royal Association for Disability and Rehabilitation, 1985.
12. Kettle M, Massie B, eds. Employers' guide to disabilities. 2nd ed. Cambridge: Woodhead-Faulkner Ltd, 1986.
13. Cooke P. The role of the Disabled Living Foundation in assisting employers of disabled people. Rehab Network no.5, Spring 1987:11-2.

3

Medication

L. Beeley and I. G. Rennie

INTRODUCTION

Many people attend work while taking medication; in fact many can only attend work because of the medication they take. Additionally, many people have to take medication because of their work, e.g. those who travel regularly to malarious areas of the world. In discussion of any effect medication may have on fitness for work the main area to be considered is whether the taking of such medication carries any risk. The point must be re-emphasized, however, that many people could not work safely without taking medication and few, if any, studies have compared how people with an untreated medical condition perform at work, as opposed to those taking medication.

It must be remembered also that we are talking about a selected group of people who, because they are able to work, will be fitter than those not at work and, in general, as a group be less likely to be on medication. In such a group, the bulk of the prescribing will be by the general practitioner and there can be little doubt that many general practitioners know very little about the working environment of their patients, while hospital doctors probably know even less. General practitioners are concerned with treating their patient and give perhaps too little thought to any potential side-effects the drugs may produce, and may omit to relate such effects to the circumstances of their patient's work. They may enquire about whether the patient drives, but few enquire about their patient's employment.

Concern over the risks first associated with alcohol has led to concern as to whether medication, particularly psychotropic drugs, might impair performance, skills, and memory in such a way as to place those taking such drugs at risk.[1] The World Health Organisation (1983) expressed further concern and gave advice and guidance on the subject in a booklet (*Drugs, driving and traffic safety*). However, such advice is relevant not only to drivers of vehicles but also to those who fly aircraft, operate machinery and perform skilled tasks, or remain vigilant at a workstation.

PREVALENCE OF MEDICATION IN SOCIETY

Consumption of medication continues to rise throughout all developed countries. In the UK, in 1963 the average number of prescriptions per head on a National Health Service list was 4.6, while in 1986 it was estimated at

7.0.[2] This figure, however, covers the entire population and the position regarding those at work has rarely been investigated. A study by Dunnell and Cartwright[3] indicated that 55 per cent of a sample city population had taken or used some medication during the 24 hours before the interview, whereas a study by Rennie in 1984[4] within a factory population indicated that 20 per cent of those interviewed were taking medication, reflecting a healthy worker effect. The commonest group of drugs taken by those in the latter study were the beta-blockers, reflecting both the older average age and preponderance of men (88 per cent) of the study population.

The prevalence of medication within a working population will be dependent upon a number of factors, in particular age and sex. Where more women are working, Lader[5] has found that more psychotropic drugs will be taken. Where there are more men, it is likely that drugs acting on the cardiovascular system, particularly the beta-blocker group, will be the drugs most frequently used. Both these groups can affect performance, and the implications of any side-effects must be considered when they are prescribed for those at work.

CLINICAL ASPECTS AFFECTING WORK CAPACITY

Unwanted effects of medication fall into two main groups: those which are predictable and usually dose-related, and those which are unpredictable and not usually dose-related (Rawlins).[6] In addition, unwanted effects may result from interactions with other drugs, with alcohol, and with other chemical substances which may be encountered at work. Of particular concern to the patient at work are the effects of drugs on performance, especially for those who operate machinery, drive vehicles or fly aircraft, or whose sound judgement is imperative. However, drugs can interfere with work capacity in other ways and some drug effects may produce particular problems for patients in specific jobs. Any doctor prescribing medication, or any occupational physician reviewing an individual returning to work, should consider whether there might be hazards to the patient from any drug effects, e.g. slowing of reacting time, drowsiness, or altered thermoregulatory systems. In addition, because of the wide individual variation that people can show, particularly in their reactions to psychoactive medicaments, any dangerous occupation should be avoided for at least a week after starting such therapy, and the situation should then be reviewed. These points will be considered in general terms initially, and then individual drug groups will be discussed.

GENERAL EFFECTS OF MEDICATION ON PERFORMANCE

Circadian rhythm

Before the effects of medication on performance are discussed, it should be mentioned that changes in performance occur spontaneously as part of the circadian rhythm. Scores for most simple tasks rise during the day to a peak or plateau between 12.00 and 21.00 hours and fall to a minimum between 03.00 and 06.00 hours,[7] correlating with body temperature. Scores for more complex tests may peak at other times of the day, dependent on the components of psychomotor function required, e.g. if short-term memory is the greatest component, the score will peak early in the day.

When a prolonged duty (e.g. of 12 hours) begins at noon, performance declines by between 10 per cent and 15 per cent of control levels, but when the same work starts at midnight the decrease may be as much as 35 per cent. During the day increased arousal partly compensates the effect of prolonged work, whereas at night the circadian decrease in alertness may add to the problem. Problems may occur with shiftwork, submarines, aircraft, and space flight, and any action of a drug which affects performance may be additive in such situations.

Furthermore, there is evidence that both the rates of absorption and elimination and the response to some drugs are dependent on circadian rhythms. For example, blood levels of amitriptyline are higher after a morning dose than after an evening dose and this is associated with greater sedative and anticholinergic effects.[8] The mechanism is unknown, as is the relevance to shift-workers.

In patients on long-term corticosteroid treatment, suppression of the hypothalamo-pituitary-adrenal axis can be minimized by giving the steroid as a single daily dose in the morning, after the diurnal peak of ACTH secretion which occurs in the early morning. In long-term night workers the diurnal rhythm is reversed, and the steroid should be given on waking.

Testing drugs to assess performance

This is complex and time consuming. Tests fall into two main categories: those that measure the effects of drugs on individual components of psychomotor function, and those which measure their effects on activities of everyday life, such as car driving. Assessing the effects of drugs on real-life activities has many problems but there is now much evidence that some laboratory tests of psychomotor function correlate well with, for example, real-life driving ability. The components of psychomotor function measured by laboratory tests include cognitive information processing, short-term memory and learning, motor function, and activities involving sensory, central, and motor abilities. Well-controlled psychopharmacological tests of this kind can now indicate reasonably reliably those drugs which may affect everyday activities such as driving and operating machinery.[9, 10]

The effects of environmental chemicals on drug response

Most drugs are inactivated by metabolism in the liver, and drug metabolism can be affected by factors which increase or reduce the activity of the hepatic enzyme systems responsible. Many environmental chemicals have been shown to be enzyme inducers and increase the rate of metabolism of many drugs in animals. They include polycyclic aromatic hydrocarbons and organochlorine and other pesticides. Studies of workers engaged in pesticide manufacture have demonstrated that enzyme induction occurs[11] but the practical importance of this is unknown.

Effects on work capacity

Drugs which primarily affect the central nervous system (CNS) and cause lethargy and drowsiness are all likely to reduce the work capacity. However, other drugs can affect the capacity to work and they include many commonly prescribed drugs, such as the beta-blockers.

Effects on adaptation to extremes of temperature

The human body temperature is maintained within $\pm 0.5°$ of 36.6°C, despite wide ambient changes in association with the circadian rhythm which are individually consistent.[12] Drugs may affect the control of body temperature and place those taking them at risk if they are working in an inhospitable environment. Drugs may act on normal body temperature either by interfering directly with effector pathways or by an action on the central control of temperature.

Effector pathways

Sweating This provides coarse control of heat loss; it is under cholinergic control and hence may be diminished by drugs with anticholinergic (atropine-like) properties. Thus anti-parkinsonism agents, antihistamines, tricyclic antidepressants, and neuroleptics such as chlorpromazine can cause heat intolerance. However, as most of these drugs cross the blood-brain barrier their effects on body temperature may involve central effects as well as peripheral mechanisms.

Cutaneous blood flow This is responsible for fine control of heat loss, and drugs—e.g. the adrenergic neurone-blocking drugs such as bethanidine, which act on the peripheral sympathetic nervous system; alpha-adrenoreceptor antagonists such as prazosin; direct vasodilators such as hydralazine; and calcium antagonists such as nifedipine—may impair the vasomotor response to cold exposure. Normally, however, reflex mechanisms compensate for these effects.

The cutaneous vasoconstriction which occurs following administration of beta-adrenoreceptor antagonists does not affect body temperature but causes local signs and symptoms, e.g. cold extremities, chilblains, Raynaud's phenomenon, and the development of ischaemic changes particularly in patients with pre-existing peripheral vascular disease. Those working in cold environments should be warned of potential side-effects, and the suitability for such work when employees require beta-blockers must be assessed.

Central mechanisms

Virtually all drugs with cerebral depressant properties may alter thermo-regulation when given in sufficient doses. Individuals become poikilothermic, that is, their body temperature is dependent on their surroundings. Mechanisms are complex and not only is there suppression of hypothalamic control, but there may also be effects on the vasomotor centre producing disturbances in cutaneous blood flow. In therapeutic doses barbiturates, benzodiazepines, and neuroleptics may all impair temperature regulation. Tricyclic antidepressants and monoamine oxidase inhibitors may precipitate hyperthermia both singly and more commonly in combination.

Effects due to occupational exposure to CNS depressants

Employees who work with solvents, e.g. in degreasing plants, printing, paint spraying, or with adhesives, and those who work in atmospheres where there may be a potential build-up of gases or fumes that can depress the CNS may be at risk if they take medications which also depress the CNS. Safe exposure levels at work are based on occupational exposure limits and these are derived from animal experiments and experiments on humans who are not on medication. Any minimal effects that such substances in the working environment may have on the CNS can be expected to summate with any CNS depressant action that medication may be producing.

HYPNOTICS AND SEDATIVES

Effects on performance

These are all CNS depressants and most have been shown to impair psychomotor function, slow down responsiveness, and impair motor skills, co-ordination, and the responses concerned with self-preservation. The duration of effect after a single dose depends on the plasma half-life of the drug and on the dose given, but most hypnotics produce residual effects the following morning. Effects on psychomotor function persist during long-term administration though some tolerance occurs. They are potentiated by alcohol, and are more marked in elderly patients. Barbiturates have a greater effect on performance than benzodiazepines and, with the exception of phenobarbitone, should not now be used in patients who drive or operate machinery.

The individual benzodiazepines differ in their effects on psychomotor performance. When used as hypnotics, the short-acting drugs such as temazepam, triazolam, and lormetazepam are less likely than nitrazepam and flurazepam to produce effects the following morning. When used during the day as anxiolytics clobazam appears to have less effect than other benzodiazepines on performance. However, all these drugs can affect performance in susceptible patients and differences between the drugs are of degree only. Benzodiazepines have amnesic effects which are only partly secondary to the reduction in arousal produced by sedation. Lorazepam and diazepam severely affect performance of memory-based tests. Less is known about other benzodiazepines but some, e.g. clobazam, appear to have less effect on memory. Effects on memory are unlikely to produce problems when benzodiazepines are used as nocturnal hypnotics but the effects of daytime use on immediate memory could affect the performance of a wide range of activities. Temazepam, because of its short activity time, is the only hypnotic approved by the Royal Air Force (RAF) for pilots.

Particular problems can arise when these drugs are stopped. Benzodiazepine withdrawal can produce a characteristic syndrome consisting of anxiety, sleeplessness, perceptual disturbances, depersonalization, and general malaise. When severe, these effects could markedly impair work performance.

Barbiturates can interfere with central thermoregulation, and this may occasionally be a problem with benzodiazepines (see p. 54).

ANTIPSYCHOTICS

This group includes the phenothiazines, such as chlorpromazine; the butyrophenones, such as haloperidol; and similar drugs, such as pimozide and fluspirilene, which are used mainly to treat schizophrenia and other psychotic illness.

Effects on performance

Many of these drugs impair psychomotor performance and the degree to which they do so probably depends on the amount of sedation they produce. Thus flupenthixol and low doses of sulpiride, which have a predominantly alerting effect, may have less effect on performance than the more sedative phenothiazines such as chlorpromazine. Psychotic patients show impairment of psychomotor function even without drugs and in some this will be improved by treatment. This needs to be considered when advising such patients about the possible risks of working or driving while taking antipsychotic medication. Lithium probably has little effect on performance, though impairment of some laboratory tests of psychomotor function has been described.[13]

The extrapyramidal side-effects of antipsychotic drugs, particularly tremor, may interfere with precision work and affect driving. Lithium rarely produces extrapyramidal effects but commonly produces tremor. Postural hypotension may produce problems, particularly in hot environments. Interference with temperature regulation is more profound than with the hypnotic/sedative drugs. The neuroleptics interfere both with hypothalamic temperature regulation and with cholinergic control of sweating. Either hyperthermia or hypothermia can occur when environmental temperatures are extreme.

ANTIDEPRESSANTS

Effects on performance

Many antidepressants produce sedation, especially when treatment is first started, and this is markedly potentiated by alcohol. Psychomotor impairment has been demonstrated and seems to be related to the sedative effect. Of the tricyclic antidepressants, amitriptyline, doxepin, and trimipramine are the most sedative and desipramine, nortriptyline, protriptyline, and clomipramine the least. Mianserin and trazodone are moderately sedative, but viloxazine does not produce sedation; and monoamine oxidase inhibitors are usually stimulant but phenelzine can sometimes be sedative. As tolerance develops to the sedative effects of antidepressants, it seems sensible to advise patients not to drive or undertake work which could be affected during the first few days of treatment with the more sedative ones.

Tremor may be a problem for some types of work. Many antidepressants produce blurring of near vision which may affect driving and the performance of other tasks. Those with anticholinergic effects interfere with sweating and can also affect central temperature regulation. All can produce postural hypotension, but this is more likely to occur with the monoamine oxidase inhibitors and with imipramine and amitriptyline than with nortriptyline and some of the newer antidepressants, e.g. mianserin.

ANTIHISTAMINES AND ANTICHOLINERGIC ANTI-EMETICS

Effects on performance

The sedative effects of these are well known, as is the potentiating effect of alcohol. The effects vary, depending on individual susceptibility and the sedative properties of the individual drugs. Astemizole and terfenadine do not usually produce sedation and are the antihistamines of choice where driving cannot be avoided. Otherwise, patients should be warned that their ability to drive or operate machinery is likely to be impaired. Hyoscine is thought to have less effect on driving skills than most antihistamines and, though it produces some sedation, it is the anti-emetic of choice for drivers with travel sickness.

Effects on performance

Amphetamines and other stimulants increase risk-taking behaviour and can be expected to affect work performance and driving adversely, especially if combined with alcohol. Fenfluramine produces sedation but its effects on psychomotor function are unknown.

Effects on performance

The more powerful narcotic analgesics, such as morphine, produce marked sedation, and patients requiring them should not drive or undertake work likely to be affected. Of the milder narcotic analgesics, codeine is known to affect driving-related skills, and others, such as dextropropoxyphene, can probably do so also. Alcohol potentiates the effects of all these analgesics and even dextropropoxyphene is likely to be dangerous when combined with alcohol. Phenylbutazone and indomethacin have been reported to impair laboratory tests of driving-related skills. The effects of other anti-inflammatory analgesics are unknown.

Effects on performance

Studies of cognitive function, both in normal volunteers and in patients on chronic anticonvulsant therapy, have shown impairment of concentration, sustained attention, and other aspects of psychomotor performance. Impairment is greater in patients on polytherapy than in those treated with a single drug, and there is some evidence that it is greater with phenytoin than with carbamazepine.[14] The importance of these effects in patients well-controlled on long-term monotherapy is unknown. Driving must be stopped if treatment is changed (see Chapter 12).

Excessive doses of phenytoin and carbamazepine produce drowsiness, tremor, and ataxia. Particular care should be taken to keep blood levels within the therapeutic range for patients at work. Sodium valproate produces a troublesome tremor in some patients.

ANAESTHETICS

As a general rule patients should not drive for 24–48 hours after anaesthesia for minor out-patient surgery, but this depends to some extent on the drug used, the duration of anaesthesia, and the response of the individual patient. More detailed information can be found in the review by Seppala *et al.*[15]

ANTIHYPERTENSIVE DRUGS

Effects on performance

Methyldopa, clonidine, and indoramin produce sedation, and methyldopa has been shown to impair driving performance. In a small proportion of patients beta-blockers produce side-effects which could impair work capacity. These effects include general fatigue, malaise, tiredness, and muscle fatigue which usually affects the limbs.[16] Reduced exercise-tolerance has been reported with all beta-blockers and there is no good evidence that the cardio-selective drugs are less likely than propranolol to produce it. For example, studies on the effect of beta-adrenoreceptor blockade on exercise tolerance in normal healthy men[17] indicate a fall of 12 per cent in cardiac output with both propranolol and metoprolol. Oxygen consumption was reduced by 3.5 per cent over the whole work range on bicycle ergometry. Endurance was reduced by 18 per cent on propranolol and 11 per cent on metoprolol compared to placebo. Both beta-blockers significantly increased the sense of fatigue during exercise compared to placebo, and a given workload appeared harder in the presence of beta-adrenoreceptor blocking drugs. Clinically, many patients complained of lack of energy, fatigue, and aching muscles while taking these drugs.

The exact mechanism is not entirely clear and several factors probably play a part. Beta-blockers reduce muscle blood flow and oxygen consumption by reducing cardiac output and partly by reducing beta-2-mediated vasodilation; they reduce the availability of substrates, such as glucose and fatty acids, necessary for muscle activity; and they may have an additional central effect on the perception of fatigue. Fatigue has been reported in about 5 per cent of patients on beta-blockers but minor unreported symptoms are probably more common, and it is important to be aware of the potential effect of these drugs on work capacity.

All antihypertensive drugs carry with them the risk of unexpected hypotension, and patients should therefore be advised not to drive or operate machinery at the beginning of treatment or when the dose is being increased. Particular care should be taken if the patient works in a hot environment.

Most antihypertensive drugs affect cutaneous blood flow and can impair the vasomotor response to cold exposure (see pp. 53–4).

Beta-blockers can produce bronchospasm in susceptible people, and this should be considered when they are prescribed for such patients working in irritant atmospheres. Lipophilic beta-blockers, e.g. propranolol, cross the blood-brain barrier and have been used to reduce the anxiety of public speaking. Studies have shown, however, that although beta-blockers may have an initial effect on psychomotor function this returns to normal after three weeks' administration. Air crew are permitted by the Civil Aviation Authority to take specified beta-blockers, but only after careful specialist evaluation and simulation testing. A period of ground duties should be undertaken first to allow stabilization and any habituation effects to occur. This subject was dealt with in greater detail by the second United Kingdom workshop in Aviation Cardiology.[18] Diuretics increase the risk of dehydration at high temperatures and are not the antihypertensive of choice for patients working in a hot environment.

ANTIDIABETIC DRUGS

Psychomotor performance may be affected by even mild hypoglycaemia and insulin-dependent diabetics should not drive or operate machinery unless they are well controlled. They should carry sugar and be warned not to drive under conditions likely to be associated with hypoglycaemia (see Chapter 13)

ANTICOAGULANTS

Consideration must be given to the suitability for employment of people taking anticoagulants. Usually the underlying condition is the limiting factor. Should bleeding occur, the guidelines given in the British National Formulary should be followed. It is advisable for employees taking such medication to carry anticoagulant treatment cards, or other means of indicating that they are receiving this treatment.

OTHER DRUGS

The muscle relaxants baclofen and dantrolene produce sedation and muscle weakness and make driving and operating machinery dangerous. Many other drugs produce sedation. They include cyproheptadine, ketotifen, pizotifen, cyproterone, procarbazine, and thiabendazole. Patients should be warned about the possible effects on driving and work when given these drugs, and that the effects are likely to be potentiated by alcohol. Mydriatic eyedrops such as homatropine, atropine, and cyclopentolate paralyse accommodation and produce blurred vision. It should also be remembered that the effects of ototoxic drugs, such as gentamicin or salicylates, on the middle ear can be expected to summate with any effects noise may have on the ear.

DRIVING

For further information referring specifically to driving, see Seppala *et al.*[15] and Ashton.[19]

MALARIA PROPHYLAXIS

The prospective traveller should consult his doctor, or a specialist in tropical diseases, who will determine the appropriate prophylactic drug and its dosage according to the area to be visited and the time to be spent away, also taking into consideration any drug intolerance. In order to avoid this last complication, it is advisable to start chemotherapy a week before departure. The recommended prophylactic drug for malaria protection varies according to the type of malaria present in the area visited and its sensitivity to drugs, the age of the traveller, the traveller's previous exposure to antimalarial drugs, the duration of stay and conditions which may prejudice the use of certain drugs.

Drug prophylaxis should begin at the latest on the day of travel to the endemic area. When drugs are taken daily or only once per week, it is advisable to take the medicament at the same time each day, or the same day each week. The correct dosage should be strictly observed. Whatever drug is taken it must be taken with unfailing regularity to be fully effective. Drugs should be taken with liquids after a meal in order to reduce the occurrence of nausea and vomiting or mild gastrointestinal upsets, particularly if chloroquine is used. Those who are to reside for periods of over six months should seek appropriate medical care on arrival in the malarious area concerned.

Further information and up-to-date advice can be obtained from:

- The Liverpool School of Tropical Medicine (Tel. 051 708 9393);

- The Malarial Reference Laboratory, The Ross Institute, London School of Hygiene and Tropical Medicine (Tel. 01 636 8636);

- The East Birmingham Hospital (Tel. 021 772 4311).

CONCLUSIONS AND RECOMMENDATIONS

Suggestions for advice to patients taking drugs which affect the CNS

1. Do not exceed the stated dose.

2. Do not drive, fly, or operate machinery until the nature and extent of any side-effects or the main effects are known.

3. Do not take any other medication or drugs while receiving this treatment unless they are prescribed for you.

General principles of prescribing for people at work

1. Always enquire into the patient's occupation, and be aware of drug effects which can be hazardous in the working environment.

2. Make sure the patient understands what to expect and what action to take.

3. Be particularly careful with all drugs which act on the CNS and avoid polypharmacy if this is likely to have unintended additive effects.

4. Keep treatment regimes simple and avoid more than two daily doses, where possible, to increase compliance.

5. If a hypnotic is required, use one with a short duration of effect.

6. Avoid repeated unsupervised use of drugs; give a minimum of repeat prescriptions and supervise regularly.

7. Avoid the use of antihistamines in those who have to operate machinery, drive, or fly. Where they are essential, favour the more recently introduced, less-sedating agents.

8. Reserves of medication must be carried by those whose occupation takes them abroad for long periods of time, e.g. those on board ship. Reserves should also be available for emergency use for those working in isolated or dangerous situations where rescue may be delayed.

Appendix

SPECIAL PROBLEMS IN SPECIFIC OCCUPATIONS

Flying (see Appendix 2 at the end of the book)

All medication that affects performance is likely to be a hazard to those who fly. In addition, environmental factors such as pressure, gravity, and temperature may all affect the performance of those flying, together with the potential effects of the medication. The Civil Aviation Authority (CAA) gives guidance to those who fly[20] and states that accidents and incidents have occurred as a result of pilots flying while medically unfit, and that the majority have been associated with minor ailments rather than overwhelming medical catastrophes. The following is an extract from the CAA information circular relating to medication:

1. *Antibiotics*: apart from any potential effects of the antibiotics, the effects of the infection will almost always mean that the pilot is not fit to fly.

2. *Tranquillisers, antidepressants, and sedatives*: because of their effects on performance those who are required to fly must not take them.

3. *Stimulants, e.g. caffeine and amphetamines*: the use of such 'pep' pills whilst flying cannot be permitted.

4. *Antihistamines*: many cause drowsiness. In many cases the condition requiring treatment precludes flying and if treatment is necessary, expert advice should be sought.

5. *Drugs for the control of high blood pressure*: if the blood pressure is such that drugs are needed the pilot must be temporarily grounded. Any treatment instituted should be discussed with an expert in Aviation Medicine before return to flying.

6. *Analgesics*: the more potent analgesics may have marked effects on performance. In any case the pain for which they are being taken indicates a condition which is a bar to flying.

7. *Anaesthetics*: following local and general dental and other anaesthetics at least 24 hours should elapse before return to flying.

8. *Other medication*: if there is any change in medication or dosage or if any other medication is taken, those flying are exhorted not to take such medication unless they are completely familiar with the effect on their own body. Those taking such medication should ask three questions, (a) do I really feel fit to fly? (b) do I really need to take medicine at all? (c) have I given this particular medication a personal trial on the ground of at least 24 hours before flying to ensure it will not have any adverse effects whatsoever on my ability to fly?

In certain selected cases, aircrew who are under the care of cardiologists and consultants in aviation medicine may be allowed beta-blockers. Additionally, the use of temazepam as a hypnotic by aircrew in the RAF has been shown by Nicholson to have no residual effects on performance.[21] It is, however, most important that, before issuing hypnotics to aircrew, the cause for the requirement should be sought as this may be work-related and possible to change, e.g. unusual work rosters.

Similar advice is given by the Civil Aviation Authority regarding medication and air traffic controllers.[22] The position regarding cabincrew is different, as these staff are unlicensed and each company sets its own health standard. However, a good general standard of health should be required for these employees as they may have to deal with emergency situations, and environmental conditions within aircraft vary, e.g., the reduced oxygen partial pressure may diminish the cardiopulmonary reserve of some individuals to a point of embarrassment. Additionally, expansion of gases on ascent and contraction on descent may cause problems, e.g., to those with otitis media or sinusitis. The question of risks from medication in this context is less relevant than the health status of the individual concerned. The same situation applies to those travelling as passengers as part of their job.

Merchant seamen (see Appendix 3 at the end of the book)

Guidance is given to medical examiners on the medical and visual standards required for serving seafarers.[23] A high standard of health and fitness is required for those entering or re-entering this industry, and it is doubtful if it is ever wise to commence seafaring if the loss of a necessary medicament could precipitate the rapid deterioration of the condition.

The same principles apply to those at sea as to those who drive, fly, or work in variable climatic conditions. Seamen with diabetes mellitus requiring insulin are classified as permanently unfit. Those requiring oral hypoglycaemic agents are classified unfit for six months for stabilization, and then reviewed. In the absence of any complications, service may be considered subject to six-monthly medical reviews. Those dependent on controlled drugs are permanently unfit to be seafarers. Hypertensive seafarers may be classified as fit for unrestricted sea service provided they are under medical surveillance and that the blood pressure can be maintained below 170/100 mm by the use of diuretics or beta-blockers.

Diving (see Appendix 4 at the end of the book)

Any medication that may affect performance will be a potential hazard to those who dive. Additionally, environmental temperature and pressure and the use of gas combinations, e.g. oxygen/helium, may cause further problems. Guidance is given on Form MAI from the Employment Medical Advisory Service (EMAS) on the medical examination of divers. In general, it is the medical condition rather than medication that is the bar to diving. Divers should, however, be asked specifically for details of any current medication.

The question of the effect and use of drugs under pressure is interesting. Cox[24] lists drugs that have been used by divers; the depths to which they have been used; and whether there were any untoward effects.

Offshore workers

Guidance is given by the United Kingdom Offshore Operators Association who refer to 'Conditions which definitely render an individual unfit for work offshore'; this section includes those taking regular drug therapy.[25] Uncomplicated hypertensives on medication which has maintained stability for six months with no manifestations of treatment side-effects may be acceptable.

Those workers in the Norwegian and Dutch sectors of the North Sea will come within the legislation of those countries.

LEGISLATION AND GUIDANCE

Driving

Ordinary driving licences

1. *Section 5 of the Road Traffic Act, 1972*: refers to 'Driving or being in charge under the influence of a drug.'

2. *Poisons Rules (1972)*: requires a number of substances containing antihistamines to be labelled with the words 'Caution, may cause drowsiness, if affected do not drive or operate machinery.'

Drivers of heavy goods vehicles (HGV), public service vehicles (PSV), and taxis

Much stricter criteria have to be applied to professional than to private drivers. As a class they have to drive for longer hours, so that the risks of adverse drugs reactions or interactions coinciding with a situation in which other road users could be injured by loss of control is far greater. Furthermore, it is not easy for a professional driver to stop if he is feeling unwell as a result of adverse effects of drugs.

Where there is a need for long-term medication, the issue of whether it is safe for vocational driving to continue may not arise as the driver will often be excluded from holding an HGV or PSV licence as a result of the medical condition requiring treatment. *Medical aspects of fitness to drive*[26] deals with the desirability or otherwise of HGV or PSV drivers being allowed to drive under treatment, and should be consulted where appropriate.

In the case of short-term medication, the safest course is to give the driver a certificate for an initial period off work in any case where it is necessary for a drug to be given which might impair his driving ability. If treatment has to continue, a decision about returning to work can then be taken in the light of any adverse reactions which may have occurred in the initial stage of treatment.

As a general rule, the taking of drugs affecting the central nervous system and medication with insulin and hypotensive drugs (except diuretics and beta-blockers) is incompatible with vocational driving.

Diving

Guidance

(1) Information and advice from the Employment Medical Advisory Service (EMAS);

(2) Form MA1 *The medical examination of divers*, Note 3: 'The diver should be asked specifically for details of any current medication.'

Offshore workers

(1) Guidelines from the UK Offshore Operators Association (applies to UK sector of the North Sea);

(2) for workers in Dutch and Norwegian sectors specific regulations apply.

Merchant shipping

The Merchant Shipping (Medical Examination) Regulations 1983 S1 1983, No. 808:

It is doubtful that it is ever wise to permit seafaring if the loss of a necessary medicament could precipitate the rapid deterioration of a condition.

Where medication is acceptable for serving seafarers, arrangements should be made for a reserve stock of the prescribed drugs to be held in a safe place, with the agreement of the ships master.

Guidance is given as to those medical conditions, and reference is made to medication, which may be a bar or cause restrictions to seafarers.

Aviation

1. *Civil Aviation Authority Aeronautical Information Circular—UK 77/1984* gives guidance on 'Medication, flying and alcohol.'

2. *Aeronautical Information Circular—UK 17/1986* gives guidance on 'Medication and air traffic control.'

3. *Air Navigation Order (1980): Article 47(2):* 'It is an offence for a person to be on board an aircraft as a member of its Flight Crew if under the influence of alcohol or a drug to an extent which will impair his/her ability to perform his/her duties.'

REFERENCES

1. Edwards F. Risks at work from medication. J R Coll Physicians Lond. 1978;**12**:219–29.
2. Office of Health Economics. Compendium of Health Statistics. 6th ed. 1986.
3. Dunnell K, Cartwright A. Medicine takers, prescribers and hoarders. London and Boston: Routledge and Kegan Paul, 1972.
4. Rennie IG. Accidents at work—risks from medication. Royal College of Physicians Faculty of Occupational Medicine, 1985. MFOM Dissertation.

5. Lader M. Benzodiazepines—long-term use and problems of withdrawal. MIMS Magazine 1985; March.

6. Rawlins MD, Thompson JW. In: Davies DM, ed. Textbook of adverse drug reactions. 3rd ed. Oxford: Oxford University Press, 1985.

7. Nicholson AM, Stone BM. Disturbance of circadian rhythms and sleep. Proc Roy Soc Edinburgh 1985;**82BL**:135–9.

8. Nakano S. Time of day effect on psychotherapeutic drug response and kinetics in man. In: Takahashi R, Holberg F, Walker CA, eds. Toward chronopharmacology. Advances in the Biosciences 1982;**41**:51–9.

9. Hindmarch I. Psychomotor function and psychoactive drugs. Br J Clin Pharmacol 1980;**10**:189–209.

10. Broadbent DE. Performance and its measurement. Br J Clin Pharmacol 1984; **18**:5S–9S. (Also rest of symposium.)

11. Hunter J, Maxwell JD, Stewart DA. Increased hepatic microsomal enzyme activity from occupational exposure to certain organochlorine pesticides. Nature 1972;**237**:399–401.

12. Blain PG, Rawlins MD. Drug-induced body temperature changes. Prescribers Journal 1981;**21**:204.

13. Linnoila M, Rudorfer MV, Dubyoski KV. Effects of one week lithium treatment on skilled performance, information processing and mood in healthy volunteers. J Clin Pharmacol 1986;**6**:356–9.

14. Reynolds EH, Trimble MR. Adverse neuropsychiatric effects of anticonvulsant drugs. Drugs 1985;**29**:570–81.

15. Seppala T, Linnoila M, Mattila MJ. Drugs, alcohol and driving. Drugs 1979; **17**:389–408.

16. Hall PE, Kendall MJ, Smith SR. Beta-blockers and fatigue, J Clin Hosp Pharm 1984;**9**:283–91.

17. Pearson SB, Banks BC, Patrick JM. The effect of beta-adrenoreceptor blockade on factors affecting exercise tolerance in normal man. Br J Clin Pharmacol 1979;**8**:143–8.

18. The Second United Kingdom Workshop in Aviation Cardiology. Eur Heart J 1988 (in press).

19. Ashton H. Drugs and driving. Adverse Drug Reaction Bulletin 1983;**98**:360–3.

20. Aeronautical Information Circular, United Kingdom. Medication alcohol and flying. Civil Aviation Authority 77/1984.

21. Nicholson AN. Long periods of work and disturbed sleep. Ergonomics 1984; **27**:629–30.

22. Aeronautical Information Circular, United Kingdom. Medication and air traffic control. Civil Aviation Authority 17/1986.

23. The Merchant Shipping (Medical Examination) Regulation 1983; SI 1983; no 808.

24. Cox RAF, (ed.) Offshore medicine: medical care of employees in the offshore oil industry. 2nd ed. Berlin: Springer-Verlag, 1987.

25. Recommended General Medical Standards of Fitness for Designated Offshore Employees. United Kingdom Offshore Operators Association Ltd, 1986.

26. Raffle A, ed. Medical aspects of Fitness to drive. 4th ed. London: Medical Commission on Accident Prevention, 1985.

4

Hearing

R. R. A. Coles and A. Sinclair

INTRODUCTION

Disorders of the ear can affect fitness for work in several ways: hearing difficulty, tinnitus, ear discharge, problems associated with barometric pressure changes, and balance disturbances.

Hearing difficulty

This may be associated with obvious conditions such as disease of the middle ear or hearing disorder present since birth. In other cases the cause is uncertain. Often the affected person may be unaware that anything is wrong; for example, in hearing loss resulting from noise exposure the deterioration progresses gradually for a period of time before the impairment becomes evident. Hearing loss may not be compatible with particular tasks at work, such as where there is a requirement for good communication or where there are exceptionally high levels of responsibility, e.g. radio operators and civil airline pilots. Fitness depends on interaction between the degree of disability and the auditory demands of the job. In severe or profound hearing loss, especially if congenital, speech production may also be impaired to such a degree that fitness for work may be adversely affected.

Tinnitus

This is often associated with hearing disorder. Although the impairment of hearing will usually be the more significant factor regarding fitness for work, tinnitus may be associated with psychological upsets, including insomnia. These can be severe and incapacitating and can impair performance of jobs that are heavily dependent upon personal skills.

Ear discharge

Most commonly this arises from a bacterial or fungal infection of the middle or external ear, but some forms of otitis externa are more akin to an eczematous dermatitis. It affects fitness for work in several ways. These are considerations of appearance and of hygiene, and of ability to use hearing protectors in high levels of noise or to use telephonic equipment. Not only might otitis media cause a conductive hearing loss, it can also result in a sensorineural loss. Hygiene considerations preclude work as a food-handler at all stages, from processing the raw food product to food retailing or catering: active or recurrent ear infections should be regarded as unacceptable in these industries.

Barometric problems

Chronic or recurrent eustachian tube insufficiency, or middle-ear disease, preclude people from certain occupations, notably flying and diving.

Balance disorders

Vestibular disturbances are covered in Chapter 5, and the non-vestibular disorders of balance in Chapter 11, but the possibility of their association with ear disorders, hearing defect, or tinnitus needs to be kept in mind when assessing fitness for work.

Hearing is vital for normal social and working communication. In contrast to a blind person whose disability is evident, the person with defective hearing has a hidden disability. His hearing aid, even if worn and visible, is usually regarded not as a sign of a major disability but as an appliance that restores normal hearing. This is not so, however, for the majority of hearing-aid users. The consequence is that when a hearing-impaired person fails to comprehend, he may be taken as mentally backward, and even ridiculed, or else he is shunned because of embarrassment and the time and effort involved in communication.

These attitudes often extend mistakenly towards the employability of hearing-impaired persons. The deaf, hard of hearing and those with ear disorders need be excluded from only a minority of jobs. For further information on the impact of defective hearing on employability and the means of reducing its effect at work see Kettle and Massie[1], MSC Booklet EPL 80,[2] and Appendix 5 at the end of the book.

PREVALENCE

As with most disabilities, the register of disabled persons gives very misleading statistics. In April 1984 the Manpower Services Commission identified just over 420 000 registered disabled persons aged between 16 and 64 years; of these, only 23 735 (under 0.1 per cent of the total population

Table 4.1 Percentage of people in seven age groups whose hearing threshold levels (averaged over 0.5, 1, 2, and 4 kHz) were at or over 25 dB, 35 dB, and 45 dB HL in the better ear[3]

Age Group	Percent with average hearing threshold level (HL) in the better ear at or greater than:		
	25 dB	35 dB	45 dB
17–20	3	2	0
21–30	1	1	0
31–40	5	2	1
41–50	10	4	2
51–60	23	10	6
61–70	34	17	12
over 70	74	49	25
All ages	17 ± 2.2	8 ± 1.5	4 ± 1.2

aged 16–64) were registered because of hearing impairment. The extent to which this is an underestimate is indicated by data from the National Study of Hearing (NSH), a nationwide epidemiological study in the UK. Of the adult population, 3–4 per cent (about 1.6 million people, including the retired) have sufficient hearing problems to possess a hearing aid, and a similar proportion has an average hearing threshold level in the better ear of 45 dB or worse.[3] A preliminary estimate of the prevalence of stated degrees of impairment (hearing loss) as a function of age is given in Table 4.1. Note that a 25 dB average hearing loss in the better ear is just beyond that commonly regarded as the lower limit of normal; 35 dB is commonly the level at which otologists start to consider surgery or a hearing aid; and 45 dB is usually distinctly handicapping.

Audiometric criteria of hearing impairment are useful, especially for hearing conservation purposes, but provide an incomplete indication of hearing disability. Data on the proportions of people experiencing various degrees of hearing difficulty, and ear discharge, are also available from the NSH and are shown in Table 4.2. It can be seen that hearing difficulties are common in the population at all ages and in both sexes, a factor which has to be taken into account in consideration of fitness for work.

CLINICAL ASPECTS AFFECTING WORK CAPACITY

Hearing disorders will seldom lead to periods off work. Their impact is related more to working efficiency and safety, employers' responsibilities for the health of their employees, and sometimes to medicolegal problems.

Table 4.2 Percentages in three working age groups of males and females with various degrees of hearing difficulty and of ear disorder (data from the National Study of Hearing; A. C. Davis, 1985, personal communication)

	Age group (years) and sex					
	17–24		25–44		45–64	
	M	F	M	F	M	F
Very difficult to hear in noise	(2859) 12	(3052) 15	(6030) 20	(6430) 19	(5709) 36	(6346) 27
Difficult to hear in quiet room: a normal voice	(1674) 1	(1881) 2	(3291) 2	(3512) 2	(2937) 7	(3178) 5
a loud voice	(1664) 1	(1842) 1	(3457) 1	(3255) 1	(2837) 3	(3051) 3
Difficulty in hearing:						
Better ear	(1980)	(2157)	(4038)	(4300)	(3734)	(4161)
none	97	98	96	97	86	92
slight	2	2	4	2	11	5
moderate	0.4	0.1	0.5	0.4	2	2
great	0.1	0.2	0.1	0.2	0.6	0.7
cannot hear at all	0.1	0.0	0.1	0.2	0.2	0.5
Worse ear	(1980)	(2157)	(4038)	(4300)	(3734)	(4161)
none	92	92	88	90	74	82
slight	6	6	9	7	15	10
moderate	1	1	2	2	7	4
great	0.7	0.5	1	1	4	3
cannot hear at all	0.5	0.1	0.2	0.4	1	2
Discharging ear (ever)	(2584) 13	(2761) 15	(5347) 15	(5762) 17	(5043) 18	(5617) 16
Hearing aid (ever)	(2603) 0.6	(2774) 0.6	(5396) 0.7	(5827) 1	(5113) 3	(5722) 3
Registered disabled (hearing impaired)	(295) 0.3	(341) 0.3	(748) 0.0	(778) 0.3	(778) 0.6	(894) 0.3

Size of samples (*n*) varies with number of phases of study in which the particular questions were asked and with number of incomplete answers.

Working efficiency and safety

There are few jobs in which perfect hearing is essential. A number of jobs can be done even by people with total or profound hearing impairment. For the majority of jobs it is sufficient that the applicant (wearing a hearing aid if appropriate) can hear what people say in the normal working environment and no special tests are therefore needed for pre-employment assessment. Where auditory requirements are more stringent, the needs for hearing and the safety aspects should be considered carefully to identify the real requirements.

Occasionally, in some quiet work environments it is essential to hear voices which may be soft, or spoken from some distance. For these, a simple clinical test for the hearing of speech (aided, if appropriate) is sufficient, e.g. voice tests carefully performed to a defined protocol (see Appendix to this chapter). Alternatively or additionally, correct identification of speech in a background of noise or of other voices may be needed. Here the critical factors are the relative level of speech and noise (the signal-to-noise or S/N ratio), together with the individual's ability to detect one sound in the presence of another (frequency resolution) or immediately preceding or following another (temporal resolution). Both of these latter functions are likely to be impaired in cochlear hearing disorders. A test of speech identification in noise (see Appendix to this chapter) is probably the most appropriate way to check the disabling effects of these and other forms of hearing dysfunction. A practical test of hearing in the workplace itself is an alternative, or may be required in addition to the voice or speech-in-noise tests.

Most conductive hearing losses are due to middle-ear disorders and result only or mainly in loss of auditory sensitivity. Sensorineural hearing losses arising from cochlear damage (e.g. by noise exposure or associated with ageing) can impair both frequency and temporal resolution as well as causing loss of sensitivity. Pure-tone audiometry will detect loss of sensitivity for a range of pure tones and is a useful diagnostic and/or monitoring procedure, but it is a very imperfect indicator of speech identification ability and might therefore be considered to be unsuitable to define fitness for many kinds of work.

Some jobs have highly specific auditory requirements, e.g. the need to hear weak pure tones over a range of possible frequencies in radio operating, to detect changes in pitch, or to identify the character of echoes in sonar operating. For such work, a practical test with the particular listening task is more appropriate. This is especially true with a trained operator, as his experience and skill in the job usually outweigh any potential disadvantage suggested by some auditory test unrelated to the task.

A more common requirement that can cause problems and thus affect employability is the need to hear warning signals or to detect the direction of their source. These sounds often occur in a background of high noise levels, when their detection is dependent primarily on the S/N ratio, although sensorineural hearing impairments make the task markedly more difficult, typically equivalent to a reduction of S/N ratio by 5–10 dB.

Communication difficulties arising from hearing protection

Earmuffs or earplugs may have to be worn in noisy occupations. Although these will reduce both signal and noise equally, they may also reduce the intrusiveness of the warning signal by altering the spectrum of the noise reaching the ear with increased masking of high frequency signals by low frequency components. Hearing protectors will interfere with speech communication in a noisy environment if the speaker is also wearing them,[4] or if the listener is hearing impaired.[5] Machinery sounds and warning signals often become more difficult to hear when hearing protectors are worn:[6] this may be due to a reduction in their intrusiveness or attention-demanding properties in those who already have hearing impairments[7, 8] or to a reduction in ability to directionalize their source.[9]

The solution is to increase as far as possible the S/N ratio of the warning signals to a target of not less than 15 dB above its masked threshold,[10, 11] and perhaps to alter the frequency spectrum of the warning signals. Until there is standardization, or regulation on the design characteristics for adequate auditory warning signals, the 'design window' approach of Coleman and his colleagues[12, 13] would seem to provide the most useful set of guidelines. In many cases the auditory signals should be supplemented by visual signals, especially when hearing-impaired persons are to be employed, whether in noise or not. Such modifications to warning and communication signal systems could qualify for financial support from the Manpower Services Commission (Chapter 2).

In general, hearing protectors should provide adequate but not excessive attenuation. Although some have been developed to assist the hearing of speech and/or warning signals, they have inherent limitations. Amplitude-sensitive earplugs[14] can protect against occasional explosive noises while interfering minimally with verbal communication, provided the intervals are quiet, a situation not often encountered in industry. Noise-attenuating communication headsets can be helpful, but either have reduced attenuation properties or are heavy and bulky. If cords are needed for signal–source connection, they are cumbersome; if cordless, using magnetic induction or radio systems, they are expensive.

Rehabilitation

Hearing aids improve sensitivity, provided that there is some residual hearing to improve. They do nothing, however, for the reductions in the frequency and temporal resolving properties of the ear associated with sensorineural hearing loss, which is the most common form of hearing disorder in the general population.[3] They also add their own distortions in greater or lesser degree. Thus, the benefit they provide falls far short of that given by spectacles for most forms of visual impairment. Because of these limitations, the fairest way to judge the employability of a hearing-aided person is to test his hearing ability in the listening conditions (aided or unaided) that would be both permissible and appropriate in his intended working environment.

Most work conditions are compatible with wearing a hearing aid. However, only certain hearing aids are acceptable as intrinsically safe for use in coal mines or other places where there may be flammable atmospheres. Only particular models, and even batches within certain models, are safe; these change from time to time so it is important to check the latest version of DHSS information sheet B200 in its series 'Services for hearing-impaired people'. If in doubt, the DHSS (Supply Division—DS82, 14 Russell Square, London WC1B 5EP) should be contacted. If the employee is dependent on a hearing aid, safety factors may need special consideration to allow for possible failure of the aid. A greater limitation on the use of hearing aids arises with work in high levels of noise, where an aid would be useless and would increase the noise hazard. Communication in such conditions often depends largely on lip-reading and hand signals, at which hearing-disordered persons are often better than those with normal hearing.

SPECIAL WORK PROBLEMS, RESTRICTIONS, OR NEEDS

Defective hearing and accidents

As far as is known, there are no statistics relating industrial accidents and hearing loss. It seems possible, however, that noise may contribute to accidents, from failure to hear shouts or warning signals.[15] Nevertheless, serious accidents due to verbal communication failure arising from deafness or noise interference appear to be uncommon.

Types of work for which people with hearing defects are unsuitable

The most critical types of work in this respect are those in which the actual task is an auditory one, such as in most forms of telephony, and where accurate hearing of speech and of other auditory signals is important. Exceptions can be made, particularly where the hearing-impaired person is already trained and experienced, or where there is some special connection with defective hearing, e.g. teachers of the deaf, social workers for the deaf. Major factors in defining acceptability include the degree of their expected responsibility for others, perhaps highest in passenger aircraft pilots, and the extent to which the impairment may undermine the public's confidence. These factors canot be quantified. It is a matter for careful consideration by each employer as to whether or not it is essential to exclude people with defective hearing from certain jobs.

LEGISLATION AND GUIDELINES FOR EMPLOYMENT

Noise

The outstanding employment problem related to hearing and the ear is that of noise exposure.

General legal background

There is at present little UK legislation governing exposure to noise. In 1981 the Health and Safety Commission's consultative document reported that in British manufacturing industry alone about 600 000 individuals work in noise levels exceeding an equivalent continuous sound level of 90 dB(A), and over 2 million more are exposed to levels over 80 dB(A).[16] This followed two earlier publications, the Department of Employment's voluntary code of practice in 1972[17] and the HSE discussion document in 1979.[18] The recent Directive of the Council of European Communities (1986) is concerned with protection from noise exposure,[19] with limited hearing conservation measures being required for equivalent continuous sound levels in excess of 85 dB(A). It does, however, allow member states to grant derogations from the requirement to use hearing protectors if their use increases the overall risk to the health and/or safety of the workers concerned. It remains to be seen to what extent the UK regulations, required by 1990 in order to comply with the Directive, may include guidelines on the employability of hearing-impaired persons.

The extent of the problem

It is difficult to obtain an accurate assessment of noise-induced hearing loss, since the prevalence will depend largely on noise levels and length of exposure. In one major manufacturing industry, however, which has been performing audiometric screening for several years, one of us (AS) has found evidence of noise damage in 40 per cent of the noise-exposed workforce, with 8 per cent reaching or exceeding a mean hearing loss of 25 dB averaged over 1, 2, and 3 kHz in at least one ear.

Current situation in industry

Until recent years, the greater part of industry has been apathetic towards hearing conservation. Effective programmes have been limited largely to those organizations with comprehensive occupational health services, and these exist in only 15 per cent of firms. For the enlightened employer the main consideration is the prevention of noise-induced hearing loss.

If a hearing impairment does not involve substantial and unpreventable hazards to the health and safety of the individual or others, there is seldom any convincing reason for excluding the individual from employment in high levels of noise, but the employer should still provide him with properly selected and fitted hearing protectors, and keep him fully informed of the importance of wearing them and when to do so. With these precautions the individual is probably at little or no risk of developing further hearing loss. This risk is probably one which, with due explanation and precautions, the individual is entitled to accept, either at pre-employment selection or in continuing employment.

The employer has a greater responsibility where the individual has only one functional ear (Chapter 2), the other ear being totally or severely impaired. This is a not uncommon condition in the general population. The person is not always aware of it, sometimes even if the asymmetry is gross, and especially if it has been present since childhood. Such individuals may therefore have to be excluded from jobs where there is an inherent and not always preventable risk of damage to the remaining ear. In some working environments good directional hearing ability may be particularly important and those with markedly asymmetrical hearing may not be acceptable. Great care is also needed in considering whether or not to employ severely hearing-impaired persons in conditions where there is a substantial risk of damage to the eyes.

Tinnitus can present greater problems. It is often exacerbated by noise and/or stress at work, being much reduced after weekends or holidays. Hearing protection is advisable for such persons when the noise level rises above about 80 dB(A) even for short periods. Even then, transfer to less noisy or stressful work has occasionally to be considered.

Medicolegal considerations

One of the arguments sometimes advanced for pre-employment audiometry is as a safeguard against possible future claims, when the damage may in fact have been present before the employment began. The question then arises as to the medicolegal risks of employing in noisy surroundings the considerable number of people likely to be revealed by audiometry as having some degree of hearing impairment. Providing the audiometry is supported by appropriate and properly conducted hearing conservation measures, including documented explanation to the employee about the hazards to hearing, the implications of hearing loss, and the means of preventing it, the medicolegal risk becomes very slight. The presence of pre-existing hearing impairment *per se* is not a valid argument against employment. Similar considerations apply to the use of serial monitoring audiometry and the action to be taken when hearing deterioration is detected.

Assessment of fitness for work

In the absence of guidelines, the position varies across industry. Many employers, particularly small firms, recruit staff without any medical screening. Conversely, there are some who are prepared to reject a potential employee if his pre-employment audiogram demonstrates a dip at or around 4 kHz. The majority of employers who perform audiometry do so to establish a baseline for the individual, particularly if he is to work in a noisy environment. In fact, very few cases are encountered in general industry where the hearing loss causes a severe enough disability to preclude employment.

Serial audiometry

Periodic audiometric testing is generally considered to form part of a comprehensive hearing conservation programme. It is best conducted at intervals of 3–5 years, with shorter intervals in the initial years of noise exposure. Its main use is to detect deterioration in the hearing status of individuals or groups, and as an aid to their effective counselling. Safety indications for redeployment are restricted to those situations where hearing impairment puts the individual, the working group, or the plant at risk. Such instances are rarely encountered in general industry Each case has to be assessed in the light of the particular job content and working conditions in order to reach an equitable decision.

Existing employment regulations and standards

Where there are particular demands on hearing in relation to occupation, organizations develop their own internal standards. Examples are given below. In some cases there are detailed and specific regulations. More commonly, the decision is left to the examining medical officer or the personnel officer, and the requirement is simply that of fitness for the job, informally and intuitively assessed.

Flying (civil)

The licensing requirements for Class 1 aircrew (professional pilots, engineers and navigators, and also air traffic control officers) and other pilots (Class 3) are laid down in this country by the Civil Aviation Authority (CAA), the UK being a contracting state in the International Civil Aviation Organisation which sets down the basic minimum medical standards. Initial and periodic medical examinations are carried out by specially trained and qualified doctors, authorized for such work by the CAA.[20] Professional pilots rarely lose their licences from hearing loss because the aircraft radios and intercom systems function rather like hearing aids. Vertigo, however, does present a risk (Chapter 5). The hearing standards are given in Table 4.3.

Armed services

Medical fitness is expressed in terms of the PULHEEMS system (Chapter 1), in which 'H' refers to the Hearing acuity. Each quality is judged on a scale

Table 4.3 Hearing standards of the Civil Aviation Authority

Audiogram	
Maximum hearing loss (dB) in either ear	Frequency (Hz)
35	500
35	1000
35	2000
50	3000

This test is required every five years up to the age of 40, and thereafter every three years.

An applicant with a hearing loss greater than the above must be able to hear an average conversational voice in a quiet room, using both ears, at a distance of 2 m from the examiner, with his/her back turned to the examiner. He or she must also pass a practical test in the air or in a suitable simulator.

1–8, where 1 is exceptionally good and 8 is unfit for service. Interpretation of PULHEEMS scales with respect to fitness for service tends to be stricter for recruits than for personnel already serving. The general entry standard is H2, but for aircrew it is H1. These standards are defined primarily by audiometry, but where this is not available forced whisper tests can be used for routine examinations of personnel already serving. Conversational voice tests are also used in conjunction with audiometry in assessment of fitness when hearing disorders have arisen during service. The audiometric standards are given in Table 4.4.

Police

The tests performed vary from one police force to another. In Nottinghamshire, for example, the screening test for hearing is the ability to hear a forced whisper at a distance of 20 feet with each ear individually. The test technique and the 'ability to hear' response criterion are not defined. Any abnormality detected by this test is referred for full audiological assessment. There is also an annual screening by a consultant ENT surgeon for members of the force who work in an environment which might lead to hearing impairment, for example firearms instructors. In another police force, there is audiometric screening of all new applicants with a maximum acceptable hearing threshold level of 30 dB in each ear averaged over any three consecutive frequencies in the range 250 Hz to 8 kHz.

Fire service

In 1970 the Home Office issued guidance on entry and periodic medical examinations. Different standards of fitness are required for recruits and for older men, who are recommended for reassessment every 3 years after the age of 40 years. The basic criterion is defined in a general way, typical of many

Table 4.4 Audiometric standards in the armed services (1981 regulations)

PULHEEMS H grade	Sum of hearing threshold levels (dB HL) at		General description
	0.5, 1 and 2 kHz	3, 4 and 6 kHz	
H1	not more than 45	not more than 45	good hearing
H2	not more than 84	not more than 123	acceptable practical hearing for service purposes
H3	not more than 150	not more than 210	impaired hearing; usually unfit for entry
H8	greater than 150	greater than 210	very poor hearing; invaliding is usually required

The assessment is recorded as a two-digit number under H, the first digit for the right ear, the second for the left. The higher digit, representing the worse ear, will determine the individual's overall hearing category. The Royal Navy has a more stringent definition of H1, and certain branches within each service have particular requirements.

occupations: that no man should engage in duties (operational fire-fighting in this case) who is not fit for those duties. While the definition is essentially circular and thus no more than a guideline, it has the merits of flexibility, adaptability, and of evident relevance. Even the specific hearing requirements for recruits go little further. These requirements include 'Ability to hear sufficiently well to serve in any capacity. (Forced whisper to be heard in each ear separately at 20 feet.) Good hearing is essential. For the hearing test an assistant is needed to ensure proper testing of each ear and in case of doubt an audiometric test is advisable.' The guidelines are currently being revised.

Merchant navy

In 1983 the Department of Transport set regulations with respect to medical examinations of merchant seafarers. The General Council of British Shipping has also embarked recently on a programme of audiometric testing of engine-room personnel, primarily for hearing conservation purposes. Some individual companies already have their own pre-employment and periodic routine audiometric tests for noise-exposed personnel. Conditions leading to 'permanently unfit' categorization include impaired hearing sufficient to interfere with communication. A unilateral hearing defect is considered in relation to the particular job. Hearing aids are allowable in certain trades provided the aided hearing is sufficient for communication and safety: they are not allowed for engine-room, electrical, and radio personnel.

British Rail

The Board has issued guidelines on medical examinations and standards, but discretion is allowed in individual cases. The hearing tests include conversational voice and pure-tone audiometry, with stricter standards for new entrants than for periodic reviews of employees. For example, for entry to footplate and safety grades the hearing losses averaged over 0.5, 1 and 2 kHz must be less than 20 dB, whereas this is relaxed to 30 dB at the periodic reviews carried out at ages 40, 45, 50, 55, 60, 62, and 64 years. It is considered unsafe to employ a man who is dependent on a hearing aid on footplate duties on main lines, or in any grade which involves working on running lines.

British Steel Corporation (BSC)

One of the major problems encountered in heavy manufacturing industries like BSC is the potential effect of excessive noise on hearing. The main initiative has therefore been the implementation of a comprehensive hearing conservation programme which consists of a number of components, e.g. noise surveys, engineering control, education, and training, in addition to screening audiometry and the provision of personal protection. Audiometry is performed on all new employees to establish a baseline and is also offered on a voluntary basis at three-yearly intervals to those employees potentially exposed to excessive noise. The incidence of cases where hearing loss is severe enough to act as a bar to employment, or where existing employees require redeployment, is minimal. A range of communication equipment is used: contact may be by means of personal radio, tannoy, visual as opposed to auditory signals, etc. The basic criteria of auditory fitness for work are those described in detail above, i.e. ability to perform the job safely and competently, with each case considered individually. Accordingly, no specific hearing standards have been laid down.

Driving

It is conceivable that defective hearing could result in failure to hear a warning sound and thus lead to an accident. However, 'There is no significant evidence that people with severe degrees of deafness have a higher accident rate than others. Deaf people qualify for an ordinary driving licence.'[21] Thus, defective hearing as such need not be declared in an application for a driving licence, or at onset of the condition in the case of the holder of a current ordinary driving licence. However, where it is symptomatic of some other disorder liable to affect fitness to drive, then that disorder must be notified to the Licensing Centre at Swansea.

For heavy goods and public service vehicle drivers the British Medical

Association advises that a hearing defect is regarded as a contraindication to vocational driving where it prevents communication by telephone in an emergency.[22] The Medical Commission on Accident Prevention recommends that heavy goods vehicle and public service vehicle drivers' driving licences shall not be granted or renewed to those whose hearing is so bad that it interferes with the proper discharge of their duties. A useful test is to determine whether a person is capable of using a telephone so as to call the emergency services.[21] Drivers of public service vehicles and taxis are usually regarded as unfit for this work if their hearing defect is such that they are unable to communicate with passengers.

Diving

Information and advice on 'The medical examination of divers' has been published by the Health and Safety Executive in relation to the Diving Operations at Work Regulations, 1981. The standards have recently been revised and are reproduced in detail below (for general discussion on fitness to dive see also Appendix 4).

Ears The diver should be able to clear his ears. Complications of otitis media such as glue ear, deafness, perforation and persistent discharge are causes for rejection. Mastoiditis would also debar.
The following points should be covered during examination:

1. *Meati* should appear normal. If wax is present, it is not necessary to disturb it unless it is excessive or obstructing the canal. Acute or chronic otitis externa is a bar to diving. Exostoses are not harmful unless the canal is occluded, when the diver should be referred for their removal.

2. *The drum* should be seen: well-healed scars are acceptable. New entrants must demonstrate the ability to clear their ears. This may also be indicated after infection or barotrauma.

3. *Hearing*. The diver must be able to hear and understand normal conversation.

4. *Audiometric examination* must be carried out at each annual examination, using equipment covering the frequencies 250 Hz–8 kHz and according to prescribed procedures. Particular attention should be given to divers who have only unilateral hearing, and the risks of further hearing damage should be discussed with the diver.

Further education

Certain universities specialize in supplementary provision for particular types of disability (Chapter 2), Durham in the case of the hearing disabled. Many colleges of further education make special arrangements for technical courses in preparation for jobs not based on interpersonal communication, where prelingually hearing-impaired students are likely to be able to fulfil the job requirements. In considering deaf and hard-of-hearing students, particularly for lecture-based curricula, proper account should be taken of the extra support which the teaching staff (who should be consulted over admissions) may need to give, and to the possible need for supplementary aids, such as a microphone and an induction loop or infra-red transmission system, to overcome poor room acoustics. An audiological assessment prior to admission, or assessment by an educationist with relevant experience, would be valuable.

Medicine and dentistry

There are no medical standards for acceptance as a student, the fitness of each applicant being judged on the individual circumstances. A medical course, however, would be particularly difficult for a student with a severe hearing impairment because of the many different teaching environments and tutors, the fact that lip-reading will not always be possible to aid hearing, the need to hear patients clearly, and the need to use a stethoscope. An electronic stethoscope has much the same limitations as a hearing aid, outlined earlier in this chapter, and would be useless for a totally deaf student and of little or no value for one who is severely hard-of-hearing.

Nursing

The final decision on acceptance rests with the employing authority, taking account of any advice from the occupational health adviser to the school or college of nursing. With respect to hearing loss, the guidance from the Royal College of Nursing of the United Kingdom for prospective applicants warns that 'Acceptance will depend on whether your hearing loss is unilateral or bilateral, total or partial. Total hearing loss on one side may lead to rejection. Partial hearing loss on both sides may create difficulties in obtaining acceptance.'

CONCLUSIONS AND RECOMMENDATIONS

Normal hearing is difficult to define in terms of either normal function or lack of perceived disability, especially as any definition is essentially arbitrary and may be ambiguous as to whether or not 'normal for age' is intended. There is wide individual variation in the degree to which a hearing impairment causes measurable hearing disability, and to which a hearing disability is perceived by the person affected. Moreover, the effect of a disability in the context of fitness for work depends greatly on the particular job requirement and working environment. These difficulties have to be seen in relation to the quite high prevalence of measurable hearing impairments (Table 4.1) and of reported hearing difficulties (Table 4.2).

Totally normal hearing, implying a stringent audiometric definition, is truly necessary in very few jobs. But there are a number of occupations in which more than a minor impairment or disability, or having monaural hearing, is not acceptable for a variety of reasons. These include high levels of responsibility to others, need for efficient and easy communication, particular listening tasks, and safety with respect to hearing warning signals especially when having to wear hearing protectors. The hearing requirements of each job have to be considered carefully when setting standards for entry or for continued employment, but care is needed to counteract natural or traditional prejudices against employing hard-of-hearing or deaf persons. The problems that their hearing difficulties cause can be much less than are widely imagined, and can often be reduced or abolished by suitable modifications in equipment and/or in work and safety procedures.

For the majority of jobs, actual tests of hearing are unnecessary, other than a simple observation of the applicant's or employee's hearing ability at interview. This can be done, as may be applicable, with or without the interviewee wearing a hearing aid if he has one, and with or without lip-reading (being able to see the interviewer's face). This is preferably coupled with some form of health declaration and statement of any disability. For those already employed, there may also be evidence as to the importance or otherwise of any problems due to hearing difficulties that may have occurred with the particular employee and job.

Where the job requires a more definite degree of hearing ability, or minimum of disability, a test of ability to hear speech would probably be sufficient in most cases. Two such tests are suggested in the Appendix to this chapter. The choice between them depends on the nature and environment of the work, particularly whether or not there is need to hear speech in a background of noise. Audiometry could be used, but is less relevant, relatively costly, and also raises problems of correct interpretation and subsequent management. It is probably best reserved for testing those in whom particularly good hearing is required and when speech tests are insufficiently sensitive to detect minor impairments of potential significance, or where a medicolegal baseline or rejection criterion is desired, or where the test has to form the baseline for periodic monitoring in support of a hearing conservation programme.

Appendix: recommended tests of hearing for assessment of fitness for work

A wide variety of hearing tests has been or could be used for assessment of auditory fitness. The three outlined below should meet most situations and are put forward in the hope of achieving greater standardization. In selecting a test, it is advisable first to define clearly the objective(s) of the test and obtain the agreement of the involved parties to this definition. It should then be a relatively simple matter to choose which test or tests are the most suitable. The final selection may also be influenced by financial, administrative, and space considerations, and by the acoustics of the proposed test environment.

TESTS OF HEARING SPEECH IN A QUIET BACKGROUND: VOICE TESTS

Free-field live-voice testing, widely used in clinical and occupational assessment of hearing ability, gives both a quantitive method of assessing hearing and one which has obvious practical relevance. It requires no instrumentation. It has, however, fallen into disrepute in recent decades due to inadequate test protocols, calibration, and interpretative criteria, as well as appearing to be overtaken in accuracy by audiometry. The principal deficiencies in live-voice tests have been:

(1) substantial inter-examiner and intra-examiner variability in voice levels;[23]

(2) tendency to raise the voice level when the ambient noise level rises,[23] or

(3) when distance from the subject increases;[24]

(4) lack of a standard technique or sufficiently detailed test protocol;[23]

(5) ambient noise;[23]

(6) too small a test space; and

(7) too narrow and reverberant a test space.

A major contribution to restoring confidence in voice tests has been made recently by Swan.[25] He showed that deficiency (1) need not be a cause of major concern given suitable interpretative criteria, and deficiencies (3), (6), and (7) can be obviated by using the near field only. He argues that deficiency (2) is rarely a problem and (5) should not be for most medical examinations rooms. He has also shown how the non-test ear can be efficiently, easily, and inexpensively masked. As a consequence, it is hoped that the recommendations below will meet the remaining need for a detailed protocol for conducting and interpreting the tests.

Test protocol for voice tests

The examiner positions himself in front of the subject at a nominal distance of 60 cm between his mouth and subject's ears. He speaks the test material clearly in a whispered voice after full expiration (WV), conversational voice (CV), or loud voice (LV). The test material consists of trios of words: a numeral, a letter, a numeral (for example, 5B6). Different combinations of

Table 4.5 Relationship between voice test results and pure-tone hearing threshold levels (after Swan[25])

Grade	Voice test result	Approximate equivalent hearing threshold level (0.5, 1, and 2 kHz average)
1	pass WV	less than 30 dB HL
2	fail WV, pass CV	20–60 dB HL
3	fail CV, pass LV	over 45 dB HL, probably over 60 dB HL

numerals and letters must be used in each trio. Two trios are used for each type of voice, and the subject is considered to have passed that voice test when he has repeated correctly at least three of the possible total of six numerals and letters. If less than three are repeated correctly, the next (louder) type of voice is used, and so on. When required, masking of the non-test ear is accomplished by pressing a finger on the tragus of the non-test ear and moving the skin over the cartilage to and fro, thus producing a continuous noise in the ear.

The hearing requirements of the job will define the other test details as follows:

(1) whether each ear is to be tested separately with masking of the non-test ear in order to detect monaural disorders, or whether the ears are to be tested together;

(2) whether the subject's hearing aid may be worn, which in turn depends on whether it is possible and permissible at work;

(3) whether the subject can make use of lip-reading (told to watch the examiner's face) or not (told to shut his eyes), which also depends on whether lip-reading is always or normally possible at work.

Swan related the results of six grades of response to such voice tests to the audiometric thresholds of the large number of clinical patients included in his study, both retrospectively and prospectively. For test distances nominally at 60 cm and for hearing by a single ear without hearing aid or lip-reading, he established the approximate equivalents shown in Table 4.5, which include the effects of inter-clinician variability in voice levels.

Since voice levels can vary considerably between examiners[25, 26] and also between occasions with the same examiner,[25] best practice would require the examiner to calibrate his own voice levels for the test materials and in the test environment, both initially and at intervals. They can then be compared with, or adjusted to, the mean voice sound pressure levels measured by Swan, which were 57, 71, and 91 dB(A) for WV, CV, and LV respectively when measured at a distance of 60 cm from the clinician's mouth with a sound-level meter set to the fast response. For such self-calibration of voice levels an inexpensive non-precision sound-level meter would be adequate.

Where the test is conducted binaurally, and/or with a hearing aid, and/or with help from lip-reading, the result of the voice tests can be expressed in functional terms equivalent as above to unaided monaural listening. Grade 1 hearing would be quite adequate for nearly all jobs; grade 2 for all jobs other than those in which there is an operational or safety requirement for good hearing *per se* or possibly when wearing ear protection and/or working in noise; with grade 3 applicants, each individual should be carefully considered in relation to the actual hearing requirements of the jobs concerned and not be excluded unnecessarily.

Finally, it is recommended that where audiometry is to be carried out, this should not replace voice tests but supplement them. For each subject, the results of voice tests can provide a very useful check on the apparent hearing ability as measured with an audiometer; and they also give information on another often more relevant dimension of hearing ability.

TEST OF ABILITY TO UNDERSTAND SPEECH IN A BACKGROUND OF NOISE: SENTENCE IDENTIFICATION IN NOISE (SIiN) TEST

In noisy conditions, someone with a substantial loss of hearing sensitivity only (such as caused by conductive hearing loss) would be at no disadvantage relative to persons with normal hearing and even at some advantage, as they often hear better in noise than in quiet, an observation resulting from the fact that the normally hearing raise their voice levels in noise. This well-known diagnostic feature (paracusis Willisii) suggests that the patient's hearing loss is probably of conductive type.

In contrast, persons with sensorineural hearing loss (SNHL) have particular difficulty in hearing in a background of noise. Lip-reading and signing is a help but cannot always be relied upon, although workers in high levels of noise tend to learn from experience how to make maximal use of their hearing.[27] These factors, together with a wide range of individual variability in the relationship between hearing sensitivity (as measured by voice tests or pure-tone audiometry) and ability to identify correctly speech sounds in noise, make it desirable to have a test of the latter. Ideally, this should be based on samples of the sort of speech to be heard under the listening conditions to be expected, or with the communication equipment likely to be used, and in the actual noise background. Unfortunately, this is usually impracticable.

A general-purpose test of hearing of speech in noise is needed. There is no such test in standard clinical use, mainly because it would have little diagnostic importance. There is a test, however, which has been used extensively in epidemiological work[3] and meets the occupational requirement. This is the Sentence Identification in Noise (SIiN) test, which has been calibrated with suitably large numbers of persons of all hearing abilities, ages, social backgrounds, and both sexes, selected from samples of the general adult population. It is proposed that this be adopted for occupational purposes if a test of hearing speech in noise is needed. The test material on reel-to-reel or cassette tape, with a test protocol, scoring sheets, and normative data, is available from Dr R. R. A. Coles, MRC Institute of Hearing Research, University of Nottingham.

Brief notes on the test

The SIiN tape recording should be delivered to the testee by earphones. Both tape recorder and earphones have to be of reasonable quality, meeting certain minimal stated specifications, but the total cost for these items could be kept under £100 (1988 prices). The test material is played to the testee at whatever level he desires, up to the maximum level available. A practice list is provided for him to determine the test level desired and for his familiarization with the test. Guidelines and suggested standards are given for interpretation of the results, taking account of the spread of results to be expected of persons of various degrees of hearing impairment and age; age *per se* of the testee being an important factor in addition to degree of impairment.[28]

The objective of this test is to meet the requirement for checking the testee's ability to identify speech in a background of noise, to whatever standard is required by the employer, and thereby to detect those who have, or who develop, a difficulty in such auditory tasks. The standard required may be based on *ad hoc* selection of a particular percentile from our statistics, but ideally should be based on test results from those working in the actual noise environment(s) in relation to their auditory adequacy in the job(s) concerned.

PURE-TONE AUDIOMETRY

In the present context, the purposes of audiometry are to obtain a frequency-specific and a more precise and diagnostic measurement of hearing ability than are provided by speech tests, although its results will usually have less practical relevance to defining fitness for work than live or recorded voice tests. It also has many disadvantages, needing costly and carefully calibrated equipment, trained operators, and (for low frequencies) particularly good acoustic conditions. The latter will require an acoustic booth which takes up more space and is heavy and expensive (£2500 or more). The acoustic requirements themselves depend on many factors. The most satisfactory published data on recommended maximum ambient noise levels for audiometry are those of Berry.[29] Despite the basic precision of the stimulus and measurement technique in audiometry, its sources of imprecision are often overlooked. Not everyone performs well at audiometry and it is not always easy to detect poor performers. There is a considerable degree of test/retest variability, which may be due to several factors.[30] Substantial uncertainties in interpretation of audiograms may lead also to mismanagement in terms of initial or continuing fitness for work. Audiometry is a two-edged tool and one not to be embarked on without careful consideration.

Further guidance on industrial audiometry equipment and techniques and interpretation of results is available from two booklets specially written for the purpose.[31,32] Since they were written, there has also been a useful standardization of technique for manually-performed audiometry.[33] However, automatic self-recording audiometry is preferred to manual audiometry in most industries,[18] particularly where there are large numbers to be tested or the audiometrician's skill is uncertain.

REFERENCES

1. Kettle M, Massie B, eds. Employers' guide to disabilities. 2nd ed. Cambridge: Woodhead-Faulkner, 1986;19–23.
2. Manpower Services Commission. Employing someone who is deaf or hard of hearing. Booklet EPL 80. Sheffield: MSC, 1984.
3. Davis AC. Hearing disorders in the population: first phase findings of the MRC National Study of Hearing. In: Lutman ME, Haggard MP, eds. Hearing Science and Hearing Disorders. London: Academic Press, 1983;35–60.
4. Howell K, Martin AM. An investigation of the effects of hearing protectors on vocal communication in noise. J Sound Vib 1975;**41**:181–96.
5. Lindeman HE. Speech intelligibility and the use of hearing protectors. Audiology 1976;**15**:348–56.
6. Karmy SJ, Coles RRA. Hearing protection: factors affecting its use. In: Rossi G, Visone M, eds. Man and noise. Torino: Edizioni Minerva Medica, 1976;260–74.
7. Wilkins PA. A field study to assess the effects of wearing hearing protectors on the perception of warning sounds in an industrial environment. Applied Acoustics 1984;**17**:413–37.
8. Wilkins PA, Martin AM. Attention demand and recognition in the perception of warning sounds and the effects of wearing hearing protection. J Sound Vib 1984;**94**:483–94.
9. Atherley GRC, Noble WG. Effect of ear-defenders (ear-muffs) on the localisation of sound. Br J Ind Med 1970;**27**:260–5.
10. Acton WI, Wilkins PA. Can noise cause accidents? Occup Safety and Hlth 1982;**12**:14–6.
11. Wilkins PA, Martin AM. The role of acoustical characteristics in the perception

of warning sounds and the effects of wearing hearing protection. J Sound Vib 1985;**100**:181–90.

12. Coleman GJ, Graves RJ, Simpson GC. Dealing with auditory communication problems in noisy environments. In: Megaw ED, ed. Contemporary ergonomics 1984. London: Taylor and Francis, 1984;227–33.
13. Coleman GJ, Graves RJ, Collier SG, et al. Communications in noisy environments. Report TM/84/1. Edinburgh: Institute of Occupational Medicine, 1984.
14. Forrest MR, Coles RRA. Problems of communication and ear protection in the Royal Marines. J R Nav Med Serv 1970;**56**:162–9.
15. Wilkins PA, Acton WI. Noise and accidents: a review. Ann Occ Hyg 1982; **25**:249–60.
16. Health and Safety Commission. Protection of Hearing at Work. Consultative Document. London: HMSO, 1981.
17. Department of Employment. Code of practice for reducing the exposure of employed persons to noise. London: HMSO, 1972.
18. Health and Safety Executive. Audiometry in industry. Discussion Document. London: HMSO, 1979.
19. Council of the European Communities. Council Directive of 12 May 1986 on the protection of workers from the risks related to exposure to noise at work. Official Journal of the European Communities, 1986; No L 137/28 of 24.5.86.
20. Harding RM, Mills FJ. Is the crew fit to fly? Br Med J 1983;**287**:114–6 and 192–5.
21. Raffle A, ed. Medical aspects of fitness to drive: a guide for medical practitioners. 4th ed. London: Medical Commission on Accident Prevention, 1985.
22. British Medical Association. Notes for guidance of doctors completing medical certificates in respect of applicants for heavy goods and public service vehicle and taxi drivers' licences. 5th ed. London: British Medical Association, 1983.
23. King PF. Some imperfections of the freefield voice tests. J Laryngol Otol 1953;**67**:358–64.
24. Fowler EP Jr. Discovery and evaluation of otic cripples. Arch Otolaryngol 1947;**45**:550–61.
25. Swan IRC. Clinical aspects of hearing aid provision. Glasgow, Scotland: University of Glasgow, 1984. MD Thesis.
26. Pearsons KS, Bennet RL, Fidell S. Speech levels in various noise environments. Report EPA-600/1-77-025. Washington DC: US Environmental Protection Agency, 1977.
27. Acton WI. Speech intelligibility in a background noise and noise-induced hearing loss. Ergonomics 1970;**13**:546–54.
28. Davis AC. The epidemiology of hearing disorders. In: Hinchcliffe R, ed. Hearing and balance in the elderly. Edinburgh: Churchill Livingstone, 1983.
29. Berry BF. Ambient noise limits for audiometry. Report Ac60. Middlesex: National Physical Laboratory, 1973.
30. Stephens SDG. Clinical audiometry Section 14. In: Beagley HA ed. Audiology and audiological medicine; vol 1. Oxford: Oxford Medical Publications, 1981.
31. Bryan ME, Tempest W. Industrial audiometry. London: PC Werth Ltd, 1976.

32. Bryan ME, Tempest W. Examples of industrial audiograms. London: PC Werth Ltd, 1978.
33. Anonymous. Recommended procedures for pure-tone audiometry using a manually operated instrument (Joint recommendations by the British Society of Audiology and the British Association of Otolaryngologists). Br J Aud 1981; 15:213–6. J Laryngol Otol 1981;95:757–61.

5

The vestibular system

R. R. A. Coles and A. Sinclair

Principal disorders

Dizziness and giddiness describe symptoms encompassing a wide variety of experiences. They may result from disorders of the vestibular, neurological, ophthalmic, cardiovascular, or orthopaedic systems, or they may be of psychological type, or some combination of these. Their cause, and even the likely system of origin, is often difficult or impossible to define. Distinction between central vestibular and general neurological (including psychological and vasovagal) disorders is often arbitrary, or unwarranted when both forms of disorder are present as is not uncommon. On the other hand, differentiation between peripheral (end-organ and 8th cranial nerve) and central neural origin is usually possible and helps to define the type of disorder, its likely prognosis, and appropriate management. Vertigo is best defined as a hallucination of movement, its occurrence usually meaning a peripheral or central disorder of the vestibular system. Two important aspects of vestibular physiology explain most of the symptoms, signs, and prognosis of peripheral vestibular disorders, as follows.

First, the vestibular end-organs have a resting rate of nerve discharge: stimuli can either increase or decrease the firing rate. The end-organs of the semicircular canals on the two sides of the head are paired, and the afferent inputs to the central nervous system from each side act in opposition. Most, but probably not all, disorders of the *peripheral vestibular system* cause a reduction in the resting rate in the corresponding part of the 8th cranial nerve. The left/right imbalance so caused results in the eyes and body being reflexly deviated towards the side of the lesion. This is often experienced as a falling, or imbalance, to that side, and seen as the slow phase of nystagmus to that side. The vertigo or sense of rotation will go in the opposite direction, to the unaffected side, in such a case.

Secondly, the *central vestibular system* has the great ability to compensate for a chronic imbalance in the neural tonus coming from the two sides, or to habituate or adapt to frequently repeated or constant stimulation, such as 'getting your sea legs' in habituation to motion sickness. Habituation and compensation are such that the acute disturbance of a severe unilateral vestibular failure is essentially self-limiting. Over a few weeks, the sufferer passes from intolerable vertigo with nausea and vomiting, to no vertigo while keeping still but subject to vertigo with movement, to some imbalance and only momentary vertigo accompanying major rotational movements of the head or body. If symptoms of dizziness last continuously for longer than 2 or 3 weeks, the cause is not vestibular.[1]

Stimulation by sound

The cochlea responds readily to faint acoustic stimuli and yet is susceptible to damage over the long term by excessive noise levels. In contrast the vestibular part of the internal ear, whose perilymph and endolymph are in direct continuity with the corresponding fluids in the cochlea, is little affected. The explanation lies in the cochlea's micro-structure which is so uniquely responsive to mechano-acoustic stimulation. On the other hand, the organization of the vestibular labyrinth is such that the cupulae or maculae are much less likely to respond to rapid to-and-fro stimulation arising from sound at ordinary levels. Nevertheless, the human vestibular system is not totally unresponsive to acoustic stimulation, in several ways.

Even in health, very high noise levels, at and above about 135 dB SPL (sound pressure level),[2] such as experienced by those very close to powerful jet engines running at high power, can cause vertigo and nausea together with other unpleasant symptoms such as fluttering of the cheeks, chest, and abdomen, and heating of hairy surfaces and in skin folds. The saccule may also function as a receptor for low-frequency acoustic signals.[3]

When a pathological disorder of the internal ear is present, however, levels of sound in the region of 110 to 120 dB SPL may cause a form of vertigo know clinically as the Tullio effect.[4] The 'sono-ocular test'[5] takes advantage of this: if such stimuli cause nystagmus in the absence of visual fixation, this is taken as evidence of internal-ear pathology. The mechanism is uncertain. Its importance in the industrial context is that industrial noise seldom stimulates giddiness unless there is some pre-existing disorder of the internal ear.

The potentially damaging effects of noise exposure on the cochlea are now recognized without question. Noise-induced damage to the vestibular part of the internal ear is much less documented, although evidence relating to this is accumulating.[6-10] Noise-induced vestibular disorders exist, but whether or not these (apart from the Tullio phenomenon) can be produced by the acoustic conditions of civilian industry has yet to be established. Further epidemiological and clinical research is required.

One form of noise damage to the vestibular labyrinth affects the saccule in particular,[7-9] producing spontaneous, positional, or cervical nystagmus.[10] The importance of this is not so much to identify a possible new form of

Table 5.1   Prevalence of history (past or present) of dizziness or giddiness according to age group (after Hinchcliffe[11])

Age group (years)	History of dizziness or giddiness (percentage of each age group)
18–24	17
25–34	20
35–44	19
45–54	23
55–64	35
65–74	29

occupational disease or group of diseases, but to warn that signs or symptoms of peripheral vestibular disorder would not necessarily imply that an accompanying disorder of the cochlea is likely to be of constitutional origin. Not only is it perfectly possible for coincident vestibular and cochlear disorders to have different aetiologies, it seems possible that the vestibular disorder itself might be due to damage by noise.

Although there may be very reasonable anxieties about the employability of people with dizziness in certain jobs, there are liable to be additional prejudices for the following reasons. Vestibular disorders rarely yield unambiguous features in the overt behaviour of the person affected, and even when evident there may be suspicion of functional origin or overlay. The disorders are seldom diagnosed with any label more precise than vertigo (which is a symptom, not a cause or disease state), are often without any reliable treatment, and may have a very uncertain prognosis.

PREVALENCE

Hinchcliffe's study[11]

Two random samples of rural populations in the Vale of Glamorgan and in mid-Annandale (Dumfries and Galloway) were studied in 1957 and 1958 respectively. The target number was 800 subjects, divided equally between males and females and between the two locations; 90 per cent and 95 per cent of the Welsh and Scottish samples respectively were actually examined. The prevalence of a history (past or present) of dizziness or giddiness as a function of age is shown in Table 5.1: overall it was 23 per cent. Most of the episodes of vertigo were transient and not troublesome, but 3 per cent of the whole sample had experienced recurrent sustained vertigo with or without other symptoms over a period of at least one year. Hinchcliffe considered that the major basis of this was probably endolymphatic hydrops and that in

Table 5.2 Prevalence of history (past or present) of giddiness, dizziness, unsteadiness, or lightheadedness according to location, sex, and age group

	Percentage of responders to question C5 who answered 'Yes'			
	Cardiff	Glasgow	Nottingham	Southampton
Sex				
males	34	34	36	33
females	47	43	50	45
Age (years)				
17–40	39	37	41	38
41–60	43	40	46	42
over 60	43	41	45	40

Answers to question C5, in Phase III of the National Study of Hearing, MRC Institute of Hearing Research, not previously published. Total postal questionnaire sample, $n = 25\,642$; $18\,677$ responded. Total responding to question C5, $n = 16\,964$.

about one third of these (1 per cent) a diagnosis of Ménière's disease would be appropriate. He surmised further that the bulk of vertiginous histories, especially the episodes of transient vertigo, may have been arteriosclerotic in origin in the older individuals but not in the younger ones.

The National Study of Hearing

This is a long-term, two-tier, three-phase epidemiological study being conducted by the Institute of Hearing Research and is concerned primarily with hearing difficulties and tinnitus (Chapter 4). An opportunity was taken to add one question (C5) on vestibular-type disorders: 'Have you ever suffered from attacks of giddiness, dizziness, unsteadiness, or lightheadedness?' Two-thirds of recipients responded to this question: 41 per cent of these answered 'Yes'. A higher proportion of women than of men responders admitted such a history (Table 5.2). A feature of both studies was that there was little age dependence in the prevalence of dizziness. This might be an artefact, due to age differences in awareness and memory, or to increasing expectancy and tolerance (and therefore non-reporting) of balance disturbances with ageing, akin to that which occurs with hearing difficulties.[12, 13] In contrast, several studies have shown a considerably increased prevalence of vertigo-like symptoms after retirement age.[14] Thus, giddiness and similar symptoms appear to occur quite frequently throughout the working age range. The possible occupational significance of this is indicated below.

A further questionnaire was sent to the 1720 people in the Nottingham subset of 'Yes' responders. Non-responders were not followed up, and only 657 (38 per cent) responded. Major biases may thus have occurred if only those with more troublesome symptoms bothered to reply, exaggerating any prevalence estimates derived from answers to the further questions by up to threefold. Nevertheless, some of the results are interesting, given due caution in their interpretation.

Only 13 per cent of these further respondents said that their dizzy symptoms caused moderate or severe restriction of their current activities. In the context of fitness for work, this suggests that perhaps 2–5 per cent of people of working age experience intermittent disturbance of their working ability from this cause.

The episodes reported were very transient, 'a few seconds' in 55 per cent of the further respondents, and fairly infrequent 'less than once a month' in 43 per cent. Responders were asked about association with other factors. These included physical events—such as transport, 10 per cent; faints or near-faints, 23 per cent; physical strain, 32 per cent—or psychological factors—such as heights, 29 per cent; open spaces, 5 per cent; enclosed spaces, 15 per cent; mental strain, 30 per cent; strong emotion, 21 per cent; anxiety, 37 per cent; when tired, 46 per cent. Episodes were brought on by various activities, notably getting up from bed or chair, 53 per cent; straightening up after bending down, 62 per cent; looking down or bending down, 41 per cent; looking around or making a sudden turn, 51 per cent.

CLINICAL ASPECTS AFFECTING WORK CAPACITY

Relation to fitness for particular types of work

Fitness for work of those suffering from dizziness has to be judged in two ways. First, those with acute disorienting episodes coming on without warning may be a potential danger to themselves or to others in some types of work (see below). Secondly, those who have due warning, whose episodes are not dangerously disorienting, or who do not work in hazardous situations but are liable to recurrent and unpredictable absences from work on account of dizziness, may be unsuitable for jobs dependent on a particular individual.

These sorts of disorder may sometimes lead to premature retirement, especially where the disabling effects are recurrent or prolonged and there seems no reasonable prospect of an acceptable degree of recovery or rehabilitation. *Per se* they seldom lead to death, although occasionally death or serious injury results from accidents due to acute and unexpected disorientation. In some cases, however, dizziness is a manifestation of a more serious underlying disorder, such as cardiovascular disease, cerebral tumour, or multiple sclerosis, which itself may have serious implications for work ability and life expectancy.

Treatment and rehabilitation

In the acute phase, the management of vestibular symptoms should be based upon vestibular suppressive drugs. In the chronic phase, vestibular rehabilitation should be based upon Cawthorne and Cooksey's head and balance exercises.[15] Dizziness may nevertheless lead to prolonged or frequent absences from work. Additionally, sedative side-effects occur with many of the drugs used, such as cinnarizine and prochlorperazine.[16] This is especially true of drugs used to prevent motion sickness, such as hyoscine, and those with antihistamine-like properties, e.g. meclozine, dimenhydrinate, or promethazine. Treatment with drugs of this sort has clear implications for work efficiency and safety, and especially for safety in driving road, rail, air, or factory vehicles, or if combined with alcohol. Special warning has also been given[16] on the treatment of unsteadiness in elderly people with phenothiazines, such as prochlorperazine; this tends to aggravate postural falls in blood pressure and, if continued for long periods, may result in Parkinsonism. Because of these side-effects, vestibular suppressive drugs should be phased out as soon as possible and replaced by a programme of vestibular rehabilitation.[17]

SPECIAL WORK PROBLEMS, RESTRICTIONS OR NEEDS

The disadvantages to the employer of workers with recurrent or prolonged periods of illness and the possible side-effects of treatment have been mentioned above. They are not specific to any particular job, but there are certain kinds of work in which an acute attack of vertigo or imbalance could be very dangerous. These are outlined below.

Work on or near potentially hazardous machinery

The degree of the hazard will depend on the size, form, and power of the machine, and the extent to which the dangerous parts are shielded. Each individual has to be considered separately, particularly the ways in which the disorder might affect him and whether he is likely to experience warning symptoms of an impending attack and can then take appropriate avoiding action.

Work at heights

Much the same considerations apply as to work near moving machinery. Some patients' attacks may be related to or induced by heights.

Work in other potentially dangerous environments

Such as those involving molten metal, caustic acids or alkalis.

Working in moving environments

The likelihood of motion sickness is increased by most forms of vestibular disorder. Preventive drugs may be used, but due thought must be given beforehand to the potential side-effects and their influence on work safety and efficiency. Probably the best solution, if possible, is to give the affected worker a conditional trial in the actual environment in question.

Diving

Chronic or recurrent vestibular disturbances are usually incompatible with work or sport as a diver, especially if of the free-swimming sort. This is because spatial orientation depends on three main factors: vestibular, pressure sense coupled with proprioceptive input, and visual. Underwater surroundings may be dark or murky, reducing or removing the visual input; there is also a much reduced pressure sense even when the diver is on the bottom, as he has a similar specific gravity to that of his environment. Orientation sense then depends heavily on the vestibular system; if that is deficient or disturbed, the diver's predicament can be highly dangerous.

Jobs with high levels of responsibility for the safety of others

Sudden onset of acute vestibular impairment while in control of a vehicle can give the operator a false impression that the vehicle has veered from its correct direction. This can lead to unnecessary corrective action which could cause an accident. An acute vertigo can also cause a reflex response which could cause the driver to pull the vehicle out of its correct direction without him initially being aware of it. Persons subject to vestibular or similar disturbances are not fit to be in control of vehicles on roads, work sites, or farms; or in the air, until they are fully recovered and have had no attacks for a long period, perhaps a year or even more.

EXISTING EMPLOYMENT REGULATIONS AND STANDARDS OF EMPLOYMENT

Medical examination

Unlike hearing, vestibular function cannot be measured quickly and easily. Therefore, tests of it have not been a subject for standardization for purposes of employment. If carried out at all, which is unusual, they are limited to simple clinical tests, such as the Romberg test or heel-toe walking in a straight line. This may be supplemented by direct observation of the eyes to check that there is no nystagmus. These procedures will only detect substantial disturbances of balance, or nystagmus due to central, or to recent and severe peripheral, vestibular disorders. Probably the history of severity, duration, frequency, nature, and effects of vestibular episodes is more important.

Regulations

Some examples from particular occupations follow.

Flying

The criteria are whether the licence holder may become incapacitated while in control of an aircraft and whether he or she can function effectively. Clearly, vertigo or imbalance arising from Ménière's disorder, vestibular neuronitis, or positional vertigo would not be compatible with flying. More borderline or uncertain conditions will occur, and the question of fitness for flying is finally decided by the Civil Aviation Authority following examination by a doctor specially qualified in aviation medicine (see Appendix 2).

Armed forces

The degree to which a vestibular disorder will affect the 'P' assessment in the PULHEEMS system depends on its nature, severity, and effects. The interpretation of the P assessment in terms of fitness for service depends on the particular branch of service, and is closely related to the actual requirements of the job and the limitations which physical disorders would place on its performance.

Police, fire, and other public services

In general, there are no specific regulations. Certification of fitness would depend on a non-specialist medical opinion on whether the vestibular symptoms were likely to incapacitate the individual for operational duty. For firemen, the latter may involve work up ladders or with minimal visibility from smoke, and so a more stringent criterion needs to be applied. Indeed, the Home Office guidelines specify 'evidence of labyrinthine disturbance, a history of vertigo or any condition which would impair a candidate's sense of balance' as rendering a recruit unsuitable.

Merchant navy

Ménière's disease is the only vestibular disorder specified in the Department of Transport regulations on medical fitness of seafarers: it implies permanent unfitness, as do transient ischaemic attacks, which often present as episodes of dizziness (see Appendix 3).

Diving

Fitness to dive is covered by statutory medical standards. With few exceptions, disorders of balance constitute an absolute bar to working as a commercial diver (see Appendix 4).

General industry

Where pre-employment screening is performed, unless there are requirements specifically related to the work, any enquiry will probably be limited to the general question: 'Do you suffer from fits, faints, blackouts, or dizzy attacks?' If the individual admits to the last, experience in industry supports the data obtained from the National Study of Hearing that it rarely interferes with work (see p. 94). Where the severity is sufficient to cause problems, the potential employer tends to err on the side of caution, sometimes to the detriment of the individual. Occupational physicians tend to be more liberal. This unsatisfactory situation arises from the difficulties in diagnosis and uncertainties in prognosis mentioned earlier.

Similar problems are encountered with existing employees. If an employee develops disabling vertigo, the employer must then consider the safety of the individual and the group with whom he works. Accordingly, restrictions on driving, work at heights or near moving machinery are common which, together with the uncertainties regarding regular attendance at work, must raise questions of employability. In such cases, as much information as possible on the aetiology, treatment, and prognosis should be obtained and weighed against the job requirements before any decision is made.

Professions

Vestibular disorders, *per se*, are unlikely to disqualify.

Driving

The Licensing Centre must be informed by the licence holder or applicant with such a disability. Persons who are liable to sudden disabling attacks of giddiness or fainting are banned from holding any motor vehicle driving licence. In the case of vertebrobasilar artery insufficiency attacks, a person is advised to stop driving and report the condition. After a first episode, the ordinary driving licence is revoked for at least three months. If there is recurrence, then driving can be resumed if there have been no episodes for a period of at least six months. In the case of vocational drivers, a single transient ischaemic episode is a permanent bar.

Ménière's disorder, vestibular neuronitis, and positional vertigo are normally regarded as a bar to ordinary motor vehicle driving until they have been adequately controlled for a reasonable period of time as a result of treatment, or by spontaneous remission. Normally any person with a persisting vestibular disorder is regarded as unfit to drive vocationally (public service vehicles, heavy goods vehicles, and taxis) (see Appendix 1).

CONCLUSIONS AND RECOMMENDATIONS

Vestibular disorders, and those masquerading as or confused with them, are common in men and women of all age groups. Most are transient and probably of vascular (including vaso-vagal) origin. Few have substantial implications for fitness for work, although in many instances they will lead to absences from work. By and large they are difficult to diagnose; in most, prognosis and treatment are also difficult.

Real work limitations may be applicable if there is liability to acute episodes of vertigo or imbalance, especially if these are unpredictable. Limitations have to be considered where the work is near unguarded moving machinery, at heights, involves driving or exposure to motion (as in ships), or is in certain jobs with a high level of responsibility or potential risk to others. Such episodes are generally incompatible with diving, or flying as aircrew, either commercially or for sport.

REFERENCES

1. McCabe BF. Physiological basis of diagnosis and treatment of the dizzy patient. In: Gibb AG, Smith MFW, eds. Otology. Butterworth International Medical Reviews, Otolaryngology 1. London: Butterworths, 1982:177–215.
2. Ades HW. BENOX Report: orientation in space, ONR Report NR 144079. University of Chicago, 1953.
3. Cazals Y, Aran J-M, Erre J-P, Guilhaume A, Aurosseau C. Vestibular acoustic reception in the guinea pig: a saccular function? Acta Otolaryngologica 1983; **95**:211–7.
4. Tullio P. Das Ohr und die Enstehung der Sprache und Schrift. Berlin-Vienna: Urban und Schwartzenberg, 1929.
5. Stephens SDG, Ballam HM. The sono-ocular test. J Laryngol Otol 1974;**88**: 1049–59.
6. Sirala U, Lahikainen E. Studies of deafness in shipyard workers. Acta Otolaryngologica 1948; suppl 67.
7. McCabe BF, Lawrence M. The effects of intense sound on the non-auditory labyrinth. Acta Otolaryngologica 1958;**49**:147–57.
8. Mangabeira-Albernaz PL, Covell WP, Eldredge DH. Changes in the vestibular labyrinths with intense sound. Laryngoscope 1959;**69**:1478–93.
9. van Eyck M. Sound produced labyrinthine trauma. Arch Otolaryngol 1974;**100**:465–6.

10. Oosterveld WJ, Polman AR, Schoonheyt P. Vestibular implications of noise-induced hearing loss. Br J Audiology 1982;**16**:227–32.
11. Hinchcliffe R. Prevalence of the commoner ear, nose and throat conditions in the adult rural population of Great Britain: a study by direct examination of two random samples. Br J Prev Soc Med 1961;**15**:128–40.
12. Merluzzi F, Hinchcliffe R. Threshold of subjective auditory handicap. Audiology 1973;**12**:65–9.
13. Lutman ME, Brown EJ, Coles RRA. Self-reported disability and handicap in the population in relation to pure-tone threshold, age, sex and type of hearing loss. Br J Audiology 1987;**21**:45–58.
14. Hinchcliffe R. Epidemiology of balance disorders in the elderly. In: Hinchcliffe R ed. Hearing and balance in the elderly. Edinburgh: Churchill Livingstone, 1983:227–50.
15. Dix MR. Rehabilitation of vertigo. In: Dix MR, Hood JD, eds. Vertigo. Chichester: John Wiley, 1984:467–79.
16. Bateman DN. Drug treatment of nausea and vomiting. Prescribers' Journal 1985;**25**:81–6. London: DHSS.
17. Beyts JP. Vestibular rehabilitation. In: Kerr AG ed. Scott-Brown's Otolaryngology; vol 2. Guildford: Butterworth Scientific, 1987:532–57.

6

Vision and eye disorders

A. G. Cross and P. A. M. Diamond

INTRODUCTION

Vision is necessary for most types of work, though there are some occupations which can be undertaken with a low degree of visual acuity and even with total blindness, if there is ability to use Braille and a keyboard. A consideration of the visual acuity is of primary importance when deciding whether on ocular grounds any particular type of work can be undertaken. The use of spectacles and of contact lenses may improve the visual acuity, but there are some occupations where the use of one or both of these aids is not possible. The extent of the visual fields, problems of binocularity and double vision, together with defective colour vision also influence decisions on the nature of work that can be undertaken.

PREVALENCE OF OCULAR DEFECTS

In both men and women vision is variable and all degrees of visual acuity occur at all ages, though serious defects are commoner in later life. Other ophthalmic defects, such as monocularity, visual field defects, and imbalance of the eyes, also occur in both sexes and throughout life. Ocular injuries may cause serious visual defects.

It is estimated that there are 135 690 people in the British Isles who are registered as blind and 67 700 who are registered as partially sighted.

CLINICAL ASPECTS AFFECTING WORK CAPACITY

Certain types of work can only be undertaken by those workers who have perfect visual function, but other work can be performed by people with a low visual standard, and even by the blind. A period of training may be required when visual function has been damaged but thereafter there is no reason why the standard of work should not be satisfactory and done, at home if necessary, without interruption. There are varying degrees of visual defect. Some people have no sight, but the register of blind persons contains others who have enough vision to walk about independently, even though they experience some difficulty and are unable to read.

People with defective vision which cannot be improved with spectacles may be helped by low vision aids. The simplest of these is a magnifying glass of about 12 dioptres which helps a person with low visual acuity to read, but it is an unsatisfactory method of reading. Some low vision aids resemble small telescopes, with compound lenses which are fitted into spectacle frames. These can be provided to give help for distance vision, but the field of vision is constricted. They can also be provided for reading. These aids give considerable magnification, but the reduced visual field is a disadvantage. They do, however, enable people with severe visual defect, not amounting to blindness, to carry on with some close work. Recent advances in closed circuit technology and computing techniques enable the visually handicapped to read and visualize information more effectively, particularly at work.

The definition of a blind person for registration purposes is that there is not sufficient sight to carry out work for which sight is essential, and for practical purposes this is considered to be a visual acuity of 3/60 or less in each eye. This is an inability to read the top letter of the standard sight testing chart at a greater distance than three metres. The state of the visual fields also influences the ability of a person with defective sight to manage independently the routine activities of daily life.

Defects of the visual fields occur in various conditions. Vascular lesions of the nervous system can result in hemianopia (loss of half the visual field) and may be bilateral, complete, or partial. It often affects the same side of each visual field (homonymous hemianopia) which causes some difficulty in walking about since one side of the vision is absent in each eye. A complete lower quadrant homonymous defect should be a bar to driving. Bitemporal hemianopia occurs in disease of the pituitary gland and results in defective vision on both sides although the vision straight ahead is satisfactory. Bitemporal hemianopia precludes the driving of any vehicle and also the performance of any work where safety would be compromised by lateral field loss. Retinitis pigmentosa, or pigmentary degeneration of the retina, causes loss of all the peripheral field of vision so that only the 5°–10° of central vision persists. This is known as tunnel vision and causes considerable disability and should be considered to be a bar to all driving. It also affects the capacity to do many other tasks safely and effectively. A similar condition occurs in advanced chronic simple glaucoma, and should be similarly regarded.

Blind persons receive instruction under the organization of the Royal National Institute for the Blind (RNIB). Braille and typing are taught, together with instruction in how to walk about independently using a stick, usually coloured white, which indicates the visual handicap. The long-cane technique, and newer devices using ultra-sound, allow even more independence. The ability to manage personal matters like eating and toilet is included in this instruction which is undertaken soon after the sight is damaged. Blindness associated with deafness causes extra problems.

Blindness has many causes. Congenital defects and trauma are usual causes in the young, while acquired defects such as cataract, glaucoma, and macular degeneration damage sight in the more elderly. The results of trauma can often be treated to prevent loss of sight, and many cases of cataract and glaucoma react satisfactorily to therapy. Macular degeneration, which damages central fixation, is fairly common in the elderly and is in many cases untreatable. Some cases can be halted by laser treatment, but the condition cannot be cured. Diabetes is the commonest cause of blindness in the western world and accounts for 7–8 per cent of all registrations.

SPECIAL WORK PROBLEMS

The main difficulty for those who have defective vision is that they are more liable to have accidents in hazardous situations. Thus people with defective vision, restricted visual fields, or imbalance of the eyes with resulting diplopia, should not work on ladders or scaffolding where they will fall if they overstep the boundaries, and they should not work among moving machinery where they might, also, suffer injury. Manifestly, people with seriously defective visual function must be barred from driving vehicles not only on the public highway, but also on construction sites and on industrial and other premises. They should not operate cranes or hoists. They cannot be employed in the armed services, the police, or the fire services.

It is particularly important that young people with ocular problems should receive advice about a suitable career after their visual state has been assessed, and it is essential that the lifetime prognosis for this should be considered when a decision is being made about their employment. Candidates for the armed services, the police force, the mercantile marine, and flying services undergo full medical examination on entry, and careful examination is undertaken for train and bus drivers. Normal vision and ocular function is required in all people who propose to spend their lives in transport or in occupations where driving is an essential component, and it is necessary that they can be given reasonable assurance that their ocular function (with correction, if necessary and allowed) will remain at a satisfactory level for their expected work-span.

Normal vision

The majority of the population falls into this category. The visual acuity is normal (6/6 in each eye), *with or without optical help*; the visual fields are full, the balance between the two eyes is normal, and colour perception is satisfactory. Such people can in general undertake any occupation, though the wearing of contact lenses or spectacles may, exceptionally, result in some difficulty. High visual standards are required for aircraft pilots, for navigators of ships at sea, and for drivers of trains and motor vehicles. Officers in the police force and members of the fire and rescue services must also have a high standard of visual acuity. Members of the armed services are required to achieve definite visual standards which differ according to the duties to be undertaken. All workers in these various occupations must undergo regular examinations to ascertain that they have not fallen below the necessary standards. Serious visual defects, such as the loss of an eye, will often lead to dismissal from their occupation.

Intermediate vision

This group comprises those who have defective sight (less than 6/6 in each eye) but who are not in the blind or partially sighted categories. Many can achieve satisfactory visual acuity with spectacles or contact lenses, but others have some degree of subnormal vision even with optical help. Some have mild defects of visual fields, ocular muscle balance, or colour vision. People in this category are ocularly fit for all occupations except those requiring the highest visual standards. They can undertake clerical work, most manufacturing and servicing tasks, and all professional occupations, and are usually fit to drive private cars. Those with marked defects of the visual fields must be regarded as being at risk if they work at heights or among moving machinery. Crane operators, fork-lift truck drivers, and drivers of electric trucks within stores and work sites all require good peripheral vision, both for the driving task and for the control and manipulation of the loads they carry. Double vision should disqualify from work in all hazardous situations, and from vocational driving. In less exacting tasks the disability can be overcome by retraining after covering one eye.

Aphakia

In this condition the lens of the eye is absent, usually as the result of an operation to remove the opaque lens of cataract. This is commonly of the senile type but it occurs also in some cases of traumatic damage to the eye and secondarily to some eye diseases. Removal of the lens alters the optical properties of that eye so that in most cases satisfactory vision can only be obtained by the use of a strong convex lens in spectacles. This alters the size of the image seen by the operated eye making it larger, so that where only one eye has been operated on, fusion of the images of the two eyes is not possible and, if there is good vision in the other eye, double vision results. This disability can be overcome by the use of a contact lens or by the implantation of a plastic lens to the eye at the time of the cataract operation. People who are aphakic in one eye and who have not been given an implanted lens or contact lens are functionally monocular. Even where both eyes have been operated on and are aphakic the enlarged image may mean that objects to the side are not easily seen, for example in walking, so that persons crossing in the pathway may suddenly spring into view and just as suddenly disappear from the field of view, a phenomenon which has been called the 'jack-in-the-box'.

Monocularity

The removal of an eye results in monocular vision, and a similar state occurs if the vision of one eye is very defective. This causes difficulty in the estimation of distance, although this improves with learning, and the visual field is reduced. An eye may have to be removed because of injury, as the result of severe and continuous pain, or as the result of the development of a malignant tumour. Damage to the vascular supply of an eye by embolus or thrombosis may cause loss of vision, as will the chronic inflammation in some patients with uveitis.

People who are monocular are at increased risk if they work in hazardous jobs, such as on scaffolding or amongst unguarded machinery. They are excluded from work as pilots of ships and as drivers of trains, heavy goods vehicles (HGV), and public service vehicles (PSV). A minimal level of binocularity is required for *all* new entrants for heavy goods and public service vehicle licences. HGV and PSV drivers who become monocular are required to surrender their licences, while such drivers who have had cataract surgery with an intraocular implant are allowed to continue two months after the surgery, provided they fulfill the necessary minimum binocular visual standard, and are subject to annual checks.

Injuries
Perforation occurs when the eye is struck by some pointed object. A common injury occurs as a result of an intraocular foreign body, often from the use of a hammer and chisel to cut a hole in a wall or cement floor. The intraocular foreign body is a chip of metal from the hammer which is made of hard but relatively brittle steel, and damage to the lens and retina is a common result. Blows on the eye with a blunt object such as a hammer may rupture the eyeball, which necessitates removal of the eye. Lesser blows, as from a fist, may cause traumatic cataract. This does not usually result in removal of the eye, but usually requires removal of the lens which, if no implant is used, causes unilateral aphakia.

Eye protection
Eyes should always be protected from high velocity particles, dust, irritant fumes, gases, radiation, and chemical splashing. Safety spectacles, or goggles where a complete seal is required, with toughened glass or plastic lenses to

British Standard specification can be supplied with correcting lenses; spectacles cannot be worn satisfactorily under goggles. Protection is particularly important where there is effective vision in only one eye, since this is doubly valuable, and monocular workers must be warned about occupational hazards. Monocular vision, however, has a considerable effect on employer liability[1] and a skilled craftsman who loses the sight in one eye may have to be moved to a less hazardous occupation. People who have a squint in early life may have an amblyopic, or lazy, eye which renders them virtually monocular. Such people, together with the monocular group, should be advised not to undertake occupations which represent a danger to the remaining eye.

Conditions causing sudden variation of vision

Sudden variation of vision may cause difficulty, especially if very fine work is being undertaken. It is unusual but may occur in migraine, sometimes associated with the sensation of flashes of light. Spasm of the central artery of the retina or its branches may cause blurred vision which is usually transitory. Blood sugar variations in diabetics who are unstable or undergoing stabilization, and medication which affects accommodation are more common iatrogenic causes.

Colour perception

Defective colour vision is inherited in the majority of cases, occurring in 8.0 per cent of men and about 0.2 per cent of women. There are different types of defect, but for practical purposes the problem is identification of red and green. Acquired defects are rare, but do exist, and may be permanent. They may be temporary in various ocular diseases such as tobacco amblyopia, toxic amblyopia due to medication, and lens opacities. Where good colour perception is necessary for safety reasons, therefore, periodic re-examination is necessary.

Only a very small proportion of occupations require perfect colour discrimination; a few others present some difficulties but are not necessarily precluded. Pre-employment rejection of workers with defective colour vision will eliminate up to 8.0 per cent of male applicants, depending on the tests used. It is therefore prudent to assess the need for perfect colour vision before instigating a screening programme. Further investigations to diagnose the type and severity of the colour defect are best left to specialists. Conditions for all tests are exacting, and findings will be useless if these are not followed. Equipment must be clean, and not left on the windowsill to collect dust and fade in the sun. The most practical acceptable ambient illumination is ordinary daylight through a north-aspect window. Artificial illumination standards must be precise, and variations in the colour of light are not acceptable. The subject should wear corrective lenses (not tinted of course) if necessary, to enable him to define the characters. There needs to be a good understanding between tester and subject; it is a fairly complex procedure.

Methods of colour vision testing

Pseudoisochromatic tests, of which the best known is the set of Ishihara plates, are the most commonly used method. It is not unknown, however, for pre-employment applicants to memorize the characters and plate numbers, and rapid random replies should be sought. Matching tests are the oldest type of colour vision examination. The Holmgren wool test, which requires the subject to match colours of various skeins of wool, was used in the railway industry until other techniques became more sophisticated. Modern matching tests, such as the Farnsworth–Munsell 100 Hue test, detect the more subtle defects. Lantern tests rely on transmitted light through filters. Ambient illumination is less critical, and lanterns more easily simulate signals for testing for navigation and transport purposes.[2] Often they use only the relevant signal colours, but they may include any colours in the range. Well-known lanterns are the Giles–Archer, Holmes–Wright, and Edridge–Green. Practice and custom usually decree which is used in any occupation or industry: for instance, the railway industry currently uses the Edridge–Green Lantern as an ancillary test to the Ishihara plates. The anomaloscope is a highly specialized diagnostic instrument which has no place in occupational screening procedures. A good comprehensive review of tests for colour vision with recommended lighting standards, etc. can be found in the recent publication *Defective colour vision* by Fletcher and Voke.[3]

Those occupations requiring normal colour perception fall into three categories:

Transport, navigation, the armed services

The need is to interpret colour signals without error, both in operating tasks and in the maintenance and wiring of these signals. There is usually no positional reference, and the signal may be at a great distance and weather conditions adverse, with fog, rain, or bright sunshine. Testing procedures evolved because accidents on the railways and in navigating were attributed to incorrect colour perception. Driving on the road, however, does not require colour perception because road traffic signals can be interpreted by the position of the lights. These are of a standard, high intensity, but other red lights of low intensity may be difficult to distinguish. There is no statistical indication that drivers with defective colour perception have more traffic accidents than those with normal vision,[4] and such people probably learn to compensate for their defect, so resulting in more vigilance in driving.

Drivers of public service and heavy goods vehicles undergo intensive training; in London Regional Transport intending bus drivers spend 10 days driving with an experienced instructor, and are expected to achieve a high standard of driving performance. This would tend to eliminate drivers who do not compensate for defective colour perception.

Occupations using colour coding for safety and technical purposes

Colour differentiation is used for hazard warning systems, cables and wiring, coding of pipelines, etc. In the concept of British Standard colour coding,[5] those with defective colour vision have not been sufficiently considered. Coding may have to be done under dirty and poorly lit conditions by people who are not aware that they have a problem. Other features which supplement the colour code (as in the pin index used with medical gas cylinders) are useful. Chemical analysis and medical diagnosis (clinical and technical) may present difficulties, such as with urinalysis and, indeed, with colour vision screening. These problems may be eliminated by screening at school so that appropriate career advice can be offered to the very small proportion of affected children who would be unable to work in these occupations.

Occupations commercially dependent on sophisticated colour selection

Examples range from fruit picking to ticket collection, but are mainly concerned with dyeing, textiles, paper, and printing. Employers in these industries may not consider formal colour vision screening until an expensive mistake has been made. Trade tests are useful, and for some less exacting tasks colour filters may help. Coloured pens can be labelled; this helped a clerk to avoid writing in green on accounts sheets, the colour reserved exclusively for audit checks within his firm. With more artistic vocations, there will be a degree of self-selection.

Visual fatigue at work

This condition does not ordinarily occur in people who have normal vision, who have satisfactory balance between the two eyes, and where there is adequate illumination. The eyes will seek relief from any exacting visual task by attempting to focus on infinity; this can be assisted by altering the desk position or with the help of a picture or mirror.

Visual display units

Rapid expansion in the use of visual display units (VDUs) has aroused concern about the ability of the eyes to cope. There is no evidence that working with VDUs can harm the eyesight, but partially sighted persons, whose sight cannot be corrected to a satisfactory standard by spectacles, may have difficulty working at normal office VDU stations. They can be helped by using VDUs with enlarged output; and the Disablement Resettlement Officer can provide low-vision aids if they are necessary. Headaches attributed to eyestrain are usually caused by lack of ergonomic consideration, with consequent awkward posture and muscular problems. Equipment should be properly mantained to avoid flicker and glare, and have sufficient flexibility in positioning of screen, keyboard, and source documents to enable the operator to adjust them to his or her particular visual requirements. Middle-aged and elderly people may experience difficulty because their ordinary reading glasses do not correspond with the distance at which they need to carry out their VDU work. They may be more comfortable with specially modified lenses which are weaker, enabling them to view the screen at 60–75 cm (2 ft. to 2 ft. 6 in.). Bifocal spectacles may not be as convenient. Excessive heat generated by electronic equipment in a confined or over-crowded space with inadequate ventilation may exacerbate dryness or soreness of the eyes.[6]

Limitations of spectacles and contact lenses at work

Circumstances can pose problems for persons who have to wear spectacles or contact lenses at work. Protective clothing, such as safety helmets, welding visors, and ear defenders can make spectacle-wearing and even the use of contact lenses uncomfortable. In such cases goggles should be provided with correcting lenses. It is seldom possible to wear spectacles with special breathing apparatus. The wearer of such apparatus may have to read warning notices, instructions and dials, and so good unaided visual acuity is necessary. Spectacles with flat temple pieces may improve compatibility with certain items of personal protection, such as earmuffs or respirators, but should not be worn with self-contained breathing apparatus unless positive pressure within the face piece is maintained. The wearing of tinted spectacles or lenses will reduce visibility, especially in dull weather and at night. Reactive lenses will not change sufficiently quickly to cope with sudden changes of illumination such as in driving through road tunnels, or passing headlights, and their use should be limited. Drivers may have to perform exacting manoeuvres as in reversing, even when spectacles have become dislodged by accident. For this reason heavy goods and public service vehicle drivers must have an unaided visual acuity in each eye of at least 3/60. For further details on visual standards and driving, particularly vocational driving, see Cross 1985.[7]

Contact lenses my be useful in occupations where spectacles may become misted, in aphakia, and where distortion occurs when looking through the marginal parts of the spectacle lenses. Some occupations are associated with the production of dust and particles which may cause irritation when trapped under the contact lenses. These particles often cannot be removed without removal of the lens, and discomfort in the form of headache or conjunctivitis may persist. This is a hazard in dirty and dusty occupations, such as railway track work, mining, and work with rescue teams, and requires constant vigilance. Ultraviolet and infra-red rays are absorbed by contact lenses, and this may cause photophobia and possible heating of the lens. Tinted lenses, however, will absorb most of the ultraviolet and infra-red energy. People who wear contact lenses at work must be identified because there are certain occupations in which they should not work, and in some cases protective measures may be required. Cosmetic considerations are the motivating factor for many people who wear contact lenses, but there is also no doubt that they give better optical correction where myopia exceeds five dioptres. Contact lenses are also useful in association with aphakia, especially unilateral aphakia. They are useful in irregular astigmatism but they do not help in high degrees of regular astigmatism. Oxygen is absorbed by the cornea and those hard contact lenses which are not gas permeable may inhibit this absorption with resulting discomfort. Soft contact lenses may absorb fumes and this can cause irritation. Working in extreme cold, as in cold stores, can cause discomfort in people who wear soft contact lenses. Contact lenses may therefore be helpful at work but there are certain disadvantages which must be considered. Individual tolerance is variable and is affected by sensitivity to lens lubricants, by photophobia, and by personal lens hygiene. The carrying of a spare pair of spectacles may be required.

Conditions of work which may be detrimental to vision

Contrary to popular opinion, the intensive use of the eyes either for distance vision or close work does not result in damage to the vision of healthy eyes. The presence of dust may cause irritation. Diminished corneal sensation may occur in a small number of workers in dusty occupations. They may be helped by wearing protective goggles, but the best solution is a change of occupation. Corneal ulcers may occur from a multiplicity of causes. They are usually treatable but there is a tendency to recurrence which may limit the usefulness of the worker in dusty atmospheres. Work with irradiation may cause lesions in the eyes and it is very important that workers who are exposed to the various forms of irradiation should have adequate protection (see below). This is particularly important for those workers using high-output laser devices where goggles of appropriate wavelength absorption should be provided. Workers under constant fluorescent lighting may complain of some discomfort but there is no evidence that this illumination damages the sight. The use of tinted spectacles may minimize the symptoms.

Non-ionizing irradiation
Ultraviolet light may cause superficial corneal lesions associated with gross discomfort, and workers who are exposed to this form of irradiation should

wear tinted spectacles. Similar corneal lesions may occur with electric flashes from short circuits and from arc lights. Infra-red rays can cause lens opacity. Heat, as from furnaces and in the glass-blowing industry, can also cause lens opacity and it is essential that ocular protection by tinted spectacles is provided. High-output pulsed and cutting laser devices pose a specific hazard for workers. Protective goggles designed specifically for work with lasers should be worn, and the working head of the laser should be enclosed. The goggles should be checked regularly for wear or damage. Stringent safety precautions should always be enforced and practised in work with lasers or with microwaves.

Ionizing irradiation

Ionizing irradiation which results from exposure to radium and X-rays can cause cataract, and workers in radiological departments should always be provided with eye protection, such as glass containing lead.

Ocular problems in older workers

It is inevitable that some older workers will suffer a degree of visual disablement and this cannot be foreseen in any particular person. Cataract, macular degeneration, and glaucoma may occur in later life without any indication of these conditions being present in earlier years. If visual acuity is reduced as a result of these diseases, treatment must be undertaken according to the current clinical findings. Cataract can be treated surgically and this may enable patients to continue at work in their chosen career. Early macular degeneration may be controlled by laser therapy. In some cases premature retirement may be necessary. Experience may override the disability, and it is not always appropriate to apply the same strict visual standards to older long-term employees. Good illumination is necessary for the maximum degree of close work in elderly persons.

The anaesthetic cornea

The cornea is normally a very sensitive part of the eyeball and with the corneal reflex reacts immediately to injury and to the presence of a foreign body. Corneal sensitivity declines in later life but the cornea still reacts even to minor trauma. Complete corneal anaesthesia is the result of injury or disease of the trigeminal nerve. It usually requires treatment by tarsorrhaphy which turns the patient effectively into a one-eyed person so that his working activities are correspondingly reduced. More recently, the use of a bandage soft contact lens instead of tarsorrhaphy has enabled binocular vision to be retained.

Some common eye diseases and their effects

A number of eye diseases occur with some frequency in all members of the population. These do not always lead to inability to work, but they may cause difficulty.

Conjunctivitis

This condition does not in most cases necessitate a cessation of work. It is characterized by discomfort rather than pain, in the absence of complications, and by a discharge from the eyes which may be muco-purulent. It yields rapidly to treatment with antibiotic drops. It may be associated with ulceration of the cornea and with inflammation of the eyelid margins (blepharitis). This latter condition is the result of inflammation of the glands at the margin of the eyelids. It requires massage of the eyelid margins and the use of antibiotic drops. Watering of the eyes due to obstruction of nasolacrimal ducts may cause annoyance at work but can be treated if necessary by surgical methods.

Uveitis

This is an inflammation of the uveal tract. A part or the whole of the uvea, which is responsible for the nourishment and focusing of the eye, may be affected. It occurs in all states of severity from the mild form, causing only a slight blurring of vision, to the acute state where there is severe pain and serious visual defect. The condition usually responds to treatment with local or systemic steroid preparations but a long period of therapy may be necessary. It is sometimes associated with secondary glaucoma, complicated cataract, and rarely with the loss of sight of the eye. It may sometimes cause severe disablement and inability to continue in employment. Ophthalmic *Herpes zoster* may cause uveitis, but this can usually be treated and this type of ocular inflammation does not usually recur.

Glaucoma

In this condition the pressure in the eyeball is higher than normal. It occurs in two forms. The acute form causes sudden severe pain and visual defect; when treated promptly long-term results are good. The chronic form, which usually occurs in later life, may cause a serious degree of visual defect with contracture of the visual fields and resulting inability to continue in employment.

Myopia

This is the condition of short-sight, which is characterized by difficulty in seeing clearly in the distance. It can be overcome by the use of spectacles or contact lenses. The large majority of short-sighted people have small degrees of the defect and are not seriously disabled. A minority of myopic people have such a big error that, even with optical correction, useful vision is not possible. Persons in occupations where spectacles or contact lenses cannot be worn are unsuitable for these forms of work. Higher degrees of myopia, such as 12 dioptres or more, may be associated with separation of the retina. This results in a sudden defect of visual acuity. Occupations which require heavy exertion, such as digging or carrying heavy weights, are unsuitable for such people.

Retinal separation

This condition occurs not infrequently, particularly in association with high degrees of myopia and after ocular trauma. It is treated surgically and in many cases good vision is restored. The prognosis depends upon the amount of retina which separates and whether or not the macula is detached. Detachment of the macula results in diminution of vision to about 6/60 even if the retina reattaches. Patients whose retina does not reattach with surgery lose all vision in that eye. Patients whose retina reattaches should subsequently avoid the heaviest manual work.

CONCLUSION

Satisfactory visual function is important in assessing the fitness of people at work. There are many occupations which require the highest standards, but defective ocular function does not necessarily prevent people from working in certain other occupations if suitable training and/or equipment are available. Career guidance should ensure that young people do not embark on unsuitable careers, where an uncorrectable or progressive disability will restrict promotional advancement in the future.

REFERENCES

1. *Paris* v. *Stepney Borough Council* (1951) AC 367, 1 All ER 42.
2. Cole BL, Vingrys AJ. A survey and evaluation of Lantern Tests of colour vision. Am J Optom, Physiol Opt 1982;**59**:346–74.
3. Fletcher R, Voke J. Defective colour vision, fundamentals, diagnosis and management. Bristol and Boston: Adam Hilger Ltd, 1985.
4. Norman LG. Medical aspects of road safety. Lancet 1960;i:989–94 and 1039–45.
5. British Standards Specification for identification of pipelines and services (BS 1710, 1984). British Standards Institution, 1984.
6. Health and Safety Executive. Visual display units. London: HMSO, 1983.
7. Cross AG. Vision. In: Raffle PAB ed. Medical aspects of fitness to drive. 4th ed. London: Medical Commission on Accident Prevention, 1985.

7

Dermatology

H. O. Engel and R. J. G. Rycroft

INTRODUCTION

Less is known about the relationship between skin conditions (dermatoses) and employment than some dermatologists and occupational physicians care to admit. In the everyday practice of dermatology and occupational medicine there are many individual exceptions to most of the current dermatological wisdom. For example Rystedt in Sweden found that, even in known high-risk jobs, about a quarter of those who had had moderate or severe atopic eczema in childhood did not develop dermatitis.[1]

This means that there is often doubt as to whether a particular individual with a dermatosis will be able to tolerate a particular job. It is frequently a sound decision to give the individual the benefit of that doubt, in the interests both of the employee and his prospective employer. The recommendations that follow should not, therefore, be treated as inflexible. A flexible approach allows individual circumstances to be considered properly and fosters good industrial relations.

Classification of skin conditions

Dermatoses can usefully be divided into two categories:

1. *Non-occupational*: not primarily caused by skin contact at work, though some (such as psoriasis) may be aggravated by it.

2. *Occupational*: primarily caused by skin contact at work, though some (such as allergic contact dermatitis from chromate in cement) may continue even if this contact ceases.

The distinction between occupational and non-occupational dermatoses is often difficult, largely because the majority of occupational dermatoses and a sizeable proportion of non-occupational dermatoses have the same clinical appearance. This clinical and histopathological entity is termed eczema or dermatitis; the two words are now used synonymously by most dermatologists. Until the distinction between occupational and non-occupational dermatoses has been made as accurately as possible, all decisions about fitness for work are severely handicapped.

The interaction between individual constitution and the occupational environment remains largely unmeasurable and unpredictable. That is to say, exogenous (contact) factors and endogenous (constitutional) factors appear to interact differently in different individuals. For example, of two individuals with the same occupational skin contacts, one might notice no adverse effects on a pre-existing psoriasis, while another might find that psoriasis was initiated on their palms for the very first time (see p. 119).

Skin conditions and employment

Dermatoses and employment may be considered from two aspects, which correspond to the above classification:

(1)   the effect of the common non-occupational dermatoses on fitness for work; and

(2)   the effect of the common occupational dermatoses on fitness for work.

Skin conditions, especially those involving the hands and face, are obvious to prospective employers and fellow-employees. They easily, therefore, provoke aversion and prejudice from fear of contagion or simply from appearing unhygienic.

Employers may need to be reassured that, contrary to popular belief, the great majority of dermatoses are not infectious or contagious and that skin conditions need only rarely be a bar to employment. The emphasis should be shifted instead towards the accurate identification of the few dermatoses that can present real problems in specific occupations.

Similarly, fellow-employees may need to be reassured, particularly about the sharing of washing and eating facilities. While the occupational physician or general practitioner may fully accept the fitness for work of a prospective employee, the personnel manager, supervisor, and fellow-employees still have to be convinced. For some of them it may be their first proper introduction to the medical facts about skin disease. The level of accurate information about skin disease in the community is still low in relation to its visibility and prevalence.

PREVALENCE

General

Probably the nearest that there has ever been to a survey of the prevalence of skin disease in the general population was that carried out on behalf of the National Center for Health Statistics in the United States.[2] Nearly one-third of a 20 000 general population sample examined were found to have 'some skin pathology that should be evaluated by a physician at least once.' The most common of the skin conditions found were acne vulgaris, tinea, benign and malignant tumours, seborrhoeic eczema, atopic eczema, and contact dermatitis.

Skin conditions prompted 22.5 per cent of attendances at general practitioner surgeries in an inner-city borough in London.[3] Yet general practitioners' training in dermatology is frequently slight in comparison with other areas of medicine which involve much smaller percentages of their patients. This may lead to inappropriate medical guidance, including those instances when it is sought by employers, and sometimes to unnecessarily prolonged absences from work.

Contact dermatitis

In industrialized countries contact dermatitis accounts for about 5 per cent of dermatological consultations in hospital out-patient departments.[4] The proportion of eczematous patients diagnosed as having contact dermatitis can differ widely, however, from one dermatologist to another.

Occupational dermatoses

The prevalence of occupational dermatoses is not as accurately known as the prevalence of the common non-occupational dermatoses. This is due both to the greater difficulty in diagnosing occupational dermatoses and to the lack of accurate reporting systems.

Agrup attributed only 11 per cent of all hand dermatoses to occupation, of which 56 per cent were found to be due to allergy.[5] Such figures, however, should not be accepted uncritically, because they are heavily dependent on the views of the individual dermatologists.

Statistics compiled by the Department of Health and Social Security (DHSS) for Great Britain show that in 1984–85 skin conditions accounted for 2.5 per cent of all periods of sickness absence from work over eight weeks (20 000 out of 758 000) and 1 per cent of all days lost from sickness absence (2.8 million out of 328 million days).[6] These figures can be regarded as only the tip of an iceberg: many patients with occupational dermatoses never lose any time from work attributed to their skin condition. During the same year, half of all diseases prescribed for industrial injury benefit by the DHSS were for 'non-infective dermatitis of external origin'.

The maximum number of certified periods off work for skin diseases occurs between the ages of 20 and 40, as is clearly illustrated by Griffiths,[7] though a second peak in the prevalence of occupational dermatoses has often been demonstrated during the last decade or so of working life.

Industrial injury benefit figures derived from DHSS sources include an element of giving the claimant the benefit of the doubt. Biasing these figures in the opposite direction, however, there must be many individuals whose occupational dermatoses are never claimed as such.

As one would expect, more males than females have occupational dermatoses. Among patients included in a joint European study of contact dermatitis, 30 per cent of men and 12 per cent of women had occupational dermatoses.[8]

The number of premature retirements due to skin disease is not known. Frequently an alternative occupation can be found. But some highly trained people such as laboratory technicians, pharmacists, and nurses, may be forced by contact sensitization to give up their work. Some atopic eczema sufferers may eventually have to give up working with unavoidable contact irritants.

CLINICAL ASPECTS AFFECTING WORK CAPACITY

All the comments that follow apply mainly to prospective employees with a past history *and* clinical signs of the skin disease in question. If their conditions have cleared and remained clear without therapy for an extended length of time, a year for example, they need not necessarily be considered a significant influence on fitness for work. When a history *alone* may have to be taken into consideration this will be specifically indicated for the dermatosis in question. Extreme conditions, such as those experienced in jungle warfare, may be contraindicated for practically any of the skin conditions listed.

Effect of the common non-occupational conditions on fitness for work[9]

Eczema

Atopic eczema renders the potential employee more susceptible to contact irritants, though not to contact sensitizers unless they are also contact irritants.[10] This increased susceptibility is probably not shared by those with asthma or hay fever only.[1]

The atopic is not immunologically more likely to develop contact sensitization; in fact there is a certain amount of evidence that the atopic is less easily contact-sensitized than the non-atopic.[11-14]

If there is any increased susceptibility to sensitization in an atopic, it is likely to be due to skin already compromised by eczema presenting a less effective barrier to the penetration of contact allergens. This is unlikely to be a relevant factor unless there is active eczema on the hands or forearms. The better such eczema is controlled with treatment the less significant even this potential susceptibility becomes.

There is undoubtedly an increased susceptibility to contact irritants in some particularly high-risk work, such as hairdressing training (shampoo), catering (wet work and detergents), and production engineering (soluble oil). In these few particular occupations a prolonged history of atopic eczema in childhood might alone be considered sufficient contraindication, though it always remains possible that a particular individual may even then escape unscathed.

In most other jobs the irritant factor is insufficient, even in employees with active atopic eczema, to constitute a bar unless the hands are currently eczematous. Examples of other occupations with irritant potential are domestic cleaning, nursing, construction work, motor-vehicle maintenance, horticulture, and agriculture. The eczema of some atopics worsens in response to hot occupational environments, over-dry as well as humid.

Involvement of the hands in atopic eczema also raises an entirely separate fitness-for-work problem in certain occupations. This is due to the potential presence of secondary infection or carriage of *Staphylococcus aureus*. This may constitute, for example, an increased risk of food poisoning from staphylococcal toxin in catering staff, and an increased risk of promoting the cross-infection of patients in hospital staff.

One further consideration may influence the advice given to atopic subjects. Rystedt[15] has pointed out that, even where their work provided no recognizable skin hazard, around half of atopics may develop exacerbations of pre-existing hand eczema, or hand eczema *de novo*. When hand eczema develops in an atopic potentially exposed to any skin hazard at all, it is often difficult for the patient, his trade union representative, or the insurer to accept that the condition is not necessarily occupational. In such cases, industrial injury assessors and expert witnesses giving evidence in claims for compensation may allow the patient the benefit of the doubt. Many essentially endogenous dermatoses are then stated to be aggravated by work exposure, especially if there is known to be a high-risk substance, such as chromate, epoxy resin, or a powerful irritant, in the occupational environment.

The prognosis in atopic eczema has to be very guarded. According to Rystedt,[15] 8 per cent of 995 atopic subjects questioned had had to change their jobs. But, as was mentioned at the beginning of the chapter, even in high-risk jobs a substantial minority never develop any form of dermatitis. Wilkinson has published some useful notes on careers advice for young people with atopic eczema.[16]

Seborrhoeic eczema   tends, as a clinical impression, to be associated with an increased susceptibility to contact irritants, but this does not appear to be as strong a factor as in atopic eczema. Spread of seborrhoeic eczema from its localized chronic sites can occur in response to hot environments, over-dry as well as humid, as previously mentioned in connection with atopic eczema. Discharging otitis externa or heavily scaling seborrhoeic eczema of the scalp may raise problems of bacterial transfer similar to those described for infected atopic hand eczema.

Stasis (varicose) eczema   can be aggravated by standing still for prolonged periods. Problematic jobs therefore exist, such as working as a waiter, a shop assistant, or a machine operator in engineering. Such postural occupational factors could probably be countered effectively, however, with correct advice about the 'muscle pump' and properly supportive legwear.

Discoid (nummular) eczema   has little, if any, implication for employment, unless associated with hand eczema, when similar considerations to those in atopic eczema apply.

It is worth stressing that differential diagnosis between the more localized forms of discoid eczema and contact dermatitis can sometimes be difficult. This can result in a diagnosis of contact dermatitis being missed, as well as in a patient with discoid eczema being given inappropriate advice to change jobs.

Psoriasis

Psoriasis, which affects around 2 per cent of the adult population of north-western Europe, can be aggravated by physical or chemical trauma (Koebner effect). It may be elicited on the hands for the first time in psoriasis-prone individuals by occupational contact factors. Psoriatics vary widely, however, in their liability to lesions on the hands.

Mild psoriasis not affecting the hands can probably safely be ignored altogether from the point of view of fitness for work, except in exceptional circumstances, such as those occupations intensely in the public gaze.

If psoriasis already involves the hands, work involving heavy manual labour such as scaffolding, or contact with irritants, such as in production engineering, may aggravate it.

If psoriasis is or has been extensive, physically or emotionally strenous jobs, such as in the armed forces, may aggravate it. When extensive and/or associated with arthropathy, tighter restrictions are applicable.

If psoriasis involves the exposed skin of the hands and forearms or the scalp, its tendency to shed scales capable of bearing pathogenic staphylococci may also be a contraindication in catering or hospital staff.

Other conditions

Chronic urticaria   may be aggravated by physically or emotionally stressful work. Its control with oral antihistamines, which tend to have the side-effect of drowsiness, raises problems in work requiring a constant level of alertness, such as driving or machine operating. Certain newer antihistamines are claimed to be non-sedative and many, though not all, patients can tolerate these safely (Chapter 3).

Photosensitive dermatoses, and to a lesser extent *vitiligo*, may be a bar to outdoor work in very sunny environments unless sufficient protection is provided by clothing or by the high-efficacy sunscreens which are now available. Dermatological advice can often assist for very light-sensitive subjects.

Severe pustular and cystic acne may be a contraindication to work involving hot climatic or microclimatic environments, such as diving, which can severely exacerbate the disorder. It also probably increases the susceptibility to oil acne, though this should be preventable by other means. Dermatological treatment can now diminish even severe acne much more effectively than in the past. Recent work has shown a generally raised unemployment level among acne sufferers, suggesting that many jobs are refused them on no more than cosmetic grounds. There is therefore a strong argument for positively guarding against this unfair discrimination when recruiting young staff, unless facial appearance is genuinely of crucial importance, as it might be for a hotel receptionist.

Multiple viral warts of the hands can be unacceptable in many occupations involving food-handling, patient-care, or frequent contact with the public. A specific group at risk are wholesale butchers, among whom viral warts can spread to become endemic. It would be unwise, therefore, to allow anyone with viral warts on the hands to start work in a large butchery without prior treatment. Viral warts on the feet (verrucae) may be contraindicated in occupations involving shared showering or bathing facilities. Dermatological referral should eventually effect the removal of all but the most stubborn warts, allowing the patient to proceed with previously contraindicated work.

Tinea pedis is endemic in occupations involving shared showering or bathing facilities, such as mining, or particularly occlusive footwear, such as diving.

Given the existence of this endemic state, it is probably not justified to keep new employees with tinea pedis out of the work until cleared with treatment, but the condition should at least be recognized and treatment initiated before employment starts.

Tinea unguium may be difficult to clear even with prolonged treatment, but, as long as skin infection is treated as needed, some residual nail infection should be allowable.

Impetigo and other more serious *primary bacterial infections* of the skin including tuberculosis, have clear implications for employability. Adequate treatment of primary bacterial infections should, however, remove the bar.

Zoonoses. It is important to be clear that zoonoses such as cattle ringworm can be transferred between animal and man, but *NOT* from man to man. A zoonosis is not therefore the risk to fellow employees that its appearance might suggest.

Hyperhidrosis of the hands may make the individual a 'ruster' in engineering, unacceptable in catering, or unsuitable for work such as in sales or public relations, where frequent hand shaking is required. Dermatological treatment can help but often only to a limit extent, which may fail to solve the occupational problem.

The question of complexion

Clinical experience suggests that those with fair complexions are more susceptible to irritants, though not to allergens. When put to the test in a survey, however, the assessment of skin complexion was an unreliable guide to susceptibility.[17] It is possible that a quick and reliable method of testing for individual sunlight sensitivity may be made available to classify skin types more accurately, but this may not turn out to be a reliable guide to individual susceptibility to skin irritants.

The question of pre-employment skin testing

Patch testing
Patch testing prior to employment can detect only previously acquired sensitization and cannot predict future sensitization. Its general recommendation is therefore often based on a misunderstanding of the fundamental principles of patch testing. Patch tests may be indicated in individual cases prior to employment if a past or present dermatitis has previously been investigated inadequately.

Prick testing
Prick testing prior to employment is not generally of great value from the dermatological point of view. It will help to detect an atopic constitution, but it is the history or presence of atopic eczema which indicates an increased susceptibility to contact irritants, rather than an atopic constitution (p. 117).

Alkali tests

These are not considered by most dermatologists to be of practical use in pre-employment screening.[18]

Effect of the common occupational dermatoses on fitness for work

Since most workers naturally prefer to continue in their own occupation, an accurate assessment of causal factors is the first essential. Once guided by an accurate diagnosis, changes in working method and other preventive measures such as protective clothing, enclosure, mechanical handling, substitution, ventilation, rotation, can be helpful. In the majority of cases of occupational dermatoses continuation in the same occupation should thus be achievable. This is particularly important in the many occupational dermatoses where prognosis is known to be little altered by change of job, such as allergic contact dermatitis caused by chromate in cement used by construction workers.[19]

In a minority of cases a change of occupation may be in the better interest of the individual. This is particularly true of special groups, such as first-year apprentices, persons sensitive to epoxy resin or the Compositae group of plants associated with airborne contact dermatitis, and those with active atopic eczema who find themselves in entirely unsuitable work. When the prognosis on avoiding further contact with the allergen is known to be almost certainly good, as it is in epoxy dermatitis, a rapid change of job may be indicated once the allergy has been demonstrated by patch testing.

When a change of occupation is decided on, it is crucially important that the new occupation should genuinely be more suitable. Clearly, the major requirement should be avoidance of the original contact factor. This may need expert guidance, particularly when the contact factor is widely distributed, such as formaldehyde among allergens, and irritants in wet work. A patient with atopic eczema may otherwise, for example, change from hairdressing to catering without benefit. Prior dermatological investigation should enable the best guidance to be given.

A list of low-risk occupations was published in 1969[20] and an updated list of irritants and allergens in various occupations in 1981.[21] These are readily consulted in Cronin's *Contact dermatitis* (pp. 879–80 and 880–5, respectively).[10]

Spurious contra-indications to employment on the grounds of common allergies are sometimes met. For example, there is a misconception that nickel sensitivity, which is acquired by about 10 per cent of all north-western European women and an increasing precentage of men, implies a generally increased risk of dermatitis in the engineering industry. This is probably not so, because of the very low percentages of available nickel in the great majority of metals used in engineering. Only prolonged contact with nickel-plated objects or nickel plating itself is likely to constitute a common risk in engineering. Few of the approximately 10 per cent of female supermarket cashiers who are allergic to nickel appear to contract any hand dermatitis from nickel-containing coins.

SPECIAL WORK PROBLEMS, RESTRICTIONS, OR NEEDS CAUSED BY SKIN CONDITIONS

Certain types of work may be considered unsuitable from the point of view of the employer, the insurer, or the safety engineer, though safety itself is never likely to be impaired by any skin condition. Public health considerations concerning canteens, food-handlers, personal hygiene, and washing facilities, may preclude the employment of certain patients, for example those with untreated otitis externa, psoriasis of the scalp, or hand eczema.

Rehabilitation

Rehabilitation of patients with occupational dermatoses rarely requires special facilities. Patients need not necessarily achieve complete clearance of their dermatosis before returning to work, especially if they can temporarily be offered alternative work away from the specific allergen or irritant which precipitated the condition. Too often patients are advised to stay off work until all trace of abnormality is gone, possibly causing unnecessary emotional and financial strain and endangering the patient's eventual chance of resettlement. This, though done for the best of reasons, can hinder rather than help the overall prognosis.

The aim of rehabilitation in occupational dermatology is to keep the patient in the same job if at all possible, and this can be irretrievably jeopardized by prolonged sickness absence.[22]

The availability of an occupational physician, nurse, and hygienist is of great advantage, because they are together best able to advise on suitable employment and on preventive skin-care programmes.

CONCLUSIONS AND RECOMMENDATIONS

Skin conditions require thorough dermatological investigation in order to diagnose them sufficiently accurately to give reliable medical advice about employment.

Even after full dermatological investigation, there can remain sufficient doubt about the prognosis to make medical advice on employment subject to error.

Because of this, it will frequently be sound medical advice to give the individual the benefit of the doubt on his fitness for work. Medicolegal considerations may prompt an over-cautious approach that is not truly in the best interests of the potential employee or employer. If possible, such prompting should be resisted in a rational manner capable of being legally defended.

Dermatological treatment of many common dermatoses has advanced considerably in recent years. A patient's fitness for work may in certain cases be transformed by dermatological referral and treatment prior to final placement.

The emphasis should be on the accurate identification of the few dermatoses that do have genuine implications for employment, rather than on a general bar on people with skin disease.

Any kind of medical report on a patient, however informal, that is requested for the purposes of pre-employment assessment should be supplied only with the patient's consent, after due consideration, and with great care not to mislead unwittingly. Uncertainty, which is always likely to exist to some extent, should not be concealed by general statements that cannot be supported either by published evidence or by experience.

REFERENCES

1. Rystedt I. Work-related hand eczema in atopics. Contact Dermatitis 1985;**12**:164–71.
2. Johnson MLT. Skin conditions and related needs for medical care among persons 1–74 years, United States 1971–1974. US Dept of Health, Education and Welfare, 1977; DHEW publications no. (PHS)79–1660. (series 11; no 212). Washington, DC.
3. Rea JN, Newhouse ML, Hall T. Skin disease in Lambeth. Br J Prev Soc Med 1976;**30**:107–14.
4. Wilkinson JD. Rycroft RJG. In: Rook A, Wilkinson DS, Ebling FJG, Champion RH, Burton JL, eds. Textbook of dermatology. 4th ed. Oxford: Blackwell, 1986:460.
5. Agrup G. Hand eczema. Acta Dermat-venereol 1969;**49**(suppl 61):59–61.
6. Department of Health and Social Security. Social Security Statistics. London: HMSO, 1986.
7. Griffiths WAD. In: Griffiths WAD, Wilkinson DS, eds. Essentials of industrial dermatology. Oxford: Blackwell, 1985:7.
8. Malten KE, Fregert S, Bandmann H-J. Occupational dermatitis in five European dermatological departments. Berufdermatosen 1971;**19**:1–14.
9. Cotterill JA. Constitutional skin disease in industry. In: Griffiths WAD, Wilkinson DS, eds. Essentials of industrial dermatology. Oxford: Blackwell, 1985:38–46.
10. Cronin E. Contact dermatitis. Edinburgh: Churchill Livingstone, 1980.

11. Cronin E, Bandmann H-J, Calnan CD. Contact dermatitis in the atopic. Acta Dermat-venereol 1970;**50**:183–7.
12. Jones HE, Lewis CW, McMarlin SL. Allergic contact sensitivity in atopic dermatitis. Arch Dermatol 1973;**107**:217–22.
13. Rudzki E, Grzywa Z. Contact sensitivity in atopic dermatitis. Contact Dermatitis 1975;**1**:285–7.
14. Forsbeck M, Hovmark A, Skog E. Patch testing, tuberculin testing and sensitization of patients with atopic dermatitis. Acta Dermat-venereol 1976;**56**:135–8.
15. Rystedt I. Factors influencing the occurrence of hand eczema in adults with a history of atopic dermatitis in childhood. Contact Dermatitis 1985;**12**:185–91.
16. Wilkinson DS. Careers advice to youths with atopic dermatitis. Contact Dermatitis 1975;**1**:11–2.
17. Rycroft RJG. Soluble oil as major cause of occupational dermatitis. University of Cambridge, 1982. 502 pp. MD thesis.
18. Foussereau J, Benezra C, Maibach HI. Occupational dermatitis. Copenhagen: Munksgaard, 1982:77.
19. Fregert S. Occupational dermatitis in a 10-year material. Contact Dermatitis 1975;**1**:96–107.
20. Fregert S, Calnan CD. Low risk occupations. Contact Dermatitis Newsletter 1969;**6**:111.
21. Fregert S. Manual of contact dermatitis. 2nd ed. Copenhagen: Munksgaard, 1981:91 8.
22. Calnan CD, Rycroft RJG. Rehabilitation in occupational skin disease. Transactions of the College of Medicine of South Africa 1981;**25** (suppl rehabilitation):136–42.

8

Orthopaedics

R. McL. Archibald, H. B. S. Kemp, L. J. Marks, and
C. B. Wynn Parry

INTRODUCTION

Orthopaedic injuries and disabilities form one of the largest and commonest groups of disabilities which are likely to be seen by the primary care physician who then has to assess their relevance to, and impact on, the patient's working capacity. They occur in the young adult as a result of sporting activities or road-traffic accidents, in the middle-aged as the result of accidents at work or in the home, and in the elderly as the result of degenerative changes in joints, ligaments, and muscles.

It is not possible to discuss each condition in more than outline and the reader should refer to one of the standard texts listed at the end of the chapter for fuller clinical details. Here we are concerned with the practical implications of many common and some less common conditions which may limit functional activity at the workplace.

Many large firms provide physiotherapy facilities or, occasionally, rehabilitation workshops or similar arrangements. Full advantage should be taken of these to speed the transition from invalidity to work, while treatment to restore and maximize function continues as the patient readjusts to his working environment.

RHEUMATOID ARTHRITIS (also discussed in Chapter 10)

This is predominantly a disease of young to middle-aged people with a female to male ratio of 3:2. Prevalence estimates are between 100–250 per 100 000. The cause remains unknown and it classically affects the small or medium sized joints. By no means all patients are doomed to severe deformity and with modern methods of treatment, in particular surgery and rehabilitation, it is perfectly feasible for the majority of patients with this disease to have a full working life.

Because the cause is unknown and the progression of the disease variable and somewhat unpredictable, a great deal of attention has been paid in recent years to indicators of possible prognosis from long-term follow-up studies. We know that some 10 per cent of patients will have one attack only and will never be troubled again. We also know that between 10 and 15 per cent pursue a relentless course with severe deformities, whereas the rest pursue a fluctuating course with remissions and relapses which can be modified or completely controlled by medical treatment and surgery.

Clinical aspects affecting work capacity

There is a variety of patterns of disease. One can distinguish for practical purposes the type of disease that affects particularly the small joints of the hands and feet and may lead to many different sorts of deformities. These include ulnar drift with subluxation of the metacarpo-phalangeal joints, the Boutonière deformity with flexion of the proximal interphalangeal joint and hyperextension of the distal joint; and the swan-neck deformity which is the reverse—hyperextension of the proximal interphalangeal joint and flexion of the distal joint. Both these deformities can seriously impair hand function. Despite the appearance of severe deformity, function may be surprisingly good and surgeons have learnt that a careful functional assessment by an occupational therapist is essential before embarking on a programme of surgery. Perhaps the key joint in the upper limb is the wrist, for if this is affected with painful limitation of movement, the whole function of the upper limb is compromised. The elbow is frequently involved in rheumatoid arthritis and lack of extension is commonly seen. This may well not result in functional disability. Severe shoulder involvement very seriously impairs function.

The knee is commonly involved in rheumatoid arthritis and can produce either varus or valgus deformity, causing marked pain and stiffness particularly on weightbearing, and severely limiting function. In addition, a painful knee prevents people standing for long periods, walking long distances, and particularly coping with stairs, and modifications that allow work to be done while sitting can help. Possibly the most difficult joint of all is the ankle. Here, swelling and limitation of movement with a valgus angle can produce marked disability and it can be extremely difficult to fit satisfactory supportive splints or provide adequate and comfortable footwear. As yet ankle replacement is in its infancy. Thus, ankle involvement may be a great deal more disabling at work than a comparable degree of severity of hip or knee involvement, for replacement of the hip joint is now routine and the success rate of total knee replacement is increasing all the time.

Management

Drug treatment is controversial and the simplest drugs possible are preferable. They can be divided into first-, second-, and third-line. First-line drugs include aspirin and non-steroidal anti-inflammatory agents, and the appropriate one for each patient must be found. Second-line drugs are those which affect the natural history of the disease, such as gold and penicillamine. Corticosteroids were the vogue 20 years ago, but it has now been learnt that there are relatively few indications for their use; on the other hand there are many patients who can be kept at work on small doses of steroids (e.g. 7.5 mg of enteric-coated prednisolone per day) who would otherwise be confined to home. Third-line drugs include the immunosuppressive agents whose use is confined to patients with severe systemic disease and who are usually incapable of work.

Much can be done to prevent deterioration of joint function in the hand by measures known as joint protection. These include the use of supportive splints for the wrist, especially while performing manual tasks; learning the correct way of handling and lifting; gadgets and aids for turning on taps, opening doors, using keys and switches, etc. Relapses and flare-ups are best treated by admission for complete rest in hospital with adequate splinting and a review of drug therapy. It is far better for patients to accept this regime than to try to continue at work and end up with a severe exacerbation of the disease.

The patient should be asked for a reasonably detailed description of his working activities in order to bring out any activities which may be exacerbating his disease and to suggest modifications to the job which may enable him to continue at work. The co-operation of the occupational health department must always be sought, and where none exists a letter to management explaining the implications of the condition and its relationship to work may be helpful.

It is emphasized that the majority of patients with this disease can be kept at work for many years, provided they have regular follow-up and careful management of their drug regime. Periodic admissions to hospital may be necessary for rest in the event of a relapse, or for surgical reconstruction. Surgery should be seen as a means of restoring function and not as an end resort, and employers should not be afraid to employ people if the therapeutic team in the hospital has shown that these patients are not at risk.

ANKYLOSING SPONDYLITIS (also discussed in Chapters 9 and 10)

This is an important cause of chronic low back pain in young adults. It is much commoner in men than women and the age of onset is between 18 and 30.

Clinical aspects affecting work capacity

The disease is characterized by inflammation of the central joints, particularly the sacroiliac joints, the lower lumbar spine, the joints of the chest, and frequently the neck. Peripheral joints are rarely involved, but the hip joints are not infrequently affected. The combination of stiffness in the hips and in the spine can lead to very severe disability, but long-term follow-up studies have shown that this disease does not lead to such severe disability as was once thought. Severe deformities such as gross kyphosis are very rarely seen now, and this may be due to the recognition that early rehabilitation is essential and may well have prevented the onset of deformity in many patients.

The disease can burn out at various stages. At one end of the spectrum is the classical textbook patient with a bamboo spine and no movement in the neck or back. At the other end is the patient who has some stiffness of the lower lumbar spine, fused sacroiliac joints, but virtually no physical disability.

In a Royal Air Force series, [1] 70 per cent of 238 patients were able to follow a full service career, and most of the patients invalided were only discharged from the service because their jobs were particularly physically demanding. Patients complain of pain which is made worse by rest and improved by activity, in sharp contrast to patients with postural and mechanical disorders, such as prolapsed discs, in which rest relieves the pain and exercise aggravates it. Patients often wake themselves up in the night or early in the morning specifically to exercise so as to loosen up in time for work. This phenomenon gives a clue to management and patients are better in work that allows them to change their position frequently, rather than in situations where they have to sit for long hours at a desk.

Limitation of chest expansion is an early sign, as is limitation of lateral flexion. It used to be thought that chest involvement led to an increased frequency of tuberculosis and of bronchitis but this is now known to be false. The diagnosis of ankylosing spondylitis is entirely consistent with a full active working life. Only if the disease causes severe limitation of movement which might interfere with work, does it become significant. Complications include iritis in some 10 per cent, and fleeting peripheral joint pains which rarely lead to deformity, except in the hips. There is also an increased association with other inflammatory disorders, such as inflammatory bowel disease (ulcerative colitis and Crohn's disease), psoriasis, and Reiter's syndrome.

Management

Modern treatment emphasizes the importance of a routine exercise regime which the patient must follow scrupulously.[2] This includes neck and spinal exercises to preserve a full range of mobility; breathing exercises to maintain chest expansion; and postural exercises to prevent kyphosis and lordosis. Patients are encouraged wherever possible to take up regular swimming for this, being a non-weightbearing exercise, does no harm to the joints of the spine and encourages cardio-respiratory development. The value of short spells of intensive in-patient rehabilitation have been amply documented, and many centres call up their patients with ankylosing spondylitis once every year or every 18 months for a short refresher burst of exercise. It is in the best interests of the patient and the employer to allow patients to take time off for such intensive programmes of rehabilitation. Occasionally there may be flare-ups of the condition causing severe back pain, and a rest may be required for a short spell. In such eventualities the patient must be off work until the symptoms have completely subsided or are well controlled by anti-inflammatory drugs.

The combination of its early onset predominantly in young men coupled with the natural history detailed above makes it essential, once the diagnosis is established, to discuss not only the immediate job but the proposed pattern of future employment, although it is not an easy task to look 30 or 40 years ahead. As in the case of rheumatoid arthritis, the employer should be warned that occasional short periods of absence are likely, but for the patient's welfare an optimistic note should be struck. At the same time it is clearly unwise to continue in any occupation which demands heavy physical effort imposing a load on the spine, or prolonged sitting, as in long-distance lorry driving.

SHOULDER CONDITIONS

Lesions of the rotator-cuff are very common and can be brought on by particular stresses at work. Repetitive movements particularly in the range 70°–100° abduction, such as in painting and decorating, and hedge-clipping, can cause inflammation of the supraspinatus and infraspinatus tendons and the tendon of subscapularis. This can cause pain on movement, particularly between 70° and 120° when the tendon abuts against the acromion. In more severe cases, pain may be spontaneous and results in gradual and progressive stiffening of the joint until there is virtually no movement and the condition known as frozen shoulder has developed. Clearly, continuing physical work with such a condition will only aggravate the situation, and patients must be encouraged to rest and have therapy which may include physical treatment and steroid injections into the joint.

The classical severe frozen shoulder where there is continuous and spontaneous pain both night and day and virtually no movement in the shoulder, is a severe condition. Strangely, it almost always clears up completely and a sound guideline is that it will take as long to get better as it took for the shoulder to become stiff; thus if from the onset of symptoms to complete stiffness of the shoulder took four months, it is likely to be at least four months before function is restored. It is a wise precaution on contemplating return to work to avoid the type of repetitive movement which might cause the condition to recur; such modification of the job should normally be necessary only for a matter of weeks, or one or two months. In these conditions, as in so many referred to in this chapter, the ergonomic aspects of the work are vitally important and can be the crucial difference between return to and continuation of work and continued absence.

CERVICAL SPONDYLOSIS

Well over half the population over the age of 40 have radiographic changes of disc degeneration and spondylosis in the neck, but many have no symptoms. Clinically the condition can cause either pain in the neck, pain in the neck with pain radiating down the arm, or referred pain down the arm alone. When the 5th cervical root is compressed, the patient feels pain in the trapezius posteriorly. When the 6th cervical root is compressed, pain is felt in the middle of the forearm; and with compression of the 7th root, along the back of the forearm and into the middle finger. Compression of C8 and T1 roots produces pain along the inner side of the forearm and into the little and ring fingers. In the acute stage the pain is continuous in the neck and is relieved only by complete rest. In the chronic stage there may be recurrent attacks of aching in the neck and paraesthesiae in the distribution of the affected root, with weakness and sensory impairment in the arm.

In the acute stage, complete rest is advised, either in bed or ambulant with a collar. This will not be consistent with professional driving as it restricts vision and, clearly, any form of physical work is contraindicated. In the chronic stage where the patient has periodic attacks of aching in the neck and pain down the arm, situations that will aggravate the condition should be avoided, particularly those where the neck has to be held in one position for any length of time, such as in driving, working in a confined space, under cars, or where there is much vibration.

BRACHIAL PLEXUS LESIONS

By far the commonest causes of traction injuries to the brachial plexus are motorcycle accidents, when acute depression of the shoulder and acute lateral flexion of the neck causes traction to the nerve roots. Mercifully, head injuries are less common since crash helmets were made compulsory, but they are still an important cause of disability. There are three types of injury: traction lesion in continuity, rupture of nerve roots, and avulsion of the roots from the spinal cord. With a *lesion in continuity* the sheath of the nerve is intact but the axis cylinder degenerates. Spontaneous recovery after 1–2 years is possible and the functional result may be quite good. When a *nerve root is ruptured* there is clear discontinuity and no hope of recovery unless the nerve is explored and repaired by nerve graft. In *avulsion injuries* the roots are torn out of the spinal cord and there is no hope either of spontaneous recovery or of repair by grafting. The incidence of ruptures and avulsions has been steadily increasing over the years.

At the Royal National Orthopaedic Hospital, which is a national referral centre for such injuries, 100 new patients are seen each year. The incidence of total avulsion lesions has steadily increased over the past 10 years and is now 50 per cent of the total. This means that there is complete and permanent paralysis, usually of the dominant arm. The incidence of these lesions is increasing because, as a result of the compulsory wearing of crash helmets and the advances in intensive care, patients are surviving with very much more severe injuries than before. For the best management of these patients, referral to a specialist centre is strongly advised to assess whether surgery is indicated or whether the lesion is beyond repair. Grafting the upper trunks of the brachial plexus may restore elbow function, adduction of the shoulder, and some protective sensation in the hands.[3] Restoration of the fine function of the hand is not possible because even if the lower trunks are reparable, by the time re-innervation has occurred the intrinsic muscles will have atrophied.

The indications for amputation are severely limited; it is only advised when the arm becomes a nuisance or the patient suffers periodic burns or trophic lesions, an exceptionally rare occurrence. The psychological effect of losing an arm must not be underestimated. It must be emphasized that amputation has no effect on the severe central pain that these patients so often suffer.

The youthfulness of the majority of patients, predominantly male, coupled with the severity of the lesion and the long-term consequences, call for a radical reappraisal of their work. In the first place, the initial absence will be prolonged if the dominant arm is affected. There will be a period of re-learning basic skills and inability to return to jobs which traditionally demand two sound upper limbs. It is here that the rehabilitation skills and mechanical ingenuity of the specialist units referred to above have a crucial role to play. Often, special functional splints can allow patients to return to work.[4] Both primary care and occupational physicians will most likely have to advise either a radical modification of a manual job, or a course of retraining.

PERIPHERAL NERVE INJURIES

Peripheral nerves are commonly injured when hands are put through windows, in crushing injuries, and in road-traffic accidents. The functional result depends on a number of factors including age, associated injuries, involvement of blood vessels, degree of crushing, and availability of expert surgical treatment. Wherever possible, primary suture is recommended and results have improved enormously since it was realized that blood vessels must be repaired as well as the nerves, for in the past it was common to ligate rather than repair a damaged artery.

Median nerve lesions

Division of the median nerve, commonly at the wrist, results in complete loss of sensation of the medial two-thirds of the hand, the thumb, index, middle finger, and half the ring finger, with loss of palmar abduction and rotation such that the fine opposition grip is lost. The results of nerve suture in children are uniformly good, for a child's nervous system is much more adaptable and can learn to recode abnormal sensations so that stereognosis can be almost perfect. In adults this is not usually possible and after median nerve suture at the wrist protective sensation is regained but stereognosis remains poor.

It has, however, been shown that it is possible to re-educate sensation by formal physiotherapy and occupational therapy techniques, resulting in a high degree of stereognostic function. Patients such as electronics experts, keyboard operators, and seamstresses, who require sensation for their work and indeed anyone who requires fine function of the fingers and the ability to recognize textures and objects rapidly, are suitable for formal re-education. It is not necessary for patients who are involved in primarily manual tasks who will not use such fine sensation. Opposition does not usually return, but a surprising degree of function can be provided by the ulnar-supplied muscles of the thumb, in particular the adductor and the deep flexor. If this is inadequate, then tendon transfers usually using the flexor sublimis of the ring finger are available to give opposition but only if some sensation is present.

Ulnar nerve lesions

Division of the ulnar nerve in the wrist leads to loss of sensation of the little finger and the ulnar half of the ring finger, and complete paralysis of the intrinsic muscles that abduct and adduct the fingers, flex the metacarpophalangeal joints, extend the interphalangeal joints, and control the pinch grip of thumb to index finger. It is thus a devastating lesion for somebody who requires finely co-ordinated finger movements. Repair of the ulnar nerve in adults usually does not result in independent action of the interossei, though with a very well motivated patient this may be possible with prolonged training. Patients, however, retain an excellent power grip, although this can be weakened by the lack of metacarpophalangeal flexion. The long flexors can to some extent substitute.

Reconstructive procedures are available to stabilize the metacarpophalangeal joints. Lively splints to prevent hyperextension deformity of these joints can be worn in the early stages of recovery. A lack of key grip can be extremely disabling, particularly in patients who need to manipulate switches and operate keys. Here, reconstructive procedures are available; the classic operation is to transfer the extensor indicis into the first dorsal interosseous muscle.

Radial nerve lesions

Damage to the radial nerve in the upper arm commonly follows fractures of the humerus where the radial nerve winds round the spiral groove. The functional disability is a wrist drop such that the patient cannot extend the wrist, or thumb. Grip is substantially reduced if the patient cannot stabilize the wrist in dorsiflexion. The radial nerve being almost entirely a motor nerve, results are good after nerve suture. If, however, too much nerve has been lost or has been embedded in callus, then repair may be impossible. Reconstructive procedures are available which give excellent function and these involve rerouting the flexors of the wrist to the extensors of the wrist and fingers. A common procedure is to put pronator teres into the extensor carpi radialis brevis to provide wrist extension, and to put flexor carpi ulnaris into the extensors of the fingers, and the palmaris longus into the extensor of the thumb. Excellent function not far short of normal is possible after this procedure.

Median and ulnar nerve lesions

Involvement of both nerves of the wrist is not uncommon and produces a devastating functional disability. Almost invariably nearly all the tendons and both arteries are cut and this means that functional results after nerve suture are less likely to be good. There may, therefore, be a vascular insufficiency and weakened grip due to weakness of the flexor tendons. However, modern surgical techniques can give the chance of good functional return but rehabilitation may be prolonged. Restoration of some protective and stereognostic function of the median distribution and a key grip between thumb and index finger are the major objectives. As in so many fields in medicine, patients adapt remarkably well to disability and can do most things with the other hand. Only in jobs requiring fine control with both hands is there a major disability and this can often be improved by rehabilitation and judicious tendon transfers. Very careful assessment in a specialist hand-unit is necessary, but the occupational physician can be a great help to the surgeon by indicating exactly what the functional problem is, and what is required of the patient to operate machinery adequately.

Sciatic nerve lesions

The sciatic nerve can be damaged in dislocations of the hip, by direct injuries and, rarely, following total hip replacement. A complete lesion of the sciatic nerve results in total paralysis of all muscles below the knee and therefore difficulty in walking. Repair of the nerve usually allows plantar flexion to return, but dorsiflexion and eversion often remain paralysed. A light ortholene orthosis worn in the shoe can stabilize the foot and allow standing and a fair degree of walking. One of the distressing features of complete sciatic nerve lesions is the relatively high incidence of paraesthesiae and burning pain with nerve regeneration; so much so that some surgeons are loth to repair the sciatic nerve, believing that the patient is better off with an insensible but painless foot than one with sensation and severe causalgic pain.

Patients with complete sciatic nerve palsies are clearly unsafe at heights and on ladders and cannot cope with long periods of standing and walking. Patients with sedentary tasks have no handicap and it is only getting to and from work that may present a problem.

INJURIES TO THE HAND

Stiff hand

A stiff hand may result from a variety of injuries, the commonest being crush injuries in which there may be fractures and dislocations of the metacarpals and phalanges, with an outpouring of tissue fluid that organizes with fibrosis and causes a stiff frozen hand. It is the soft tissue damage rather than the bony damage that is the most important feature of this condition. A stiff hand can follow from multiple tendon involvement, vascular insufficiency (particularly after tight plasters) causing Volkmann's ischaemic contracture, after burns, and in the relatively rare but important condition known as Sudeck's atrophy or algodystrophy. This is a curious condition which often follows quite trivial injuries, such as a sprain or a minor fracture. The hand becomes suddenly extremely painful and swollen and progresses to complete stiffness with atrophy of the skin and nails, a shiny blue skin, and a stiff and useless hand. If a patient presents after a trivial injury with sudden swelling and pain he should be referred immediately for expert treatment, for it is known that early treatment of this condition gives the best results. If the patient presents with a stiff frozen hand some weeks or months after injury the prognosis is poor.

Pain in the hand following nerve damage

Severe pain in the hand can also follow partial damage to nerves (causalgia) in which the patient complains of severe spontaneous burning pain with hyperpathia (an abnormal response to light touch, such that the patient feels severe pain).

Clearly there has been a profound disorder of peripheral nerve function and the pain may spread outside the autonomous zone of the damaged nerve. A variety of effects follow nerve damage—including spontaneous firing of damaged nerve ends; cross-talk between damaged and normal segments of the nerve, in particular the sprouts that form after nerve recovery; hypersensitivity to circulating noradrenaline; and profound central nervous changes. Intensive skilled treatment can often materially improve the situation, and this will involve application of transcutaneous electrical stimulation, serial sympathetic nerve block using guanethidine, and intensive rehabilitation to try to restore normal movement patterns centrally. The development of these symptoms after nerve injury should lead to immediate referral to a specialist centre, for these patients do not respond to analgesics and rest.[5]

The full potential disability caused by this type of injury is not immediately apparent, and a successive series of recommendations will often be made about modifying working conditions. When the full extent of the disability unfolds it is necessary to make a radical reappraisal to ensure, on the one hand, specialist assessment and, on the other, continuity of employment of an individual who has become, to all intents and purposes, virtually one-handed.

INJURIES TO THE KNEE

Chronic traumatic synovitis (beat knee)

This may result from repeated minor trauma to the knee, usually a sequel to working in cramped, damp, cold conditions, such as a low coal-face, and can occur in work involving kneeling, for instance in carpet-layers. These lesions respond well to physiotherapy, such as ultrasonics and quadriceps exercises, but rapidly recur when subjected to the same work. Using thick foam knee-pads may prevent this condition.

Cartilage injuries

These commonly occur in workers who, by virtue of activity, repeatedly rotate on flexed knees. Tears of the anterior horn usually occur and there may be a peripheral detachment. Miners and others working in a squatting position frequently sustain tears of the posterior horn.

Ligament injuries

Amongst manual workers these generally result from direct trauma. Commonest injuries are forced rotation and valgus strain, resulting in a tear of the medial meniscus with or without tears of the medial collateral ligament and tear of the anterior cruciate. Falls from heights coupled with such rotational strains may also cause depressed fractures of the tibial table, usually the lateral plateau.

Management

Meniscal tears

These are fashionably treated by arthroscopic resection, particularly in sportsmen. In the hands of experts it is not unreasonable for patients to return to work within 1–2 weeks. More orthodox meniscectomies performed by arthrotomy will return sedentary workers to employment in 4–6 weeks. Manual workers will not return to full employment for three months due to lack of adequate quadriceps control and knee flexion.

Ligamentous injuries

These will require formal repair, spending 6–8 weeks in plaster and a further three months of physiotherapy. Sedentary workers can be expected to return to work within three months but manual workers may need at least six months' sick leave. The latter cannot be expected to have the normal knee function required for certain forms of heavy employment.

Fractures of the tibial table

Such fractures require elevation, grafting, and internal fixation, and are usually associated with internal derangement of the knee. Patients are immobilized for three months and need 6–12 weeks' rehabilitation. Again, these patients cannot be expected to return to heavy employment.

Osteoarthritis

This may be secondary to injuries to the knee, although not exclusively so. *Knee replacement*, which is still in the experimental stage, will demand an absence of 3–4 months and considerable restriction of mobility on return to work.

OSTEOARTHRITIS OF THE HIP

Osteoarthritis of the hip may be idiopathic or secondary to a predisposing cause, such as congenital dislocation, acetabular dysplasia, coxa valga, Perthes' disease, slipped upper femoral epiphysis, and subclinical juvenile rheumatoid disease.

Prevention

Patients with a history of such diseases should be discouraged from employment in heavy manual occupations as functional expectancy is unlikely to exceed the age of 45. Gross disease will preclude individuals from applying because of existing disability, but the individual will not necessarily be aware of acetabular dysplasia and other subclinical conditions. In acetabular dysplasia both the femoral head and acetabular surfaces may be congruous, but the acetabular element is shallow and therefore weightbearing stresses are increased.

Perthes' disease is more common in males. It is often silent in its presentation, and the patient may be unaware of the condition during childhood. Due to transient ischaemic changes in the femoral head, the capital epiphysis may necrose. Consequently, unless healing is complete, the acetabulum and epiphysis may be discongruous and early breakdown of acetabular surfaces may occur. Slipped upper femoral epiphysis occurs in adolescence, predominantly in males, with a sex ratio of approximately 4:1. Discongruity can again produce similar changes.

Prosthetic replacement

Total hip replacement is one of the outstanding success stories in contemporary orthopaedics. The success rate is now between 94 and 96 per cent. The average patient can return to work in 6–8 weeks. Failures are essentially due to loosening. Six per cent of all cases require revision during the first 15 years. Loosening occurs predominantly in patients with rheumatoid arthritis. Far more serious from the patient's point of view is infection. This occurs variously in 0.5–2.0 per cent of all cases. Despite claims by Buchholz et al.,[6] the majority need to be converted to the modified Girdlestone.

Stress fractures of prostheses are extremely rare, not higher than 1.5 per 1000 for those of reputable manufacture. Patients are capable of returning to all but the heaviest duties, but it is logical to restrict climbing, lifting, and similar activities.

THE FOOT

While there are numerous disabilities of the foot which give rise to industrial problems, the two commonest are hallux rigidus and hallux valgus.

Hallux rigidus

This occurs in the first metatarsophalangeal joint in certain athletes and in manual workers who do not wear protective footwear. It is due to repeated minor injuries of the joint. Early osteoarthritic changes will lead to a planoid joint, loss of movement, and disabling pain. It may be controlled by conservative measures, such as surgical footwear, but usually requires surgical treatment such as a Keller's procedure.

Hallux valgus

This is a deformity of the first metatarsophalangeal joint, occurring predominantly in females; it is rarely due to a congenital short first metatarsal, more

Table 8.1 Causes of amputation

Lower limb	%		Upper limb	%
Vascular	60.3	}81.3	Trauma	80.0
Diabetic	21.0		Congenital	10–15.0
Trauma	9.0		Tumours, and other	5.0
Malignancy	4.5			
Neurogenic deformity	3.6			
Infection, and other	1.5			

commonly to nylon stockings, less frequently to fashionable footwear.

If the joint is not degenerate it is best treated by corrective osteotomy. If secondary osteoarthritis is present, a salvage procedure such as a Keller's operation is advised. Osteotomies require six weeks in plaster, with return to work in three months. Patients can return to work in two months after Keller's and similar procedures.

AMPUTATIONS

There are approximately 5500 new amputations performed per year in this country. Lower limb amputations are much more frequent than upper-limb amputations, the ratio in 1983 being 15.7:1.[7] The causes of lower- and upper-limb amputations are quite different and are shown in Table 8.1.

In 1983 the overall ratio of male to female amputees was 2.04:1, but males predominate more noticeably in the 10–59 age group and females are beginning to predominate in the over-80s.

Functionally, the effect of an amputation is a problem of mobility for lower-limb amputees or dexterity for upper-limb amputees. The extent of disturbance of function will depend mainly on the level of amputation: the more proximal the greater the disturbance. As a rough guide, lower-limb amputees will need six months before returning to work and upper-limb amputees three months.

Complications of amputation

Complications of amputation can be divided into 'immediate' and 'late' complications. These are shown in Table 8.2, with the appropriate treatment for each condition. Each of these complications can not only delay return to work, but can also limit working effectiveness or lead to further absence with associated social and psychological problems.

In addition to these medical complications there is the inconvenience of relying on a mechanical device, which itself requires maintenance and repairs to provide reliable service.

Table 8.2   The complications of amputation and their management

Immediate
  Delayed healing
    Infection (antibiotics)
    Ischaemia (stop smoking, vasodilators, sympathectomy, higher amputation)
  Post-operative oedema (stump elevation, exercises, stump bandaging or
  elasticated stump sock, treatment with PPAM Aid)
  Phantom pain (massage, analgesics, carbamazepine, transcutaneous nerve
  stimulation)
  Psychological (counselling)

Late
  Changes in stump volume (adjust or refit socket)
  Stump abrasions: blisters, corns, boils (adjust socket)
  Infected epidermoid cysts (socket fit, stump hygiene, ? surgical excision)
  Neuromata (adjust socket, neurectomy)
  Stress on other parts of the body: in lower-limb amputees there is an increased
  incidence of premature degenerative change in the joints of the contralateral
  limb, knee more than hip; in upper-limb amputees there appears to be an
  increased incidence of shoulder and neck problems

Prosthetics

The satisfactory fitting of a prosthesis, which must be tailored to the individual needs of each patient, is a highly skilled job and requires full knowledge and consideration of the traditional materials such as leather, metal, and wood as well as of a wide range of modern plastics. Cleverly engineered joints are indispensable. Regarding upper-limb prostheses, these can be either body-powered or externally powered. Body-powered limbs can be adapted to a wide range of functions and very fine movements can be achieved. Externally powered arms are usually designed on an individual basis at specialist units and, although myoelectric prostheses are more widely available, they tend to be heavy with relatively crude movements.

Employment adjustments

A number of general and specific points should be borne in mind when advising both the amputee and employers about working conditions. In general, employers should be made aware that the patient has an artificial limb. It is particularly important that adequate washing facilities can allow the amputee to attend to the limb and stump in reasonable privacy.

Lower-limb amputees will be restricted and should avoid working at heights, climbing ladders, and habitually walking over uneven ground. They may well not be able to stand all day, but equally it is inadvisable to sit all day without periodically stretching the legs. In the case of upper-limb amputation there is little or no restriction on the clerical worker. Manual workers have considerable ability to minimize this type of disability and it will often be a case of 'try and see' before giving a definite opinion.

CONCLUSIONS

Although this chapter has dealt with many common and some less common conditions, sight must not be lost of the whole man or woman who is the patient. In no other branch of medical practice in relation to work is it easier to see the practical efforts of the well-motivated patient overcoming formidable anatomical problems and exercising ingenuity in the use of residual ability. It is better, with the consent and co-operation of all concerned, always provided no breach of safety is involved, to attempt and fail rather than consistently to underachieve. This is where the co-operation of primary care physician, occupational health services, hospital specialist, and not least management and fellow-workers, can be invaluable.

REFERENCES

1. Wynn Parry CB. Management of ankylosing spondylitis. Proc Roy Soc Med 1966;**59**:619.
2. Wynn Parry CB, Deary JB, In: Moll JMH ed. Ankylosing spondylitis. London: Churchill Livingstone, 1980: 214–24.
3. Birch R. Traction lesions of the brachial plexus. Br J Hosp Med 1984;**32**:140–3.
4. Wynn Parry CB. Traction lesions of the brachial plexus. Br J Hosp Med 1984;**32**:130–9.
5. Witherington RW, Wynn Parry CB. Painful disorders of peripheral nerves. Postgrad Med J 1984;**60**:869–75.
6. Buchholz HW, Elson RA, Engelbrecht E, *et al.* Management of deep infection of total hip replacement. J Bone Joint Surg 1981;**63B**:342–53.
7. DHSS. On the state of the public health for the year 1983. London: HMSO, 1984.

General reading

Harris N ed. Postgraduate textbook of clinical orthopaedics. London: Wright PSG, 1983.

9

Back pain

R. J. Blow and M. I. V. Jayson

INTRODUCTION

Back pain is a very common complaint. Most of us can expect at least one episode during our lifetime. This will probably be of short duration, get better without professional advice, and cause little interruption of work or recreation. But in a small proportion of people back pain may be more severe and can persist, so having a long-standing social and financial impact.

PREVALENCE AND MORBIDITY

Prevalence

Most episodes of back pain last a few days and in only 10 per cent of instances do patients need advice or treatment from a general practitioner.[1] Nevertheless, back pain occupies a great deal of a general practitioner's time and about 4 per cent of those on a doctor's list can be expected to seek advice on the subject in any year. This amounts to 2.2 million consultations. The peak rate of consultation is in middle age (45–64) and there is a slight excess of males to females.[2] Of those visiting their doctor, between 10 per cent and 20 per cent will be referred to hospital and 30 per cent of these will be admitted to a hospital bed at some stage of their treatment. Where a specific diagnosis is made, the commonest reason for referral to hospital is an intervertebral disc disorder. Combined back-pain diagnoses accounted for 62 572 admissions to hospitals in Great Britain during 1982. About 50 per cent of 'disc' patients seen at hospital are under 45 and an operative procedure is performed on perhaps one-fifth.[2]

The estimated impact of back pain is summarized in Fig. 9.1. The care and treatment of back pain is estimated to have cost the NHS £156 millions in 1982. For the year 1982–83 there were 361 million days of certified incapacity for work and, of this, 33.3 million were for back problems, with a diagnosis of spondylosis and allied disorders and intervertebral disc disorders making up 50 per cent of the total.[2] It is likely that at least an equivalent amount of incapacity occurred in the non-insured population. Back problems have a significant economic impact, with lost production in 1982–83 being in excess of £1000 million.[2]

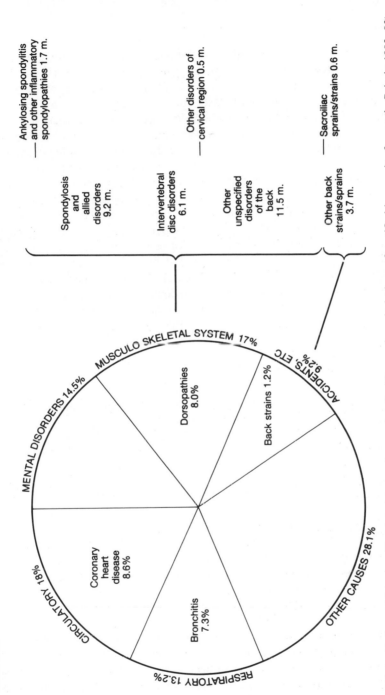

Fig. 9.1 Estimated impact of back pain over the course of a 12-month period (days of certified incapacity for work, Britain 1982–83) (from Wells[2]).

Morbidity

Because of the wide variety of causes of back pain there is great variation in prognosis. Most problems are of mechanical origin. Following a lift or a twist the patient develops acute back pain. The vast majority of these incidents are trivial: the pain lasts for a few days only and then ceases completely. Because many patients do not seek medical advice, it is difficult to estimate the prevalence of this problem, but it is very common. Many studies are referred to in the Office of Health Economics publication on back pain.[2] In one study in general practice, an episode of back pain had resolved within four weeks in between 80 per cent and 90 per cent of those affected.[3] Even in subjects referred to hospital rheumatology and orthopaedic clinics, spontaneous resolution of symptoms occurred in between 70 per cent and 80 per cent of the patients. Because back pain is such an extremely common complaint, even though the proportion of people who do not improve is low, a substantial number of people still fall into that category. The greater problem is the relapsing nature of back pain, in that the patient who has had one attack is at risk of another. In particular, a disc that has prolapsed is permanently damaged and the patient who has had back pain and/or sciatica from this cause is always at risk of further prolapse (see below).

CAUSES OF BACK PAIN

Introduction

Back pain is a symptom, not a diagnosis. Although mechanical disorders produce the majority of back-pain problems, there are many other important causes and it is essential to consider these in assessing patients, particularly when pain develops for the first time. In many episodes of back pain a definite link with an event at work may be recognized, while in other instances pain in the back may present at work and yet be a symptom of an underlying disorder.

Problems of mechanical origin

Strains of muscles, tendons, or ligaments

These are very common; most resolve quickly with rest, support, and simple analgesics.

Prolapsed intervertebral disc

Among mechanical problems, recognition of the prolapsed intervertebral disc is relatively easy. The patient gives a history of back pain followed by pain in the leg (sciatica), usually in the distribution of the L5 or S1 nerve root. Examination may show a lumbar scoliosis, limitation of straight leg raising and associated muscle weakness, reflex changes, and sensory loss. The diagnosis is confirmed by radiological examination. Many patients relate the onset of acute sciatica to some mechanical event and in particular to lifting, especially if combined with twisting of the spine. Loads which are unexpectedly heavy often lead to back pain and are a very potent cause of litigation. It is not rare for an employer to be sued after such an event. There is often doubt whether the actual incident is truly responsible for the problem or whether it merely acts as the final precipitating event leading to prolapse in a previously damaged disc that is likely to prolapse sooner or later anyway. In general, *in vitro* mechanical studies show that the vertebral end plates are more likely to fail under load than the annulus fibrosus, and it is only a disc showing degenerative changes that will prolapse readily.[4] In many instances the prolapse follows some trivial stress or movement performed many times before by the same person without difficulty. This fits in with the concept of previous damage.

Lumbar spondylosis

This is a common diagnosis in patients with back pain. The history is of pain in the back aggravated by physical activity and relieved by rest, often with acute exacerbations. Radiographs show evidence of disc-space narrowing, usually at the L4/L5 and L5/S1 levels, with osteophytes and osteoarthrosis of the posterior interfacetal joints. The problem in making this diagnosis is that these changes are remarkably frequent in symptom-free individuals. Pathological changes of spondylosis can be found in virtually the whole adult population. Radiological evidence occurs in about two-thirds and, although back pain is common, it correlates poorly with the radiological features.[5] Even in the back-pain sufferer the symptoms are often intermittent, with long intervening periods without any pain, yet the radiological and pathological changes will not disappear. This means that it is extremely difficult to incriminate spondylosis as the cause of back pain in individual subjects. Lawrence[5] undertook detailed epidemiological surveys and found back pain to be only 12 per cent more prevalent in those with the grossest evidence of lumbar spondylosis, compared to those with normal or virtually normal radiographs.

Spinal stenosis

This is another, although rarer, mechanical problem which should be identified and is suggested when the patient presents with a pattern of back pain which is relieved by flexion and aggravated by extension. Pain, numbness, paraesthesiae and a 'woolly' feeling occur in the lower limbs. These symptoms develop on exercise and are relieved by rest. They resemble intermittent claudication and many patients are misdiagnosed as such. The condition is one in which there is narrowing of the vertebral canal and, in particular, of the lateral recesses. If this clinical problem is suspected a CAT scan will be required to confirm the diagnosis.

Other mechanical problems

These include spondylolisthesis, small spinal fractures, and congenital anomalies.

Problems of inflammatory origin

These must always be identified and include common arthropathies, such as ankylosing spondylitis, less commonly rheumatoid arthritis, and rarely infections.

Ankylosing spondylitis (also discussed in Chapters 8 and 10)

It is important to recognize the condition early as appropriate physical treatment is effective in relieving symptoms and preventing the development of permanent stiffness and deformity. There are implications for employers to pay attention to the working posture, encourage physical activity, and those with physiotherapists to supervise an aggressive exercise programme at least once a week as this encourages the daily performance of home exercises. Intensive bouts of treatment lasting one week have also been shown to be of great benefit and liaison between employer and NHS physiotherapy departments, when the firm does not employ physiotherapists, is important. Ideally physiotherapy departments should offer time for physiotherapy outside normal office hours.

Rheumatoid arthritis

This can occasionally involve the lumbar spine. It is easy to recognize because of the presence of peripheral features of the disease (see Chapters 8 and 10).

Infective arthritis

In infections involving the spine the patient is usually ill and has a pyrexia with localized pain and tenderness. Such problems are not usually confused with pain of mechanical origin.

Neoplasms

These can affect the spine. Metastases are more common than primary tumours, but reticuloses may occur. The history of gradual onset of back pain, perhaps associated with feeling unwell, loss of weight, etc. should alert one to the possibility.

Metabolic disorders

The commonest disorder is osteoporosis with vertebral fractures. This usually occurs in elderly women and is rare in the working population. Osteomalacia is not uncommon in the Asian immigrant population of working age and, although usually associated with generalized bone pain, may present with pain in the back.

Referred pain

Referred pain in the back may arise from abdominal or pelvic disorders. The back moves normally and painlessly and there is usually clear evidence of an underlying abdominal or pelvic problem.

Psychological problems and back pain

Psychological factors confuse the diagnosis in many patients. Particularly in patients with chronic back pain, the symptoms and disability may be largely of psychological origin, the actual damage within the spine playing a relatively minor role. Several different psychological mechanisms have been identified.[6]

Malingering undoubtedly occurs but it is impossible to obtain any real estimate of the magnitude of this problem.

'Compensation neurosis' is sometimes found in patients pursuing medico-legal claims. In some there may be a deliberate aggravation of symptoms but, for the majority, subtle psychological mechanisms may reinforce the severity of the pain and the perpetuation of disability. This can be an example of 'operant conditioning', or 'secondary gain', in which the patient obtains psychological or physical rewards because of the problem. Over-solicitous relatives or friends, whose lives revolve round the suffering of the back pain patient, may act as reinforcers and prolong back-pain disability. Absence from work may also be prolonged unnecessarily, sometimes on the re-commendation of health care practitioners who are misled by the patient or his relatives.

Not infrequently, episodes of cervical or low back pain may become prolonged, or more severe than can be accounted for by the assessment of the patient's physical state. In these situations, psychological or social factors that may predate or postdate the onset of spinal pain may become the dominant problem in the patient's life and be expressed as physical pain. Such patients may become severely depressed or have symptoms reflecting an anxiety state. More rarely, depression or anxiety states themselves may manifest as back pain.

When the cause of the back pain is uncertain, it is all too easy to suggest that it is of psychological origin and miss a physical cause. It is important both to exclude an underlying physical condition and also to make a positive diagnosis of the psychological disorder if there is evidence of this. Waddell has identified a number of 'non-organic physical signs' that help in the recognition of a likely psychological origin. These include pain in the back brought on by simulated rotation of the spine, pain produced by pressure on the vertex of the skull, superficial skin tenderness, normal straight leg raising when the patient's attention is distracted, a non-anatomical distribution of lower-limb symptoms and over-reaction throughout the examination.[6]

PREVENTION OF BACK PAIN

There is a vast literature on the relationship between occupation, lifting, and back pain. There is no doubt that many cases which present at work are related to occupation and a direct result of work activity. Under the most recent Health and Safety Executive reporting structure, two out of every three accidents reported under the category 'strenuous movements, etc.' (the nearest approximation to the former 'handling' category) in the last few years result in sprains and strains and other injuries to the back, and there are back injuries in other categories.[7] In general, the heavier the work the greater the risk of back injury. Young workers appear to be more at risk.[8] There are more reports of disc degeneration in those engaged in heavy work, and in this group the older worker is more affected, as might be expected.

Legislation

Most legislation attempts to protect workers from manual handling injury by general statements, because of the difficulties in being more specific.

The Factories Act, 1961 states that 'a person shall not be employed to lift, carry or move, any load so heavy as to be likely to cause injury to him' and there is a virtually identical statement in the Offices, Shops and Railway Premises Act, 1963. Specific regulations also apply in some industries (including the woollen and worsted textiles, jute, pottery, agriculture, and construction industries) and there are also some provisions applying to young people. The current legislation is listed in the review of manual handling published by the Health and Safety Executive in 1985.[7]

Quite apart from specific regulations, however, all employers now have a duty under Section 2 of the Health and Safety at Work etc Act, 1974, to provide and maintain a system of work that is safe and without risks to health of all their employees, so far as is reasonably practicable. This Act therefore covers employees engaged in any form of work, including manual handling and lifting. The Act also requires that an employer should provide 'such information, instruction, training and supervision as is necessary to ensure, as far as is reasonably practicable, the health and safety of his employees'. The Health and Safety Commission is currently considering ways to improve and rationalize the existing range of legislation, and to provide framework guidance, with a view to reducing the number and severity of manual handling injuries.

The International Labour Conference in 1967 adopted ILO Convention 127 recommendation 'concerning the maximum permissible weight to be lifted by one person'. It was suggested that a man should not lift more than 55 kg, with lower figures for women and young people. This recommendation was not ratified by the UK and many other countries.

Accident investigation

If an employee sustains a back injury, it is essential to investigate the circumstances in which it occurred and, if possible, to correct any adverse personal or environmental factors which can be identified. This should help to prevent a recurrence and the experience can be incorporated into training programmes.

Assessing the job

The conditions under which people work influence the risk of accident and the possibility of developing a back problem. In some occupations, such as dock work, certain aspects of the working conditions may be outside the control of the employer, for example, they may depend on the layout of the ship and the nature and packing of the cargo to be unloaded. But in most work situations potential hazards can be identified and controlled. Redesign on ergonomic lines can make a safer environment and improve output with less demand on the employees. The aspects which need to be considered include the physical demands, the task itself, and the working posture.

Physical demands of the work

This will involve assessment of the load to be moved or carried, its physical characteristics and location, as well as the type, frequency, and duration of the effort involved.

An interesting approach, developed at the University of Michigan, USA, compares the maximum force involved in a particular lift with the maximum that could be achieved by a strong male worker in that same position.[9] This provides a lift strength ratio (LSR) which is defined as follows:

$$LSR = \frac{\text{Maximum load lifted on job}}{\text{Predicted strength of a large strong male in the same position}}$$

The research provides charts showing the predicted maximum lifting strength of a strong male worker representing the strongest 2.5 per cent of men in various lifting positions. If the LSR required is 0.2 or more for an employee in the same lifting position, there is a significant increase in the incidence of low back pain and the job should be modified to be physically less demanding. Personal computer programmes have now been produced by the Michigan group to assist in evaluating the strength requirements of manual tasks in industry. Further research has also shown that if jobs require manual exertion that exceeds the isometric strength of individuals tested with reference to standardized protocols, such individuals are three times more likely to develop low back pain than stronger individuals. There is added risk if the weaker individuals have a history of previous back-pain incidents. This approach provides a real advance in understanding the physical requirements of various types of manual labour and in matching worker strength to jobs. More widespread application of the principles should lead to the elimination of hazardous tasks and to their replacement by more acceptable procedures.[10] A sample chart is shown in Fig. 9.2.

The work task

Little attention has been given to this in the past. The first priority should be to consider if the job can be mechanized and thus remove the lifting hazard. The use of mechanical aids such as levers, barrows, and trollies will often reduce the demands of the job. Fork-lift trucks may be appropriate. Simple rollers and conveyors will assist loading and unloading, for example. Redesign of existing equipment and working layout may well reduce the risk of back injury and, although redesign is often thought to be impracticable, simple changes can be effective. An awkward task may well be a hazardous task, with an increased accident risk. Nevertheless, significant reduction in the risk can frequently be achieved at relatively low cost. Considerations will include:

(1)   the use of mechanical aids;

(2)   reduction in the size and weight of the load;

(3)   ensuring that it can be handled easily, providing hand grips if necessary;

(4)   ensuring that goods are stored in easily accessible positions at a reasonable height;

(5)   good, spacious working conditions in which floors, lighting, etc. allow the task to be carried out safely.

Although the mass of the load is a major contributor to the likelihood of a back injury, there is particular risk to the lumbar spine when load bearing is

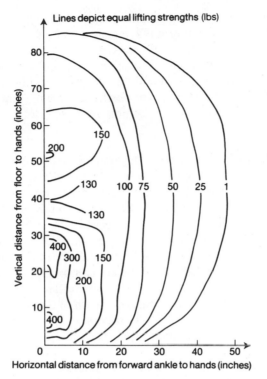

Lines depict equal lifting strengths (lbs)

Fig. 9.2 Predicted lifting strength of the strongest 2.5 per cent of men[9]

combined with flexion and rotation of the back. Situations such as the following occur frequently:

(1) lifting goods out of high sided boxes, or bins;

(2) two men loading heavy sacks onto a lorry or platform;

(3) removing goods stored under benches;

(4) lifting a load from the side while sitting on a chair;

and there are many other examples.

Such actions should be avoided and alternative handling methods devised.

Working posture
Quite apart from applying good handling techniques when undertaking heavy manual work, the posture adopted by any worker in carrying out a task may contribute to the future development of back pain or aggravate an existing condition.

Standing Prolonged standing in one position should be avoided. Many factory jobs require standing at a bench which is often too low and encourages a slouched posture. Perhaps the bench could be raised or the work itself lifted onto a box. The ideal height for a bench is about 8 cm below the elbow when standing upright and there must be enough room below the bench for the feet, so that they can be positioned one in front of the other to aid balance. Frequent changes in position are important and there must be room to move about.

Sitting Much research has been devoted to improving the comfort of chairs, and a well-designed chair will reduce fatigue and improve productivity. A badly designed chair may cause backache as a result of ligament strain and will certainly aggravate an existing back condition. The seat height should allow the feet to rest flat on the floor. If the seat height needs to be raised to allow work to be carried out at a bench, a suitable foot rest must be provided. The seat itself should be horizontal or tilting slightly back and firm, but not hard, so that the body weight can be supported on the ischial tuberosities without discomfort. Too soft a seat will spread the load to other areas not intended for weightbearing. The depth of the seat should allow the back of the calves to be free when the sacrum is against the back rest. The back rest should support the lumbar spine in its natural curve, with its upper margin just below the lower border of the scapulae.[11] Many therapists believe that the ideal chair tilts so that the anterior part of the seat is lower than the posterior. Chairs of Scandinavian design with a tilted seat and knee rests are now widely available. Since many patients with low back pain will have co-existing cervical problems, chairs with arm rests will be helpful to this group and will probably also encourage better posture. There is no perfect chair because individual dimensions vary. Chairs should be adjustable so that changes can be made to suit most people.

There are many misconceptions about sitting. The layman usually thinks that a sitting job must be good for back pain sufferers, but a poor posture can be harmful, by increasing intradiscal pressures and stretching the sciatic nerve. Some people find that 'lodging' on the edge of a stool or bench is comfortable and avoids the strain of prolonged standing. This is all right if the seat is deep enough for the weight to be borne by the ischial tuberosities. Frequent changes of posture are helpful and job rotation may contribute to the patient's comfort. A useful review of ergonomic and other aspects of design has recently been published.[12]

Driving

Some people's work will, in whole or in part, involve driving, and the working posture will be dictated by the driving seat. In general, the more positions into which the seat may be adjusted the better, particularly changing the incline of the seat back. Simple additional back rests which support the lumbar curve are cheap and may be very helpful. Some more expensive cars incorporate an adjustable lumbar support into the seat design. Power steering can help some people with cervico-brachial pain. Long journeys often aggravate back pain and frequent breaks, with change of posture, are recommended. If driving also requires loading and unloading goods from the boot of the car, the use of a hatchback or shooting brake with a low sill is likely to reduce the risk of back pain.

Training

Ideally, instruction in protecting the back should begin at school. This could well be incorporated into physical education periods. Most large organizations have training programmes for employees, especially recruits. Apprentices and trainees are probably more receptive than older workers to the educational aspect of training in lifting. Nurses are particularly at risk. Many patients are unable to assist when they need to be lifted and it is difficult to apply the principles for safe lifting when a patient is in bed. The Back Pain Association in collaboration with the Royal College of Nursing has produced a useful guide for nurses on the handling of patients, which explains safe techniques and emphasizes the importance of ergonomics and aids to lifting.[13] The Health and Safety Commission has also published guidance on lifting patients.[14]

The Health and Safety at Work, etc. Act, 1974 requires training in the widest sense, although smaller firms may do this on the job. Glover and Davies[15] introduced a training programme into a factory employing 6000 people, and there were short-term benefits from increased awareness of the hazards of lifting. Manual handling instruction in an electronics factory was shown to be cost effective, with a significant reduction of sickness absence attributed to back pain during the next year (Blow, personal communication). A number of studies have shown an initial benefit from training in lifting, but the benefit diminishes with time. Any kind of instruction or publicity (e.g. posters) should be repeated at intervals to remain effective.

The kinetic lift method is believed to be the optimum way of lifting and is now taught in many industries. The technique involves keeping the back straight although not necessarily upright, the chin in, appropriate foot position, a good grip on the object with the arms close to the body, and using the body weight to assist in moving the object. This can be demonstrated with a heavy, awkward object such as a large oil drum, and common faults such as poor grip, the free-style lift, and the effects of a poor foot position can be illustrated.

In applying this to a particular workplace, the first step is to size up the job and consider whether or not the object is too heavy or bulky to be moved by one person. If so, the task should be divided into two or more parts, a colleague should be asked to help, or a mechanical means of lifting should be used. The position of the feet is all important. They should be spread about 50 cm (20 in.) apart, with one foot behind the object and the other by the side of the object, pointing in the direction in which it is to be moved. This has two benefits: the broad base is very stable and avoids balancing problems, while by pointing the forward foot in the direction of travel, it will not be necessary to twist the spine when the object is lifted but simply to move the rear foot forward. The worker squats down with the hips, knees, and ankles flexed and the chin in. The back is kept straight and usually inclined forward as necessary. The object is positioned between the knees and as close to the body as possible. A good grip is essential and, if not readily available, the object should be tilted onto one corner and gripped firmly at a free bottom corner on the opposite side. The grip should be performed with the palm of the hand and the roots of the fingers and thumb and not with the fingers alone as they are much weaker. Finally, the lift itself should be performed using the leg muscles. The load is set down by repeating these steps in reverse. The worker must avoid twisting the back throughout the lift, the carry, and the set-down. The load should be kept close to the body. A load at arms' length puts greater strain on the spine.

These instructions cannot, however, be rigidly applied to all lifting activities irrespective of the task and work conditions. But keeping a straight back reduces spinal stresses in many lifting situations and instruction is believed to reduce the accident risk. The most important point is to keep the load as close to the body as possible when lifting.

HEALTH SCREENING

Pre-employment screening

There is a degree of self-selection in many job applications. Those of stocky or muscular build are more likely to apply for manual work than those of light build and short stature. There is some evidence that fit people are less likely to develop back problems and have a greater tolerance of minor injuries.

Routine medical examination is not justified except in special circumstances, such as work in heavy industry, or where there are particular hazards to the health of the employee, or where litigation has identified a particular need. It is uneconomic in medical manpower and probably unnecessary. Although most large organizations can be expected to have a nurse or doctor, the majority of industry has no direct access to professional occupational health advice on a day-to-day basis. It is likely that recruitment will be the responsibility of the personnel officer, or the manager or foreman in a small organization. A good relationship with local general practitioners is important in these circumstances. A nurse trained in occupational health is the ideal person for this sort of health screening and ideally she should have access to a doctor to whom she can refer problems. If there is no doctor at the workplace she should liaise with the employee's family doctor.

The Health and Safety Executive's Guidance Note MS 20 deals with pre-employment health screening.[16] A simple self-administered questionnaire, to be completed before attending for screening, is a useful method of collecting health information. Many managers have a sixth sense for health problems and, if these are suspected, further advice on job placement should be sought. The minimum information required is:

1. A detailed medical history. Has the recruit had any major illness, injury, or operation which has resulted in reduced ability to undertake manual work?

2. A detailed occupational history. Has there been a back injury or prolonged or recurrent absence from work due to back pain or other medical condition?

3. Does the individual appear to be fit to do the job on offer?

In general, if a recruit has a normal range of movement of the spine and limbs, unimpaired exercise tolerance, absence of musculoskeletal deformity, and does not have a hernia (see Chapter 20), he is usually acceptable for manual work.

It might seem sensible that people who apply to work in heavy industry should have a radiograph of their spine to exclude any abnormality. However, there is abundant evidence that routine lumbar radiographs have *no* value in predicting those likely to develop back pain at work.[17] The possible radiation hazard is therefore unacceptable. Heavy industries, such as docks and coal-mining, do not now undertake routine spine radiographs.

The most useful single item of information in predicting potential back problems is a history of back pain, particularly if severe enough to have caused some absence from work.[18]

Screening after sickness absence

Any employee engaged in heavy manual work should be screened on return to work after sickness absence. This is particularly important if the absence was due to back or sciatic pain, but other conditions such as a chest infection or recovery from an operation, are relevant to manual handling. The absence may have been certified by a general practitioner, or by the worker himself if the absence was of short duration. Many general practitioners and hospital doctors have little experience of working conditions in industry and the decision to return to work will often be on the advice of the patient himself. Sometimes economic or other factors encourage people to return to work before they are fit to undertake the physical demands of their normal job without risk. It is likely that back or sciatic pain will recur if the following are identified at screening:[18]

(1) *from the history:*

    (a)   residual pain in the leg on return to work;

    (b)   sickness absence of five or more weeks in the current attack;

    (c)   a fall on the buttocks or back as a cause of back injury;

    (d)   two or more previous attacks.

(2) *from the examination:*

    (a)   restriction of the painfree range of straight leg raising to 45° or less;

    (b)   inability to 'sit-up' from lying flat;

    (c)   pain or weakness on resisted hip flexion;

    (d)   back pain on lumbar extension, induced by passive flexion of the knees and extension of the hips with the patient in the prone position.

If any of these factors is present, the patient should either be employed initially on lighter work or arrangements made for further active rehabilitation. The more factors that are positive the greater the risk of recurring disability. The opportunity should also be taken to review the employee's knowledge of handling techniques.

TREATMENT OF BACK PAIN

There is considerable doubt as to the value of many forms of treatment. Controlled trials have produced little evidence that many of the procedures used make any difference to prognosis or do more than pass the time until natural remission occurs. The most important element in initial management would seem to be rest during the acute phase and then active rehabilitation.

Bed rest

A well-recognized routine in acute back pain is a period of complete bed rest, with a board under the mattress if this seems to sag, and only one pillow. The patient is allowed up for toilet, washing, and meals as this produces less strain on the spine than attempting these manœuvres while lying flat. A commode by the bed may be required. Patients who have struggled on without specific advice often report improvement on this regime.

A recent report from Canada suggests that patients presenting to their family physicians with acute low back pain, and treated with analgesics only, recovered as quickly as those treated with either bed rest or physiotherapy combined with education. More specific treatment did not shorten the time of disability. There was doubt, however, whether patients complied strictly with the prescribed routines, and both physiotherapy and education may have been inadequate.[19] In Texas, a randomized trial involving 203 patients presenting with 'mechanical' low back pain compared the results of treatment with either two or seven days bed rest. Those patients treated with two days bed rest missed 45 per cent fewer days off work than the other group.[20] Many UK physicians believe that adequate bed rest, with increased activity as soon as reduction of symptoms allows, is the treatment of choice.

Spinal support

The spine can be rested in a lumbar corset. Pain relief is thought to occur as a result of splinting the spine in a good posture, increase in intra-abdominal pressure, local warmth to the back, and stimulation of mechano-receptors in the back. The use of a corset should be restricted to patients recovering from prolapse of an intervertebral disc, and used only for a few weeks to enable the subject to gain confidence. Long-term use of a support produces spinal stiffness and can lead to further back problems. In some patients a corset can usefully be worn when undertaking 'at risk' tasks.

Medication

Pain relieving drugs, such as analgesics and anti-inflammatory agents, are often needed. Occasionally, for some subjects, symptoms can be exacerbated by bed rest, with an element of morning stiffness. There is some evidence that in these patients secondary inflammatory changes related to the mechanical problem may occur in the spine, and a long-acting non-steroid anti-inflammatory drug last thing at night can be very effective. Antidepressant drugs may be helpful in the management of some patients with long-standing pain.

Physiotherapy

There is a wide variety of physiotherapy techniques. Massage, ice, shortwave, radiant heat, traction, etc. seem of temporary benefit and usually provide relief only while they are being given and for a few hours afterwards.

Exercises are often prescribed but many patients find that these make their backs worse. In general, mobilizing exercises, flexion exercises, and extension exercises are contraindicated. The emphasis over the long term should be on isometric exercises to strengthen the paraspinal and abdominal muscles.

Manipulation

Manipulation is practised by physicians, surgeons, physiotherapists, osteopaths, chiropractors, and others. Despite the widespread use of this technique, there are no firm data to suggest that it is of real value. Controlled trials have failed to indicate that it makes any difference to the long-term outlook,[21] although it may hasten the resolution of acute back symptoms.

Injections

Several injection procedures may prove helpful. These include local injections at focal tender points and epidural injections for patients with persistent sciatic pain. The latter are probably most effective for the patient who fails to make a complete recovery following a prolonged period of bed rest for sciatica.

Surgery

Surgery is seldom required. There are probably less than 10 000 operations for back pain each year although the incidence of back problems may be as high as 20 million episodes.[2] It has been suggested that 10–15 per cent of operations are unsuccessful.[2] In general, procedures such as laminectomy and discectomy are more effective for nerve-root pain than for back pain. Chemonucleolysis, in which the nucleus is 'dissolved' by an enzyme injection, may be an alternative to discectomy for some patients. Surgery should be considered only for patients with persistent severe problems following an adequate period of conservative therapy, including bed rest. Patients with lesser problems but with recurrent disability present difficult decisions about treatment. Such a person may lose a lot of time from work or have difficulty in performing his job adequately and yet not be in severe pain or totally disabled. If there is any evidence of cauda equina compression, with loss of bladder and bowel control, surgical decompression becomes an emergency.

REHABILITATION

Most back injuries recover fully but, once a back injury has been sustained, there is a greater risk of recurrence. This is particularly so with disorders of the intervertebral disc.

After an initial period of rest, and appropriate treatment if indicated, early mobilization is important. This is usually in the hands of the general practitioner and direct access to physiotherapy is available in many areas. The physiotherapist should concentrate on strengthening the paraspinal and abdominal muscles and on teaching patients to understand their backs and how to avoid future problems.

Many employees have mechanical skills. Understanding the structure and function of the spine gives workers insight into the stresses the spine will meet in various postures and working conditions, and considerably reinforces the value of instruction on manual handling techniques. In Sweden this has been formalized into a 'Back School' in which workers with back pain have three or four lessons from a physiotherapist trained in communication methods. The lessons explain the structure of the spine using a human skeleton, the stresses that are met in various positions, illustrate what can go wrong with the spine, and then show how appropriate handling techniques will prevent this.[22] Simple programmes in back education have been shown to be effective in the United Kingdom as well as in Sweden.[23]

If recovery is slow, or if a significant spinal problem is recognized, referral to a hospital clinic is the usual practice. The problem is often compounded by delay in getting an appointment and a condition can become chronic while the patient is waiting for this. Some health districts have back pain clinics but, surprisingly, these are often underused.

Recovery is slow in some patients and incomplete in others. Where alternative lighter work is available it is beneficial to most patients to return to some form of work at the earliest opportunity. It is usually desirable to arrange reduced working hours initially, and enable the patient to travel to and from work outside the rush hours for perhaps two or three weeks. This is often a significant part of the total rehabilitation and speeds return to the former level of work.

Medical Rehabilitation Units exist in some areas and, if one is reasonably accessible for the patient, treatment is available for several hours each day. Activity is graded and progressive under expert medical supervision and equipment is often available to rehabilitate patients in conditions simulating their own working environment. This graded activity restores confidence after injury. Re-education is an important part of the programme.

RECOMMENDATIONS

Despite the magnitude of the problem, relatively limited resources have been directed at improving our understanding of the pathogenesis, prevention, and treatment of back pain. In part, this is due to difficulties in understanding the causes of the problem, assessing its severity and in determining the value of different forms of treatment. In recent years this challenge has acted

as the stimulus to many groups and, in particular, led to co-operation between physicians, surgeons, bio-engineers, biochemists, etc. and to inter-
disciplinary approaches and co-operative studies, but there is still a need for
well-structured investigations.

Many industries could do more to study the ergonomics of the working
environment and take action to reduce the risk of back injuries. This should
include careful choice and specifications for new equipment and the layout of
the workplace.

Ideally, general practitioners and consultants should take the opportunity
of visiting local workplaces to see their patients' conditions of work. Where
visits have been arranged, the doctor has usually benefited from an increased
understanding of manual handling problems and is therefore better equipped
to advise his patients with back pain.

REFERENCES

1. Dixon A StJ. Diagnosis of low back pain—sorting the complainers. In: Jayson MIV, ed. The lumbar spine and back pain. 2nd ed. London: Pitman Medical, 1980:135–55.
2. Wells N. Back pain. Studies of current health problems, no. 78. London: Office of Health Economics, 1985.
3. Simms-Williams H, Jayson MIV, Young SMS, Baddeley H, Collins E. Controlled trial of mobilisation and manipulation for patients with low back pain in general practice. Br Med J 1978;2:1338–40.
4. Jayson MIV, Barks JS. Intervertebral discs: nuclear morphology and bursting pressure. Ann Rheum Dis 1973;32:308–15.
5. Lawrence JS. Rheumatism in populations. London: Heinemann, 1977:68–97.
6. Waddell G, McCulloch JA, Kummel EG, Venner RM. Non-organic physical signs in low back pain. Spine 1980;5:117–25.
7. Troup JDG, Edwards FC. Manual handling and lifting. An information and literature review with special reference to the back. London: HMSO, 1985.
8. Blow RJ, Jackson JM. An analysis of back injuries in registered dock workers. Proc Roy Soc Med 1971;64:753–7.
9. Chaffin DB. Human strength capability and low back pain. J Occup Med 1974;16:248–54.
10. Chaffin DB, Park KS. A longitudinal study of low-back pain as associated with occupational weight lifting factors. Am Ind Hyg Ass J 1973;34:513–25.
11. Pheasant ST. Anthropometric estimates for British civilian adults. Ergonomics 1982;25:993–1001.
12. Pheasant ST. Bodyspace. Anthropometry, ergonomics and design. London: Taylor and Francis, 1986.
13. Lloyd P, Tarling C, Troup JDG, Wright B. The handling of patients: a guide for nurses. 2nd ed. London: The Back Pain Association in collaboration with the Royal College of Nursing, 1987.
14. The lifting of patients in the Health Services. Health and Safety Commission and Health Services Advisory Committee. London: HMSO, 1984.

15. Glover JR, Davies BT. Manual handling and lifting: its introduction into a 6000 employee works. J Ind Nurs 1961;**13**:289–300.
16. Health and Safety Executive. Pre-employment health screening. Guidance Note MS 20. London: HMSO, 1982.
17. Rowe ML. Are routine spine films on workers in industry cost or risk-benefit effective? J Occup Med 1982;**24**:41–3.
18. Lloyd DCEF, Troup JDG. Recurrent back pain and its prediction. J Soc Occup Med 1983;**33**:66–74.
19. Gilbert JR, Taylor DW, Hildebrand A, Evans C. Clinical trial of common treatments for low back pain in family practice. Br Med J 1985;**291**:791–4.
20. Deyo RA, Diehl AK, Rosenthal M. How many days of bed rest for acute low back pain? N Engl J Med 1986;**315**:1064–70.
21. Jayson MIV. A limited role for manipulation (editorial). Br Med J 1986; **293**:1454–5.
22. Lidström A, Zachrisson M. Ryggbesvär och arbetssoförmaga Ryggskolan. Ett Försok till mer rationell fysikalist terapi. Socialmed T 1973;**7**:419–22.
23. Klaber Moffett JA, Chase SM, Portek I, Ennis JR. A controlled prospective study to evaluate the effectiveness of the back pain school in the relief of chronic low back pain. Spine 1986;**11**(2):120–2.

10

Locomotor disorders

G.M. Cochrane and E.B. Macdonald

INTRODUCTION

This chapter is about some of the disabilities of movement—the rheumatic diseases which are painful and the diseases of muscle and of the nervous system which cause weakness. Some are rare and others affect millions, and together they are the most widespread and crippling conditions to which our population is subject.

Diseases of the musculoskeletal system and connective tissues with congenital anomalies accounted for the loss of 62 million days through certified incapacity in 1982–83—over 17 per cent of all days lost.[1]

As might be expected, the loss is greater in heavy industry than among those doing sedentary work, and the consultation rate in general practice is over three times higher for patients in Social Class V compared with those in Social Class 1.[2]

The locomotor disorders which are described here belong to four ages:

1. Present in infancy and persisting throughout life:

   - dwarfism;

   - haemophilia with arthritis;

   - osteogenesis imperfecta;

   - spina bifida with paraplegia.

2. Developing during childhood, interfering with education, and substantially restricting the choices of career:

   - juvenile chronic arthritis;

   - muscular dystrophies.

3. Occurring in late adolesence and during the early years at work:

   - ankylosing spondylitis;

   - chondromalacia patellae;

   - spinal injuries.

4. Coming in the middle- and later years at work:

- rheumatoid arthritis;

- soft tissue rheumatism—bursitis, enthesiopathies, fibrositis, 'frozen shoulder', over-use injuries, and tenosynovitis;

- cervical spondylosis;

- generalized osteoarthrosis;

- Paget's disease.

Each disease will be discussed separately, observing its prevalence, its features and treatment which may alter in some way the worker's abilities and performance. The selection of suitable work and training, the conditions of the workplace and how disabled school-leavers may be helped in choosing their careers are also discussed.

While some occupations—such as coal-mining; diving; the armed forces; the police, fire, ambulance, and nursing services; and the merchant navy and others—demand locomotor normality at entry, the development of loco-motor disability in the individual already employed is not necessarily a ban on further employment and most can be accommodated. If in doubt, approach to the appropriate employer's medical adviser is recommended: unsuitability should not be assumed.

Often the degree of physical disability bears little relationship to the patient's eventual success in rehabilitation and occupation. The physician, employer, and union may be apprehensive about the ability of an individual to fulfil any particular job and caution prevails. It is a common experience of occupational physicians, when health screening is introduced in a working population for the first time, to find that there are many workers in jobs for which they would normally be considered unsuitable for physical reasons—yet these individuals will often have performed their tasks competently and without excessive sickness absence. The problem of employers' attitudes is even more pronounced with the so-called 'aversive handicaps'[3] referring to those with unsightly defects or distortions of the body, or abnormal movements such as tics, athetosis, or abnormalities causing socially unacceptable sight, sound, or smell.

Employers are often reluctant to hire those with locomotor handicap. This tends to be because of the associated need to overcome the architectural barriers and to provide aids and adapt the workplace and tools for such employees. However, it has been shown that when the possibility of financial aid for these very problems is explained to employers then their attitude can become more positive.[4] Such help is available through the Manpower Services Commission (see Chapter 2).

Trained disabled youths are much more readily accepted by the labour market than unskilled workers. Every effort must be made to improve the vocational training of the young disabled[5] and it has been shown, for example, that providing that adequate training is given, and with a certain amount of education of employers, computer-competent programmers and systems analysts will succeed in open employment in high-technology industry.[6]

Indeed, the disabled may often display greater motivation and commitment to their job. The US Chamber of Commerce, in a survey of 279 companies, found that 90 per cent had experienced no increase in insurance costs as a result of employing handicapped workers,[7] and in a review of their 1400 handicapped employees the Du Pont Corporation found that 96 per cent had better safety records than their able-bodied colleagues.[8]

The advising physician is encouraged to adopt a policy of erring towards the over-optimistic assessment of functional ability and job potential.

LOCOMOTOR DISORDERS SINCE INFANCY

Dwarfism

Growth is retarded because of an inherited defect or a disorder which develops during childhood. Well-known genetic causes of dwarfism are achondroplasia and diastrophic dysplasia. Examples of childhood illnesses which stunt growth are coeliac disease, rickets, renal failure, juvenile chronic arthritis, and protein–calorie malnutrition.

Dwarfs' capacity for work

There is some evidence that besides the complications peculiar to each form, all dwarfs are likely to experience difficulty in obtaining employment. People meeting those of small stature intuitively and impulsively gear their attitude to the size and not to the age of the person.[9] Through ridicule and isolation their education and the opportunities for further education may have been diminished though their intelligence is normal. Such antipathy may persist, limiting their choices of friends, partners, recreation, and work.

There are numerous occupations which have height requirements such that dwarfs may be excluded. Small limbs with short reach and arm span may create specific problems with machine-control operations and some manual tasks. Heavy manual work is not likely to be suitable, though many dwarfs find that their height has little effect on their ability to do their jobs and in some instances may be an advantage. In general, only those with severe physical abnormalities are handicapped in obtaining education and employment, and in one survey of dwarfs in employment[10] 75 per cent of males and 45 per cent of females gained employment—most in the tradesmen and clerical occupational groups, and fewer in the professional and supervisory groups. Show business and circuses are not the main employers as is often thought.

The Manpower Services Commission can assist in providing individual seating, desk or work-bench at the appropriate height, equipment within restricted reach and, where necessary, assistance with transport to work and parking. With modification to the workplace, dwarfs are able to perform most jobs.

Haemophilia and arthritis (Haemophilia is also discussed in Chapter 18)

Deficiency of Factor VIII is the commonest heritable disorder of blood clotting, inherited as an X-linked recessive character. Bleeding into joints is the most frequent and painful complication and usually follows injury which may be trivial. After childhood the frequency of bleeding into joints diminishes. In each episode usually one joint is involved: the knees, ankles, subtalar joints, and elbows are most often affected. In about half of those who have suffered repeated haemarthroses permanent joint damage and deformity occur. Bleeding may also occur into bone and muscle, most often in the leg, causing severe pain, swelling, and neurovascular compression. Chronic damage is most common in the knee (70 per cent) causing permanent limitation of movement, flexion contracture, and muscle wasting with severely limited mobility.

Concentrated preparations of plasma coagulation factors are available to control bleeding, and regular administration of small amounts of concentrate can maintain the Factor VIII activity above the critical level of 3 per cent of normal.

The risk of occurrence of haemophilia due to Factor VIII deficiency is one in 2500 live male births. If the mother is a carrier, the risk of her sons being affected is one in two and, similarly, the risk of her daughters being carriers is one in two.

Prognosis

Ignorance and time-honoured misconceptions have kept affected boys from school and men from work. The introduction of replacement therapy with Factor VIII concentrates has led to active lives. Haemophiliacs take reasonable care to avoid trauma, recognize the first signs of bleeding, and know how to achieve immediate control. Since there have been Haemophilia Centres in all regions of Britain, haemophiliacs have relied less on local hospitals and enjoy an increased independence and morale.[11] In some haemophiliacs the disease is mild, causing little inconvenience, but in others there may be recurrent joint haemorrhages and troublesome bleeding from minor cuts, with life tainted by the fear of haemorrhage. Those on self-treatment have been shown to have improved attendance at school and subsequently higher academic achievement.[12] The prospects for the delay, if not the prevention, of chronic arthropathy are now good.[13] Markova and Forbes[14] found that many haemophiliacs lived in undesirable accommodation, and one-third had missed more than two years of schooling due to their disease and consequently were educationally disadvantaged. Twenty-nine per cent were unemployed at a time when local unemployment in men was 5.2 per cent and, in a later study,[15] 12 of 23 haemophiliacs were unemployed when the local unemployment of men was 12.7 per cent. Six of the 11 in work felt that their performance had improved since self-treatment was introduced, but only 2 of 11 had facilities at work for self-treatment. About 30 per cent of jobs had some inherent defects for the haemophiliac, demanding too much standing, heavy loading and unloading, stair climbing, and difficulties with transport. The most severely affected had the lower-qualified jobs. The special needs of the workplace depend upon the severity of the deficiency of the clotting factor and the damage that has resulted from haemorrhage into joints.

One-third of 225 haemophiliacs were preoccupied with whether or not to tell their employers.[16] Employers know little about haemophilia and the benefits of self-treatment. While, traditionally, haemophiliacs have been advised to avoid heavy manual jobs such as mining, heavy labouring, work involving prolonged physical effort in awkward situations or remote from medical facilities, the evidence is that most accidents precipitating bleeding have been caused by sudden impact with doors or furniture, or falls.

In a major study[12] of 429 haemophiliacs throughout the United Kingdom their overall unemployment rate was 17.5 per cent against a national rate of 6.9 per cent. Of those employed, 89 per cent reported no problems with their job or travelling; did not have special facilities or privileges at work; had usually obtained the job on their own initiative; and 75 per cent considered they had received no advice leading to employment from doctors, teachers, careers officers, or Disablement Resettlement Officers. Three in four had been in their job for over three years.

Only a 15-minute break from work in a reasonably clean environment is required for self-treatment if necessary, and potential employers need to be appropriately educated about the good prospects for the haemophiliac at work. Good haemophilia care has been demonstrated as leading to a twofold reduction in days lost from school and a threefold reduction in days lost from work.[12]

Osteogenesis imperfecta

Osteogenesis imperfecta or the brittle bone syndrome[17] is a rare inherited disorder of connective tissue with defective formation of collagen by osteoblasts and fibroblasts, for which there is no cure. The overall incidence is around 5 per 100 000 births. Osteogenesis imperfecta tarda, the commoner and milder form, is dominantly inherited and has extra-skeletal features of blue sclerae, deafness, abnormal teeth, lax ligaments, and hypermobile joints. The less common form frequently occurs in the absence of family history, is more severe, and is not accompanied by extra-skeletal features except for discoloured and deformed teeth. As a result of recurrent fractures, the limbs and spine may be severely deformed. The fracture rate declines with age.[18]

Commonly, those with osteogenesis imperfecta are affable, intelligent, extrovert, willing to seek higher education, and achieving additional training and a high rate of employment.[19] The severely affected need to attend a special school. In all cases further education and training should be encouraged.

If the disease and deformities are mild, work involving strenuous exertion or agility should best be avoided and, if the disease is more severe, limitations will be obvious and assistance from a special career adviser should be sought. In job placement, care should be taken to avoid excessive exposure to noise because of the risk of deafness.

Spina bifida with paraplegia

Spina bifida with myelomeningocoele is the commonest of all central nervous system malformations. The midline defect of fusion of the vertebral arches with herniation of meninges and nerve tissue occurs in 1 in 200 to 1 in 500 live births, and most often in the lumbo-sacral area. Neurological deficit is usually of the lower motor neurone type with flaccid paralysis of the legs, absent reflexes, segmental sensory loss, and paralysis of the urinary and anal sphincters. An enlarged head indicates hydrocephaly which may be associated with Arnold-Chiari malformation. Other common complications are hydronephrosis due to back pressure from the bladder to the renal pelvis and ascending urinary tract infections, hip dislocations related to the unopposed action of the hip flexors, and associated congenital defects of the heart, cleft palate, and genito-urinary tract. The prognosis depends upon the severity of the neurological defects: it is good when neural deficiency is slight and there is no hydrocephaly and poor if there are complete lower-limb paralysis, severe hydrocephaly, and other congenital abnormalities.

Urinary incontinence in boys is commonly managed by condom connected to a plastic bag secured to one leg: urinary incontinence in girls may be managed by intermittent self-catheterization or by urinary diversion by an ileal loop with an abdominal stoma. Faecal incontinence may be controlled by diet, aperients, and suppositories before defaecation. Digital evacuation of the lower bowel or occasional enemas may be necessary. Young people with spina bifida and hydrocephalus commonly have more verbal than practical abilities, and frequently they are inattentive to their paralysed and insensitive buttocks and lower limbs.

Advances in antibiotic and surgical management of infants and young children have resulted in an increasing number of individuals surviving through childhood and adolescence.[20]

More than ever before, children with spina bifida and paraplegia are receiving education in ordinary schools in place of special schools for the physically handicapped. Some will choose to continue their education beyond the age of 16 in local or residential colleges. Those with paraplegia rely on a wheelchair for their mobility and outside drive a car or electrically powered outdoor wheelchair. The special careers advisers for the disabled and the Disablement Resettlement Officers will seek out open or sheltered work to match the physical and mental abilities, and they rely upon detailed accounts given by the child and parents, school staff, educational psychologist, social worker, family doctor, and hospital specialists.

Work and future employment are a great source of anxiety for young people with spina bifida and their families. In one study of 100 school children with spina bifida 39 per cent had an IQ below 80, 64 per cent had visual defects, 27 per cent had epilepsy, and many had learning difficulties such that they required a period of education and training beyond their usual school-leaving age.[21] Some managed a repetitive sedentary job in a sheltered environment. Occupational potential of adults with spina bifida thus depends very much on the severity of the condition, the educational attainment and degree of independence, and the management of urinary and faecal incontinence and associated disorders of the nervous system. Castree and Walker[22] found that 33 per cent of 45 patients were in open employment, 36 per cent were in further education or sheltered employment, and 31 per cent were unemployed. A major factor influencing employment is the ability to travel. Schoolteachers and employers are likely to know little about the condition, and need the support and advice of the physician to overcome their misconceptions and anxieties about the capacity for work of those with spina bifida.

In a survey of 187 adults with spina bifida in Sheffield, only 23 per cent of 115 respondents with full clinical records were in work, although 45 per cent had been employed at some time. Most of those employed had skilled, non-manual jobs, such as typist, clerk, receptionist, or telephonist. Some of the more suitable jobs were those in which accuracy was more important than speed and in which a high degree of manual skill was not required. Some needed altered desks and chairs, others ramps and adapted toilets.[23]

Their hindrances are in mobility and toileting, in eye-hand co-ordination, and in slowness of manipulation through generalized and specific neurological deficits.

While it has been suggested that those with spina bifida have lower work potentials and poorer work attendance, of those in work 4 per cent will enter a profession and about 10 per cent achieve semi-professional status.[24]

LOCOMOTOR DISORDERS DEVELOPING DURING CHILDHOOD

Juvenile chronic arthritis

Juvenile chronic arthritis is a relatively common systemic disorder affecting one in a thousand children. There are two periods of high incidence, the ages of 2–4 and 11–13. Girls are affected more often than boys. Arthritis may affect many joints symmetrically, and this polyarticular distribution occurs in 34 per cent; or arthritis may be limited to a few joints (pauciarticular) and be asymmetrical.

Some children with pauciarticular disease develop iridocyclitis with risks of cataract, adhesions of the iris, secondary glaucoma, visual impairment, and sometimes blindness. In another subset, arthritis begins later, affects mainly boys, carries the risk of iridocyclitis, involves the sacro-iliac joints, hips, and knees, and may proceed to ankylosing spondylitis. Other serious complications of juvenile chronic arthritis are retarded growth, muscle atrophy, joint contractures, underdevelopment of the lower jaw, fusion of the joints of the cervical spine, and destruction of the joints of the hips and knees.

About 20 per cent of those with juvenile chronic arthritis are severely disabled and the prevalence of this form of severe disability is about one in 20 000 of the population. Females are affected twice as often as males. One in 10 has defective vision. Education is commonly interrupted and a prolonged absence from school was recorded in 31 per cent of those with severe disease,[25] but in other studies[26, 27] the educational achievements have compared favourably with those of the general population.

Emotional and social problems occur, especially in adolescent girls: anxiety or depression centre on feelings of inferiority, small stature, absence of sexual attraction, retarded mobility, physical dependence, and fear of the future. Segregation through special school and parental anxiety and overprotection can cause fewer friends and dependence on the family.

The entry of young people to work entails careful matching of their abilities and opportunities. At school emphasis should be laid on broadening and extending education to the highest standard, as permanent disability is likely. Counselling of children and parents is important: Wilkinson[28] found that five of 17 school-leavers with juvenile chronic arthritis did not know what they wanted to do, and among those who did many were unrealistic. Ansell and Wood[29] found that 83 per cent were able to work 15 years after the onset of their illness. Hill *et al.*[25] found that 62 per cent of 58 adults were

competitively employed and their arthritis had not affected their employment, while 14 per cent were active home-makers: two-thirds had mild
disease and one-third had progressive disablement.

Muscular dystrophies

Seventeen different forms of muscular dystrophy have three features in
common: their hereditary nature, primary involvement of voluntary muscle,
and tendency to progressive deterioration. Each can be distinguished by the
mode of inheritance, age of onset, rate of progression, and constant familial
pattern of muscles affected. The diagnosis is confirmed by electromyography,
microscopic and electron microscopic examinations of muscle, and abnormally raised levels of creatine kinase in the serum. The commonest types
of muscular dystrophy are the X-linked recessive Duchenne and Becker
dystrophies,[30] with prevalences in the population of 3 per 100 000 and 1 per
100 000 respectively; the autosomal dominant facio-scapulo-humeral dystrophy (0.5 per 100 000); and myotonic muscular dystrophy (5 per 100 000).

Duchenne muscular dystrophy
This is the most severe, and death comes to the majority in late adolescence,
usually from overwhelming respiratory infection and heart failure resulting
from cardiomyopathy, and few survive to be 25 years old. Some may proceed
to further education but none will work.

Becker muscular dystrophy
This is a distinct X-linked disorder and progression is much slower: some live
to draw the old-age pension. In most affected boys muscular weakness is
obvious before they leave school and will worsen inexorably but all will be
capable of chosen employment for 20 years or longer. Whenever appropriate,
further education should be encouraged towards a career that will not
require strength but administrative, literary, and numeracy skills.

Facio-scapulo-humeral dystrophy
This is inherited as an autosomal dominant trait with wide variation of
expression. Some patients become too weak to walk before their late teens,
some may show only slight weakness of the facial and scapular muscles in
middle life, and most fall between these extremes. Weakness progresses
slowly and life expectancy is close to normal. Work should be chosen
according to the severity of the weakness and the anticipated rate of
progression. Thoraco-lumbar scoliosis and foot drop are usual, causing
difficulties in walking over rough ground or climbing steps or ladders and
there will be increasing difficulty in raising the arms.

Myotonic muscular dystrophy

This form of muscular dystrophy is inherited as an autosomal dominant trait. In myotonic dystrophy there is wasting of the facial, temporal, sternomastoid, shoulder girdle, quadriceps, and leg muscles and ptosis is prominent. Cataracts are present in 90 per cent, cardiac conduction defects, frontal baldness, syncope, gonadal atrophy, impotence and sterility, constipation, mental retardation, and social decline are usual. Up to 20 per cent may have hearing loss. Myotonia can be relieved by procainamide, quinine sulphate, or diphenylhydantoin. Most are substantially disabled within 20 years of the first symptoms, yet a characteristic feature of the disease is the denial of symptoms and the reluctance to seek or take advice despite obvious disablement.

Weakness and inability to relax the grip make heavy manual work impracticable. Sometimes dysphonia, dysarthria, and a withdrawn affect make jobs which demand communication with the public less suitable, whereas office employment is usually apt. The disease presents at different ages and progresses at different rates. Many who are affected will change occupations during the course of the disease. They should always be encouraged to remain in their jobs as long as possible.

Disabled school-leavers

About 11 000 disabled adolescents leave special schools and more than this number leave ordinary schools in Britain each year. They have much poorer chances of being employed or receiving training and further education than able-bodied school-leavers. Hirst in 1983 showed that of 934 16–21-year-olds with 'severe disability' 51 per cent were in employment:[31] in 1973, 64 per cent of physically handicapped school-leavers obtained work.[32] Full appreciation of their cognitive, motor, and education potentials is required at least a year before they are due to leave school. Warnock[33] urges continuing discussion between the young person, his parents, the school and special career advisory service, and all who can contribute in establishing objectives and designing a flexible programme from education to open or sheltered employment.

Early in the final year at school a school leavers' conference encourages exchange of opinions.[34] The Disablement Resettlement Officer will assume responsibility from the careers adviser when the young person is 18 and it is best that he should enter the discussion at its beginning. At the conference the nature of the locomotor disorder, the prognosis, and any complications are made plain. Manipulative skills, speed and dexterity of movements, the degree of personal independence, the type of outdoor transport, and the need for orthoses, aids, and equipment are defined. The child's aptitudes and preferences, intellect, and educational achievements are established, as are the integrity of the home and the reliability of parental backing.

To prevent the physical and psychological deterioration which accompanies unemployment it is essential to think ahead.[35] The child may choose to apply for higher academic training at university, polytechnic, or college of further education; for a place in a technical college to prepare for a selected occupation such as office management, secretarial and clerical work, accounting, or computer studies; for work which needs no specific preliminary training or provides training within the firm; for admission to a residential training centre run independently or by the MSC's Training Services; through a work opportunities course at the local employment rehabilitation centre; or for sheltered work (see Chapter 2). It is absolutely clear that young disabled people who are trained are much more readily accepted by the labour market.[36] If work is not feasible, the school-leaver becomes eligible for invalidity benefit at the age of 16 and may attend a day centre provided by the local authority.

LOCOMOTOR DISORDERS OCCURRING IN EARLY ADULT YEARS

Ankylosing spondylitis (also discussed in Chapters 8 and 9)

Ankylosing spondylitis is predominantly a disease of young people that causes pain and stiffness of the spine due to inflammation and may lead to fusion of the sacro-iliac and spinal joints. Women often have fewer symptoms, giving a clinical male to female ratio of about 4:1. Overall the prevalence is about 1 per cent and many remain undiagnosed. There is a family history in 6 per cent. The disease is chronic and the age of onset of low backache is about 20. In many the disease causes little discomfort and no time is lost from work. The description which follows belongs to those in whom the disease is more severe.

The sacro-iliac joints are involved early and the entire spine may become affected, with restriction of spinal movement and of chest expansion. When there is thoracic kyphosis and the head pokes forwards, vision becomes restricted. The hips and shoulders are affected in 40 per cent and the peripheral joints in 25 per cent. Iritis occurs in 25 per cent and less common complications are: cardiac conduction defects, aortic incompetence, atlanto-axial subluxation, fracture of rigid segments of the spine, apical pulmonary fibrosis, and cauda equina syndrome.

Chronic discomfort for many years, stiffness, spinal and limb pain, and feeling tired and unwell may restrict the choices of both men and women, and deny the opportunities for physically demanding work. Nine of 25 men and 11 of 25 women felt that they were financially adversely affected by the disease[37] and, in another series,[38] 49 per cent of those engaged in full-time employment believed that the disease had influenced their career decisions.

The predictors of a poor functional outcome are involvement of the hips, ossification of the thoracic spine in a position of flexion, and severe peripheral polyarthritis. About 80 per cent can work full-time. Unless lumbar mobility is severely restricted or hip surgery is undertaken or there are complications, most will continue in full-time employment, nearly all in sedentary, light manual, professional, or domestic work. Eventually only 10 per cent will be in heavy manual work.[39] After 30 years of ankylosing spondylitis, 31 per cent were still working in their original jobs and 22 per cent changed to lighter work.[40] Even in the forces, of 170 ankylosing spondylitics 63 were able to continue in their work.[41]

For the majority their working ability is good for at least 20 years and minimal work adjustments are required. The physical activity of work is therapeutic. Limited spinal ability interferes with driving[38]; nearly 50 per cent of the patients reviewed acknowledged restriction of all-round vision, and three of them admitted accidents which had been directly attributed to this. Panoramic rear-view mirrors, such as 'Panamirror' obtainable from Combined Optical Instruments Ltd, 200 Bath Road, Slough SL1 4DW, are necessary to drivers who have limited neck movement. Better patient education, non-steroidal anti-inflammatory drugs, and continuing physical activity are major factors in successful management. The National Ankylosing Spondylitis Society propagates knowledge about the disease. There are also local branches and self-help groups. Some national and regional centres for rheumatic diseases, such as those at Harrogate and Bath, arrange two- or three-week courses of in-patient treatment, generally in classes, for those suffering from ankylosing spondylitis: employers are often most co-operative in allowing this. Evening physiotherapy classes and educational programmes may also be arranged.

Chondromalacia patellae

Chrondromalacia patellae mostly affects young adults, girls outnumbering boys in the ratio of 3:2, and causes pain behind the kneecap, soreness, and grating, aggravated by dynamic compressive forces of the patella against the femur, as in going up and down stairs. Sometimes this condition occurs when the young person is seeking employment and may have his or her opportunities restricted at a critical time. Many will recover spontaneously but in some disabling pain persists for years. Only seven of 71 men previously diagnosed were found later to have mild osteoarthritic changes.[42] Until discomfort abates, activities have to be restrained and work should be at a bench or desk and not demand crouching, climbing many stairs, or heavy lifting and carrying. When conservative treatments fail, localized chondrectomy usually succeeds.[43]

Spinal cord injuries

The incidence of spinal cord injuries in Britain is about 3 per 100 000 of the population. Motor vehicle accidents account for 50 per cent. Spinal cord injury occurs most often in teenagers and young adults at the beginning of their careers.

The functional independence which may be achieved in the end depends upon the level and completeness of the lesion and the adequacy of training (see Table 10.1). Excluding those with a high cord lesion, paraplegics should be able to lead an independent life, though this is only achieved by rehabilitation in a special unit where there is rigorous training in self-care and no concessions to dependence or invalidism.

Spinal cord injury is not simply a malady of the spine—physical, psychological, and social adjustment continue indefinitely. Paraplegics are likely to stay in the spinal injury centre for 4–6 months and quadriplegics about eight months. Quadriplegics are liable to:

(1) orthostatic hypotension;

(2) autonomic hyper-reflexia with increased sympathetic activity usually provoked by over-distention of a viscus causing hypertension, severe headache, flushing, goose-flesh, and sweating;

(3) thromboembolism;

(4) spasticity; and

(5) impaired respiratory function.

All with spinal injuries lose control of the bladder and bowels, have impaired genital function, and are liable to pressure sores and successive emotional reactions of shock, denial, depression, and hostility before gradual acceptance. After spinal injury, capacity for physical work is low at first. Endurance and muscle strength are regained by physical training. Subsequently, medical complications and social isolation are lessened.[44] The goals of rehabilitation may not be reached for several years. Return to work may be delayed by psychological, physical, environmental, and opportunity constraints, and by claims for compensation. Vocational counsellors in the spinal injury centres work closely with the Disablement Resettlement Officer, previous employer, training services, and institutions for further education. Rehabilitation must include the acquisition of new skills. Open employment may prove difficult for many, especially quadriplegics, who may consider sheltered employment where productivity is geared to capabilities. Rather than severity of disability, the best predictors of successful occupational resettlement in rank order are previous employment status and ability, previous attitudes towards work, maturity, and verbal ability.[45]

Table 10.1 Functional expectations at different levels of spinal injury

Level of injury	Functional expectation
Above C5	Totally dependent: special respiratory equipment is required; speech is restrained; a powered wheelchair may be controlled by head or mouth micro-switches
C5	Some assistance is needed in all activities
C6	Can propel manual wheelchair with difficulty; a powered wheelchair is needed on slopes; sometimes driving is possible; in males, bladder drainage is to a leg bag after bladder outlet surgery
C7–T1	May achieve bladder evacuation by reflex bladder contraction; bowel evacuation is by suppository and rectal stimulation; can be completely independent from a wheelchair
T2–T6	Fully independent with a wheelchair
T7–T12	By using a wheelchair is completely independent; can 'walk' wearing orthoses to brace the lower trunk and legs, but not far
L1–L3	Can walk using knee-ankle-foot orthoses and crutches
L4–S1	Can walk using ankle/foot orthoses and two sticks or crutches; bladder is emptied by straining and applying suprapubic pressure; lower bowel is emptied by straining or manual removal of faeces
S2–S4	Only urinary control is difficult

If attention is paid to removing the architectural barriers to employment and maintaining a positive attitude throughout, many should be able to return to useful employment. In one large series of 2012 paraplegics and tetraplegics, 65 per cent were in employment and 20 per cent in some home occupation; only 14.6 per cent were not working.[46]

In assessing paraplegics who depend on wheelchairs, their abilities to propel, open, go through and close doors, go up and down ramps, transfer from wheelchair to lavatory, chair, or bed must be ascertained. Their independence in dressing and the time taken to prepare for work in the morning should be measured.

LOCOMOTOR DISORDERS COMING IN THE MIDDLE AND LATER YEARS

Rheumatoid arthritis (also discussed in Chapter 8)

Rheumatoid arthritis is a chronic systemic inflammatory disorder which is world-wide, involves all races and ethnic groups, and affects women 2–3 times more often than men. The total prevalence in the adult population is about 3 per cent. Most people who develop rheumatoid arthritis are already well established in their careers. The age of onset reaches a peak in the fifth decade and for both sexes the prevalence increases with advancing years. Arthritis is initially polyarticular in 75 per cent of cases, sometimes remits, but usually progresses to varying extents and may damage the joints of the hands and feet, wrists, ankles, knees, elbows, shoulders, cervical spine, and hips.

Common extra-articular features which are part of the disease are tenosynovitis, rheumatoid nodules, muscle wasting, anaemia, scleritis, arteritis, neuropathy, leg ulcers, pericarditis, granulomatous lesions of the heart, lung involvement, lymphadenopathy, oedema, osteoporosis, and infections. The clinical course ranges from a pauciarticular illness of brief duration to a relentlessly progressive destruction of many joints. Signs of an unfavourable prognosis are insidious onset, early involvement of large joints, persisting active disease without remission beyond one year, eosinophilia, raised sedimentation rate and C reactive protein, and the early appearance of extra-articular features.

The symptoms of pain, stiffness, malaise, weakness, tiredness, and limited mobility vary from day to day and within a day. Morning stiffness makes the first hour to two after waking particularly punishing. Those engaged in heavy manual work are forced, before others, to seek less demanding work. Town people have a better chance of finding work than country people for a greater proportion of those in rural areas have heavier occupations, limited opportunities to change, and must travel to obtain selected work in town.

Treatment

The management of rheumatoid arthritis hinges upon the stage of the disease. Acute pain, swelling and stiffness of the joints, and systemic illness may be expected to subside with rest in bed, splints to rest the affected joints, and non-steroidal anti-inflammatory drugs. Chronic rheumatoid disease is treated symptomatically. The differences in anti-inflammatory potencies between salicylates and the wide choice of other non-steroidal anti-inflammatory drugs are small, but there are substantial variations in the patient response and in the incidence, type, and severities of side-effects. When the disease does not remit, the family doctor and hospital consultant may endeavour to change the course of the disease by sulphasalazine, gold, penicillamine, chloroquine or hydroxychloroquine, azathioprine or other immunosuppressive drug, or a corticosteroid. Other treatments which may be required for joints and tendon sheaths which are persistently inflamed or damaged are orthoses, intra-synovial injections of corticosteroids, surgical synovectomies, tendon repairs, excision arthroplasties or joint replacements; and appropriate technical aids, personal assistance, and alterations of employment may also be needed.

Robinson and Walters[47] concluded that there were three critical factors in patients with rheumatoid arthritis returning to competitive employment:

1. The level of education. Eighty-one per cent of those who continued in education beyond the 12-year-old level returned to work, compared with 44 per cent with less education.

2. Previous employment. Those in supervisory or executive positions or who were self-employed competed more successfully: they earned more, could afford the personal and technical assistance they required, could work flexible hours, and the attitudes of senior colleagues were more likely to be favourable.

3. Geography. Sixty-five per cent of city-dwellers and 50 per cent of those living in rural areas were working full- or part-time.

Sheppeard,[48] in comparing arthritic patients employed and unemployed one year after counselling by Disablement Resettlement Officers, also found that successful employment depended more on social and environmental factors than on the degree of disability. The married are more likely to be employed than the single, those living in towns are twice as likely to be employed as those living in the country, the shorter the interval since work the greater the chance of returning to it, and the best jobs are those indoors which call for skill not strength. Starting vocational rehabilitation at an early stage of the disease could improve the prognosis of functional competence and capacity for work.[49] The ability to work is the best indication of the value of treatment.[50] Every time that work is interrupted during exacerbations of the disease or for surgery, all those concerned should agree the programme of treatment and when return to work is likely. It is imperative to hold on to work whenever possible, modifying it if necessary or changing the form of work within the firm but avoiding becoming unemployed without the chance to return. In a time of high unemployment, few employers will be willing to take on a patient with arthritis with progressive disease, physical limitations, chequered work record, and uncertain future. Enlightened legislation in Sweden favours part-time work and economic support for those unable to continue in full-time employment, and assistance with the cost of transport.[51] Many patients with arthritis continue at work despite active disease, feeling sure that if they were to stop they would give into their disease and become crippled. Their income is likely to be diminished. Thirty of 38 earners with stage III rheumatoid arthritis suffered a substantial loss of earnings.[52] Men severely disabled by arthritis suffered a 37 per cent drop in earnings, while a matched control group received a 90 per cent rise.[53]

Cervical spondylosis (also discussed on pp. 131 and 195)

Cervical spondylosis is the commonest cause of persisting pain in the neck and restriction of its movements. By middle age, radiographs of the cervical spine of most people show narrowing of one or more intervertebral disc spaces in the middle or lower cervical regions with osteophytic outgrowths and subchondral sclerosis: commonly, the apophyseal and neurocentral joints are similarly affected. The correlation between the degree of radiographic change and the severity of symptoms is rather poor. Radiography is helpful after neck injuries and for the investigation of possible malignant disease or infections of bone, but is otherwise little guide to prognosis, treatment, or fitness for work. The pain of cervical spondylosis is usually situated in the neck, over the shoulders and down the arms; it may come in bouts of several weeks and then clear. Movements are restricted and are often accompanied by crepitus. There may be compression of one or more cervical nerve roots, producing weakness of the muscles supplied by those nerves, pain and spontaneous tingling and diminished sensation over the cutaneous territory of the nerves. The 6th cervical nerve root is the most commonly affected.

The symptoms and severity of disability caused by cervical spondylosis vary a lot. Jobs that demand free movements of the neck, as in driving a motor vehicle, crane or fork-lift truck, or those where there is restricted headroom, are likely to exacerbate the pain. Strenuous work using the arms may aggravate neck stiffness, pain in the neck and arms, and paraesthesiae.

Pain and disability caused by cervical spondylosis may affect not only those in heavy occupations but also those bent over keyboards and visual display units. On return to work after exacerbation it is prudent to avoid tasks which involve heavy carrying, lifting, shovelling, manual loading and unloading, violent vibration, and working with the arms raised and the neck extended. Clerical workers can be helped by having raised and tilted work surfaces so that their papers are laid out in front of them at chest height and flexion of the neck over long periods is avoided.

Generalized osteoarthritis (also discussed in Chapters 8 and 9)

Degenerative joint disease is the most common affliction of synovial joints of spine and limbs. Pervalence increases with age and by the time of retirement the radiological evidence is almost universal, though not all are troubled by pain and stiffness. In the Leigh and Wensleydale study[54] in the 35–44-year-old age-group, 38 per cent of men and 39 per cent of women had at least one joint affected and, with the exception of the lumbar joints of the spine and the sacro-iliac joints, there was a significant association between the radiographic evidence of osteoarthrosis and symptoms in the joint examined. The knees (75 per cent), hands (60 per cent), lumbar spine (30 per cent), and hips (25 per cent) are most commonly affected. Pain is worse towards the evening and aggravated by particular activities, and stiffness follows resting. The course is slowly progressive with exacerbations and remissions. Movements are restricted at affected joints which may become deformed or unstable. Primary generalized osteoarthritis, which occurs mainly in middle-aged females, has a familial trait, affects the terminal interphalangeal joints of the fingers with Heberden's nodes, the carpo-metacarpal joint at the base of the thumb, apophyseal spinal joints, and the weightbearing joints of the hips, knees, and ankles.

Repeated occupational trauma causes osteoarthrosis. In miners the lumbar spine and knees are frequently affected[55, 56] and, at the age of 50, 36 per cent had radiological evidence of osteoarthrosis in the knee, compared with 11 per cent of dockers and light manual workers and 7 per cent of sedentary workers. Heavy manual work predisposes to osteoarthrosis at the elbow and this had occurred in 31 per cent of miners by the age of 50.[55] Repeated minor injuries, strains, and repetitive movements can predispose to osteoarthrosis, as in the fingers of seamstresses, hands of bricklayers, wrists and elbows of drillers, the cervical spine of market porters, and the shoulders and lumbar spine of manual labourers.

The pathological changes are irreversible. In selecting work the aim is to lessen stress on the damaged joints, and discussion can help to disclose the parts of the job which are most difficult. Usually employment can continue often with minor modifications.[57] A change of occupation or a transfer within the place of work usually allows work to continue without loss of time. Work which avoids awkward postures, heavy labouring, and much climbing is best. Walking long distances, particularly over rough ground, and carrying loads may aggravate pain in the back and lower limbs and sometimes in the upper limbs and neck. Function is improved by loss of excess weight and treatments which relieve pain, mobilize joints, and strengthen the muscles.

Paget's disease (osteitis deformans)

Paget's disease is a common metabolic disorder of bone. The incidence rises towards the end of working life from 0.5 per cent at 40 to 2 per cent at 65, and men are affected twice as often as women. A family history is common. One or many bones may be affected, most often the pelvis, femur, skull, tibia, and vertebrae. The distribution is irregular. The pathological features are increased activity of osteoblast and osteoclast cells leading to irregular areas of increased bone formation and areas of rarefied bone next to normal bone. In most people with Paget's disease the disorder is recognized only on radiography, but in others aching and pain may be severe and the bones become deformed. Paget's disease of the skull may cause headache and loss of hearing and Paget's disease of the spine causes aching, stiffness after rest, kyphosis and, rarely, compression of the spinal cord or nerve roots. Arthritis of the hips and knees may become severe. Autopsy studies have shown that

3.5 per cent of men and 2.4 per cent of women over the age of 45 have the disease.[58, 59] There are geographical differences, the highest prevalence in the United Kingdom being in Leeds, where 1.8 per cent of the population over 35 have been found to be affected. There are also genetic differences. The disease is asymptomatic in 29 per cent of cases.[59]

Most people with Paget's disease are able to continue their usual work, but those having headache, backache, and arthritis should be spared strenuous physical activity, given mainly sedentary work, and enabled to change their posture as they want. They should be allowed to park close to their workplace and climb stairs seldom.

Gout

Gout is a disorder of men of all ages and of women after the menopause and is a complication of a prolonged abnormally raised level of urate in the serum. In the elderly, gout may be precipitated by thiazide diuretics. The prevalence is 4 per 1000 and the incidence is about 0.9 per 1000 per annum.[60] Deposits of urate may form around the joints and in the kidneys. Paroxysms of acute inflammation are provoked by lysosomal enzymes released in the cavity of the joint from ruptured leucocytes which have engulfed micro-crystals of urate. The management has two distinct objectives: immediate control of acute arthritis and the long-term treatment of hyperuricaemia to prevent complications such as tophaceous deposits, joint destruction, and renal calculi. Uric acid kidney stones occur in 10–20 per cent of people with gout. Occasionally one encounters people in whom failure to diagnose and treat properly have resulted in full expression of the disease, but gout can now be treated so effectively that activities and work need not be restricted. Gout often affects bar-tenders, brewery workers, and business executives. They should be advised to limit their alcohol intake.

Non-articular rheumatism

Non-articular rheumatism is common and most people will suffer musculo-skeletal pains at some time in their lives. The industrial survey unit of the Arthritis and Rheumatism Council[61] found that in 1396 male manual workers with rheumatic complaints the diagnoses were undetermined in more than half. 'Fibrositis' is a term sometimes applied to unexplained aching and tenderness. Common underlying disorders are mechanical stresses in the neck and lower back, often associated with cervical and lumbar spondylosis, and with poor posture, and emotional stress.

Occupational rheumatic disorders are common, despite the gradual replacement of physical work by machines. In one study in Finland,[62] the upper limbs were affected in 93 per cent of 3090 cases analysed; 69.2 per cent

Table 10.2 Conditions associated with occupational over-use

Tenosynovitis

Stenosing tenosynovitis, examples are:
  De Quervain's disease and 'gamekeeper's thumb'

Ganglionic cyst

Enthesiopathies, examples are:
  epicondylitis, tendinitis and 'frozen shoulder' (adhesive capsulitis)

Bursitis

Entrapment neuropathies, examples are:
  carpal tunnel syndrome, cubital tunnel syndrome,
  Guyon's canal syndrome and compression of the common peroneal nerve

Thoracic outlet syndrome

Raynaud's syndrome

Repetitive strain injury

---

were in females, the mean age being 40.7 years; tenosynovitis was the most common disorder (58 per cent) and epicondylitis was second (24 per cent). Numerous other conditions, however, have been associated with work (Table 10.2) and when any of these are present the physician should enquire about the nature of both work and hobbies.

Prolonged tissue loading due to awkward postures or to frequent repetitive movements may cause muscle fatigue and pain, or damage tendons by ischaemia,[63] and peripheral nerves may be compressed in a ligamentous bony canal or squeezed between muscle edges.

Workers at particular risk are those using high forces with frequent repetition,[64] and both wrist and forearm tendon lesions are more likely if the work involves flexion, hyperextension or deviation of the wrist, with the fingers either clenched or spread widely. Thus up to 53 per cent of Finnish butchers had carpal tunnel syndrome and 18 per cent of Swedish scissor workers and 56 per cent of Swedish packers had tendon lesions.[64] In a poultry-processing plant 12.8 per cent of workers had cumulative trauma disorders over one year.[65]

Terminology can be confusing and there is a plethora of titles which have found their way into lay usage, e.g. repetitive strain injury, occupational overuse injuries, and cumulative trauma disorders. These categories have been poorly defined, there is a dearth of epidemiology and it may be difficult to separate physical and psychosocial causal factors. While some syndromes may readily be identified, frequently symptoms may be vague and physical signs few.

Although these diseases account for a substantial proportion of medical consultations and heavy costs in prescribed medicines, sickness benefit, and lost productivity, they are often poorly understood, diagnosed with uncertainty, and treated inadequately with rest and anti-inflammatory analgesic medicines in the hope of spontaneous resolution. Prompt and correct diagnosis and treatment result in reduced morbidity and early return to work. Accurate steroid injections, physiotherapy, and, if necessary, surgical decompression can bring speedy relief. Individuals with inadequately treated lesions who continue with the precipitating activity may develop chronic lesions and disability.

If an occupational component has been identified, then assessment of the workplace ergonomics will be necessary. Problems may be due either to poor job design or to the worker's technique. Frequently, simple modifications to the task will be all that are required. Equal attention should be focused on hobbies and leisure activities.

Enthesiopathies

Repetitive movements often cause inflammation of entheses, which are the insertions of tendons, ligaments and articular capsules into bone, and the pain and disability may cause the patient to miss work. Relief comes quickly after accurate intra-lesional injection of corticosteroid, such as methylprednisolone or triamcinolone hexacetonide with 2 per cent lignocaine. Common examples of enthesiopathies are: plantar fasciitis, causing pain and tenderness under the heel; tennis elbow at the attachment of the common extensor tendon to the lateral epicondyle of the humerus; golfer's elbow at the attachment of the common flexor tendon to the medial epicondyle of the humerus; and painful arc syndrome at the shoulder, due to rotator cuff injuries.

Calcific tendinitis

Calcific tendinitis at the shoulder arises because trauma, often repeated, causes fraying and irregularity of bundles of collagen in the rotator cuff, sometimes leading to the deposits of large plaques of hydroxyapatite. Pain may occur suddenly or more gradually and may become chronic. Peak incidence is between the ages of 40 and 45, females are affected more often than males, and the dominant arm is more often affected. It is important in disorders of the shoulder to avoid carrying heavy loads and this has an impact on work. The range of motion becomes restricted. The treatment is intralesional injection of corticosteroid and to obtain high levels of success the technique has to be learned.

Frozen shoulder or adhesive capsulitis most often affects people in their middle years and is caused either by disease of the shoulder, such as calcific tendinitis, bursitis, trauma, or rotator cuff tears, or is secondary to pain referred to the shoulder from disease elsewhere; common examples are cervical spondylosis with radiculopathy, acute cerebrovascular disease, and coronary thrombosis. Exercises as early as possible to mobilize the shoulder prevent progressive stiffness and lead to earlier resolution. Without treatment adhesive capsulitis causing pain and stiffness is likely to persist for two years or longer, and even with treatment the range of movement is often diminished for many months but that will not necessarily limit activities.

Bursitis

This may be caused by repeated injury, and certain occupations predispose to the inflammation of bursae. Olecranon bursitis has been called miner's or student's elbow, ischial bursitis occurred in weavers, and pre-patellar bursitis may be provoked by excessive kneeling. Inflamed bursae may be aspirated and the fluid cultured. Aspiration relieves pain and, if infection is excluded, intrasynovial injection of corticosteroid will accelerate cure. Chronic and recurrent inflamed bursae may have to be excised. Beat knee in miners is caused by chronic trauma and infection, and protective rubber knee-pads should be worn.

Entrapment neuropathies

Entrapment neuropathies may be caused by direct pressure on the nerve, as by leaning on the ulnar nerve in its groove on the back of the medial condyle of the humerus, or thumping the nerve near the hook of the hamate in the heel of the hand, or pressing on the common peroneal nerve as it winds round the lateral surface of the neck of the fibula, or compression of the median nerve in the carpal tunnel at the wrist. Carpal tunnel syndrome is the commonest of these neuropathies and usually presents with unpleasant tingling in the median nerve territory of the hand, but the pain may radiate to the whole hand and up to the elbow and disturb sleep in the early hours. Often the person shakes the hand for a few minutes before the pain subsides. There are paraesthesiae and there may be diminished sensibility over the thumb, index, and middle fingers, and weakness and wasting of the thenar muscles. In mild cases the pain may be relieved by wearing a resting wrist and hand splint and, if symptoms and signs continue, the correct treatment is surgical decompression of the nerve by section of the flexor retinaculum.

A claim for compensation commonly delays return to work, yet early return to work need not prejudice the settlement. In one recent study, significantly more patients who were directed to return to work during the treatment programme did so (60 per cent) than in another group similarly treated but for whom return to work was not a component of therapy (25 per cent). At review 9½ months later, 90 per cent of those in the first group were still working, were receiving fewer compensation benefits, and had received less additional treatment for their pain than the other group.[66]

The disabled worker towards the end of his career faces decline and looks not for cure but for a sufficient income or pension, medical attention, and self-respect. The number of applications for premature retirement on the grounds of sickness and disability increases.

TRANSPORT TO WORK

Disabled people must be advised correctly on whether they should drive, which car to choose, and what modifications they require. Careful physical examination, tests of cognitive function, and practical driving tests for disabled people who want to start or restart driving are essential. Much can be done to help the mechanical difficulties of the disabled person;[67] since much less can be done to overcome possible intellectual difficulties, it is particularly important that their presence should be detected.

Mobility allowance is a non-means-tested weekly cash benefit which is designed to help severely disabled people become more mobile. To qualify for mobility allowance, ability to walk must be so limited that the person is virtually unable to walk without severe discomfort. The mobility allowance enables disabled people to choose and afford the form of transport which is best for them, and large numbers of disabled people own and use cars as drivers or passengers.

Motability was launched in 1978 for disabled drivers or passengers to procure cheap finance, discounts, and insurance. A disabled person applies to Motability to lease, buy, or hire-purchase a new or second-hand car. Outdoor powered wheelchairs can also be bought through Motability at favourable rates.

Most of the difficulties experienced by disabled drivers can be overcome by simple accessories, powered steering, automatic transmission, standard adaptations, and by other conversions.[68] The spatial difficulties of those with ankylosing spondylitis and osteoarthritis may be overcome by the use of rotating or sliding seats, but a small proportion will need extensive structural conversion of the car to enlarge the doorway. Individual conversions may be expensive and the initial choice of vehicle to adapt is crucial. The disabled driver or passenger needs informed and impartial advice when considering the purchase of a car and the requirements for conversion. The Department of Transport's Mobility Advice and Vehicle Information Service (MAVIS) offers assessment and advice on driving ability, on car adaptations, and on any aspect of transport and outdoor mobility for people with disabilities. Advice may also be obtained from the British School of Motoring, Banstead Place Mobility Centre, Derbyshire Royal Infirmary, and Astley Ainslie Hospital, Edinburgh.

REFERENCES

1. Annual Abstract of Statistics no 121, Central Statistical Office, London: HMSO, 1985.
2. Anderson JAD. In: Jayson MIV and Million, R ed. Locomotor disability in general practice. Oxford: Oxford University Press, 1983.
3. Agerholm M. Handicaps and the handicapped—a nomenclature and classification of intrinsic handicaps. Roy Soc Hlth J 1975;**95**:3–8.
4. Florian V. Objective obstacles in hiring disabled persons: the employer's point of view. Int J Rehab Res 1981;**4**:167–74.
5. Lotze R. Evaluation of long-term efforts to place disabled young people in work. Int J Rehab Res 1981;**4**:198–9.
6. Stephenson J. Employment opportunities for physically disabled people in computing in Britain. Int J Rehab Res 1983;**6**:483–5.
7. Guide for employers in hiring the physically handicapped. New York National Association for Manufacturing, 1985.
8. Sears JH. The able disabled. *J. Rehabilitation*. 1975;**42**:19–22.
9. Money J, Pollitt E. Studies in the psychology of dwarfism. J Pediatr 1966; **68**:381–90.
10. Folstein SE. Impairment, psychiatric symptoms and handicap in dwarfs. The Johns Hopkins Medical Journal 1981;**148**:273–7.
11. Ingram GIC, Dykes SR, Crease AL, et al. Home treatment in haemophilia: clinical, social and economic advantages. Clin Lab Haematol 1979;**1**:13–27.
12. Stuart J, Forbes CD, Jones P, Lane G, Rizza CR, Wilkes S. Improving prospects for employment of the haemophiliac. Br Med J 1980;**280**:1169–72.
13. Levine PH. Efficiency of self therapy in haemophilia. N Engl J Med 1974; **291**:1381–4.
14. Markova I, Forbes C. The social and psychological effects of haemophilia on patients and their families. Int J Rehab Res 1979;**2**:515–17.
15. Markova I, Forbes CD, Rowlands A, Pettigrew A, Willoughby M. The haemophiliac patient's self-perception of changes in health and lifestyle arising from self-treatment. Int J Rehab Res 1983;**6**:11–18.
16. Forbes CD, Markova I, Stuart J, Jones P. To tell or not to tell: haemophiliacs' views on their employment prospects. Int J Rehab Res 1982;**5**:13–8.
17. Smith R, Francis MJO, Houghton GR. The brittle bone syndrome. London: Butterworths, 1983.
18. Moorfield WC, Miller GR. Aftermath of osteogenesis imperfecta—the disease in adulthood. J Bone Joint Surg (Am) 1980;**62A**:113–19.
19. King JD, Bobechko WP. Osteogenesis imperfecta: an orthopaedic description and surgical review. J Bone Joint Surg (Br) 1971;**53B**:72–90.
20. Blum RW. The adolescent with spina bifida. Clin Pediatr 1983;**22**:331–5.
21. Hunt GM. Spina bifida: implications for 100 children at school. Dev Med Child Neurol 1981;**23**:160–72.
22. Castree BJ, Walker JH. The young adult with spina bifida. Br Med J 1981;**283**:1040–2.
23. Lonton AP, Loughlin AM, O'Sullivan AM. The employment of adults with spina bifida. z. Kinderchir 1984;**39**(suppl 2, Dec):132–4.

24. Smith AD. Adult spina bifida survey in Scotland: educational attainment and employment. z. Kinderchir 1983;**38**(suppl 2, Dec): 107–9.

25. Hill RH, Herstein A, Walters K. Juvenile rheumatoid arthritis: follow-up into adulthood—medical, sexual and social status. Can Med Assoc J 1976; **114**(a):790–6.

26. Laaksonen AL. A prognostic study of juvenile rheumatoid arthritis. Acta Paediatr Scand 1966;(suppl 166):1–168.

27. Morse J. Aspirations and achievements of patients with juvenile rheumatoid arthritis: a study of 100 patients with juvenile rheumatoid arthritis. Rehab Lit 1972;**33**:290–303.

28. Wilkinson VA. Juvenile chronic arthritis in adolescence: facing the reality. Int Rehab Med 1981;**3**:11–7.

29. Ansell BM, Wood PHN. Prognosis in juvenile chronic polyarthritis. Clin Rheum Dis 1976;**2**(2):397–412.

30. Emery AEH, Skinner R. Clinical studies in benign (Becker type) X-linked muscular dystrophy. Clin Genet 1976;**10**:189–201.

31. Hirst MA. Young people with disabilities: what happens after 16? Child Care Health Develop 1983;**9**:273–84.

32. Tuckey L, Parfitt J. Tuckey B. Handicapped school leavers: their further education, training and employment. Windsor: National Foundation for Education Research, 1973.

33. Special Educational Needs. Report of the Committee of Enquiry into the Education of Handicapped Children and Young People (Warnock Report). Cmnd 721164. London: HMSO; 1978.

34. Cochrane GM. Rheumatoid arthritis: vocational rehabilitation. Int Rehab Med 1982;**4**:148–53.

35. Glendinning C, Hirst M, Baldwin S, Parker G. After school—what next? York: Family Fund, Joseph Rowntree Memorial Trust, 1984.

36. Pugh G, Walker A. Employment experiences of handicapped school-leavers. Int J Rehab Res 1981;**4**:231.

37. Chamberlain MA. Socioeconomic effects of ankylosing spondylitis. Int Rehab Med 1983;**5**:149–53.

38. Wordsworth BP, Mowat, AG. A review of 100 patients with ankylosing spondylitis with particular reference to its socioeconomic effects. Br J Rheumatol 1986;**25**:175–80.

39. McGuigan LE, Hart HH, Gow PJ, et al. Employment in ankylosing spondylitis. Ann Rheum Dis 1984;**43**:604–6.

40. Lehtinen K. Working ability of 76 patients with ankylosing spondylitis. Scand J Rheumatol 1981;**10**:263–5.

41. Wynn Party CB. Some problems in rehabilitation in the services. Management of ankylosing spondylitis. Proc Roy Soc Med 1966;**59**:619.

42. Karlson S. Chondromalacia patellae. Acta Chir Scand 1939;**83**:347–81.

43. Goodfellow J, Hungerford DS, Woods C. Patello-femoral joint mechanics and pathology: 2. Chondromalacia patellae. J Bone Joint Surg (Br) 1976;**56B**:291–9.

44. Hjeltnes N. Capacity for physical work and training after spinal injuries and stroke. Scand J Soc Med 1982;**10**(suppl 29):245–51.

45. Goldberg RT, Freed MM. Vocational adjustment, interests, work values and career plans of persons with spinal cord injuries; Scand J Rehab Med 1973; **5**:3–11.

46. Guttman L. Spinal cord injuries. Oxford: Blackwell Scientific Publications, 1973.

47. Robinson H, Walters K. Patterns of work in rheumatoid arthritis. Int Rehab Med 1979;**1**:121–5.

48. Sheppeard H, Bulgen D, Ward DJ. Rheumatoid arthritis: returning patients to work. Rheumatol Rehab 1981;**20**:160–3.

49. Makisara GL, Makisara P. Progression of functional capacity and work capacity in rheumatoid arthritis. Clin Rheumatol 1982;**1**:117–25.

50. Savage O, Copeman WSC, Chapman L, Wells MV, Treadwell BLJ. Pituitary and adrenal hormones in rheumatoid arthritis. Lancet 1962;**i**:232–5.

51. Bratstrom M, Larsson B-M. The arthritic at work. Int J Rehab Res 1983; **6**:79–81.

52. Meenan RF, Yelin EH, Henke CJ, et al. The costs of rheumatoid arthritis: a patient orientated study of chronic disease costs. Arthritis Rheum 1978;**21**: 827–33.

53. Allender E. A population survey of rheumatoid arthritis. Acta Rheumatol Scand 1979;suppl 15.

54. Lawrence JS. Rheumatism in populations. London: Heinemann, 1977.

55. Lawrence JS. Rheumatism in coalminers. III: Occupational factors. Br J Ind Med 1955;**12**:249–61.

56. Kellgren JH, Lawrence JS. Osteoarthritis and disk degeneration in an urban population. Ann Rheum Dis 1958;**17**:388–97.

57. Tarasov AN, Zabolotnykh TV, Orlova TV, et al. The time course of invalidism and specialised employment of patients with deforming osteoarthrosis. Ter-Arkh 1985;**57**:93–6.

58. Schmorl G. Über Osteitus deformans Paget. Virchow's Arch Path Anat 1932;283:694.

59. Collins DH. Paget's disease of bones: incidence and subclinical forms. Lancet 1956;**2**:51–7.

60. Hall AP, Barry PE, Dunbar TR, McNamara PM. Epidemiology of gout and hyperuricaemia. Am J Med 1967;**42**:27–37.

61. Anderson JAD. Occupational factors in arthritis and rheumatism. Reports on Rheumatic Diseases (1959–1977). London: Arthritis and Rheumatism Council, 1978:134–7.

62. Kivi P. Rheumatic disorders of the upper limbs associated with repetitive occupational tasks in Finland in 1975–1979. Scand J Rheumatol 1984;**13**:101–7.

63. Brown CD, Nolan BM, Faithfull DK. Occupational repetition strain injuries. Med J Aust 1984;**140**:329–32.

64. Silverstein BA, Fine LJ, Armstrong TJ. Hand wrist cumulative trauma disorders in industry. Br J Ind Med 1986;**43**:779–84.

65. Armstrong TJ, Chaffin DB, Joseph BS, Goldstein SA. Analysis of cumulative trauma disorders in a poultry processing plant. Am Ind Hyg Assoc J 1982;**45**:103–16.

66. Catchlove R, Cohen K. Effects of directive return to work approach in the treatment of workmen's compensation in patients with chronic pain. Pain 1982;**14**:181–91.
67. Raffle A, ed. Medical aspects of fitness to drive: a guide for medical practitioners. 4th ed. London: Medical Commission on Accident Prevention, 1985.
68. Cochrane GM, Wilshire ER, eds. Outdoor transport. 6th Ed. Equipment for the disabled. Oxford: Oxfordshire Health Authority, 1987.

Sources of information and advice

Code of good practice on the employment of disabled people. Sheffield: Manpower Services Commission, 1984.

Employment aids and adaptations for disabled people. Sheffield: Manpower Services Commission, 1983.

11

Neurological disorders

M. L. E. Espir and R. B. Godwin-Austen

INTRODUCTION

Data on the size of neurological problems at work are limited. Information is available on the incidence and prevalence of individual neurological disorders in the general population,[1] but little is known about their overall impact or the extent of the difficulties that they may present at work. In a survey of civil servants with health problems referred to the Civil Service Medical Advisory Service, about 7 per cent had neurological disorders (including strokes), 1.3 per cent had epilepsy, and 1.8 per cent alcohol problems.[2]

Each job has its own specific requirements. Some are mainly physical, e.g. stamina, strength, mobility, dexterity, while others make demands mainly on intellectual or perceptual functions, e.g. writing, designing, management, and many jobs require combinations of physical and mental capabilities. Thus someone with a permanent paraplegia (for example, due to a spinal injury) should be able to do a writing, desk or bench job, and a variety of jobs can be performed very satisfactorily by blind or deaf people. Those of low intelligence may be able to manage the more physical types of work of a routine nature with limited requirements for initiative, calculation, or mental concentration.

The effect of a neurological disorder on fitness to work will therefore depend on the particular work requirements and also on which part or function of the nervous system is affected, on its severity, and also on its course, i.e. whether it is:

(1) episodic or transient but likely to recur;

(2) acute or subacute in onset, followed by improvement;

(3) progressive, deteriorating;

(4) static or of long standing.

Examples of neurological disorders classified in this way and the medical factors influencing fitness to work are shown in Table 11.1.[3]

Jobs that involve driving a motor vehicle require the ability to perform

Table 11.1 Conditions affecting the nervous system and medical factors influencing fitness to work classified according to the mode of onset and course (modified from Espir and Godwin-Austen 1985[3])

Onset/course	Cause	Medical factors influencing fitness to work	Decision required
Episodic, transient, reversible	Attacks of impaired consciousness whether or not the cause is known Epilepsy Syncope Vertigo Transient ischaemic attacks Migraine Hypoglycaemia Narcolepsy Drugs	Freedom from attacks due to remission or response to treatment	To comply with the regulations or requirements for the job
Acute or subacute onset, with improvement	Stroke Encephalitis Head injury Neurosurgery	Degree and rate of recovery	If and when fit to resume work
Progressive deterioration	Parkinson's disease Motor neurone disease Dementia	Degree and rate of deterioration	When work is no longer safe or possible and must be stopped
Long-standing static	Paraplegia (e.g. due to spinal injury) Cerebral palsy Poliomyelitis	Type and severity of disability Residual function and ability	How to adapt or modify conditions to make work possible

precise complex actions in response to a continually changing environment. Any disease process or drug which temporarily or permanently affects those functions of the nervous system governing the driver's perception, judgement, or alertness, or ability to carry out the movements necessary to control his vehicle, may impair his fitness to drive. Practically every neurological disease if sufficiently severe, comes into this category, and some patients will be precluded from driving by the driving licence regulations.[4]

Whatever the type of work, regular attendance and efficiency are dependent not only on health but also on motivation and on individual characteristics such as personality, temperament, and behaviour.

The age of onset is of special importance. Fitness for work may be restricted if disability is due to a congenital disorder or to one that develops during childhood, particularly if it interferes with schooling and academic achievement, or limits training and acquisition of the skills and experience which are likely to be vital for success with job applications and career.

For some jobs there are strict medical standards that may be statutory or non-statutory which will influence recruitment of those with certain neurological conditions. If a disease develops during employment, modification of duties, change to a different job, and sometimes retirement on medical grounds may be needed.

In general, fitness for work will depend on the nature and severity of the disease process, the effect of the illness on the individual's character, skills, and motivation, the type of work and the duties involved, the working environment and its location, and sometimes on the attitude and sympathetic understanding of the employer to help and enable those with disabilities to work. Objective assessment of physical disability from neurological disease, for example impairment of strength, mobility or co-ordination, and its effect on working capacity, is generally straightforward in the context of a specific job. On the other hand, stamina and fatiguability are often subjective and more difficult to assess. The possibility of a functional overlay or frank hysteria must be borne in mind.

Diseases causing intellectual impairment and perceptual deficits are not readily understood by most employers or co-workers, and in such cases thorough medical investigation of the individual and his working environment may be necessary to make appropriate recommendations. Similar assessment may also be necessary in cases of inefficiency at work, particularly to determine whether deterioration of performance is due to a neurological or other medical problem. A number of neurological diseases involving the brain may present with impairment of memory, judgement, and cognitive functions, or of speech and the ability to read and write, or of topographical skills and perceptual abilities.

Certain neurological disorders are associated with changes in mood, most often depression, but occasionally with euphoria or disinhibition. Lethargy, somnolence, or inability to sustain concentration will be incompatible with most forms of employment.

Disorders of the special senses, such as loss of the sense of smell or taste, or colour vision defects (see Chapter 6) will not usually be relevant but clearly will be critical for the few jobs in which one or more of these functions are essential.

The ability of someone with a neurological disorder to retain employment will depend on whether the disability interferes with the exercise of professional or technical skills or with the ability to use previous experience. The possibility of retraining will depend upon the age of onset of the disease, the nature of the disability and prognosis, the relevance of the faculties and skills preserved, and, of course, motivation.

The nature of the job and its physical and intellectual demands may determine whether someone with a neurological disease can continue at work. Jobs are extremely varied and each has to be considered individually. For example, the degree of mobility required, the need to deal with the public, the attitude of the employer and his perception of the disease may be relevant. Stigma may be a significant factor. Although the employment of disabled persons should be encouraged,[5] consideration has to be given to the Health and Safety at Work etc. Act to protect the individual and fellow-employees from accidents at work. Certain disabilities such as impaired co-ordination or balance, or episodes of giddiness or loss of consciousness, will preclude individuals from jobs with special hazards[6] (Table 11.2). However, if there is no special danger in the workplace, then employers should be advised that even though unsteadiness, for example, may increase the risk of falling or accidental injury, this need not prevent the individual's employment, provided that reasonable precautions are taken. Thus, a secretary in an office whose balance is impaired may be more likely to slip, fall, and injure herself than her able-bodied colleagues. But this should not justify non-employment or retirement unless the disability (whether it is unsteadiness, weakness, epilepsy, or another) affects the individual's ability to do the job.

The sympathetic and caring employer will also wish to consider the effect of work on the employee's condition, e.g. stress, strenuous duties such as heavy lifting, exposure to heat or chemicals. Occasionally, remoteness from medical facilities, abroad for instance, may be an important constraint. After certain illnesses, for example an episode of multiple sclerosis, an individual should be given the opportunity to return to work as soon as he is capable of working without danger to himself or others. A period of part-time work with a programme of increasing hours and duties over a limited period may be most important for rehabilitation, and can help to restore working capacity more quickly and completely than when, as not infrequently happens, an employee is told 'don't come back to work until you have made

Table 11.2 Examples of jobs with special hazards (from Espir and Floyd 1986[6])

Vocational drivers, i.e. of heavy goods and public service vehicles, and taxis
Drivers of trains, cranes, straddle carriers
Aircraft pilots, seamen, coastguards
Work at unprotected heights, e.g. scaffolders, steeplejacks, and firemen
Work with high-voltage electricity
Work with dangerous unguarded machinery, e.g. chainsaws
Work with valuable fragile objects and equipment
Work near tanks of water or chemical fluids

a 100 per cent recovery'. Employment should not be regarded as occupational therapy however, for nowadays few firms have room for passengers at work. At the same time employers must realize that disability does not inevitably imply impaired efficiency or high rates of sickness absence and accidents, but rather that the converse is often true.

Adaptation of the working environment for the disabled person should always be considered, for example the provision of wheelchair and special toilet facilities, flexitime to avoid rush-hour travelling, the use of mechanical, electrical or electronic aids, modification of duties, and appropriate evacuation arrangements in case of emergency.

In this chapter it will not be possible to cover the whole range of neurological disease, and attention is focused on the effect of some of the commoner organic disorders of the nervous system on fitness to work, with the exclusion of epilepsy (Chapter 12), muscular dystrophies and spinal injuries (Chapter 10), peripheral nerve injuries and brachial plexus lesions (Chapter 8). Disorders of hearing and vision are also dealt with in Chapters 4 and 6 respectively, and the effects of alcohol and drugs of abuse in Chapter 21.

Migraine and other types of headache

Prevalence

In the working population about 10 per cent of females and 5 per cent of males have migraine and a higher proportion suffer from other types of headache, which may interfere with both work and leisure, and cause high rates of sickness absence. People who have severe migraine usually have to stop work and rest while having an attack or may be prevented from coming into work by an attack on waking. A visual aura may cause transient, partial, and occasionally total loss of vision, and basilar migraine may be associated with impairment of consciousness, although this is rare. Obviously this will interfere with work and driving. Those whose attacks occur at work may not be able to function efficiently until the symptoms clear. They may leave work early and go home to rest so that they can lie in a quiet darkened room. Consideration should be given to providing facilities for this at the workplace, together with a simple treatment schedule along the lines suggested by Jones and Harrop.[7] Between attacks the individual should be perfectly well and capable of maximum work output and efficiency. Stress, environmental factors, and dissatisfaction with conditions at work may be aggravating factors in some cases. Other known provocative factors, e.g. dietary, alcohol, or hormonal, may be important. Attention given to the working environment, e.g. to ergonomic factors, lighting, appropriate breaks from VDU work, smoke-free areas, and adequate ventilation, is likely to be helpful.

In a recent questionnaire study of civil servants,[8] 77 per cent of 747 responders reported having headaches in the last year, and 34 per cent said that they had interfered with their work, either by impairing performance, making them leave work early, or stopping them coming into work. Twenty-two per cent reported that their headaches had interfered with leisure, social, or domestic activities as well as with work, indicating that the condition was truly disabling. In this study no attempt was made to separate migrainous from non-migrainous headaches, or to distinguish between those whose primary symptom was headache and those in whom it was secondary to other conditions, such as influenza, sinusitis, or cervical spondylosis. Headaches associated with anxiety or depression, tension headaches, and muscle contraction headaches sometimes cause frequent short spells of sickness absence, but other non-medical factors, e.g. psychosocial, poor morale, or motivation, may also contribute to the problem.

Medication

Many sufferers from migraine and other forms of headache rely on self-medication. Occasionally the drugs used cause side-effects, such as drowsiness or impaired concentration, and there is a danger of interaction with alcohol. Jones and Harrop[7] found that approximately 6 per cent of the workforce of a marketing research company had suffered from migraine during an eight-month period. They treated acute attacks at work with metoclopramide (10 mg) orally, followed 10 minutes later by soluble paracetamol (500 mg × 2), and one hour's rest in a dark quiet room. The result of this was that 35 out of 36 employees were able to return to work to undertake their normal job after the lapse of one hour. Prophylactic medication is also effective in some cases, and by avoiding the possible precipitating factors mentioned above, interference with work may be kept to the minimum.

Cervical spondylosis (also discussed in Chapters 8 and 10)

Cervical spondylosis may interfere with work in several ways. It may simply cause pain at the back of the head and neck[9] and across the shoulders, and there may be nerve-root involvement affecting one or both arms. It can also cause spinal cord involvement (myelopathy) resulting in various degrees of spastic paraparesis or tetraparesis with bladder and bowel dysfunction, and surgical treatment may be necessary. A collar may help for a time, and the extent to which work is affected will depend partly on the severity of the condition and partly on the nature of the job. In many mild cases the condition is self-limiting, but persistent or severe disability is likely to necessitate modification of duties or retirement on medical grounds.

Cerebrovascular disease

Transient ischaemic attacks (TIAs)
Those involving the carotid or vertebro-basilar artery territory may cause impairment of consciousness, confusion or sudden vertigo, or disturbances of speech, vision, or limb function. These are not only contraindications to driving, but may also preclude work, depending on their frequency and the disability caused by the attacks, and also on the nature of the job and the working environment.

The possibility that transient ischaemic attacks may be due to a primary cardiac arrhythmia, or that there is some other coincidental cardiac disorder, must also be considered (see Chapter 15).

Completed stroke
The incidence of stroke rises with age from about 60 per 100 000 per year at age 45 to 600 per 100 000 per year at 65.[10] The prevalence is uncertain, but about 59 per cent have residual neurological signs after a stroke[11] and in a study by Holbrook[12] only 5 out of 30 patients who were working before their stroke were working two years afterwards.

Employers are often concerned about the stress of work as a risk factor in the recurrence of stroke, but this can be discounted and reassurance given.[13]

The range of severity of disability following a stroke is enormously variable, and here we shall consider just three of the common sequelae and their relevance to employment. The problems with resuming work are similar whether the stroke was due to haemorrhage from an aneurysm or angioma, or to infarction.

Hemiplegia
A completed stroke causing persistent hemiplegia is likely to make work and driving impossible. If there is some degree of recovery and the residual

hemiparesis is on the left side, the patient may be able to control a car satisfactorily or to resume work if various modifications or aids are provided. Most measurable recovery is achieved within six months.[14] Recovery is both intrinsic and adaptive, emphasis on adaptive recovery being particularly important for successful return to work.

Weakness and reduced mobility following a stroke will affect ability to work (especially in manual jobs) according to their severity. Loss of dexterity is particularly relevant to fine and rapid manipulative work, and to employment involving hand skills, such as those required for machine or computer operators, typists, etc. Careful clinical assessment may be necessary to distinguish disability due to dyspraxia, otherwise this may easily be misinterpreted and regarded as non-organic.

Impairment of language and cognitive functions

About 40 per cent of strokes cause dysphasia which is often, although not invariably, accompanied by dysgraphia and dyslexia, or by other neurological deficits such as hemiplegia, homonymous hemianopia, visual neglect and spatial disorientation, dyspraxia, anosognosia, and various degrees of impairment of cognitive function. The distinction from dementia is very important, as is the level of language that remains intact so that it is put to maximum use to compensate for residual difficulties. Just as dysphasia can occur with or without hemiplegia, so recovery of speech and power do not necessarily proceed in parallel. Generally, the younger the patient and the more anterior the lesion, the better the recovery of speech.

For some jobs, assessment of the ability to understand spoken and written instructions may be all that is necessary; but for other jobs, for example involving the interpretation of complicated plans or diagrams, specialized assessment will probably be required. There may be defects of memory and orientation, and the patient's general manner and behaviour should be observed. Further evidence should be obtained if possible from relatives and friends as to whether there is any evidence of periods of confusion or momentary inattention which could have serious consequences in certain types of work and particularly if there is a question of driving.

Visual field defects

An homonymous hemianopia results if the optic tract, radiation or visual cortex is involved on one side. There may also be visual inattention in the homonymous fields. Such impairment is frequently overlooked after a stroke. It may occur as an isolated deficit or be associated with other more obvious manifestations such as a hemiplegia or dysphasia. It is of serious significance in that it precludes driving and may also interfere with safety in various other work situations.

It should be remembered that dyslexia can occur without any associated visual field defect and, although it is usually associated with some degree of dysphasia, this is not invariably the case.

Loss of vision in one eye may result from retinal or carotid artery lesions. Other visual disturbances and their effect on work are considered in Chapter 6.

Head injury

Prevalence

There are remarkably few data on the prevalence of disability from head injury in the working population. The incidence of survival after serious head injuries in the UK has risen during recent years and the resulting neurological deficits are important causes of reduced working capacity or unemployment.[15,16] Recovery from the effects of head injuries sufficient to allow return to work may be considered under the following four headings:

1. Residual physical deficits where similar considerations apply to those described under the heading of 'stroke'.

2. Cognitive or behavioural disturbances, especially of memory, attention, and concentration, and frontal lobe deficits, e.g. disinhibition, childishness, apathy, and lack of insight.

3. Post-traumatic symptoms such as recurrent headache, dizziness, impaired concentration, and fatiguability.

4. Post-traumatic epilepsy, which is discussed in Chapter 12.

Miller and Stern[17] reported 85 severely head-injured patients who were disabled from an occupational standpoint. Ten were totally disabled because of epilepsy. Despite head injuries with prolonged post-traumatic amnesia (i.e. more than 24 hours), 45 of the 85 patients had suffered no loss of occupational status. Miller and Stern found that cranial nerve lesions from head injury involving sense of smell, vision, and hearing carried a poor prognosis and were associated with specific occupational hazards (e.g. failure to detect gas or fumes in the case of olfaction). Traumatic dysphasia, diplopia, and spastic pareses, however, carried a good prognosis and seldom led to permanent occupational disablement.

Cognitive and behavioural disturbances form a significant group of disabilities. Problems may arise from defects of short-term memory, unreliability and inability to grasp instructions or take messages. Frontal lobe defects may interfere with motivation and judgement, with lack of insight and apathy. There is controversy regarding the prognosis of post-traumatic symptomatology and compensation neurosis. Some believe that a pending compensation claim may have an adverse effect on recovery and return to work. Kelly and Smith,[18] however, contend that patients suffering from the post-traumatic syndrome do recover and return to full-time work before litigation is settled. Failure to have returned to work by the time of settlement indicates a bad prognosis, and such patients rarely return to work afterwards; the older the patient the worse the prognosis.

A recent study by Johnson[19] showed that the most important factors influencing the chances of successful return to work after severe head injury were the opportunity to go back to the previous job and the provision by the employer of special conditions, such as a work trial or easier work, and a lengthy period of support when the individual first returns to work.

Intracranial tumours

The development of an intracranial tumour (or other structural lesion) will sooner or later interfere with working capacity, depending on its site and extent, rate of progression, and whether or not it causes epilepsy.

Neurosurgical treatment, possibly with radiotherapy, may result in complete or partial recovery so that work and driving can be resumed, but the considerably increased risk of epilepsy in the first year after craniotomy must be borne in mind.[20]

Assessment of fitness to resume work and driving after a stroke, head injury, or craniotomy

Assessment as to whether and when a patient is fit to resume work and driving after a serious stroke, head injury, or craniotomy is not easy. The main problems to be considered are the nature and severity of both the physical disabilities and degree of mental impairment. The disorders due to cerebral damage may include intellectual deficits, dysphasia, varying degrees of hemiparesis, homonymous visual field defects, perceptual difficulties, dyspraxia, and epilepsy. Disorders due to brain-stem involvement include ataxia, vertigo, and diplopia.

A marked degree of dysphasia and dyslexia may preclude work and driving, particularly if comprehension is defective. Other cerebral deficits, such as parietal lobe syndromes and visual field defects may not be recognized by the patient who is lacking in insight and judgement. Homonymous visual field defects and visual inattention should call for advice to stop driving immediately and to notify the condition to the DVLC, and fitness to work will need careful assessment.

Fitness to resume work and driving in these patients will also depend on whether they have had one or more epileptic attacks, or have a high risk of developing epilepsy (see Chapter 12).

Apart from these, fitness to resume work and driving will depend on the degree of recovery, as well as the age and general condition of the patient, and the type of work required. Very careful assessment is necessary if resumption of work and driving is contemplated, and the patient should be subject to regular review.

Cerebral palsy

Definition

Cerebral palsy is not a specific disease but is the term used to cover a variety of non-progressive disorders of the brain resulting from maldevelopment, injury, or disease, which are either congenital or present in early infancy. The abnormalities of brain function are reflected most obviously in defects of movement, i.e. the spastic, athetoid, or ataxic types. There are often, but not always, failure of development of intellect and speech, and disturbances of behaviour and emotional control. All grades of severity are encountered; at one extreme cerebral palsy merges into minimal cerebral dysfunction, at the other into profound mental retardation with severe educational subnormality and physical handicap.

There is difficulty in assessing the incidence and prevalence rates, due to variations in definition and recognition of the syndromes, and in completeness of ascertainment of cases. The estimated prevalence also depends on the age of the children examined: for example, it appears less in surveys of children under the age of 4 than in those between 5 and 15 years old, as the problems increase and may only come to light when the child goes to school. Cerebral palsy occurs in approximately 7 per 1000 births, and between 1 and 2 of every 1000 schoolchildren have some form of cerebral palsy. A few do well at school, obtain university degrees, and manage to obtain employment. The relatively small proportion with a high IQ are able to perform useful jobs provided that they have learnt to cope with their physical disability. Types of jobs that can be done are obviously limited and special consideration may have to be given to wheelchair facilities and emergency exit arrangements.

Multiple sclerosis

Prevalence

This is 50–125 per 100 000.[21] In 197 Post Office employees with multiple sclerosis[22] there was a female to male ratio of 2.4:1. There was a more than even chance of remaining at work for as long as 15 or more years after diagnosis. The availability of sedentary work was as important as the amount of sickness absence in determining prospects for continued employment. Onset usually occurs during working life, and in view of the unpredictable prognosis, 'here and now' fitness to work assessment is important. It must be emphasized that in many patients the disease is relatively benign, with mild and infrequent relapses causing little or no interference with work or other activities.

Fluctuations in degree of disability and particularly fatigue were features identified in a study organized by the Multiple Sclerosis Society[23] as affecting working capacity. Other manifestations causing difficulties at work and unemployment included loss of manual dexterity, impaired vision, loss of sphincter control and, rarely, speech disturbances. Other reasons for unemployment were mobility difficulties, commuting problems, and prolonged or frequent periods of sickness absence.

Disturbances of co-ordination and dexterity due to cerebellar dysfunction may vary in severity and affect either one or both arms. This will interfere with a wide range of work activities, e.g. those undertaken by scientists, musicians, bench and assembly workers, machinists or packers, typists, accounts clerks, etc. Disturbances of balance are also common in multiple sclerosis, and employers may confuse this with alcoholic intoxication. Suitability for work using ladders and scaffolding, or steps and stairs, may be a problem for librarians and store keepers, as well as for those in the construction industry, for safety reasons. Depression is the commonest change in mood and may require treatment. Euphoria and intellectual impairment are rare but may occur in the later stages, although probably only after severe physical disability has already made employment impossible.

Employer's support

In the Post Office, the overriding factor in continuing employment was willingness on the part of the employer to supply help and support in job changes or by modifying working conditions, particularly to sedentary work which alleviates the fatigue from which many patients can suffer. The Multiple Sclerosis Society study concluded that many of the patients could have worked reduced hours but there was a general lack of opportunity for part-time work. Those with higher education or basic training showed the lowest level of unemployment, whereas manual workers, who required specialized retraining, and those living in rural areas showed the highest levels.

Continuation in the same job is usually easier and better than seeking a new one, even if modification of duties and responsibilities or of the work situation is necessary to compensate for any disability. Standing for long periods, overtime and heavy work are likely to become impracticable. Steps and stairs may render some jobs impossible, unless ramps, lifts, or work at one level can be arranged. Those unable to walk, or only just able to do so, are eligible for a wheelchair (electrically operated if necessary) both at home and at work. Provision will have to be made for the special needs of the wheelchair-bound if they are to be employed, e.g. ramps, wide doorways, car-park access, modified working heights and toilet facilities. Financial help for some alterations is available from the Department of Employment (Chapter 2).

Type of work
In general, service work is most suitable, particularly if a part-time option is available, e.g. accountancy, personnel, records, research and development, statistics analysis, design, and computing. If job suitability is carefully considered and matched to an individual's disability, patients with multiple sclerosis are likely to have the same or even lower rates of sickness absence and accidents than their able-bodied counterparts and to be at least as productive. A small proportion of patients will have severe or catastrophic episodes which preclude continued employment. When the patient can no longer either get to work or do the jobs available once there, the possibility of taking on some form of employment at home should be considered. There is a clear need for a scheme to increase the opportunities for home-based employment for the severely disabled.

Prognosis
The employer will probably wish to know the cause, and prognosis, of any obvious disability. Some employers may have misconceptions about multiple sclerosis and think the disease is always severe or progressive. Thus, if the employer is informed about the diagnosis in an early case, it is important to make sure he is aware that the course may be benign and that working capacity may not be seriously affected.

Motor neurone disease

Prevalence
This is about 5 per 100 000, the disease usually starting between the ages of 50 and 70, although it can occur at any age. Males are affected more often than females, in the proportion of 1.5:1, and in rare instances the condition may be familial.

The cause is unknown, but the pathological process is characterized by progressive degeneration of both upper and lower motor neurones and their fibre tracts. The pattern of the disease varies and may include bulbar or pseudobulbar palsy with speech and swallowing difficulties, spinal muscular atrophy (in which lower motor neurone features dominate), or amyotrophic lateral sclerosis (ALS) with both upper and lower motor neurone features causing weakness of the limbs and trunk. These syndromes are progressive and may occur either singly or in combination, with one or other pre-dominating. The generic term for the disease (ALS) is favoured by some, particularly in the USA.

The initial signs may be unilateral but with progression of the disease usually become bilateral and more or less symmetrical. The onset is gradual and the clinical picture depends on which motor neurones are affected first, whether they are upper or lower motor neurones or both. Commonly, the weakness and wasting start in the small muscles of one hand, gradually increasing and becoming more extensive. When the upper motor neurones are involved first, the weakness is associated with spasticity. Impairment of speech may be an early sign of the disease and when this becomes so slurred and weak, or when more than a mild degree of weakness in the limbs and trunk has developed, work will no longer be possible.

Ability to work will be affected according to the distribution of the initial weakness and type of job, and will then depend on the rate of progression of the disease. Sooner or later work and travelling will become impossible, and medical retirement will then be appropriate. But continuation at work for as long as possible will not accelerate the course of the disease and may be psychologically beneficial.

Prognosis

The disease is not associated with any disturbance of higher mental functions or awareness, and does not cause incontinence. It is usually fatal within 3–4 years of the onset, but when progressive bulbar and pseudobulbar palsy occur early, death may ensue within two years. Some cases of progressive spinal muscular atrophy, however, have survived for more than 10 years. No specific treatment is available for the condition.

Parkinson's disease

Prevalence

This is about 160 per 100 000 and the onset is usually between the ages of 45 and 65 years. Although the disease tends to be progressive, in the early stages continuation at work is usually possible, and with modern drug treatment incapacity may not develop for several years. The employer may make the mistaken assumption that the disease will be exacerbated by work and that the diagnosis indicates the need for immediate retirement. In fact, continuing work within his or her capabilities has a salutary effect both physically and mentally. The onset of slight unilateral tremor may not initially be accompanied by slowness of movement and reactions. When the disease has progressed, however, these additional features may interfere with the patient's ability to react quickly. Apart from the impairment of manual dexterity and fine movements, the tremor is often more disabling by virtue of the embarrassment engendered, for example in those dealing with the public, teaching, or doing committee work.

The slowing of movements (bradykinesia) and stiffness causes specific difficulty not only with manual dexterity (for example with assembly work), but also with repetitive movements such as polishing, cleaning, and decorating. Sometimes there is also impairment of initiative and motivation, with lethargy and depression.

Treatment and prognosis

Although modern treatment may abolish disability at least for a time, side-effects of the drugs may also interfere with work. Involuntary, usually choreiform, movements may be particularly troublesome and the patient sometimes has less insight or awareness of these than of the tremor. Fluctuations in performance, the 'on-off' phenomenon and 'freezing' are often critical factors in compelling retirement. When the disease is progressive, the patient may come to realize that work and driving will have to be given up, although the timing of such a decision is seldom easy. Practical testing may be necessary, but patients with this condition tend not to overestimate their ability to continue at work and will usually opt for elective retirement on medical grounds before being compelled to do so by the employer.

Other diseases with involuntary movements

Essential tremor

This is likely to interfere with jobs requiring fine finger and hand movements. Response to drug treatment is variable and usually limited, and the condition may deteriorate with age so that any form of office or manual work becomes impossible.

Huntington's disease

This is a rare hereditary condition which usually starts in the forties or fifties and causes progressive dementia with involuntary movements, and will sooner rather than later make continuation of work impossible.

Blepharospasm, spasmodic torticollis and writer's cramp

These are conditions which also respond very poorly to treatment and, although relatively uncommon, will prevent work when severe.

Dementia

Dementia is not a diagnosis but a syndrome whose aetiology must be ascertained in order to recognize the reversible or modifiable causes. It is no longer considered to be caused just by senility but is increasingly common with advancing age. Most of those affected will therefore have completed the employment stage of their life. Nevertheless, dementia can develop before the age of 60 or 65 and, although this has been referred to as pre-senile dementia, this term serves only to indicate the relatively early age of onset, as the pathological causes may be the same as in the elderly.

The commonest cause of dementia without other neurological signs is Alzheimer's disease, and the second most common type is vascular or so-called multi-infarct dementia. The differential diagnosis includes depression and drug toxicity, including alcoholism. The other causes which can develop during working age, usually with other typical features, are normal pressure hydrocephalus, Huntington's disease, the dementia of Parkinsonism, hypo-thyroidism, neurosyphilis, and vitamin B_{12} deficiency, hepatic encephalo-pathy, Creutzfeldt–Jakob disease, and the acquired immune deficiency syndrome (AIDS).

These various causes of dementia result in impairment of memory and cognitive function, disturbances of mood and behaviour, or periods of confusion, all of which may lead to dangerous errors of judgement, and seriously affect the ability to work and drive. Early dementia may be difficult to detect but the decision about fitness to work and drive should be based on common sense and simple tests of mental function and co-ordination. The assessment should involve checking orientation in time and space, making sure, for example, that the purpose and function of any machinery or instructions are understood. Memory should be assessed with a few simple questions on work procedures, current events, and general knowledge.

Sleep disorders

Narcolepsy and other causes of daytime drowsiness such as nocturnal obstructive apnoea may affect performance and efficiency at work and can have serious consequences if the job involves driving or other hazardous duties.[24] The dangers of people driving when sleepy, and particularly those known to have narcolepsy, are obvious and these conditions are probably a commoner cause of accidents than is generally realized. Their importance as a cause of road traffic accidents has been described by Parkes,[25,26] and the consequences of falling asleep at work may be just as serious as when driving, depending on the nature of the duties and the events at the time.

Oversleeping causing late arrival at work and falling asleep at work are more likely to be due to the effects of alcohol or drugs than to organic neurological disease. A social report may be informative and, although medical assessment may be necessary to determine whether there is a health problem, a strict attitude by management and disciplinary rather than medical measures are likely to be most helpful sooner than later.

Vertigo

Sudden unpredictable and recurrent attacks of vertigo have the same implications for work as epilepsy (see Chapter 12). The causes include

Ménière's disease which may be associated with progressive deafness usually in one but sometimes in both ears. This may seriously affect fitness for work, as well as driving, but treatment is often effective (see Chapter 5).

Labyrinthitis and benign positional vertigo, whether post-traumatic, infective, or idiopathic, will generally interfere with work. These conditions are usually self-limited and may be relieved by treatment so that the individual may be able to resume duties within a matter of weeks or, occasionally, months.

Disorders of co-ordination and balance

Clumsiness of voluntary movements and ataxia result from cerebellar dysfunction. Multiple sclerosis is the commonest condition causing this (see p. 200). Other conditions include cerebellar degenerations, the hereditary ataxias of which Friedreich's is the best known, and posterior fossa tumours (including acoustic neuromas).

Intention tremor in one or both upper limbs will obviously interfere with many jobs, as will ataxia of stance or gait. Occasionally nystagmus may interfere with vision (oscillopsia), and titubation of the head, or trunk ataxia may cause additional difficulty.

Driving will be a particular problem, although it is important to note that severe degrees of ataxia do not necessarily prevent driving with safety, and a practical test may be the best arbiter. Smoking and alcohol may aggravate cerebellar inco-ordination; even small quantities of alcohol may erroneously be regarded as the cause of the physical disability, and this particularly applies to people with a staggering gait and slurring of speech.

Weakness and sensory loss

Muscular dystrophies, and injuries to peripheral nerves, brachial plexus, and spinal cord are dealt with in other chapters but weakness and sensory disturbances, particularly in the limbs, due to other causes need to be considered here.

Myasthenia gravis
This is a rare autoimmune disease with symptoms due to a disorder of neuromuscular transmission at the myo-neural junction. This results in the increased fatiguability which is characteristic of this condition; the muscles tire sooner than normal and become progressively weaker as they are used, with recovery after a period of rest. The condition may occur at any age but usually between 20 and 50 years; it is slightly more frequent in females. The commonest mode of presentation in about 80 per cent of cases is with diplopia or ptosis. In some cases, after talking for some time, the voice becomes weaker and speech may become slurred and indistinct. Weakness of

the limbs may increase as they are used at work, becoming worse towards the end of the day and relieved by rest. Modern methods of treatment, which may include thymectomy, are often effective and most patients, other than those with persistent weakness, should be able to resume their work provided that this is not particularly strenuous.

Other disorders causing weakness

The effect on working capacity will depend on the distribution and severity of weakness. The prospects for future employment will depend on the cause and thus the prognosis of the underlying disorder, the degree of any improvement, as well as the possibility of compensating for residual disability by using unaffected functions, retraining, modification of duties, or transfer to a different type of work. Mobility and travelling may be all important, and are discussed in Chapter 10.

Sensory loss

Sensory loss in the hands and/or feet, when severe, is likely to interfere with work and driving. Proprioceptive defects causing so-called sensory ataxia will cause special difficulties if visual control of co-ordination is incompatible with the duties required.

Speech, voice, and communication problems

Speech defects have already been considered under the headings of stroke and head injury, but there are many other neurological causes. The ability to communicate is probably a prerequisite for most jobs and anything more than a mild degree of expressive or receptive dysphasia may preclude employment.

Developmental dyslexia seems to be a more frequent problem than is generally realized, and requires early recognition and specialized treatment if education, training, and employment are not to be jeopardized.

Stammering is likely to be an embarrassing handicap in all spheres of employment. Speech therapy may help in some cases.

Dysarthria, i.e. difficulty with articulation due to neuromuscular disorders, may be due to many causes. Its effect on work will depend on its severity and the extent to which clear speech is necessary for efficient performance of duties.

Dysphonia will also create difficulties at work if severe and if duties are dependent on a strong voice. There is a variety of non-neurological causes, e.g. hysteria, local laryngeal disorders, and post-laryngectomy cases, as well as neurological causes, e.g. myasthenia gravis, recurrent laryngeal nerve lesions, and motor neurone disease.

Communication aids such as a laryngeal microphone and more sophisticated electronic devices with microprocessor-based aids are now available and may help with the employment of those whose speech is impaired.

CONCLUSIONS AND RECOMMENDATIONS

Exact diagnosis is essential in determining prognosis, although functional ability to do the job may depend more on the nature, severity, and extent of the resulting disability than on the cause. Onset of neurological deficit at an early age is likely to be important because of its effect on education, training, experience, and skills.

There can be no substitute for precise knowledge of the job and the working environment in question. These details must be known when considering either recruitment or resumption of work following neurological illness, and also in assessing whether a health problem contributes to inefficiency and whether there is any alternative to medical retirement.

Health education has an important role in ensuring that the individual, employer, and colleagues are appropriately informed, as many a job has been lost unjustifiably or put into serious jeopardy by misconceptions or lack of understanding about the medical condition.

Although the provision of aids and modification of duties, part-time or flexihours, help with travelling, or even change of job have all been emphasized, it is also very important that premature resumption of work is avoided. An unsatisfactory impression or failure to achieve during the recovery stage may be far worse than delaying another week or month when, with a little more patience, all should be well. It may also be a mistake to allow continuation at work or to delay retirement when deterioration is likely to lead to inefficiency or lack of judgement. Efforts to keep someone at work under these circumstances may be misguided, especially as sometimes the individual himself will not have the insight or confidence to know what is best. For some people it may just 'go against the grain' to retire gracefully, even though they really know that it would be better for them not to continue. They may need their medical adviser to make the decision for them, and contrary to expectations they may then be grateful, rather than resentful, when told that the time has come to retire.

REFERENCES

1. Wade DT, Hewer RL. Epidemiology of some neurological diseases with special reference to work load on the NHS. Int Rehabil Med 1987;**8**:129–37.

2.   The Health of the Civil Service. London: HMSO, 1985.
3.   Espir MLE, Godwin-Austen R. Disorders of the nervous system. In: Raffle A ed. Medical aspects of fitness to drive. 4th ed. London: Medical Commission on Accident Prevention, 1985: 39–48.
4.   Raffle A, ed. Medical aspects of fitness to drive, 4th ed. London: Medical Commission on Accident Prevention, 1985.
5.   Manpower Services Commission. Code of practice on the employment of disabled people. Sheffield: Manpower Services Commission, 1984.
6.   Espir M, Floyd M. Epilepsy and recruitment. In: Edwards F, Espir M, Oxley J, eds. Epilepsy and employment. London: Royal Society of Medicine, 1986: 39–46.
7.   Jones A, Harrop C. Study of migraine and the treatment of acute attacks in industry. J Int Med Res 1980;**8**:321–5.
8.   Espir MLE, Thomason J, Blau JN, Kurtz Z. Headaches in civil servants: effect on work and leisure. Br J Ind Med 1988;**45**:336–40.
9.   Leading article. Third-nerve headache. Lancet 1986;**2**:374.
10. Wade DT, Hewer RL, Skilbeck CE, David RM. Stroke. London: Chapman and Hall, 1985.
11. Sorensen PS, Boysen G, Jensen G, Schnohr P. Prevalence of stroke in a district in Copenhagen. Acta Neurol Scand 1982;**66**:68–81.
12. Holbrook M. Stroke: social and emotional outcome. J R Coll Physicians Lond 1982;**16**:100–4.
13. Gentry WD, Jenkins CD, Kaplan BH, Heyman A, Breslin MS, Gianturco DT. Type A behaviour pattern and ischemic cerebrovascular disease. Heart and Lung 1979;**8**:1113–6.
14. Skilbeck CE, Wade DT, Hewer RL, Wood VA. Recovery after stroke. J Neurol Neurosurg Psychiatry 1983;**46**:5–8.
15. Roberts AH. Severe accidental head injury. An assessment of longterm prognosis. London: Macmillan, 1979.
16. Jennett B, MacMillan R. Epidemiology of head injury. Br Med J 1981; **282**:101–4.
17. Miller H, Stern G. The long-term prognosis of severe head injury. Lancet 1965;**1**:225–9.
18. Kelly R, Smith BN. Post-traumatic syndrome: another myth discredited. J R Soc Med 1981;**74**:275–7.
19. Johnson R. Return to work after severe head injury. Int Disabil Studies 1987;**9**:49–54.
20. Jennett B. Epilepsy (2)—After head injury and craniotomy. In: Raffle A ed. Medical aspects of fitness to drive. 4th ed. London: Medical Commission on Accident Prevention, 1985:35–7.
21. Williams ES, McKeran RO. The prevalence of multiple sclerosis in a south London borough. Br Med J 1986;**293**:237–9.
22. Mitchell JN. Multiple sclerosis and the prospects for employment. J Soc Occup Med 1981;**31**:134–8.
23. Davoud N, Kettle M. Multiple sclerosis and its effect on employment. Multiple Sclerosis Society, 1980.

24. Parkes JD, Langdon N, Lock C. Narcolepsy and immunity. Br Med J 1986;**292**:359–60.
25. Parkes JD. The sleepy patient. Lancet 1977;**1**:990–3.
26. Parkes JD. The sleepy driver. In: Godwin-Austen RB, Espir MLE, eds. Driving and epilepsy—and other causes of impaired consciousness. Royal Society of Medicine International Congress and Symposium Series no 60. London: Academic Press and the Royal Society of Medicine, 1983:23–7.

12

Epilepsy

I. Brown and A. P. Hopkins

INTRODUCTION

This chapter reviews the definition and epidemiology of epilepsy, clinical factors affecting capacity for work, the special problems that arise at work, and current legislation of particular relevance to epilepsy, particularly the regulations relating to driving.

A practical epidemiological definition of epilepsy

A useful operational definition of epilepsy, used in many international studies, is the occurrence of more than one non-febrile seizure at any time. There is no great difficulty in excluding previous febrile convulsions as irrelevant, especially in an occupational context, to the diagnosis of epilepsy. Numerous epidemiological studies have shown that febrile convulsions affect about 2.3 per cent of all healthy children between the ages of 18 months and five years,[1] but are not usually followed by epilepsy. This is more likely, however, if they arise on the basis of pre-existing neurological handicap, or if they are unusually prolonged or asymmetrical.

The use of the words 'more than one' non-febrile seizure begs the question as to what happens after one non-febrile seizure. Anyone suffering from recurrent epileptic seizures must at some stage have had his first, of many. It is therefore not possible to say of any individual that his first seizure is not epileptic.

A number of follow-up studies have shown high recurrence rates, of up to 70 per cent in the three years following the first seizure.[2-6a] This last high figure is biased by the particular nature of the sample, a retrospective analysis of the interseizure intervals of those referred to a neurologist with a known interest in epilepsy.[5] A similar figure of 63 per cent recurrence, however, was found in a US Navy study in which 77 young Navy personnel aged between 18 and 30 were followed prospectively for approximately four years after their first seizure.[2] All the studies show that the chances of recurrence are highest in the first 12 months after an attack (Fig. 12.1). Faced with these statistics, there seem no grounds for distinguishing first seizures as non-epileptic.

No controlled trial has as yet been undertaken to show that the recurrence

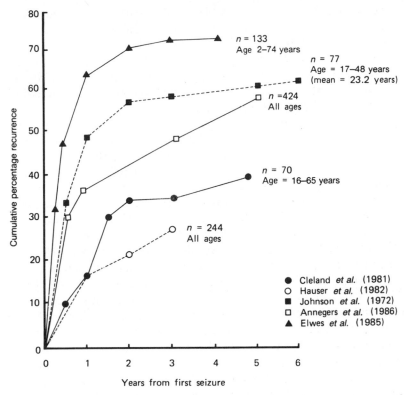

Fig. 12.1 The risk of recurrence of further seizures, data from five separate studies.[2-6]

rate after a first seizure is reduced by the prescription of an anticonvulsant drug, but as the figures described above become more widely known, it is probable that the present 'wait and see' policy adopted by most practitioners will give way to more active prophylactic therapy.

Cessation of epilepsy is also difficult to define. Take the example of a youth who had many seizures in adolescence, and then none after the age of 21. When does he stop having epilepsy: after an interval of five years free from seizures, or 10 years, or should he be regarded throughout his life as 'an epileptic'? It seems best to record this patient as being in remission for *x* years, as undoubtedly he is at greater risk from recurrent seizures in later life than is someone who has never had a single seizure.

Incidence and prevalence of epileptic seizures

The inception rate of epilepsy is best studied in family care practice, although one survey has shown that 95 per cent of all those with seizures are referred to hospital soon after onset.[7] Crombie *et al.* 1960[8] recorded first seizures occurring in 57 general practices, and found an annual incidence, across all ages, of 0.63 per 1000, a rate very similar to that reported from Olmsted County in the United States.[9] Both studies found that the age-specific incidence was highest in the first few years of life, and in old age. Throughout the ages of employment, from 16–65, first seizures occur at a rate of approximately 0.4 per 1000 per year.

The paper by Crombie *et al.*[8] was novel in so far as for the first time a calculation was made of the number of persons who are likely to have a fit of some sort during their lifetime, based upon the age-specific incidence rate and the number at risk in any age group. The total risk throughout life was calculated to be just over 4 per cent. The impact of this figure was diminished by the paper being unclear as to whether febrile convulsions were included. Such a figure, however, has been supported by the work of Goodridge and Shorvon[10] who reviewed the entire medical records of one general practice. They found a lifetime 'some-time' prevalence of 17.0 per 1000 (1.7 per cent) of two or more non-febrile seizures. As many of the population had many years to live, and as medical records may be mislaid or incomplete, this figure must be a minimum estimate of lifetime 'some-time' prevalence. Indeed, Hauser and his colleagues[11] quote a cumulative incidence through life to age 80 of 3.2 per cent. These figures indicate that epilepsy is not a rare and unusual affliction but one that affects at some time a substantial minority of the population.

The prevalence of active epilepsy depends upon the definition of activity. Most epidemiologists have included those who have had a seizure during the last two years. In the English general practice surveys already quoted, the prevalence of active epilepsy so defined ranged between 2.3 per 1000 and 5.3 per 1000. A further 1.1–2.5 per 1000 remained on anticonvulsant drugs, even though no seizure had occurred for two years or more.[12]

The prevalence of different types of seizure might, it may be thought, best be studied in community surveys, but accurate classification of types of seizure is dependent upon high-technology medicine, including video recording and simultaneous EEG monitoring of seizures, and various types of imaging. Seizures with a local origin in one part of the brain (partial seizures) were identified in 29 per cent of all patients with seizures when general practitioner records alone were inspected, but 56 per cent when hospital records were inspected as well.[7] Neurologists who have the facilities for long-term EEG recording and imaging techniques estimate that between 80 and 90 per cent of all seizures in adult life have a partial origin, though progression to a generalized tonic–clonic seizure may be so rapid that the original partial onset is only identified electrically. The typical absences of primary generalized epilepsy (petit mal) reflect an illness of childhood, and are unusual in adult life. Most minor epileptic attacks are complex partial seizures arising in one or other temporal lobe.

Chances of remission of epilepsy

The very fact that the cumulative lifetime incidence of epilepsy is up to 3.2 per cent,[11] and yet the prevalence of active epilepsy at any time is of the order of 0.2 per cent (5 per 1000) indicates that, in the majority of cases, epileptic seizures cease. As most work on the prognosis of epilepsy has been published from hospital clinics specializing in this disorder,[13] physicians, and hence the population at large, have had a pessimistic view of the outcome. There have been only two community studies on prognosis, one from the United States,[14] and one from England.[10] Both these studies show that many patients achieve a lasting remission within the first few years after onset. For example, in the Minnesota study,[14] one year after diagnosis, 42 per cent of the subjects had entered a seizure-free period that was to extend for at least five years. The net probability of being currently in remission (five years or more, and continuing) was 61 per cent at 10 years after diagnosis and 70 per cent at 20 years after diagnosis. Relapse once a long remission had been achieved was rare. The prospects for long-term remission are thus better than is widely appreciated.

Not everyone is so fortunate, and a number of factors have been identified that indicate a poor prognosis in spite of energetic treatment.[13] The most important of these is the duration of uncontrolled epilepsy to date: the longer epilepsy has continued, the less likely it is to stop. Other unfavourable features include combinations of different types of seizure (usually temporal lobe and tonic–clonic seizures), a tendency for seizures to cluster over a few days, with intervals of freedom, and the presence of associated neurological deficits such as may follow a birth injury or meningo-encephalitis. Conversely, young people who have focal seizures in association with central spikes on the EEG have a particularly good prognosis.

The physician should direct his most energetic efforts to an intermediate group, those whose epilepsy is continuing solely because of inadequate therapy. The definition of the therapeutic range of serum concentrations of anticonvulsant drugs and the ready availability of laboratory facilities for measuring these means that such patients should be rare. Inertia on the part of the doctor and patient, however, and failure of compliance may prevent the attainment of therapeutic levels.

Causes of epilepsy

Many people attribute their seizures to distinct illnesses, accidents, or other unfavourable events in their lives, but epidemiological studies[9,12] have shown that a cause can be defined, with any degree of confidence, in only about 25 per cent of all cases of epilepsy. This quarter is made up of roughly equal proportions of patients with epilepsy due to birth injury or anoxia; to the late effects of cranial injury or of surgery; to the late effects of infections; and to tumours, to vascular events, and in association with congenital lesions such as hydrocephalus.

Toxic causes of epilepsy are rare. Seizures may occur as a result of lead encephalopathy, almost always in children. Seizures have occurred in employees over-exposed during the manufacture of chlorinated hydrocarbons. EEG abnormalities have been recorded in the absence of any clinical abnormality in workers exposed to methylene chloride, methyl bromide, carbon disulphide, benzene, and styrene, though the significance of these observations is uncertain.

A review of the inheritance of epilepsy is outside the scope of this chapter, but probably only about 10 per cent of adults with seizures have true primary generalized (idiopathic) epilepsy. The cause of the epilepsy of the remaining 65 per cent of adults cannot be assigned with confidence.

PREVENTION OF EPILEPSY IN THE WORKPLACE

Primary prevention

The prevention of head injuries is undoubtedly the most important preventive action and is fundamental to safety at work. The measures used are largely common sense. Epilepsy does not follow a trivial head injury. However, if the head injury is associated with a depressed fracture (especially if the dura is torn) or an intracranial haematoma, or focal neurological signs, then there is a significant risk of later epilepsy.[15]

The introduction of a comfortable and strong safety helmet is the obvious first measure, although this somewhat reverses the usual order of safety steps used in occupational health, making personal protection top of the list. Making the working environment safe should be the first step, but often the unpredictability of events makes this impossible. It should be compulsory that safety helmets are worn at all times in areas specified by the work's safety team. As a second step, the workforce should be made aware of areas above which other employees are operating at heights, so that these can be avoided if possible. A safety helmet will not protect the individual from serious head injury if anything heayy is dropped from a great height. If work has to be performed underneath such a hazard, it is well worth rigging steel netting to catch anything that falls.

Secondary prevention

Patients who have had penetrating head injuries, or a cerebral abscess, have such a significant risk of seizures in the first two years after the acute event that there are good arguments for choosing work for them during this period along the same lines as for someone who has already had a seizure, and they should not drive. Although it is customary to give prophylactic anticon-vulsants after a head injury of the type that is likely to be followed by epilepsy, controlled trials have yet to show an advantage.[16] The other main preventive measure is the avoidance of precipitating factors.[17] Some of these are discussed below.

Shiftwork

Seizures are common just before and just after waking, so it might be felt that the introduction of a shift system into the work programme of a person with well-controlled epilepsy would predispose him to an increased frequency of seizures, although firm documentary evidence of an alteration in seizure frequency is not to be found. This may be due to people with epilepsy opting out of shiftwork, as indicated by Dasgupta, Saunders and Dick.[18] Many people with well-controlled epilepsy, however, can work rotating shifts without problems.

Patterns of sleep are disturbed by night-work and to a lesser extent by other types of shiftwork. Night-workers sleep for shorter periods during their working week and sleep longer on rest days, to make up the deficit.[19] Sleep deprivation is an important precipitant of seizures for some individuals, and is best avoided by those with epilepsy.

A drug with a short half-life, such as carbamazepine, may have to be taken up to four times per day to maintain satisfactory serum levels and control of seizures. A dose may be overlooked if the employee is attempting one of the popular rapidly rotating shift regimes, with the result that serum drug levels may drop below the therapeutic range, allowing a seizure to occur.

Stress

An association between stress and seizures has been recognized for many years on the basis of clinical observation. Until recently little scientific evidence for this was to be found. A study by Temkin and Davis[20] demonstrated an association, although the number of subjects in the study was small and the period of observation only three months. None the less, the possibility that stress may have an adverse effect should be considered when employees with epilepsy are moved to different areas of responsibility, or promoted.

Photosensitivity

Photosensitive epilepsy is rare, but worthy of consideration in a situation where a light-source flickers. The overall prevalence is 1 in 10 000 but it is twice as common in females. Ninety per cent of patients have suffered their first convulsion due to photosensitivity before the age of 22 years.[21] Photosensitivity may be increased following deprivation of sleep.

The diagnosis of photosensitive epilepsy is supported by performing an EEG recording with photic stimulation and eliciting a photo-convulsive response. This is usually a generalized discharge of spike-wave activity elicited by the flickering stimulus, persisting after the stimulus has ceased. Spontaneous seizures may occur in photosensitive subjects. It must be remembered that some individuals have a paroxysmal EEG response to photic stimulation, without any evidence of having had a seizure.[21]

Television is a common precipitant of photosensitive epilepsy.[22] The provocative stimulus is the pattern of interlacing lines formed by the flying spot from the electron gun. Nearness to the set appears to be an important factor, as this enables the viewer to discriminate the line pattern. Background illumination is another factor.[23] Flickering sunlight (e.g. through the leaves of a tree), faulty and flickering artificial lights, and glare are also occasional precipitants. It would be unwise for a person with photosensitive epilepsy to work in a situation where television or video screens are in common use. Swimming in bright sunlight may constitute some risk because of glare and flicker patterns on the water surface. Helicopter rotor blades and aeroplane propellers may provoke episodes.

The use of a visual display unit (VDU) in employment constitutes a much smaller risk than that incurred while viewing television. The majority of VDUs have relatively slow phosphors in the tubes to reduce apparent flicker, and, in addition, they usually do not use an interlaced line pattern. The probability of a first fit being induced by a VDU is exceedingly small and, even in the established photosensitive subject, unlikely to occur.

The Civil Aviation Authority has recognized the special risks that may be related to flying, especially to the slow flicker that is visible through helicopter blades. This body performs an EEG investigation as part of its routine medical screen on pilots applying for commercial licences.

Other types of reflex epilepsy

Although reflex epilepsy may occasionally be induced by reading or concentrating, or by hearing music or bells, this is rare.[17]

Alcohol and drugs

Alcohol taken as beer seems to be a particularly potent precipitant, possibly because of the associated overhydration. Moderate overhydration may similarly be the reason for an increase in convulsions just before menstruation, although hormonal factors may also play a part.

A number of drugs have been incriminated as epileptogenic agents.[17] By far the commonest are the tricyclic antidepressants. Others include isoniazid, bronchodilators such as theophylline and terbutaline, and anti-psychotic drugs such as haloperidol and chlorpromazine.

Fluctuating levels of anticonvulsant drugs, due to failure of compliance or interaction with other drugs may also result in seizures.

WHAT TO DO IF A SEIZURE OCCURS[1][2]

Supervisors and colleagues should be instructed in appropriate first-aid measures. These are that the subject be moved away from immediate danger, for example away from hot metal or moving machinery, and that he be placed in the coma position after convulsions have ceased until consciousness is recovered. No attempts should be made to open the mouth to prevent the tongue being bitten, as, if damaged, this occurs in the first tonic contraction. Unwise attempts to force objects into the mouth may result in broken teeth.

As the subject recovers consciousness, he is usually confused, and a quiet yet firm manner from one or two supportive colleagues seems to be helpful.

The responsibility of the physician at the workplace

The first task is to establish without doubt that a seizure has occurred. The employee should attend the occupational health service as soon as possible and remain off work in the interim period. A detailed history of the event should be obtained and information sought from the patient and any reliable witness to try and establish the nature of the attack. Interviewing work colleagues and relatives who witnessed the event can be extremely useful, as the subject himself usually remembers very little beyond the first few seconds. It is very unwise to rely solely on written reports and second-hand information. Relevant points about a possible family history and consumption of drugs or alcohol, should also be obtained. The patient should be fully examined, as a seizure may occasionally be the first symptom of an important systemic illness such as meningitis, or of a local cerebral condition; detailed medical assessment is always necessary.

Permission to contact both family doctor and hospital consultant (if referral has taken place) should be obtained from the patient. It is often useful to contact these physicians informally and discuss the situation that has arisen. This should be followed by a formal letter giving a concise account of events, the examination findings, and requesting any further relevant information.

Not all episodes of unconsciousness are epileptic seizures: other possible diagnoses include syncope, drug overdose, paroxysmal cardiac arrhythmia, transient cerebral ischaemia (TIA), and simulated attacks.

Prolonged cerebral anoxia due to syncope may produce some twitching and even incontinence, although a generalized seizure is unusual. The focal ischaemia of a TIA does not usually involve loss of consciousness and is often a neurologically negative event, causing loss of function such as aphasia, and producing a convulsion only rarely. The possibility of a simulated attack may need to be considered.

Once it has been established as far as possible that a single, unprovoked, convulsion has taken place at work, the following procedure should be adopted:

1. The medical notes must state clearly the course of events and that a single seizure has taken place.

2. Management should be contacted and given clear and concise recommendations, in writing, regarding placement of the employee, without any breach of confidentiality. Such written recommendations should be constructed with the agreement of the employee. Some employees prefer to inform their immediate supervisor that they suffer from epilepsy and that this is well controlled with medication; it is worth discussing the possibility of such disclosure.

3. The occupational physician and occupational health nurse must become familiar with any anticonvulsant prescribed and have a sound knowledge of both unwanted and toxic effects.

Sensible restrictions on the work of people with epilepsy

Restrictions must be discussed fully with the employee and with management. Clear written instructions should be given regarding placement, responsibilities, and review. Confidentiality must not be breached. Restrictions should be no more than is necessary on common-sense grounds, as would apply equally to any individual subject to sudden and unexpected lapses in consciousness or concentration, however infrequent.

In the United States it is illegal, provided the disability does not impair health and safety standards at the workplace, to deny employment to an otherwise qualified applicant because of disability. However, this begs the question 'for what type of work is someone with epilepsy qualified?' The Epilepsy Foundation of America (EFA) has developed a comprehensive interview guide summarized by Masland.[24] The guide helps define the important characteristics of a person's epilepsy, and draws attention to both advantageous and disadvantageous features. A consistent warning of attacks is certainly an advantageous feature, but is unusual. Conversely, sudden loss of consciousness without warning must be considered disadvantageous. The frequency of attacks is another important consideration and the success rate in placing a person with epilepsy is far greater if they have fewer than six seizures per year.

In general, minor attacks are less disruptive than major ones, but periods of automatism may upset colleagues. Other particularly disadvantageous characteristics are prolonged periods of post-ictal confusion, and sudden akinetic attacks where the possibility of serious injury is increased.

It is impossible to be dogmatic for all occasions, as individuals and industries are infinitely variable. Sensible restrictions, however, include the following: climbing and working unprotected at heights, driving or operating motorized vehicles, working around unguarded machinery, working near fire or water, working for long periods in an isolated situation. Hand-held power tools may be a hazard if they can be fixed in the 'on' position.

There are certain jobs with special hazards where the risk of even one seizure may give rise to catastrophic consequences. These jobs fall into two groups. First, mainly in transport, are vocational drivers, train drivers, drivers of large container-terminal vehicles, and crane operators; aircraft pilots; seamen and coastguards; and commercial divers. For further details see the appendices at the end of this book. Second are jobs that include work at unprotected heights, e.g. scaffolders, steeplejacks and firemen; work on mainline railways; with high-voltage electricity, hot metal, or dangerous unguarded machinery, e.g. chain saws; or near open tanks of chemical fluids (see Table 11.2).

The working environment and any equipment to be used by the employee with epilepsy should be inspected by the occupational physician, if there is one. The safety officer and the employee's immediate supervisor should be involved in any decisions.

It is important to remind the employee that contravention of agreed restrictions may not only put his own life in danger, but also those of his colleagues and friends. The employee should also be reminded that it may be impossible to make any insurance claim for financial compensation for personal injuries should an accident occur as a result of evasion of agreed restrictions.

A policy should be established for terminating any restrictions on work. This policy should be made known to the affected employee and not altered unless circumstances are exceptional. There is little place for partial lifting of restrictions: the employee is either considered safe or not. If a work restriction is removed after a period of freedom from seizures, the employee should be instructed to report any further attack to occupational health staff or to a personnel officer or manager. If anticonvulsant medication is stopped or changed, consideration should be given to closer monitoring at work for a period, or to the temporary re-introduction of a suitable work restriction.

It may be found that following the introduction of medication, control is still poor with an unacceptable rate of seizure recurrence. It is important that every effort is made to improve control before the individual is rejected for employment or promotion. Perhaps there are certain precipitating factors that can easily be avoided, e.g. alcohol (p. 216). Has an appropriate anticonvulsant been chosen, and an adequate serum level been achieved?

Perhaps the employee is forgetful or actively non-compliant? Is there a correctable structural cause? All these possibilities should be explored and the occupational physician or occupational health nurse should co-ordinate their efforts with the family doctor and hospital consultant.

There should be a specified time-scale for the removal of restrictions. A de-restriction review date should be offered, as this will ensure that the employee's future is being seriously considered and confirm that he or she is still a valuable member of the workforce. In this respect it seems reasonable to follow, for employment, those guidelines used by the Department of Transport for ordinary driving licences (p. 226). If an employee is safe to drive an instrument as dangerous as a car, he should be safe to undertake virtually all industrial duties. Jobs with special hazards are listed on p. 219 and in Table 11.2. After an initial seizure, the Department of Transport advises that a subject may not drive a motor car for one year, and it would seem reasonable to follow the same practice for restrictions in industry.

The effect of anticonvulsant drugs upon work performance

A clear distinction must be made between the toxic effects of anticonvulsant drugs and the predictable side-effects of these agents. Toxicity occurs when the serum levels increase beyond the often narrow therapeutic range. Because of the pharmacokinetics of phenytoin, even a small increase in dose may well push serum levels into the toxic range. To make matters even more complicated, each patient will have an individual dose–serum-level curve and those with a particularly steep curve will have problems in establishing an optimum dose of the anticonvulsant. Anticonvulsant drugs within the therapeutic range may have a deleterious effect on cognitive and motor function but, unfortunately, there have been few studies which have demonstrated adequate experimental design to prove this controversial assumption. The interpretation of results has been confounded by the lack of balanced cross-over with placebo drugs, and tests which are subject to practise effects.

Thompson and colleagues[25-7] examined the influence of phenytoin (100 mg, three times a day), carbamazepine (200 mg, three times a day) and sodium valproate (1000 mg per day) on a variety of cognitive functions. The results demonstrated that phenytoin significantly impaired ability across most aspects of higher cognitive function, although it did not influence the visuomotor response. The other two drugs impaired cognitive function less than phenytoin, in particular with regard to any influence on perceptual and motor speed.

Behavioural changes such as aggression and irritability can be produced by most anticonvulsants, but these are far more common in the brain-damaged patient. Dystonia, orofacial dyskinesis, and chorea can be produced by phenytoin, carbamazepine, valproate, and ethosuximide, but these are usually idiosyncratic and dose dependent. Mood changes have also been noted, especially an increase in symptoms of depression.

Nystagmus, dysarthria, ataxia, and vertigo are common dose-related toxic side-effects of most anticonvulsant drugs, although a permanent cerebellar syndrome has been attributed to long-term phenytoin therapy. Reversible visual blurring and diplopia are commonly seen with high doses of carbamazepine. All such effects require a reduction in dosage. Unusual reactions are occasionally seen when combination therapy is attempted.

Opportunities for sheltered work

The majority of people with epilepsy are capable of normal employment without need for supervision or major restrictions. There exists a minority group with additional handicap who may only be able to work in a more sheltered environment. Such additional handicap often includes poorly controlled seizures, physical disability, low intelligence, and poor social adaptive skills. The appendix to this chapter gives further information on the facilities available.

SPECIAL WORK PROBLEMS

Disclosure of epilepsy

In an ideal world, an individual with epilepsy would start work armed with an account of how his seizures affect him, how often and when they occur, details of his medication (and possible side-effects), and an estimate of likely prognosis. The occupational physician could then, from his own knowledge of the work processes at the factory or office, advise employment in a sector which maximized the employee's production and opportunities for promotion, and minimized any risk to him or to his colleagues.

Only about a third of the working population have even a nominal contact with an occupational physician, however, and in reality the situation is often quite different. The person with epilepsy is aware that in open competition his opportunities of employment are impaired, and that his choice of vocation is limited. His opportunities of mobility and promotion within a company may also be limited. He may have suspicions that he will not be allowed to join the pension fund. Finally, he has to face the possible condescension of his fellow workers who, he feels, may have been told to watch out for his fits.

From this perspective, therefore, it is not surprising if epilepsy is often concealed from an employer or a potential employer. A survey of people in London with epilepsy[28] showed that over half of those who had had two or more full-time jobs after the onset of epilepsy had *never* disclosed their epilepsy to their employer, and only 1 in 10 had *always* revealed it. If seizures were infrequent, or usually nocturnal, so that the applicant considered that he had a good chance of getting away with concealment, then the employer was virtually never informed. Two variables in this survey correlated with failure to gain employment: frequent seizures, and lack of any special skill. This state of affairs will be improved only slowly by educational programmes. Another possible way forward includes a clearer definition of jobs that can safely be done by people with epilepsy.

Accident and absence records of those with epilepsy

It is widely held that people with epilepsy are more accident prone and have worse attendance records than other workers. This view cannot be substantiated from the literature, although few data are available. Many studies must be inherently biased, however, as the person already known to have epilepsy has declared his condition, either voluntarily or involuntarily by having a seizure at work, and therefore eliminated himself from many potentially hazardous jobs which in themselves lead to increased accidents and sickness absence. The most significant study of work performance which attempted to eliminate this bias was conducted by the United States Department of Labor 40 years ago.[29] A statistical comparison was made of 10 groups with different disabilities, including people with epilepsy, with matched unimpaired controls. Within the epilepsy group, no differences were found in absenteeism, but the incidence of work injuries was slightly higher among people with epilepsy. The differences noted in accident rates were not, however, statistically significant. The general conclusion of this study was that people with epilepsy perform as well as matched unimpaired workers in manufacturing industries.

The study by Udell[30] hypothesized that people with epilepsy were capable of normal work performance. Although the sample was small, this work demonstrated that discriminatory practices against the recruitment of people with epilepsy is unwarranted, if based on the notion that as a group they have high accident rates, poor absence records and low production efficiency. Udell also made the point that any applicant with epilepsy must be appraised individually with regard to the degree of seizure control, and any other associated handicap. He also added that employers should have a receptive policy for recruitment and job security. This may encourage employees to admit the problem, and allow industry an opportunity to appraise their abilities and place them most appropriately.

The more recent study of epilepsy in the British Steel Corporation (BSC)[18] generally supports these previous findings. There was no significant difference between epilepsy and control groups with regard to overall sickness absence and accident records. This report also analysed job performance, and showed that there was no major overall difference between epilepsy and control groups using five job-performance factors. Work performance, however, was significantly reduced when people with epilepsy and an associated personality disorder were compared with the remainder of the epilepsy group. The BSC study emphasized that, although some degree of selection has to be applied when employing people with epilepsy, the overall performance of those with epilepsy compared with that of their colleagues was satisfactory.

The major problem is not to prove that performance at work is satisfactory, but to challenge and change the firmly held and deeply entrenched prejudices of employers.

Current employment practices in the nationalized industries, the armed forces, the teaching profession, and the National Health Service

An informal survey of current attitudes and practices with respect to epilepsy within these services revealed an interesting dual approach adopted by most occupational health departments. There was often a carefully worded and apparently inflexible regulation, yet many occupational physicians used a more sympathetic approach. This was usually only obvious, however, if the physician was contacted personally. Such manoeuvres were only undertaken by doctors in industries and services that could allow the flexibility of relocation to different jobs.

Not unreasonably, the *armed forces* were found to be the least flexible. Proven cases of epilepsy were not accepted for service. Epilepsy which developed during service was fully investigated and, if proved, the individual was discharged from the service (personal communication to I.B.).

Epilepsy is also a contraindication for employment in the *police force*. The police expect all their officers to be fit for all duties. Officers developing epilepsy in service are usually discharged, but only after careful individual assessment (personal communication to I.B.).

The *nationalized industries* all follow a code of practice similar to each other, and are able to pursue a more sympathetic approach. Epilepsy declared at the pre-employment stage may be a contraindication to employment, but is not an absolute bar. The discretion of the examining physician allows some compromise to be achieved if the applicant has a special skill or quality to offer, and if the job is suitable. Epilepsy developing in service can often be accommodated if the employee is willing to be relocated, but this often involves loss of earnings and status. If unacceptable, retirement on grounds of ill-health is usually offered. A good example of such practices is demonstrated by the current policy of British Coal's medical service.

The *Department of Education and Science* has a flexible policy for the employment of school teachers with epilepsy and allows its locally appointed part-time Medical Officers to use reasonable discretion. Difficult cases are referred to the Department's Medical Advisers, and each is judged on its own merits.

The *National Health Service (NHS)* presents an interesting enigma. The NHS employs more people than any other single employer, and yet has no national guidelines regarding the employment of those with epilepsy.[31] The lack of clear guidelines is manifestly unsatisfactory. Attitudes vary from one Regional Health Authority to another and, within one Authority, between different Districts. Such a state of affairs is confusing both to potential employees and employment advisers. Consultant physicians in occupational medicine have been appointed by some Health Authorities and it is to be hoped that they will formulate guidelines for the recruitment and employment of people with epilepsy. Because NHS employees frequently change Regions for promotion and experience, it is essential that such guidelines are standardized on a national basis.

Getting employers to understand about epilepsy

Many of those with epilepsy are unemployed. Even if employed, many workers with epilepsy are frequently denied promotion because of their disability or because of misconceptions about it. In a survey of employers in the USA[32] it was found that few would employ persons known by them to have had a generalized seizure within the previous year. In this study, Hicks and Hicks recorded a consistent reason given for the failure to offer people with epilepsy employment, that 'they create safety problems for themselves and other workers.'[32] Such reasoning has not varied for more than two decades. These authors point out that this assumption is misconceived, and not supported by published data. An encouraging feature of this study was evidence of a positive change in attitude. Although the cause remains uncertain, changes in the law in the USA and the continued efforts of public and private agencies may well be responsible.

Regular informal health education seminars could take place at work. A well-thought-out programme that involves the personnel department, occupational health team, and interested union representatives may prevent some problems occurring. Subjects such as epilepsy, stress, or alcohol abuse could be discussed openly, with the benefit of expert advice immediately available. The occupational physician or occupational health nurse can play a major role in informal health education and in changing attitudes. Health education is concerned not only with the prevention of disease, but in the understanding of disease in others. Problems such as epilepsy are often shrouded in mystery, or considered as too unsavoury to discuss in detail. For such a common complaint, a prevalence of about 1 in 200 of the population, the ignorance demonstrated is astonishing. Many employees, both on the shop-floor and in management, consider that someone with epilepsy also has some degree of mental handicap combined with a lesser or greater physical infirmity. Certainly such problems may co-exist, but they are the exception rather than the rule. It is of paramount importance that health professionals should dispel myths and give a sense of proportion to problems.

The hard work of agencies such as the British Epilepsy Association, the National Society for Epilepsy, and the Employment Medical Advisory Service has done much to inform employers. Misconceptions about epilepsy are slowly disappearing and attitudes changing.

The relationship between the occupational physician, consultant neurologist, and family practitioner

Recommendations received from the neurologist may differ from those acceptable to the occupational physician, who must consider the best interests of the patient in his particular working environment. The family doctor, who may have cogent views and is likely to have closer knowledge of the patient can liaise with both these two specialists. It is advantageous if all the physicians involved work together to avoid conflicting advice.

In firms with an occupational health service, an employee with epilepsy should be encouraged to contact the nurse and discuss problems as they arise. The nursing service at work is often readily accessible to the employee and has a special role in counselling and health education. Confidential notes should be kept and the case discussed with the occupational physician at the earliest opportunity. Employees with epilepsy should be reviewed regularly by the occupational health service.

GUIDELINES FOR EMPLOYMENT: THE LEGAL CONSIDERATIONS

Employment legislation

For a more detailed discussion of legal aspects, see Chapter 2, and also Carter.[33]

The Health and Safety at Work etc Act 1974 makes no specific references to the disabled, and applies to all employees regardless of their health.[34] The dual responsibility of employer and employee is entirely reasonable, but may create problems. Many people with epilepsy do not disclose it to their employer for fear of losing their job, or to a prospective employer for fear of not being offered the job.[28] Under these circumstances the employee with epilepsy may contravene Section 7 of the Health and Safety at Work etc Act, if he knowingly accepts a job that is unsuitable for a person with epilepsy. An employer, however, may legally refuse to employ an applicant for a job on any grounds except those of sex and race (see Chapter 2).

What are the legal implications if a worker develops epilepsy while in service? All employees are covered by the Employment Protection (Consolidation) Act 1978. This Act protects against unfair dismissal, but such protection is only operable after two years continuous employment. Is dismissal on medical grounds unfair? The employer is obliged to justify his decision to a tribunal on at least one of five fair reasons for dismissal. Is the employee capable of performing his duties safely and efficiently? Has it become impossible for the employee to continue to work without contravening a statutory duty or restriction? Incapability and illegality are both fair grounds for dismissal. The Employment Appeal Tribunal makes the final decision, but will emphasize that the employer should discuss with the worker his state of health if possible, and make absolutely sure that the employee is incapable of doing the job in question, and that an alternative job is not available.

Some employers are under the misconception that an applicant with a history of epilepsy will not be accepted into the Pension Fund. The view of the Occupational Pensions Board, however, succinctly states the situation: 'Fit for employment—fit for the pension fund.'[35]

No special insurance arrangements are necessary for a worker with epilepsy. The Employer's Liability Insurance covers everyone in the workplace, provided that the employer has taken the disability into account when allocating the individual to a particular job.

To summarize the legal position, the employee with epilepsy is protected by the same legislation and should enjoy the same pension rights as any other employee. He can be dismissed from employment if the disability interferes with his capability to perform his duties satisfactorily. Dismissal can also take place if the employee's medical condition contravenes statutory regulations governing the job.[33] It is unfortunate that employers can discriminate against a suitably qualified applicant with epilepsy purely on the grounds of potential disability. A satisfactory solution to the employment of someone whose epilepsy is well controlled is unlikely to be achieved by legislation alone. Changing the legal position on discrimination would help, particularly if the employer had to justify his decision to reject an applicant, if such a decision were made purely on medical grounds unrelated to the job in question.

The Driving Licence Regulations and their effects

Under the Road Traffic Acts, 1972 and 1974, epilepsy is a disability under section 87 (3) (b), but an ordinary driving licence for a limited period may be granted if an applicant suffering from epilepsy satisfies the following conditions:

(a) he shall have been free from any epileptic attack during the period of two years immediately preceding the date when the licence is to have effect; or

(b) in the case of an applicant who has had such attacks whilst asleep during the last two years, he shall have had such attacks only whilst asleep during a period of at least three years immediately preceding the date when the licence is to have effect; and

(c) the driving of a vehicle by him in pursuance of the licence is not likely to be a source of danger to the public.

The broad intention is to allow driving licences to be granted, in suitable cases, to people with epilepsy who have been free of any attacks for two years with or without treatment, or who have a history of at least three years of attacks only during sleep.

Those who need to drive to work when public transport is not available may get assisted taxi fares from the Manpower Services Commission. The Public Transport Acts make provision for local authorities to give subsidized bus transport to people with epilepsy deprived of a driving licence, although not all authorities exercise their power to make this provision. It may also be possible to help maintain employment by arranging work nearer to home, or by encouraging other employees to provide a lift to work. No driving licence is necessary to ride a bicycle but, before advising this, care needs to be taken to assess the risks involved and discuss them with the patient.

Van, crane and mini-bus drivers will need to be found alternative employment within the company, as will those whose job involves driving. The safety of fork-lift truck drivers will depend upon individual circumstances.

A single fit, as defined on page 210 is not epilepsy, but the subject is still obliged by law to inform the Driver and Vehicle Licensing Centre, Swansea (DVLC) of the event as it clearly is, in view of the high recurrence rate, a 'disability which is or may become likely to affect your fitness as a driver'.[36] DVLC will invariably advise at least one year of ineligibility to hold a licence. Initial seizures are commonly followed by others (p. 210).

Heavy goods and public service vehicle drivers come into a special category. Under the Heavy Goods Vehicles (Drivers Licences) (Amendment Regulations, 1982), a person cannot hold such a licence if he has 'suffered an epileptic attack since attaining the age of five'.

Finally, there is a group of people who are at risk from seizures, but who have not yet had one. Such patients are those who have had a severe cranial injury, particularly if associated with a depressed fracture, or those who have had a craniotomy, cerebral abscess, or subarachnoid haemorrhage complicated by an intracerebral haematoma.[16]*

CONCLUSIONS AND RECOMMENDATIONS

Many people do not disclose a past or present medical history of convulsions when applying for a job, or during a routine examination at the workplace.[28] This may well cause major problems for the individual and the employer and may, on occasions, inadvertently contravene the Health and Safety at Work etc. Act or invalidate insurance cover. The unenlightened attitudes of some employers have led understandably to such secrecy or even denial by the employee or applicant. The possibility of dangerous situations arising at work, or dismissal without recourse to appeal may be the outcome. A competent occupational health service, trusted by both shop floor and management, can be invaluable in sorting out conflicts and giving advice.

Responsibility for the employment and placement of a person with epilepsy rests with the employer; he should have appropriate medical advice. Each case must be judged on its merits in the light of all available information. Any attempt to advise management without a sound and complete understanding of the employee's personal and medical circumstances and of the exact requirements of the job is unfair to both employee and employer. Each employee with epilepsy must be regularly reviewed. The development of good rapport and mutual trust will encourage the employee to report any changes in his condition or medication and discuss any anxieties that have developed.

A sensible approach by management, with access to medical advice, should help the individual to come to terms with his condition, to appreciate the reasons for any restrictions, and to understand that decisions taken on the basis of such medical advice are in his best interests. The employer should drop old prejudices in favour of current concepts about epilepsy. This will only occur when all those concerned with epilepsy undertake the responsibility of educating employers, the general public, and perhaps some members of the medical profession.

Appendix

CENTRES FOR EPILEPSY

In Britain there are a number of schools and centres for epilepsy which incorporate sheltered workshops. Their origins are diverse and their support

---

*The Department of Transport's Medical Advisory Branch will usually advise one year's abstention from non-professional driving, but a bar on professional driving. However, advice should be sought from them on individual patients in this group [Dr J. Taylor, DOT].

similarly varied. Although all are independent of the British Epilepsy Association (p. 230), this body collates information about them and will advise on the appropriateness of a centre to the needs of an individual patient. A description of one centre follows.

The Chalfont Centre for Epilepsy

This centre is associated with the National Hospital for Nervous Diseases, Queen Square, London, and the National Society for Epilepsy. Referrals are usually from hospital consultants. The main function is assessment, rehabilitation, and support. A therapeutic work-centre operates as an assessment unit and is fully staffed with instructors. This unit trains people to work situations rather than specific skills. The majority work according to their abilities and inclinations on the farm, in the market gardens, or in the service departments, such as laundry, catering, maintenance, and domestic cleaning. The residents perform useful and satisfying jobs while reducing the financial burden on the local authority.

The National Society for Epilepsy (NSE)

The National Society for Epilepsy (NSE) was established in 1892 and is one of the oldest British charities devoted to furthering the interests and welfare of people with epilepsy. The headquarters of the NSE are situated at the Chalfont Centre and the society is funded largely from maintenance fees paid by local authorities, the DHSS, and fund-raising projects. The NSE provides support for epilepsy research, and current projects include the assessment of newly developed anticonvulsants and the prevention of drug toxicity. In June 1982 an Education and Information Service was established. This now provides well-thought-out information packages for health care professionals and teachers.

Many other special centres exist through the country and provide a similar range of activities (Appendix 5).

Most of these specialized centres are residential. Facilities also exist for sheltered work in a non-residential setting. Expert advice is obtainable about these from the Area Disablement Resettlement Officer (DRO) or the local Employment Medical Advisory Service (EMAS). The DRO can be contacted through the job centre; he will give advice about local authority sheltered workshops which are usually attached to psychiatric hospitals, as well as work in the Remploy network, or Employment Rehabilitation Centres (see Chapter 2).

Many of these organizations allow the patient to adjust to a work routine and gain useful skills. The less severely affected may eventually graduate into a non-sheltered, fully commercial job.

Regardless of education and skill, many people with epilepsy still require considerable help in obtaining employment. An example of this is the work of the Epilepsy Foundation of America which sponsors a Training and Placement Service especially for people with epilepsy. This service recognizes two major factors which hold back the skilled and educated person with epilepsy from employment. The first is a combination of a poor attitude demonstrated by the candidate, and inefficient job seeking skills. Many job applicants with epilepsy are found to be hostile, suspicious, and inexperienced in interview techniques. The second factor is the actual job-finding and placement efforts of the rehabilitation programme. Employers will recruit applicants with epilepsy if they can be assured of appropriate referrals. It is also desirable for the referral agency to maintain continued contact with their employed clients. Sheltered workshops and rehabilitation programmes must concentrate on these two factors, in addition to the more traditional ones, if they hope to integrate their clients into the working community.

THE WORK OF THE BRITISH EPILEPSY ASSOCIATION

Established in 1950, the British Epilepsy Association is concerned with the interests of people with epilepsy, their families, and professionals working with them. Services are provided by highly competent staff based at headquarters in Leeds and regional offices in Belfast, Birmingham, and Cardiff. The Epilepsy Research Fund supports scientific work in epilepsy. The Association is governed by a Board elected from the membership, and is a registered charity and limited company. Government and local authorities provide some financial help, and support is also received from trusts and companies. Members support the Association through their individual subscriptions and donations. Contact with the Association can be made by visits, telephone, or letter. The Association is able to undertake domiciliary visiting, mainly for the purpose of counselling. The professional members of the Association are competent, experienced, and enthusiastic. Much of their time is spent dealing with problems that result from ignorance and prejudice, not only from employers, teachers, parents, and relatives, but often from the sufferers themselves. The Association's major task is the field of education about epilepsy. It is 'attitudes towards epilepsy' that it is attempting to modify: these are frequently a much greater problem than the medical management of the disorder itself.

The Association provides useful literature at little cost, and produces a magazine with topical news and informative articles. Expert and specific advice is also freely available on employment, schooling, treatment, welfare rights, driving licence applications, holidays, and financial aid. If staff are unable to answer a query immediately, every effort is made to uncover the information required without delay.

REFERENCES

1. Verity CM, Butler NR, Golding J. Febrile convulsions in a national cohort followed up from birth. Br Med J 1985;**290**:1307–14.
2. Johnson LC, de Bolt WL, Long MT, et al. Diagnostic factors in adult males following initial seizures: a three year follow up. Arch Neurol 1972;**27**:193–7.
3. Cleland PJ, Mosquera I, Steward WP, et al. Prognosis of isolated seizures in adult life. Br Med J 1981;**283**:1364.
4. Hauser WA, Anderson VE, Lowenson RB, et al. Seizure recurrence after a first unprovoked seizure. N Engl J Med 1982;**307**:522–8.
5. Elwes RDC, Chesterman P, Reynolds EH. Prognosis after a first untreated tonic-clonic seizure. Lancet 1977;**i**:183–6.
6. Annegers JF, Shirts SB, Hauser WA, Kurland LT. Risk of recurrence after an initial unprovoked seizure. Epilepsia 1986;**27**:43–50.
6a. Hopkins A, Garman A, Clarke C. The first seizure in adult life: value of clinical features, electroencephalography and computerised tomographic scanning in prediction of seizure recurrence. Lancet 1988;**i**:721–6.
7. Hopkins A, Scambler G. How doctors deal with epilepsy. Lancet 1985;**ii**:183–6.
8. Research Committee of the Royal College of General Practitioners. A survey of the epilepsies in general practice. Br Med J 1960;**ii**:416–22.
9. Hauser WA, Kurland LT. The epidemiology of epilepsy in Rochester, Minnesota through 1967. Epilepsia 1975;**16**:1–66.
10. Goodridge DMG, Shorvon SD. Epileptic seizures in a population of 6000. Br Med J 1983;**287**:641–4.
11. Hauser WA, Annegers JF, Anderson VE. Epidemiology and the genetics of epilepsy. In: Ward AA, Penry JK, Purpura D, eds. Epilepsy. New York: Raven, 1983.
12. Hopkins AP. Epilepsy—the facts. Oxford: Oxford University Press, 1981.
13. Rodin EA. The prognosis of patients with epilepsy. Springfield: Charles Thomas, 1968.
14. Annegers JF, Hauser WA, Elveback LR. Remission of seizures and relapse in patients with epilepsy. Epilepsia 1979;**20**:729–37.
15. Jennett WB. Epilepsy after non-missile head injuries. 2nd ed. London: William Heinemann, 1975.
16. Jennett WB. Epilepsy after head injury and intracranial surgery. In: Hopkins A ed. Epilepsy. London: Chapman and Hall, 1987:399–409.
17. Hopkins A, Garman A. The causes and precipitation of seizures. In: Hopkins A, ed. Epilepsy. London: Chapman and Hall, 1987:116–36.
18. Dasgupta AK, Saunders M, Dick DJ. Epilepsy in the British Steel Corporation: an evaluation of sickness, accident, and work records. Br J Ind Med 1982;**39**:146–8.
19. Wilkinson RT. Hours of work and the 24 hour cycle of rest and activity. In: Warr PB ed. Psychology at work. Harmondsworth: Penguin, 1971:31–54.
20. Temkin NR, Davis GR. Stress as a risk factor of seizures among adults with epilepsy. Epilepsia 1984;**25**:450–6.
21. Jeavons PM, Harding GFA. Photosensitive epilepsy: a review of the literature and a study of 460 patients. Clinics in developmental medicine; Spastics International Publications, no 56. London: Heinemann, 1975.

22.   Wilkins AJ, Binnie CD, Darby CE. Visually induced seizures. Prog Neurobiol 1980;**15**:85–117.
23.   Binnie CD. Electroencephalography and epilepsy. In: Hopkins A ed. Epilepsy. London: Chapman and Hall, 1987:169–99.
24.   Masland RL. Employability, Part VIII, Social aspects. In: Rose C ed. Research progress in epilepsy. London: Pitman, 1983:527–32.
25.   Thompson PJ. The effects of anticonvulsant drugs on the cognitive functioning of normal volunteers and patients with epilepsy. London: University of London, 1981. Ph.D. thesis.
26.   Thompson PJ, Trimble MR. Sodium valproate and cognitive functioning in normal volunteers. Br J Clin Pharmacol 1981;**12**:819–24.
27.   Thompson PJ, Huppert FA, Trimble MR. Phenytoin and cognitive function: effects on normal volunteers and implications for epilepsy. Br J Clin Psychol 1981;**20**:155–62.
28.   Scambler G, Hopkins AP. Social class, epileptic activity and disadvantage at work. J Epidemiol Community Health 1980;**34**:129–33.
29.   The performance of physically impaired workers in manufacturing industries. US Dept of Labor Bulletin no 293. Washington: US Government Printing Office, 1948.
30.   Udell MM. The work performance of epileptics in industry. Arch Environ Health 1960;**1**:257–64.
31.   Betts T. Employment of people with epilepsy within the National Health Service. In: Edwards F, Espir M, Oxley J, eds. Epilepsy and employment. International Congress and Symposium Series no 86. London: Royal Society of Medicine Services, 1986:59–65.
32.   Hicks RA, Hicks MJ. The attitudes of major companies towards the employment of epileptics: an assessment of 2 decades of change. Am Correct Ther J 1978;**32**:180–2.
33.   Carter T. Health and safety at work: implications of current legislation. In: Edwards F, Espir M, Oxley J, eds. Epilepsy and employment. International Congress and Symposium Series no 86. London: Royal Society of Medicine Services, 1986:9–17.
34.   Health and Safety at Work etc. Act. London: HMSO, 1974: Chapter 37.
35.   Occupational Pensions Board. Occupational pension scheme cover for disabled people. London: HMSO, 1977. (Cmnd 6849).
36.   Conditions on UK Driving Licence. London: Department of Transport, 1982.

13

Diabetes mellitus

R. H. Greenwood and P. A. B. Raffle

Classification of diabetes

For practical clinical purposes there are two types of diabetes:

1. *Insulin-dependent diabetes mellitus (IDDM)*, or type I diabetes. The cause is not known but it may result from viral damage to pancreatic islet beta cells in genetically susceptible individuals. Autoimmunity may also play a part and islet cell antibodies can be demonstrated in most subjects. It can occur at any age, although most of those diagnosed under 20 years of age are of this type.

2. *Non-insulin-dependent diabetes mellitus (NIDDM)*, or type II diabetes. It has a strong genetic component but the cause in most cases is not known. It affects predominantly those over 30 years of age. Approximately two-thirds of diabetics are of this type.

Diabetes and employment

Diabetes remains poorly understood and is sometimes feared by employers and even by their medical advisers. As a result, significant numbers of diabetics encounter largely unjustifiable difficulties in finding work because of their condition.[1] There is an almost total absence of recently published data on the work implications for diabetics in general or in particular situations, for example in shift work. There is an urgent need to familiarize employers both with the condition itself and also with such published data as are available which suggest that the work record of diabetics is good and that they make perfectly satisfactory employees in a wide variety of occupations.[2]

PREVALENCE, MORBIDITY, AND MORTALITY

Prevalence of diabetes

The overall prevalence of insulin-dependent diabetes in the United Kingdom is of the order of 3.5 per 1000 population.[3] It increases with age: for children below the age of 16 the prevalence is around 1.42 per 1000.[4] Most series show some preponderance of males, but this sex difference is not marked. The prevalence of non-insulin-dependent diabetes is 10–12 per 1000.[5,6] Its annual incidence has been found to be between 10 and 23 per 100 000, the higher figures being found in areas with poor socio-economic conditions.[7]

Morbidity and mortality of diabetes

The scale of the morbidity of diabetes cannot be estimated accurately, although it is said to be the commonest cause of blindness in the working age-group.[8] Heart disease and stroke are increased by a factor of two to three; diabetes is the second leading cause of fatal kidney disease; and a diabetic is twenty times more likely to need an amputation than a non-diabetic.[9] It should be emphasized, however, that only a minority of diabetics develop disabling complications. Nevertheless, life expectancy is reduced in all age-groups, mainly as a result of renal failure and vascular disease.[10] There is great variation, however, and many diabetics live for 40 years or more after the onset of the disease without developing serious complications. Improved methods of control of diabetes and more effective treatment for end-stage renal failure are likely to improve the prognosis, but some years must elapse before the extent of the benefit is known.

CLINICAL ASPECTS AFFECTING WORK CAPACITY

Management of insulin-dependent diabetics

For most insulin-dependent diabetics, acceptable control of blood glucose should be possible throughout 24 hours by adjusting the relative proportion of short- and medium-acting insulins, a combination of which is usually injected twice a day before meals. In older individuals, and in those in whom the condition is unusually mild, a single daily injection of a long-acting insulin may suffice. It has so far proved impossible in routine clinical practice to administer insulin by any route other than subcutaneous injection. However, the use of miniature electric infusion pumps and pen-injector devices to deliver insulin more accurately in relation to meals offers the prospect of better diabetic control, more flexibility with regard to eating patterns, and may possibly reduce the risk of complications. The use of pen-injector devices is becoming more widespread and this could have an important impact on some employment problems: for example, variations in routine resulting from shiftwork might become easier to manage.

Management of non-insulin-dependent diabetics

Non-insulin-dependent diabetics are managed with diet alone or diet and oral hypoglycaemic drugs. They are frequently obese: the main objective of diet is to reduce body-weight, principally by controlling fat intake, although excessive intake of refined carbohydrates is not advisable. High fibre intake seems to be beneficial for all diabetics, as fibre appears to delay glucose absorption and reduce blood glucose excursions. Oral hypoglycaemic drugs are of two types:

1. *Biguanides*, for example metformin. Biguanides appear to act by reducing glucose absorption from the gut, reducing glucose release from the liver, and enhancing glucose uptake by the tissues. They are not very potent and they do not cause symptomatic hypoglycaemia.

2. *Sulphonylureas*, for example glibenclamide, chlorpropamide, tolbutamide, glipizide. The sulphonylureas act mainly by stimulating insulin release, although they also enhance tissue uptake of glucose. They are more powerful and chlorpropamide and glibenclamide may cause mild hypoglycaemia, especially after unaccustomed exercise, high alcohol consumption, and/or inadequate food intake. This appears to be less common with shorter-acting sulphonylureas, such as tolbutamide or glipizide.

Newer concepts of control

With the realization that careful control of diabetes can reduce the risk of long-term complications[11] increasing emphasis is now placed on achieving not only clinical well-being but also near-normal blood glucose levels. Self-monitoring of blood glucose is replacing time-honoured urine testing, especially in younger insulin-treated diabetics. The main advantages of blood testing are that it more accurately reflects diabetic control and is not subject to variations in the renal threshold for glucose; and that it gives information on low blood glucose levels, as well as high, and can thus give warning of impending hypoglycaemia. It is also more aesthetically acceptable to many patients. Blood glucose strips have recently been included in the drug tariff and will become more readily available than at present. Careful regulation of insulin dosage together with blood glucose monitoring should reduce the risk of hypoglycaemia and enable individuals to cope more easily with variations in daily work patterns. It may also reduce the incidence of long-term complications. For these reasons, blood glucose testing should be valuable for some insulin-treated patients who might otherwise experience difficulty in coping with certain types of employment, for example those involving shiftwork.

SPECIAL WORK PROBLEMS CAUSED BY DIABETES

The work record of diabetics

Accurate information on the effect of diabetes on attendance at work and work performance is difficult to obtain. Like all occupational populations, diabetics studied in industry are to a certain extent self-selected, in that those who continue in a given workforce are less likely to have developed disabling complications than those who leave it. Because of concealment of the disease it is seldom possible to be sure that all diabetics in a given population have been recognized, while conversely some diabetics attribute all unfavourable events in their lives to the disease. These difficulties should always be remembered when appraising published work on the subject.

The results of the first major survey of diabetics in employment was published over 30 years ago.[12] In a survey of 63 American companies, widespread ignorance and prejudice was encountered. The authors made a plea for more education of management, unions, and patients; they also called for closer co-operation between the diabetics' own physicians and the occupational health services.

In a questionnaire survey of 3430 members of the British Diabetic Association in a wide variety of occupations,[13] Jackson established that 46 per cent of men and 35 per cent of women had no sick leave during the previous year; amongst the remainder many had time off for reasons unrelated to their diabetes. Some studies have indicated that the work record of diabetics compares favourably with that of non-diabetics,[14,15] while others have indicated an increased rate of sickness absence amongst diabetics in industry.[16-18] The majority of diabetics seem to have good work records. Indeed in a study of 108 diabetics amongst 8000 employees of a chemical firm in the USA,[19] diabetics had *less* sickness absence than non-diabetics, perhaps because they were more strongly motivated to work normally. The apparent excess of sickness absence in some studies may be attributable to a small number of diabetics with serious complications.[12]

Working patterns and diabetic treatment

Irregular working hours have been considered to be a hazard for diabetics. Some employers feel that those treated with insulin are not able to cope with changing patterns of shiftwork. This has, for example, been given as a reason for not admitting diabetic girls to schools of nursing.[20] However, most sensible and well-motivated diabetics rapidly learn how to adjust their treatment, especially if they are measuring their own blood glucose levels and using multiple insulin-injection techniques. Thus, shiftwork should not be an automatic bar to the employment of diabetics. One development worth watching, however, is the introduction, mainly at the behest of the unions, of shorter and shorter shift cycles, when, for instance, day, evening, and night shifts can follow each other at two-day intervals. This may test the ingenuity of the most intelligent insulin-dependent diabetic. These problems can occur in different types and grades of employment, for example supervisors and managers may also be required to undertake shiftwork or work irregular hours.

Diabetic coma

Many of the more important employment problems in diabetics can be related, directly or indirectly, to the fear of diabetic coma. This unsatisfactory term covers both diabetic ketoacidosis and hypoglycaemia.

Diabetic ketoacidosis

This may occur if there is serious loss of control of diabetes, resulting in hyperglycaemia, dehydration, and acidosis due to the accumulation of ketones. The onset is usually gradual and it is not a cause of sudden collapse at work. It is the cause of significant sickness absence in a small number of individuals.

Hypoglycaemia

Hypoglycaemia can cause confusion and loss of consciousness and so it is a much more serious problem from the work standpoint. The majority of insulin-treated diabetics receive ample warning of impending hypoglycaemia, take preventive steps (i.e. take glucose) and experience neither loss of control nor unconsciousness. Yet in some insulin-treated diabetics, hypoglycaemia can develop suddenly and may lead to irrational behaviour, aggression, or even unconsciousness. For this reason many employers have reservations about diabetics working in potentially hazardous situations, for example at heights or near dangerous moving machinery. The majority of insulin-dependent diabetics very rarely experience serious hypoglycaemia and they usually carry glucose tablets which will rapidly restore the blood glucose level to normal. The risk of hypoglycaemia has certainly been exaggerated. Nevertheless, it is a factor which has to be considered by employers and occupational physicians when deciding on the placement of diabetics at work and ensuring that they are aware of appropriate preventive measures. It may be important for some diabetics to have regular work breaks when they can carry out blood or urine tests, consume snacks, or take insulin; and it may be sensible to avoid situations where an insulin-taking diabetic in a responsible position would be working entirely alone for long periods of time. Oral hypoglycaemic agents rarely cause significant hypoglycaemia and thus non-insulin-dependent diabetics are capable of most occupations. Sulphonylureas can, however, occasionally induce mild hypoglycaemia, especially after unaccustomed exercise or if a meal is missed. Because judgement or responses may be impaired, tablet-treated diabetics are currently barred from a few occupations, for example flying commercial aeroplanes and driving main-line passenger trains, unless they satisfy very stringent criteria with regard to diabetic control (see p. 241). The guiding principle must always be to assess whether or not the development of hypoglycaemia might put the diabetic himself or others at risk.

Complications of diabetes

A relatively small proportion of diabetics develop long-term complications, usually after many years of diabetes. From the employment viewpoint the most important are cataracts and retinopathy which can lead to visual impairment and blindness; neuropathy, either sensory or autonomic (which may occasionally cause postural hypotension); nephropathy which can lead to renal failure, and foot ulceration which occasionally necessitates amputation. Furthermore, there is an increased incidence of cardiovascular disease in diabetics which can lead to heart attacks, strokes, and peripheral vascular disease. Even some treatment may cause problems: for example, pan-retinal photocoagulation, sometimes used in the treatment of retinopathy, may cause significant diminution in peripheral visual fields. However, few diabetics of working age develop these severe and disabling complications. Recent evidence suggests that careful control of the diabetes from the outset, along the lines discussed above, will reduce their incidence and severity. Those individuals who hold driving licences and develop significant complications should be advised to notify these to the licensing authorities. They are, however, often able to continue employment.

Superannuation

Difficulty in arranging associated life insurance is sometimes given as a reason for not employing a diabetic. This is not usually a problem in medium or larger sized organizations, where group life insurance schemes can include diabetics without requiring any medical evidence or additional premium. Problems may arise in smaller firms where employees have to be assessed individually, or in larger organizations where the salary of a highly paid executive may rise above the 'free cover level' and attract additional premiums. The attitude of different insurance companies to diabetes can vary considerably.[21] If a diabetic is penalized by a particular insurance company or scheme and this is a major obstacle to his employment, then he should be able to opt out and arrange his own cover with another company, if necessary paying additional insurance premiums himself. Unfortunately, however, many employers are not prepared to offer this flexibility with regard to insurance and superannuation and this remains a cause of employment problems for some diabetics. The British Diabetic Association can give useful advice on insurance matters.

Advisory services

The diabetic specialists, family practitioners, and occupational health services should be able to give advice in cases of employment difficulty. The specialist and/or family practitioner can provide detailed medical information, whilst the occupational physician is in a unique position to assess the suitability of a diabetic for a particular occupation, or of a particular occupation for a diabetic. In some instances, problems might be prevented if blood glucose testing facilities were provided by the occupational health service so that monitoring could be continued at the workplace. Some diabetic clinics have specialist nurses, who can liaise directly with occupational health services. The British Diabetic Association may be able to assist both diabetics and employers by clarifying the employment implications of diabetes in specific situations. Disablement Resettlement Officers and the Manpower Services Commission may be able to help the minority of diabetics with disabling complications. Careers officers and teachers should be able to advise diabetic school leavers about employment and the British Diabetic Association is currently attempting to familiarise careers advisers more fully with the condition.

EXISTING LEGISLATION AND GUIDELINES FOR EMPLOYMENT

Road Traffic Acts and diabetes

British Statutory Law places an obligation on all British applicants for a driving licence to notify their condition and also on British licence holders to inform DVLC, Swansea, as soon as the diagnosis is confirmed, if it has been confirmed previously and has not been notified, or if any complications develop which may affect driving. Late notifications to the Licensing Centre are not prosecuted, but failure to notify can have serious implications for motor insurance. Doctors have a responsibility to remind their patients of these obligations which stem from the 1972 Road Traffic Act (amended 1974). The Courts, including the Court of Appeal, treat insulin as a drug within the meaning of the Road Traffic Act 1972, so that an insulin-treated diabetic driving while hypoglycaemic runs the risk of being found guilty of driving under the influence of drugs.

Heavy goods and public service vehicle licences and diabetes

Drivers of heavy goods vehicles and public service vehicles (vocational drivers) must obtain an additional licence (HGV or PSV) from the licensing authorities in the traffic areas in which they live. The authorities have discretion in the application of standards for vocational licences to individual cases, but usually follow international agreements. The WHO Expert Committee on Diabetes Mellitus (second Report 1980) recommends that insulin-treated diabetics should not drive vocationally.[9] The EEC Driving Licence Directive (80/1263/EEC), which incorporates the United Nations

Agreement on minimum requirements for the issue and validity of driving permits (Geneva 1975), states that a Group 2 (vocational) driving licence 'shall not be granted ... for applicants ... who are diabetics needing insulin treatment': its terms are binding on the UK. This standard is also the policy of the licensing authorities. The British Diabetic Association strongly advises insulin-treated diabetics against attempting to take employment requiring a vocational licence. There is no comparable policy for diabetics not taking insulin.

Professional drivers and diabetes

Apart from vocational drivers, many other individuals drive for a living. Local authorities and the Metropolitan Police have their own licensing requirements for taxi drivers and car hire drivers: a substantial number apply medical standards, similar to those for public service vehicle drivers. The standard of fitness of emergency police, fire engine, and ambulance drivers is the special responsibility of their employing authorities, most of which would apply the vocational (HGV and PSV) licence standards.

Vocational drivers who develop diabetes

The situation for existing vocational drivers depends again on the type of diabetes and whether the licence was issued before or after 1 January 1983. A vocational driver who has uncomplicated diabetes which is treated with diet or with oral anti-diabetic preparations would usually be expected to continue driving vocationally. The British Diabetic Association believes that insulin-treated diabetics who currently hold vocational licences should be reviewed individually when they apply for renewal, where necessary with the help of specialist advice. The EEC Directive states, however, that vocational licences 'shall not be ... renewed for ... drivers who are diabetics requiring insulin treatment' and its terms are binding on the United Kingdom. This provision does not apply, however, to the renewal of licences first granted before the directive came into force on 1 January 1983, so that a licence may be renewed under the conditions prevailing at the time it was first issued. The non-insulin-dependent vocational driver who has to change over to insulin should stop driving and report the fact to the licensing authority who will consider whether the circumstances justify the exercise of discretion.

Ordinary driving licences and diabetes

Ordinary driving licence holders not receiving insulin injections, who are free of diabetic complications, and not otherwise impaired, can expect to continue to hold licences. The status of such patients may alter, however, if they develop complications or change to insulin therapy. Even insulin-dependent diabetics can reasonably expect to be issued with and continue to hold an ordinary driving licence, although it will be restricted to three years' duration and subject to certain conditions: they must not be disqualified by other conditions or by complications of diabetes, their diabetes must be under reasonable control, their understanding of the condition and its treatment must be adequate, and they must not be subject to attacks of disabling hypoglycaemia.

Concealment of diabetes

No driver should conceal diabetes from an employer or from the employer's insurance company: in the event of an accident, failure to have declared the condition may have serious legal or financial consequences. Whatever the type of diabetes and whatever the class of driving, a licence holder must notify the development of a complication, a deterioration in health, or a deterioration in diabetic control to the licensing authority so that his fitness to continue holding a licence can be considered.

Existing guidance for employers and occupational health services

Broadly similar guidance has been published both by the British Diabetic Association[22] and the American Diabetes Association.[23] The current situation can be summarized as follows:

1. Diabetics treated with diet alone should be able to undertake virtually any occupation.

2. Diabetics treated with diet and tablets can undertake most occupations although they are not currently allowed to join the armed services, the police, the fire brigade, and not usually to pilot transport aeroplanes. The criteria relating to main line train driving have recently been relaxed. This occupation is now permitted to diabetics on oral treatment, who are well controlled, under regular specialist supervision, who monitor their blood glucose levels, and who do not suffer from any significant complication or experience hypoglycaemia. Vocational drivers with uncomplicated diabetes which is well controlled by diet alone or with oral anti-diabetic preparations are usually able to continue driving heavy goods vehicles and public service vehicles. Serving merchant seamen may be allowed to remain at sea subject to six-monthly medical review.

3. Diabetics treated with insulin may be prone to hypoglycaemia: in most patients this does not cause problems. They should not, however, work in situations where sudden attacks could endanger themselves or others. For

this reason they are not usually permitted to hold HGV or PSV licences, nor may they fly airplanes, drive trains, or continue as seafarers or divers. It may be undesirable for them to work in potentially hazardous surroundings, for example at heights or near dangerous moving machinery (although this should be interpreted with caution because almost any machine could be construed as potentially dangerous). They may be barred from certain occupations (for instance railway signalman, electricity generating station operator) because of the risk to the safety of the operation of diminished vigilance while working alone in such critical situations for long periods.

CONCLUSIONS AND RECOMMENDATIONS

Although the sickness record of diabetics is comparable to that of non-diabetics, there is evidence of continuing employment prejudice against diabetics. This seems to be due in part to ignorance and fear of the condition among employers and their medical and personnel advisers.

Much of the published information on the work record of diabetics is at least 10 years old and most of it originates from the United States.[12,14-19] Very little information about employment and diabetes has been obtained in the United Kingdom[1,13] and there is a need for up-to-date surveys in this country. Moreover, information is needed on the impact of particular work activities on diabetic control and vice versa: shiftwork and driving are important examples. Because of the paucity of definitive information, the advice given to diabetics is often arbitrary and decisions are made with little supporting evidence.

The introduction of finger-prick blood glucose testing and new methods of treatment which result in improved control, for example insulin pumps and pen-injectors, may enable diabetics to cope more easily with irregular work patterns and may in time reduce morbidity and mortality.

Careers officers and teachers need to become more knowledgeable about diabetes so that they can give school-leavers accurate advice and enable them to make sensible career plans.

A concerted effort should be made to educate employers and persuade them to take a more compassionate view of diabetics.

Many pension schemes still exclude diabetics and this is a frequent cause of employment difficulties. Many insurance companies now take a more liberal view of diabetics and so an individual should be able to make his own pension arrangements if rejected by a group scheme. Employers should be encouraged to allow more flexible pension arrangements and this should reduce the occurrence of this distressing problem.

It is essential that each individual case be assessed on its own merits with full consultation between all medical advisers. Diabetes *per se* should not limit employment prospects, for the majority of diabetics have few, if any, problems arising from the condition and make perfectly satisfactory employees in a wide variety of occupations.

REFERENCES

1. Hutchison SJ, Kesson CM, Slater SD. Does diabetes affect employment prospects? Br Med J 1983;**287**:349–50.
2. Lister J. The employment of diabetics. J Soc Occ Med 1982;**32**:153–8.
3. Hedley AJ, Jones RB, Gale EAM, Tattersall RB. Prevalence of insulin treated diabetes mellitus. Br Med J 1982;**285**:509.
4. Calnan M, Peckham CS. The incidence of insulin-dependent diabetes in the first sixteen years of life. Lancet 1977;**i**:589–90.
5. Reid DD, Brett GZ, Hamilton PJS, Jarrett RJ, Keen H, Rose GA. Cardio-respiratory disease and diabetes among middle-aged civil servants. Lancet 1974;**i**:469–73.
6. Yudkin JS, Boucher BJ, Scopfein KE, *et al.* The quality of diabetic care in a London Health District. J Epidemiol and Community Health 1980;**34**:277–80.
7. Barker DJP, Gardner MJ, Power C. Incidence of diabetes amongst people aged 18–50 years in nine British towns; a collaborative study. Diabetologia 1982;**22**:421–5.
8. Kohner EM, McCleod D, Marshall J. Diabetic eye disease. In: Keen H, Jarrett J, eds. Complications of Diabetes. 2nd ed. London: Edward Arnold, 1982: 14–95.
9. World Health Organization. Expert Committee on Diabetes Mellitus, second report. Technical Report Series 646. Geneva: World Health Organization, 1980.
10. Goodkin G. Mortality factors in diabetes. J Occ Med 1975;**17**:716–21.
11. West KM. Hyperglycaemia as a cause of long-term complications. In: Keen H, Jarrett J, eds. Complications of diabetes. 2nd ed. London: Edward Arnold, 1982: 13–18.
12. Brandaleone H, Friedman GJ. Diabetes in industry. Diabetes 1953;**2**:448–53.
13. Jackson JGL. Employment Survey. London: British Diabetic Association, 1961.
14. Beardwood J. Industry's role in the employment of diabetics. Ind Med and Surg 1950;**19**:271–277.
15. Dublin LI, Marks HH. The diabetic in industry and his employer. Ind Med and Surg 1950;**19**:279–82.
16. Pell S, D'Alonzo CA. Sickness and injury experience of employed diabetics. Diabetes 1960;**9**:303–10.
17. Nasr ANM, Block DL, Magnuson HJ. Absenteeism experience in a group of employed diabetics. J Occ Med 1966;**8**:621–5.
18. Pell, S, D'Alonzo CA. Sickness absenteeism in employed diabetics. Am J Public Health 1967;**57**:253–60.
19. Moore RH, Buschbom RL. Work absenteeism in diabetics. Diabetes 1974;**23**:957–61.
20. Bagshaw E. Careers for diabetic girls in nursing. Br Med J 1980;**280**:1227.

21. Frier B, Sullivan FM, Stewart EJC. Diabetes and insurance: a survey of patient experience. Diabetic Medicine 1984;1:127–30.
22. The employment of diabetics. Diabetic Medicine 1984;1:308.
23. Mastbaum L, Tetrick L, Alexander RW. Physicians guidelines for employment and placement of the diabetic in industry—an update. J Occ Med 1980;22: 601–2.

14

Gastrointestinal and liver disorders

C. White and R. J. Wyke

INTRODUCTION

The gastrointestinal tract and liver are subject to many disease processes, several of which can affect employment and result in large numbers of consultations with general practitioners, referrals to hospital specialists, and hospital admissions. Digestive diseases were responsible for 11.5 million days of sickness or invalidity absence in Great Britain between June 1984 and May 1985. Men experienced more lost days (9.4 m.) than women (2.1 m.). Levels of incapacity were highest in Scotland and lowest in East Anglia.

Despite this, there have been very few studies of the influence of diseases of the gastrointestinal tract or liver on work. The opinions expressed in this chapter are derived from the limited published work, our own experience in clinical and occupational medicine, and detailed discussions with specialist colleagues. Conditions likely to cause employment problems, or risks to individuals and the public, are:

- gastro-oesophageal reflux and hiatus hernia,
- peptic ulceration,
- acute and chronic liver disease,
- inflammatory bowel disease,
- ileostomy and colostomy,
- gastroenteritis and infestations of the gut,
- functional disorders (non-ulcer dyspepsia, irritable bowel syndrome),
- coeliac disease,
- chronic pancreatitis.

OESOPHAGEAL REFLUX AND HIATUS HERNIA

The most common conditions affecting the oesophagus are oesophageal reflux and hiatus hernia. Oesophageal reflux is experienced at some time by

10 per cent of Americans and, with appropriate positioning during barium meal, most people over 40 can be shown to have a hiatus hernia.[1] Only a small number of these patients have symptoms and the precise relation between hiatus hernia and reflux is not clear. Morbidity is difficult to estimate but mortality is extremely low.

Oesophageal reflux and heartburn are made worse by bending, especially when this is accompanied by heavy lifting. Symptoms often improve with simple measures such as stopping smoking, weight reduction, wearing looser clothes, and antacid therapy. Patients with severe persistent reflux may develop oesophagitis and oesophageal strictures which, if symptomatic, may require dilation under sedation or, in extreme cases, surgery. Surgery is also undertaken to control severe persistent reflux in severely incapacitated cases unresponsive to intensive medical therapy. Time off work will depend on the incision used and type of work and is discussed in Chapter 20.

Special work problems

The following types of work may produce symptoms in some individuals with these conditions:

(1)   frequent bending;

(2)   lifting and carrying heavy or awkward loads;

(3)   pulling and pushing of heavy loads;

(4)   work involving stooping, crouching, or working in confined spaces, e.g. maintenance fitters, plumbers.

Although the effects of increases in intra-abdominal pressure and stooping can be reduced by correct lifting or adaptation of the work place, the effect on symptoms is variable.

PEPTIC ULCERATION

Prevalence and incidence

Peptic ulceration is the most important organic gastrointestinal disease in many western countries, affecting at some time approximately 10 per cent of all adult males. During the 1970s there was a fall in hospital admissions and in deaths from peptic ulcer, both of which occur mainly in the elderly patient.[2] The reasons for this change are not clear but it may be due to the influence of modern treatment. Although declining, the resultant sickness absence, morbidity, and mortality are still substantial. In the year 1982–83, 2.7 million working days were lost in England and Wales as a result of ulcer of the stomach and duodenum.[3] Such certification may not be based on an accurate diagnosis and could include functional disorder of the gut. There is no evidence of any link between occupation and peptic ulceration.[4]

Prevalence of peptic ulcers is difficult to obtain as the only accurate way would be to perform endoscopy or barium meals on the whole population. Data from 13 000 autopsies in Leeds, reported in 1960, showed that 13 per cent of men and 5 per cent of women over the age of 35 suffered from duodenal ulceration, and 3.9 per cent and 2.9 per cent respectively from gastric ulceration.[5] Doll and Avery-Jones'[6] survey of factory workers in London (1951) showed that 5.8 per cent of men and 1.9 per cent of women aged 15–64 years had peptic ulceration. A study of a static population in Aberdeen (1968) showed that 8 per cent of males aged 15–64 years had peptic ulcers.[7]

During this century the incidence of gastric ulcer has declined and that of duodenal ulcer has risen. The ratio of men to women affected has also decreased and currently stands at 2:1 for duodenal and 0.9:1 for gastric ulcer.[8] The incidence of perforation of a gastric ulcer has decreased; this now occurs chiefly in the elderly, and may be associated with ingestion of non-steroidal anti-inflammatory drugs.

The annual incidence rates for gastric ulcer are 42 per 100 000 in men and 45 per 100 000 in women, while duodenal ulcer occurs in 180 and 85 per 100 000 respectively.[8,9] There is a tendency for the incidence of peptic ulcers to increase with age. Prevalence rates are higher due to the finding of acute and chronic ulcers. Peptic ulcer disease is more prevalent in the North of England and Scotland[10] and among Social Classes IV and V.

Mortality

During the past 30 years there has been a decline in mortality from peptic ulceration among younger people. In 1984 in England and Wales death rates from ulcers of the stomach and duodenum were 85 per million for men and 95 per million for women.[11] Mortality was highest in elderly patients, rising from three deaths per million for men and one per million for women aged 15–34 years, to 115 and 55 per million respectively for those aged 55–64 years. There were more deaths from gastric ulcer among women than men, with a ratio of 1.6:1, but deaths from duodenal ulcer were about equal at 0.9:1. Although deaths are related to bleeding or perforation, more than half occur after surgery, especially in the elderly patient with intercurrent illness.[12]

Clinical aspects of peptic ulceration affecting work[13,14]

The most common complaint of patients with peptic ulceration is epigastric pain; less common are vomiting (more frequent with duodenal or pyloric ulceration), gastrointestinal bleeding, and perforation. Gastric and duodenal ulcers cannot be distinguished from the history alone and so barium meal radiography or endoscopic examination is necessary to establish the diagnosis. In patients with gastric ulcer, endoscopy has the advantage of enabling cytological and histological specimens to be obtained to exclude malignancy. Only a few hours off work is required for a barium meal radiographic examination, or for endoscopy performed without sedation (not so common in this country). If endoscopy is performed with sedation, and if the patient's work involves heavy machinery or driving duties, then 36 hours should be allowed before resuming normal work.

The clinical course of duodenal ulceration is one of spontaneous relapse and remission which can vary from a single episode to a progressive disease with few remissions and major complications. Major complications including haemorrhage, perforation, or pyloric stenosis, occur in 1 per cent per year of patients followed, and are commoner in the elderly. The clinical course of gastric ulceration tends to be more continuous and is more often associated with weight loss.

Work may be affected by episodes of abdominal pain, consequent loss of sleep, vomiting, and anaemia. The use of modern drug therapy, in particular histamine H2 antagonists, results in healing of 80 per cent of peptic ulcers in six weeks and should avoid loss of time from work. A course of medical treatment relieves symptoms and heals ulceration, but does not prevent further ulceration. Ulcers recur in 50 per cent of treated patients within two years, mainly in the first six months, and 25 per cent of these ulcers are asymptomatic.[13,14] Since most recurrent ulcers heal with further courses of drug treatment, how should these patients be managed over the long term?

Surgery should be considered if a gastric ulcer either fails to heal or recurs after a full course of eight weeks' medical therapy, as there is a fear of undiagnosed malignancy. With duodenal ulcer the choice is between treating each relapse with a course of medical treatment, or long-term maintenance treatment, and will depend on the individual patient. Hence, the otherwise fit patient who has three or four well-defined relapses of ulceration per year could be managed with a course of treatment for each relapse. On the other hand, long-term maintenance treatment might be more appropriate for patients with continuous symptoms or with short intervals between relapses. Patients with chronic medical conditions, particularly those requiring treatment with non-steroidal anti-inflammatory drugs or corticosteroids should also receive maintenance treatment. Even on maintenance therapy, approximately 10 per cent of duodenal ulcers relapse within one year.

Surgery is seldom necessary nowadays for uncomplicated duodenal ulcers and is reserved for the small proportion of patients who develop complications, or have symptomatic ulcers unresponsive to medical treatment, or for gastric ulcers which fail to heal. Surgical treatment (Chapter 20) may require from six weeks to three months absence from work, depending on the type of operation and the work. The most widely used operation is proximal gastric vagotomy or truncal vagotomy and drainage, with a mortality of 1 per cent or less and an ulcer recurrence of under 5 per cent.[15,16] In comparison, partial gastrectomy has a mortality of 4 per cent and a similar recurrence rate. Long-term complications of surgery are less common after proximal gastric vagotomy, but include dumping syndrome and intractable diarrhoea after eating, which can have serious consequences for work.[17] Patients may benefit from eating small dry meals and avoiding drinks containing carbohydrate. Other long-term complications, especially of partial gastrectomy, include anaemia, osteomalacia, and, with increasing time, a low risk of carcinoma of the gastric remnant.

Predisposing factors

Smoking and peptic ulceration

Smoking increases the susceptibility to ulcer diseases, impairs spontaneous and drug-induced healing, increases the risk and rapidity of recurrence and the likelihood of surgery.[18] Thus, patients with peptic ulcer should stop smoking.

Other conditions

Ingestion of aspirin, non-steroidal anti-inflammatory drugs (see above), and corticosteroids in high dose are generally accepted clinically as predisposing to the complications of peptic ulcer and dyspepsia, but evidence for causing ulceration is not conclusive. Patients with chronic renal failure on dialysis or following transplantation, however, have an increased frequency of peptic ulceration and there is probably an association with hepatic cirrhosis and hyperparathyroidism.

Special work problems

Generally, patients with peptic ulceration can pursue any type of work. There is no clear relation between peptic ulceration and stress but some patients experience exacerbations of symptoms during periods of stress and some may require long-term maintenance drug treatment or even surgery. A recent study suggests that men with peptic ulcers tend to perceive stressful life events more negatively and may exhibit more emotional distress in the form of anxiety.[19] If a patient works in isolation he may benefit from having other workers around him.

Shiftwork

Although there has been a steady increase in the number of people working shifts,[20] such work probably does not cause peptic ulcers[21] but in certain individuals may exacerbate symptoms. It has been suggested[22] that a person with a history of digestive tract disorder should be excluded from shiftwork because of irregular meals and other psychological problems, but this seems a rather extreme attitude especially in the context of modern drug therapy. Furthermore, although many shiftworkers report gastrointestinal disturbances, fewer than the expected number of deaths from gastrointestinal complaints were observed among shiftworkers when compared with national rates.[23] Perhaps shiftworkers are a self-selected group and people with significant gastrointestinal problems which tend to deteriorate with disturbed routine seek different work.

A not uncommon problem arises when someone has to work shifts either temporarily as part of in-service training, or due to unforeseen circumstances. Also, the financial rewards for working unsocial hours may make an employee with an exacerbation of peptic ulceration reluctant to change to less well paid but regular hours. Where peptic ulceration arises in a shiftworker consideration must be given to the advisability of returning to a normal shift, a period of medical treatment or, if repeated relapses occur, maintenance drug therapy or, if intractable, surgery.

Work in remote areas, in particular at sea

The question of work in remote places is difficult, as healed ulcers can recur. The risk is around one complication per 10 patient years but nearly zero for compliant patients on treatment. This suggests that such patients should be considered for maintenance treatment while working in remote areas. Under the Merchant Shipping Regulations,[24] seafaring should not be resumed until patients are free from symptoms without treatment for at least three months, have endoscopic evidence of healing, and are on a normal diet. Where there has been gastrointestinal bleeding, perforation, or recurrent peptic ulceration in spite of maintenance treatment with H2 blockers, or an unsatisfactory operation, the seafarer will be permanently unfit.[24] (See Appendix 3.)

ACUTE LIVER DISEASE

Acute viral hepatitis[25]

Hepatitis type A is responsible for 60 per cent of episodes of acute viral hepatitis in the UK, type B 27 per cent and non-A non-B 13 per cent.[26,27] There is confusion among lay people and some doctors as to modes of transmission and the relative hazard posed by patients with different types of hepatitis, as well as a lack of understanding of the interpretation of serological tests for hepatitis B which can result in people being regarded incorrectly as infectious.

Hepatitis A (infectious hepatitis)

This is caused by an enterovirus transmitted by the faecal-oral route and affects chiefly children, with only 20 per cent of cases in patients over 16 years of age.[27]

Prevalence

Children in institutions and adults in communities with poor sanitation, as in the Third World, are at highest risk. The prevalence is decreasing world-wide with improved standards of sanitation. Serological evidence of previous infection is found in 45 per cent of adults, and increases with age from less than 20 per cent in people under 30 to nearly 60 per cent in those over 45.[28] Most of them do not give a history of jaundice. Sporadic cases and epidemics are caused by eating virus-containing shellfish or cold food (particularly dairy products) contaminated by food-handlers during the prodrome of acute or anicteric hepatitis.

Clinical aspects affecting work

Hepatitis is anicteric in 50 per cent of cases and has an excellent prognosis with a mortality of less than 0.15 per cent, no progression to chronic liver disease and no carrier state.[25]

The incubation period is 21–40 days and the patient is infectious while virus is in the stools, i.e. two to three weeks before until not more than eight days after jaundice is apparent (Fig. 14.1). Hence the period of maximal infectivity occurs before the patient is symptomatic. Patients feel unwell during the prodrome but often improve with the onset of jaundice. Lethargy may continue for six weeks or as long as three months. Diagnosis is based on the detection in the serum of the IgM antibody to hepatitis A. The presence of the IgG type of antibody indicates either previous exposure to the virus or passive immunity from immune serum globulin or blood transfusion.

Special work problems

With the exception of food-handlers, patients can resume or continue all forms of work as soon as they feel fit.

Food-handlers must stay off work until jaundice has disappeared, or for one week after the onset of jaundice, whichever is the longer. Those with anicteric hepatitis should remain off work for one week after serum transaminases have reached a peak. It must be recognized that the patient will have been infectious during the asymptomatic phase and special efforts should be made to monitor other staff to detect contact cases. The most practical approach is to ask staff to report even minor indisposition, and to perform liver function

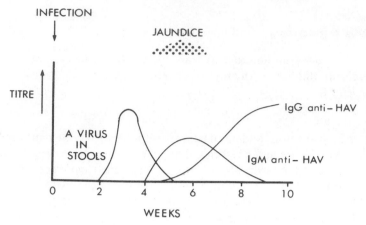

Fig. 14.1 Sequential appearance and disappearance of hepatitis A virus in stool and antibody (IgM and IgG anti-HAV) in the serum of a patient with acute hepatitis A. The infectious period (excretion of the virus) is normally before the development of jaundice.

tests and IgM hepatitis A serology on anyone with suspicious symptoms. This surveillance should be continued for 10 weeks after the index case is diagnosed. It is probably unnecessary to give unaffected staff immune globulin since this may attenuate symptoms without preventing virus excretion, but this should be discussed with the community physician.

Hepatitis A immune serum

Prophylaxis is appropriate for employees travelling to an endemic area and for close personal contacts of a sufferer, but not for office or work contacts. If possible, the potential recipient should be tested for serological evidence of previous infection (IgG HAV) as this makes immune serum unnecessary. This is important, as immune serum prophylaxis must be repeated every six months and one injection can cost more than serological screening.[29]

Hepatitis B (serum hepatitis)

This results from the transfer of the hepatitis virus in blood, blood products, or body fluids and secretions from an infected to a susceptible individual.[25] Transmission by blood transfusion is extremely rare in this country but drug addiction, tattooing, acupuncture, dental treatment, and homosexual practices are well-recognized means of transmission.

Horizontal transmission from person to person may result from sexual contact or sharing the same razor blade, toothbrush, or syringe. *Vertical transmission* from mother to child is particularly important in highly endemic areas such as the Far East. If the mother is a carrier of hepatitis B or suffers acute hepatitis during the third trimester, infection of the newborn infant is likely.

Incidence

In England and Wales approximately 2000 cases of acute hepatitis B were reported in 1984, 70 per cent in males.[30] Few cases occur in children and the elderly, with 50 per cent of cases aged 15–34 years. The incidence of acute hepatitis B in adults aged 15–65 years has been calculated at 6 per 100 000 for men and 2 per 100 000 for women.[30] The incidence is increasing in men but not in women. In the former this may in part be due to homosexual spread.

Mortality

Mortality from acute hepatitis B among adults aged 15–64 is about 0.6 per cent for men and 0.3 per cent for women, and tends to increase with age.

In the UK, approximately 3 per cent of the normal population have serological markers of previous exposure to hepatitis B. Approximately 10 per cent of patients, mainly men, progress to the carrier state with persisting hepatitis B viraemia. World-wide, however, there are estimated to be 200 million carriers, varying from less than 0.15 per cent of the UK population to 15 per cent in the Far East. The risk of becoming a carrier is highest after hepatitis in neonates.

Clinical aspects affecting work capacity

Acute hepatitis B has an incubation period of 3–6 months, with maximum infectivity during the late incubation and prodromal periods (Fig. 14.2). Clinical illness tends to be more severe than in hepatitis A, but over half of infections are mild and often anicteric. In addition to the normal features of hepatitis an urticarial rash and arthropathy, part of a serum sickness-like syndrome, are occasionally seen.

Serological markers of the hepatitis B virus indicate the stage of infection and the degree of infectivity. Serological findings in a typical case of acute type B hepatitis and progression to chronic infection are shown in Figures 14.2 and 14.3. The presence in patients' serum of hepatitis B surface (Australia) antigen (HBsAg) should be followed by clinical examination for features of acute or chronic liver disease and further tests for other serological markers of hepatitis B. The presence of antibody to the surface antigen (HBsAb) indicates previous contact with the hepatitis B virus or vaccination with development of immunity, but the patient is not infectious. High titres of the IgM antibody to core (IgM anti-HBc) denote an acute type B viral hepatitis (Fig. 14.2). The finding of hepatitis e antigen correlates with a high degree of infectivity, while antibody to e shows seroconversion with a low degree of infectivity. From a practical point of view the patient with a

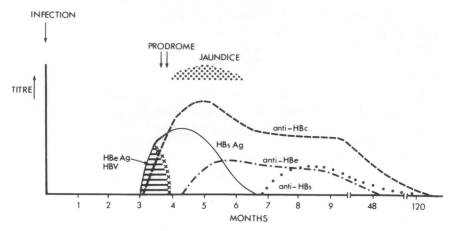

Fig. 14.2 Relation of serological markers and symptoms of hepatitis to infection with hepatitis B in an uncomplicated acute case. The period of maximum infectivity (shaded area) during which hepatitis B, viral DNA and HBe antigen are found in the serum is mainly immediately before jaundice develops. Note clearance of surface (HBsAg) and e antigens with formation of antibodies (anti-HBe and anti-HBs).

resolving acute hepatitis is not infectious once hepatitis B surface antigen (HBsAg) is no longer detectable in the blood.

Chronic carriers are those patients who fail to clear the surface antigen from the blood six months after acute hepatitis B (Fig. 14.3) and can be subdivided into:

1. *Simple carriers*: blood contains hepatitis B surface antigen in low titre and antibody to hepatitis e, but hepatitis B virus and DNA polymerase activity are absent. Such cases have a low infectivity.

2. *Super carriers*: blood contains high titre of hepatitis B surface antigen, e antigen, DNA polymerase activity, and hepatitis B viral DNA and is highly infectious.

Prognosis of carriers

Most carriers are in good health and able to work normally but should be referred to a hepatologist as 70 per cent have histological evidence of chronic liver disease, mainly chronic persistent hepatitis, and 10 per cent have cirrhosis.[31] In the long term they may seroconvert and liver diseases improve, but cases with persistent infection have a high risk of developing cirrhosis and hepatocellular carcinoma, which has a bad prognosis.[32] Strenuous efforts are being made to develop treatments for chronic carriers and make them clear the virus by means of immunotherapy and antiviral agents.[33]

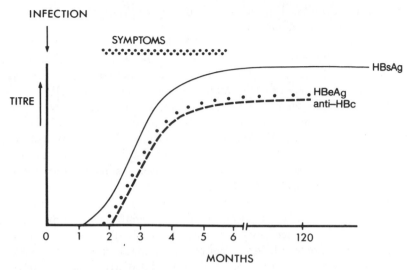

Fig. 14.3 Development of a hepatitis B carrier after acute hepatitis B. Note persistence in very high titre of surface (HBsAg) and e antigens, and antibody to core (anti-HBc); also absence of antibodies to hepatitis B surface (anti-HBs) and e (anti-HBe) antigens.

Time off work

During the acute phase the symptomatic patient will not feel well enough to work and usually rests at home. Convalescence should be approximately twice the period of bed rest.

Risk of spread of infection

There is no evidence of transmission of hepatitis B by casual contact in the workplace, or from contaminated food, water, or via airborne or faecal-oral routes. Spread of infection is likely only through intimate contact with the patient's blood, or body secretions, as occurs during sexual intercourse.

Prevention of hepatitis B[25]

Passive immunity can be provided by hepatitis B hyperimmune serum globulin but is only of value if administered prophylactically or within hours of infection (0.06 mg/kg IM). Such treatment is indicated only for victims of parenteral (needle stick) exposure to HBsAg-positive blood or body fluids, babies born to HBsAg-positive mothers, and sexual contacts of acute sufferers. The former are a particular hazard for health care workers. Blood from the victim and donor should be tested for serological markers of hepatitis B but do *not* wait for the result before instituting treatment with hyperimmune globulin. If possible, hepatitis B vaccination should be started at the same time as passive immunization.

Active immunization can be achieved by hepatitis B vaccine.[34] Although prepared from the plasma of hepatitis B carriers, the stringent purification processes make the vaccine totally safe and, in particular, there is no risk of transmission of the acquired immune deficiency syndrome (AIDS).[35] The vaccine should be given to people who are exposed regularly to, or at increased risk of contracting, hepatitis B; in particular certain health care personnel[36,37] (Table 14.1). However, vaccination of people at risk is not necessary if their serum contains antibody to hepatitis B surface (anti-HBs) or core (anti-HBc) antigen. The cost of vaccination is currently over £50 for a course of three injections but the recently introduced genetically engineered vaccine costs under £37. The costs must be considered in the context of preventing long-term complications and potential liability for compensation. Revaccination may be necessary in some individuals after five years, as levels of antibody are undetectable in 15 per cent or inadequate in 27 per cent after this time.[38] Injections should be made into the deltoid and not into the buttocks as there is less subcutaneous fat and a higher antibody response is obtained.

Special work problems of the hepatitis B carrier

The hepatitis B carrier is usually in good health and should not be treated as a hepatitis leper or barred from any type of work provided that simple measures are taken. The only risk is of accidental inoculation of his blood or body secretions into other people. Carriers should exercise care to avoid injury to hands, especially when preparing food, and must appreciate the importance of covering cuts and abrasions.

First aid

Concern is sometimes expressed over the action to be taken if carriers cut themselves. Like any normal individual, they should dress the wound and clean up any spilt blood with warm soapy water, then wipe the object or area thoroughly with a solution of household bleach to kill the virus. Food contaminated with blood as a result of the accident should be discarded for both hygienic and aesthetic reasons. With these provisos, the carrier can continue to work in all jobs including food-handling, catering, hairdressing, and teaching but should, of course, not act as a blood donor. Carriers should not be barred from using office equipment, toilets, shower, or eating facilities.

The specific problem of health care workers is more difficult.[39] Staff who are hepatitis B carriers are seldom a risk to their patients but should be excluded from renal dialysis and transplantation units. The case of dentists and surgeons requires special consideration, but for the former the wearing of rubber gloves has been shown to prevent transmission to patients. If the

Table 14.1 General indications for vaccination against hepatitis B[36, 37]

Health care staff
Surgical and dental staff
Hospital and laboratory staff in regular contact with blood or needles
Necropsy staff
Direct carers of hepatitis B carriers, including genitourinary, endoscopy, and
  accident and emergency staff
Staff in oncology, haemodialysis, haemophilia, and liver units
Staff providing maintenance treatment with blood or blood products
Accidental exposure to hepatitis B material
Staff on secondment to areas of the world with a high prevalence of hepatitis B

Patients
First entrants to residential care for mentally handicapped
On maintenance haemodialysis or with chronic renal failure before dialysis or
  transplantation
Requiring multiple blood transfusions or injections of blood products—e.g.
  haemophilia
Natural or acquired immune deficiency

Contacts of patients with hepatitis B
Sexual partners of patients with acute hepatitis B or carriers
Other family members in close contact
Infants born to women with acute hepatitis B or who are hepatitis B carriers,
  especially those with e antigen

Other staff
Ambulance and rescue services
Staff at reception centres for people from high endemic areas (SE Asia)

Others at high risk
Promiscuous homosexuals or prostitutes (male or female)
Intravenous drug abusers

Lower risk
Long-term men prisoners
Staff of custodial institutions
Some police personnel

People living in intermediate and high prevalence areas
Women
Infants
Children
Susceptible individuals

---

*In general, people in low-risk careers or those in administrative posts, out-patient
sections, and those working in the community will not require vaccination.*

chronic carrier develops chronic liver disease with cirrhosis (see below) this may affect his work.

Non-A non-B hepatitis[25]

Acute hepatitis without serological markers of viruses known to cause hepatitis in man (hepatitis A, hepatitis B, hepatitis delta virus, cytomegalovirus, or Epstein Barr virus) is termed non-A non-B hepatitis. Such cases constitute 13 per cent of sporadic hepatitis in England and more than 75 per cent of post-transfusion hepatitis.[26] Epidemiologically it resembles hepatitis B, being transmitted parenterally but also in an epidemic form. The incubation period is usually about seven weeks, although a short incubation type (1–4 weeks) has been observed. The hepatitis is usually mild and frequently sub-clinical. A mild chronic hepatitis develops in 20 per cent of patients but normally improves. There must be a carrier state but screening tests are not currently available and infectivity is presumed to be low.

In the present state of knowledge there is no reason why a patient who has had this type of hepatitis should be barred from any type of work, but he should not donate blood.

CHRONIC LIVER DISEASE

Cirrhosis

Cirrhosis results from chronic liver injury as a result of which inflammation and necrosis of liver cells leads to fibrosis and nodule formation. There are many causes of cirrhosis (Table 14.2) the most common of which is alcohol, but not all cirrhotics are alcoholics.[40] The crucial results of cirrhosis are hepatocellular failure and portal hypertension. These cause serious complications including the development of ascites, encephalopathy, jaundice, gastrointestinal bleeding from oesophageal varices, and malnutrition. Any of these complications can have serious consequences for work. This section will deal with the problems of patients with cirrhosis, in particular the alcoholic type.

Prevalence

The prevalence of cirrhosis in the UK is 15 per 100 000 and 60 per cent are due to alcohol, 30 per cent cryptogenic, and 6 per cent chronic active hepatitis.[41] The mean age of diagnosis of alcoholic cirrhosis is 47 years in women compared to 52 years in men.

Alcoholism is an increasing problem: in the UK the number of problem drinkers is estimated at 700 000 with 200 000 addicted to alcohol. One in five men and one in 14 young women aged 18–24 years are heavy drinkers.

Table 14.2   Some common causes of cirrhosis

Alcohol
Viral hepatitis type B, or non-A non-B
Chronic active (lupoid) hepatitis
Metabolic, e.g. haemochromatosis
   Wilson's disease
   α_1-anti-trypsin deficiency
Drugs, e.g. methotrexate
Hepatic venous outflow obstruction
   Budd–Chiari syndrome
Chronic cholestasis, e.g. primary biliary cirrhosis
Cryptogenic

Alcoholic liver disease has been increasing in women, with a changing ratio of men to women from 5:1 in 1976 to 2:1 in 1981. Not only do women develop alcoholic liver disease at an earlier age than men but they also have a worse prognosis.[41]

Prognosis

In the most acute form of liver injury, alcohol causes acute alcoholic hepatitis which is a precirrhotic condition. The overall five-year survival depends on the severity of the liver inflammation and on whether the patient stops drinking; for those who stop drinking it is 70 per cent, compared to 34 per cent for those who continue.[42] The number of deaths per year in the UK from alcoholic liver disease is 5 per 100 000, but this is an underestimate by as much as a third owing to the reluctance of doctors prior to 1984 to report alcohol-related deaths to a coroner.[43] Prognosis is worst for women and patients with bleeding oesophageal varices and best for cases with well-compensated liver disease.

Clinical aspects affecting work

Time off work for treatment depends on the severity of the liver disease, ranging from none to several months for severe hepatic decompensation such as occurs in alcoholic hepatitis. Follow-up is likely to vary according to whether the patient is attending an alcohol-dependency clinic or medical out-patients. In the extreme case of a patient at work but undergoing endoscopic injection sclerotherapy to obliterate oesophageal varices, appointments, often with overnight stay, may be necessary every 2–3 weeks for up to six months. Such treatment reduces the risk of bleeding and improves prognosis.[44]

The effect of chronic liver disease, regardless of the aetiology, depends on the degree of hepatic decompensation, in particular on hepatic encephalopathy, ascites, and gastrointestinal bleeding.

Hepatic encephalopathy. Mental impairment, reduced physical fitness, and tremor may all reduce work capacity. The development of hepatic (portal-systemic) encephalopathy is usually a feature of severe liver disease or a complication of the now unfashionable operation of porta-caval shunt. Some patients with cirrhosis but without clinical features of encephalopathy have impairment of psychomotor function on testing sufficient to disrupt their every-day life and even render them unfit to drive.[45] This condition has been termed 'latent encephalopathy'. Encephalopathy can be chronic or intermittent and precipitated by a number of causes including a high protein meal, infection, drugs, or bleeding into the gut. Some patients are very susceptible to meals high in animal protein and have to take a special diet and/or lactulose to alter the bowel flora.

Ascites. The presence of ascites may limit physical performance both by virtue of the mechanical effect of the large (up to 30 litres) volume of fluid and the associated malnutrition. Fortunately, ascites can usually be controlled with diuretics and hence problems with work can be avoided.

Bleeding from oesophageal varices. The prognosis of patients with bleeding from oesophageal varices depends on the severity of the underlying liver disease and on further episodes of bleeding. Rebleeding occurs in 60 per cent of patients within one year.

Varices secondary to extrahepatic portal venous obstruction. Oesophageal varices also occur in patients without cirrhosis, in whom obstruction, for example from thrombosis to the portal venous system, results in portal hypertension. Such patients commonly present as a child with variceal bleeding which can recur during childhood but becomes less frequent after puberty. They have an excellent prognosis, unlike patients with portal hypertension secondary to cirrhosis.

Associated conditions. Other conditions associated with cirrhosis[40] include diabetes mellitus (which is 2–4 times commoner than in the normal population), malnutrition, and peptic ulceration (although this association has been refuted by some). Bone disease, especially affecting the back, is a problem for patients with chronic cholestasis, e.g. primary biliary cirrhosis; they may also be troubled by pruritis which can be so distressing and intractable as to result in suicide. In those with alcoholic liver disease, other systemic effects of alcohol (such as on the central nervous system including acute withdrawal; peripheral neuropathy; cerebrovascular accident; or cardiomyopathy) may all affect work.

Special work problems

Ideally, patients with complications of cirrhosis, that is ascites, encephalopathy, or bleeding from oesophageal varices, should have been managed by a specialist before resuming work.

Certain occupations are particularly associated with the *risks of alcoholism*. They include those working in the manufacture, distribution, and sale of alcohol; commercial travellers; seamen and those in the armed forces; and journalists, doctors, and entertainers.[46] To employ someone with an alcohol problem in one of these jobs would seem inadvisable. Whether alcohol is a problem to the individual can be assessed quickly by the use of four 'CAGE' questions.[47] (see also Chapter 21).

Overt encephalopathy is uncommon but such patients may be a hazard to themselves and others and should not be relied upon for jobs requiring a high degree of vigilance, including driving. The presence of *latent encephalopathy* (see p. 260) is more difficult to identify but may have equally serious consequences for work.[45] Individual suitability for driving duties should be discussed with the medical branch of the Driver and Vehicle Licensing Centre (DVLC) (see Appendix 1). Patients who are dependent on alcohol are barred from holding a vocational licence until they have been abstinent for five years and have a normal level of gamma glutamyltransferase.

There is no evidence that *bleeding from oesophageal varices* is precipitated by particular occupations or activities. Patients who have suffered episodes of bleeding from varices will normally have undergone injection sclerotherapy to obliterate the varices by the time they resume work. If treatment has not been completed or undertaken, it would seem prudent for them to avoid jobs involving heavy lifting as the associated increase in intra-abdominal pressure might rupture the varix. They should probably also avoid contact sports and would be unwise to travel to remote places where medical services are limited. Once sclerosis of the varices is completed there is no reason why their work should be restricted.

Patients with *ascites* may experience difficulty with strenuous lifting, or with bending and stooping.

Handling of hepatotoxic substances by patients with liver disease

Many substances, including drugs, are known to cause liver damage[48] but by far the most important environmental hepatotoxin is alcohol. Data on these substances are derived from the accidental or deliberate exposure of animals or humans with normal liver function to toxic substances. For obvious ethical reasons, there are virtually no data on the effect of these toxins on patients with liver diseases. Unfortunately, even a knowledge of the mode of action of these substances and the potential influence of liver disease cannot predict accurately the outcome of exposure on the individual patient with liver disease.

Hepatotoxic substances exert their effect in one of two ways:

1. By the action of a toxic metabolite, produced by the microsomal enzymes in the liver, which binds to liver macromolecules and results in the necrosis of the cell.

2. The other chief mode of action is immunological: the metabolite binds to the liver cell and results in a change of antigenicity of the cell membrane with destruction of the cell by the immune system.

Susceptibility to liver damage depends on whether the rate at which the toxic metabolite is formed is greater than the rate of the detoxification, usually by conjugation with compounds such as glutathione. Once the stores of these protective compounds are exhausted, liver necrosis will follow. Chronic exposure to certain substances, such as anticonvulsants, results in induction of the liver microsomal enzymes with increased production of hepatotoxic metabolites. But, paradoxically, these enzyme-inducers may stimulate other pathways for the production of non-toxic metabolites. Although alcohol induces hepatic enzymes, the effect on the handling of hepatotoxins is variable and inconsistent. Thus, chronic alcohol exposure can potentiate the toxic effect of paracetamol, while acute exposure protects against paracetamol damage but potentiates carbon tetrachloride hepatotoxicity.[49,50] It is impossible to predict the result of exposure to hepatotoxic agents of a patient with a normal liver, who is also taking an enzyme-inducing agent.

Influence of liver disease

There are great variations in the metabolism of toxic substances by patients with liver disease. These are related not only to the severity of the liver disease but also to genetic and environmental factors which result in changes in the activity of liver enzymes. The reduced hepatic mass may result in reduced conversion of the substance to a toxic metabolite and so protect against damage. But protective co-factors and detoxifying enzymes are likely to be reduced and will tend to potentiate liver damage. The outcome of exposure depends on the relative balance between these two effects of the liver disease.

Guidelines for the employment of workers with hepatotoxins

The previous paragraphs show the unpredictability of hepatotoxins in patients with liver disease and explain the need for restricting the exposure of such people to hepatotoxins. However, statements such as 'Workers who have any disorder of the liver or gall bladder, or a past history of jaundice, should not handle or be exposed to potentially hepatotoxic agents'[51] are too sweeping for the 1980s and need qualification. True, patients with chronic liver disease or active acute liver disease should not work or be exposed to hepatotoxins, but there are other categories who can. These are patients who have had hepatitis A; resolved acute viral hepatitis B, or non-A non-B hepatitis in whom liver function tests and liver histology have returned to normal; patients with gall stones unless they are jaundiced or have developed secondary biliary cirrhosis which is very rare. All people working with hepatotoxic agents should avoid alcohol and enzyme-inducing agents such as anticonvulsants, in particular phenobarbitone and phenytoin.

INFLAMMATORY BOWEL DISEASE[52]

The most common types of inflammatory bowel disease in the UK are ulcerative colitis and Crohn's disease, both of which are of unknown aetiology. Inflammation is limited to the mucosa of the colon in ulcerative colitis, while in Crohn's disease the whole of the gastrointestinal tract from the lips to the anus may be affected by transmural inflammation. Both diseases are characterized primarily by diarrhoea, but abdominal pain and the formation of abscesses, gut perforation, and fistulae are features of Crohn's disease.

Inflammatory bowel disease and employment

Inflammatory bowel disease remains poorly understood by employers and doctors, many of whom remember from their student days the sight of a young patient with extensive, progressive, and disabling Crohn's disease. Such cases are the exception rather than the rule, and most patients with controlled inflammatory bowel disease lead a normal life and work with little sickness absence. Nevertheless, unnecessary concern is expressed over their employment, especially of those with stomas, and employers must learn that most will make perfectly satisfactory employees capable of most occupations.

Prevalence and incidence

The prevalence of these diseases varies in different parts of the UK. A survey from Oxford between 1951 and 1960 estimated that there were 80 cases of ulcerative colitis and nine of Crohn's disease per 100 000 population, with an incidence of 6.5 and 1.8 respectively.[53] Crohn's disease is becoming more common, due in part to increased familiarity with the condition: recent estimates put the prevalence at 30 per 100 000 with an incidence of 4–5 per 100 000.[54,55]

Men and women are equally affected by Crohn's disease, while ulcerative colitis is more common in women. Both diseases can start at any age with a peak from 15 to 40 years and a secondary peak at 55.

Mortality and morbidity of inflammatory bowel disease
Both types of disease are associated with diarrhoea which can result in intermittent or persistent morbidity that is difficult to estimate accurately. The occasional patient experiences one isolated episode only, while conversely a fulminating presentation may require early emergency surgery.

Ulcerative colitis[52]

Patients with ulcerative proctitis have a normal life expectancy but may have considerable urgency of defaecation and diarrhoea. Such distal disease may extend to affect the whole colon; 10 per cent in 10 years. Patients with more extensive ulcerative colitis have an increased mortality during the first year after diagnosis, but after this mortality is the same as for the general population. Surgery is necessary for patients who fail to respond to medical treatment and is likely in 1 in 50 patients within five years of onset of proctitis, 1 in 20 with left-sided, and 1 in 3 with total colitis.[56] The most common type of surgery is panproctocolectomy with creation of an ileostomy, which has a mortality of less than 1 per cent in experienced hands. Such patients have a normal life expectancy with only minor limitations of their work.[57] Patients with total colitis of more than 10 years' duration, especially those in whom disease commenced before the age of 20, have an increased risk of carcinoma of the colon and colectomy may be undertaken prophylactically.

Crohn's disease

Morbidity of Crohn's disease[58,59]
The transmural inflammation of the bowel can result in thickening, obstruction, and perforation of the bowel wall, with liability to fistulae or abscess formation. Such complications can cause major morbidity requiring surgery or may be relatively asymptomatic. The natural history of the disease is not related to the age of onset but depends on the extent and site of disease. Thus, disease limited to the terminal ileum has a better prognosis than diffuse inflammation of the small bowel. Disease of the colon and rectum will result in distressing symptoms of diarrhoea and urgency, while small bowel disease can have a profound nutritional effect. Exacerbations of the disease occur at variable intervals after presentation, with 70 per cent of patients experiencing relapse within five years.

Mortality of Crohn's disease[58, 59]

The risk of dying does not increase with duration of disease and is highest for patients whose disease began before the age of 40. Late mortality is only slightly in excess of the expected mortality. Deaths are related to complications of surgery and development of carcinoma of the bowel.

Clinical aspects of inflammatory bowel disease affecting work

The main problems for patients irrespective of the type of inflammatory bowel disease are frequency and urgency of defaecation. Urgency is related to inflammation and reduced capacity of the rectum and is as major a problem for someone with proctitis as with inflammation involving the whole of the colon. The urgency and resultant incontinence are very disabling and cause serious restrictions to patients' life and work. The National Association for Colitis and Crohn's Disease issues members with a card which they can use to help gain access to a toilet in public places.

Most patients with a mild attack of inflammatory bowel disease without constitutional upset can be treated as out-patients and usually without loss of time from work. Treatment of moderate or severe attacks generally requires rest in bed, or in hospital in the case of severe attacks with constitutional upset. Time off work for relapses treated medically varies from two weeks to two months.

Side-effects of medical treatment
Systemic steroids are seldom used long term in the management of patients with inflammatory bowel disease, with the exception of the small number of cases with extensive Crohn's disease of the small bowel. Large doses used in an acute severe attack can cause greater side-effects than in a normal person, owing to the low serum albumin. Salazopyrine, used to reduce the frequency and severity of relapse in ulcerative colitis, can cause distressing headaches and rashes but side-effects are less frequent with newer preparations.[60]

Surgical treatment
Surgical treatment is necessary for patients with ulcerative colitis who fail to respond to aggressive medical treatment or who are at risk of developing carcinoma of the colon. For Crohn's disease, surgery is indicated for relief of mechanical problems such as strictures or fistulae, or for resection of severely diseased segments of bowel which fail to respond to intensive medical therapy.

Time off work for bowel surgery
This depends on the type of operation and ranges from two weeks for a minor procedure to up to six months for panproctocolectomy and ileostomy.

Employers should be encouraged to be supportive of patients during this time. Surgical treatment, especially the formation of an ileostomy, usually restores patients' general health to normal with greater energy, fewer problems at work, and less sickness absence. It is often only after surgery that everyone appreciates just how debilitating the inflammatory bowel disease has been. An ileostomy may require surgical refashioning especially during the first year after creation but thereafter should be relatively trouble free.

Patients with ulcerative colitis are usually restored to normal health once the colon has been removed. Crohn's disease, however, is frequently characterized by recurrence of disease despite surgical resection. Thus, 55 per cent of cases develop recurrent disease 10 years after resection of affected bowel.[58] The patient with Crohn's disease affecting long segments of small bowel can be a particular problem, as surgical resection is undesirable. Such cases are uncommon and may require long-term corticosteroid therapy.

Other conditions associated with inflammatory bowel disease

Arthritis occurs in 10 per cent of patients with ulcerative colitis and in 20 per cent with Crohn's disease, tends to affect the lower limbs, and is associated with active bowel disease.

Sacroiliitis occurs in 15 per cent of patients with inflammatory bowel disease but is usually not severe and seldom progresses to involve the lumbar and thoracic spine. Unlike peripheral arthritis, sacroiliitis is not related to the extent or severity of underlying bowel disease and can antedate the onset of the latter. These problems may cause some limitation of activity.

Iritis is an uncommon (0.5–3 per cent) but serious complication of inflammatory bowel disease, causing painful blurred vision and headaches. It is usually associated with exacerbations of disease and with other extra-intestinal manifestations, such as arthritis and erythema nodosum. Steroid therapy may be required, but colectomy does not always result in resolution.

Skin problems, the most severe of which are pyoderma gangrenosum and erythema nodosum, occur in up to 9 per cent of patients, mainly those with ulcerative colitis. Lesions tend to occur on the legs, are associated with active bowel disease in the case of erythema nodosum, and often require steroid therapy.

Special work problems

Despite the potential for ill health, most patients with chronic inflammatory bowel disease are able to contine to work. A recent survey from the General Hospital, Birmingham, found 70 per cent of 170 out-patients to be working with good continuity of employment over a six-year period of follow-up. Sickness absence was not high, with 70 per cent of patients having lost no time off work in the preceding year. Irrespective of the type of inflammatory bowel disease, patients with an ileostomy took less sickness absence and experienced fewer problems at work, than those without.

Changes of work due to health

Premature retirement on account of ill health had been taken by 4 per cent of patients in the Birmingham survey and was often due to associated conditions (arthritis and renal failure due to amyloidosis) rather than to the inflammatory bowel disease itself. However, 42 per cent of patients had had to change their work because of their health, 12 per cent had modified their work or hours, and 4 per cent had retrained.

Effect of surgery on work

Seventy per cent of patients in the Birmingham survey had undergone surgery which had resulted in 4 per cent retiring prematurely and 10 per cent having to change their work. Although 12 per cent had altered their work or hours, 20 per cent had been able to resume work, often after long periods of sickness absence. Time off work was longer for patients who had undergone panproctocolectomy and ileostomy than for colectomy and ileorectal anastomosis or for resections of segments of bowel. These differences are presumably related to the delayed healing of the perineal wound of panproctocolectomy.

Unsuitable work for patients with inflammatory bowel disease

Most work is suitable for patients with inflammatory bowel disease. Some patients, however, do experience more problems with their disease during periods of increased stress. Thus, shiftwork may be a problem to some patients, especially those with active or severe disease. Patients are often a good judge of what work is suitable for them. In the Birmingham survey the main problems that patients experienced that affected their work were general fatigue, frequent bowel action, arthritis, and leakage from their stomas.

General fatigue is a very common complaint of patients with active inflammatory bowel disease. For some patients this may require a change to less strenuous work. Fortunately, energy improves after effective medical or surgical treatment of the diseased bowel.

Frequent bowel action may present problems for patients with limited access to toilets. These include people:

(1) working out of doors;

(2) with restricted toilet access;

(3) with restricted mobility due to wearing protective clothing;

(4)   with severe arthritis;

(5)   who are production-line workers, especially on paced work.

Hence it may be important to consider the siting of work to provide easy and adequate toilet access.

Sacroiliitis and arthritis are usually mild but can cause varying degrees of limitation which will have to be assessed individually.

Food-handling and preparation

Once inflammatory bowel disease has been diagnosed and an infectious cause for the diarrhoea excluded, there is no reason why the patient should not work as a food-handler, providing that the normal standards of personal hygiene expected of such a worker are satisfied. Although such patients may always have loose stools, they are usually able to recognize any changes from their normal pattern which would indicate a superimposed gastroenteritis. If this happens, the patient should be investigated in the usual way.

Special facilities

The only provision needed for patients with inflammatory bowel disease is unrestricted access to adequate toilet and washing facilities, which should include some privacy for those with an ileostomy.

ILEOSTOMY OR COLOSTOMY

Ileostomies and colostomies are created either as a permanent stoma, or temporarily to enable an acute bowel problem to resolve following which the normal route for bowel function is re-established. Such patients have to adjust to their new body image and functions but are generally able to lead a full and normal life. Unfortunately, some of them experience problems and discrimination in obtaining or continuing work, in part due to prejudice and ignorance by both employers and doctors.[61]

In England and Wales there are around 10 000 people with an ileostomy and 250 to 300 permanent stomas are created each year from this population.[62,63] The majority of ileostomies are created in young people for inflammatory bowel disease. In comparison, there are probably 100 000 people in England and Wales with a permanent colostomy. They tend to be older (peak age incidence 65 years) and with a male to female ratio of 1.1 : 1. In contrast, the stoma is often created for cancer of the colon or rectum.

Clinical aspects affecting work capacity

The capacity of someone with a stoma to work will depend both on the reason for surgery and on his general health after convalescence. Hence, the patient with ulcerative colitis who has had an ileostomy created as part of a colectomy should be returned to full fitness with a near normal life expectancy, while the prospects of a patient with a colostomy for carcinoma of the colon may be less favourable.[64]

Time off work for creation of the stoma ranges from three to six months but in the case of a permanent stoma very little further surgery is usually necessary. Complications include electrolyte imbalance, dehydration, and intestinal obstruction, and in the long term an increased risk of biliary and renal stones.[64]

A recent survey of 1033 members of the Ileostomy Association of Great Britain and Ireland found 79 per cent of women and 96 per cent of men to be working after their operation. Of these, 6 per cent began work for the first time after the operation. Continuity of employment was good.[61] (Appendix 5.)

Special work problems

While it is true that people with an ileostomy or colostomy can be found performing almost every type of work including deep-sea diving, certain jobs are more likely to cause problems. It is generally considered that excessive stooping or bending, especially if accompanied by heavy lifting or carrying loads close to the abdominal wall, and working in a very confined space, may result in leakage from the appliance or injury to the stoma. Modern appliances and a better understanding of optimum siting of the stoma have resulted in the appliance being more stable and less vulnerable. Work in the emergency services, which generally combines the problem of heavy lifting close to the body with the use of restrictive clothing, tends to be difficult for the person with a stoma, although there are a few patients working in this capacity. Miners with stomas who work at the coal face find the hot, dirty, sweaty environment combined with the heavy work and poor toilet facilities unsuitable.

Food-handling
The bacterial content of ileostomy effluent is one-twentieth that of normal faeces.[65] Hence, provided the patient has good personal hygiene, the risk of spread of infection should be no greater, and possibly less than in a normal person, and in these circumstances a patient with an ileostomy should not be barred from working as a food-handler[66]. Colostomy effluent has a bacterial content more akin to normal faeces.[67] Patients with colostomies tend to be older, and are sometimes less dexterous, and so the question of food-handling is more contentious but again a decision should depend on the level of personal hygiene.[66]

Hot environments
Dehydration is a potential problem for anyone with an ileostomy as the stoma results in loss of water and salt such that the total body water is

reduced by 10 per cent and salt by 7 per cent,[68] compared to a normal person. People with an ileostomy are thus more susceptible to dehydration when in extremely hot environments or during periods of gastrointestinal upset. Work in hot environments is not contraindicated for the ileostomist, provided that fluid and salt intake is maintained. If the patient is visiting the tropics, he should be instructed on the use of oral rehydration solutions.

Work in remote places

Concern has been expressed over someone with an ileostomy working in very remote places with limited medical and surgical back-up in case of emergency. This should be taken into account and each case will have to be considered on its merits. Factors to be considered are the reason for the ileostomy, any previous problems, and the length of time since the stoma was created. For example, a person with an ileostomy as part of a panproctocolectomy for ulcerative colitis will not suffer further problems from the colitis, while patients with Crohn's disease may still develop recurrent disease. The need for further surgery to the stoma, regardless of the type of underlying bowel disease, tends to be greatest during the first year after its formation.

Handling of hazardous substances

The handling of toxic chemicals and/or pathogenic material should not be a risk to people with an ileostomy provided that they maintain normal safety standards and safe working practices.

Air travel

Air travel results in reduced outside pressure. Gas in the bag expands and unless vented can burst the appliance. People with a stoma should wear an appliance with a flatus valve and avoid aerated drinks before and during the flight.

Special facilities

The patient with a stoma needs good toilet and washing facilities with privacy so that the appliance can be changed or leakage cleaned up. If a medical department is readily available, staff will help and also keep an eye on any problems.

GASTROENTERITIS AND INFESTATIONS OF THE GUT

Gastrointestinal infections can result in diarrhoea and ill health which may impair work capacity, but the main concern is the risk of spread of infection, in particular by food-handlers. Fortunately, most of the infections encountered in this country are self-limiting but travellers from abroad may contract more serious chronic infection.

Because of limited space we have dealt only with the most common and with those of particular consequence to the occupational physician. They are:

(1) *Staphylococcus aureus*;

(2) *Campylobacter enteritis*;

(3) *Salmonella* infections;

(4) amoebiasis and gay bowel syndrome.

Staphylococcus aureus

Infected food-handlers do not normally play a significant role in bacterial food poisoning except for this variety. This organism may be found in septic lesions and as a commensal in the nose and on the skin. If transferred to food that is not at adequately low storage temperature, the organism will multiply, producing an enterotoxin that is not inactivated by further cooking. If ingested, it will lead to an abrupt onset of severe nausea, vomiting, abdominal cramps, and diarrhoea. The incubation period is short, usually 2–4 hours and the duration of the illness is less than 48 hours. Deaths are rare.

Campylobacter enteritis[69]

Campylobacter (*jejuni* and *intestinalis*) enteritis is now the most common cause of gastroenteritis in adults in Britain and has increased from 12 000 cases in 1981 to 24 400 in 1986. Infection is more common in the summer months.

The most common source of infection is eating inadequately cooked poultry, or food contaminated from poultry by poor kitchen hygiene. After 3–5 days' incubation period, a prodrome is followed by a systemic upset, with abdominal pain, and diarrhoea. Mortality is extremely low, occurring mainly in the young or elderly. Infection is usually self-limiting, although patients may excrete the organism in the stool for up to five weeks. Person to person transmission is only a problem between young children and siblings to parents. Thus, there is no significant occupational health hazard and even food-handlers can resume work once fit.

Salmonella infection[70]

Although there are more than 1700 types of Salmonellae, from a practical point of view only a relatively small number cause problems for man. *Salmonella typhi* and *S. paratyphi* A, B, and C are primarily human pathogens causing enteric fever. Other Salmonellae are primarily animal pathogens causing illness in man usually localized to the gastrointestinal tract; most infections are caused by a small number of different serotypes. The most common presentation is an acute gastroenteritis and/or septicaemia which can result in dissemination of infection to other sites, e.g. chest and bone.

The source of most *Salmonella* infection is poultry and agricultural animals, or food contaminated during preparation. Person to person spread can occur in closed communities. Watery diarrhoea occurs 12–72 hours after infection, accompanied by abdominal pain, vomiting, and fever. The illness lasts a few days and is usually self-limiting.

Antibiotics are indicated for patients with septicaemia or focal sepsis but should be avoided in less severe cases as they result in a prolonged clinical course and drug resistance. Patients who have undergone gastric surgery, those with achlorhydria or on antacid therapy seem to have an increased susceptibility to infection. Fatalities are rare but occur in the young or elderly. Adults excrete the organism for 4–8 weeks, but most patients can resume work once fit, the exceptions being food-handlers[66] (Table 14.3) and water workers.

Typhoid and paratyphoid

These infections occur throughout the world but are endemic in the Far East, Central and South America, and Africa, a reflection of poor hygiene and sanitation. There were 135 cases of typhoid and 98 of paratyphoid in the UK in 1985. Typhoid is contracted from food or drink contaminated with faeces or urine from a carrier or patient. The incubation period of 10–14 days can result in patients developing symptoms once they have returned to Britain. Common presenting features are mild abdominal pain and constipation rather than diarrhoea, which develops later in only 20 per cent of cases. The rash and hepatosplenomegaly develop in the second week. Diagnosis rests on isolation of the organism from blood, stool, or urine. Serological tests are unhelpful. Patients are barrier-nursed in hospital and treated with antibiotics. Complications include septicaemia, hyperpyrexia, haemolysis, and perforation of the gut. Relapse occurs in approximately 20 per cent of cases, usually two weeks after stopping antibiotic treatment and an attack confers no effective immunity.

Carriers of Salmonella typhi
Patients usually cease to excrete *Salmonella typhi* after three months, but 3 per cent of cases become chronic carriers excreting the organism for more than one year in their stools and/or urine. The number of recognized carriers in the UK is around 1 in 100 000, 90 per cent of whom excrete the organism in their stools, sometimes intermittently. Serological tests are unreliable for detecting the carrier state.

Table 14.3 Microbiological surveillance and implications of infections and infestations in food-handlers[66]

Type of organism	Requirement for resumption of work as a food-handler (criteria for clearance once symptom-free)
Campylobacter *Bacillus cereus* *Clostridium botulinum* *Clostridium perfringens* *Vibrio parahaemolyticus* *Giardia lamblia*	none

Cholera
Dysentery—amoebic
Dysentery—bacillary
Enteropathogenic *E. coli*
  (outbreaks only)
Salmonellosis (excluding
  paratyphoid A and typhoid
  infections)
Paratyphoid B
	3 consecutive negative faeces specimens at 48-hour intervals

Paratyphoid A Typhoid	12 negative faeces specimens over 6 months Permanently unfit to work as a food-handler

Viral gastroenteritis
  Rotavirus
  Other viruses
Worms (threadworm and
  Taenia Solium)
Hepatitis A
Staphylococcus aureus
	
	7 days after recovery
	None
	Once treated
	
	7 days after onset of jaundice
	Once septic lesions are treated and healed

Treatment of the carrier state is difficult, especially in the presence of biliary disease which, in extreme cases, may necessitate cholecystectomy. For less severe cases amoxycillin and cotrimoxazole therapy may be successful. Salmonella carriers are barred from work as food-handlers (see Table 14.3).[66]

Immunization against Salmonella typhi
This should be considered for travellers to endemic areas, people living with a chronic carrier, and laboratory staff who may handle *S. typhi*. Immunization with a heat-killed phenolized vaccine does not reduce the severity of attacks but reduces the rate of infection to 20 per cent and provides protection for up

to two years. Two subcutaneous injections one month apart (not less than 10 days in emergency cases) are necessary.

Amoebiasis and the gay bowel syndrome

Until 10 years ago amoebiasis was thought to be transmitted by ingestion of contaminated food or water, and was principally a problem of underdeveloped countries with poor sanitation.[71] While the highest incidence is still in South America and Southern Asia, in the United States and Europe amoebiasis has become far more common as a sexually transmitted disease, mainly among male homosexuals. Such patients may also be infected with one or more other enteric organisms including *Giardia lamblia*, *Campylobacter*, Salmonellae, and Shigellae, a condition termed the gay bowel syndrome.[72,73] Cysts of *E. histolytica* are endemic among homosexual males, being excreted by 4 per cent of those attending clinics for sexually transmitted diseases in the UK. As patients are usually asymptomatic and the amoebae of non-pathogenic types, the place of treatment is controversial. The risk of spread of infection during every-day contact rather than sexual contact is not known but it is probably low. However, there is evidence from the United States of transmission among homosexuals of *Shigella* dysentery and isolated cases of *Salmonella typhi* probably by oral–anal contact.[73] The acquired immune deficiency syndrome (AIDS) is discussed in Chapter 22.

Food-handlers

The growth of ready prepared foods and more facilities for eating out mean that food poisoning can affect all sections of the population with serious and even fatal consequences, especially in the very young or weakened individual.[74] In spite of increased legislation, inspection, and education, there has been a steady increase in food-borne infections and intoxications (Table 14.4).

Between 1981–85 there were 18 major outbreaks of food poisoning in the UK, resulting in 37 deaths. Many home-produced and imported food items are heavily contaminated with *Salmonella* organisms, frozen chicken being the commonest vector.[75] Infected food-handlers account for only a small proportion of *Salmonella* outbreaks. The majority of bacterial food poisonings emanate from contaminated raw food, from tasting during food preparation, and from eating contaminated left-over food.

Doctors have a duty to ensure that food-handlers under their care are fit to resume food-handling duties following an infectious illness.

Definition of a food-handler

A food-handler handles food itself, containers in which it is packed, or machines or implements with which it comes into contact. Included in this definition,

Table 14.4 Number of reported cases of bacterial food poisoning and Salmonella infection in England and Wales 1981–84[75]

Year	Salmonella	C. perfringens	S. aureus	B. cereus & Bacillus sp.	Total
1981	9532	918	143	72	10665
1982	11099	1455	89	41	12684
1983	13250	1624	160	134	15168
1984	13201	1716	181	214	15312

therefore, are engineers, maintenance fitters, hygiene and cleaning workers in the food industry, as well as those engaged in the preparation or serving of food within catering establishments or retail food outlets. Greater care has to be taken when the food is likely to support bacterial growth and where it will be eaten without further and adequate cooking.

The Food Hygiene (General) Regulations (1970) (SI 970 WO1172)

These require that any food-handler shall immediately notify the Medical Officer of Environmental Health if suffering from any *Salmonella* infection, amoebic or bacillary dysentery, or any staphylococcal infection likely to cause food poisoning. As many food-handlers fail to notify these illnesses, medical practitioners must be alert to the dangers. Problems frequently arise when individuals contract gastroenteritis, especially on holiday in tropical or semi-tropical areas. In the latter instance, this is often expected by the patient and is not recognized as a potential hazard. Medical practitioners responsible for the health of employees in food factories, in hotels, and canteen workers, should ensure that food-handlers report any episode affecting them or close family contacts before resuming work. Cases should be seen and investigated by the occupational physician, general practitioner or the Medical Officer of Environmental Health.

Food-handlers with vomiting and/or diarrhoea should be excluded from work until they are symptom-free, and have normal formed stools. If there are clinical grounds for believing that they may have or have had, typhoid, paratyphoid, cholera, amoebic or bacillary dysentery, salmonellosis, or intestinal worms, appropriate clearance procedures must be followed (see Table 14.3).[66]

Symptomless contacts of cases of food-borne disease

Typhoid fever will have to be investigated in conjunction with the Medical Officer of Environmental Health, the Public Health Laboratory Service, or a consultant microbiologist. Laboratories isolating Salmonellae are obliged to inform the Environmental Health Officer who will issue an exclusion order if the individual is a food-handler.

For all other conditions there is no need to investigate unless the contacts develop symptoms. Advice should be given daily to all food-handlers to report any symptoms promptly, and to practise a good standard of personal hygiene.

Selection of food-handlers

The pre-employment examination frequently presents problems. The following conditions would normally exclude an individual from food-handling duties:

(1) history of paratyphoid or typhoid disease;

(2) history of recurrent attacks of gastroenteritis, unless carrier state has been excluded by bacteriological tests (Table 14.3);

(3) history and presence of persistent and recurring staphylococcal infections of the skin;

(4) chronic infections of the ears, eyes, nose or throat;

(5) poor oral hygiene;

(6) conditions of the upper or lower respiratory tract which cause coughing and production of purulent sputum during normal working hours;

(7) low standards of personal hygiene, including nail-biters.

Chest radiography and Widal tests are not now considered to be a necessary part of the pre-employment examination, unless there are indications that either is required.

Meat-workers

These are covered by Food Hygiene Regulations (1970) and EEC Council Directive 79/784/EEC. The latter requires that work on fresh meat, meat-based products, and chicken must be prohibited to persons likely to contaminate them, in particular to persons:

(1) either infected or suspected of being infected with abdominal typhoid, paratyphoid A and B, infectious enteritis (salmonellosis), dysentery, infectious hepatitis A or scarlet fever, or who are carriers of these same diseases;

(2) infected or suspected of being infected with contagious tuberculosis;

(3) infected or suspected of being infected with contagious skin disease;

(4) carrying out another, parallel activity whereby organisms are likely to be transmitted to fresh meat or meat-based products;

(5) the wearing of a dressing on the hands, with the exception of an adhesive plaster dressing protecting a fresh uninfected finger wound.

These regulations also require that the worker shall provide medical evidence of fitness for employment in handling meat-products, and that this certificate shall be renewed annually or at any time that the regional meat hygiene adviser of the Ministry of Agriculture, Fisheries and Food requests (EEC Council Directive 85/327/EEC). The community physician may also wish to inspect meat-workers.

Doctors working in the UK food industry consider such certificates to be of doubtful value, and there is little epidemiological evidence that they will reduce the incidence of food poisoning.[76]

FUNCTIONAL DISORDERS

Non-ulcer dyspepsia

The widespread use of endoscopy and double-contrast barium-meal radiography has revealed that many people with dyspepsia do not have peptic ulceration. Most of these patients are aged between 20 and 40 years, with a predominance of men. A recent survey from Sweden estimated that patients with non-ulcer dyspepsia suffered 2.6 times more sickness absence than the general population.[77] Their condition also results in substantial numbers of both in- and out-patient consultations, and inappropriate use of anti-ulcer medication. Although some of these patients improve initially on anti-ulcer treatment, this is probably largely a placebo response and may result in psychological dependence. Dyspepsia is more likely to be due to other causes, such as the irritable bowel syndrome and/or gastro-oesophageal reflux, but in a quarter of cases no explanation can be found.

Irritable bowel (spastic colon) syndrome

This is a disorder of unknown aetiology characterized by abdominal pain, distension, and bowel upset (diarrhoea and/or constipation) in the absence of demonstrable organic disease.[78,79] It is the most common disorder of the gastrointesinal tract, affecting one-third of the general population, yet only 20 per cent of sufferers seek medical advice.[80] Many general practitioners' awareness and understanding of the condition is poor, and doctors should appreciate the diverse clinical features (Table 14.5). Many of these patients are treated inappropriately for dyspepsia and some with severe pain may even have a normal appendix or gall bladder removed without relief of symptoms. Recent work has shown that for two-thirds of patients, the onset of symptoms is often preceded by an anxiety-provoking life situation or an episode of psychiatric illness, such as depression.[81] It seems likely that the syndrome is a normal somatic response to stress rather than a disease.

Table 14.5 Clinical features of the irritable bowel syndrome

	% affected
Abdominal pain, often left lower quadrant	98
Disordered bowel habit	80
Flatus/distension	65
Weight usually steady or increasing/modest reduction	20
Nausea with occasional vomiting	50
Dyspepsia (and occasional dysphagia)	25–50
Previous 'normal' appendicectomy	33
Cancer phobia	Up to 50
Urinary symptoms—frequency and dysuria	20
Gynaecological symptoms	
dysmenorrhoea	90
dyspareunia	33

Prevalence

Although only the more severe or chronic cases tend to be referred to a specialist, they account for approximately 50 per cent of gastroenterology out-patient work.[81,82] There are twice as many women as men amongst those referred.

The onset of symptoms is generally from late adolescence to the 30s, and is slightly later in men. The syndrome is rare in the over 60s and should only be diagnosed after other causes of gastrointestinal upset have been excluded, especially in the older patient.

The most incapacitating symptoms are diarrhoea and abdominal pain, which are usually intermittent but can have a profound effect on capacity to work. Data on sickness absence, however, are not available.

The response to treatment, especially of those seeking specialist advice, is often transient and variable, with 25 per cent deriving no benefit or even deteriorating. For some patients with food intolerance, dietary manipulation can prove beneficial but for many this is short lived. There is often a strong psychological component and symptoms are worse during periods of stress. Reassurance and explanation of the nature of the condition and its relation to stress can be helpful.

The majority of patients manage to work unaffected by the condition but for a small number work may be severely affected by severe or chronic diarrhoea and/or abdominal pain. For patients with frequent bowel action, toilet access can be a problem. Avoidance of excessive stress may be helpful for some patients, although as a group they will tend to worry excessively.

COELIAC DISEASE

This is due to an allergy to gluten in wheat and results in atrophy of the small bowel mucosa especially the jejunum. Most patients present in childhood with failure to grow and/or diarrhoea, but a small number present as adults. Exclusion of gluten from the diet usually results in complete restoration of normal health. Relapse of symptoms usually occurs only if gluten is inadvertently or deliberately introduced into the diet. Thus, the only restriction for employment of someone with coeliac disease is if they have to consume gluten-containing food as part of their work (i.e. food-tester). Travel is not usually a problem provided that gluten-containing foods are avoided.

CHRONIC PANCREATITIS

Chronic pancreatitis· is a rare disorder characterized by chronic severe epigastric pain, steatorrhoea, and diabetes due to damage to the pancreas. Alcohol is a common cause and has obvious consequences for work. The chronic pain may be so severe as to require opiate analgesia or even pain control by nerve block. Fortunately, with time the condition tends to burn out. There are no special restrictions for work apart from those related to coexistent diabetes mellitus and/or alcoholism (Chapters 13 and 21).

REFERENCES

1. Atkinson M. The pathophysiology of gastro-oesophageal reflux. In: Truelove SC, Ritchie JK, eds. Topics in gastroenterology. Vol. 4. Oxford: Blackwell, 1984:67–83.
2. Coggon D, Lambert P, Langman MJS. 20 years of hospital admissions for peptic ulcer in England and Wales. Lancet 1981;i:1302–4.
3. Department of Health and Social Security. Social Security Statistics 1986, Table 3.75. London: HMSO, 1987.
4. Langman MJS & Logan RFA. Gastrointestinal disease. In: Holland WW, Detels R, Knox G, eds. Oxford Textbook of Public Health. Vol. IV. Oxford: Oxford University Press, 1985:167–80.
5. Watkinson G. The incidence of chronic peptic ulcer found at necropsy. Gut 1960;1:14–31.
6. Doll R, Avery-Jones F. Occupational factors in the aetiology of gastric and duodenal ulcer. MRC Special Report 1951, Series 276. London: HMSO.
7. Weir RD, Backett EM. Studies of the epidemiology of peptic ulcer in a rural community: prevalence and natural history of dyspepsia and peptic ulcer. Gut 1968;9:75–83.
8. Langman MJS. The epidemiology of chronic digestive disease. London: Edward Arnold, 1979:9–39.

9. Glynn MJ, Kane SP. Benign gastric ulceration in a Health District: incidence and presentation. Postgrad Med J 1985;**61**:695–700.
10. Brown RC, Langman MJS, Lambert PM. Hospital admissions for peptic ulcer during 1958–1972. Br Med J 1976;**1**:35–7.
11. Office of Population Censuses and Surveys. Mortality statistics for England and Wales 1984,DH2 no. 11. London: HMSO.
12. Bonnevie O. Causes of death in duodenal and gastric ulcer. Gastroenterology 1977;**73**:1000–4.
13. Morgan AG. Chronic gastric ulcer. In: Bouchier IAD, Allan RN, Hodgson JF, Keighley MRB, eds. Textbook of gastroenterology. London: Baillière Tindall, 1984:134–40.
14. Pounder RE. Chronic duodenal ulcer. In: Bouchier IAD, Allan RN, Hodgson JF, Keighley MRB, eds. Textbook of gastroenterology. London: Baillière Tindall, 1984:165–8.
15. Venables CW. Chronic peptic ulcer: surgical treatment. In: Bouchier IAD, Allan RN, Hodgson JF, Keighley MRB, eds. Textbook of gastroenterology. London: Baillière Tindall, 1984:156–65.
16. Johnston D, Blackett RL. Chronic duodenal ulcer: surgical treatment. In: Bouchier IAD, Allan RN, Hodgson JF, Keighley MRB, eds. Textbook of gastroenterology. London: Baillière Tindall, 1984:176–90.
17. Alexander-Williams JA. Chronic peptic ulcer: complications of gastric surgery. In: Bouchier IAD, Allan RN, Hodgson JF, Keighley MRB, eds. Textbook of gastroenterology. London: Baillière Tindall, 1984:201–17.
18. Piper DW, Nasiry R, McIntosh J, Shy CM, Pierce J, Byth K. Smoking, alcohol, analgesics, and chronic duodenal ulcer: a controlled study of habits before first symptoms and before diagnosis. Scand J Med 1984;**19**:1015–21.
19. Feldman M, Walker P, Green JL, Weingarden K. Life events, stress and psychosocial factors in men with peptic ulcer disease. Gastroenterology 1986;**91**: 1370–79.
20. Bosworth DL, Dawkins PJ. Work patterns. An economical analysis. New York: Gower Press Publications, 1981.
21. Rutenfranz J. Arbeitsphysiologische aspeckte de nacht und schichtarbeit. Arbeitsmed Sozialmed Arbeitshyg 1967;**2**:17–23.
22. Wolf S, Almy TP, Bachrach WH, Spiro HM, Sturdevant RA, Weiner H. The role of stress in peptic ulcer disease. J Human Stress 1979;**5**:27–39.
23. Taylor PJ, Pocock SJ. Mortality of shift and day workers. Br J Ind Med 1972;**29**:201–7.
24. Merchant Shipping (Medical Examination) Regulations 1983,S11983 no. 808. London: HMSO.
25. Sherlock S. Viral hepatitis. In: Diseases of the liver and biliary system. 7th ed. London: Blackwell, 1985:251–79.
26. Farrow LJ, Stewart JS, Stern H, Clifford RE, Smith HG, Zuckerman AJ. Non A, non B hepatitis in West London. Lancet 1981;i:982–84.
27. Cossart YE. Virus hepatitis and its control. London: Baillière Tindall, 1977: Ch. 3.

28. Hepatitis A antibodies. In: The health of the civil service. Cabinet Office (Management and Personnel Office), Civil Service Medical Advisory Service. London: HMSO, 1985:78–9.

29. Cossar JH, Reid D. Not all travellers need immunoglobulin for hepatitis A. Br Med J 1987;1:294:1503.

30. Polakoff S. Acute viral hepatitis B: Laboratory report 1980–84. Br Med J 1986;**293**:37–8.

31. Wright R. Type B hepatitis: progression to chronic hepatitis. Clin Gastroenterology 1980;**9**:97–115.

32. Beasley RP, Hwang LY. Hepatocellular carcinoma and hepatitis B virus. Semin Liver Dis 1984;**4**:113–26.

33. Alexander G, Williams R. Antiviral treatment in chronic infection with hepatitis B. Br Med J 1986;**292**:915–17.

34. Finch RG. Time for action on hepatitis B vaccination. Br Med J 1987;**294**: 197–8.

35. Stevens CE, Taylor PE, Rubinstein P, et al. Safety of hepatitis B vaccine. N Engl J Med 1985;**312**:375–6.

36. Zuckerman AJ. Who should be immunised against hepatitis B? Br Med J 1984;**289**:1243–4.

37. British Medical Association: Report of the Board of Science and Education. Immunisation against hepatitis B. London: British Medical Association, 1987.

38. Hadler SC, Francis DP, Maynard JE, et al. Long term immunogenicity and efficacy of hepatitis B vaccine in homosexual men. N Engl J Med 1986; **315**:209–14.

39. Galambos JT. Transmission of hepatitis B from provider to patients: how big is the risk? Hepatology 1986;**6**:320–5.

40. Sherlock S. Diseases of the liver and biliary system. 7th ed. Oxford: Blackwell, 1985:334–45.

41. Saunders JB, Walters JRF, Davies P, Paton A. A 20 year prospective study of cirrhosis. Br Med J 1981;**282**:263–6.

42. Brunt PW, Kew MC, Scheuer PJ, et al. Studies of alcoholic liver disease in Britain: I Clinical and pathological patterns related to natural history. Gut 1974;**15**:52–8.

43. Maxwell JD, Knapman P. Effect of coroners' rules on death certification for alcoholic liver disease. Br Med J 1985;**291**:708.

44. Westaby D, Williams R. Injection sclerotherapy for the long term management of variceal bleeding. World J Surgery 1984;**8**:667–72.

45. Shomerus H, Hamster W, Blunk H, Reinhard U, Mayer K, Dolle W. Latent portasystemic encephalopathy. 1. Nature of cerebral functional defects and their effect on fitness to drive. Dig Dis Sci 1981;**26**:622–30.

46. Murray RM. Alcoholism and employment. J Alcoholism 1973;**10**:23–6.

47. Mayfield D, McLeod G, Hall P. The CAGE questionnaire: validation of a new alcoholism screening instrument. Am J Psychiatry 1974;**131**:1121–3.

48. Tamburro CH. Chemical hepatitis. Pathogenesis, detection and management. Med Clin North Am 1979;**63**:545–66.

49. Seeff LB, Cucherini BA, Zimmerman HJ, Adler E, Benjamin SB. Acetamino-phen hepatotoxicity in alcoholics. A therapeutic misadventure. Ann Intern Med 1986;**104**:399–404.
50. Sato C, Nakano M, Lieber CS. Prevention of acetaminophen-induced hepa-totoxicity by acute ethanol administration in the rat: comparison with carbon tetrachloride-induced hepatotoxicity. J Pharmacol Exp Therap 1981;**215**: 805–10.
51. Kazantzis G. Liver—preventive measures. In: Parmeggiani L ed. Encyclopaedia of Occupational Health and Safety. Geneva: International Labour Office, 1983:1238.
52. Allan RN, Keighley MRB, Alexander-Williams J, Hawkins C. Inflammatory bowel diseases. Edinburgh: Churchill Livingstone, 1983.
53. Evans JG, Acheson ED. An epidemiological study of ulcerative colitis and regional enteritis in the Oxford area. Gut 1965;**6**:311–24.
54. Devlin HB, Datta D, Dellipiani AW. The incidence and prevalence of in-flammatory bowel disease in North Tees Health District. World J of Surgery 1980;**4**:183–93.
55. Mayberry J, Rhodes J, Hughes LE. Incidence of Crohn's disease in Cardiff between 1934 and 1977. Gut 1979;**20**:602–8.
56. Ritchie JK, Powell-Tuck J, Lennard-Jones JE. Clinical outcome of the first 10 years of ulcerative colitis and proctitis. Lancet 1978;**1**:1140–3.
57. Daly DW, Brooke BN. Ileostomy and excision of the large intestine for ulcerative colitis. Lancet 1967;**2**:62–4.
58. Sircus W. Natural history of Crohn's disease—overview. In: Allan RN, Keighley MRB, Alexander-Williams J, Hawkins C, eds. Inflammatory bowel diseases. Edinburgh: Churchill Livingstone, 1983:289–98.
59. Allan RN, Steinberg DM, Alexander-Williams J, Cooke WT. Crohn's disease involving the colon: an audit of clinical management. Gastroenterology 1977;**73**:723–32.
60. Hawkey CJ. Salicylates for the sulfa-sensitive patient with ulcerative colitis (editorial). Gastroenterology 1986;**90**:1082–4.
61. Whates PD, Irving M. Return to work following ileostomy. Br J Surg 1984;**71**:619–22.
62. Hawkley PR, Ritchie JK. Complications of ileostomy and colostomy following excisional surgery. Clin Gastroenterology 1979;**8**:403–14.
63. Office of Population Censuses and Surveys (1970–1983). Report on Hospital Inpatient Enquiry for the years 1967–1980. London: HMSO.
64. Kennedy HJ, Lee ECG, Claridge G, Truelove SC. The health of subjects living with a permanent ileostomy. Quart J Med 1982;**203**:341–57.
65. Gorbach SL, Nahas L, Weinstein L, Levitan R, Patterson JF. Studies of intestinal microflora. Gastroenterology 1967;**53**:874–80.
66. Report of Food Industry Medical Officers working group. Health standards for work in the food industry, food retailing and in establishments involved in catering. J Soc Occ Med 1987;**37**:4–9.
67. Finegold SM, Sutter VL, Boyle JD, Shimada K. The normal flora of ileostomy and transverse colostomy effluents. J Infect Dis 1970;**122**:376–81.

68. Clarke AM, Chirnside A, Hill GL, Pope G, Stewart MK. Chronic dehydration and salt depletion in patients with established ileostomies. Lancet 1967;2:740–3.
69. Skirrow MB. Campylobacter enteritis: a "new" disease. Br Med J 1977;ii:9–11.
70. Turnbull PCB. Food poisoning with special reference to salmonella—its epidemiology, pathogenesis and control. Clin Gastroenterology 1977;6:663–714.
71. Zaidman I. Intestinal amoebiasis. In: Bouchier IAD, Allan RN, Hodgson JF, Keighley MRB, eds. Textbook of gastroenterology. London: Baillière Tindall, 1984:1118–26.
72. Kazal HL, Sohn N, Carrasco JI, Robilotti JG, et al. The gay bowel syndrome. Clinicopathologic correlation in 260 cases. Ann Clin Lab Sci 1976;6:184–92.
73. Weller IVD. Gay gastroenterology. In: Pounder RE ed. Recent advances in gastroenterology. Vol. 6. Edinburgh: Churchill Livingstone, 1986:161–80.
74. Report of the Committee of Inquiry into an outbreak of food poisoning at Stanley Royd Hospital. DHSS. London: HMSO, 1986.
75. Gilbert RJ, Roberts D. *Salmonella*—food hygiene, aspects and laboratory methods. Public Health Laboratory Service Microbiology Digest 1986;3:32–4.
76. Winter J. Certification of Food Handlers. A system to fulfil EEC requirements. J Soc Occ Med 1983;33:93–7.
77. Nyren O, Adami HO, Gustavsson S, Loof L, Nyberg A. Social and economic effects of non-ulcer dyspepsia. Scand J Gastroenterology 1985;20(suppl 109):41–5.
78. Heaton KW. Irritable bowel syndrome. In: Bouchier IAD, Allan RN, Hodgson JF, Keighley MRB, eds. Textbook of gastroenterology. London: Baillière Tindall, 1984:867–74.
79. Fielding JF. The irritable bowel syndrome. Clin Gastroenterology 1977;6:607–22.
80. Thompson WG, Heaton KW. Functional bowel disorders in apparently healthy people. Gastroenterology 1980;79:283–88.
81. Ford MJ, Miller PMcC, Eastwood J, Eastwood MA. Life events, psychiatric illness and the irritable bowel syndrome. Gut 1987;28:160–5.
82. Harvey RF, Salik SY, Read AE. Organic and functional disorders in 2000 gastroenterological out-patients. Lancet 1983;i:632–4.

15

Cardiovascular disease

M. C. Petch and I. Picton-Robinson

INTRODUCTION

Individuals suffering from congenital heart disease will generally be detected in childhood and should seek cardiological advice before entering employment. Employers should not be deterred from taking on young people who have undergone cardiac surgery for the correction of congenital defects in childhood, as many lead a normal life and are capable of full-time employment. Acquired valve disease (which remains important despite the disappearance of rheumatic fever), endocarditis, cardiomyopathy, and cardiac arrhythmias are responsible for a small but troublesome morbidity and mortality. The greatest scourge affecting the working population, however, is undoubtedly ischaemic heart disease (IHD), with a prevalence that has been estimated at 24.7 per cent of men aged 40–59 years[1] and that is greater in social classes IV and V than in classes I, II, and III.[2] Some IHD is preventable; employers have an opportunity to support and reinforce community measures by discouraging smoking, encouraging healthy activities during rest and recreational hours, and by providing a healthy diet at work.

Some victims of IHD die suddenly and unpredictably from ventricular fibrillation. In the WHO Tower Hamlets study[3] 40 per cent of heart attacks were fatal and 60 per cent of deaths occurred within one hour of the onset of any symptoms. This fact is widely recognized and naturally makes employers reluctant to take on employees known to be, or suspected of, suffering from IHD.

Effective treatment is now available for many forms of cardiovascular disease. Drug therapy (beta-adrenergic antagonists, diuretics, anticoagulants) is discussed elsewhere (Chapter 3). Coronary bypass surgery can allow patients to resume normal work early, at a level of fitness higher than that achieved before the operation.[4] Housewives are often more able to cope without help after operation.[5] Improved cardiovascular fitness can also result from cardiac pacing, valve replacement, and cardiac transplantation. Unfortunately, waiting times, particularly for coronary arteriography and bypass surgery are such that many patients do not return to work. One study[5] showed that of those who had lost more than six months before operation, fewer (35 per cent) returned to work than those who had lost less than six months (73 per cent).

IHD usually presents as chest pain, either myocardial infarction or angina; it may also present with symptoms resulting from arrhythmias, or heart failure, or be detected incidentally by electrocardiography. After myocardial infarction, there may be complete physiological and psychological recovery, even to the extent of permitting heavy physical work and marathon running.[6] The likelihood of returning to work is affected by physical, psychological, and social factors;[7] these should be carefully assessed in the weeks following the acute event. Manifestations of major cardiac damage are associated with delay in, or prevention of return to work. Minor problems are unreliable predictors, being overwhelmed by the effects of anxiety, depression, inappropriate medical advice, or lack of awareness of the possibility of being able to return to work.

Chronic physical disability from heart disease is due to limitation of exercise tolerance through angina pectoris, dyspnoea, and fatigue. Rarely, patients may continue to experience sudden attacks of disability, e.g. faintness, despite treatment. The severity of angina, however, does not seem to be a clear guide to the possibility of return to work. Inability to find work that is neither physically nor mentally stressful, and the anxieties of family and close relatives, may also increase apparent disability.

There are many jobs, with a variety of physical or mental demands, and people with varying disabilities can often be accommodated, especially in large working groups. The safe performance of some work, however, would be severely compromised by the risk of giddiness or sudden unconsciousness even in the presence of an apparently high standard of present fitness; thus individuals with those symptoms are not accepted in certain occupations such as airline pilot, or driver of heavy goods and public service vehicles (see Appendices 1 and 2). This will be discussed more fully later.

Employers whose help is needed to find suitable work for cardiac patients will need specific advice in every-day terms about physical strength and endurance, tolerance of mental stress, work pace, and responsibility, as well as ability to manage night- or shiftwork and possible need for adjusted hours of work. Any information disclosed to employers, however, should first be discussed and agreeed with the patient so that confidentiality is preserved.

Employers can usefully contribute toward reducing the amount of heart disease in their workforce by actively encouraging employees to stop smoking. The potential benefits of reduced ill health are likely to be worth the effort of running a vigorous and comprehensive campaign.

PREVALENCE

In developed countries, about one-quarter of all deaths are due to IHD. In England and Wales in recent years, there were approximately 156 000 deaths and 115 000 hospital discharges per annum with the diagnosis of IHD. The Royal College of Practitioners' third national study confirmed the high morbidity.[8] Thus IHD is very common. Congenital heart disease affects approximately 8 per 1000 live births. Accurate figures for other forms of heart disease are not available, but there are at present approximately 620 patients with cardiac pacemakers per 1 million population, many of them past working age.

Of patients with myocardial infarction who have survived to reach hospital, half can expect to be back at work by five months and virtually all who will return eventually will be back by 12 months.[9] At four months, only one-quarter with evidence of serious heart damage,[7] as assessed during the hospital stay, will manage to return, while two-thirds of the rest, whether with minor heart damage or no heart damage, will manage to return. About 40 per cent of those with angina are likely to return, the severity not influencing this very much. In a stable working population those that have returned can expect to form some 1.7 per cent of the workforce.[10] If the record of work attendance is poor before the illness, perhaps only 40 per cent will have returned by four months, against 75 per cent of those whose work record was previously good.[11]

CLINICAL ASPECTS AFFECTING WORK CAPACITY

The risk of sudden disability, and death through ventricular fibrillation, is the major factor affecting work capacity among victims of heart disease. The risk is greatest in those with most myocardial damage. Thus subjects should be carefully examined, with particular reference to evidence of heart failure, cardiomegaly on chest radiography, and electrocardiographic change. The prognosis may be further refined using investigations such as ambulatory electrocardiography, radionuclide ventriculography, and coronary arteriography in selected cases. Exercise testing on a treadmill or bicycle ergometer with multiple clinical and electrocardiographic observations may be helpful in defining high- and low-risk groups. Furthermore, this investigation will permit accurate assessment of the physical working capacity of patients with IHD.

Subjects with continuing severe disability, sinister arrhythmias, or poor left ventricular function should generally be advised to retire, whatever the cause of their cardiac disease. This also applies to many patients with a progressive cardiac disorder, e.g. dilated cardiomyopathy. In contrast, subjects with good ventricular function, a stable cardiac rhythm, and minimal disability, whatever the cause, will usually fare well and should be encouraged to work. If the cause of the disability was corrected by surgical treatment, e.g. valve disease, then return to work 2–3 months after surgery can be expected.

Following myocardial infarction, assessment of prognosis along the lines outlined above is recommended: those with no complications and good exercise tolerance may return to work in 4–6 weeks. Others will take longer.

Patients with IHD and persistent angina despite medical treatment should be assessed with a view to coronary bypass surgery. Return to work, when possible, is usually 2–3 months after the operation (see p. 293). Following less traumatic procedures, such as the implantation of a pacemaker or coronary angioplasty, return to work is much quicker. In all cases, when work is resumed, the levels and duration of activity should be increased progressively; returning to work implies a level of sustained activity well above that achieved by most who are recovering at home or who are undertaking hospital rehabilitation programmes.

Psychological difficulties may be experienced even by those with no signs of cardiac damage. Anxieties of both the patient and wife have been shown to affect the ability of men surviving myocardial infarction to return to work; half may have some anxiety or depression and, of those, half may have severe symptoms persisting, if untreated, a year later.[11]

Cardiac rehabilitation has an important psychological effect, but the physiological benefits may be slight. Few hospitals and very few employers have formal programmes of rehabilitation. Where disability is uncertain and merits assessment, then the Manpower Services Commission's Employment Rehabilitation Centres serve a valuable role. Many companies, however, contribute to rehabilitation by arranging, on medical advice, for employees to return initially to less strenuous work. Employers will need to be advised what improvement can be expected and when to progress their employees towards normal working.

In general, physical activity is good for the heart. The degree of physical activity must take into account patients' previous fitness and the results of exercise testing, etc. Patients with stable angina pectoris can safely work within their limitations of fitness but should not be put in situations where their angina may readily be provoked. Although it is possible to give dogmatic advice about physical work, guidance about the psychological stresses associated with managerial duties needs individual attention. Personality has little influence on survival following myocardial infarction.[12]

Transient cardiac arrhythmias (e.g. extrasystoles) are extremely common and do not usually indicate heart disease. Assessment by a physician is recommended for those with persisting symptoms. A few individuals will suffer recurrent paroxysms of tachycardia which necessitate drug treatment; for some, an opportunity to withdraw from work and rest for a short period may be required. Symptomatic bradycardia is usually treated by permanent cardiac pacing. Pacemakers are generally implanted by physicians using local anaesthesia. Recovery is rapid. Pacemakers are very reliable and the batteries last more than five years. All pacemaker patients remain under the care of a cardiac centre. The indications for cardiac pacing are widening, as the efficacy of this form of treatment improves; some paroxysmal tachycardias can be controlled by pacemaker therapy, and automatic implantable defibrillators are now available, though at present they are very expensive.

Modern pacemaker technology allows pacing of atria and ventricles, variation in the rate and output of the generator, facilities for telemetry etc. Virtually all pacemakers have the capacity to sense and be inhibited by the patient's own ventricular electrical activity (demand mode). This can be mimicked by extraneous electrical activity. In theory, therefore, they may be subject to electrical interference, but in practice most pacemakers have good discrimination. In the presence of an extraneous signal, pacemakers may also stimulate the heart at a relatively fast rate which is felt by the patient so that he moves away from the source of interference (see p. 292).

Uncontrolled high blood pressure carries the risk of sudden disabling illness (e.g. stroke), yet may be silent until the onset of catastrophe. Screening for hypertension by occupational health staff is to be encouraged. Some antihypertensive drugs may provoke a tendency to faintness; diuretics and beta-blocking drugs are deemed relatively safe.

Peripheral vascular disease causes intermittent claudication which limits the victim's mobility. Medical treatment is relatively unsatisfactory, though surgical treatment can be very successful. The prognosis depends upon any associated coronary artery disease. The presence of an aortic aneurysm also indicates arterial disease and a liability to vascular catastrophe. Both these groups of patients should be carefully assessed in hospital, both clinically and by modern investigative techniques (ultrasound, Doppler, etc.) and particular attention should be paid to the likelihood of cardiac involvement. Raynaud's phenomenon on the other hand is a benign, albeit distressing, complaint. Underlying disorders, e.g. collagen disease, should be excluded; and occupational trauma, such as from chain saws or pneumatic hammer devices, must be avoided. Sufferers should work in a warm environment and be allowed to wear gloves and heated socks if indicated.

SPECIAL WORK PROBLEMS AND RESTRICTIONS

For most forms of heart disease the general rule is that activities causing no undue symptoms can be undertaken safely. Artificial restrictions are, therefore, unnecessary.

Most problems occur in patients with ischaemic heart disease. Not everyone would be able to go back to their own work after a coronary event. Some will require modifications to their job or a complete job change. In light engineering it has been observed that in one year about half those returning were fully fit, requiring no job change. The remainder had some limitation of fitness. Half their number required a job change; about one-tenth of all returning to work had severe limitations of fitness requiring a change of work.[9]

If recovery has been less than complete, circumstances at work will tend to affect the ability of patients to return. Work responding to emergency calls may place unacceptable demands on the cardiovascular system, rendering the individual liable to arrhythmias; such duties should be avoided. Heavy physical work, the need to climb up and down stairs, rapid and tight pacing of repetitive operations, such as component assembly, and the stress of responsibility and skill will all be relevant.

In most situations a full working day must be managed from the day of restarting. Tiredness that will often be burdensome initially usually resolves over the subsequent days or weeks. It may be helpful to arrange temporary shorter hours, perhaps curtailing both ends of the day so as to avoid rush-hour travelling. This recommendation can usefully be accompanied by a defined time through which the hours can be extended toward the full working day. By defining this time period, the perceived stress on the organization is notably less than leaving the period open-ended.

Shortness of breath and angina will require a consideration of the physical activity undertaken during the working day, including the amount of walking, sitting, and standing that is undertaken and what adaptations the employee can make within his own working routine. The speed of work, weights to be carried, and work pace will also be a significant stress which may well require temporarily easing for the not yet fully fit, or permanently adjusting for the permanently disabled.

The stress of managing or supervising may be significant and consideration will need to be given to the time necessary to catch up with events that the employee will have missed while being away, and to allow a gradual resumption of responsibilities. Consideration should be given to the requirements for overtime, meetings that occur early or late in the day, and the managerial responsibility that may be exercised. For all these, shortening the hours of work temporarily signals to the organization that the employee is not yet fully recovered, and perhaps encourages those who have been managing in the employee's absence to continue to do so for a further period of time. Permanent short-time work is not usually available, although some Local Authorities do operate, in conjunction with The Manpower Services Commission, sheltered placement schemes (see Chapter 2).

Psychological stress may arise from a variety of circumstances peculiar to the patient, his relatives, friends (and others), or his particular working circumstances. Commonly these factors are the source of encouragement and promote recovery. Work contact is often anticipated with pleasure after a long spell out of work and the consequent social isolation.

In some jobs, sudden collapse could be disastrous and the likelihood of a further sudden illness such as a ventricular arrhythmia needs careful assessment. Airline pilots, heavy goods and public service vehicle drivers, and those at sea in merchant shipping are rarely allowed to resume their employment following a myocardial infarction, and then only after extensive cardiovascular testing including angiography to demonstrate minimum risk.

Policemen, fire brigade officers and railway main line locomotive drivers normally have to discontinue their occupations following cardiac infarction.

Liability to sudden dizziness or unconsciousness can present hazards in many types of work. Driving any vehicle including life trucks and cranes, and the control of some machinery, is likely to be unsafe if the risk is at all significant. Working at unguarded heights, or with hot or corrosive liquids would present serious risks. Working alone, remote from contact with other people, may be hazardous. Thus those with arrhythmias and those with poorly controlled hypertension may need to have their work suitably altered.

Paroxysmal tachycardia and arrhythmias present problems if they are severe enough to induce symptoms of faintness, or angina, or if they could reasonably carry a risk of doing so. Judgement of the degree of risk needs to be made if the condition is mild, occurs infrequently, or is associated with other activities which allow prediction of its occurrence so that sudden disability could be avoided in dangerous situations.

The weights to be lifted regularly in manufacturing industries have tended to reduce in recent years and can usefully be considered on the scale indicated by the United States Department of Labor 1981[13] (see Chapter 1). Only the very fit and confident might reasonably attempt heavy work, such as lifting 50–100 pounds (23–45 kg). Many employees may manage quite comfortably medium work, such as lifting 25–50 pounds perhaps at the rate of one a minute, providing they do not have any evident physical limitations. The presence of support for the weights, keeping them at waist height, eases the strain considerably and if the task only requires the weights to be slid along benches or roller tracks, then the strain can be considered to be reduced by some 50 per cent. Those with moderate to severe restrictions may need to be confined to a maximum of 10 pounds (4.5 kg) or an equivalent degree of force on levers, turning wheels and similar machine controls. In any work organization there may be a few jobs requiring light-weight detailed work or simple checking which are suitable for those who are quite severely disabled. Some patients have sufficient skills to be able to learn inspection tasks which may be physically much less stressful. Other opportunities may be found in material and production control, progress chasing, recording, indexing, etc., which may allow continued working in basically fairly heavy industries. Exercise requirements well above normal, such as in foundries and forges, may well be reasons for debarring the employment of patients with or without shortness of breath or angina.

Rapid and tightly controlled pacing of work such as on assembly lines will not automatically be a problem to employees already adapted to it. If they were managing satisfactorily beforehand, they may well manage subsequent to the illness, if they are not severely disabled. Returning to their own work may be less of a problem than trying a new task, and more social support is provided by former rather than by new colleagues.

Similar arrangements apply to shiftwork and to the long-term coping with responsibility of those in supervisory and management work. If all has been well before the illness, returning to the same job may be the least stressful option. Permanent night-working can be easier if it has been managed well previously. At night, organizations tend to function along more routine patterns with less interference from peripheral parts of the organization. The co-operation amongst members of a team may well be higher and productivity can appear better. Those who have shortness of breath or angina find it an advantage to be able to rise from their bed during the day when the weather may be warm, or at least the house warm, to have some contact with their family and to travel to and from work in quieter times than their day-shift colleagues. New work can bring new situations, different personalities, different tasks and different sorts of components, all of which can be difficult to cope with even without the presence of heart disease. As detailed previously, working reduced hours on a temporary basis may be all that is required.

Rearranging work on a permanent basis for management and supervisory staff ideally requires considerable knowledge of the organization for which they work. In attempting to reduce stress, it helps to know how particular jobs are regarded in respect of decision-making, pushing events forward, advising on matters of experience and skill, or merely following routine procedures. Understandably, if the employee's perceived skills and strengths, or possible weaknesses, and inter-personal relationships may be relevant to making a successful placement, telephone contact with an employer, the personnel/welfare department of an organization, or with company occupational health medical and nursing staff may illuminate some of these matters so that a confirmatory written recommendation is seen as practical and helpful.

Solvents

It is now recognized that some volatile substances, such as halogenated or unsubstituted hydrocarbons, can affect the heart.[14] Although this is usually associated with 'glue-sniffing', it has been associated with the industrial use of trichlorethane. The usual medical problem is the development of cardiac arrhythmias, but it is possible that sustained exposure to these substances may produce the picture of dilated cardiomyopathy. Exposure to high levels of solvent fumes and chlorinated solvents, such as trichlorethylene, trichlorethane, or carbon tetrachloride, may thus lead to sudden irregular heart action, perhaps to a greater degree in those who have suffered heart damage or who are already prone to arrhythmias. Degreasing tanks, for example, should be properly designed, with adequate ventilation, but it is true to say that sometimes they are not.

Hot conditions

Working in hot conditions may prove difficult for some patients with heart disease. High ambient temperatures or significant heat radiation from hot surfaces or liquid metal, added to the physical strain of heavy work will produce quite profound vasodilatation of muscle and skin vessels. Compensatory vascular and cardiac reactions to maintain central blood pressure may be inadequate and lead to reduced cerebral or coronary artery blood flow. The resulting weakness or giddiness could prove dangerous.

Implanted cardiac pacemakers

The presence of an implanted pacemaker designed to maintain regular heart action is entirely compatible with normal or even strenuous exercise. The underlying heart condition for which the pacemaker was fitted may, however, impose its own restrictions. If the heart is otherwise healthy, then it is reasonable for strength and endurance to be explored gradually and for activity to be progressively increased. Effort tolerance is more likely to be maintained in patients fully dependent on pacing if they have one of the newer types of unit that preserves atrio-ventricular synchrony.

Muscle action-potentials can occasionally interfere with the pacemaker, causing temporary cessation of pacing that may induce faintness. Usually the interference will be brief, but sustained heavy work should not normally be attempted in these circumstances.

Cardiac pacemakers are vulnerable to electrical interference, but the number of documented cases is only about three per annum.[15,16] Industrial electrical sources such as arc welding, faulty domestic equipment, engines, anti-theft devices, airport weapon detectors, radar, and citizens-band radio can all potentially affect pacemakers but, in general, the patient has to be very close to the power source before any interference can be demonstrated, and the pacemaker abnormality is confined to one or two missed beats or reversion to the fixed rate mode. If pacemaker patients are expected to work in the vicinity of a high-energy electrical field capable of producing signals at a rate and pattern similar to a QRS complex (e.g. power stations, welding equipment), then formal testing is recommended. The cardiac centre responsible for implanting the pacemaker will usually provide a technical service for this purpose, thus enabling the risk of interference to be defined precisely. If a pacemaker patient should experience untoward symptoms while near electrical apparatus, then he should move away. In the event of collapse the patient should be moved but other causes for the collapse should also be sought. Pacemaker patients carry cards which identify the type of pace-maker, the supervising cardiac centre, etc. Further advice is readily available from the cardiac centre or, if this information is not available, from the British Pacing and Electrophysiology Group (see Appendix 5 for address).

Cardiac surgery

Replacement of the aortic and mitral valves by mechanical or biological prostheses is a common and safe procedure. Patients generally recover rapidly and fully to resume work at 2–3 months after the operation. Those with mechanical valves need to take anticoagulants indefinitely and are thus at risk from bleeding. Sudden failure of mechanical valves is extremely uncommon but nevertheless they are a bar to professional vehicle and mainline locomotive driving. Most biological valves undergo slow deterioration some years after implantation but professional driving, including public service vehicles, heavy goods vehicles, and mainline locomotives, is permitted if the drivers are fit in other respects, but subject to regular medical surveillance.

Coronary artery bypass grafting also allows most patients with ischaemic heart disease to resume work within 2–3 months of surgery. Most patients are relieved of their angina and for many the prognosis is improved, i.e. there is less chance of sudden incapacity from ventricular fibrillation. Patients who are able to work before operation should generally be able to work afterwards, and restrictions that may have been appropriate previously should no longer be relevant. Similarly, many who could not work before surgery because of their disability should be able to do so afterwards. Unfortunately, surgery constitutes a rather dramatic event that may generate inappropriate anxiety in patients, spouses, employers, or even medical advisers. Many individuals who could and should return to work fail to do so for this reason rather than because of continuing incapacity. No special restrictions are usually necessary after return to work.

Graft stenosis and occlusion, however, does lead to recurrence of angina at a rate of about 4 per cent per annum. This is seldom severe but may affect long-term occupational planning. Similar comments apply to patients following successful coronary angioplasty. The criteria for fitness to resume heavy goods vehicle driving after coronary artery bypass grafting are set out in *Medical aspects of fitness to drive* (see p. 296). British Rail, however, do not at present allow any patients who have had coronary grafting or angioplasty to resume main line driving.

Cardiac transplantation may allow dramatic improvement in working capacity but recipients do have to be maintained on immunosuppressants and other drugs. For advice about work the transplantation centre should be consulted.

Hypertension

Untreated hypertension carries the risk of sudden disability from heart attack or stroke; discovery of this condition may require immediate cessation of some employments where a serious accident risk exists (pp. 289–90). Controlled hypertension must be regarded in the same light and the risks carefully assessed against details of the individual's work content. Risks to self may be weighted a little less than risks to others. When considering the need to continue in employment well-controlled hypertension may be risk-free, especially if control is by diet only or with small doses of mild diuretic. Control with stronger drugs may carry the risk of side-effects such as hypotension with resultant giddiness or fatigue, limited effort and endurance. Central nervous system side-effects may affect judgement and the performance of skilled tasks.

Controlled hypertensives can expect to manage most varieties of working activity. Frequent postural changes may prove troublesome due to altered central and peripheral vascular responses. Very heavy physical work and exposure to very warm or hot conditions with high humidity may not be managed because of dilatation of muscle vessels and of skin vessels, to aid cooling; blood pressure control may be severely embarrassed. Such work should not be attempted if these ill-effects might prove dangerous either to health or because of the associated accident risk; they may be cautiously attempted if the work is safe, and patients should be give due warning of what effects may occur and what to look out for. Provided blood pressure readings can be maintained under satisfactory control and are checked regularly, heavy goods and public service vehicle driving is now allowed on some other drugs, as well as on beta-blockers and diuretics, provided that the cardiothoracic ratio on radiography is less than 0.55, there is no evidence on investigation of coronary heart disease, and there are no disabling side-effects.

Other cardiovascular problems

Postural hypotension occasionally troubles the young and fit and may also be recognized as a complication of neuropathy affecting autonomic nerves, as may occur occasionally in diabetes (see Chapter 13). The circumstances and frequency of postural hypotension would need to be assessed against job requirements and environment.

Circulatory restriction of internal carotid vertebral and cerebral vessels will produce disturbance of consciousness and other neurological effects (see Chapter 11).

Restriction of circulation to limbs will result in muscular claudication, especially in cold and wet, risk of damage to skin (frostbite), and poor recovery from accidental injury to skin and deeper structures. Raynaud's phenomenon can be provoked by the use of vibrating tools and work processes that transmit vibration to the fingers. Common situations are the use of power saws, pneumatic chisels, rough grinding by hand of metal objects. Clearly those with symptoms should avoid such work.

Outdoor work and work in cold stores or cold test rooms (some with moving air increasing the chill factor) may prove unsafe if peripheral circulation is significantly restricted and may also provoke angina. The risk of frostbite and gangrene would be high in cases where a serious circulatory restriction existed. Poor clothing may prove inadequate if limbs are likely to get wet as well as cold; such clothing relies on trapped air for insulation which is lost if the garments become soaked with water or sweat. Wind chill equivalent to a temperature of less than -10 °C is unlikely to be safe, but temperatures from 10-0°C using good protection may be coped with.

Intermittent claudication may significantly affect leg muscles, limiting walking distance, climbing stairs, and negotiating other obstacles such as assembly lines, climbing in and out of vehicles, etc. The pace of work will determine whether or not a patient can allow sufficient time to cope with his claudication by intermittent rest spells. Production work may not be as static as it appears at first; moving between machines and work stations, fetching and delivering components, may require more standing and walking than can be managed. Conversely, some machine work is sufficiently automated to allow frequent sitting down during the work cycle. Claudication of other muscles used frequently and heavily may occasionally occur and need detailed consideration. Muscle of the hand may be affected, especially by prolonged writing, which perhaps could be alleviated by the use of typewriting or computer-entry record-keeping and composing.

Cuts and bruises from accidental contact with furniture, machinery, etc., or from dropped objects, may not heal at all well in the presence of circulatory restriction, and there could be the risk of the onset of gangrene and the subsequent need for disabling operations. Limbs at risk need adequate protection continuously while at work.

Varicose veins of the legs present similar problems; accidental injury may lead to severe blood loss and protection is essential. Work routines involving standing still are difficult to cope with but some walking is helpful. Sitting for long uninterrupted periods may aggravate ankle swelling and, if the hip and knee are awkwardly flexed, there could be some risk of vascular thrombosis.

Individual limitations need to be set against the individual requirements for continuing at work. Quite often serious disability proves not to present the expected difficulty because the particular work circumstance is sufficiently favourable.

LEGISLATION AND GUIDANCE

Driving (see also Appendix 1)

The Road Traffic Acts[17] require notification by an applicant or licence-holder to the DVLC at Swansea immediately on diagnosis of any disability that is likely to affect safe driving either at the time of diagnosis or in the future, except in the case of disabilities, such as fractures, which will be completely cured within three months. The medical practitioner's role is to advise the patient on the basis of the severity of the condition. If the driver's fitness is so severely affected as to present a significant hazard to other people, and if the driver fails to carry out this duty, there may be grounds for the doctor to consider whether or not he should notify the DVLC directly. This must be judged in the context of ethical standards prevailing.[18] Those heart conditions likely to produce sudden incapacity would be grounds for notification to DVLC. *For HGV and PSV driving* (including ambulance, fire, police, taxi, and hire car) quite specific advice is given in *Medical aspects of fitness to drive*[19] and is the standard applied by local authorities. Advice is given about angina, heart attack, ECG abnormalities, cardiac enlargement, aortic aneurysm, paroxysmal arrhythmias, hypertension, peripheral artery disease, syncope, and cardiac surgery. This document should be consulted in detail.

Aviation (see also Appendix 2)

Aircraft pilots must meet the standards of the Civil Aviation Authority. These are higher for professional pilots than for private pilots and call for good cardiovascular function and a low risk of sudden incapacitation. The Civil Aviation Authority appoints doctors to carry out medical examinations on those applying for pilot's licences. Patients can be referred to these appointed doctors. Further advice and information on aviation and cardio-vascular disease can be found in the published proceedings of the second United Kingdom Workshop in Aviation Cardiology.[20]

Merchant Shipping (see also Appendix 3)

The Merchant Shipping Regulations 1983[21] required that those with a history of coronary thrombosis be declared permanently unfit, but the regulations do now allow people with a history of coronary thrombosis to resume seafaring on appeal, subject to undergoing rigorous cardiovascular testing. Those patients with valvular disease of the heart causing significant impairment or having required surgery are deemed unfit, as are those with intermittent claudication. Merchant seamen with hypertension are allowed more potent hypotensive agents now in addition to beta-blockers and/or diuretics, subject to their blood pressure being controlled to below 170/100 without any significant side-effects and without cardiac complications.

SUMMARY

The high incidence of ischaemic heart disease over the past few decades has been accompanied by greater accuracy of diagnosis (and hence prognosis). Improvements in treatment, medical and surgical, have allowed much higher expectation of recovery and ultimate fitness. Those with other heart conditions have shared in these improvements and expectations.

Those returning to work show a much improved fitness in recent years compared with those some 20 years ago. Considerable numbers are returning to employment, some with help from rehabilitation and resettlement services, many getting back to their own work.

It is possible to give clear recommendations for helping patients to return to normal active life and to work. These recommendations help not only patients and their doctors, but also employers, who should understand what is happening to their employees to be able to assist them in their return to work.

The probability of sudden disabling attacks of giddiness and loss of consciousness represents the most difficult disability to accommodate, but improvements in workplace safety allow more people to be suitably employed.

Limitation of exercise tolerance may prevent patients managing their transport to and from work. For many, the work itself can be organized to avoid undue extra stress. Developments towards automation and robotic manufacturing promise to reduce the physical content of a day's work, perhaps improving the opportunities for continued working by those disabled with cardiac conditions.

REFERENCES

1. Shaper AG, Cook DG, Walker M, Macfarlane PW. Prevalence of ischaemic heart disease in middle-aged British men. Br Heart J 1984;**51**:595–605.
2. Rose G, Marmot MG. Social class and coronary heart disease. Br Heart J 1981;**45**:13–9.
3. Tunstall-Pedoe H, Clayton D, Morris JN, Bridgden W, MacDonald L. Coronary heart attacks in East London. Lancet 1975;**2**:833–8.
4. Oakley CM. Clinical aspects of cardiac rehabilitation. In: Cardiac rehabilitation. Proceedings of the Society of Occupational Medicine Research Panel Symposium. London: Society of Occupational Medicine, 1983:2–9.
5. Clarke DB, Edwards FC, Williams WG. Cardiac surgery and return to work in the West Midlands. In: Cardiac rehabilitation. Proceedings of the Society of

Occupational Medicine Research Panel Symposium. London: Soc Occ Med, 1983:61–70.

6. Gloag D. Rehabilitation of patients with cardiac conditions. Br Med J 1984; **288**:615–20.

7. Nagle R, Gangola R, Picton-Robinson I. Factors influencing return to work after myocardial infarction. Lancet 1971;**2**:454–6.

8. Morbidity statistics from general practice 1981–2. Third National Study. Royal College of General Practitioners. London: HMSO, 1986.

9. Picton-Robinson I. Rehabilitation at work, opinion and overview. In: Cardiac rehabilitation. Proceedings of the Society of Occupational Medicine Research Panel Symposium. London: Soc Occ Med, 1983:90–9.

10. Kemble HR. Occupational aspects of cardiac rehabilitation. In: Cardiac rehabilitation. Ibid 26–41.

11. Cay EL. The influence of psychological problems in returning to work after a myocardial infarction. In: Cardiac rehabilitation. Ibid 42–60.

12. Case RB, Heller SS, Case NB, Moss AJ, and the Multicenter Post-Infarction Research Group. Type A behavior and survival after acute myocardial infarction. N Engl J Med 1985;**312**:737–41.

13. Selected characteristics of occupations defined in the Dictionary of Occupational Titles. United States Department of Labor. Washington: US Government Printing Office, 1981.

14. Boon NA. Solvent abuse of the heart (editorial). Br Med J 1987;**294**:722.

15. Gold RG. Interference to cardiac pacemakers—how often is it a problem? Prescribers Jl 1984;**24**:115–23.

16. Sowton E. Environmental hazards and pacemaker patients. J R Coll Physicians Lond 1982;**16**:159–64.

17. Road Traffic Act. London: HMSO, 1972.

18. British Medical Association. Handbook of medical ethics. London: British Medical Association, 1981.

19. Raffle PAB, ed. Medical aspects of fitness to drive. 4th ed. Medical Commission on Accident Prevention. London: Royal College of Surgeons, 1985.

20. Joy M, Bennett G, eds. The second United Kingdom workshop in aviation cardiology. Eur Heart J, 1988 (in press).

21. Merchant Shipping (Medical Examinations) Regulations 1983. S.I. 1983 no. 808. London: HMSO, 1984.

16

Respiratory disease

J. A. Dick and A. J. Newman Taylor

INTRODUCTION

Improved social conditions and the advent of effective drug therapy have caused a remarkable change in the pattern of respiratory disease during this century. Previously common causes of illness and unfitness for work, such as pneumonia, tuberculosis, and bronchiectasis, are now unusual. Nevertheless, respiratory disease remains an important cause of ill health during the years of working life; it accounts for 25 per cent of all consultations in general practice[1] and is responsible for 14 per cent of all days off work.[2] The infections and their sequelae have now been replaced as causes of lung disease, mainly by lung cancer and conditions whose dominant effect is on airway function: chronic bronchitis, asthma, and emphysema.

Pulmonary tuberculosis remains a problem in the immigrant population particularly in Asians, and in elderly men. Spontaneous pneumothorax, which may recur, occurs predominantly in otherwise healthy young men. Improved treatment for cystic fibrosis has considerably increased the number with the disease who survive into their twenties and thirties and who are therefore eligible for employment. Sarcoidosis only rarely causes lung fibrosis; fibrosing alveolitis, although usually leading to progressive lung fibrosis, is an uncommon disease.

Classical occupational lung diseases, the inorganic dust pneumoconioses, and occupational lung cancer are becoming less common, reflecting improvements in occupational hygiene and reduction of working life time. Mesothelioma incidence however has remained unchanged for several years, reflecting the long latent period which may elapse between exposure to asbestos and the development of this disease. Occupational asthma is increasingly recognized, but this is probably as much a reflection of increased awareness as of a rising incidence.

Lung function is commonly and easily measured by assessment of the ventilatory function of the lungs and, in the laboratory, by the measurement of gas transfer, usually as the fractional uptake from the lungs of a small concentration of carbon monoxide added to inspired air. The most frequently used method to assess ventilatory function is measurement of forced vital capacity (FVC) and forced expiratory volume in one second (FEV_1), measurements which are easily made with a portable spirometer which prints out the data. The method is dependent upon a forced expiration and, therefore, on the co-operation of the individual tested. For this reason, demonstration of the reliability of the test result is essential and it is usual to require three comparable measurements to be made. The FVC is the total volume of air which can be expelled from the lungs after a maximum inspiration, and the FEV_1 is the volume of air expelled during the first second of this manoeuvre. The values of these measurements differ between men and women, and vary with their age and stature. The measurements obtained in any individual must therefore be interpreted by comparison with the predicted normal values for someone of similar sex, age, and height. The distribution of values has been established by examining normal populations and is readily available. As a rule of thumb, FEV_1 increases with growth of the lungs up to about the age of 20–25 years, following which it declines by 25–30 ml/yr. In cigarette smokers susceptible to the effects of inhaled smoke the rate of decline is accelerated some three fold, such that they may lose an additional half litre each decade.[3]

Chronic bronchitis and emphysema and asthma cause narrowing of the intrapulmonary airways. For this reason, the effect on FEV_1 is greater than the effect on FVC, and the ratio of FEV_1 to FVC, normally some 2:3 to 3:4 is reduced, an obstructive ventilatory impairment. The obstructive defect in asthma is distinguished from that of chronic bronchitis and emphysema by the improvement (15 to 20 per cent or more) which follows the inhalation of a bronchodilator such as salbutamol or following treatment with corticosteroid drugs such as prednisolone. This is described as a reversible obstructive ventilatory impairment to distinguish it from the relatively irreversible obstruction which occurs in chronic bronchitis and emphysema. The disability caused by these diseases is primarily the result of inability to increase expiratory flow rates sufficiently to meet the demands of exercise. In addition, asthmatic airways are hyperresponsive to a variety of inhaled irritants, and acute airway narrowing may be provoked by many non-specific stimuli including exercise and cold air. FEV_1 is a powerful predictor of life expectancy. A reduction of 2 SDs or greater was associated in a 20-year follow-up period with a fourfold increase in overall mortality and fortyfold increase in mortality from respiratory disease.[4]

Diseases which cause inflammation and thickening of alveolar walls, such as fibrosing alveolitis, allergic alveolitis, and sarcoidosis, cause stiffening of the lungs with impairment of gas transfer across the alveolar membrane. By increasing the ventilation rate the lungs are able to maintain the excretion of carbon dioxide but, because of the different shapes of the oxygen and carbon dioxide dissociation curves, this is not possible for oxygen and so arterial pO_2 falls while pCO_2 is maintained or reduced. The stiffness of the lungs increases the work of breathing and this is probably the major contributory factor in the breathlessness which occurs at lower than normal work loads in individuals with these diseases. Increased stiffness of the lungs reduces the volume of air which can be taken into the lungs but does not diminish the rate at which air can be expelled. FVC and FEV_1 are reduced to a similar extent and the FEV_1/FVC ratio maintained. This is referred to as a restrictive ventilatory impairment and is characteristic of inflammatory and fibrosing diseases of the interstitium of the lungs. The associated impairment of gas transfer can be demonstrated by diminution in the uptake of CO from inspired air (transfer factor or DLCO). A restrictive pattern of ventilatory impairment also occurs in circumstances where the lung is compressed by air in the pleural space (pneumothorax) or fluid in the pleural space (pleural effusion).

The degree of impairment of lung function is, however, only one of the factors which will determine exercise capacity. The degree of breathlessness perceived by an individual as caused by a particular work load is closely related to the distance walked in a particular time, e.g. 6 or 12 minutes. The distance walked in 12 minutes was originally introduced because it is the time anticipated for an infantryman in full kit to walk 1000 metres. Walking speed varies little during the 12-minute period and a 6-minute walk is now more commonly used. These tests have the advantage over more formal exercise tests using treadmills or bicycles in that they use 'every-day exercise' and are very much more convenient to undertake.[5]

The determinants of the distance walked during a timed period include the severity of respiratory impairment; FVC and transfer factor (DLCO) are better predictors than FEV_1. However, equally powerful predictors are mood (depression and anxiety) and attitudes and beliefs about ill health, its social and financial consequences, and the chances of improvement with treatment. Some of the blame for the poor outlook seen in many patients with respiratory disease, in particular chronic bronchitis and emphysema, lies with their medical advisers who may transmit their own pessimism to their patients, possibly not surprisingly in view of the words we use to describe these diseases: *chronic* bronchitis, *irreversible* airways obstruction, and respiratory *failure*. In fact, although normal lung function cannot be restored, some improvement can often be obtained with the use of inhaled drugs and the rate of decline in lung function can be slowed by stopping smoking. A more optimistic perception of the illness causes significant amelioration of disablement.

Of the major causes of respiratory disease, chronic bronchitis, asthma, emphysema, and lung cancer, only asthma is significantly amenable to drug treatment although airflow limitation in chronic bronchitis and emphysema may be partially reversible in some cases. The introduction of inhaled steroids and bronchodilators has provided a safe and effective treatment which, when used correctly, allows the great majority of asthmatics to lead normal lives. Airflow limitation in chronic bronchitis and emphysema can be partially improved with inhaled bronchodilators, both sympathomimetics and anticholinergics. Chronic bronchitis, emphysema, and lung cancer are mainly attributable to cigarette smoking and therefore largely preventable. Employers can contribute considerably to community preventive pro- grammes by discouraging smoking. Stopping smoking reduces both mucus hypersecretion and the risk of infective exacerbations of bronchitis at times of viral upper respiratory tract infections, as well as reducing to normal the accelerated rate of decline in lung function which occurs in susceptible smokers. If a smoker stops smoking his risk of dying of lung cancer decreases with the duration of stopping over a 15-year period.[6]

Unlike chronic bronchitis, emphysema, and lung cancer, which usually develop from middle age onwards, the onset of asthma is frequently in childhood, when it may be one manifestation of an allergic diathesis. It may be present in school- or university-leavers applying for jobs.

PREVALENCE

Respiratory diseases are second only to cardiovascular diseases in shortening life. The 1977 report *Smoking OR Health* from the Royal College of Physicians of London[7] focuses on the effects of the smoking-related diseases, chronic bronchitis, emphysema, and lung cancer, during working life and describes mortality from these causes in men and women under the age of 65 years. In 1974 lung cancer caused some 37 000 deaths in men under the age of 65 years and 14 500 deaths in women under the age of 65 years. The death rate is declining in men, but increasing in women to the extent that with breast cancer it is now the major cause of death from malignancy. The number of person days lost from work in 1976/77 because of bronchitis, chronic bronchitis, and emphysema was recorded as 26 million for men and 2.6 million for women. Chronic bronchitis and emphysema cause about 30 000 deaths a year, 5500 in those under the age of 65 years. The number of deaths caused by chronic bronchitis and emphysema has been falling since 1965, in part because of cleaner air but also because of improved treatment of chest infections. Deaths from these diseases are five times commoner in unskilled labourers than in professional men. Occupations where exposure to dust and fumes occurs, such as work with coal and cotton, are also contributory causes of chronic bronchitis, although of less importance than cigarette smoking.

Asthma

Difficulty in the identification of asthma has led to uncertainty about its prevalence. In one survey of an NHS general practice in north London, which used reversibility of airways obstruction of at least 30 per cent as the criterion for diagnosis, the prevalence in adults was found to be 5.4 per cent.[8] A more recently published survey of general practices in England and Wales in 1970–1 and 1980–1 reported the prevalence of asthma in men to have increased between these dates from 11.6 to 20.5 persons consulting per 1000 population, and in women from 8.8 to 15.9 per 1000 population.[9] The prevalence between the ages of 15 and 25 in men had increased from about 10 to nearly 20 persons consulting per 1000 population and in women from nearly 10 to 15 per 1000 population.

Occupational lung diseases

The prevalence of occupational lung diseases has decreased in recent years, and their nature as identified by claims accepted for compensation by the Department of Health and Social Security has changed. Whereas in 1960 the total number of new certified cases of pneumoconiosis was 3654, of which 3279 were coal workers' pneumoconiosis and 29 were asbestosis, in 1985 the total number of new certified cases of pneumoconiosis was 739 of which 364 were coal workers' pneumoconiosis and 273 asbestosis; in addition in 1985 405 cases of mesothelioma and 166 cases of occupational asthma were certified. Neither of these diseases was prescribed in 1960. The changing prevalence of various forms of pneumoconiosis is shown in Table 16.1.

CLINICAL ASPECTS AFFECTING WORK CAPACITY

Airflow limitation

The major factor affecting the work capacity of individuals with the chronic non-malignant respiratory diseases, chronic bronchitis, emphysema, asthma, and pulmonary fibrosis, is the reduced capacity to increase alveolar ventilation and gas exchange sufficiently to meet the increased demands of exercise. The greatest effect of these diseases therefore occurs in those in physically demanding jobs.

Airway function can be stabilized in the majority of cases of bronchial asthma by currently available inhaled steroids, cromoglycate, and bronchodilators. Vigorous exertion, particularly in cold air, may provoke acute airway narrowing in otherwise controlled asthmatics, 'exercise-induced asthma'.

Airflow limitation in chronic bronchitis and emphysema and established pulmonary fibrosis are generally not greatly improved by treatment. Airflow limitation in chronic bronchitis and emphysema increases with age, more rapidly in those who continue to smoke cigarettes. Lung function in patients with pulmonary fibrosis caused by sarcoidosis can be improved with corticosteroids, but they are usually less successful in the treatment of cryptogenic fibrosing alveolitis.

Table 16.1   New cases certified by Pneumoconiosis Panels (Medical Boarding Centres)

Industry	1956	1968	1980
Coal mining	4853	774	461
Pottery	432	31	18
Foundry work	290	51	21
Cotton	238	126	148
Steel dressing	64	11	3
Refractories	47	10	6
Asbestos	31	130	144
Furnace dismantling	29	4	—
Slate mining and splitting	27	42	47
Quarrying	16	6	8

Viral infections of the upper respiratory tract

Individuals with chronic bronchitis, emphysema, asthma, cystic fibrosis, and pulmonary fibrosis are susceptible to viral infections of the upper respiratory tract which are frequently followed by acute bronchitis and, on occasion, pneumonia. Repeated attacks of acute bronchitis associated with viral upper respiratory tract infections occur in patients with chronic bronchitis and emphysema causing loss of time from work particularly during the last 10 years of life. On average both males and females who smoke 20 or more cigarettes a day lose twice as much time from work as non-smokers.[7] Asthmatics are also susceptible to the effects of viral respiratory tract infections which increase both nonspecific airway hyperresponsiveness and the severity of the asthma, which may persist for weeks.

Exposure of asthmatics to workplace allergens

The majority of asthmatics need little restriction in their choice of occupation. Clearly, it is unwise to enter employment in any occupation in which the asthmatic is exposed to specific allergens to which he is sensitive; an individual who is allergic to cats or dogs would be unwise to consider employment as a veterinary surgeon. Similarly, on more general grounds individuals with asthma should avoid exposure to agents known to cause occupational asthma (some causes listed in Table 16.2). Although for many of the causes of occupational asthma they may be no more likely than others to be sensitized, the consequences for someone with pre-existing asthma may be considerably more severe. The same argument does not apply to individuals who are atopic, which is the predisposition to produce IgE antibody to common environmental allergens such as grass pollen, house dust mite, or cat hair. Atopy is identified by an immediate skin-prick test response to extracts of one or more of these. Atopics have a greater risk than non-atopics of developing asthma from some causes of occupational asthma (Table 16.2), for instance the secreta and excreta of laboratory animals. However, the risk of developing asthma in those exposed is 5–10 per cent and the prevalence of atopy is high (about one-third of the adult population). If adopted as a pre-employment screen for potential laboratory animal workers, atopy would probably exclude some three to four times as many individuals who would not develop asthma as those who would. Furthermore, asthma may develop in some of the non-atopics who have been accepted for employment.

Cystic fibrosis

The improved outlook for patients with cystic fibrosis, largely attributable to physiotherapy and antibiotic treatment, means that some 75 per cent of patients survive to adult life. Having lived to the age of 16 years, their probability of survival to 30 years is now 0.46. Recurrent chest infections mean that these patients frequently require intensive antibiotic treatment. Time lost from school may leave them less well qualified than their peers when applying for jobs and time away from work requires understanding from their employers. None the less, their work record is remarkably good Of 183 patients attending the Brompton Hospital in 1982, 61 were at school or in further education, 97 in gainful employment, and 13 unemployed. Nine were housewives. Only three were incapable of work because of their illness.[10]

Lung cancer

The poor outlook for patients with lung cancer, of whom only 5 per cent survive five years or more, and for patients with mesothelioma, which has a median survival of some 18 months, makes the prospects for continuing employment difficult and uncertain. Patients with small-cell carcinoma of lung treated with chemotherapy require frequent short in-patient admissions for chemotherapy but longer periods to recover from its effects. Patients with resectable lung cancer (some 20 per cent) will usually need a period of one month or more for investigation, operation, and post-operative recovery. Patients with non-resectable disease are likely to suffer the effects of local or distant spread of the disease within one to two years.

Pneumonia

Pneumonia occurring in otherwise healthy young persons is usually amenable to specific antimicrobial therapy and should not recur. Recurrent

Table 16.2   Some causes of occupational asthma

	Proteins	Haptens
Animal	Excreta of: rats, mice, etc. locusts, grain mites	
Vegetable	Grain/flour Castor bean Green coffee bean Ispaghula	Plicatic acid (western red cedar) Colophony (pinewood resin)
Microbial	Harvest moulds *Bacillus subtilis* enzymes	Antibiotics, e.g. penicillins, cephalosporins
'Mineral'		Acid anhydrides Isocyanates Complex platinum salts Polyamines Reactive dyes

pneumonia occurs in patients with chronic airway disease, including bronchiectasis and cystic fibrosis, and in the immunosuppressed.

Pulmonary tuberculosis

Pulmonary tuberculosis is curable provided regular and adequate chemotherapy, which should now include rifampicin and isoniazid and possibly also pyrazinamide, is taken for 6 or 9 months depending on the particular drug regimen. For practical purposes only persons with pulmonary tuberculosis who have tubercle bacilli in sufficient numbers to be visible in their sputum on direct smear are infectious. Patients with non-pulmonary tuberculosis, and with pulmonary tuberculosis who have three sputa which are smear-negative for acid-fast bacilli, can be regarded as non-infectious and, provided their general condition is satisfactory, they can continue to work while having treatment. Patients whose treatment includes rifampicin can be regarded as non-infectious after 2 weeks therapy but may not remain so if regular treatment is not continued.

   Contacts who share accommodation with index cases who are smear-positive are at greatest risk of subsequently developing active tuberculosis. Both they and domestic contacts of smear-negative cases should be identified and contacted in order to offer treatment where necessary. Nine per cent of Asian and 12 per cent of non-Asian domestic contacts of smear-positive cases subsequently develop active disease. On the other hand, only 2.5 per cent of Asian and 0.5 per cent of non-Asian domestic contacts of smear-negative cases will subsequently develop active disease. The risk of subsequently developing active disease is much lower (about 0.3 per cent) for non-household contacts and, unless they are unusually susceptible, such as schoolchildren or the immunosuppressed, they are not normally examined. In schools contact procedures are required only if the index case has pulmonary tuberculosis. If the index case, teacher or child, is smear-negative, only the classmates need examination; if a child is smear-positive, all children in the same year should be examined to allow for the mobility of a child in different classrooms. If a teacher is smear-positive, all other members of staff should be examined as well as the children.[11]

Protection against pulmonary tuberculosis among NHS staff and teachers and local authority staff is based upon a pre-employment chest radiograph and the response to tuberculin. If tuberculin negative an individial should be given BCG. For NHS staff at high risk because of contacts with patients with tuberculosis, or with tuberculous material the site of BCG vaccination should be inspected 6 weeks after the vaccination to ensure a satisfactory reaction, and annual chest radiographs should be taken. Staff beginning work with infants and children must produce a satisfactory chest radiograph taken within the previous 12 months to prevent those with infectious pulmonary tuberculosis coming into contact with this susceptible age group.[11]

Influenza

Influenza is an extremely infectious disease of the respiratory tract caused by the influenza group of viruses, A, B, and C. It is endemic throughout the world with irregular outbreaks caused by A or B virus. Pandemics due to mutation of the influenza A virus occur about every 30 years. The only protection against influenza is immunization with vaccine containing the relevant virus strains, which confers about 70 per cent protection. Immunization is only recommended for persons at special risk from severe consequences of influenza virus infection and in whom vaccination is not contraindicated by egg allergy. Special high-risk groups include particularly the elderly and those who suffer from chronic lung and heart diseases, chronic kidney disease, and diabetes mellitus. Unless there is a major epidemic, protection for health care staff should also be limited to those with these illnesses.

Pneumothorax

Spontaneous pneumothorax in young adults is rapidly relieved by aspiration of air from the pleural space. Relapse can be anticipated in about 30 per cent of cases; one or two recurrences are an indication for curative treatment by pleurectomy.

SPECIAL WORK PROBLEMS

In the assessment of fitness for work of patients with respiratory disease a number of general factors should be considered.

The physical demands of a job and its component tasks need to be assessed in relation to the individual's capacity to meet them. How much physical effort is required in terms of lifting, carrying, or walking upstairs? Those with lung disease may be unable to meet the exercise demands of heavy physical work. Where respiratory disease is progressive, as lung function deteriorates the capacity for exercise will become increasingly limited. This can be a particular problem for patients in physically demanding, relatively unskilled work, who become increasingly less able to cope with it in the middle years of life.

Similar considerations apply to the use of respiratory protection: reduction in ventilatory reserve will make breathing through a high-resistance filter increasingly difficult. This problem may be overcome by the use of laminar flow equipment, provided this gives adequate protection.

Heat and cold and high and low humidity are poorly tolerated by many individuals with asthma (a reflection of airway hyperresponsiveness) and with other chronic airway diseases. Work in cold rooms or outdoors in the winter months can be particularly difficult for those with asthma, chronic bronchitis, emphysema, and cystic fibrosis.

Dusty conditions and exposure to irritant gases, such as SO_2 and organic solvents are similarly poorly tolerated by patients with chronic airway diseases.

The severity of respiratory symptoms in patients with asthma is often greatest in the night, on waking, and in the evening; and with chronic bronchitis on waking in the morning. Patients with bronchiectasis and cystic fibrosis need time for postural drainage on first waking up in order to clear secretions which have accumulated during the night. The diurnal pattern of symptoms and treatment requirements places severe constraints on the ability of those suffering from these diseases to undertake shift work when it involves work in the night or early morning. Arranging for these patients to have an afternoon shift can be very helpful. When flexi-time but not shift work is available, the individual should be advised to start work at the latest permitted time.

Non- or poorly communicating airspaces in the thorax, such as a pneumothorax or emphysematous bullae, may rupture when ambient pressure changes rapidly. For this reason individuals with these conditions must be excluded from any work involving diving or flying.

The loss of lung function and associated disablement following resection for lung cancer will depend upon the volume of lung removed and the age of the patient. The consequences of pneumonectomy are clearly greater than those of lobectomy, and both are more severe in the elderly. The loss of lung volume after a pneumonectomy is about 30 per cent and after a lobectomy about 15 per cent. The capacity for exercise is likely to be diminished, but, following successful resection, many patients are able to lead lives appropriate for their age. The risk of cerebral metastases in patients with lung cancer is sufficiently high and unpredictable to make it necessary to debar those in whom this diagnosis has been made from driving HGV or PSV vehicles and from working at heights.

Occupational lung diseases

Lung diseases caused by occupation pose special problems. Agents inhaled at work can cause many different diseases of the lungs. Acute chemical pneumonia is the consequence of inhaling reactive chemicals, such as chlorine gas, oxides of nitrogen, or cadmium fume, in toxic concentrations. In general, if the acute illness is survived, full recovery of lung function is to be anticipated. Chemical pneumonitis caused by oxides of nitrogen may run a relapsing course with the development of bronchiolitis. Inhalation of respirable mineral dusts can, depending on the fibrogenicity of the dust and the dose inhaled, cause varying degrees of pulmonary fibrosis (pneumoconiosis). The most important pneumoconioses are asbestosis, coal workers' pneumoconiosis, and silicosis. Asbestos can cause diffuse interstitial fibrosis with severe respiratory disability. Coal workers' pneumoconiosis and silicosis may progress to the complicated form progressive massive fibrosis (PMF) which can also cause considerable respiratory disability. In silicosis tuberculosis is an important complication. Asbestos also causes mesothelioma and like other chemicals, such as bischloromethyl ether (BCME), products of nickel refining (possibly nickel subsulphide), as well as radon daughters, may cause lung cancer. A wide variety of agents inhaled at work may stimulate a specific hypersensitivity response (usually immunologically mediated) to cause asthma (Table 16.2), extrinsic allergic alveolitis (Table 16.3). Beryllium causes a form of sarcoidosis.

The restrictions which the development of these diseases will impose on future employment are dependent upon the risk of progression of the disease if exposure continues and the adequacy of dust control at the job, tempered by awareness of the financial, psychological, and social consequences that can ensue when avoidance of exposure means job loss. Restrictions are not usually necessary for those who have recovered from acute chemical pneumonia. Management of occupational lung cancer is determined by the nature of the cancer, not its cause.

Table 16.3 Some causes of extrinsic allergic alveolitis

Disease	Antigen source	Antigen
Farmer's lung	Mouldy hay, etc.	*Micropolyspora faeni*
Pigeon fancier's lung } Budgerigar fancier's lung }	Avian excreta and bloom	Avian serum proteins
Bagassosis	Mouldy bagasse	*Thermoactinomycetes sacchari*
Malt worker's lung	Mouldy maltings	*Aspergillus clavatus*
Mushroom worker's lung	Spores generated during mushroom spawning	*Thermophilic actinomycetes*
Maple bark stripper's lung	Removing bark from stored maple, sycamore, etc.	*Cryptostroma corticale*
'Ventilation pneumonitis'	Contaminated air-conditioning systems	*Thermophilic actinomycetes*

The precise cause of the development of complicated pneumoconiosis is not yet understood, but it is known that the risk increases with increasing exposure to respirable dust. For this reason young men (36 years old or less), men who show exceptionally rapid progression, and all men with pneumoconiosis of Category 2 or more are advised to work in approved low dust conditions (on average 3 mg/m³ of inspired air). Suitable financial arrangements are made by the coal-mining industry so that if a change of job is necessary there is no significant loss of income.

Any individual who develops radiological evidence of simple silicosis should be protected from further silica exposure. Regular sputum examination for acid-fast bacilli is also worthwhile because of the risk of complicating tuberculosis.

The general advice given to those who develop asbestosis is to avoid all further work with asbestos. However, the evidence that progression is affected by further exposure is limited and current control limits are such that the dose of asbestos inhaled in the future is likely to be minimal in comparison to the current fibre burden in the lungs, the consequence of past less controlled exposures, which has caused the pulmonary fibrosis. Cigarette smoking interacts with inhaled asbestos to increase the risk of lung cancer in a manner more than additive but less than multiplicative. At present lung cancer is the cause of death in some 40 per cent of cases of asbestosis.[12] Asbestos workers should be strongly advised to stop smoking; in those with asbestosis this will reduce the risk of developing lung cancer some tenfold over a 10-year period.

Occupational asthma, extrinsic allergic alveolitis (Table 16.3), and beryllium sarcoidosis are diseases caused by an acquired hypersensitivity (allergy) to a specific agent inhaled at work. Continuing exposure to the causes of these diseases provokes both reversible inflammation with acute asthma or alveolitis and increases the chance of developing irreversible damage, either chronic asthma or fibrosis, so that further exposure to the cause of the disease must be prevented. Respiratory protection can be effective where asthma or alveolitis is due to a dust, e.g. laboratory animal urine contaminating cage dust, the manufacture of antibiotics and other drugs, and thermophilic actinomyces spores in mouldy hay. It is essential where respiratory protection is used in these situations that its effectiveness is monitored by serial measurement of lung function. Where possible, substitution of materials or relocation away from exposure are the most appropriate solutions, although often, as for farmers, this may not be feasible.

Cigarette smoking has interesting and opposite effects on the risk of developing specific IgE antibody and occupational asthma, and specific IgG antibody and extrinsic allergic alveolitis. It increases the risk of developing IgE antibody and reduces the risk of developing IgG antibody. The reasons for this are unclear, but the increased risk of IgE production may reflect damage to the barrier between airway lumen and submucosal immunocompetent cells, whereas the reduced risk of IgG production may be the result of a direct toxic effect of cigarette smoke on alveolar macrophages, impairing their ability to handle and present antigen to T lymphocytes.[13]

LEGISLATION AND GUIDANCE

There are no statutory limitations on work for individuals with respiratory disease.

The compensation legislation for occupational respiratory diseases is, however, considerable.[14] Those who develop any of the listed 'prescribed diseases' are eligible for compensation under the provisions of the Social Security Act (1975). The decision on both diagnosis and disablement assessment is made by a specialist adjudicating medical authority (AMA) which is constituted by two doctors of a Medical Boarding Centre (Respiratory Diseases) (MBC). If a prescribed disease is diagnosed the claimant is entitled to a disablement allowance the level of which is based on the AMA's disablement assessment, as well as other allowances. The most important of these is reduced earnings allowance which is intended to compensate for loss of income where, because of the prescribed disease, persons cannot continue in their regular occupation. Details of the benefits available can be found in DHSS leaflets *N13* and *N16*. The list of prescribed diseases can be found in the DHSS leaflet *Pneumoconiosis and related occupational diseases*, which is at present being updated to include the more recently prescribed diseases including occupational asthma.

The currently prescribed respiratory diseases are:

B5   Tuberculosis
B6   Extrinsic allergic alveolitis (including Farmer's lung)
C14   Poisoning by nickel carbonyl
C15   Poisoning by oxides of nitrogen
C17   Poisoning by beryllium or a compound of beryllium
C18   Poisoning by cadmium
C22b   Primary carcinoma of a bronchus or of a lung (in nickel production)
D1   Pneumoconiosis
        Coal-workers' pneumoconiosis
        Silicosis
        Asbestosis
D2   Byssinosis
D3   Diffuse mesothelioma (primary neoplasm of the pleura or the pericardium or of the peritoneum)
D7   Asthma which is due to exposure to any of the following agents:

(a) Isocyanates;
(b) Platinum salts;
(c) Fumes or dusts arising from the manufacture, transport, or use of hardening agents (including epoxy resin curing agents) based on phthalic anhydride, tetrachlorophthalic anhydride, trimellitic anhydride, or triethylenetetramine;
(d) Fumes arising from the use of rosin as a soldering flux;
(e) Proteolytic enzymes;
(f) Animals or insects used for the purposes of research or education in laboratories;
(g) Dusts arising from the sowing, cultivation, harvesting, drying, handling, milling, transport, or storage of barley, oats, rye, wheat, or maize, or the handling, milling, transport, or storage of meal or flour made therefrom (occupational asthma);
(h) Antibiotics;
(i) Cimetidine;
(j) Wood dust—such as cedar, oak, and mahogany;
(k) Ispaghula—used in the manufacture of bulk laxatives;
(l) Castor bean dust—merchant seamen, laboratory workers, and felt makers may be exposed;
(m) Ipecacuanha;

(n) Azodicarbonamide—used as a blowing agent in the manufacture of foam plastics

D8 Primary carcinoma of the lung where there is accompanying evidence of one or more of the following:

(a) Asbestosis;
(b) Bilateral diffuse pleural thickening related to asbestos exposure.

Primary lung cancer in the following workers:

(a) Those whose occupations involve exposure to bischloromethyl ether (BCME) produced during the manufacture of chloromethyl methyl ether (CMME);
(b) Those whose occupations involve the use or handling of or exposure to the dust of zinc chromate, calcium chromate, or strontium chromate;
(c) Tin miners.

SUMMARY AND CONCLUSIONS

The major cause of disablement both in the common chronic bronchitis, emphysema, and asthma and the less common pulmonary fibrosis is loss of ventilatory reserve, limiting the ability of the lungs to cope with the increased demands of exercise. The impact of these diseases on the capacity for work will, therefore, primarily occur in those whose work is physically demanding. With the exception of bronchial asthma among the diseases causing airflow limitation, the scope for improvement of ventilatory function with bronchodilator drugs is limited. None the less, other simple measures can enable an individual to continue to work. Exercise capacity in those with chronic airflow limitation seems influenced as much by mood and motivation as by lung function and continuing employment will contribute to maintenance of these. Relocation to less demanding work, avoidance of cold, dust, and irritants, and optimal shift times will help to enable an individual to remain in employment.

Bronchial asthma should be considered as a reason for exclusion from employment only in a limited number of specific circumstances such as work with allergens to which the individual is sensitive, or with agents known to cause occupational asthma, or work in an environment which is liable to provoke recurrent attacks of asthma (e.g. extreme cold). Although cystic fibrosis causes limitation of life span and liability to recurrent chest infections, those with the disease who reach an employable age enjoy a good work record.

The contribution of specific occupational causes to the burden of respiratory disease in the community, although small, is important. Avoidance of further exposure to the cause of some occupational lung diseases can prevent progression to an irreversible stage. Where respiratory protection is used, its effectiveness must be monitored by regular measurement of lung function.

REFERENCES

1. Morrell DC. Expressions of morbidity in general practice. Br Med J 1971;**2**:454–8.
2. Office of Health Economics. Compendium of Health Statistics. London: Office of Health Economics, 1984.
3. Fletcher C, Peto R. The natural history of chronic airflow obstruction. Br Med J 1977;**1**:1645–8.
4. Peto R, Speizer FE, Cochrane AL, *et al.* The relevance in adults of airflow obstruction, but not of mucus hypersecretion, to mortality from chronic lung disease: results from 20 years of prospective observation. Am Rev Resp Dis 1983;**128**:491–500.
5. Geddes D. Chronic airways obstruction. Postgrad Med J 1984;**60**:194–200.
6. Doll R, Peto R. Mortality in relation to smoking: 20 years observations on male British doctors. Br Med J 1976;**2**:1525–36.
7. Smoking *OR* Health. Royal College of Physicians of London. London: Pitman, 1977.
8. Gregg I. Epidemiological aspects. In: Clark T, Godfrey S, eds. Asthma, 2nd edition. London: Chapman and Hall, 1983:242–84.
9. Fleming DM, Crombie DL. Prevalence of asthma and hay fever in England and Wales. Br Med J 1987;**294**:279–83.
10. Batten JC. Cystic fibrosis in the adult. In: Flenley D, Petty TL, eds. Recent Advances in Respiratory Medicine 3. London: Churchill Livingstone, 1983: 115–30.
11. Joint Tuberculosis Committee of the British Thoracic Society. Control and prevention of tuberculosis: a code of practice. Br Med J 1983;**287**:1118–21.
12. Berry G. Mortality of workers certified by Pneumoconiosis Medical Panels as having asbestos. Br J Ind Med 1981;**38**:130–7.
13. Newman Taylor AJ, Venables KM. Editorial: Smoking, occupation and allergic lung disease. Lancet 1985;**i**:965.
14. Ward F. Industrial benefits and respiratory diseases. Thorax 1986;**41**:257–60.

Further reading

Disabling chest disease: prevention and care. A report of the Royal College of Physicians by the College Committee on Thoracic Medicine. J Roy Coll Phys Lond 1981;**15**:69–87.
Health *OR* Smoking. Royal College of Physicians of London. London: Pitman, 1983.
Elmes PC. Relative importance of cigarette smoking in occupational lung disease. Br J Ind Med 1981;**38**:1–13.

17

Renal disease

R. Gokal and C. A. Veys

Classification

The kidney has the vital function of excretion, and controls acid-base, fluid, and electrolyte balance. It also acts as an endocrine organ. Renal failure, with severe impairment of these functions, results from a number of different disease processes, most of which are acquired although some may be inherited. Chronic renal failure implies permanent renal damage which is likely to be progressive.

Glomerular involvement (usually an immunological insult) gives rise to glomerulonephritis, which presents with proteinuria, haematuria, or both, and may be accompanied by hypertension and impaired renal function. If proteinuria is gross, it can lead to the nephrotic syndrome. Pyelonephritis with renal scarring is the end result of infective disorders with or without anatomical abnormalities of the urinary tract. Systemic diseases, such as diabetes mellitus, hypertension, and collagen disorders, can affect the kidney, while polycystic kidney disease is the commonest inherited disorder leading to renal failure. The renal tract can also be affected by problems of an anatomical nature, such as stones, strictures, obstruction, and tumour.

For the purpose of this chapter, the disorders considered are chronic renal failure and renal replacement therapy, urinary tract infections, renal calculi, tumours of the renal tract, and some of the complications and sequelae of renal disease.

End-stage renal failure

Often of insidious onset, end-stage renal failure is reached when the glomerular filtration rate is irreversibly reduced to less than 5 ml/min. Without renal replacement therapy, death is inevitable. The main causes of renal failure are glomerulonephritis and pyelonephritis (50–60 per cent), followed by polycystic kidney disease and hypertension (10 per cent each).[1] Diabetes mellitus is becoming an important cause of renal failure, accounting for 15–20 per cent of cases.

Renal replacement therapy can be achieved in one of three ways:

(1) *haemodialysis* performed at home, hospital, or specialized minimal care units;

(2) *continuous ambulatory peritoneal dialysis*, a home (or self) dialysis technique;

(3) *renal transplantation* (cadaveric, or living related donor).

In the United Kingdom (UK) the aim has been to place patients on home therapy whenever possible.

Urinary tract infections

Symptoms related to these are very common, but of serious import only when there is an underlying anatomical abnormality, which may require a urinary diversion procedure (ileal conduit) or permanent urethral catheterization. A small percentage of women suffer from repeated infections and remain symptomatic in spite of antibiotic therapy. Repeated infections in the presence of an anatomical abnormality (such as uretero-vesical reflux, or outflow obstruction) can lead to chronic renal failure later in life.

Renal stones

The predominant composition of idiopathic renal calculi is calcium oxalate. Urolithiasis of the upper urinary tract is a fairly common condition in the UK, with a recurrence rate of over 60 per cent.[2,3]

Tumours of the renal tract

Adenocarcinoma of the kidney is the commonest adult renal tumour. In the bladder more than 95 per cent of tumours are urothelial in origin. About 4–7 per cent are occupational and associated with previous work in the chemical, dye-stuffs, rubber, cable, and other industries where exposure to carcinogenic aromatic amines has occurred.[4]

Complications and sequelae of renal disease

These include hypertension, incontinence, haematuria, and proteinuria.

PREVALENCE, MORBIDITY, AND MORTALITY

End-stage renal failure

Currently, in the UK, 43 new patients are accepted for renal replacement therapy per million of the population per year, well below the 45–80 new patients/million/year of comparable western nations.[5] The number of patients on therapy in the UK (December 1985) was 215 per million of the population, in contrast to 305 and 291 for West Germany and France respectively.[5] These differences reflect the relative lack of facilities in the UK, and reveal discrimination against older patients and those who also have systemic diseases, such as diabetes mellitus, in selection for treatment.[6] In 1984, there were 3523 deaths in England and Wales from chronic and unspecified renal failure (ICD 585–6), 1517 in males and 2006 in females.[7] Most of these deaths were in patients over 55 years old. The total represents 0.6 per cent of all deaths, but 60 per cent of deaths from renal tract disease (ICD 580–99).

In Europe, patients maintained on hospital haemodialysis have an actuarial survival of 50 per cent at five years and 35 per cent at 10 years after starting dialysis.[1] Survival, however, is age-related, and is higher in younger age groups. Overall survival for home haemodialysis patients is 74 per cent at five years and 55 per cent at 10 years.[1] The five-year survival of cadaveric transplant patients is 58 per cent, and 71 per cent for those with a transplant from a living relative. Continuous ambulatory peritoneal dialysis has an 80 per cent two-year survival.[8] Overall survival statistics for the UK have shown a progressive improvement over the past decade, with similar age-related changes: in the 15–35-year age-group, five-year survival has increased from 70 per cent (1972–76) to 82 per cent (1977–81) for all renal replacement therapy patients.[9]

Death, as well as some morbidity, is related to premature atherosclerosis, hypertension, and vascular disease, and to infections and haemorrhage.[1]

The main reasons for hospital admission in patients on peritoneal dialysis are peritonitis and catheter problems; and vascular access problems in haemodialysis patients.[8] Hospitalization is much commoner in patients with other conditions such as diabetes, and in those with cerebro-cardiovascular diseases. Data for home haemodialysis and successful transplant patients show considerably less hospitalization.

Patients receiving dialysis, or having a successful transplant, need frequent out-patient visits at first, but stabilize to a visit every 2–3 months (dialysis patients) and every 4–6 months (transplant patients).

Morbidity statistics from general practice in 1971–72 revealed that for nephritis and nephrosis the number of episodes and consultations per 1000 population was only 0.2 in both men and women.[10]

Urinary tract infections

Although most infections are symptomless, there is much morbidity from these conditions. The size of the problem is difficult to ascertain. The incidence of symptomatic infections rises after puberty, and up to 50 per cent of females have such symptoms at some stage in their lives.[11] It is much less frequent in males but rises sharply after the age of 60 years as a result of prostatic enlargement.

It has been estimated that between 12 and 60 per 1000 consultations in general practice are for symptoms suggesting a urinary tract infection,[12] while some 45 days per 100 people per year are lost from work from the same cause.[13] Chronic pyelonephritis, the supposed end result of urinary tract infection, is the second most frequent cause of end-stage renal failure, and accounts for 20 per cent of all those requiring renal replacement therapy. In numerical terms, however, this is a very small proportion of those with urinary tract infections.

Renal stones

Ten years ago, the prevalence in the UK was 3.5–4 per hundred[14] but the incidence appears to be increasing. The peak incidence occurs in males at age 35.[2] Renal stones cause much morbidity, often require extensive surgery, a lengthy convalescence, and in consequence much time off work. Deaths directly from renal and ureteric calculi (ICD 592) are few: males 53 and females 95 in 1984.[7]

Urinary tract tumours

In England and Wales, bladder cancer accounts for 7 per cent of all cancer in men but only 2.5 per cent in women; similar figures for renal tumours are 2 per cent and 1 per cent respectively.[15] The mean annual age-standardized incidence of renal cancer in men in the UK is about 3.5 per 100 000, while it is under 2 for women. In 1984, 3156 deaths from bladder cancer (ICD 188) were registered for men and 1432 for women. Carcinoma of the body of the kidney (ICD 189) caused 1265 deaths in men and 753 deaths in women.[7]

CLINICAL ASPECTS AFFECTING WORK CAPACITY

Haematuria and proteinuria

The discovery of asymptomatic haematuria, whether macroscopic or microscopic, and not related to urinary tract infection, requires further investigation. Initially, microscopy and culture should be undertaken. If this is negative, then nephro-urological investigations are necessary to ascertain any underlying pathology and thus to make decisions about treatment, reassurance, and employment.[16]

Significant proteinuria needs to be quantified and, if confirmed, inevitably requires referral for further nephrological investigation. Postural or exercise proteinuria should be excluded first, for it is not in itself a contraindication to employment.

Hypertension

Hypertension is a common sequel of renal parenchymatous disease, but is itself a cause of chronic renal failure in 8–10 per cent of cases.[1] Antihypertensive therapy, together with salt and water restriction is usually necessary. The condition can sometimes be difficult to control and the drugs used may cause side-effects. This is discussed more fully in Chapters 3 and 15.

Transplantation

In successfully transplanted patients renal function returns to normal, as does the haemoglobin level. These patients can lead a normal life to all intents and purposes, but need immunosuppressive therapy (prednisolone, azathioprine, cyclosporin A) on a daily basis. Because of this the transplant patient is more prone to unusual infections, and should avoid contact with people who have acute respiratory and other infections.

Chronic renal failure and dialysis

Impaired renal function leads to a progressive anaemia with haemoglobin values around 8–10 g/dl. Consequently, patients may be chronically tired and are more easily fatigued, which can impair work performance. However the availability within the next year or so of recombinant human erythropoietin may well make symptoms of anaemia a thing of the past, with substantial improvement in well being and employment prospects.[16a] In spite of regular dialysis, the biochemistry at no time returns to normal; at best, dialysis therapy imparts a renal function equivalent to a glomerular filtration rate of 5–7 ml/min. Dietary modifications of protein, fat, carbohydrate, sodium, potassium, phosphate, and vitamin intake, and restriction of fluid intake are therefore necessary. With such dietary and fluid intake control, and with good dialysis it is unusual to experience uraemic symptoms (nausea, vomiting, itching, cramps, and diarrhoea) but some surveillance at work may be needed.

Several complications other than the anaemia can affect dialysis patients. In a minority, disordered metabolism of vitamin D, parathyroid hormone, calcium, and phosphate lead to renal osteodystrophy which can present with bone pain, proximal myopathy, and, rarely, pathological fractures.[17] Vascular disease is a commoner problem, with angina, hypertension, peripheral vascular complications, and cardiovascular accidents;[18] these set-backs are more marked in the elderly and in those with other systemic disease.

Dialysis routines
Selecting the dialysis routine and adapting it to the job can be the vital factor

in deciding whether a patient is successful in gaining or keeping a job. It is here that co-operation between renal unit staff (particularly the specialist nurse), family practitioner, and occupational health staff can reap most reward.

Haemodialysis Patients must undergo dialysis three times a week for 4–8 hours on each occasion. For those working full-time, home dialysis is done in the evenings and at weekends, while those dialysing in hospital during the day may only be able to manage part-time employment on non-dialysis days. It is not unusual for a haemodialysis patient to feel 'washed out' after a session of dialysis. This is related to the rapid removal of fluid and uraemic toxins (disequilibration).[19] Although this usually passes off completely by the next day, it may linger and affect the patient's performance at work. Machine failure at home may also mean a return to hospital dialysis, requiring more time off work.

Continuous ambulatory peritoneal dialysis entails 3–4 daily exchanges of about 2 litres of fluid drained in and out of the peritoneal cavity, each taking about 30 minutes to perform and being spaced out over the day. This usually means that at least one exchange must be done at work; this can most easily be fitted in to the lunch break, but needs to be performed in a suitably clean area. Continuous cyclic peritoneal dialysis is a modification of the dialysis routine, in which all the exchanges of fluid are done at night using a cycler machine, thus obviating the need for daytime exchanges. The apparatus is expensive, but can help those in some occupations that involve much travel, such as company representatives and salesmen.

After starting haemodialysis, people may be unable to work for some 3–4 months while undergoing training for home therapy. A similar absence may be needed following transplantation. This is the period needed for very frequent out-patient visits to monitor renal function and treat rejection episodes, which are more likely in the first three months. Most employers will understand this and be sympathetic if the reasons are explained, and will accommodate the delay. The training time for peritoneal dialysis, however, is usually about four weeks and work can thus start much sooner.

Although few figures are published, the hospitalization rate for dialysis patients is about 15 days per patient year of treatment.[8] This would be the minimum time off work, as the figures do not include out-patient visits.

Those on renal dialysis who can manage only part-time work (i.e. less than 30 hours per week) may obtain an extra Needs Allowance if already receiving Supplementary Benefit (Regulations 13(1)(a) and 14 of Schedule 4 of Supplementary Benefits (requirements) Regulations, SI 1983 No. 1399). Otherwise there are no special Social Security Benefits for dialysis patients.

The main work contraindications for dialysis patients are shown in Table 17.1. Fatigue and a tendency to tire quickly make heavy manual and other

Table 17.1 Haemodialysis and continuous ambulatory peritoneal dialysis and types of employment

1 (unsuitable) Contraindications	2 (possible) Relative contraindications	3 (suitable) No contraindications
Heavy labouring or heavy manual work	Printing*	Light manufacturing industry
Construction/building/ scaffolding	Motor repair (care with fistula in HD patients)	Driving (unless other medical problems)
Refuse collection*	Welding*	Clerical/secretarial
Furnace/smelting	Painting and decorating*	Light assembly
Mining	Horticultural work	Light maintenance/ repair
Chemical exposure to renal toxins	Catering trades*	Packing
Work in very hot environments	Nursing*	Supervising
Farm labouring*	Shiftwork	Middle and senior management Law, accountancy Retail trade Sales Receptionist Teaching Medicine

* not contraindicated in haemodialysis.

For patients on haemodialysis, shiftwork and long hours may present problems requiring greater adaptation. Some patients have learnt to dialyse while asleep using the built-in warning devices on the machine.

Should occupations in column 2 entail heavy lifting, labouring, or manual work, they are unsuitable. However this may change with improvement in anaemia from administration of erythropoietin.[16a]

physically demanding work unsuitable. Apart from problems posed by fatigue, patients may also have visual impairment related to diabetes or hypertension, which may need special provisions and surveillance.

Dialysis, and to some extent transplant patients, live a stressful life.[20, 21] Although most patients adjust to dialysis regimes, some may have psychological problems related to the stress of the dialysis itself. Additionally, the altered quality of life, and other problems such as loss of libido and impotence, understandably cause further stress and such patients may overreact to any small difficulties in their work situation. Nevertheless, there is no doubt that satisfactory rehabilitation can be achieved by those who learn to adapt to their condition.

Urinary tract infections

Most episodes are short lived and respond to therapy. Those with frequent episodes, however, may succumb to chronic illness with backache, dysuria, and frequency in spite of long-term antibiotic therapy. These problems are difficult to manage and may result in frequent absences from work.[13]

Renal stones

The newer treatments of percutaneous nephrolithotomy, and especially extracorporeal shock-wave lithotripsy for stones of over 2 cm in diameter, offer the prospect of dramatically improving the previous picture of long periods off work and poor attendance. The average in-patient stay for extracorporeal shock-wave lithotripsy is 3–7 days, with minimal post-operative discomfort, and generally a resumption of normal activity within a day or so after discharge.[22]

Because of the relative dehydration and possible recurrent renal stone formation, it is probably unwise either to encourage long overseas postings in tropical climates, or to pass applicants with a strong history of stone formation as fit for furnace or other very hot work.

Urinary incontinence

Improved incontinence devices and more thorough investigation now offer those afflicted better prospects for staying at work. Urinary diversion procedures for incontinence are becoming more acceptable.[23] The specialist incontinence nurse can help to improve work attendance by giving advice, reassurance, practical help, and support.

SPECIAL EMPLOYMENT PROBLEMS

Work record

The work record of patients with renal disease remains largely unreported in the medical literature.

Many patients with end-stage renal failure remain unemployed because of the problems imposed by their demanding treatment regimes and the need to undergo haemodialysis in the renal unit or at home during the day. Their real difficulty is to find suitable work when they are available for it. Sometimes a rearrangement of dialysis regimes will give the flexibility needed for a particular job. Patients who are not able to continue in their original work may need further training once treatment has been started.

Some dialysis patients are faced with the additional costs of frequent trips to the clinic or renal unit for treatment and review, and this may impose an extra burden on their employability. If reasonable adaptation cannot be effected, a special rehabilitation programme should be considered in conjunction with the social worker and the Disablement Resettlement Officer. Further details of help with return to work are given in Chapter 2.

Renal failure and employment

Many employers, although sympathetic, misunderstand what can be achieved by patients with chronic renal failure and this may preclude a successful outcome. There is thus a real need to educate both doctors and employers about the work capabilities of people with renal failure. The close co-operation of all concerned (the renal unit, the patient, the general practitioner, occupational health staff, and the employer) is often needed to effect a successful placement. The occupational physician is usually best placed to catalyse the necessary adjustments. There is sometimes a dilemma in advising a patient to become a Registered Disabled Person, because some patients feel strongly that they are not really disabled. Pressing for registration in these circumstances can have an adverse psychological effect without compensatory advantages.

The work record of those who have received a successful transplant is especially good.[20] A transplant cannot now be accepted as a reason for denying employment or of restricting work content, for transplant patients are capable of virtually any normal work.

The main problems surround those on dialysis. The needs of these patients and their capabilities are less well understood and, thus far, little studied. A recent joint study from the Manchester and Oxford renal units, however, found that over half of those working before the start of continuous ambulatory peritoneal dialysis or of haemodialysis were in employment after 6–12 months of therapy.[21] The figure for transplant patients is much higher. Recent surveys in the USA show employment figures of 74 per cent (transplant), 60 per cent (haemodialysis), and 30 per cent (peritoneal dialysis).[20] These statistics do not take into account patient selection, which favours fitter patients for transplant and usually means high-risk patients receiving peritoneal dialysis. It is worth pointing out that one of the most arduous jobs is performed by housewives, and there are many women on dialysis coping with both a home and a family successfully.

Other renal conditions and employment

Two situations arise with respect to the employment of someone with renal tract cancer. For the patient with an existing tumour who is seeking employment, the extent of the pathology and the patient's general condition dictate employability. On the other hand, someone already in employment, perhaps in one of the relevant at-risk industries, may be included in a cytology screening programme. There are thus advantages for them in continuing their surveillance at work for as long as they are able to remain at their job. Thereafter, on leaving or retirement, a postal cytology service can ensure continuity.

There are few contraindications to employment for those with renal stones, except perhaps very hot work, such as in tropical climates. Patients with repeated urinary tract infections may lose time from work, but this should not be a bar to employment. Those with a urinary diversion may work, but should be kept under review to detect early onset of possible complications.[24]

Shiftwork

Shiftwork is not an absolute contraindication to the employment of dialysis patients, for their treatment can often be rescheduled to fit in with a regular shift rota. Rapidly rotating shift systems can be more difficult to accommodate because of their constantly changing patterns, especially for patients on haemodialysis.

Work restrictions and contraindications

Patients in irreversible renal failure are unsuited for work as firemen, police on the beat, rescue personnel, or the armed forces on active service, because of the high energy demands and the flexibility required for the extended hours, on call and call-out duty imposed by such strenuous and demanding jobs. Similar restrictions may apply to stressful jobs demanding a very high degree of vigilance (e.g. air traffic controllers). Jobs with a high radiant heat burden and work in the tropics may also be contraindicated.

Such patients are likely to be rejected for diving and for underground work. They are also unlikely to meet the standards required for Merchant Shipping, as this may require lengthy periods in tropical and sub-tropical climates. Additionally, most seafarers nowadays will need to join and leave ships by air travel. Because of absence from home, fatigue, and long hours at the driving wheel, heavy goods vehicle driving may also be precluded. Again, the physical demands of loading and unloading wagons, climbing in and out of cabs, may mean that similar work in transportation, such as removals, warehouse storage, or dockyard labouring, is unsuitable.

Patients who are students when dialysis starts will certainly experience an interruption in studies and may fall behind contemporaries. Their long-term future and the suitability of a particular course should be considered in relation to proposed dialysis regimes. Nevertheless, firm encouragement to continue should be given, for much can be achieved with motivation and support.[25,26]

Usually there are no restrictions to employment for persons with only one kidney (Chapter 20).

Holidays

Most patients on peritoneal dialysis can holiday without restrictions, but haemodialysis patients either need to make arrangements with a dialysis facility at the holiday centre, or arrange for the use of portable machines. Such provisions need to be planned well beforehand.

Special provisions

It is essential for those on peritoneal dialysis to avoid work in dirty or dusty environments and also work which requires heavy lifting or constant bending (Table 17.1). Tight or restrictive clothing should not be worn. Such patients also need a clean area for performing their midday fluid exchange, as it is essential to prevent infection. The suitability, both of the work and of an area at the workplace for the exchange, should preferably be assessed on site by the renal unit specialist nurse, together with occupational heath staff and the employer.

Patients on haemodialysis need to be within reach of a dialysis facility, so work involving much travel and frequent periods away from home may not be suitable.

Those with a successful transplant can lead a normal life at home and at work. The work situation should, however, carry no undue risk of blows or trauma to the lower abdomen, for there is need to protect the area of transplant. The arteriovenous fistula can be injured by sharp projections or tools, and cutting instruments need to be carefully handled.

If there are canteen facilities, it can be helpful to ensure that the necessary low salt and high/low protein foodstuffs are available.

Those with incontinence, repeated urinary infections, ileal conduits, or catheterization need good toilet facilities and nearby access. Ileostomy bags may be pressed on by low benches or the sides of bins or boxes, and excess bending or crouching may inhibit the free flow of urine in the bag, or damage it, causing leakage.

Superannuation

Difficulty in arranging associated life insurance is sometimes given as a reason for not employing someone in end-stage renal failure. This is not usually a problem in medium- or larger-sized organizations, where group life insurance schemes can include patients on dialysis without requiring any medical evidence or additional premium.

Problems may arise in smaller firms where employees have to be assessed individually. Understandably, the attitude of insurance companies to end-stage renal failure is likely to be adverse. For someone already in a scheme who develops renal failure, it is sometimes possible to obtain extended life insurance cover in the advent of early retirement or redundancy. The occupational physician can help in these circumstances, with the consent of the patient, and everything should be done to obtain the most favourable terms.

Advisory services

The staff of renal units, general practitioners, occupational health services, the Manpower Services Commission's Disablement Resettlement Officers, and the Employment Medical Advisory Service should be able to advise on all employment matters. The approach is usually spearheaded by members of the renal unit team: physician, specialist nurse, social worker, home dialysis administrator, and transplant co-ordinator. An occupational health physician or nurse is uniquely qualified to assess the suitability of a patient with renal disease for a particular job, as well as ways and means to adapt it. The advice, guidance, and contacts of the social workers attached to renal units may be indispensable. The British Kidney Patients Association and the National Federation of Kidney Patients Associations both offer useful advice and support. Their addresses are given in Appendix 5.

EXISTING LEGISLATION

Restrictions on the employment of persons with diseases of the genito-urinary tract are imposed by the Merchant Shipping (Medical Examination Regulations) 1983 SI: 1983 808, which require a statutory examination for fitness to work. The medical standards for service in the tropics, or other conditions of high ambient temperature, would not be met by those with recurrent infections, stone formation, urinary obstruction, renal transplant, or intractable incontinence.

Patients on peritoneal dialysis could seek an exemption under the Motor Vehicle (Wearing of Seat Belt) Regulations 1982, SI: 1982 Regulation 5, by obtaining a valid medical certificate from a registered medical practitioner, but the hazards of not wearing a seat belt must be weighed up against any relatively minor inconvenience and restrictions. Adaptations to seat belt mountings can often solve this problem.

CONCLUSIONS AND RECOMMENDATIONS

Because of the great advances in dialysis treatment and the results of renal transplant, most people with renal failure can now achieve significant rehabilitation and often a degree of independence and quality of life sufficient to allow useful, gainful, and active employment.

For the younger patient with good family and hospital support, and without other serious medical problems, dialysis now offers the chance of increased longevity and a better prospect of employment. Physicians advising on fitness for work and on specific employment must actively seek out ways and means whereby successful job placement can be achieved, rather than just looking for the contraindications. They should also take every opportunity to educate both employers and medical colleagues alike into a more postive approach.

With flexibility, adaptation, careful planning and support, and often with a change of attitude on the part of some employers, many more dialysis patients could work successfully. The aim should be to adapt both ways: the work to the patient's needs and the patient's treatment regime to the work, whichever direction best achieves a satisfactory outcome.

Physicians should recall that haemodialysis has kept patients alive for up to 20 years, with 60 per cent of those aged 15–34 surviving at least 10 years. Whether peritoneal dialysis is as good a long-term treatment is not yet fully clear,[27] but either treatment increases the chance of longevity and decreases the likelihood of serious morbidity. Although the final goal is a successful renal transplant which offers the opportunity of a full and normal working life, dialysis treatment is fully compatible with many types of employment. It is worth re-emphasizing that the time off needed to learn to cope independently with haemodialysis is no more than that required for a medium to major operation, and should therefore be considered as sympathetically by both medical advisers and employers.

Medical surveillance at the workplace and close liaison with personnel and management can help to maintain satisfactory work for employees with renal disease. Complications can be watched for, remedial action taken and any further adjustments to the job can be anticipated. Such surveillance also benefits patients with hypertension complicating renal pathology, and those with urinary tract infections, or renal tract tumours.

There are few absolute contraindications to specific types of work for those with renal pathology.

REFERENCES

1. Brynger H, Brunner FP, Chantler C, et al. Combined report on regular dialysis and transplantation in Europe 1979. Proc Eur Dial Transplant Assoc 1980;**17**:4–86.

2. Robertson WG, Peacock M, Heyburn PJ. Practical implications for urologists from epidemiological studies on stone formation. Proc 18th Cong Int Soc Urol 1979;**1**:138.

3. Williams RE. Long term survey of 538 patients with upper urinary tract stones. Br J Urol 1963;**35**:416.

4. Davies JM. Occupational and environmental factors in bladder cancer. In: Williams D, Chisholm GD, eds. Scientific foundations of urology. London: Heinemann, 1982:723–6.

5. Broyer M, Brunner FP, Brynger H, et al. Demography of dialysis and transplantation in Europe. Nephrol Dial Transplant 1987;**2**:475–87.

6. Wing AJ. Why don't the British treat more patients with kidney failure? Br Med J 1983;**287**:1157–8.

7. Office of Population Censuses and Surveys (OPCS). Mortality Statistics (Cause) 1984; Series DH2, 11. England and Wales. London: HMSO, 1985.

8. Gokal R, Baillod R, Bogle S, et al. Multicentre study on outcome of treatment in patients on CAPD and HD. Nephrol Dial Transplant 1987;**2**:172–8.

9. Wing AJ, Broyer M, Brunner FP, et al. Treatment of end stage renal failure in the UK. In: Bradley B, Moras D, eds. UK Transplant Service Review. Bristol: UK Transplant Service, 1982:33–65.

10. Morbidity Statistics from General Practice 1971–2. Second National Study. RCGP, OPCS, DHSS. Studies on medical and population subjects, no. 36. London: HMSO, 1979:Table 8.

11. Asscher AW. Incidence, prevalence, morbidity and mortality—urinary tract infections. London: Update publications, 1982:2.

12. Logan WPD, Cusheon AA. Morbidity statistics from general practice. Vol 1. General studies on medical and population subjects, no 14. London: HMSO, 1985.

13. Kunin CM. Detection, prevention and management of urinary tract infections. 3rd ed. Philadelphia: Lea and Febiger, 1980:3.

14. Scott R, Freeland R, Mowatt W, et al. The prevalence of calcified upper urinary tract stone disease in a random population. Cumberland Health Survey. Br J Urol 1977;**49**(7):589–95.

15. Skeet RG. Epidemiology of urogenital tumours. In: Williams DL, Chisholm GD, eds. Scientific foundations of urology. London: Heinemann, 1982:579–88.

16. Ritchie CD, Bevan EA, Collier St. J. Importance of occult haematuria found at screening. Br Med J 1986;**292**:681–3.

16a. Eschbach JW, Egne JC, Downing MR et al. Correction of anaemia of end stage renal disease with recombinant human erythropoietin: results of a Phase I and II clinical trial. N Engl. J. Med. 1987;**316**:73–78.

17. Coburn JW, Slatopolsky E. Vitamin D, parathyroid hormone and renal osteodystrophy. In: Brenner BM, Rector FC, eds. The kidney. Philadelphia: WB Saunders, 1981:2213–305.

18. Lindner A, Charra B, Sharrad DJ, Scribner BH. Accelerated atherosclerosis in prolonged maintenance haemodialysis. N Engl J Med 1974;**290**:697–701.
19. Cerra FB, Anthone R, Anthone S. Colloid osmotic pressure fluctuations and the disequilibrium syndrome during haemodialysis. Nephron 1974;**13**:245–9.
20. Evans RW, Mannien DL, Gramson LP, et al. The quality of life of patients with end stage renal disease. N Engl J Med 1985;**312**:553–9.
21. Gokal R, Stout JP, Auer J, et al. The quality of life of high risk and elderly dialysis patients. In: Khanna R et al, eds. Advances in CAPD 1987. Toronto: University of Toronto Press, 1987:56–60.
22. Wickham JE, Webb DR, Payne SR, et al. Extracorporeal shock wave lithotripsy: the first 50 patients treated in Britain. Br Med J 1985;**290**:1188–9.
23. Anonymous. Urinary diversion for incontinence (leading article). Lancet 1986;**i**:363–4.
24. Neal DE. Complications of ileal conduit diversion in adults with cancer followed up for at least 5 years. Br Med J 1985;**290**:1695–7.
25. Anonymous. Disabilities and how to live with them. Haemodialysis. Lancet 1981;**ii**:800–1.
26. Anonymous. Disabilities and how to live with them. Continuous Ambulatory Peritoneal Dialysis. Lancet 1982;**i**:556.
27. Coles GA. Is peritoneal dialysis a good long term treatment? Br Med J 1985;**290**:1164–5.

Further reading

1. Renal failure: a priority in health. London: Office of Health Economics, April 1978.
2. End stage renal failure. Briefing no 11. London: Office of Health Economics, April 1980.
3. Kettle M, Massie B, eds. Employers guide to disabilities. 2nd ed. Cambridge: Woodhead-Faulkner, in association with RADAR, 1986.
4. Gokal R, ed. Continuous ambulatory peritoneal dialysis. Edinburgh: Churchill Livingstone, 1986.
5. Drukker W, Parsons F, Maher HF, eds. Replacement of renal function by dialysis. Hague: Martinus Nijhoff, 1984.

18

Haematological disorders

J. A. Bonnell and P. M. Emerson

INTRODUCTION

In the context of employment, haematological problems arise either as the result of incidental findings during routine health screening procedures in industry or during the course of specific investigations of ill health by general practitioners or hospital consultants. Screening procedures in industry may be required statutorily because of exposure to toxic chemical substances or potentially harmful physical agents, e.g. lead, chemical solvents, or ionizing radiation. Alternatively, many large industries have well-established policies for routine health screening of staff for various reasons.

Haematological disorders are common and it is beyond the scope of this chapter to encompass the full range. Some conditions, e.g. pernicious anaemia, are easily diagnosed, treatable and curable, and these will not be described as they have little relevance to fitness to work. We have therefore concentrated on those conditions, mainly of a subacute or chronic nature where work performance, types of employment, or sickness absence are a problem, with special reference to up-to-date therapy and advances in treatment over the last two decades.

Before proceeding to specific conditions a general word on the anaemic patient is relevant. Chronically anaemic patients may remain asymptomatic even with extremely low haemoglobin levels, particularly in the case of some of the congenital anaemias where a compensatory right shift in the oxygen dissociation curve allows patients with very low haemoglobin levels to have functional haemoglobins of several grams higher. For this reason it is absolutely essential to assess every patient individually with regard to employment: i.e. a low haemoglobin detected in an asymptomatic patient as part of a routine screening procedure obviously needs investigation and diagnosis, but is not *per se* a contraindication for employment.

IRON DEFICIENCY

No results of up-to-date surveys are available, but a randomized study in Wales in 1965 showed that 3 per cent of adult men and 14 per cent of post-menopausal women were anaemic[1] and the prevalence has probably remained relatively constant.[2] Iron deficiency should be considered not as a diagnosis but rather as a symptom of an underlying disorder; certainly, treatment with iron is not sufficient and the cause should be sought assiduously. These causes are not listed as they are well known, but it is as well to remind readers that dietary lack, except in physiological states of increased need such as pregnancy, is unusual with the high quality foods now available, which are often fortified with iron. The most likely cause of iron deficiency in a previously healthy individual is occult bleeding from the gastrointestinal tract from such lesions as hiatus hernia, peptic ulceration, carcinoma of the colon, diverticulitis, and angiodysplasia. Aspirin and non-steroidal anti-inflammatory drugs may also cause gastrointestinal bleeding.

Iron deficiency may be detected as part of a routine screen in an individual who feels perfectly fit, but adequate investigation is still required. Patients who present to their doctor with symptoms of iron deficiency which are non-specific, i.e. lethargy, easy fatigue, mild dyspnoea on effort, are often quite severely anaemic and it is not unusual for the haemoglobin to fall to below 9.0 g/dl and 7.0 g/dl in males and females respectively before help is sought. Iron therapy can be started immediately while other investigations are in progress, but should be continued long enough (at least three months) to replenish the depleted body stores after the haemoglobin has risen to normal (males: 13.0–18.0 g/dl; females: 11.5–16.0 g/dl). It should also be remembered that patients with α or β Thalassaemia trait may have very low red cell indices (MCH and MCV) due to lack of the globin component of haemoglobin. Although these patients are usually iron replete (p. 342) they can suffer from associated iron deficiency and this possibility should be considered in a previously healthy individual who complains of new symptoms.

It is difficult to assess how much iron deficiency affects work capacity but it should be remembered that iron is an essential cellular component for all tissues of the body in addition to haemopoiesis. There are often no problems at rest but these may occur while at work; the venesection of 800 ml of blood in healthy volunteers produced a 30 per cent reduction in exercise efficiency two days later.[2] Surveys of agricultural workers in Sri Lanka and Guatemala showed considerable impairment of activity even in mildly anaemic individuals.[3,4] In the former survey, haemoglobin levels ranged from 6.0 to 13 g/dl; none of the most anaemic group was able to reach the peak workload in a given exercise test, and work time in the marginally anaemic group (Hb 11.0–11.9 g/dl) was 20 per cent less than that of women with haemoglobin values greater than 13.0 g/dl, thus emphasizing that work capacity and productivity will be sub-maximal, though not necessarily overtly so, in employees with early signs of iron deficiency.

POLYCYTHAEMIA

A high haematocrit gives rise to problems which are potentially more hazardous than an equivalent fall in haemoglobin. The blood viscosity rises sharply if the packed-cell volume (PCV) is 50 or more, and transient ischaemic attacks, visual disturbances, peripheral vascular disease, and other manifestations of ischaemia are common if the PCV is above 55. Thus, the polycythaemic patient is more likely to have accidents at work or put his colleagues at risk than a moderately anaemic one. The upper limits of normal for adult males and females are a PCV of 0.54 and 0.48 respectively (Hb 18.0 g/dl and 16.0 g/dl).

Polycythaemia is classified as primary (polycythaemia rubra vera (PRV), primary proliferative polycythaemia (PPP)) or secondary, the latter being far more common. Polycythaemia rubra vera is a clonal myeloproliferative disorder in which the red-cell mass (RCM) is increased, and which requires therapy to keep the haematocrit and/or platelet count within the normal range. Treatment is essential (the median survival in untreated patients is under 18 months) and is either by regular venesection, ^{32}P, or oral chemotherapy. Patients can continue at full-time work and the condition runs a protracted course, the median survival being 11 years.[5] Treatment with either ^{32}P or alkylating agents has resulted in a higher incidence of associated leukaemia than with other forms of therapy.

Secondary polycythaemia, in which there is also an absolute increase in the red-cell mass, is associated with conditions in which there is either a reduction in arterial oxygen, inappropriate secretion of erythropoietin, or rarely, an abnormal haemoglobin. Treatment consists of reducing the packed-cell volume to safe levels by venesection, the level depending on the nature of the associated condition, e.g. cyanotic heart disease, or removing the underlying cause, e.g. renal tumour or fibroids. Work limitation depends on the severity of the associated condition. It should be stressed that patients presenting with either primary or secondary polycythaemia are at high risk from thromboembolic complications and no time should be lost in referring the patient to the appropriate centre. Occasionally a high haemoglobin is found in normal individuals who have returned from working abroad at high altitude; these require no special treatment as the haematocrit rapidly returns to normal.

Particular attention should be paid to the individual with what is now termed apparent or relative polycythaemia. Other terms used for this condition are Geisbock's syndrome, stress-, spurious-, or pseudo-polycythaemia. These individuals are found to have a high packed-cell volume (PCV) or Hb on routine blood count; measurement of the red-cell mass (RCM) gives a normal value but the plasma volume (PV) is reduced more than 12.5 per cent below the predicted normal value. The condition is much commoner in males, with a maximum prevalence in the 40–70-year age group. The cause is not known; contributory factors may be hypertension, smoking, diuretics, alcohol, and obesity but treatment or an improvement in lifestyle is not always followed by a fall in haematocrit. Suggestions that the condition is due to stress, inappropriate secretion of antidiuretic hormone, sleep hypoxia, or low aldosterone levels have not been confirmed.[6] Some individuals with minor elevations of the haematocrit probably represent one extreme of the normal range. In the majority of patients the values for the PCV, RCM, and PV tend to remain unchanged, but some patients revert to normal and an occasional one develops a true polycythaemia.[6] One retrospective study has concluded that there is a higher risk of vascular complications in this group[7] but this was not confirmed in a second retrospective study where hypertension was found to be of more importance.[8] It is hoped that the question of whether regular venesection is needed will be answered by the Royal College of Physicians Research Group,[9] but until then it is inadvisable to give any definite prediction which may affect work prospects or life insurance.

THE HIGH MEAN CELL VOLUME

Since the introduction of modern automated equipment, the mean cell volume (MCV) is available as part of the routine blood profile, but the normal range varies slightly with the equipment used. Generally speaking, however, a patient's red cells can be said to be macrocytic if the value exceeds 100 fl. As with iron deficiency and polycythaemia, abnormal values may be picked up on a routine blood count and discretion as to when to investigate must be left with the physician, as it is not unusual to find a raised MCV in the presence of a normal haemoglobin. Having excluded the well-known causes, such as B_{12} and folate deficiency, the commonest cause is excessive alcohol intake. Alcohol causes many haematological problems, ranging from the complications of liver disease, such as bleeding from varices, coagulation disturbances, hypersplenism and often associated with dietary folate deficiency, to the direct effect on the bone marrow itself. This is probably the cause of the macrocytosis in excessive drinkers who are otherwise healthy, as the index rapidly returns to normal on alcohol withdrawal. Alcohol is a direct tissue toxin and there is considerable evidence of a direct suppressive action on erythropoiesis, granulopoiesis, and platelet production, both *in vivo* and *in vitro*.[10] Physicians encountering a raised MCV as an isolated finding should take a thorough alcohol history from the patient, especially if work performance is in doubt, and appropriate help should be offered if needed. A persistently raised MCV suggests permanent liver damage or continued drinking.[11] (Alcohol is also discussed in Chapters 14 and 21.)

In patients with no history of excessive alcohol intake, macrocytic red cells may be due to early myxoedema or myelodysplastic conditions. The latter have increasingly been recognized over the past decade as pre-leukaemic states; this state may last for several years and is usually followed by cytopenias of varying severity before the development of overt leukaemia.[12] Specialized investigations are required to confirm the diagnosis.

THE LOW PLATELET COUNT

One of the problems which is continually encountered by the haematologist is the patient, usually with refractory idiopathic thrombocytopenic purpura (ITP), who runs a persistently low platelet count. These patients are often young and may be concerned about the nature of their employment. Generally speaking, patients with a count of $> 100 \times 10^9/l$ will be symptom free and not bleed excessively following trauma; between 50 and $100 \times 10^9/l$ there may be haemorrhagic manifestations following trauma, but otherwise few problems. The patient with a count persistently below this level and certainly below $25 \times 10^9/l$ may suffer from spontaneous bleeding, usually purpuric, the major risk to life being intracranial haemorrhage. This group is at risk and employment involving heavy manual work is best avoided and should be replaced by more sedentary occupations. It should be stressed, however, that some patients with counts in the $25-50 \times 10^9/l$ range rarely bleed or even bruise easily and few restrictions on employment are necessary in such patients. There is an often quoted statement by haematologists to the effect that the patient and not the platelet count should be treated.

A small proportion of patients with chronic idiopathic thrombocytopenic purpura may be receiving steroid or immunosuppressive therapy or have been subjected to splenectomy in the past. The latter group are prone to the development of overwhelming potentially fatal bacterial infections, especially from the pneumococcus, and there should be no delay in referring the patient to hospital if this is suspected. A pneumococcal vaccine which gives protection against many but not all strains is available, and it is also generally recommended that twice daily prophylactic penicillin should be prescribed for splenectomized patients.

MALIGNANT DISEASE

Incidence and meaning of remission

Table 18.1 shows the latest available figures for the incidence of haematological malignant disease in the employable age group 16–64.[13] These conditions are rare when compared with other forms of malignant disease and until twenty years ago their often rapidly fatal outcome precluded any

Table 18.1 Annual incidence of haematological malignant disease in the population of working age (16–64 years)[13]

Type	Number
All leukaemias	1350
acute myeloid leukaemia	452
acute lymphoblastic leukaemia	191
chronic myeloid leukaemia	177
chronic lymphatic leukaemia	224
other leukaemias	306
All lymphomas	2807
Hodgkin's disease	930
non-Hodgkin's lymphoma	1877
Multiple myeloma	578

consideration of return to work. The discovery of effective chemotherapeutic agents in the 1950s and 1960s, however, and the knowledge of how best to use them, together with improvements in supportive care in the past two decades, has led to increase in remission rates and in length of survival and to the possibility of a 'cure' in some conditions. *The definition of remission* is of considerable importance concerning fitness to work. Generally speaking, a patient can be said to be in complete remission if abnormal cells cannot be detected either clinically or *in vitro*, i.e. the patient feels well, has no organomegaly, a normal cerebrospinal fluid and bone marrow, and a blood count within the normal range except when depressed by chemotherapy. During complete remission there is no reason why a patient should not return to any type of previous employment and many do, but there is inevitably, especially with the acute leukaemias and some lymphomas, a period of absence from work during induction of remission. It is current clinical practice for a patient to be informed of the nature of his condition, the objectives of treatment, and given some idea of prognosis. Medical practitioners can be extremely helpful during this period by reassuring both the patient and his employer that the aim is to return the patient to normal life and to full-time employment as soon as possible.

Aim of treatment and general effects of chemotherapy

Modern treatment consists mainly of the administration of cytotoxic drugs with the aim of destroying as many abnormal cells as possible and allowing the marrow to repopulate with normal cells. Radiotherapy, however, may be given as the treatment of choice or as an additional form of therapy. All chemotherapeutic agents have side-effects and are frequently used in combination, thus compounding these effects. The drugs are not specific for tumour cells and some damage to normal tissues is inevitable with adequate therapeutic dosage. Different drug combinations are used for the different conditions and a detailed description is outside the scope of this chapter. Broadly speaking, the more acute or high grade the malignancy the more likely the patient is to receive combination chemotherapy with up to four or more drugs.

Acute myeloid leukaemia (AML)

In the age-group 15–65 years, acute myeloid leukaemia (AML) and its variants are approximately twice as common as acute lymphoblastic leukaemia (ALL). The majority of patients in the UK are entered into one of the Medical Research Council's (MRC) trials of therapy. Treatment can be divided into four phases:

(1)   induction of remission;

(2)   consolidation of remission;

(3)   maintenance therapy;

(4)   period of observation off treatment.

The patient is likely to be in hospital during the initial induction and intermittently during the consolidation period; these two phases together can last anything up to six months or longer, but if the patient feels well enough he should be encouraged to return to part-time or even full-time work. During maintenance therapy which lasts up to two years, depending on the trial, blocks of therapy are given at approximately monthly to six-weekly intervals and it should be anticipated that a few days will be lost from work during these periods, the main problems being nausea and vomiting which vary with the individual but can be prostrating in some cases. It is useful to give the patient and his family doctor a schedule of treatment so that times off work can be anticipated. Absence from work may also occur due to intercurrent infections as a result of immunosuppression, or the need for blood transfusion; the latter can often be arranged over weekends, as can the blocks of chemotherapy, in order to minimize time lost from work.

Between 1978 and 1983, 1127 patients, between the ages of 0 and 83 years, were entered into the 8th MRC acute myeloid leukaemia trial and of these an average of 74 per cent patients in the employable age-group attained a complete remission.[14] The projected five-year survival for the entire group was 18 per cent and the overall probability of patients attaining a second remission was assessed at 29 per cent. Patients receiving an allogeneic marrow transplant from a compatible sibling have an estimated 54 per cent chance of survival at five years and this is currently the treatment of choice in remitting patients under the age of 40 years.[15]

Acute lymphoblastic leukaemia (ALL)

This is the commonest leukaemia in childhood but constitutes only 20 per cent of adult acute leukaemia; in adults, unfortunately, the disease does not carry the excellent prognosis of childhood leukaemia, where a 'cure' can be expected in 75 per cent of cases in some sub-groups, as adults have lower remission rates and shorter survival times. Of the four currently recognized forms of ALL (common, null-cell, T-cell, and the rare B-cell type) there is a greater incidence of null-cell and T-cell ALL in adults than in children. In addition, approximately 12 per cent of adult patients have the Philadelphia chromosome on presentation and their prognosis is the same as patients entering the ALL blast-cell crisis of chronic myeloid leukaemia (p. 338). The remission rate for all cases is reported as from 70 per cent in various series and the median survival is between 2–3 years from diagnosis.[16] Treatment is on the same lines as that currently in use for childhood ALL and central nervous system prophylaxis is necessary. Intensive induction and post-remission intensive consolidation have produced better survival results[17] and longer periods of in-patient treatment are to be expected, but the majority of patients return to work early in the course of their disease. Maintenance therapy lasts for about two years and is almost entirely given on an out-patient basis. Bone marrow transplantation from a compatible sibling for high-risk patients in their first or second remission gives reported disease-free survival varying from 30–50 per cent at 2–4 years; marrow transplantation in ALL, however, particularly in first remission, is still a controversial issue.[18]

Chronic lymphatic leukaemia (CLL)

This is a disease of the middle-aged and elderly and is often diagnosed incidentally during routine screening; 72 per cent in one recent series.[19] These individuals feel fit and may not need therapy for many years and, once it has been assessed that the disease is not progressing, all that is required is a blood count check at regular intervals. Progressive disease as diagnosed by commencement of symptoms, anaemia or thrombocytopenia, and increase in size of lymph nodes or spleen, requires therapy. This will vary with the physician and may range from gentle oral therapy with chlorambucil and prednisolone to more aggressive combined chemotherapy or splenic irradiation. Whatever the treatment, the main problems are recurrent infections, usually respiratory in nature, which require early antibiotic therapy and are often prolonged because of the associated immunosuppression. It is of considerable importance to recognize the relatively benign nature of the condition in many individuals, particularly in terms of employment, pension schemes, and life insurance. At one time it was thought that younger patients had a more aggressive form of the disease but recent data have shown this not to be the case, the mean (50 per cent) survival for patients aged under 55 years at the time of diagnosis being 12 years.[19,20] Death is likely to occur from the same medical conditions as in the general population. Attempts have been made to stage the disease but the most important poor prognostic signs are anaemia (Hb < 10 g/dl) and/or thrombocytopenia (platelet count < 100 × 10^9/l) at presentation, when the median survival is two years.[21] The nature of the lymphocytic cell-surface immunoglobulin is also of prognostic significance.[19]

Chronic myeloid leukaemia (CML)

This may also be diagnosed on a routine screening procedure either as a result of a blood count or the presence of splenomegaly, but once diagnosed therapy is commenced immediately. The condition has been designated a pre-leukaemic state by some authors, as progression to an accelerated phase and ultimately transformation into an acute leukaemia (blast-cell crisis) is the usual course of the disease.[22] The condition is due to a mutation in a pluripotential stem cell and the blast-cell crisis may be either myeloid or lymphoblastic in nature. During the chronic phase the disease is usually treated by oral chemotherapy with either busulphan or hydroxyurea, and the majority of patients continue in full-time work during this period, which lasts on average under four years.[23] Once patients enter the accelerated phase, however, thrombocytopenia and increasing splenomegaly present problems requiring regular supportive therapy, and loss of time from work is inevitable. In the absence of a compatible sibling for bone marrow transplantation the condition is incurable, but some patients remain in the chronic phase for 10 years or longer. Once acute transformation has occurred the prognosis is poor. Patients are treated with a regime according to the type of transformation, the median survival for patients in lymphoblastic transformation being 12 months, compared with two months for those with myeloid markers.[22]

Hodgkin's disease (HD)

This has proved one of the most rewarding conditions to treat over the past 20 years. Eighty per cent of all patients can be expected to obtain a complete remission and of these approximately 65 per cent will remain disease-free at 10 years.[24] The condition is staged histologically and clinically before therapy and the poor prognostic signs are lymphocyte depletion (now rarer than originally thought) and the presence of B symptoms, i.e. loss of weight and night sweats. Age and sex are not important prognostic indicators.[25] The need for staging laparotomy and splenectomy prior to therapy has decreased since the use of computerized axial tomography, but still remains a debatable issue.[26] Treatment is either by radiotherapy or quadruple chemotherapy, depending on the clinical staging at presentation; radiotherapy alone is invariably used for Stage I and IIA patients.

Most males and 15 per cent of females are sterile following combination chemotherapy, and the recognition of a relatively high incidence of secondary neoplasia associated with drug therapy has led to the reappraisal of the use of this form of therapy in some Stage II and III patients.[27] Recurrent disease still remains a problem but the best series show a median survival rate of greater than five years from the time of relapse.[24] Chemotherapy usually lasts for about six months to a year and the patient may be fit enough to work throughout treatment apart from a few days every month; others experience side-effects which limit activity, but the high 'cure' rate of this condition means that patients should not be barred from employment of any type, nor be given heavy insurance loading. It is important that all physicians and employers are aware of the excellent prognosis of this condition compared with the 100 per cent mortality at five years in all groups before 1964, the year in which combination chemotherapy was introduced.

Non-Hodgkin's lymphoma

The ability to give accurate statistics regarding remission rates and survival in this group of tumours has been bedevilled by the number of histological classifications (of which at least six are in international use at the present time) and also by the lack of properly controlled clinical trials. The tumours consist of monoclonal proliferations of B cells, T cells, or histiocytes, the first being the most common and the latter the rarest. They may occur at almost any site and are highly sensitive to irradiation and chemotherapy.[28] The simplest classification for the purposes of this chapter is to divide them into low-grade, intermediate-grade and high-grade lymphomas.[29] The treatment and prognosis vary with each group and it is important to stress that there is now a possibility of cure of some cases within each group. As with Hodgkin's disease, the lymphomas are staged clinically from I to IV. Approximately 40 per cent of all cases of lymphoma are *low-grade tumours*. They have a long clinical course and occur in the older age-groups. Stage I and II tumours are usually treated by radiotherapy and Stage III and IV by chemotherapy, often with a single agent. Few patients are 'cured' in this group but very long remission rates (> 10 years) have occurred. The median time of relapse is approximately four years and survival is 7–10 years in most series.[30] When relapse occurs it is often to a more aggressive (intermediate) form. *Intermediate-grade tumours* comprise about 45 per cent of cases and patients require early therapy, most being treated with combined chemotherapy except some in Stage I for whom radiotherapy is adequate. About 80 per cent of patients will attain a complete remission, with 60–70 per cent going on to long-term survival. Relapse after two years is uncommon.[31] The *high-grade group*, which also contains the youngest patients, comprises 15–20 per cent of all cases. Early spread to the bone marrow and central nervous system is common, thus resembling leukaemia in many respects. This group of patients is always treated aggressively with combined chemotherapy, and 'cures' are possible, especially with T cell tumours where up to 45 per cent long-term survivors have been described.[32]

Multiple myeloma

This condition affects mainly the middle-aged and elderly but there are over 500 cases per annum in those of working age. Response to chemotherapy has not been as satisfactory as in other forms of leukaemia and lymphoma and has improved very little in the past decade.[33] Complete remissions are unusual and a greater than 75 per cent reduction in tumour burden is classed as a good response. The main clinical problems are bone pain, infection, and bone marrow suppression, either due to the disease or as a result of treatment. Poor prognostic indicators are a presenting pancytopenia and renal failure which cannot be reversed by rehydration. The severity of the condition varies greatly with individuals and some patients lead a relatively normal life for many months or even years and are capable of full work. Recent trials have been concerned mainly with comparing gentle oral therapy (melphelan and prednisolone) with more aggressive regimes using four or more drugs in combination, and results have shown the latter to have a marginal advantage.[33] Intractable bone pain can often be relieved by radiotherapy. The median survival in most large studies has been less than three years from diagnosis.

General comments on malignant disease

There is little in the current literature about patients' attitudes to haematological malignant disease and their employment prospects. In a paper entitled *The cancer patient at work* a survey of 29 sufferers from lymphoma showed that 89 per cent of patients felt capable of returning to work, and of these 64 per cent had returned to their normal job.[34] Where career goals had been changed it had largely been because of unrelated factors. In the case of leukaemia, a larger proportion were still receiving treatment but 63 per cent had sought work and 40 per cent returned to their pre-illness employment. Half the patients in both groups had lost up to 13 weeks from work initially but subsequent leave was remarkably low, averaging 1–4 weeks per annum in

70 per cent of the patients. In an earlier study of adult leukaemia, 13 of 19 patients had gone back to work within the first year.[35] One of the main problems encountered was job rejection, which 45 per cent of patients attributed to their condition. About one-fifth of patients reported special problems on their return to work, due mainly to the negative attitude of employers who were felt to be ignorant of modern advances in treatment.[34] It was generally concluded that return to work improved the self-esteem of the patient and most took a positive attitude. A proportion who were unhappy in their work used their condition as a reason for early retirement. It must be stressed that the acute leukaemias are unlike other forms of disseminated malignancy in that the patient in complete remission is clinically disease free and there is unlikely to be a slowly progressive down-hill course preceding relapse, which is usually of sudden onset.

The attitude of the physician in encouraging patients to return to work is highly important; patients place great reliance on this advice, as optimistic attitudes encourage shattered morale and improve self-esteem. Practical advice on life insurance, pension prospects, and estates is also extremely helpful as individuals often feel greatly relieved if they have settled their affairs even though their condition carries a good prognosis. Close communication between all doctors involved in the patient's care (at work, hospitals, and family practice) is necessary and every effort should be made to organize chemotherapy and supportive treatment in such a way as to minimize interruption to the normal work routine wherever possible.

THALASSAEMIA AND THE HAEMOGLOBINOPATHIES

Of the many presently described variants of haemoglobin production and structure, only two present problems which are likely to be encountered by prospective employers and the occupational health service.

Thalassaemia major

In this condition there is insufficient production of adult haemoglobin because of the inability to manufacture the β chains of the haemoglobin A molecule. It is inherited as an autosomal recessive disorder, i.e. both parents are carriers and there is a $1:4$ chance that a child will be affected. There are about 350 patients in the UK of whom 60 per cent are over the age of 16, most being the offspring of immigrants from Mediterranean and Asian countries. Antenatal diagnosis by means of trophoblast sampling (chorionic villous sampling (CVS)) and recombinant DNA techniques early in pregnancy, followed by abortion, has led to a substantial reduction in the number of patients under 10 years of age. Affected individuals present in the first year and require regular transfusions to maintain their haemoglobin at a level compatible with life; these repeated transfusions produce massive iron overload which ultimately affects vital organs producing cardiac, hepatic, and endocrine failure. The introduction of intensive iron chelation by the administration of desferrioxamine on five days of each week has extended the life span of patients. A retrospective review in 1982 of chelated and unchelated patients showed that the majority of the former had reached adult life, whereas the unchelated group had all died.[36] The need for regular transfusion at monthly or six-weekly intervals necessitates some absence from work, but many centres arrange treatment over weekends so that time lost is minimal. Most British thalassaemia patients have not encountered major difficulties in obtaining employment, though most are employed below their potential because of previous loss of schooling.[36]

Thalassaemia trait

As mentioned on page 331, affected individuals show a blood picture resembling iron deficiency. It is of considerable importance that these patients are not disadvantaged or advised wrongly about their work prospects, as the vast majority are symptom-free healthy individuals.

Sickle-cell disease

Sickle-cell disease has arisen as a clinical problem in the UK in the past 30 years, mainly as a result of the large influx of immigrants of African ancestry. It is estimated that there are at least 4500 sufferers in the UK at the present time.[37] Like thalassaemia major, it is inherited as an autosomal condition; heterozygotes are symptom free but homozygous patients present with a severe and potentially crippling and life threatening condition. Affected individuals have a point mutation resulting in the substitution of valine for glutamic acid on the β chain of haemoglobin A. The resulting haemoglobin S polymerizes under conditions of lower oxygen tension into rigid units which deform the red cell and produce the classical sickle or holly-leaf cell which can be seen microscopically. These abnormal cells give rise to the clinical effects, namely chronic anaemia (Hb 7.0–9.0 g/dl) due to haemolysis, painful episodic crises from stasis and infarction in small vessels, aplastic crises due to intercurrent viral infections, and sequestration crises when there is massive pooling of blood in the spleen in infants and, more rarely, in the liver in older patients. These latter three events should be treated as acute medical emergencies and the patient should be referred to hospital immediately if symptoms arise at work.

The incidence of sickle-cell trait in the UK is about 8 per cent among the Afro-Caribbean community and approximately 1:600 births in this population group will produce a homozygous individual.[38] Antenatal screening is routine in this country and parents can be counselled about the possibility of producing an affected child. It is extremely important to differentiate between heterozygote carriers and patients with sickle-cell disease, as the former should be treated no differently from other members of the community with the exception that work in environments with the risks of low oxygen tension (e.g. aircraft, diving operations, and submarines) is best avoided.

Patients with sickle-cell disease should be given careful consideration when selecting a working environment. Because of the factors mentioned in the introduction they tolerate their anaemia remarkably well and a low haemoglobin level is not a contraindication to employment. Factors which may have an adverse effect on their condition are hypoxia, acidosis, extremes of temperature, dehydration, and atmospheric pressure. There is no reason, however, why most forms of employment should not be undertaken, including outside and relatively heavy work. Modern airlines have cabin pressures adjusted such that holiday travel is safe, but sufferers should not be accepted as aircraft pilots or divers. It is of considerable importance that a few patients with sickle-cell disease are remarkably free from any form of complication and they should be assessed separately.

There is little information about the employment prospects of patients with sickle-cell disease. Advances in supportive care rather than specific prevention of sickling, which is still a major therapeutic problem, has allowed many patients with sickle-cell disease to reach adult life and enter the job market. A recent survey has highlighted many problems: 13 patients over the age of 16 were interviewed and 61 per cent found to be unemployed; two patients had never had a job, and the 8 patients who had been in some form of employment previously thought they had lost their job because of intercurrent illness; only one patient was considered unfit for work because of chronic illness.[38] In the same study 22 major employers were approached about their attitude towards employing individuals with sickle-cell disease. Eleven replies were received, showing a wide range in attitude, from a company who routinely screened applicants to one firm who did not consider anyone with sickle-cell disease suitable for employment. Six companies stated that every applicant would be considered individually. The article concluded that sufferers are severely disadvantaged when trying to obtain employment, particularly as most patients are members of a community which already has a high level of unemployment.

GLUCOSE-6-PHOSPHATE DEHYDROGENASE DEFICIENCY

This sex-linked condition affects approximately the same number of individuals and is present in the same ethnic groups as haemoglobin S and thalassaemia. Most sufferers are entirely symptom free and are unaware that they have the condition. Once diagnosed they should carry a list of drugs to be avoided as most problems arise as a result of haemolysis due to the ingestion of oxidative agents. From the point of view of employment they should be advised not to work in chemical plants manufacturing naphthalene and trinitrotoluene, as haemolysis following exposure to the latter has been described in at least six workers.[39] If there is a history of favism, agricultural work involving broad-bean cultivation or processing should be avoided; otherwise there should be no problem in employment.

COAGULATION DISORDERS

Haemophilia A and B (see also Chapter 10)

There are approximately 5000 individuals with haemophilia A and 1000 with haemophilia B (Christmas disease) in the United Kingdom; these two disorders will be discussed together as their clinical presentation and treatment are similar. Both are sex-linked disorders and female homozygotes are extremely rare (estimated 1 per 50 million population) so, in practice, all patients are male. The condition varies in severity from mild cases who may not be diagnosed until adult life, to very severely affected individuals who require regular replacement therapy. The severity of the condition tends to run true in families and is assessed by measuring the blood coagulant activity of either Factor VIII or Factor IX. Haemophiliacs are classed as *severe* (Factor VIII C < 1 unit/ml), *moderate* ($1-5$ units/ml), or *mild* (> 5 units/ml). The clinical presentation varies according to the level of activity, the most severely affected individuals suffering repeated haemorrhages into joints, deep tissues, and occasionally externally. These episodic bleeds can cause severe arthroses and contractures which, before the advent of modern treatment, led to crippling disability early in life. Mildly affected haemophiliacs, with Factor VIII C levels of > 5 units/ml, escape these deformities and tend to bleed only after accidental trauma, surgery, or dental extraction.

Modern therapy has greatly improved the prognosis with regard to mobility, motivation, education, employment, social activities, and life expectancy. Treatment consists of replacing the missing factor by intravenous injection as necessary, a procedure which takes about 15 minutes. There are designated Haemophilia Centres throughout the UK where programmes of replacement therapy are arranged to suit individuals. Home therapy, whereby patients are instructed to inject themselves with Factor VIII, has been of major benefit in limiting the severity of bleeds and reducing travelling and waiting time at hospital. Other problems related to haemophilia are associated with chronic pain (there is a relatively high degree of drug dependency), unavoidable absence from school or college, and the psychological aspects of suffering from an inherited and potentially crippling condition.

The occupations which haemophiliacs can be expected to follow vary according to the severity of the condition. There are no limitations in obtaining driving licences unless debarred by associated medical conditions. Haemophiliacs are not accepted into the armed forces nor usually allowed to fly passenger aircraft. In one instance a patient with a Factor VIII C value of 2 per cent (2 units/ml), who had previously flown in Australia, was accepted as a commercial airline pilot in the UK but could not take up the position as insurance cover was refused (personal communication, 1987). Apart from these, no occupations are unsuitable for mildly affected individuals but severely affected patients are best suited to sedentary jobs, such as office or clerical work, and heavy manual labour should be avoided. There is no fixed rule, however, as some haemophiliacs with extremely low coagulant activity seldom bleed, while some patients classed as moderately affected may suffer repeat haemorrhages.[40]

There is relatively little recent literature about employment prospects and problems, and this has been concerned mainly with the results of the introduction of self-treatment. In 1980 a survey of 429 patients between the ages of 16 and 65, of whom 72 per cent were classed as severely or moderately affected, showed that 48 per cent had followed a course of further education and 15 per cent had a degree or diploma.[41] Ninety per cent did not require extra privileges at work and 50 per cent had been with their present employer for more than 10 years. One-third considered that self-treatment had increased their potential range of work. Over half the group had lost an appreciable amount of schooling (>1 month per year) and 48 per cent had registered as disabled with the Department of Employment. One of the major problems encountered was a lack of suitable facilities for self-treatment at work. Many patients leave a refrigerated pack at their place of work (there is remarkable self-perception of early bleeds by haemophiliacs), but in those places without a first-aid room (60 per cent) the treatment had to be administered in offices or kitchens, and treatment kits were sometimes stored alongside food. Bleeds at work had mainly resulted from accidental impact injuries rather than as a result of heavy work or machinery.[41] The occupational physician has a vital role to play both in assessing suitable work for the haemophiliac and in making suitable arrangements for his self-treatment.

Unemployment among haemophiliacs is, as expected, greater than the national average and there is marked geographical variation, unemployment being much higher in the North of England and Scotland. Though self-treatment would have been expected to reduce unemployment because of lack of time off work, this was not shown to be the case in a small survey of 23 adults in Scotland between 1981 and 1983, comparing unemployment rates before and after the start of this form of therapy.[42] A disturbingly high proportion (30 per cent) had found that attendance at employment rehabilitation centres was of no use, a fact reflected in results of referrals of patients with other conditions.[43]

One of the major problems facing haemophiliacs is whether to tell prospective employers of their condition. In a survey of 225 patients in 1982, approximately one-third of haemophiliacs had reservations about imparting the information, mainly because they felt that many employers were ignorant about the condition and had little knowledge of recent advances in therapy; but where employers had been told they had generally been sympathetic and helpful.[44] Some haemophiliacs have experienced problems with life insurance and there is usually a 2 per cent loading. Advice on employers' insurance and pension schemes is available from the Haemophilia Society, and the Disablement Resettlement Officer can advise employers.[45] In conclusion, although modern treatment has improved the general well-being of haemophiliacs it has not been shown to have reduced unemployment, but it has reduced absenteeism in employed haemophiliacs and probably increased the potential range of work. Better facilities for self-treatment at work are required, and ignorance among employers about the condition is still encountered. The recent finding that at least 50 per cent of haemophiliacs are antibody positive to the AIDS virus is a separate major issue (Chapter 22).

ANTICOAGULANT THERAPY

The exact number of patients on long-term anticoagulant therapy in the UK is unknown but the number is substantial: it has been estimated that up to 10 million coagulation control tests are performed per annum. At the John Radcliffe Hospital, tests are performed currently on 1350 patients in a population of half a million. The major problems encountered are with dose control as response to therapy varies with changes in diet, alcohol intake, intercurrent illness, and changes in other medication. It is essential that the doctor responsible for prescribing anticoagulants is informed of any alterations to other therapy, as many drugs potentiate and some inhibit the action of anticoagulants. A full list is available in the British National Formulary.[46] Patients are encouraged to continue in their present employment and no occupations are barred except those needing strenuous physical work. In practice, however, the patient's lifestyle may already have changed as a result of the underlying condition necessitating anticoagulant therapy, e.g. coronary artery bypass.

REFERENCES

1. Jacobs A, Kilpatrick GS, Withey JL. Iron deficiency in adults: prevalence and prevention. Postgrad Med J 1965;**41**:418–24.

2. Dallman PR. Manifestations of iron deficiency. Semin Haematol 1982;**19**:19-30.
3. Gardner GW, Edgerton VR, Barnard RJ, et al. Cardiorespiratory, haematological and physical performance responses of anaemic subjects to iron treatment. Am J Clin Nutr 1975;**28**:982-8.
4. Viteri FE, Torun B. Anaemia and physical work capacity. Clin Haemat 1974;**3**:609-26.
5. Berk PD, Goldberg J, Donovan PB, Fruchtman SM, et al. Therapeutic recommendations in polycythaemia vera based on polycythaemia vera study group protocols. Semin Haematol 1986;**23**:132-43.
6. Pearson TC. Stress polycythaemia (in press).
7. Burge PS, Johnson WS, Prankerd TAJ. Morbidity and mortality in pseudo-polycythaemia. Lancet 1975;**i**:1266-9.
8. Weinreb NJ, Shih C-F. Spurious polycythaemia. Semin Haematol 1975;**12**: 397-407.
9. Wetherley-Mein G, Pearson TC, Burney PGJ, Morris RW. Polycythaemia study. A project of the Royal College of Physicians Research Unit. J R Coll Physicians Lond 1987;**21**:7-15.
10. Colman N, Herbert V. Haematological complications of alcoholism: overview. Semin Haematol 1980;**17**:164-76.
11. Allsop DT. Dealing with problems of alcohol in an employment setting. Health Services Manpower Review 1987;**12**:20-2.
12. Bennett JM, Catovsky D, Daniel MT, Flandrin G, et al. Proposals for the classification of the myelodysplastic syndromes. Br J Haem 1982;**51**:189-99.
13. Cancer Statistics Registration. Office of Population Censuses and Surveys. Series MB1 no 15. London: HMSO, 1983:22-3:45-7.
14. Rees JKH, Gray RG, Swirsky D, Hayhoe FGJ. Principal results of the Medical Research Council's 8th acute myeloid leukaemia trial. Lancet 1986;**ii**:1234-41.
15. Gratwohl A, Zwaan F, Hermans J, Lyklemaa A. Bone marrow transplantation for leukaemia in Europe: Report from the Leukaemia Working Party. Bone Marrow Transplant 1986;**1**:177-81.
16. Jacobs AD, Gale RP. Recent advances in the biology and treatment of acute lymphoblastic leukaemia in adults. N Engl J Med 1984;**311**:1219-31.
17. Hoelzer D. Current status of ALL/AML therapy in adults. Recent Results in Cancer Research 1984;**93**:182-223.
18. Hoelzer D, Gale RP. Acute lymphoblastic leukaemia in adults: recent progress, future directions. Semin Haematol 1987;**24**:27-39.
19. Hamblin TJ, Oscier DG, Stevens JR, Smith JL. Long survival in B-CLL correlates with surface IgMK phenotype. Br J Haem 1987;**66**:21-6.
20. Hamblin TJ. Chronic lymphatic leukaemia. Baillière's Clinical and Laboratory Haematology 1987;**1**:449-91.
21. Chastang C, Travade P, Auquier A. Critical discussion of the assessment of a three-stage prognostic classification for chronic lymphatic leukaemia. Statistics in Medicine 1985;**4**:287-93.
22. Griffin JD. Management of chronic myelogenous leukaemia. Semin Haematol 1986;**23**:20-4.

23. Medical Research Council's working party for therapeutic trials in leukaemia. Randomized trial of splenectomy in ph¹-positive chronic granulocytic leukaemia, including an analysis of prognostic features. Br J Haem 1983;**54**:415–30.

24. Longo DL, Young RC, Vincent T de V. Chemotherapy for Hodgkin's disease; the remaining challenges. Cancer Treatment Reports 1982;**66**:925–36.

25. Should we bother subclassifying Hodgkin's disease? [Editorial]. J Clin Oncol 1986;**4**:275–7.

26. Laparotomy and splenectomy in Hodgkin's disease: a reappraisal after twenty years. Annotation Scand J Haematol 1985;**34**:289–92.

27. Hodgkin's disease IIB or not to be—using irradiation alone or in combination with chemotherapy? That is the question! [Editorial]. J Clin Oncol 1986;**4**:455–7.

28. Mead GM, Whitehouse JMA. Modern management of non-Hodgkin's lymphoma. Br Med J 1986;**293**:577–80.

29. The non-Hodgkin's Lymphoma Pathologic Classification Project. National Cancer Institute sponsored study of classification of non-Hodgkin's lymphomas: summary and description of a working formulation for clinical usage. Cancer 1982;**49**:2112–35.

30. Horning SJ, Rosenberg SA. The natural history of initially untreated low grade non-Hodgkin's lymphoma. N Engl J Med 1984;**322**:1471–5.

31. Mead GM, Mackintosh FR, Burke JS, Rosenberg SA. Late relapse from complete remission in nodular and diffusing histiocytic lymphoma. Cancer 1983;**52**:1536–9.

32. Slater DE, Mertelsmann R, Koziner B, et al. Lymphoblastic lymphoma in adults. J Clin Oncol 1986;**4**:57–67.

33. Durie BGM, Dixon DO, Caxten S, Stephens R, et al. Improved survival duration with combination chemotherapy induction for multiple myeloma: a Southwest Oncology Group Study—1986. J Clin Oncol 1986;**4**:1227–37.

34. Melette SJ. The cancer patient at work. CA-A. Cancer Journal for Clinicians 1985;**35**:360–73.

35. Hann A. Study of employment problems encountered by leukaemic patients in remission. Proceedings of a national forum on comprehensive cancer rehabilitation and its vocational implications. Department of rehabilitation services and cancer rehabilitation programme. Richmond, Va.: Medical College of Virginia, 1980;7–12.

36. Modell B. The management of the improved prognosis of thalassaemia major. Birth Defects 1982;**18**:329–37.

37. Brozović M, Davies SC, Brownell AI. Acute admissions of patients with sickle cell disease who live in Britain. Br Med J 1987;**294**:1206–8.

38. Franklin IM, Atkin K. Employment of patients with sickle cell disease and sickle cell trait. J Soc Occup Med 1986;**36**:76–9.

39. Beutler E. Haemolytic anaemia in disorders of red cell metabolism. Plenium Medical 1978:84–90.

40. Hardisty RM, Weatherall DJ, eds. Blood and its disorders. Oxford: Blackwell Scientific Publications, 1982:1105–59.

41. Stuart J, Forbes CD, Jones P, Lane G, Rizza CR, Wilkes S. Improving prospects for employment of the haemophiliac. Br Med J 1980;**280**:1169–72.

42. Markova I, Forbes CD, Rowlands A, Pettigrew A, Willoughby M. The haemophiliac patient's self-perception of changes in health and life-style arising from self-treatment. Int J Rehab Research 1983;**6**:11–8.

43. Employment of the disabled [Editorial]. Br Med J 1980;**281**:891–2.
44. Forbes CD, Markova I, Stuart J, Jones P. To tell or not to tell: haemophiliacs' views on their employment prospects. Int J Rehab Res 1982;**5**:13–8.
45. Employing someone with haemophilia. Sheffield: Manpower Services Commission, 1980.
46. British National Formulary no 12. London: British Medical Association and The Pharmaceutical Society of Great Britain, 1986:421–2.

19

Obstetrics and gynaecology

G. V. P. Chamberlain and D. M. Miller

Introduction

About 9 million women are in employment in the UK: about 3 million in office work, 2 million in service jobs, and over a million in the health services and in education. There are now more women who are pregnant and working in paid employment outside the home than there were 40 years ago; 75 per cent of these are in paid work in the last trimester of pregnancy.[1,2] This produces potential problems in the workplace, though they are not usually major ones.[3]

Hazards

A few specific hazards exist, such as radiation and certain chemicals (Table 19.1); these obviously should be avoided in pregnancy, particularly in the first few weeks. They are well reviewed by Murray.[4] It must be emphasized that all these hazards are relevant to very few working women. Because of the risks in the very early stages of pregnancy, when a woman may not realize that she is actually pregnant, advice may be needed for those jobs at higher risk. This needs to be given specifically, and should include plans to restrict these known hazards for women who are planning to become pregnant.

Problems

There are some general, non-specific problems which apply to all pregnant women. Fatigue comes on easily in pregnancy and non-specific backache follows with the altered centre of gravity of the body; the woman's bulk may make certain tasks difficult as she is forced further and further away from her work. Concentration may be affected by the metabolic changes of pregnancy. It is important to review all aspects of an employee's job as soon as she becomes pregnant to see if they require modification.

Most pregnant women can work the usual working hours, but provision of a time to rest after lunch may be required; in other instances shorter working

Table 19.1 Potential hazards at work in pregnancy

Chemical	Physical	Biological
Mercury, lead, copper	Noise and vibration	Rubella
Anaesthetic agents	Thermal stress	
Chemicals in specific industries, e.g. leather work and dry cleaning	Ionizing radiation	

hours or flexitime may be recommended to avoid tiring rush-hour travel. Often, a sedentary worker is happy to have the opportunity of a standing job for short periods as her pregnancy advances, to avoid or alleviate backache or abdominal discomfort.

When work involves standing in a fixed position at a production line, or as a sales assistant in a retail outlet, alternative work should be considered to allow mobility in standing work, possibly with part-time sedentary work as well. Any employer who is keen to maintain the best productivity from the employees is likely to suggest less arduous work for a pregnant member of staff, if at all possible. Repetitive lifting tasks should be avoided in pregnancy, as should the work associated with climbing ladders which often involves carrying merchandise and placing it in storage bins. Since the centre of gravity of a pregnant woman is progressively altered as pregnancy advances, the safety aspects of the work should discourage any employer from keeping her in this type of work (Health and Safety at Work Act 1974).[5]

Through modifications of such aspects of the pregnant employee's work, most women should be able to continue working until the last weeks of pregnancy if desired and if the load is light. Although fatigue, and repetitive or boring jobs have been shown to be associated with an increased risk of preterm labour and low-birth-weight babies,[6] by adopting the above policy of care these, and other risk factors, will be minimized.

Many women leave work after 28 weeks of gestation (12 weeks before the expected date of delivery) which is the time when maternity benefits may first be claimed (see below). However, more women are extending their working lives into late pregnancy quite safely but needing greater understanding from their employer.

Visual display units

Many of the fears which women hold in pregnancy cannot be substantiated scientifically. A typical example is the recent spurt of interest in visual display units (VDUs). Existing fears about X-rays and other electromagnetic radiation being linked to problems in pregnancy have arisen from sporadic reports of spontaneous abortions, birth defects, and preterm labours in women VDU operators. These reports have been mostly uncontrolled, small, and anecdotal. It would be surprising if there was anything emitted by a VDU which would affect pregnancy. The energy output of X-rays from VDUs is about 25 keV and is not detectable beyond the glass screen of the tube.[7] Other electromagnetic radiations are at background levels, well below acknowledged international safety standards.[8]

Anxieties about working with VDUs will not be resolved until a randomized controlled trial is mounted, but the difficulties of doing this are many. Variations in age, previous pregnancy outcome, intensity of exposure, smoking habits, and selection bias are some of the problems to overcome. Kurppa *et al.* reported in 1984 that in a comparison with paired controls of 1500 mothers who had given birth to malformed children, there was no evidence that exposure to VDUs was associated with birth defect.[9] Macdonald and her colleagues (1986), reporting the results of their Montreal study, reviewed women whose occupation might require VDU usage.[10] Of the 2500 pregnancies in which no VDU had been used, the spontaneous abortion rate was 5.7 per cent; among 600 women using a VDU for less than 15 hours weekly it was 8.2 per cent, and in 700 women using a VDU for more than 15 hours a week it was 9.3 per cent. The greatest spontaneous abortion rate among almost 6000 pregnancies in workers not using VDUs was 7.8 per cent. The authors themselves caution that these results may be biased both by selection and response. The subject was reviewed by Lee in 1985.[11]

In view of uncertainty of the effects of VDUs in early pregnancy, it may therefore be advisable for those trying to get pregnant and those in early pregnancy to work only part-time at these machines. If an employee in early pregnancy is particularly anxious about working with VDUs, then alternative work may need to be considered on account of the anxiety itself.

Diet

During pregnancy a woman should take a nutritious diet which is not necessarily bulky or very calorific. In some places of work, canteens are provided and provision is made for a pregnant woman to select appropriate food. However, in many instances employees buy their own lunches or snacks in nearby shops. Employers would do well to look at this area of good employee relations and health promotion by providing good catering facilities, if many women of reproductive age are employed.

Maternity rights and benefits

During pregnancy a woman has certain rights to maternity benefits which are usually obtained in return for a certificate of expected delivery completed by her obstetrician or family practitioner. These rights and benefits often change, and are well laid out in current DHSS pamphlets. The woman also has a right to absent herself from work to attend antenatal clinics.

In some places of work, the employer may encourage antenatal care to be carried out on the premises by the occupational health nurse in association with the community midwife. The convenience is considerable for the employees, and the employer benefits from the reduced time lost from work.

After leaving work to have a child a woman has the right to return to a job up to six months postpartum. Most women, however, are keen to breast feed and look after their child for much longer after delivery before returning to full-time employment. Some employers can provide a crèche and so ease the return to work; in other cases the woman may return part-time. In most instances, this is between six and 16 weeks after birth. The World Health Organization Expert Group on Conditions in the Work Place recommended in 1985 that facilities be provided at the place of work to allow women to breast feed their children for at least six months.[12]

Health education

Increasingly, the place of work is being considered as a valuable site for health education. The development of occupational health services within companies or on industrial estates as group services, provides opportunities for health education programmes for employees about smoking and diet, for instance.

The benefits to female employees of providing literature with information about gynaecological problems and pregnancy are considerable, particularly if there is an occupational health nurse available to give specific advice, e.g. pre-pregnancy counselling or antenatal care.

In this way employees will be able to prepare themselves for the changes which may accompany or follow the natural progress of pregnancy. Fear and anxiety are allayed and as a result the woman is likely to be more efficient and productive at work, although this is difficult to show as a clear financial benefit.

GYNAECOLOGY

Introduction

The workforce in the United Kingdom contains an increasing number of women, from all social classes and all age groups. The General Household Survey (1981) reports that 33 per cent of all women between 16 and 59 are working full-time and another 25 per cent part-time.[13]

It is probable that women who are working have a lower morbidity rate than those who are not employed[14] (the healthy worker effect), but anyone employing women is likely to come in contact with women who between them experience a full range of gynaecological conditions.

Pelvic pain

Between 10 and 20 per cent of young women may get *primary dysmenorrhoea*. This is due to spasm of uterine muscle and usually presents as a dull pain in the lower abdomen and pelvis before the period. It can be quite severe and tends to last for 24–48 hours only. Treatments provided for primary dysmenorrhoea are multiple and include analgesics and antispasmodics. Antiprostaglandins may help and the suppression of ovulation with combined oral contraceptives is commonly used. The latter is one of the most effective treatments.

When a woman has primary dysmenorrhoea at work, she may be able to overcome the symptoms with rest and simple analgesia, in a rest room if available. Some women with very severe symptoms, however, may have to take time off work for a few days each menstrual cycle, although this happens only rarely. If treated appropriately, little or no time off work should be lost nowadays because of this. Where an occupational health service exists, recurrent absence from work or repeated visits to the occupational health nurse or physician on account of period pain may prompt further investigation, through referral to the general practitioner and a gynaecologist. Often symptoms which the woman has tolerated for months can be alleviated by this action. The benefit is two-fold; the employee is relieved of anxiety and discomfort and is therefore able to concentrate on the job more easily; the employer benefits from this by reduction in absenteeism.

Dysmenorrhoea is now a less common symptom and usually only causes an occasional day's absence from work; the wider use of the contraceptive pill has probably contributed to this current picture.

In older women, *secondary dysmenorrhoea* may occur; this pain usually occurs during the period and one should seek signs of organic disease such as chronic pelvic infection, fibroids, or endometriosis. These need treatment in their own right.

Left or right iliac fossa pain

This is often caused by gynaecological conditions. Should any specific point of tenderness be discovered on examination, this may call for a laparoscopy so that the source can be found more precisely. Adhesions and ovarian cysts are treated surgically. Sometimes recurrent pelvic infections may present with pain more on one side than the other, as can endometriosis, a common source of pain. Surgery may be of use for localized areas but is not much help with widespread disease. Antibiotics and heat are used for the former and anti-oestrogens for the latter.

Menstrual upset

Amenorrhoea and *oligomenorrhoea* represent an absence of, or scanty, periods. These symptoms often cause anxiety, particularly if an unplanned pregnancy is suspected.

Amenorrhoea is not uncommon when first coming off the oral contraceptive pill, but may also be the result of external stresses, depression, exercise, or the effects of travelling. Excess weight gain or weight loss may be relevant, as can be thyroid and prolactin disorders. The symptoms may also reflect a work or marital problem.

Where amenorrhoea is the presenting symptom of anorexia nervosa, counselling from an occupational health service doctor or nurse may enable the woman to continue working and avoid a lengthy absence.

The employee may not seek further advice from her own doctor, unless the nurse at work encourages her to do so, for the working woman's criteria for visiting her doctor are pain and illness. Time off work may be needed for investigations of either her hormone state or the accompanying infertility.

Menorrhagia or *metrorrhagia*, too heavy or too prolonged periods, can also interfere with work. They may sometimes occur in the younger woman (18–25 years) in which case they are probably due to anovulation allowing unopposed oestrogenic effect on the endometrium, or to the stimulating effect of an intra-uterine device (IUD). These symptoms require investigation and, if the diagnosis is confirmed, treatment by stimulating ovulation (if the woman wishes to become pregnant) or by giving progestogens in the second half of the menstrual cycle.

In the latter part of reproductive life (35–45 years), heavy or prolonged periods can make the woman anaemic and may be associated with organic disease such as fibroids as well as hormonal upsets. Such a condition needs investigation and it may be treated with progestogens if it is thought there is a deficiency, or with antiprostaglandin synthetase activators or antifibrinolytic agents to cope with a local aspect of the problem.

The ultimate treatment of these problems in the older woman is a hysterectomy. This does not automatically mean that the ovaries have to be removed. Such surgery needs 6–12 weeks away from work for, although the hospital stay may be only 7–10 days, the woman needs time to recover mentally and physically afterwards.

It is important to appreciate that the psychological effects of hysterectomy may often be considerable. The value of counselling with an occupational health physician or nurse before the operation is obvious. Return to work may be eased, since the employee knows that the doctor or nurse understands both her work and the medical problem: for example, the duties that she can perform safely on her return to work following the operation can be defined. She may be advised to return to work on a short-time or part-time basis for the first week or two, to allow a gentle reintroduction. Work involving lifting, or prolonged standing, should be avoided for at least three months postoperatively.

Intermenstrual bleeding is not strictly a menstrual upset, but signals some irregularity or hypertrophy of the surface of the genital tract in the uterus, cervix, or vagina. It deserves full investigation by a gynaecologist and may require a curettage to elucidate its cause. Treatment will depend upon the cause and should not be undertaken on a symptomatic basis. Causes include polyps of the endometrium or cervix, malignancies of either site, erosions of the cervix or, in later life, atrophic vaginitis. It may also be caused by an IUD.

Infections of the genital tract

Genital tract infections may be of the upper genital tract: ovaries, Fallopian tubes, and uterus; or of the lower tract: cervix, vagina, and vulva. The former may present with pain or change of menstrual function, as discussed previously; the latter are associated with discharge, vulval irritation, or urinary symptoms.

Both *moniliasis* and *trichomoniasis* are very common in young women. Sometimes the conditions are symptomless and are only detected by cervical cytology screening. Both conditions are commonly spread by sexual intercourse. The specific cause must be identified by microbiological investigation and treated with the appropriate antibiotic.

Sexually transmitted diseases in women are often asymptomatic and are first detected after testing an infected partner. *Gonorrhoea* and *Chlamydia* may produce a thin, greenish-white vaginal discharge and gross dysuria, as may *Herpes simplex* lesions of the genital tract. These infections need specific treatment with antibiotics according to sensitivity or, in the case of herpes, acyclovir which reduces the infectivity and the phase of shedding virus. Women who have had a sexually transmitted disease should be advised to have an annual cervical smear. It is unlikely that these conditions will cause absence from work unless, in the case of certain organisms, they affect the upper genital tact. Then they can lead to salpingo-oophoritis, causing abdominal pain.

Human papilloma virus

The human papilloma virus (HPV) has now been found to have a very strong link with carcinoma of the cervix. There are 32 sub-types and each sub-type is associated with a particular clinical and pathological condition and varying malignant potential, e.g. types 1, 2, 4, and 7 are benign and found in skin conditions; types 16 and 18 are associated with a risk of developing carcinoma of the cervix; and types 6, 10, and 11 are also associated with carcinoma of the cervix but with a lower risk.

Ninety per cent of cervical carcinomas contain HPV DNA, and this is similar to that found by serological studies. The lesions caused by the HPV infections on the cervix resemble mild dysplasia and this has linked the cervical intraepithelial neoplasia (CIN) to HPV infections of the cervical squamous epithelium.

Cancer

Gynaecological cancer usually affects women over 40 years old. Figures for new cases in England and Wales for 1981 are shown in Table 19.2.[15] Considered seriatim down the genital tract:

Cancer of the ovary

This is one of the commoner fatal cancers of women aged 50–70 in England and Wales. It is often asymptomatic in the early stages but may present with poorly defined ill health and swelling of the lower abdomen. It is most often diagnosed by feeling the mass on abdominal or bimanual examination and confirmed at laparotomy. Ultrasound screening may reveal pathology at an earlier stage. Following treatment, women are likely to be off work for some weeks and may require time off for further follow-up.

Survival rates vary greatly, depending on the spread of the tumour at the time of first treatment. Unfortunately, the growth has often already spread widely when it is diagnosed and so this tumour is often associated with a very poor prognosis.

Cancer of the endometrium

This presents with post-menopausal bleeding in two-thirds of cases, or with prolonged or irregular menstrual bleeding before the menopause. The diagnosis is confirmed at curettage; surgical treatment is usually followed by radiotherapy. In a few cases, progestogens are given to reduce distant spread. This condition has a good prognosis and many women are back at work within 6–12 weeks of therapy. Again, the range of survival rates is wide, but

Table 19.2   New cases of malignant disease of the genital tract diagnosed (England and Wales, 1981)[15]

Site	Number
Vulva	785
Cervix	3720
Uterus	3469
Ovary	4346

this tumour is commonly slow to metastasize and is detected early; thus the prognosis is generally good.

Cancer of the cervix
This presents in the younger woman, commonly between 35 and 50 years. It is characterized by postcoital or intermenstrual vaginal bleeding and the diagnosis is made on examination (colposcopy) and confirmed by biopsy. Depending on the stage of the disease, treatment may be by radical pelvic surgery or by radiotherapy.

Screening programmes   Of all gynaecological cancers, cervical cancer has the best chance of being prevented, by the use of cervical smears to detect the condition in its pre-invasive stage. Cervical cytology screening programmes are essential and the benefits to the working woman of providing this examination at the workplace are obvious. Good communication between the examining doctor and the general practitioner about results avoids misunderstandings. If screening is available at work, the working woman herself should be allowed to decide whether she will have this at work, or at another clinic, or with her general practitioner.

In 1984, a survey of companies offering cervical cytology was carried out by writing to the members of the Society of Occupational Medicine (personal communication). Some 435 companies replied, a 29 per cent response rate. Of the responding companies, 42 per cent undertook cervical cytology screening programmes and, in 78 per cent of these, this was done at the place of work either by the company occupational health service or by using the mobile caravans supplied by the Women's National Cancer Control Campaign. Some 49 per cent of the companies undertaking cervical cytology screening offered the test to all female employees, irrespective of age at three-yearly intervals; 20 per cent five-yearly, and 10 per cent annually.

Cancer of the vulva
This occurs in a much older age group (60 years plus). The diagnosis is confirmed by biopsy and then usually treated with radical surgery. The

woman may expect to be off work for several months. The prognosis is good, for this is a slow-growing tumour, with good survival rates for those with early tumours.

Problems arising from contraception

Most women of reproductive age will be using some form of contraception; in this country the commonest method used by married couples is still the sheath and this has no medical complications. Of the methods used by the woman, the following may give rise to problems at the workplace.

Oral contraceptives
These are taken by 50 per cent of women who attend for family planning, either as a combined oestrogen/progesterone pill or one of progesterone only. Some women develop irregular bleeding, particularly on the latter. Others may have nausea, oedema of the limbs due to water retention, and, more seriously, deep-vein thrombosis. The last occurs more often in older women who are overweight and who smoke cigarettes. Such problems are strictly the concern of the family-planning clinic or general practitioner issuing the oral contraception, but they may cause ill health and so absence from work.

Intra-uterine devices
These (IUD) are usually fitted by general practitioners or at a family-planning clinic and are used by 15 per cent of those who attend family-planning clinics. Common complications are intermenstrual bleeding or heavy periods, while a smaller proportion of users report increased dysmenorrhoea. The treatment is often removal of the IUD but some who have heavier menstruation are helped by prostaglandin inhibitors and antifibrinolytic agents. While pregnancy rates are very low with IUDs, a proportion of the pregnancies that occur are ectopic.

Sterilization
Sterilization is becoming more popular among women in some parts of the country. About 6 per cent of couples attending a family-planning clinic elect for this. Female sterilization is usually done through a laparoscope when the Fallopian tube is either cauterized by diathermy, banded, or clipped; the operation means the woman is off work for a week or two. In up to 20 per cent of women, the periods are reported as being heavier after the operation. This may settle down or may lead to further treatment as discussed in the section on menstrual disorders.

Abortion

The exact incidence of spontaneous abortion is not recorded. Probably up to 50 per cent of fertilized ova either do not implant or do not develop. Between 10 and 20 per cent of women who realize they are pregnant undergo a spontaneous abortion characterized by vaginal bleeding and lower abdominal cramping pains. This can be serious and a small number of women still die from spontaneous abortion. Treatment must be in hospital, with evacuation of the uterus. A woman who has had a spontaneous abortion will probably return to work between one and two weeks after the evacuation, unless complications occur.

In the United Kingdom, over 130 000 women have a therapeutic termination of pregnancy each year. If this is done early (before 10–12 weeks' gestation), it is a very simple operation, performed through the cervix, which involves the woman being off work for three or four days only. The psychological effects, however, may last longer. After 10–12 weeks' gestation, difficulties in performing a termination increase in parallel with the delay; some women will require 2–3 weeks off for a prostaglandin termination performed at around 20 weeks gestation.

Prolapse and stress incontinence

After 40 years of age, many women who have had children may develop some atrophy of the ligaments supporting the pelvic organs and develop a genital prolapse. Symptoms may be non-specific, such as backache or a low dragging pain; more specifically there may be an associated stress incontinence of urine. The diagnosis is made by examination and assessment of the degree of laxity. A few women who are unfit (or those in the younger age-group wishing for further pregnancies) may elect for a vaginal pessary to try to compensate for the weakness of muscles and ligaments. Such pessaries need changing at intervals and vaginal hygiene has to be strict. The occupational health nurse may be of assistance in helping the woman to adjust to this and in advising her on hygiene procedures. Occupational health staff may recommend to management that employees with prolapse should avoid jobs which involve heavy lifting or standing in one position for long periods.

More commonly, reparative surgery is performed to reduce and support the prolapse. A vaginal hysterectomy is often required, but alternatively an anterior and posterior wall buttress operation will support the organs. These operations will involve the woman being off work for 6–12 weeks. On return to work she should be advised to avoid duties involving repetitive lifting, or standing in a fixed position without an opportunity to sit down periodically. These recommendations may need to continue for three months and possibly longer.

Infertility

Infertility affects 10–15% of couples in this country. It does not produce physical symptoms but emotional stress is considerable, particularly at the time of the monthly bleed, when the woman is often depressed and disappointed that no pregnancy has occurred. Infertility does not intrude on a woman's work physically, but the mental stress and the time off for the repeated and difficult investigations may affect productivity and become noticeable to the employer.

Menopause

Eighty per cent of women stop their menses with no major problems. The remainder have a varying degree of symptoms following oestrogen withdrawal. The two that intrude most are hot flushes and sweats, and dryness of the vagina. The former may lead a woman to withdraw from her companions at work if she is embarrassed by the flushing and sweating which occur. Treatment with hormonal replacement can be offered; this should, however, be under strict medical supervision.

The occupational health nurse or physician may be the first to identify troublesome flushes and sexual problems related to the menopause. The employee should be encouraged to seek help from her own doctor where necessary, and her progress should be reviewed.

Backache

Backache at work is an important symptom which must be investigated carefully. Commonly, the causes are not gynaecological but from ligamentous or muscular strain associated with activity at home or at work. The diagnosis must be considered with care and causes elucidated. Back pain is discussed in Chapter 9.

There is a need for ergonomic studies to evaluate the benefits of improved design of workstations and equipment for women when undertaking sedentary or standing jobs. The occupational health physician or nurse may advise on the use of a suitable chair or back rest—for example in cars, if employees are travelling extensively on business.

REFERENCES

1. Douglas WB. Maternity in Great Britain. Oxford: Oxford University Press, 1948.
2. Daniels WW. Maternity rights: the experience of women. London: Policy Studies Institute, 1980.

3. Chamberlain G. Women at work in Pregnancy. In: Chamberlain G ed. Pregnant women at work. London: Royal Society of Medicine and Macmillan Press, 1984:3–13.
4. Murray R. The hazards of work in pregnancy. In: Chamberlain G ed. Pregnant women at work. London: Royal Society of Medicine and Macmillan Press, 1984:27–34.
5. Health and Safety at Work etc. Act. London: HMSO, 1974: Chapter 37.
6. Mamelle N, Laumon B. Occupational fatigue and preterm birth. In: Chamberlain G ed. Pregnant women at work. London: Royal Society of Medicine and Macmillan Press, 1984:105–15.
7. Pomroy C, Noel L. Low background radiation measurements on video display terminals. Health Physics 1984;**46**:413–7.
8. Cox EA. Electromagnetic radiation emissions from visual display units: a review. Display Technology and Application 1983;**4**:7–10.
9. Kurppa K, Holmberg PC, Rantala K, Nurminen T. Birth defects and video display terminals. Lancet 1984;**ii**:1339.
10. McDonald AD, Cherry NM, Delorme C, McDonald JC. Visual display units and pregnancy: evidence from the Montreal Survey. J Occup Med 1986;**28**:1226–31.
11. Lee WR. Working with visual display units. Br Med J 1985;**291**:989–91.
12. World Health Organization. Conditions in the work place. In: WHO Press Release 1985:WHO/13.
13. Office of Population Censuses and Surveys. General Household Survey 1980. London: HMSO, 1982.
14. Murphy JF, Dauncey M, Newcombe R, Garcia J, Elbourne D. Employment in pregnancy: prevalence, maternal characteristics, perinatal outcome. Lancet 1984;**i**:1163–6.
15. Office of Population Censuses and Surveys. Cancer Statistics 1979–81. Registrations Series MB1 86/2. London: HMSO, 1986.

20

Surgery

I. McColl and D. P. Manning

The incidence of abdominal and hernia operations

The Hospital Inpatient Enquiry[1] records the number of patients undergoing surgery in England and Wales. In 1983 there were approximately 63 600 operations for inguinal hernia and 19 300 operations for other abdominal herniae. In addition, at least 200 000 operations involved incision of the abdominal wall. Every year some quarter of a million patients require advice about the degree of activity and exertion which may safely be undertaken during convalescence, and many of them need guidance on the length of absence from work and on the type of work compatible with their surgical operations.

Factors influencing return to work following abdominal surgery and hernia operation

Wound strength

There is no general agreement amongst surgeons about the time interval between operation, ambulation, hospital discharge, and return to employment, but the trend towards early activity continues. Farquharson[2] recorded that during the Second World War an army order decreed that all patients must be kept in bed for 21 days after inguinal herniorrhaphy, but by the fifties early ambulation had become popular.[3]

The Shouldice clinic in Toronto has advocated early activity since 1945, and in 1972 Iles described the procedure followed for 75 000 abdominal herniorrhaphies.[4] Repairs were carried out under local anaesthesia and early activity was encouraged. Patients were discharged from hospital 72 hours later and advised to resume immediately any activities they could carry out in reasonable comfort. By the fourth week, the most strenuous activity was permitted, including piano-moving. The Shouldice technique consists of a double-breasted repair of the fascia transversalis, followed by a Bassini-type procedure using a continuous suture. Glassow[5] reported in 1984 that survivors to 10 years whose hernia had been repaired by a consultant using this technique had a 99 per cent expectation that the hernia will remain sound. Use of non-absorbable sutures is essential for early ambulation and also for early return to work.

A study of wound healing revealed that wound strength was 70 per cent of normal immediately after operation, provided that non-absorbable sutures were used, whereas scar tissue strength improved slowly and after eight weeks was only 41 per cent of normal.[6] Three further studies in the literature confirm that return to any kind of employment one month after an operation for unilateral inguinal hernia does not increase the risk of a recurrence.[7-9] Advice to patients is discussed on p. 365.

Size and location of scar

A small scar from a gridiron incision for appendicectomy can be expected to reach maximum strength quickly due to the crossing layers of the abdominal wall. A paramedian incision, in which the rectus abdominis muscle is sandwiched between two layers of connective tissue, may also be expected to heal soundly with more strength than midline abdominal scars. Transverse or oblique incisions involve fewer nerve segments, even though muscle is divided and are therefore less painful. A mid-line incision through the rectus aponeurosis leaves a weak scar, but current surgical practice is to use a continuous nylon suture four times the length of the wound, with 2 cm bites, and this technique reduces the incidence of incisional hernia to the same order as that for paramedian incisions.[10]

Wound dehiscence

Partial or complete disruption of the deeper layers of a wound can occur in the early post-operative period and may be symptomless. Unless the wound is immediately re-sutured an incisional hernia will develop and seriously prejudice the permanent strength of the abdominal wall (p. 367).

Wound infection/haematoma

Superficial wound infection should not weaken the wound, but infection of the deep fascia and lower layers of the wound will delay healing and may lead to permanent weakness and recurrence. A haematoma of the deep layers of a wound also considerably delays healing.

Persistent pain or paraesthesia

Pain and tenderness in the scar or paraesthesia or hypoaesthesia usually resolve rapidly following most surgical operations. Transverse abdominal incisions which divide few sensory nerves are the least painful in the post-operative period, whereas vertical incisions dividing numerous nerve branches are more painful and the occurrence of painful neuromas is more likely. Operations for inguinal hernia sometimes divide or trap the scrotal branch of the ilioinguinal nerve and cause pain or hypoaesthesia which may delay a return to full activity. Some occupations involve leaning across benches or against machine guards, and tenderness of abdominal scars may delay a return to work.

Occupation

In many occupations the intra-abdominal pressure arising from exertion and the forces applied to the scar by muscular contraction are unlikely to exceed the forces generated by normal physiological functions such as defaecation and coughing. In occupations which involve manual handling of loads or other forms of muscular effort, the force applied to the scar will be considerable.

Advice to patients

The most important factor determining the interval between surgical treatment and return to work is motivation. Some patients who have a keen interest in their work or career, or who cannot afford to lose money, will return to work very soon after an operation, sometimes on the next day. Others are more cautious and may appreciate professional advice; some will require persuasion. In practice, most patients will delay their return to work until it suits them, but pre-operative advice is important in determining not only length of stay, but also time off work. For instance, if a patient is told that the operation will require three days in-patient treatment he or she will be champing at the bit if kept any longer. Conversely, if told beforehand that the expected length of stay in hospital is 10 days, the patient will be disgruntled if discharged after three days. The same principle applies to time off work, and much unnecessary absence from work could be avoided by counselling patients appropriately before their operation about expected time off work.

The following guidelines are proposed. It should be borne in mind throughout that, except where complications are mentioned, they refer to patients who have made a normal recovery. Surgeons may sometimes deviate from these guidelines because of strong personal preferences or variations in surgical technique.

Unilateral inguinal herniorrhaphy/Epigastric hernia operations

The two long-term studies by Bourke *et al.*[8] and Taylor and Dewar[9] recommended a return to full activity and normal work within 28 and 21 days respectively. A leading article in the Lancet in 1985[11] stated that 'we should therefore recommend return to work within two weeks for sedentary workers and after four weeks for those in more strenuous occupations', but 'any physical activity that causes pain should be avoided.' Since most surgeons now use a nylon darn or a Bassini-type operation for repair of inguinal herniae, these recommedations are reasonable and evidence from the Shouldice clinic[4,5] is most convincing that any occupation may be resumed safely after four weeks. Patients should be advised not to drive for two weeks following inguinal herniorrhaphy, as they may be slower to operate the brake due to wound discomfort.

Reassurance It is traditional for some doctors to recommend a period off work of up to three months, and of light work for 3–6 months, following operations for inguinal hernia. There is no evidence, however, of clinical benefit from such a prolonged period of inactivity, and patients should be reassured that they are not increasing the risk of recurrence, or of other complications arising, if they return to normal work after a shorter interval. Patients who have residual discomfort in the scar due to peripheral nerve involvement will need an explanation and reassurance that the discomfort can be ignored.

Femoral hernia operations/Uncomplicated appendicectomy with gridiron incision

The majority of patients should be able to resume sedentary work after two weeks, and heavy occupations after three weeks.

Umbilical hernia operations/Bilateral inguinal herniae operations

The period of restriction should be longer, with a return to work and normal activity after six weeks. This may be extended to three months for a large umbilical hernia.

Hernia scars weakened by infection or haematoma

The scar may be permanently weakened and healing will certainly be delayed. Those employed in heavy occupations or indulging in strenuous leisure pursuits should be advised to avoid heavy exertion if they wish to reduce the risk of developing a hernia, but for those who must return to heavy work there appears to be no advantage in reducing activity more than three months from the time of operation.

Operations for recurrent inguinal hernia

A second repair of an inguinal hernia is less likely to produce a sound scar than the primary repair. Patients will also be more reluctant to risk a further recurrence due to heavy exertion. There is no reason why the patient should remain inactive during the post-operative period, but he should be advised against heavy exertion for a period of three months.

Operations for incisional hernia

Incisional herniae vary in size. Return to a sedentary occupation should be possible within two weeks following repair of the smallest herniae, and to more strenuous occupations after six weeks. Repair of a large incisional hernia is unlikely to achieve sufficient strength to withstand heavy manual exertion and there will remain a high probability of further breakdown of the scar. Heavy exertion should, ideally, be avoided permanently and return to manual work delayed for three months. Use of a suitable corset, however, can give very good protection for those who must undertake heavy exertion.

Cholecystectomy

Activity is usually restricted for about six weeks due to pain in the wound. Most patients will remain absent from work for six weeks, and those in heavy manual occupations may not be able to resume full activity for three months from the time of operation.

Operations on the stomach and duodenum

Operation wounds usually become pain-free within a month, enabling patients to resume employment, with progression to heavy manual work within three months. Following partial gastrectomy small frequent meals are necessary and patients must take regular meal-breaks. Shiftworkers should remain on regular days for a few weeks or longer if any digestive symptoms occur. This is not an absolute requirement for all patients as there are those who obtain more rest during daylight hours.

Post-gastrectomy syndromes

Post-operative abdominal and vasomotor symptoms are seen in the majority of patients following gastric surgery, but they usually diminish with time. Early symptoms occurring shortly after a meal may persist in 5–12 per cent of patients, who must be able to eat small meals separate from drinks,[12] and this may require concessions by management when the patient returns to work. Patients should also avoid sugar. Late symptoms occurring about two hours after a meal are treated by taking food, and here too when the patient returns to work he or she must be able to obtain food when required. Following gastric surgery it is common for patients to lose weight and to suffer from nutritional disturbances which may limit their capacity for physically strenuous work. Placement in alternative, less active work is sometimes desirable.

Resection of the colon and other major abdominal operations

The recommendations are similar to those for cholecystectomy, namely a return to sedentary occupations in six weeks, with a maximum of three months avoidance of heavy exertion in the manual occupations. Alteration of bowel function, causing more frequent bowel actions, sometimes requires immediate access to a toilet which should be taken into consideration. This applies especially to operations in which the ileocaecal valve has been removed.[13] Extensive intestinal resection for Crohn's disease and other pathology frequently results in malabsorption and loss of weight. Nevertheless, working capacity may be retained in half of the patients.[14] Permanent colostomy is discussed in Chapter 14.

Cholecystitis

Acute cholecystitis usually resolves in several weeks and a period of convalescence of two weeks may be required before the patient returns to work. If cholecystectomy is advised the patient should be able to return to full employment while waiting for surgery (see below).

Pancreatitis

The course is so variable that each patient needs individual assessment.

Patients waiting for operations

Patients waiting for surgery may be receiving treatment and may be unfit for work due to the symptoms of the illness. Those waiting for hernia repair or for cholecystectomy, however, will usually be capable of attending work. In the early stages during the development of an inguinal hernia patients may experience aching discomfort due to stretching of tissue as the hernia enlarges, and symptoms are increased by exertion. During this time the patient may be able to attend work if he can avoid manual exertion and excessive walking. As the hernia enlarges, symptoms may disappear and a return to any kind of work is possible, although it is usual to avoid heavy work while waiting for operation. The patient should be warned, however, that if pain occurs in the hernia or abdomen, he should immediately lie down and reduce the hernia. If this is not possible or if the pain continues, medical advice must be obtained without delay. A truss is an acceptable aid to some patients waiting for repair of an inguinal hernia.

Occupations involving travel

The Merchant Shipping (Medical Examinations) Regulations 1983 provide guidelines on surgical conditions which render seamen unfit for work.[15] The following notes relate to surgical conditions mentioned in this section. See also Appendix 3.

- *Hernia*: unfit for seagoing duties until repaired.

- *Peptic ulceration* (see also Chapter 14): where there has been gastrointestinal bleeding, perforation, or recurrent peptic ulceration (in spite of maintenance H2 blocker treatment), or an unsatisfactory operation result, patients are normally unfit for work at sea.

- *Recurrent attacks of appendicitis*: patients are unfit for seagoing duties pending surgical removal.

- *Biliary tract disease*: not fit for work at sea until after complete surgical cure.

- *Pancreatitis*: patients with recurrent pancreatitis, and all cases where alcohol is an aetiological factor, are permanently unfit for work at sea.

- *General advice*: it is prudent for all patients awaiting hernia operations or gall bladder operations to remain within easy reach of a hospital and avoid long journeys, particularly by sea, because of the danger of acute complications including strangulation or acute cholecystitis.

ANAL REGION AND PILONIDAL SINUS

Incidence of operations

More than 12 000 operations for haemorrhoids and a further 29 000 in the anal region are carried out per annum.[1]

Haemorrhoids

Perianal haematoma has been described as the five-day painful self-curing lesion of Milligan, and most patients present after a week and need no treatment. Discomfort is increased by walking and sitting on hard surfaces. Absence from work is usually not justified, but alternative employment may be necessary for a few days.

Prolapsing *internal* haemorrhoids may cause disability. Usually symptoms can be prevented by immediate reduction, but if strangulation and/or thrombosis occur the patient will be unable to attend work. A high roughage diet will reduce the incidence of symptoms.

Patients who suffer from recurrent prolapse of piles often assume that the condition will be aggravated by sitting on hard or warm surfaces. They should be reassured that their fears are groundless.

Operative treatment

Anal dilation or injections cause little discomfort and the patient can return to any form of employment next day. Following haemorrhoidectomy the patient should be able to return to work without a restriction on activity or exertion after one month. A high roughage diet will expedite recovery.

Ischio-rectal abscess and perianal abscess

Following surgery, symptoms should rapidly disappear and return to work will be determined by availability of dressing facilities. If there is an occupational health unit at the place of work, the patient could be referred there by letter for wound dressings. Otherwise a return to work should be postponed until the patient can cope with wound treatment. In occupations involving prolonged sitting, the patient should be advised to sit on a soft foam pad.

Fissure-in-ano and fistula-in-ano

Following anal dilation for a fissure the patient will be able to return to normal work within two or three days.

Most fistulae are low and patients can return to work in a week or two. Earlier return may be possible if dressing facilities are available at work. Higher fistulae will need a much longer period of absence from work.

Pilonidal sinus

During the Second World War, pilonidal sinus was known as 'jeep bottom' and assumed to be caused by hard seats and frequent jolts to the lower spine, causing hairs to be pushed through the skin. There is no published evidence that prolonged sitting is likely to cause infection of a pilonidal sinus, but during the acute phase and following surgery, pressure over the coccyx should be avoided by sitting on a soft foam pad. Patients are more likely to return to work at an early date if they are reassured that the inflammation is not caused by walking or sitting, and if dressing facilities are available at work.

Regulations applying to employment

Merchant seamen suffering from haemorrhoids are excluded from seagoing duties until satisfactory treatment has been obtained.[15]

ARTERIAL SYSTEM

Incidence of cardiovascular operations

The number of operations undertaken on the heart and intrathoracic vessels every year in England and Wales is 36 000, together with an additional 17 000 operations on other arteries.[1]

Aortic aneurysm

It is possible for patients in sedentary occupations to continue in employment while waiting for surgery, providing they are otherwise well, blood pressure is controlled, and they avoid driving. Those employed on manual tasks which might raise blood pressure should not work.

Aortic grafts and aorto-iliac grafts

Patients should avoid all physical exertion for four weeks and be able to return to sedentary work after six weeks and any other work after three months.

The results of aorto-iliac grafts are excellent and should enable the patient to return to any form of employment. However, there may be a restriction on activity due to the underlying arterial disease. Cessation of smoking, control of weight and blood pressure, and a healthy low-fat diet are thought to improve the prospects for a full recovery.

Femoro-popliteal grafts

Patients who are disabled by claudication may be offered a femoro-popliteal graft. The results of surgery are less successful than for aorto-iliac grafts, but patients may be able to resume sedentary work in four weeks, and more active occupations in 12 weeks, depending on the symptoms and the degree of atherosclerosis affecting other organs. They should not return to occupations involving crouching and repetitive knee flexing.

Coronary bypass surgery

Successful coronary bypass surgery enables patients to return to most kinds of work. For example, Jenkins *et al.* reported in 1983 that of 197 patients employed pre-operatively, 75 per cent were gainfully employed at six months follow-up (73 per cent of them within three months), while 20 per cent of 89 patients not working in the year before surgery re-entered work.[16] Following coronary bypass surgery patients may be anxious that physical activity and exertion could be harmful. Clear advice from the surgeons about suitable exercise and the type of employment which may safely be undertaken will help to reassure patients and encourage early return to full employment. For further discussion see Chapter 15.

Carotid stenosis

Ability to work is liable to be determined by the underlying arterial disease and residual symptoms. Recovery from surgical operations on the internal carotid artery should be complete in four or five weeks.

Research

A study of 255 employed persons undergoing major vascular surgery revealed that 64 per cent resumed full employment. The ability to work following abdominal aortic aneurysm was statistically related to the age of the patient. The ability to return to work following carotid endarterectomy, aorto-femoral bypass, femoral distal and femoro-popliteal bypass was statistically related to the degree of success of surgery.[17]

Regulations affecting employment

The Merchant Shipping (Medical Regulations) state that patients with intermittent claudication or any who require vascular surgery are permanently unfit for seagoing duties.[15] (Intermittent claudication is discussed in Chapter 15.)

BREAST

Incidence of operations on the breast

The Hospital Inpatient Enquiry[1] reported that in 1983, 38 000 mastectomies were performed, together with an additional 13 000 other operations.

Biopsy and surgery for innocent cysts and swellings

Aspiration of cysts need not lead to absence from work, but operations involving an incision may require an absence of a few days.

Simple mastectomy

Following simple mastectomy, the principal obstacle to resuming normal activity and work is motivation. It is usually in the patient's best interest to return to work as soon as the wound is healed. Breast reconstruction or fitting a prosthesis immediately after the operation will assist the patient to adjust to the disfigurement.[18] Psychological support by a nurse has been shown to assist social recovery and return to work.[19]

Following simple mastectomy, it is common for serous discharge to drain from the wound for up to one week or more. Patients should be warned about this, provided with suitable dressings and reassured that it has no serious import.

Radical mastectomy

Radical mastectomy is not often undertaken, but the operation sometimes leads to oedema of the arm and shoulder stiffness which may interfere with employment. Patients will usually require a period of absence extending to at least two months.

Radiotherapy

Radiotherapy and adjuvant therapy with either endocrine or cytotoxic drugs, are likely to delay a return to full activity owing to systemic disturbance.

GENITO-URINARY TRACT

Incidence of surgical operations

Altogether 620 000 genito-urinary operations were recorded during 1983 for England and Wales: 3000 were for removal of a kidney.[1]

Nephrectomy

Patients frequently complain of discomfort in the scar which is aggravated by bending and twisting movements. A return to clerical-type work should be possible within six weeks, but avoidance of repetitive stooping and heavy lifting for a further period of six weeks would be reasonable in some manual occupations.

Patients having lost one kidney are anxious about possible injury to the remaining kidney. In practice the risk of injury to a kidney at work is remote. Patients can be reassured that loss of a kidney does not prevent manual work in any occupation (Chapter 17).

Prostatectomy

Following transurethral prostatectomy patients usually leave hospital after 1–2 weeks and will require at least a similar period of convalescence before resuming work. The chief consideration regarding return to work is adequate control of micturition and ready access to a toilet. The type of work is of less importance.

Testicular torsion

The patient will be able to return to any kind of work when scar tenderness settles, usually within two weeks.

Hydrocoele

Aspiration treatment should not lead to absence from work. Following operation the scar will be tender, which will reduce activity for one or two weeks.

Orchidectomy

Orchidectomy should only require a reduction in activities such as walking until tenderness has diminished to an acceptable level—say two or three weeks. Treatment of the underlying disease, for example by cytotoxic drugs or radiotherapy. may delay return to work.

Vasectomy

One study showed that 46 per cent of patients do not lose time from work following vasectomy, and the percentage could be much higher if the operation is performed on a Friday.[20] Those who were absent lost an average of 5.12 days. It is possible that patients with more active manual occupations find it necessary to take time off work. The occurrence of a haematoma or of infection may require an absence of 10 days.

HEAD AND NECK

Incidence of head and neck operations

The number of operations on the thyroid performed in 1983 was 8500. There were, in addition, 3400 intracranial operations and more than 23 000 other operations on the head and neck.[1]

Thyroidectomy

Patients usually make a rapid recovery from thyroidectomy, but convalescence may be prolonged by debility from hyperthyroidism, especially if there have been symptoms of cardiac involvement. Most patients will be capable of normal work after two weeks, with a further restriction on heavy physical exertion for two months in all.

Operations on the salivary glands

Removal of stones from the ducts of salivary glands causes few post-operative problems, and patients should be capable of any type of work within two weeks.

Operations for malignant tumours

Depending on the site of the malignancy there is likely to be disfigurement and disability.[21] Radical surgery for tumours of the sinuses and mandible are especially disfiguring, and early fitting of a prosthesis will be highly beneficial.

Excision of laryngeal tumours causes partial or complete loss of voice which may damage promotion prospects in some occupations.[22] Reacquisition of speech has been shown to be an important factor for employment.[23] Laryngectomy is usually performed on patients in their late fifties or older; nevertheless 24 of 62 patients returned to competitive employment in one series.[23]

Craniotomy and operations on the circle of Willis

Subarachnoid haemorrhage and operations to clip a berry aneurysm

Disability following surgical treatment varies considerably. There may be residual neurological disability from the haemorrhage or from the surgery. This varies from minor symptoms from which the patients may recover in a few weeks to more serious disability, but most patients will require lengthy rehabilitation. A minimum absence of two months is to be expected.

Successful operations to clip the aneurysm will eliminate the need for any restriction on physical activity, but for a period of some two years the safety of the patient should be considered as there is an increased risk of an epileptic seizure. Employers should be advised that the patient could fall without warning and should not, therefore, work at heights, work with unguarded moving machinery, or drive vehicles during this period (Chapter 12).

On returning to work, patients with a post-operative skull defect who are liable to strike their heads against structures may require protection in the form of a padded cap or safety helmet.

INGROWING TOENAILS

Incidence of operations on the nails

The Hospital Inpatient Enquiry for 1983 records 8550 operations on nails.[1] The number is probably much higher, however, as many are carried out in accident and emergency departments.

Treatment of ingrowing toenails

Ingrowing toenails lead to a great deal of needless absence from work;[24] absence for more than 24 hours is quite unnecessary for the majority of patients with ingrowing toenails. Symptoms are relieved almost immediately by excising a triangle of nail where it is irritating the nail fold; avulsion of the nail causes tenderness of the nail bed and absence from work of at least one week. Recurrent ingrowing toenails requiring additional treatment, such as cryotherapy[25] or excision of a strip of nail and ablation of a small piece of the nail bed with phenol,[26] justify an absence of a few days until tenderness has cleared and the wound is healing. Complete removal of the nail bed requires an absence of at least two weeks and probably longer for patients who have to walk continuously.

THORAX

Incidence of thoracic operations

In addition to operations on the heart and intrathoracic vessels mentioned on p. 370, at least 26 000 thoracic operations were recorded in England and Wales in 1983.[1]

Thoracotomy scars

Incisions for pulmonary operations usually follow the dermatome, but injury to the sensory branches of intercostal nerves sometimes leaves residual tenderness and paraesthesia which may interfere with employment. An explanation of the cause of symptoms should help to convince the patient that there is no need to restrict activity or avoid heavy exertion.

Partial and total pneumonectomy

In addition to symptoms from scar tissue, exercise tolerance may be limited, particularly following total pneumonectomy. Pneumonectomy is commonly undertaken in middle life or in older persons whose pulmonary reserve has already been compromised by smoking. Dyspnoea at rest or on very slight exertion will prevent travel to work or any physical activity. Nevertheless, a long-term study in the Netherlands revealed that of 37 male pneumonectomy patients 14 resumed full-time work and 9 part-time work.[27] Patients have a better prospect of re-employment following partial pneumonectomy.[28] The minimum period of absence is likely to be two months, extending to six months for the most disabled.

Hiatus hernia

Patients waiting for operation should be able to attend work providing that there is no requirement to stoop to waist level or lower; symptoms are aggravated by reflux of acid while stooping. Surgery will frequently eliminate symptoms from reflux. Operations for hiatus hernia may involve an abdominal incision or a thoracotomy, and post-operative progress is mentioned on pp. 364–5 and p. 376, respectively. A minimum absence of six weeks is to be anticipated for sedentary workers and up to three months for manual workers (see also Chapter 14).

Operations on the oesophagus

Operations on the oesophagus will usually require a transthoracic approach, and the factors described on p. 376 may apply. Post-operative disability depends on the extent of the operation and will be maximal following resection of a carcinoma. This usually entails a combined abdominal and thoracic approach, together with radiotherapy. Very few patients will return to work.

Spontaneous pneumothorax

Following spontaneous pneumothorax the patient is advised to avoid exertion for at least two weeks to allow full expansion of the lung. A further period of restriction is sensible to permit sound healing of the defect. An absence of six weeks would be reasonable for manual workers. Recurrent pneumothorax will require a longer period of protection from heavy physical activity, for up to 12 months, and operative intervention may be indicated. Factors discussed on p. 376 may apply following operation.

Regulations

Merchant seamen are not permitted to sail for at least one year following pneumothorax. A recurrent pneumothorax permanently excludes seagoing duties.[15]

VARICOSE VEINS AND VENOUS THROMBOSIS

Incidence of operations on veins

More than 42 000 patients are admitted annually for operations on varicose veins.[1] In addition, several times this number of patients are treated as outpatients by injection with sclerosing agents. The majority are thought to be employed and will, therefore, require advice about the effect of occupation on varicose veins and of surgery on employment.

Varicose veins

There is no general agreement about the symptomatology of varicose veins, but patients frequently complain of aching legs. They should be reassured that walking and general activity is beneficial to the circulation; muscular movement in the leg helps to empty the veins. Conversely, standing still or sitting still may increase symptoms, but there are few occupations in which a person stands still; any movement of the feet is beneficial. Elastic stockings may be preferable or supplementary to operative treatment. Thus, there is no need for patients to lose time from work while waiting for hospital assessment or treatment.

Patients who are liable to strike their legs against objects at work should wear a protective covering to prevent haemorrhage from rupture of a varicose vein. They should also be instructed that bleeding from a ruptured varicose vein is easily stopped by raising the leg and the application of gentle pressure over a clean dressing.

Injection of varicose veins

Following injection of a sclerosing agent, the patient is usually advised to walk at least three miles per day, hence there is no reason to lose time from work. Nevertheless, a study in 1972 revealed that the average number of days absence from work following injection was 6.4.[29]

Operations to ligate or strip varicose veins

Scars sometimes remain tender for several weeks, but most patients should be able to return to work within 14 days, and 90 per cent within three weeks. The average number of days lost from work in the study mentioned above was 31.3.[29]

Superficial thrombophlebitis

A small area of thrombophlebitis may be treated while the patient attends work, but if there is evidence of spread the patient should rest at home while undergoing treatment. It would be unusual to lose more than two weeks from work unless ligation of the vein is required; in such circumstances an absence of one month may be necessary, with the possibility of some restriction on walking until tenderness resolves.

Deep vein thrombosis (phlebothrombosis) and white leg

Thrombosis of the deep veins has far more serious implications. Initially the patient will require observation and treatment for a minimum of four weeks prior to return to work to permit stabilization of the prothrombin level, but the period of disability is liable to be greater. Persistent swelling of the leg, even with an elastic support, is likely to limit the amount of walking, although patients do need to exercise the leg as much as possible. Those employed in occupations requiring continuous walking may need alternative work. Similarly, prolonged standing is not practicable. Patients receiving continuous anticoagulation treatment could profitably be instructed on methods of stopping bleeding should they receive an open wound at work.

Ulceration of the lower leg

Although this is mainly a problem with the elderly, some employed persons may suffer from a leg ulcer. The first essential is to prevent trauma to the leg as a minor blow may precipitate an ulcer. An elastic stocking will normally be required to help prevent a recurrence. Treatment of the ulcer in an occupational health department is quite feasible if staff are provided with dressings and advice on the recommended method of treatment.

Pulmonary embolism

The size of an embolism will be the chief determinant of disability. Small infarcts heal with no long-term disability. Large infarcts may limit exercise tolerance and possibly lead to persistent pleural pains and prolonged absence from work.

Axillary vein thrombosis

Axillary vein thrombosis is rare, but may cause prolonged disability due to swelling of the limb, with associated clumsiness of movement. Patients will usually be reluctant to use the arm, fearing that exercise may cause a relapse. Following the initial period of treatment, normal use of the arm should be encouraged, while avoiding situations which would apply pressure to the axilla.

Regulations

Merchant seamen may be certified as being temporarily unfit for seagoing duties while waiting for treatment of varicose veins. Those with varicose ulceration, thin unhealthy scars, or varicose eczema are permanently unfit for employment at sea.[15]

REFERENCES

1. Hospital Inpatient Enquiry, summary tables. Series MB4 no 22. Table S.10. London: HMSO, 1983.

2. Farquharson EL. Early ambulation with special reference to herniorrhaphy as an outpatient procedure. Lancet 1955;**2**:517–9.

3. Gold D. Early ambulation and return to full duty in the United States Air Force. Ann NY Acad Sci 1958;**73**:517–23.

4. Iles JDH. Convalescence after herniorrhaphy. JAMA 1972;**219**(3):385–8.

5. Glassow F. Inguinal hernia repair using local anaesthesia. Ann R Coll Surg Eng 1984;**66**:382–7.

6. Lichtenstein IL, Herzikoff S, Shore JM, Jiron MW, Stuart S, Mizuno L. The dynamics of wound healing. Surg Gynecol Obstet 1970;**130**:685–90.

7. Ross APJ. Incidence of inguinal hernia recurrence. Effect of time off work after repair. Ann R Coll Surg Eng 1975;**57**:326–8.

8. Bourke JB, Lear PA, Taylor M. Effect of early return to work after elective repair of inguinal hernia: clinical and financial consequences at one year and three years. Lancet 1981;**2**:623–5.

9. Taylor EW, Dewar EP. Early return to work after repair of a unilateral inguinal hernia. Br J Surg 1983;**70**:599–600.

10. Jenkins TPN. The burst abdominal wound: a mechanical approach. Br J Surg 1976;**63**:873–6.

11. British Hernias [Editorial]. Lancet 1985;**1**:1080–1.

12. Bailey H, Love M. Short practice of surgery. 19th ed. London: HK Lewis, 1984:844.

13. Cooke SAR. Large bowel surgery: aftercare. Update 1973;**7**(6):703–7.

14. Kristensen M, Lenz K, Nielsen OV, Jarnum S. Short bowel syndrome following resection for Crohn's disease. Scand J Gastroent 1974;**9**(6):559–65.

15. Merchant Shipping Notice No. M.1144. The Merchant Shipping (Medical Examination) Regulations 1983, SI 1983, no 808. London: Dept of Transport, Marine Directorate.

16. Jenkins CD, Stanton BA, Savageau JA, Denlinger P, Klein MD. Coronary artery bypass surgery. Physical, psychological, social and economic outcomes six months later. JAMA 1983;**250**(6):782–8.

17. Glickman MH, Hurwitz RL, Kimmins SA, Evans WE. Employment following peripheral vascular surgery: an increasingly critical issue. Surgery 1983;**93**(1):50–3.

18. Taylor SE, Lichtman RR, Wood JV, Bluming AZ, Dosik GM, Leibowitz RL. Illness-related and treatment-related factors in psychological adjustment to breast cancer. Cancer 1985;**55**(10):2506–13.

19. Maguire P, Brooke M, Tait A, Thomas C, Sellwood R. The effect of counselling on physical disability and social recovery after mastectomy. Clin Oncol 1983;**9**:319–24.

20. Randall PE, Marcuson RW. Absence from work following vasectomy. J Soc Occup Med 1985;**35**:77–8.

21. Olson ML, Shedd DP. Disability and rehabilitation in head and neck cancer patients after treatment. Head Neck Surg 1978;**1**:52–8.

22. Brøndbo K, Alberti PW, Crowson N. Adult recurrent multiple laryngeal papilloma: laser management and socioeconomic effects. Acta Otolaryngol 1983;**95**:431–9.

23. Goldberg RT. Vocational and social adjustment after laryngectomy. Scand J Rehabil Med 1975;7:1–8.
24. Miller SS. Ingrowing toenails. Br Med J 1985;**291**:91–2.
25. Sonnex S, Dawber RPR. Treatment of ingrowing toenails with liquid nitrogen spray cryotherapy. Br Med J 1985;**291**:173–5.
26. Robb JE, Murray WR. Phenol cauterisation in the management of ingrowing toenails. Scot Med J 1982;**27**:236–9.
27. Laros CD. The patient after total pneumonectomy. A long-term study. Selected Papers 1979, Vol. 19. The Royal Netherlands Tuberculosis Association, 7 Riouwstraat, The Hague, Holland.
28. Kurpat D, Anstett K. Disablement, invalidity and vocational rehabilitation after surgical treatment because of bronchial carcinoma. Z-Erkr Atmungsorgane 1977;**147**(3):223–7.
29. Piachaud D, Weddell JM. The economics of treating varicose veins. Int J Epidemiol 1972;**1**(3):287–94.

21

Psychiatric disorders, alcohol, and drug abuse

H. G. Egdell, F. A. Horrocks, K. Lee, and J. W. Warburton

PSYCHIATRIC DISORDERS

Introduction

This chapter provides a brief account of the implications for work of psychiatric illness. The emphasis is on detection and management at the workplace only and it is not intended to give a summary of psychiatric illness and its treatment.

Prejudice towards psychiatric illness is as common in the workplace as in society as a whole. Such unreasonable and unprofessional reactions arise from ignorance and fear. Health staff can provide informed advice in the workplace and achieve a balance between unreasonable anxiety or rejection of the sick worker on the one hand and too high an expectation on the other. Emotional illness and stress affect not only feelings but also physical state, performance, behaviour, and ways of thinking. Inevitably, colleagues and management are affected.

The psychological benefits of work have been listed by Warr[1] as provision of money, activity, variety, a structure to daily life, social contacts and status, and identity. He finds the disadvantages of work less easy to identify but includes boredom, low job satisfaction, lack of feeling of personal control of work activity, overload, conflict, role ambiguity, excess responsibility, bad working conditions, and troubled relationships. Management structure, skills, and activity can have a positive or negative effect. The workers' perception of the work situation and their coping abilities together with other stresses will interact with these factors.

The aetiology of most disease is multifactorial and this includes work factors. In psychiatric illness there is a complex interaction between physical, personal, social, and environmental influences. It is conventional to divide aetiology into three main headings: predisposing, precipitating, and maintaining. Precipitating factors are the triggers. These include adverse life events such as physical illness, the effects of drugs, and stress at work. Maintaining factors perpetuate the disorder, e.g. unemployment or the secondary advantages of being ill.

It is important at an early stage to raise the issue of a planned return to work, if necessary modifying any working conditions which have aggravated the problems. This can allay fears of immediate dismissal. In planning return to work the health adviser should consider if changes in the work, counselling, re-training, or a job more suitable for the individual can lessen the risk of relapse and improve performance.

Awareness of particular vulnerable groups is important, for example young married women with children, middle-aged persons susceptible to depression, and workers in specially stressful occupations (e.g. dealing with child abuse; intensive care; air traffic controllers). It is also useful to be aware of the large number of self-help organizations for assisting vulnerable groups and patients.[2]

Fear of violence in psychiatric illness is largely unfounded. The highest risk lies with alcoholic intoxication. Health staff also fear that involvement may lead them into overwhelming responsibility for a psychiatric problem. In reality, their primary contribution is that of detection and assessment, and helping the individual to plan further care. The counselling role is, of course, crucial. Expectations of immediate cure are unrealistic as treatment is unlikely to produce immediate results.

The time-scale for response to treatment varies from weeks, in the case of depression, to months or even years, in the case of schizophrenia. Although this is a source of disappointment, pessimism is inappropriate as most conditions can be improved.

The individual syndromes in the chapter are classified according to the International Classification of Diseases[3] and given in that order rather than the order of importance in the workplace. In the use of this it is important to remember that the issue is not simply one of illness but of a worker and person who has a problem. A key area of concern for occupational health staff is stress at work. This is considered under adjustment reaction (p. 399). Relevant existing legislation for psychiatric conditions will be considered later in the chapter.

Prevalence of psychiatric disorders

The prevalence of psychiatric morbidity in the workplace is not known. The nearest approximation is that occurring in general practice. The national study of general practice morbidity statistics 1981–82 found consultation rates per 1000 persons at risk to be: neurotic depression 72, anxiety state 56, transient situational disturbance 16, sleep disorders 13, affective psychosis 8, senile and pre-senile conditions 6, schizophrenia 6, tension headaches and psychogenic pains 6. Medical categories of unemployed disabled persons (1981) showed that 13.9 per cent were due to neurosis and psychosis and 7.1 per cent to mental handicap.

Further information on psychiatric diagnosis and treatment is available in Gelder *et al.*[4] and Dubovsky and Weissberg.[5]

Classification and terminology

While emphasis is given to those conditions of particular importance in the workplace, they need to be seen against a generally accepted psychiatric classification. The Ninth Revision of the International Classification of Diseases (Appendix, p. 421) will be used, as it is widely accepted even though not yet perfect. The American alternative, the DSM III,[6] is not used in this chapter although it has the advantage of detailed descriptive definitions.

A number of problems not yet fully resolved in psychiatric classification should be borne in mind in reading this chapter. These include:

1. The commonest problems presenting in the workplace are anxiety and depression. These terms also describe the normal range of feelings, whereas illness is present when anxiety and/or depression are severe, persistent, and disabling.

2. Normal anxiety can be beneficial by increasing arousal, improving effectiveness, and preparing for a challenge. If, however, it is severe and prolonged, the effectiveness reaches a plateau and then steadily falls off.

3. The terms 'psychosis' and 'neurosis' are still in common use despite continuing controversy about their use and difficulties in precise definition.

The definitions used in this chapter are reproduced from the *Mental disorders glossary* by permission of WHO, Geneva.

(a) Psychoses are 'mental disorders in which impairment of mental function has developed to a degree that interferes grossly with insight, ability to meet some ordinary demands of life or to maintain adequate contact with reality' (ICD 9 290–9). The person has difficulty in distinguishing between the experiences arising from his illness and the reality of the world about him. He may not realize he is ill even when it is clearly evident to others on the grounds of common sense. His complaints and behaviour are not understandable to those around him. Examples would be a person having frightening or suspicious misinterpretations of normal or neutral events, or having delusions (a false, unshakeable belief out of keeping with an individual's personal, social, and cultural background) or hallucinations (perceptions without an adequate external stimulus), for example 'voices'. There may or may not be an underlying physical illness, e.g. an alcohol withdrawal state.

(b) Neurotic disorders are 'mental disorders without any demonstrable organic basis in which the patient may have considerable insight and has unimpaired reality testing in that he does not confuse his morbid subjective experiences and fantasies with external reality. Behaviour may be greatly affected, although usually remaining within socially acceptable limits, but personality is not disorganized. The principal manifestations include excessive anxiety, hysterical symptoms, phobias, obsessional and compulsive symptoms, and depression' (ICD 9 300). The lay person can understand, if not always sympathize with, neurotic disorders as he or she will have had the same experiences though in a less severe and disabling manner.

(c) Both depression and anxiety can occur in the psychoses and neuroses.

DEMENTIA: (ICD 9 290) SENILE AND PRESENILE ORGANIC PSYCHOTIC CONDITIONS

Introduction

Dementia is a generalized impairment of intellect, memory, and personality occurring in the absence of clouding of consciousness. Although mainly older age-groups are affected in post-retirement years, some working groups can continue to work into old age. These will include many self-employed people and others, for example politicians, judges, and doctors.

Although dementia is usually a progressive illness, it is important to remember that a few causes are non-progressive or reversible, and that the forgetfulness and falling productivity of depression may be mistaken for dementia. The main causes are multi-infarct (atherosclerotic) dementia and Alzheimer's disease. Together they account for 90 per cent of cases. Over 65 years the term 'senile dementia of the Alzheimer type' (SDAT) is used. Rarer causes in a younger age-group include Pick's disease, Huntington's chorea, Kreutzfeld-Jacob disease, normal pressure hydrocephalus, subcortical dementia, punch drunk syndrome, alcohol, and heavy-metal poisoning, e.g. mercury, lead, arsenic, and thallium.

As a general rule the onset of dementia is insidious. In the early stages minor forgetfulness is the first sign with loss of short-term memory while distant memory is intact. The disease progresses with general intellectual decline. This is paralleled by declining social behaviour and self-care with an increasing tendency to emotional lability, particularly when the patient is aware of failing abilities. Focal signs, such as dysphasia, impairment of numerical skills and motor dexterity, and epilepsy may be present.

It is unfortunate that the term 'senile' refers to the age-group 65 and over. The implication is that intellectual decline is to be expected. The elderly do not perform as well on IQ tests as the young, but this may be because it is the tests themselves that are inappropriate. Old people are cognitively slower than the young, and short-term memory is not as good. Whether or not this is pathological is a matter of debate. The experience and wisdom of maturity must be set against the mental agility of youth. Older workers find adjustment to change more difficult and need longer to learn new techniques. Becoming old brings with it an increasing incidence of other degenerative diseases, e.g. in the joints, which have more impact on working capacity than cognitive decline. Ageing affects individuals at different rates. Some are sprightly well into their seventies while others are slowing down and becoming rigid in outlook in late middle-age. A retirement age of 60 or 65 reflects social policy and not the intellectual ability of those retiring.

Prevalence

The incidence of dementia in our society is increasing as a consequence of our ageing population. The prevalence of dementia in the 65–70 age-group is 5 per cent, doubling in the 75–85 range. The commonest cause of dementia is Alzheimer's disease, accounting for 55 per cent of cases. The age of onset may be anywhere between 40 to 90 but the commonest group affected is between 70 and 90. It is twice as common in women.

Clinical aspects affecting work capacity

Selection for work is influenced by the lack of prospect of improvement except when the worker suffers from one of the uncommon treatable dementias. Well-established routine work skills will, however, be maintained for much longer when the dementing process is slow. Placement in less demanding levels of work may be planned. Abstract thinking, dealing with new concepts and practices, judgement of work tasks, or relationships may be impaired. Skills practised over many years tend to be preserved, and disability may only be evident when the patient is confronted with a new problem. It is clear that work requiring a high intellectual capacity and involving complex judgements and decisions will be affected much earlier than that of workers with routine and repetitive unskilled or semi-skilled tasks.

Special work problems

Difficulties can occur with potentially dangerous machinery, and tasks requiring frequent and difficult decisions should be avoided. Long-term safety habits will probably be preserved but tasks demanding critical judgements to prevent accident or loss of productivity should be avoided. Regular reviews with the worker, seniors, and possibly fellow-workers will be necessary to monitor clinical progress and performance.

ACUTE CONFUSIONAL STATE (ICD 9 293.0)

There is 'clouded consciousness, confusion, disorientation, illusions and often vivid hallucinations. They are usually due to some intra- or extra-cerebral toxic, infectious, metabolic or other systemic disturbance and are generally reversible.' The key diagnostic feature of clouding of consciousness is an impaired awareness of self and surroundings, and an inability to grasp the meaning of events or current experiences. There may be disorientation of time, place, and person as well as misinterpretation and hallucinations. Emotional lability, fearfulness, and perhaps agitation are present. Attention, recent memory, abstract thinking, problem-solving ability, and judgement are all impaired. All these clinical features tend to fluctuate.

The underlying organic cause may arise from intoxication (e.g. prescribed and other drugs, alcohol, and industrial chemicals, such as carbon monoxide, heavy metals, organic poisons), drug and alcohol withdrawal, head injury, epilepsy, and infectious, vascular, or metabolic diseases affecting brain function.

Prevalence

They are common. The overall prevalence is not known but it has been estimated that between 20–30 per cent of all patients on surgical intensive care units and between 5–15 per cent of those on general surgical and medical wards are at some time confused.

Clinical aspects affecting work capacity

Selection should be guided by the frequency and severity of past episodes and treatability of the underlying cause. However, anyone may develop delirium when ill and most incidents are transient with full recovery. Work with dangerous machinery and driving should be judged against the risk of recurrence.

Special work problems

Difficulties include sudden inability to work effectively. In lay terms the normally functioning worker is confused and may or may not be obviously physically ill. This is basically a general medical emergency and requires prompt referral for diagnosis and physical treatment.

If self-induced drug or alcohol intoxication has occurred, consider future prevention. Suspected industrial poisoning will require special investigations.

SCHIZOPHRENIC PSYCHOSIS (ICD 9 295)

Introduction

Schizophrenic psychoses are:

> A group of psychoses in which there is a fundamental disturbance of personality, a characteristic distortion of thinking, often a sense of being controlled by alien forces, delusions which may be bizarre, disturbed perception, abnormal affect out of keeping with the real situation, and autism. Nevertheless, clear consciousness and intellectual capacity are usually maintained.... Hallucinations, especially of hearing, are common and may comment on the patient or address him.... Thinking becomes vague, elliptical and obscure and its expression in speech sometimes incomprehensible.

In the United Kingdom schizophrenia is usually diagnosed clinically when Schneider's first-rank symptoms are present in the absence of cognitive impairment and physical illness affecting brain function. These symptoms include: hearing one's own thoughts spoken aloud; third-person hallucinations (i.e. hearing two voices talking to each other about the individual), hallucinatory voices commenting on the person's activities, somatic hallucinations, thought withdrawal or insertion, thought broadcasting, delusional perception (attributing a new meaning of importance to the individual of a normally perceived object), feelings or actions experienced as being made or influenced by others.

It is helpful in clinical practice to divide schizophrenia into the acute and chronic. The acute episode may be short lived or progress to a chronic state. Chronic schizophrenia, however, may have an insidious onset. Acute schizophrenia (Table 21.1) is characterized by Schneider's first-rank symptoms while chronic schizophrenia (Table 21.2) has many negative symptoms such as lack of drive, energy, spontaneity, and volition.

Lay fears of schizophrenia arise mainly from fear of aggression but also because the thinking, feeling, and behaviour of the individual are not understandable. In acute schizophrenia the individual may well be frightened by his hallucinations and delusions and physically defend himself but this is uncommon. A much greater risk is self-harm and suicide.

Prevalence

Schizophrenia can manifest itself at any age but is commonest in the young adult. The annual prevalence is probably between 0.1 and 0.2 per thousand of the population with a lifetime risk of between 7 and 9 per thousand.

Clinical aspects affecting work capacity

Selection for work will depend upon the prognosis of the particular individual's illness and compliance with measures to prevent relapse, especially medication. Good and poor prognostic factors are listed in Table 21.3.

A 14-year follow-up study of patients with schizophrenia published in 1978 found that 50 per cent were managing with little or no disability, 25 per cent had moderate to marked disability, and the remaining 25 per cent were disabled psychiatrically, socially, and in their occupation.[9]

Two important factors lessen the risk of relapse. First, regular compliance with medication such as slowly absorbed depot injections of long-acting neuroleptics. The second protective factor is a characteristic of the relationship with those around them, namely 'low expressed emotion'.[10] 'High expressed emotion' occurs when there is critical comment, high social demands, and high involvement and has been shown to be associated with relapse.

Placement will aim to provide working conditions with low demanding relationships and encouragement to comply with medication.

Special work problems

Difficulties may be due to an acute episode or to chronic illness.

Acute schizophrenia frequently presents with withdrawal from social contacts. Fellow-workers notice that a person has 'gone into himself' and yet they can provide no reason for this. There may be associated lack of self-care. Routine work is continued but there are periods when the individual is in a world of his own and not concentrating on work and becomes inefficient. Unusual remarks or actions are incomprehensible to those around. These have a disconcerting effect upon fellow-workers and interrupt work. When asked for reasons for the change, the individual may become increasingly suspicious and evasive.

When the individual's feelings are affected work may be impaired by loss of drive, inappropriate laughter, anxiety, or anger, with incoherence, illogicality, and vagueness. Thinking may become unclear. Delusions, hallucinations, and the distress arising from these is very distracting. Hallucinations may be complicated by the individual misinterpreting the origin of these symptoms and angrily blaming fellow workers.

A combination of a varying number of these features in acute schizophrenia are indications for urgent withdrawal from work and referral for psychiatric assessment and treatment. Paradoxically the more florid acute schizophrenic disturbance tends to settle quickly.

Table 21.1   The most frequent symptoms of acute schizophrenia

Symptom	Frequency (%)
Lack of insight	97
Auditory hallucinations	74
Ideas of reference	70
Suspiciousness	66
Flatness of affect	66
Voices speaking to the patient	65
Delusional mood	64
Delusions of persecution	64
Thought alienation	52
Thoughts spoken aloud	50

Chronic schizophrenia with its greater liability to present the negative symptoms with some of the above features is less intrusive and can be compatible with work. Lay impressions of chronic schizophrenia leading to total unemployability are false. Some sufferers are able to encapsulate their strange beliefs and experiences and perform normally and effectively in the other parts of their lives.

It is important that superiors and colleagues understand the condition. The person suffers from a genuine illness and is not being lazy, awkward, or putting it on. Although at times withdrawn, this is related to the high physiological arousal and it appears that such persons need more time on their own with minimal social stimuli. Hallucinations are very real experiences with feelings similar to our own when hearing good, bad, or frightening news by telephone. If strange ideas are expressed, it is unproductive to argue and they are best ignored. It may, however, be necessary to remind the worker of the reasonable expectations of work and of those around him. This may achieve satisfactory work despite the continuing background of strange ideas.

Arrangements for time off to have the depot medication, perhaps every three or four weeks, may be crucial in preventing relapse. This can be a major contribution to the individual's welfare. Avoidance of high expressed emotion can be met by superiors and colleagues by arranging work which allows for a measured social withdrawal and avoids pressures to perform to very high standards or urgent deadlines. A trial period can clarify both work ability and the level of pressure tolerated.

The community psychiatric nurse is the key professional in the satisfactory maintenance of persons with chronic schizophrenia. Advice especially in crises, reviews, and possibly depot medication at work may be arranged. Marked withdrawal, persisting depression, agitation, or threats of self-harm are indications for urgent assessment (pp. 410–11).

Table 21.2   Behavioural characteristics of chronic schizophrenia

Symptom	Frequency (%)
Social withdrawal	74
Underactivity	56
Lack of conversation	54
Few leisure activities	50
Slowness	48
Overactivity	41
Odd ideas	34
Depression	34
Odd behaviour	34
Neglect of appearance	30

Table 21.3   Prognostic features in schizophrenia

Good prognosis	Poor prognosis
Sudden onset	Insidious onset
Short episode	Long episode
No previous psychiatric history	Previous psychiatric history
Prominent affective symptoms	Blunted affect
Older age at onset	Young age at onset
Married	Single, separated, widowed, or divorced
Good psychosexual adjustment	Poor psychosexual adjustment
Stable premorbid personality	Abnormal premorbid personality
Stable work record	Poor work record
Supportive social relationships	Social isolation
Compliance with medication	Poor compliance with medication

AFFECTIVE PSYCHOSIS (MANIC-DEPRESSIVE PSYCHOSIS) (ICD 9 296)

Introduction

'Mental disorders, usually recurrent, in which there is a severe disturbance of mood, e.g. depression, anxiety, elation, excitement. Accompanied by one or more of the following: delusions, perplexity, disturbed attitude to self, disorder of perception and behaviour; these are all in keeping with the prevailing mood ... there is a strong tendency to suicide.' (ICD 9 296).

They may be mild or severe. Recurrent depression is more common than recurrent mania or episodes of both forms. There is a genetic predisposition, although attacks may be precipitated by emotional or physical stress such as illness or some medications.

The *manic* type shows 'states of elation or excitement out of keeping with the person's circumstances.' (ICD 9 296.0). Typical presentation is over-activity, garrulousness, and an elated mood with unreasonable optimism and self-important ideas. There is a feeling of well-being and increased energy. A history of several almost sleepless nights is significant. Bursts of irritability are common. Denial of illness is frequent and refusal of medication, advice, and treatment can make management difficult.

The *depressive* type shows low mood, often for no obvious reason, and characteristically worse in the morning. A few questions may reveal early morning wakening, loss of interest, energy, concentration, appetite, weight, and libido. The patient appears depressed and may think and react slowly. The depression may affect judgement, with low self-esteem, feelings of hopelessness, pessimism, and suicidal behaviour. Anxieties are common as a secondary feature. The depression may be aggravated and associated with physical illness or the use of various medication, e.g. cardiovascular drugs.

Prevalence

Annual incidence is approximately 12 per 100 000 for men and 18.3 per 100 000 for women. The lifetime morbidity risk is 0.6–1 per cent.

Clinical aspects affecting work capacity

Selection for employment will require consideration of frequency, severity, and length of attacks; the effect of and compliance with preventive medication (especially lithium); and behaviour at work when previously ill. A crucial feature is that between attacks the individual almost always fully recovers his former abilities and relationships. Placement should involve consideration of the potential risk of sudden changes of mood, especially a recurrence of hypomania, e.g. with pilots and professional drivers.

Special problems at work

Difficulties arise mainly from the severity of the depression. Guilt, self-blame, and hopelessness may accompany the obvious misery which severely impairs working ability.

Suicidal risk must be assessed. Discussion of suicidal behaviour does not imply that the health staff are then totally responsible for the situation but it does provide them with a guide to the degree of urgency for further referral. It is not true that the person talking of suicide will not attempt it. The following series of questions can help: ask for loss of interest in life, thoughts of wishing they were dead, thoughts that others would be better off without them, thoughts of self-harm, any plans of self-harm or preparation for it, has there already been an attempt at self-harm? Negative replies mean that later questions are probably not necessary. More positive answers indicate a greater risk. The individual is often relieved to be able to share these distressing thoughts and questioning does not provoke suicidal behaviour.

The risk is increased if there is a previous suicidal attempt; the individual is a male over 55; is isolated; has drink, drug, or chronic physical problems; there is severe personal or work failure; there are severe family problems; or there is a possibility of some public disgrace. The combination of two or more of these factors increase the risk. Those with high risk factors will need an escort to an arranged medical or psychiatric review. Acute mania and its management is covered on p. 410–11.

ANXIETY STATES (ICD 9 300.0)

Introduction

Anxiety states are 'Various combinations of physical and mental manifestations of anxiety, not attributable to real danger occurring either in attacks or as a persisting state. The anxiety is usually diffuse and may extend to panic. Other neurotic features such as obsessional or hysterical symptoms may be present but do not dominate the clinical picture.' (ICD 9 300.0).

These are understandable to the lay person but out of proportion to the external threat. Not only is there the unpleasant and intense feeling of anticipation but also physical aspects which may affect every bodily system. Examples would be palpitations, breathlessness, chest pain, sweating, faintness, trembling, dizziness, difficulty in swallowing, frequency of micturition, tension, irritability, easily startled, feelings of unreality, fears of collapse or of acute physical or mental illness. Behaviour may be affected by indecision, the avoidance of difficult tasks or feared circumstances, or even failure to go to work. Thinking may be affected by impaired concentration, unreasonable fears of the future, misfortune, or making mistakes. Patterns of abnormal or illogical thinking may be present, such as a minor failure being interpreted as a catastrophe, or an error in one aspect of work being interpreted as all aspects of work being mistaken. Acute anxiety and panic attacks interfere with work, particularly in delicate or potentially dangerous tasks or sequences of work which cannot be interrupted.

Prevalence

Generalized anxiety states occur more commonly in women and usually start in early adulthood. The prevalence has been estimated as between 2 and 4 per cent of the population. Phobic anxiety commonly starts between the ages of 15 and 35. The overall prevalence is considered to be about 1 per cent. The sex incidence is equal, with the exception of animal phobias where women predominate.

Clinical aspects affecting work capacity

Selection for work is only a problem if the anxiety is very severe and disabling or panic attacks are frequent. Highly stressful posts, especially with responsibilities affecting lives or involving public scrutiny, may aggravate the anxiety. Nevertheless, many chronically anxious individuals cope very effectively with such work and most anxious workers are productive. Placement may involve a period of assessment or a step-by-step increase of responsibility.

Anxious feelings may impair working ability by unreasonable fearfulness in the work situation, for example by exaggerating real but minor safety issues. The physical aspects of anxiety are often misinterpreted as illness, having effects ranging from distraction to being absent from work. Particular physical symptoms such as tremor or tension may interfere with delicate tasks, and chronic muscle tension leads to feelings of exhaustion. Restlessness or frequent visits to the toilet will disturb the individual's work and possibly that of others. Hyperventilation, perhaps complicated by paraesthesia of hands and face or even tetany, is a benign though alarming experience often misinterpreted as a heart attack or stroke. Adequate first aid includes an explanation of the symptoms combined with reassurance. Chest pain in anxiety will probably need investigation to exclude organic causes. The pale, shaky, tense, irritable, and easily startled worker is a source of concern and distraction to others.

Behaviour can be seriously affected by severe anxiety and panic attacks, perhaps leading to abrupt cessation of a task, needing a period of rest at work or sick leave. Fear of recurring panics can prevent return to work.

The disturbance of thinking in anxiety states is important and often overlooked. Recent developments in cognitive therapy are providing methods of influencing this.[11,12] Poor concentration, forgetfulness, and preoccupation with physical symptoms and fears of organic illness or madness, can be seriously distracting.

Special work problems

Difficulties due to anxiety states may be recognized from the direct complaints of disturbed feelings or from physical symptoms thought to be due to organic illness, as well as from impaired performance and relationships, or repeated absences from work. Anxiety at work may develop slowly, and insidiously impair efficiency, or may present as a panic attack.

Assessment includes the need to judge whether work should be stopped immediately for the individual's welfare or for general safety, followed by an initial clarification of the precipitating factors. There will then need to be a plan for further, more detailed, assessment. This will include exclusion of physical illness and other underlying psychiatric problems, e.g. depression. Health staff will need to consider what should be done for those work factors causing or exacerbating the problem. There may be direct factors such as noise, personal relationships, or productivity expectations; or they may be indirect such as the need for a supporting nursery arrangement for mothers of young children, or planning shiftwork to accommodate the management of a family crisis or attendance for treatment.

Time off work in severe anxiety states is measured in weeks. A few days' break is usually insufficient and may simply postpone recovery. Continued contact with the worker on sick-leave by health staff and the firm's personnel department can have therapeutic value, and at least may help contain fears of job loss. Return to work is a further stress for those with anxiety states as confidence is usually impaired, and avoidance behaviour (see phobic states) may occur. The occupational physician, personnel staff, and the worker's immediate superior may need to plan a step-by-step return to responsibility and full working capacity. This is usually amply repaid by improved performance. Are there work factors needing adjustment? Can future work stresses be anticipated? Factors precipitating anxiety can never be totally avoided but may be diminished, and plans can be made to support the worker when under pressure. A judgement will need to be made of the degree of support available and how much can reasonably be expected of colleagues. Interpersonal relationships may be impaired if fellow-workers feel they are having to perform the anxious person's work for him/her or if there is serious interference with their own tasks. Most will be sympathetic when there is a foreseeable end to the need for their extra support, particularly when the individual had good relationships previously and was an effective worker. If it appears unending, then irritable rejection or an unproductive atmosphere may occur.

Driving, and working with potentially dangerous machinery, are inappropriate during panic attacks or severe anxiety states but they can be resumed when these symptoms are controlled. The side-effects of psychotropic drugs (e.g. the benzodiazepines) producing drowsiness and minor degrees of inco-ordination may be a problem. Alternative methods of anxiety control should be encouraged, for example relaxation and cognitive therapy.[13] These aim at the person gaining mastery over anxiety without the use of drugs. The National Health Service and university departments of clinical psychology are particularly helpful sources of such treatments.

Individuals with long-term anxiety may have secondary drink problems which effect work (p. 413). Drug treatment of anxiety may impair performance at the onset of treatment or in long-term use. The longer acting benzodiazepines such as diazepam and chlordiaxepoxide (used for daytime tranquillization) and nitrazepam (used for night sedation) tend to accumulate.

PHOBIC STATES (ICD 9 300.2)

'Neurotic states with abnormally intense dread of certain objects or specific situations which would not normally have that effect.' There is anxiety and possibly panic attacks.

Problems in selection and placement depend on whether regular attendance at work can be achieved and how any symptoms occurring at the work place can be overcome. Work problems may arise from avoidance of feared situations, e.g. open spaces, closed spaces, tunnels, public transport, and may result in absence from work. Behavioural treatments and help from a community psychiatric nurse are often very effective. Even with persisting symptoms regular work may be possible if transport is arranged.

NEUROTIC DEPRESSION (ICD 9 300.4)

Introduction

A neurotic disorder characterized by disproportionate depression which is usually recognizable ensued on a distressing experience; it does not include among its features, delusions or hallucinations; there is often preoccupation with the psychic trauma which preceded the illness, e.g. loss of a cherished person or possession. Anxiety is frequently present and mixed states of anxiety and depression should be included here. The distinction between depressive neurosis and psychosis should be made, not upon the degree of depression, but on the presence or absence of other neurotic and psychotic characteristics and upon the degree of disturbance of the patient's behaviour.

As in anxiety states, the distinction from normal depression is that in neurotic depression the illness is severe, persistent (i.e. in weeks), and disabling, yet it lacks the clear patterns of sleep disturbance and diurnal severity of affective disorders.

There are low spirits, 'feeling blue', loss of interest, energy, activity and drive, enjoyment in life, and possibly suicidal ideas (see below). More difficult to recognize is masked depression presenting with physical symptoms, e.g. tiredness, backache, chest pain. A vicious circle of pain–depression–more pain may occur. Thinking is coloured by unreasonable pessimism. Finally, there may be a clear precipitant, at home or at work, such as bereavement or failure to obtain promotion, or subtle work changes perceived as detrimental. Lay intolerance of persistent depression appears as 'pull yourself together' or 'you should be over it by now'.

Prevalence

The point prevalence of the symptom depression is 13–20 per cent of the population, whereas depressive illness has a point prevalence of 3 per cent for men and 7 per cent for women.

Clinical aspects affecting work capacity

Selection for work is guided by the general practice finding that a quarter of such depressions recover rapidly, half run a fluctuating course, and a quarter become chronic. Placement can include reviews to monitor the risk of chronic depression.

Impairment of concentration and attention, and forgetfulness, insomnia, and chronic tiredness may seriously affect driving, working with machinery, and the ability to persist at tasks. Decision making and judgement may be impaired. Poor self-esteem, lack of confidence, feelings of failure, and pessimism can affect output. Work relationships can be affected by the unattractive features of withdrawal, irritability, and preoccupation with personal problems or the original psychological trauma. Despite these features workers may hide their depression and detection is difficult.

Special work problems

Detection is difficult and the first evidence may be falling production, lateness or absences, accidents or mistakes, or impaired relationships. A minor problem may present out of proportion, or the individual may feel over-whelmed and impulsively resign. This should not be accepted, as depression impairs judgement and all major decisions should be postponed until full recovery. Work complications may arise from heavy drinking or self-treatment with minor tranquillizers. These aggravate depressive symptoms and cause drowsiness, impaired concentration and co-ordination.

Treatment includes management of personal and social problems and possibly antidepressants. There may be a work factor which needs to be modified.

The course of depression is over weeks and the benefits of antidepressants only occur after two or three weeks of treatment. The individual may need to be advised firmly to take two or three weeks off work. The person starting antidepressant treatment must be cautious of the minor degrees of impairment of concentration and co-ordination which might affect driving ability. Other side-effects, including dry mouth, sweating, constipation, hesitation in micturition, and difficulties in accommodation, are a nuisance rather than serious. Side-effects, fears of drug dependence, and lack of conviction that drugs are appropriate may all impair compliance.

On recovery, full working ability should return. If not, then there may be persistent depression, drug side-effects, or some other factor.

HYPOCHONDRIASIS (ICD 9 300.7)

'A neurotic disorder in which conspicuous features are excessive concern with one's health in general or the integrity and functioning of some part of one's body or, less frequently, one's mind. It is usually associated with anxiety and depression.' The unrealistic fears persist despite medical explanation and reassurance and tend to be long standing.

Selection will depend upon an estimate of future absences and medical attendances. Many sufferers, however, do not allow their symptoms to interfere with work.

Problems at work are usually no more than a minor distraction. Frequent absences or medical attendances may be reduced by planned reviews rather than in response to symptoms. If symptoms seriously interfere with work or are disabling, then underlying major psychiatric illness must be excluded, for example depression. The excessive bodily concern tends to persist when this illness is relieved.

Hysteria, obsessive compulsive disorders, neurasthenia, and the depersonalization syndrome are uncommon and should be referred for a further medical opinion.

PERSONALITY DISORDERS (ICD 9 301)

Introduction

Personality disorders are 'deeply ingrained maladaptive patterns of behaviour generally recognizable at the time of adolescence or earlier and continuing throughout most of adult life, although often becoming less obvious in middle or old age.... the patient suffers or others have to suffer and there is an adverse effect on the individual or on society.'

Although not ill, these individuals are a major problem to health staff or others. They do not fit in with other people and they are often their own worst enemy. They do not learn from their mistakes and persist in inappropriate behaviour. Interpersonal problems at work are frequent and health staff cannot expect good relationships or gratitude for their intervention. Drink problems may exacerbate irritability. Family, drink, and antisocial problems may spill into the work situation. Anankastic (obsessional) personalities, on the other hand, have some very useful work qualities.

Prevalence

No reliable data are available on the prevalence of personality disorders.

Clinical aspects affecting work capacity

Selection issues will more often occur at a non-medical level, for example in references (especially verbal) to past behaviour problems. The balance between the person's positive and negative qualities must be assessed. High levels of drive and achievement may be at the expense of poor interpersonal relationships and stress for fellow-workers.

The *paranoid* personality tends to be a source of complaint and friction, is very suspicious, easily offended, and tends to blame others. Such workers need clear instructions, careful explanations, opportunities to vent their feelings, and should be advised that any difficulties arising are not meant to be personal.

The *explosive* personality disorder has 'instability of mood with liability to intemperate outbursts of anger, hate, violence or affection. Aggression may be expressed in words or in physical violence.' (ICD 9 301.3). The individual is usually apologetic after the outburst and may not be difficult or anti-social at other times. The outbursts naturally upset others, interfere with work, and can be dangerous when driving. The individual may be counselled to recognize triggers for this behaviour and plan how to respond more appropriately. Alcohol usually aggravates the problem. A working community is entitled to expect reasonable conduct and the organization's usual disciplinary procedure may be required.

The *anankastic* personality disorder is 'characterized by feelings of personal insecurity, doubt and incompleteness leading to excessive conscientiousness, checking, stubbornness and caution'. . . . 'There is perfectionism and meticulous accuracy and a need to check repeatedly.' . . . 'Rigidity and excessive doubt may be conspicuous.' (ICD 9 301.4). Some of the more emotionally secure obsessional personalities are in fact very productive and use their perfectionist drives to produce a meticulously accurate, reliable high output of work. They are an asset when a high degree of accuracy in work is essential. Such workers can be very productive with routine work for which they have received clear instructions. Difficulties arise when doubt, checking, and excessive attention to detail leads to impaired output. They are less able to deal with rapid and major decision-making and may, in the face of change, fall back on rigidity. They need particularly clear explanation, support, and guidance.

Personality disorder with predominantly *sociopathic* or *asocial* manifestation is characterized 'by disregard for social obligations, lack of feeling for others, and impetuous violence or callous unconcern'. . . . 'Behaviour is not readily modified by experience, including punishment . . . and may be abnormally aggressive or irresponsible'. (ICD 9 301.7).

Other forms of personality disorder do not usually produce problems at work.

ADJUSTMENT REACTIONS (ICD 9 309)

Introduction

Adjustment reactions are mild or transient disorders lasting longer than acute stress reactions which occur in individuals of any age without any apparent pre-existing mental disorder. Such disorders are often relatively circumscribed or situation-specific, generally reversible and usually last only a few months. They are usually closely related in time and content to stresses such as bereavement, migration or separation experiences. Reactions to major stresses that last longer than a few days are also included here.

Presentation is usually with depression or anxiety already described under neurotic disorders. Stresses at work are of particular relevance. As in normal anxiety, stress can have a range of effects from a beneficial alertness, to a feeling of stimulation and challenge, to a sense of strain, to a feeling of being overwhelmed and helpless. In the workplace this can be a loss of job satisfaction, status, prospects of pay and promotion, interpersonal relationships, etc. A depressive adjustment reaction can often helpfully be understood as a reaction to a loss. A form of grief reaction may occur. On the other hand, a total lack of stress or monotony at work can be harmful in leading to loss of alertness and perhaps dangerous somnolence. Boredom due to underpromotion can be stressful.

Physical stresses in the workplace are listed by Poulton[14] as poor visibility, noise, vibration, heat, cold, humidity, wind, motion, perceived dangers, overwork or underload, night-shifts, and combinations of these. Each of these can also be a psychological stress either through its physiological effect, the individual's perception of it, or both. Individual variations in both physiology and perception make elimination of such stresses difficult.

Cooper and Marshall[15] estimate that there are at least 40 sources of managerial stress and some of these are illustrated in Fig. 21.1.

Kahn *et al.*[16] suggest that the main causes of stress on the individual by the organization are due to *role problems*. First, *role load*, i.e. the burden of demands on the individual derived from the need to perform a particular task. It may be either too great or too small. Secondly, *role ambiguity*, a discrepancy between the information available to the person and that required for the performance of his job. Thirdly, *role conflict*, that is incompatible demands made upon an individual by two or more others whose jobs dovetail with his. Gardell[17] considers mental strain is greatest in workers whose jobs are severely circumscribed as to autonomy, variety, skill, and social interaction. Finally work, personal and domestic stress may have a cumulative effect.

Prevalence

It is very difficult to be precise about this. It may be increasing with the effects of fear of unemployment, changing methods of production, increased automation, and use of new techniques. There is certainly an increased awareness in recent years. There is a need for study into the prevalence of work stress, especially in women,[18] and also its effects on productivity.

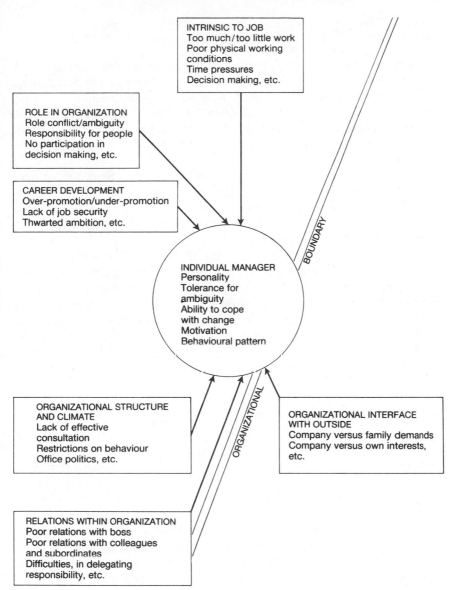

Fig. 21.1 Sources of managerial stress.[15]

Clinical aspects affecting work capacity

Selection and placement issues are similar to those of anxiety and depression (discussed on pp. 393–397), incorporating a knowledge of job descriptions and the structure and 'climate' of the total work organization.

Probably the first effects are impairment of productivity, of relationships, or repeated absences with minor illnesses. Increased smoking, drinking, and over-eating are very common, with their own physical and psychological complications and effects on working ability.

Psychosomatic disorders such as migraine, asthma, peptic ulcer may appear, or be exacerbated. There may be an aggravation of physical or psychiatric conditions already present, such as the pain of chronic arthritis or a relapse of depression. There may be less specific physical symptoms such as backache, chest pain, or indigestion. Finally, they may present as anxiety states and neurotic depression with all the effects already described.

Individual care will be based on an analysis of the interactions of the worker and his job. Clinical management will be along the lines discussed under anxiety states and neurotic depression. A review of working conditions may indicate those changes necessary in the individual's job and/or the general organization of the whole work setting. Clarke describes the limitations of psychiatric care for such individuals.[19] This underlines the importance of the counselling role of occupational health staff.

Special work problems

Difficulties are mainly in detection or the identification of the underlying cause of physical and psychological symptoms. The alertness of health staff can reduce symptoms and improve performance.

Tasks involving high stress should be identified in the organization. Jobs involving heavy responsibilities for the care of persons at physical risk are particularly onerous. Examples would be firemen, and accident and emergency and junior hospital medical staff, and nurses working on intensive care units. A constant exposure to emotional distress in clients, as in social workers and social security receptionists, is exhausting. Decision making under public scrutiny, or work constantly under criticism is very stressful. Severe and persistent stress at work may lead to the development of the burn out syndrome[20] with incapacity at work, prolonged absence, high turnover of workers, or drop out. Depersonalization with excessive detachment, too little concern for clients, and cynicism is a risk reported in the caring services.[21] On the other hand, the worker's own view of risk and stress may be more important than that which is obvious to others. This can be sought by discussion with the staff themselves as well as with unions and management.

Health advisers need to consider how they can prevent work stress by influencing the relationship between the individual and the organization as well as the organization itself. The occupational physician or occupational health nurse can draw the attention of senior managers to unhealthy areas in the organization which adversely affect both workers and productivity. Helpful changes include: involving the worker in the planning and detailed arrangements in the job, responding to suggestions, and providing both positive and negative feedback to workers. There can be anticipation of stressful times, e.g. when change or new techniques are introduced, or when staff are under pressure from absences of colleagues. Cooper and Marshall[15] suggest that stress may be reduced by increased autonomy, creating active links between work and home life, clarifying roles, improving interpersonal relationships, and creating a climate of good communication, openness, and trust.

Accidents at work may be followed by a persisting anxiety or depressive reaction, particularly if the incident was very alarming with fears of serious injury. There may be vivid memories of the incident, nightmares, or sleep disturbance. The need to discuss any upset feelings with understanding is often overlooked and the result may be prolonged disability.

AFTER SEVERE HEAD INJURY

Placement and timing of return to work normally depend upon both physical and psychological recovery. A period of assessment, perhaps arranged by the Disablement Resettlement Officer, can show how working ability is affected by impaired memory, concentration, noise intolerance, and irritability. These patients may be easily fatigued and anxious or depressed. Family attitudes and support are important. (See also Chapter 11.)

POST-CONCUSSIONAL SYNDROME (ICD 9 310.2)

Introduction

A head injury with slight or no brain damage may result in 'headache, giddiness, fatigue, insomnia' ... 'exaggerated fear and apprehension' ... 'intolerance of mental or physical exertion, undue sensitivity to noise and hypochondriacal pre-occupation.' (ICD 9 310.2). There may be associated neurotic features, with poor concentration; irritability; loss of interest in work, hobbies, and relationships; and sleep disturbance. Frequently vivid recollections or nightmares about the original injury may occur. Aggravating factors may be feelings of anger, blame, and injustice about the circumstances of the original injury and how others, especially management, have reacted subsequently. There may be avoidance of similar situations to those responsible for the original injury. Current relationships at work and in the family may help or exacerbate the situation. Compensation may be a preoccupation but follow-up studies have shown that the syndrome usually persists after the medico-legal aspects have been settled. Although symptoms tend to diminish with time, a significant proportion continue to have an impaired quality of life despite treatment.

Prevalence

No prevalence data are available.

Clinical aspects affecting work capacity

Selection should be based on how persisting symptoms, especially poor concentration, noise intolerance, and irritability may impair fulfilment of job requirements.

Special work problems

Difficulties at work can arise from symptoms interfering with performance, and temporary placement in a less demanding post may help.

MENTAL HANDICAP (MILD MENTAL RETARDATION) (ICD 9 317)

Introduction

People with mild mental handicap form an important problem-free component of the working population. Their intelligence quotient (IQ) ranges from 50–70. Problems in mental handicap arise when it is severe and there is greater intellectual impairment, or there is some additional disability or social handicap. These include problems such as reading or handling money, speech disorders, or lack of social skills.

The worker with mild mental handicap will have been a slow learner at school, and is slow in learning skills at work. Many such individuals are reliable and conscientious workers. Some are aware of their limitations and deliberately compensate for them by working harder.

Prevalence

Mild mental handicap is estimated as 20–30 per 1000 of the population. Less than half of this population need special services.

Clinical aspects affecting work capacity

Selection poses difficulties as at interview limited verbal abilities and social competence may give a poor impression. Previous assessments may underestimate working ability.[22] Much more important is the ability to fulfil the job description requirements. This can be assessed from previous employment records and references, disablement resettlement officers' reports, and the use of trial attachments. Examples are the Job Introduction Scheme under the Manpower Services Commission which allows a six-week trial period of a disabled person to allow assessment of skills and abilities. The Youth Training Scheme, funded by the Manpower Services Commission, allows young persons places on two-year courses where they may gain work skills, experience, and further education. (See also Chapter 2). MENCAP (Royal Society for Mentally Handicapped Children and Adults) has a Pathway Scheme in which their officer arranges a six-month trial placement without commitment. If selection is not appropriate, the applicant should be referred to the Disablement Resettlement Officer at the local jobcentre.

Mentally handicapped people need longer to learn new skills and to become adjusted to a new social life at work. Literacy and numeracy limitations are common. Changes in behaviour and difficulties in interpersonal relationships may arise from frustration with the inability to adjust quickly or to cope with some new issues at work. The worker may have difficulty in putting his problems and feelings into words.

The community psychiatric nurse for the mental handicap services can help with the clarification and resolution of such problems.

Broader aspects of employment in mental illness
CRITERIA FOR SELECTION FOR EMPLOYMENT

Much more important than the signs and symptoms of a particular condition is the prognosis. This will include natural history, severity, the individual's reaction to the illness, other stresses, treatability, and compliance with treatment. Functional disability arising from the illness should be judged against the requirements in the job description. It is not easy to match a list of psychiatric disorders with a list of unsuitable work tasks. The reader is therefore recommended to take account of the whole chapter and not to limit his reference to one particular heading. Would employment promote or undermine the individual's psychological health? All these factors need to be integrated into an assessment of a person's suitability for employment where there is a past or current history of psychiatric illness.

Disclosure

The prospective employee may not reveal all the details of his illness. This may be unintentional as some patients do not recall their illness, others do not recognize that they were ill, and some are afraid of revealing too much. The assessing doctor needs as much information as possible to predict an individual's work performance. The individual's own expectations may be under- or over-optimistic. Research into this whole area is scant, but some ex-psychiatric in-patients are a poor risk from the point of view of attendance, ability, and reliability.[23] Perhaps this says more about the pre-employment selection than about the individuals themselves. The restriction of the length of probation under the Employment Protection Act was found to be to the disadvantage of persons with schizophrenia.[24]

It would, however, be unjust to reject an applicant for a job just because he has a psychiatric label. There is no good reason why a person with a mental illness should not be treated, rehabilitated, and then employed, as happens in physical illness. Some posts should entail more detailed enquiry into past medical, personal, and job histories (for example, a residential-care worker) in contrast with assessment for an unskilled labouring job. A system of liaison with management for more details in the reference will be needed with the former.

If an applicant is turned down for an appointment for medical (psychiatric) reasons, then, as with any other disability, he should be told and given the reasons why. If the job for which he was aiming was unsuitable for him, he is at least entitled to advice on how to seek more suitable work. The help of the DRO could be sought.

PROBLEMS ARISING AT WORK

Any decline in attendance or work performance, or misbehaviour or disruption at work will cause concern to management. The employee should be told about any failings. The worker with neurosis will usually understand, whereas some with psychosis may not. All of us find criticism painful, but, nevertheless, the worker should know if he is underachieving at work and should be counselled to seek advice. If there is an occupational physician, he should be informed of any problems by management; he will interview and counsel the employee and, within appropriate ethical principles, will communicate with the employee's consultant and general practitioner. Everything must be done to see that treatment is given and taken, and that the employee has help with any difficult domestic, social, or welfare problem. All too often, management will send an employee along for a medical examination without either the physician or the employee being told the reason why. The physician cannot fully understand the employee's problems unless he is briefed on the nature and degree of the failures which have been observed. The patient may present very acceptably in the consulting room, but what the physician will want to know is how he is performing at work, and how he is relating to people at work.

Management will have some tolerance for failure if the employee's illness is understood. Temporary relapses can be accommodated with extended sick-leave; permanent or long-term decline of performance may be accommodated by suitable redeployment. But there are limits to these resources; the employer runs his enterprise primarily for commercial success, not as a rehabilitation centre. If the employee demonstrates that he is incapable of holding ordinary employment, even with some carefully designed adjustments, then he should be considered for retraining or sheltered employment and offered appropriate counselling. The resources of the Manpower Services Commission will be helpful in this respect.

SHELTERED EMPLOYMENT

This term implies employment where the employee is sheltered from normal commercial and management pressures. In one form of sheltered employment, in a sheltered workshop, the enterprise will receive some subsidy but there will be a desire for it to be commercially successful. Such sheltered workshops may be set up by the local authorities or by the Government (e.g. Remploy). The work is usually contracted from local larger employers who require small or relatively straightforward tasks to be done, for example, the manufacture of wooden pallets for transporting products. The men have to attend as regularly as they would for any other factory, but the staff are selected and trained and there is less commercial pressure (see Chapter 2).

There are often more people requiring this sort of work than there are special workshops for them. This can be overcome by employing small groups of people requiring sheltered working conditions within ordinary industry. The Government (Manpower Services Commission) pays half the wage, and the company pays the other half. This recognizes the fact that their performance and attendance may not be very good, and yet they are still capable of attending and performing sufficiently to complete a task. An efficiency of not less than 50 per cent is required.

If there is no sheltered placement available, the patient may be able to work in a group along with other psychiatric patients. Such a scheme, called the Industrial Therapy Organization, was started in Bristol some years ago. A number of psychiatric patients were successfully employed in small teams in depots for providing car washing and valeting services. An extension of this scheme is to attempt reintegration into open industry by employing people in small groups in open employment. Although there is extra supervision, one endeavours to make the sheltered employment approach as close as possible to ordinary working conditions. These small groups, called 'enclaves' have been successful in bringing former patients in mental hospitals back to ordinary working life.

If the patient is unsuitable for any of the above types of gainful employment, then at least attempts should be made to occupy him in some way, and to provide him with some social contacts. Social services provide Adult Training Centres where some craft work, such as pottery, woodwork, picture framing, or needlework, can be done, and where the patient can attend daily. If he is not suitable for this, then at least he should be encouraged to attend a Day Centre for a few days a week. There may also be some resources for providing out-patient occupational therapy at some of the larger hospitals.

ILL-HEALTH RETIREMENT

Just as employment can be seen as an important part of treatment, so retirement is often seen as an easy way out from some difficult problems. It must be considered with extreme care and only when other measures have failed.

Sometimes the patient requests ill-health retirement. The desire may be expressed during a stage of deep depression when the patient thinks he is useless, during a stage of prolonged anxiety where he believes work is the cause, or during a schizophrenic illness when attitudes are influenced by abnormal ideas. If the request comes from the patient, it must be carefully talked over with him and the implications must be fully understood, for it is unlikely that he will be able to obtain other employment. The general practitioner should certainly be consulted and it might also be useful to ask the spouse or another member of the family to enter into the discussion. Sometimes the decision to retire is right, but there is usually no need to rush into it. A judicious delay may save the patient from making a decision which he comes to regret bitterly.

Ill-health retirement is also the measure frequently sought by management who feel that they have had enough, they have tolerated all they can, and the time has come to part company, but this must be done only on clear and substantiated evidence. Ability, performance, and attendance are more important than the psychiatric label. If management feel that problems are arising, each incident must be carefully documented. The patient must also be told of the concern, and warned at each stage. Only when it is clear that everything has been done to remedy the deficiencies should ill-health retirement be considered.

Difficulties may arise with a psychotic patient who does not appreciate (or denies) his deficiencies, and fails to grasp the seriousness of his position. If he then does not agree to ill-health retirement, the employer may have to terminate employment on the grounds that the patient can no longer fulfil his contract.

Before employment is terminated there should be full discussions with the general practitioner, the psychiatric social worker, social services, and any other resource which may help the patient to remain in the community, look after himself to some extent, and have social support.

LEGISLATION AND GUIDELINES FOR EMPLOYMENT

Driving

In the acute stage of mental illness, with emotional instability, doubt, and indecision, driving will represent a risk. When treated, the effects of medication may impair performance. There are some absolute rules for professional drivers.[25] Further medical advice is available from the Medical Branch of the Driver and Vehicle Licensing Centre, Swansea, Tel. 0792 42731 (see Appendix 1).

Other occupations

Many employment organizations have their own medical criteria for recruitment and there may still be some prejudice regarding mental illness. However, the physician should give practical advice to the patient; some occupations are best avoided, such as the armed services and police, fire, and ambulance services; the caring professions, and aircraft piloting.

The uniformed services

Many psychiatric illnesses will be a bar to entry into the armed services and the police force. The strict discipline required, and the physical and emotional stresses of fire and ambulance work will also require a high degree of psychological stability.

The caring professions

Sometimes those with a history of psychiatric illness maintain that they will make excellent care workers. They may say this either because they have had to solve so many problems of their own that they feel they can help others, or that by helping others they will find a solution to their own problems.

Professional carers, whether for the elderly or emotionally disturbed children in homes, in the probation service, or in nursing or teaching need to have strong and resilient personalities to cope with the many vulnerable, depressed, awkward, abusive, manipulative, or aggressive people with whom they will have to deal. Just as physical fitness is desirable in a job where physical exertion and a good physical build are necessary, so psychological fitness should be desirable in a job where mental exertion and emotional stability are necessary. The placing of a vulnerable person in such a stressful post could lead to problems for both that person and those for whom he cares.

Aircraft Pilots

Although there is no statutory rule regarding psychiatric illness, the International Civil Aviation organization publishes guidelines in their Manual of

Civil Aviation Medicine. If any case gives rise to doubt, the medical branch of the Civil Aviation Authority should be consulted (Aviation House, 45–49 Kingsway, London W12 6TE [Tel. 01 379 7311]). Mental illness is second only to cardiovascular disease as a cause of disasters through pilot failure. (see Appendix 2).

TREATMENT IN PSYCHIATRY

Psychiatric care consists of combinations of pharmacological, physical, psychological, and social treatments.

Psychotropic drugs include neuroleptics (e.g. chlorpromazine, haloperidol, and trifluoperazine), anxiolytics (e.g. diazepam, chlordiazepoxide), and antidepressants (e.g. imipramine, amitriptyline, and dothiepin). Neuroleptic preparations are used to treat mania and acute schizophrenia. The depot forms (flupenthixol and fluphenazine) are slowly absorbed and reduce relapse in schizophrenia. Side-effects such as tremor, incoordination, drowsiness, and postural hypotension may be significant at work. There may be cumulative effects and interaction with other drugs, and long-term night-sedation may have daytime side-effects. Psychological treatment includes counselling, so that all health staff need to develop counselling skills.[26] Individual and group psychotherapy and behaviour therapy treatments in out-patient or day hospitals will involve health staff and management in negotiating realistic time off work for the patient.

MANAGEMENT OF THE DISTURBED AND VIOLENT EMPLOYEE

There are many causes of violence and in the context of this chapter they include personality disorders, alcohol, confusional states, mania, acute schizophrenia, and states arising from drug abuse. Explosive and sociopathic personality disorders tend to aggressive outbursts under stress or frustration. Alcoholic intoxication may release aggression. Confusional states alter the patient's grasp of his environment so that he may interpret normal events as threatening. Mania often includes flashes of anger. The experiences of acute schizophrenia may lead to self-protective violence. Drug abuse can induce both confusion and psychotic experiences.

The prime responsibility of health staff is to protect the individual and others from harm. Bystanders are best kept away, but help must be sent for and this may include the police. Threats of violence must be heeded and potential weapons should be removed. Attempts at physical restraint will usually produce violent reactions making the situation worse. The doctor should keep his distance from the dangerous and disturbed person and ensure that at all times he has unobstructed access to a route of physical escape.

The approach is, if at all possible, to talk the person down, remembering that he is frightened by his experiences. He should be encouraged to talk by the use of open questioning, which will help to reduce the violence of his actions. Statements, however unreasonable or bizarre, should be left unchallenged and encouraged to flow. This will allow evaluation of the mental state, and must not be hurried. Occasionally a minor tranquilliser, e.g. diazepam 5–10 mg, may be offered to help regain emotional control. The person would then be unfit to drive home.

The further management will depend on the cause and outcome of the crisis, but particular problems arise when the person is suffering from a mental disorder and is refusing help. Two sections of the Mental Health Act, 1983 apply here. Scotland has parallel legislation.

The police have powers under Section 136 to remove a person from a public place, who, in the opinion of a police officer, 'is suffering from a mental disorder' and is 'in need of care and control'. The police are empowered to take that person to a 'place of safety' in order that he can be examined by a medical practitioner and an approved social worker for 'any necessary arrangements' to be made for care or treatment.

Section 4 of the Mental Health Act, 1983 applies where it is of 'urgent necessity' for the patient to be detained in hospital and where more lengthy formal procedures would involve 'undesirable delay'. The application is made by an approved social worker and a medical recommendation by a doctor who, if practical, should have had previous knowledge of the patient. All Social Services Departments have a 24-hour emergency team. MIND has produced an excellent synopsis of the Mental Health Act.[27]

The person with acute anxiety or depression who is disturbing others should be advised firmly to go home. If necessary, he should be escorted home preferably by a sympathetic and trusted colleague. His family should be asked to ensure that he seeks medical advice and treatment. If he displays awkward behaviour and refuses to go home, then direct management action backed up by the threat of disciplinary measures may be needed. These threats of discipline should be removed as soon as he seeks medical treatment.

Finally, consider if there are any remediable work factors which have been the last straw added to the underlying psychiatric problem.

ALCOHOL ABUSE: PROBLEM DRINKING

Introduction

The term 'problem drinking' is preferred to that of alcoholism, which is difficult to define and may be rejected by those who have drink problems. A lay definition is when someone 'must stop but can't'. Another classification is: excessive drinking, the alcohol-dependence syndrome, and alcohol-related disabilities.

The alcohol-dependence syndrome (ICD 9 303) follows the consumption of large quantities of alcohol over a long period, when physical dependence develops. If alcohol intake is then stopped, withdrawal symptoms occur after a number of hours. These symptoms vary through a range of severity including tremors, morning vomiting (eased by drink), nightmares which may progress to visual hallucinations and delirium tremens (an organic confusional state). These symptoms are related to falling levels of alcohol in the body. They are eased by taking more alcohol. There is often reluctance to accept help.

Alcohol-related disabilities are physical (affecting all systems of the body), psychological (preoccupation with drink, problem-solving by drink, and high risk of suicide), and social (at work, in the family, and home; accidents at home, work, or in traffic; and police problems). These disabilities are common in heavy drinkers, estimated at 8 per cent of the population.[28]

A bout of heavy drinking at night may lead to blood alcohol levels the next day of over 80 mg%. Fortunately, a significant proportion of heavy drinkers can be influenced to stop or cut down.

A clear overview of drink problems is given in a series of articles entitled 'Alcohol problems', published by the British Medical Journal.[29] Physical complications are well described in 'The medical consequences of alcohol abuse. A great and growing evil.'[30]

In the workplace, drink problems are extremely common. The individual costs can be high and families can lose security and income. Employers lose potentially valuable members of staff in whom investment has been made. The financial cost to industry has been estimated at over £1300 million per annum at 1983 prices.[31] Though usually unrecognized, they affect all levels of staff: manual, management, and professional. Despite common beliefs, heavy drinkers with secondary problems can be helped. Health staff, whether at work, in general practice, or hospital, are very poor at detecting alcohol problems. If recognized, staff may still fail to provide a constructive response. Important accounts of problems and effective programmes in the workplace are given by Hore and Plant[32] and by Smith.[33] Risk factors in employment are listed by Plant:[34]

(1) availability of alcohol—drink and catering trades, entertainment of customers;

(2) social pressures to drink—coal miners, seamen, service personnel, medical students, drink trade;

(3) separation from normal social or sexual relationships—working away from home, domestic servants;

(4) freedom from supervision—company directors, lawyers, doctors, community nurses;

(5) extremes of income—the high-income group having ample finance after paying for basic necessities, and the low-income group seeking comfort in drink;

(6) collusion by colleagues—covering up inefficiencies and absences;

(7) stresses and hazards—high-risk jobs, seeking release from tension;

(8) pre-selection of high-risk people, choosing to enter medicine, merchant navy, drink trade.

An indicator of occupational risk is from statistics of liver cirrhosis mortality: publicans have 10 times the standard mortality. Seamen, barmen, and hotel managers have 3–8 times the basic rate. Restaurateurs, lorry drivers' mates, cooks, authors, journalists, and writers have 2–3 times the basic rate[34] (see Chapter 14).

Prevalence

It is estimated that 8 per cent of the population are heavy drinkers, 2 per cent are problem drinkers, and 0.4 per cent are alcohol dependent.[28] Of all male admissions to hospital, 20–30 per cent are problem drinkers. The proportion of female admissions is 5–10 per cent.

Clinical aspects affecting work capacity

Selection

All potential staff should be asked about their drinking habits. Subjective accounts are usually underestimates. Past drink–driving offences, accidents (including those in the home), a history of family break-up, and frequent absences and lateness may be clues to a drink problem. A heavy drinker, however, may have become tolerant to alcohol and show signs of unexplained trauma or forgetfulness. The currently intoxicated person may have alcohol on the breath, injected conjunctivae, or tremor. Some persons with drink problems choose to work in occupations where there is an increased risk, and may need to be guided elsewhere. If the person is selected, the company's alcohol policy should be carefully explained, and he should be warned that a lapse will lead to disciplinary warning of dismissal.

Special work problems

Identification

Absenteeism and accidents at work are the commonest indicators. Medical certification usually only refers to a complication. Only 3 per cent of a series of admissions to an alcohol unit had been issued with medical certificates of sickness giving a diagnosis of alcoholism.[35]

Other clues are lateness in the mornings or after lunch, sleepiness or other behaviour change after lunch, long lunch breaks, impaired efficiency, procrastination, attempts to avoid authority, intolerance of criticism or discussion about drinking, increased sensitivity ('prickly'), drinking excessively at work or social functions, unexplained financial difficulty, accidents at home, moonlighting to pay for drink, frequent change of job, and suffering those physical illnesses associated with excess drinking.

Problems are complicated by the drinking person's false belief of functioning normally, the development of tolerance and cumulative effects with psychotropic drugs.

The majority of excessive drinkers are young men in their teens and early twenties, particularly the single, divorced, or separated. It is this group which are still learning skills in driving and management of machinery. Lack of skill and the effects of alcohol are a dangerous combination.

Detection in professional drivers is crucial as one-third of drivers killed in road traffic accidents have blood alcohol levels of over 80 mg %. A similar risk applies to operators of dangerous machinery.

Identification by blood tests is limited, but a combination of AST, γGT, and MCV will reveal a high proportion of those with high alcohol intake. These tests are most valuable in monitoring progress.

Management

A written policy on alcohol misuse is the key measure. This should combine education, counselling, and discipline. The discipline is to provide the motivation to accept and comply with treatment. The employer should use the consultation machinery to lay down a policy with is agreed by management and unions. The key points in the policy should be:

1. Education of the workforce about the dangers of alcohol misuse and the important of early diagnosis and treatment.

2. Management will deal with impaired performance, attendance, or behaviour. When this is thought to be due to drink problems the employee is then invited to seek treatment from a appropriate source, e.g. occupational health physician, general practitioner, counselling service, specialist alcohol unit, etc. Every encouragement will be given at this stage and no disciplinary measure will be taken.

3. Provided the employee seeks treatment and succeeds in complying with it the whole matter will be dealt with as one of illness and a company sick-pay scheme or rehabilitation scheme may be used.

4. Continuing failure at work will be dealt with by normal disciplinary measures.

5. The essential points of this policy are detection and, through discipline, motivation to seek treatment and to overcome the problem. If the employee is just dismissed, he is likely to go from one employer to another without help, and without motivation to seek it. He will be likely to seek solace from continued drinking.

From the employer's and other employees' point of view, drunkenness at work is dangerous under the Health and Safety at Work etc. Act, 1974, and is a disciplinary matter.

Hore reports the claim that a 50–70 per cent success rate is possible in industry, compared with 30 per cent for hospital treatment. Problems may arise from poor co-operation by management or unions, or an agreed policy not being implemented. Those unemployed because of drink problems need a plan for rehabilitation. The preparation and success of these policies have been discussed by Smith[33] and their effect on work and industry considered by Hore and Plant.[32]

Prevention

This includes reduction of availability of alcohol at the workplace and on social occasions at work (dry sites), and education of the workforce in safer drinking. Alcohol consumption is measured in units—where one unit is the equivalent of half a pint of beer, one single measure of spirit, or a glass of wine, and contains 8 g of pure ethanol. Safe drinking is possible: the Royal College of Physicians of London[30] recommends a maximum of 21 units per week for men and 14 units per week for women. Keeping a diary of drink for a week can be revealing. Methods other than alcohol should be used to unwind.[26] Drinking behaviour can be modified by avoiding doubles and trebles at home, taking sips instead of gulps, interspersing with non-alcoholic drinks, planning one drink-free day a week, and following any excessive drinking by two or three days abstinence. Counselling by non-specialists has been shown to be effective.[36, 37]

Involvement of spouse, family members, community agencies such as Alcoholics Anonymous, Al-Anon (for spouses), Al-teen (for teenage children), and counsellors from local alcohol agencies is important. For a list of national agencies, see Appendix 5. Self-help literature is very valuable.[38, 39]

DRUG DEPENDENCE AND ABUSE (ICD 9 304 and 9 305)

Introduction

A drug is defined as any substance which when taken into the body affects its functioning. ICD 9 refers to drug dependence as 'a state psychic, and usually also physical resulting from taking a drug, characterized by behavioural and other responses that always include a compulsion to take the drug on a continuous or periodic basis in order to experience its psychic effect and sometimes to avoid the discomfort of its absence.' Drug abuse is referred to as 'the taking of drugs to the detriment of the person's health or social functioning but without evidence of dependence.'

Drug users are often male, young, and unemployed, but drug abuse can occur at any age. There is often a background of poor school achievement, delinquency, intolerance to authority, peer-group pressure, and availability.

Of the illicit street drugs, heroin is the most important and highly addictive. Some users smoke heroin (chasing the dragon), but most addicts use the drug intravenously (shoot or mainline). Amphetamines (speed) and cocaine (coke) are psychostimulants, and LSD (acid), psilocybin (magic mushrooms), and cannabis produce abnormal cognitive and perceptual states. The addictive nature of barbiturates was recognized years ago. There is increasing evidence of dependence on other sedatives and hypnotics, in particular chlormethiazole (heminevrin) and the wide range of benzodiazepines. Benzodiazepine-withdrawal syndrome presents anxiety, restlessness, insomnia, depression, depersonalization, and perceptual distortions. This may persist for months. More than one drug may be abused, including alcohol.

Clinical aspects affecting work capacity

The acute effects of intoxication can severely affect work performance. Heroin produces a state of detached mild euphoria with analgesia. Withdrawal phenomena (cold turkey) are uncomfortable but rarely life-threatening. They include apprehension, abdominal discomfort, lacrimation, piloerection, shivers, rhinorrhoea, and sleeplessness. LSD produces hallucinations (usually visual), intense emotions, and perceptual distortions. Occasionally there are flashbacks. The effects of cannabis depend on the state of mind and the expectations of the user, but often produce relaxation. A pronounced impairment of time and distance estimation has been noted, together with diminished attention and short-term memory.

Special work problems

Principles similar to those relating to alcoholism will apply. It is for management to detect that an individual's performance, behaviour, or attendance is failing and, whether drug misuse is suspected or not, medical advice should be sought.

There are important legal differences from alcohol, however, and Acts of Parliament are particularly relevant.

1. The Medicines Act, relating to the manufacture and supply of drugs for medical purposes.

2. The Misuse of Drugs Act, 1971, designed to prevent the non-medical use of certain drugs, known as controlled drugs. For practical purposes, employees need to be aware only of the more common offences described by the Misuse of Drugs Act.

The following key sections of the Act are relevant to employees in general, unless the person or the activity has been expressly licensed:

1. Section 4 makes it unlawful to supply another person (with or without monetary gain) with a drug specified by the Act.

2. Section 5 makes it unlawful to possess a controlled drug unless this has been prescribed by a doctor.

3. Section 6 makes it unlawful to grow cannabis.

4. Section 8 makes it unlawful for anybody concerned with the management of premises to permit or suffer controlled drugs to be produced, supplied, or used unlawfully on the premises.

Controlled drugs

Under the Misuse of Drugs Act, controlled drugs are divided into three classes. In addition, by means of regulations under the Act, schedules of drugs are drawn up according to their chemical and medical properties. The regulations classify the offences which may be committed in respect of the drugs. The classes A, B, and C determine the maximum and minimum penalties for these offences, class A attracting the severest penalties. The main categories of drugs in each class are listed below:

Class A. Cocaine; opiates, including heroin, morphine, and opium; hallucinogenics and psychotomimetics, including LSD and mescalin PCP (angel dust).

Class B. Drugs prepared for injection. Amphetamines in Schedule 2. Barbiturates: methaqualone (mandrax), cannabis.

Class C. Mild amphetamines (in Schedule 3). Frequent changes in the schedule are made as new preparations appear, and in the light of research and experience. From the beginning of April 1986, 33 names of benzodiazepines were scheduled, including many of the more common tranquillizers (such as diazepam) and sleeping tablets, and it is expected that these preparations will become Class C drugs.

It is an offence under the Act to offer any of these drugs, in classes A, B, and C to a person for whom they have not been prescribed, but it is not an offence to possess them.

Implications for employees and employers

The Misuse of Drugs Act, 1971 lays down penalties, therefore, for illegal possession of and trafficking in drugs. Any employee exposed to situations where an offence has been or is likely to be committed, and conscious of this, should raise the matter urgently with his manager who must consider if it is his duty to inform the police. Failure to do so will make the employee liable to prosecution. It is expressly not an offence, however, to take possession of a controlled drug with a view to handing it to the police at the earliest possible opportunity. Allowing anyone on your premises to produce or supply (give away or sell) illegal drugs to another person is an offence. The employer, therefore, has very strong legal as well as moral responsibilities.

As with alcohol, it is best to have a drugs misuse policy, agreed between management and unions, and that policy should include education, early recognition, treatment, and discipline, with the addition of compliance with the law. A specimen drug policy is outlined below.

DRUG MISUSE POLICY

Introduction

A good employer seeks to identify and help any employee with a drug-related problem at the earliest opportunity. This will be done with a proper regard to confidentiality, job security, promotion prospects, and all other benefits. Any employee who has a drug problem will be helped back into employment after treatment. In certain circumstances disciplinary action may be needed, especially where an employee has not sought help voluntarily.

Procedure

Voluntary cases

The employer will take all reasonable steps to ensure that any employee with a drug problem will get advice, help, and the necessary treatment. Employees who think they have such a problem should be encouraged to seek help voluntarily. Such requests will be treated as confidential medical matters, and will be referred to the company's occupational health adviser (or other appropriate medical authority). The employer's sick-pay scheme and policies on ill health will be used if necessary.

All employees co-operating with treatment and counselling will be seen regularly by the occupational health physician, who may refer the employee for further specialist advice and may request random screening of urine for evidence of drugs. Time off for advice and treatment will be in accordance with the normal sick-pay arrangements.

Involuntary cases or failure to co-operate with treatment

An employee's refusal of help or of treatment and screening will not be automatic grounds for dismissal, but unacceptable behaviour or performance thereafter will be subject to normal disciplinary procedures.

Rehabilitation

Employees who have been successfully treated for a drug problem will, if possible, return to their previous employment. If this is not possible, every effort will be made to find suitable redeployment within the company.

Disciplinary action including convictions for drug offences

The employer recognizes the sensitive and responsible nature of jobs in some departments. Therefore, in certain circumstances where an employee is convicted for an offence related to drug abuse, or when an employee is found either to be actively involved personally in drug abuse, or assists others in the misuse of drugs, disciplinary action will be taken. Depending on the circumstances of each individual case, such unlawful activities might well constitute gross misconduct, for which immediate dismissal would be the likely outcome.

Representation

All employees have the right to be represented at any stage during these procedures by their union representative or friend. Any dispute over the policy will be dealt with by the employer's normal appeal procedures.

Confidentiality

In certain cases of serious addiction, the doctor has to pass information about an individual patient to the Home Office (Misuse of Drugs Act, 1971). Except for this legal requirement, there will not be any breach of medical confidentiality. For the purpose of furthering research, the employer reserves the right to record and disclose, where proper, the number and job level of those who have received such treatment while in his employ, without disclosing the names or personal details.

Training and education

The employer will make provision for training those involved in implementing this policy, and for establishing links with suitable sources of professional advice and treatment. As part of the health education programme, the employer will provide, for employees, educational material on the dangers of drug-taking.

Sources of help and advice

Help can be obtained from the Drug and Alcohol Unit at the local psychiatric hospital, or at the local office of the Health Education Council. Some police drug squads offer a confidential source of help and advice. Further advice can be obtained from the following organizations (addresses given in Appendix 5):

1. The Institute for the Study of Drug Dependency. This is a leading organization for research information and educational materials on all aspects of drug use.

2. Royal Society for the Prevention of Accidents (ROSPA). ROSPA covers all kinds of accidents, at work, at home, or on the road, and provides training courses and educational materials relating to the misuse of drugs.

3. Standing Conference on Drug Abuse.

4. Turning Point. This is a leading service provider in the field of drug and alcohol misuse and is able to supply details of local resources. It also runs training courses for companies and for people in industry and commerce, as well as for professionals.

GENERAL CONCLUSIONS AND RECOMMENDATIONS

Because there is prejudice about mental illness, and because such illness often affects behaviour and relationships, it is all the more important for the physician to take care with advice on employment. It is essential to have a good knowledge of the demands and circumstances of the proposed work.

Work can be therapeutic and a good placement will help the patient. The employer will also be helped by careful selection and placement. A bad placement could have adverse effects on the patient and it would reinforce the employer's prejudices.

An applicant should not be turned down out of hand for employment because of a psychological illness. For example, it would be ridiculous to refuse employment to someone depressed because of unemployment.

If a psychological illness occurs during employment, the physician has the task of interpreting the patient's needs and trying to match these with the employer's resources. Within ethical guidelines, it is helpful for the physician to be ready to discuss these points with the employer and possibly with the patient's trade union and workmates.

Anyone who is rejected for employment, or who is required to change or leave his job, should be counselled. Reference to the resources of the Manpower Services Commission will be very helpful.

Appendix

INTERNATIONAL CLASSIFICATION OF DISEASES[40]

Mental disorders

Organic psychotic conditions (290–294)

290 Senile and presenile organic psychotic conditions
291 Alcoholic psychoses
292 Drug psychoses
293 Transient organic psychotic conditions
294 Other organic psychotic conditions (chronic)

Other psychoses (295–299)

295 Schizophrenic psychoses
296 Affective psychoses
297 Paranoid states
298 Other non-organic psychoses
299 Psychoses with origin specific to childhood

Neurotic disorders, personality disorders and other non-psychotic mental disorders (300–316)

300 Neurotic disorders
301 Personality disorders
302 Sexual deviations and disorders
303 Alcohol dependence syndrome
304 Drug dependence
305 Non-dependent abuse of drugs
306 Physiological malfunction arising from mental factors
307 Special symptoms or syndromes not elsewhere classified
308 Acute reaction to stress
309 Adjustment reaction
310 Specific non-psychotic mental disorders following organic brain damage
311 Depressive disorder, not elsewhere classified
312 Disturbance of conduct not elsewhere classified
313 Disturbance of emotions specific to childhood and adolescence
314 Hyperkinetic syndrome of childhood
315 Specific delays in development
316 Psychic factors associated with diseases classified elsewhere

Mental retardation (317–319)

317 Mild mental retardation
318 Other specified mental retardation

ACKNOWLEDGEMENTS

Dr J. Spencer Madden has kindly advised on the alcohol and drug sections. We are indebted to Dr Susan Robson for permission to quote the Drug Misuse Policy (pp. 418–19).

REFERENCES

1. Warr P. Psychological aspects of employment and unemployment. Psychol Med 1982;**12**:7–11.
2. Someone to Talk To Directory. London: Routledge and Kegan Paul, 1985.
3. Mental disorders: classification in accordance with ICD. 9. Geneva: World Health Organization, 1978.
4. Gelder M, Gath D, Mayou R. Oxford textbook of psychiatry. Oxford: Oxford University Press, 1983.
5. Dubovsky SL, Weissberg MP. Clinical psychiatry in primary care. Baltimore, Ind.: Williams and Wilkins, 1978.
6. Diagnostic and Statistical Manual (DSM III). Washington, DC: American Psychiatric Association, 1980.
7. Sartorius N, Shapiro R, Jablensky A. The International Pilot Study of Schizophrenia. Geneva: World Health Organization, 1973.
8. Creer C. Social work with patients and their families. In: Wing JK ed. Schizophrenia; towards a new synthesis. London: Academic Press, 1978.
9. Bland RC, Orn H. 14-year outcome in early schizophrenia. Acta Psychiat Scand 1978;**58**:327–38.
10. Vaughn CE, Leff JP. Influence of family and social factors on the course of psychiatric illness. Br J Psychiatry 1976;**129**:125–37.
11. Meichenbaum D. Cognitive behaviour modification. London: Plenum Press, 1977.
12. Meichenbaum D. Coping with stress. London: Century Publishing, 1983.
13. Godfried MR, Davison GC. Clinical behaviour therapy. New York: Holt Rinehart & Winston, 1976.
14. Poulton EC. Blue collar stressors. In: Cooper CL, Payne R, eds. Stress at work. Chichester: John Wiley & Sons, 1978.
15. Cooper CL, Marshall J. In: Cooper CL, Payne R, eds. Stress at work. Chichester: John Wiley & Sons, 1978.
16. Kahn RL, Wolfe DM, Quinn RP, Snoek JD, Rosenthal RA. Organizational stress; studies in role conflict and ambiguity. New York: Wiley, 1964. Quoted in Kearns J. Stress, work and management. Practitioner 1982;**226**:1600–5.
17. Gardell B. Scandinavian research on stress in working life. Int J Health Serv 1982;**12**:1.
18. Haw MA. Women, work and stress. A review and agenda for the future. J Health Soc Behav 1982;**23**:132–44.
19. Clarke I. Business men and mental illness. Bull Coll Psychiatry 1987;**11**:366–9.
20. Roberts RA. Burn out. Psychobabble or valuable concept? Br J Hosp Med 1986;**36**(3):194–7.

21. Jackson et al. Toward an understanding of the 'burn out' phenomenon. J App Psychol 1986;**71**(4):630–40.
22. Porterfield J, Gathercole C. The employment of people with mental handicap. Progress towards an ordinary life. Kings Fund Centre, 126 Albert Street, London NW1 7NF, 1985.
23. Wansbrough N. The employment of ex-psychiatric hosptial in-patients. A content analysis of open-ended comment received in recent correspondence with members of the Society of Occupational Medicine. J Soc Occup Med 1974; **24**:130–3.
24. Sergeant H. Pre-employment psychiatric examinations. Lancet 1984;**2**:212–4.
25. Raffle A ed. Medical aspects of fitness to drive. The Medical Commission on Accident Prevention, 34–43 Lincoln's Inn Fields, London WC2A 3PN, 1985.
26. Murgatroyd S. Counselling and helping, London: Methuen, 1985.
27. Gostin L ed. A practical guide to Mental Health Law. MIND (National Association for Mental Health), 22 Harley Street, London W1N 2ED, 1983.
28. Alcohol—reducing the harm. London: Office of Health Economics, 1981.
29. Alcohol problems. London: Br Med J, Tavistock Square, London WC1H 9JR, 1982.
30. Medical consequences of alcohol abuse. A great and growing evil. London: Royal College of Physicians, 1987.
31. McDonnell R, Maynard A. The costs of alcohol misuse. Br J Addict 1985; **80**:27–35.
32. Hore BD, Plant MA, eds. Alcohol problems in employment. London: Croom Helm, 1981.
33. Smith R. Alcohol and work. In: Alcohol problems. London: Br Med J, 1982.
34. Plant MA. Drugs in perspective. Sevenoaks: Hodder and Stoughton educational, 1987:92–3.
35. Saad ESN, Madden JS. Certified incapacity and unemployment in alcoholics. Br J Psychiat 1976;**128**:340.
36. Chick J. Management of the problem drinker. Med. Int. 1985;**2**:641–4.
37. Edwards G, Orford J, Egerts G. A controlled trial of treatment and advice in alcoholism. J Stud Alcohol 1977;**38**:1004–31.
38. Chick J, Chick J. Drinking problems. Information and advice for the individual, family and friends. Edinburgh: Churchill Livingstone, 1984.
39. Miller WR, Munoz RE. How to control your drinking. Englewood Cliff: Prentice Hall, 1976.
40. Manual of the international statistical classification of diseases, injuries, and causes of death, 9th Rev. 1975. Geneva: World Health Organization, 1977.

22

Acquired Immune Deficiency Syndrome

P. J. Baylis and J. M. Gallwey

None of us should adopt a rigid and uncaring stance towards patients with H.I.V. infection and AIDS; that might mean we look back at our professional lives with a feeling of shame rather than one of endeavour and, I hope, achievement.

M. W. Adler (1987)[1]

INTRODUCTION

It is perhaps the general public's perception of human immunodeficiency virus (HIV) disease which causes the greatest problem for the HIV-infected employee in the workplace. No health problem has encountered such wide publicity or created such fear and anxiety in modern times.[2] There is still considerable ignorance regarding the risks from this virus. It is still widely perceived as being contagious—transmissible by casual and accidental contact in every-day life—despite good evidence to the contrary. Additionally, in the Western world it is presently most prevalent amongst groups of people whose behaviour is seen by many as alien and indeed by some as morally reprehensible.[3] HIV has become not just a disease but a judgemental issue. HIV infection allows prejudice and bigotry to become respectable.

In fact, the virus is only transmissible by certain limited means. In the vast majority of jobs there is no risk of infection. Even where the virus or materials containing the virus are handled at work, the authors' experience and several prospective studies[4] of such occupational groups show that the risk of infection is extremely low and that the virus can be handled very safely.

Nevertheless, health professionals must recognize and play a part in successfully managing the ignorance, fear, and prejudice which still surround HIV disease. If employees discover or suspect that a colleague is HIV-infected, or even suspect that he or she is at greater risk, experience shows that considerable problems and disruption can occur.[5,6] Stigmatization and ostracism of such individuals increase the already existing burden on physical and mental well-being where infection exists. In our experience, such problems can be prevented by pre-emptive action in the workplace. This should include a programme of information and education aimed at all employees.[7,8] The employer should consider how to tackle HIV infection in an employee and review existing policies and procedures relating to ill health to ensure that they are robust enough to cope with HIV disease should it arise.

The HIV epidemic is a problem for everyone. Workplace initiatives can have a considerable influence in helping the community accept the need for the changes in attitude and behaviour necessary to control spread of infection and provide adequate care for those who are or will become infected.

SPECTRUM OF DISEASE: CLINICAL ASPECTS AFFECTING WORK CAPACITY

In order to understand the special problems related to HIV disease it is necessary to recognize that a spectrum of disease results from infection, over a variable but prolonged time span (Fig. 22.1). People with HIV will remain well for long periods and spend little time in hospital, even when constitutional illness appears. Most can and should be in employment.

Most HIV infected individuals remain in an asymptomatic carrier state for a considerable period. Infected and potentially infectious, there is probably a risk of constitutional illness appearing throughout life. Asymptomatic carriers have an unaltered potential for work. There are no areas of employment (other than prostitution) from which they should be excluded nor any modification of their working practices which should be imposed.

An initial, acute retroviral illness occurs in an unknown proportion of those infected within two to eight weeks.[9] It is probably frequently unrecognized, resembling viral infections such as influenza when mild, and glandular fever when more prolonged and severe. Within three months antibodies, which are only weakly protective, are produced in 95 per cent or more and provide a means of determining that infection has occurred.[10] In a small minority antibodies develop later or apparently not at all.[11]

After infection, persistent generalized lymphadenopathy (PGL) may develop.[12,13] Defined as swollen lymph glands in excess of 1 cm in two or more extra-inguinal sites and persisting beyond three months, it may be associated with a degree of fatigue which will limit work capacity. The presence of significant symptoms or signs beyond fatigue lead to classification as AIDS-related complex (ARC). Glandular enlargement is often multiple and appears in many sites, particularly the axillae and posterior cervical triangles. The size of the glands in the latter site may make them obvious to visual inspection. Glandular enlargement tends to fluctuate but complete disappearance has a bad prognostic significance.

ARC is characterized by symptoms and signs including fever, night sweats, significant and rapid weight loss, malaise, minor skin conditions, or oppor-

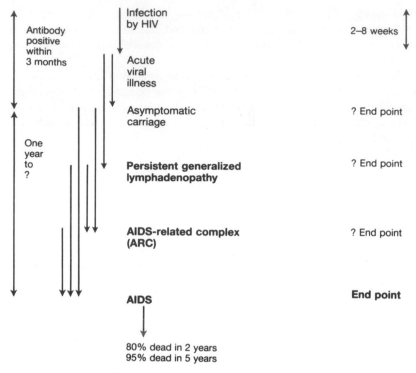

Fig. 22.1   Spectrum of HIV disease.

tunistic infections such as oral candidiasis, and fatigue.[14] ARC may well remit and relapse over a variable time span, with periods of relatively good health when work may be possible. Serious fatigue which limits work capacity is, however, a common persistent symptom.

Full blown AIDS[15] may appear from the asymptomatic, PGL, or ARC groups, in that HIV disease is not necessarily progressive with an individual passing through each category. The appearance of AIDS may be relatively sudden in a person hitherto quite unaware of being infected. Figure 22.2 demonstrates the three possible presentations of full blown AIDS although these are not mutually exclusive.

The prognosis of AIDS is bad with 75 per cent, or probably more, dying within two years.[16] The use of drugs may improve the prognosis. At the time of writing, only zidovudine has shown to be of definite clinical benefit in patients with advanced HIV infection.[17] A full evaluation of the ultimate benefits must await longer-term follow-up. The present concern about toxicity is perhaps due to its limited use in very sick patients and in large part related to the bone marrow damage already produced by disease. Further

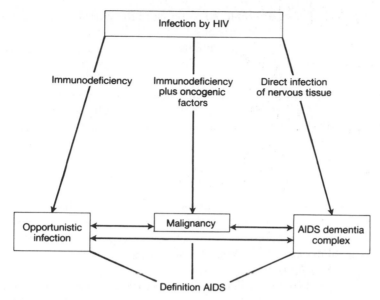

Fig. 22.2 HIV infection—presentations of AIDS.

investigations of this drug's wider application, including its use in asymptomatic seropositive patients, are now under way. Lack of information on possible benefits at present limit universal use.

Predictions of future ill health in an infected individual are controversial. Cohort studies indicate that between 8 per cent and 34 per cent will develop AIDS within three years.[18] There is an increasing feeling that most of those infected will suffer significant ill health as a result of their infection but whilst various international 'experts' prognosticate, only time can provide concrete evidence either way. There is no doubt that the longer the natural history is observed the greater the porportion who progress from seroconversion to AIDS.

Knowledge of being infected inevitably leads to considerable anxiety and possibly significant psychological morbidity.[19,20] Such problems are likely to be particularly severe if the patient is denied the support of adequate counselling before and after diagnosis.[21] Insecurity about future health and knowing they may develop life-threatening disease frequently lead to intolerable levels of fear. Anxiety, depression, and hypochondriacal preoccupation may diminish the capacity for intellectual and physical work, even in the absence of any physical illness. This will be further exacerbated if the employer or fellow employees show unsympathetic attitudes.

Confidentiality is particularly important in HIV disease.[22] It must be strictly preserved. Maintaining confidentiality can be complicated, but particular precautions are required to reassure the patient of confidentiality and limit unwarranted disclosure of information.[23-25] All patients will require adequate medical follow-up, continuing psychological support, guidance on avoidance of transmission, and advice on a number of practical issues such as dental treatment, life insurance, and, of course, work. Being HIV positive is no bar to work; indeed, the continuing support which being in work gives can bring considerable benefits. Even patients with AIDS can enjoy useful employment during periods of remission preceding final severe debilitating or incapacitating illness.

PREVALENCE: THE DEVELOPING EPIDEMIC

The prevalence of HIV infection in the UK (Table 22.1) has been greatest among homosexual men with a gradually increasing proportion of injecting drug-abusers. The potential for infection by heterosexual contact, well demonstrated in Central and West Africa,[26] indicates the need to consider at risk activities rather than at risk groups.

Table 22.2 demonstrates that a high proportion of those infected are in young, productive age-groups. The years of potential working life lost for those developing disease will be great (Curran, J. W., personal communication at 3rd International Conference on AIDS, Washington, June 1987).

Table 22.3 illustrates the risk characteristics of AIDS cases up to 31 October 1987.

At the end of June 1987 it was apparent that the number of reports of AIDS cases was continuing to double every 10 or 11 months. Figure 22.3 illustrates the observed AIDS cases reported to the Public Health Laboratory Services Communicable Diseases Surveillance Centre and Communicable Diseases (Scotland) Unit at 30th June 1987. Projections of cases by date of report are also shown.

The true incidence of HIV infection is unknown. The total of infections given in Table 22.1 represents the tip of a iceberg. The true total is variously estimated as between 30 000 and 100 000 but there is no solid basis for these figures.[27]

RISKS OF TRANSMISSION AND THEIR CONTROL IN THE WORKPLACE

The modes of transmission of HIV are shown in Table 22.4. By far the commonest mode of transmission throughout the world has been by sexual contacts, both heterosexual and homosexual, the emphasis being on the latter in the Western World. Significant spread is occurring in Europe, including the United Kingdom, by the sharing of injection equipment by drug misusers.[28,29]

Table 22.1 Cumulative totals of HIV antibody positive persons reported by transmission characteristic, to week 87/38 (England, Wales, and Northern Ireland)

Transmission characteristic	Male	Female	Unknown	Total
Homosexual/bisexual	3181	—	—	3181
Intravenous drug abuser (IVDA)	280	143	5	428
Homosexual & IVDA	42	—	—	42
Haemophiliac	981	4	1	986
Recipient of blood	36	24	—	60
Heterosexual contact*				
Contact of above groups	4	51	1	56
Contact of other groups	95	60	—	155
No information	30	21	6	57
Child of HIV antibody positive parent	9	7	2	18
Several risks	8	—	—	8
No information	1114	48	93	1255
Totals	5780	358	108	6246

PHLS Communicable Disease Surveillance Centre (Unpublished).

Table 22.2 Cumulative totals of HIV antibody positive persons reported, by age and sex, to week 87/38 (England, Wales, and Northern Ireland)

Age (years)	Male	Female	Unknown	Total
0–4	22	8	4	34
5–9	46	1	—	47
10–14	65	—	—	65
15–24	902	106	10	1018
25–44	2807	171	31	3009
45–64	476	8	4	488
>65	29	5	—	34
Not stated	1433	59	59	1551
Totals	5780	358	108	6246

PHLS Communicable Disease Surveillance Centre (Unpublished).

Table 22.3 Cumulative totals of UK reports of AIDS cases (deaths) to 31 October 1987

Transmission characteristic	Male		Female		Total	
Homosexual/bisexual	944	(517)	—		944	(517)
Intravenous drug abuser (IVDA)	12	(6)	4	(2)	16	(8)
Homosexual & IVDA	17	(8)	—		17	(8)
Haemophiliac	65	(49)	1	(—)	66	(49)
Recipient of blood: abroad	9	(6)	6	(3)	15	(9)
• UK	6	(5)	2	(2)	8	(7)
Heterosexual:						
possibly infected abroad	22	(7)	11	(6)	33	(13)
UK (no evidence of being infected abroad)	3	(2)	6	(4)	9	(6)
Child of HIV antibody positive or						
high risk parent	5	(2)	8	(4)	13	(6)
Other	—		1	(1)	1	(1)
Undetermined	1	(—)	—		1	(—)
Totals	1084	(602)	39	(22)	1123	(624)

PHLS Communicable Disease Surveillance Centre (Unpublished).

Detailed guidance on the relative risks of various sexual practices and methods of safer sex are readily available in a number of health education publications.[30-32]

In the workplace risks appear very low. They are confined to accidental exposures involving material containing live virus, namely:

inoculation injuries by sharps (e.g. needlestick); contamination of skin where its integrity is breached; possibly contamination of mucous membranes.

Unlike hepatitis B virus, HIV is of low infectivity and accidental infection rare.[33,34]

The relationship between workplace exposure to blood and body fluids from HIV infected persons and possible subsequent occupational infection is being closely monitored in the United Kingdom and United States. The results have been reviewed and reveal seven confirmed cases of occupational infection and unproven or anecdotal reports of a further nine.[4,35,36] The seven confirmed cases reported up to June 1987 include four needlestick injuries and three involving contamination of skin or mucous membranes. Since these reviews there have been reports of two laboratory workers handling concentrated virus becoming infected. There were some apparent failures in virus containment and safety procedures in the first case[37] and contamination of a cut hand in the second.[38]

These figures must be set against the thousands of AIDS patients being

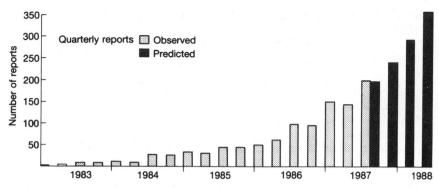

Fig. 22.3 Prediction of AIDS by date of report (at end of June 1987) (from PHLS Communicable Disease Surveillance Centre and Communicable Disease (Scotland) Unit, unpublished).

cared for by health care workers and the tens of thousands of invasive procedures and sampling procedures being carried out.[39] Prospective studies of known risk events indicate that the chance of infection, even by parenteral exposure to heavily infected materials, is small, probably less than 1 per cent.[35]

It is always very difficult to prove a negative, but there is much evidence that spread of infection does not occur through casual, social or work contact. Within the families of HIV-infected persons there is no evidence of horizontal spread other than through the three modes of transmission listed in Table 22.4.[40–43]

The virus is easily destroyed outside the body being sensitive to many commonly used disinfectants such as dilute household bleach.[44,45]

It is clear, however, that workplace standards of hygiene should be maintained at a high level and clear guidelines should exist for the safe handling of body fluids and blood. First-aiders should be trained in safe handling of body fluids and reassured that mouth-to-mouth resuscitation is safe.[46] Guidance for workers handling the virus or blood and other materials which might be infected will need to be far more specific and detailed.[47–52]

With such general guidance being applied, there is no need to lay down any special guidelines for HIV-infected individuals. For example, the HIV-infected haemophiliac should be treated in the same way as any other haemophiliac employee.

WORKFORCE EDUCATION AND COPING WITH PREJUDICE

As indicated in our introduction, the main problem in the workplace is not likely to arise from those who have the condition, but from those who do not.

Table 22.4   The modes of transmission of HIV

1. By blood or blood products

2. By sexual contact*

3. By an infected pregnant woman, to the fetus or at delivery, or in the neonatal period by breast milk

* Certain activities such as unprotected vaginal and anal intercourse carry a high risk of transmission. Orogenital contacts almost certainly carry a much lower risk. Transmission by other sexual contact has not been established.

Unreasonable and irrelevant demands may result from lack of accurate information, fear, or prejudice.[53] The demands can relate not only to known infected individuals but also to individuals perceived to be at risk. Examples of such demands included refusal to work with HIV-infected employees, with haemophiliacs, with gay men, or those thought to be gay, and requests for separate work equipment, toilet facilities, or canteens.[54]

In the authors' experience there is value in taking action in the workplace before problems arise. This requires more than just drawing up a policy. Such actions should aim to correct the misconceptions which exist about AIDS and deal with the human and industrial relations issues which may arise.

The unprecedented public health campaigns on AIDS in the United Kingdom have been deliberately designed to heighten awareness and concern about the actual risks of transmission and epidemic spread.[55] By contrast, the appropriate messages in the workplace are ones of reassurance, accurate information, and a plea for compassion and understanding.[56]

The method adopted by one company involved the collaboration of personnel, occupational health advisers, and media professionals.[7] Well-known public figures in the field of AIDS were interviewed and these interviews used as the basis for a short video with simple, easy to understand messages. This acted as a vehicle for an information programme aimed at all employees. With the help of clear briefing notes outlining the purpose and approach to the briefing, line managers headed a series of small group sessions where the video was shown and health education leaflets given to all employees.

The aim was to give the facts and also address the emotional reactions to the facts and get these on the table for discussion, i.e. to encourage an interactive response. The programme included a review of all company policies and procedures concerning ill health. This was to ensure that they were robust enough to cope with HIV disease in an employee.

There was a clear statement of company intent consistent with views expressed by health professionals, health educators, and trade unions.[56-58]

Statement of intent: Generally we will not treat anyone with AIDS any differently from anyone with any other serious illness.

Key points in programme:

- The disease is transmitted sexually or blood to blood.

- You cannot catch it from normal day-to-day social and work contact.

- People with AIDS should be treated in the same way as anyone else who has a serious illness—with compassion and understanding.

CARE OF THE HIV-INFECTED EMPLOYEE

From what has already been said, it is clear that modification of working practices are not necessary with any infected employee to protect the rest of the work force. Modifications may be required to enable constitutionally ill infected individuals to continue as useful employees.

By definition, the asymptomatic HIV-infected require no modification of working practices. As with all stages of HIV infection and disease, however, the high incidence of psychological distress and morbidity associated with uncertainty, anxiety, and hypochondriacal preoccupation must be recognized. This may diminish an employee's capabilities and functioning. Encouragement towards and access to any counselling agencies, including occupational physicians and nurses, genito-urinary medicine clinics and support organizations will be of considerable value (Appendix 5).

Persistent generalized lymphadenopathy (PGL) may lead to a significant degree of fatigue which may limit the individual's capacity for prolonged physical and intellectual exertion.

AIDS-related complex (ARC) as a remitting and relapsing condition of varying severity may require allowance for diminished work capacity because of malaise and fatigue. There are likely to be periods of ill health requiring absence from work and indeed hospitalization. The availability of work during periods of remission has an important morale-boosting function. Reduction of stress in an individual may well be an important factor in minimizing viral activation and consequent progression towards immune deficiency.

People with actual AIDS suffer a series of serious events, such as opportunistic infections, which require specialist care and usually hospital admission. Between events they may well be capable of useful employment for significant periods of time. The level of employment will depend on those factors well known in debilitating illness, but, on humanitarian grounds, work of a suitable physical and intellectual nature should be offered. Physical changes, including gross weight loss and disfiguring skin lesions, may occur.

It may be kinder to consider recommending redeployment, in the interests of the patient, where work involves much face-to-face contact with the public.

Direct infection of nervous tissue by HIV may lead, in the presence or absence of immune deficiency manifestations, to neurological disorders.[59] In particular, insidious deterioration of intellectual function leading to eventual dementia is being recorded. This must be taken into consideration in monitoring the suitability of particular work for infected individuals. Early signs of neurological disorder obviously have great significance where the health or safety of the employee or others is at stake.

PRE-EMPLOYMENT SCREENING AND HIV TESTING

Mention must be made of the controversial idea of HIV antibody testing as a condition of employment.[60] In support of such a policy, it is argued that this enables the employer to reject prospective employees who are infected, thus avoiding the eventual problems associated with future morbidity or mortality as well as trouble caused by other employees.

However, the test has its limitations, false negatives can occur, and tested employees may become infected after employment. Should such discrimination be extended to exclude so-called at risk groups, for example haemophiliacs or homosexuals? To be logical, those indulging in at risk activities might be excluded, i.e. the sexually promiscuous. Being HIV-infected does not necessarily affect work capacity and there is no accurate way of determining prognosis regarding work capacity. To be consistent, employers enacting such a policy would have to consider excluding other candidates where a higher risk of morbidity existed, e.g. heavy smokers or candidates who consume excessive alcohol.

Occupational physicians and nurses have a duty of care towards candidates. Screening for HIV offers little advantage to the employer and may have definite disadvantages to the candidate at present, with the likelihood of damage, both psychological and social.[21] Any testing must always be preceded by competent counselling and informed consent. The candidate must be informed of the test result, strict confidentiality maintained, and post-test counselling undertaken[21,61] Such routine testing is not ethically acceptable and occupational physicians should not lend themselves to such a policy.

Whilst blood donors are all tested by the HIV antibody test each time they donate blood for use by the blood transfusion services, it is of paramount importance that those who have been at real risk of infection should not donate. Such a self-exclusory policy will reduce the risk of donations within the incubation window or by those in whom antibody does not appear.

Blood donation sessions at work may lead to peer pressure on at risk employees to donate. Undue pressure to donate, such as attempts to achieve a 100 per cent contribution, should be avoided.

EXISTING LEGISLATION AND GUIDANCE

No legislation exists specifically in relation to HIV infection. There is, however, a wide range of guidance available. This covers AIDS and employment,[7,8,56] guidance on protection of employees handling the virus or caring for patients,[47-52,58,62] guidance to health professionals,[63-66] local authority employees,[67] schools,[68] and prison services.[8] A wide range of health education information has been produced by government departments,[30,55,56,69] trade unions,[57,58] and voluntary organizations.[31,32,61] In particular, The Terrence Higgins trust and the Haemophilia Society have included in their literature advice on employment (Appendix 5).

INFECTED HEALTH CARE WORKERS

Since the chapter was submitted a High Court case[70] in which the *News of the World* was prevented from naming two general practitioners with AIDS has received wide media coverage. As a result considerable public anxiety has been expressed about the risk to patients from infected doctors. While statements on this issue from the General Medical Council (GMC), and the Chief Medical Officer (CMO) of the DHSS, relate to medical practitioners, similar principles will apply to any health care worker in clinical contact with patients.

It is important to emphasize that there is no known case where HIV has been transmitted by an infected health care worker to a patient in the course of medical treatment.

Infection of health care workers as a result of their clinical work has been shown (p. 430) to be extremely uncommon, to be unrelated to casual contact, and to result only from needle stick injury or contamination of broken skin or mucous membrane. Even in those circumstances the risk is in the order of 1 per cent or less. Similarly, the risk to patients from infected health care workers would only theoretically arise in performing invasive procedures where, as a result of injury to an infected operator, blood enters the patient.

Although this theoretical risk is very low it is clearly important that an infected health care worker should avoid any situation where this could occur. The instructions from the CMO and the GMC are that any doctor infected by HIV or who considers he may have been so infected should seek advice and counselling. If found to be infected he should have regular medical supervision. Counselling must include the extent to which medical practice should be limited in order to protect patients. The GMC statement[71] (see appendix) specifically states 'It is unethical for doctors, who know or believe themselves to be infected with HIV to put patients at risk by failing to seek appropriate counselling or to act upon it when given ... No [such] doctors should continue in clinical practice on the basis of their own assessment of the risk to patients.' It also makes clear that a doctor providing counselling for an HIV infected colleague and who is aware that his advice on professional practice modification is not being followed, has a duty to inform an appropriate body that the doctor's fitness to practise may be seriously impaired.

Advice on limitation of practice needs to be determined on an individual basis and directed toward protection of the patient from accidental infection by HIV or by an opportunistic organism such as *Mycobacterium species* which could be carried by an immunodeficient health care worker. Consideration must also be given to the protection of an immunodeficient health care worker from opportunistic organisms which could be carried by patients. The CMO is expected to issue guidelines, in the near future, on this issue.

Occupational physicians with responsibility for health care workers have a duty to create an environment in which management of an infected health care worker is possible.[72] Clear circulated guidelines will pre-empt the development of problems and should include the following elements:

(1)   that there is an ethical requirement for health care workers who know or believe themselves to be infected to inform an appropriate authority;

(2)   that specialist advice must be obtained on the extent to which they should limit clinical practice;

(3)   that regular medical supervision is required;

(4)   the local arrangements for provision of counselling;

(5)   that confidentiality is guaranteed.

Occupational physicians should be prepared to provide such counselling or to refer the health care worker to an appropriate counselling and care agency.

The authors recognize a special situation in the health care worker–patient relationship where a risk, albeit 'slightly more than negligible',[70] exists of accidental infection. They also recognize the need for retaining public confidence in the safety of medical care. Confidentiality remains, however, of paramount importance. As Mr. Justice Rose said in the *News of the World* trial 'If patients [including doctors] had reason for believing that [confidentiality] might be breached they would be reluctant to come forward for and to continue with treatment and, in particular, counselling.' The authors do not believe that the special situation of health care workers justifies opening the door to widespread requirement of identification or disclosure of antibody status in other occupations.

CONCLUSIONS AND RECOMMENDATIONS

The background, natural history, and potential risks to life associated with HIV infection and disease have predisposed to discrimination within the workplace and stigmatization of potentially at risk individuals. Pre-emptive efforts to educate and inform correctly may prevent or diminish employment disruption and reduce distress to infected individuals and those at significant risk. Occupational physicians must play their part.[73]

The continued employment of infected workers, with or without constitutional illness, is feasible. It is an important factor in the successful management of their condition and should be strongly encouraged. The modifications of work and enviroment which may be needed are, in principle, no different from those likely to be needed for any employee with a progressive and debilitating condition. The possibility of neuropsychological manifestations requires consideration in certain occupations, particularly as they may appear relatively rapidly in a younger than usual age group.

In this disease, perhaps more than any other at the present time, strict adherence to the normal professional duty of confidentiality is of the utmost importance in care.

APPENDIX: STATEMENT OF GENERAL MEDICAL COUNCIL (GMC)[71]

There is no known case anywhere in the world of the human immunodeficiency virus (HIV) having been transmitted by an infected doctor to a patient in the course of medical treatment.

Nevertheless it is imperative, both in the public interest and on ethical grounds, that any doctors who consider that they may have been infected with HIV should seek appropriate diagnostic testing and counselling, and, if found to be infected, should have regular medical supervision. They should also seek specialist advice on the extent to which they should limit their professional practice in order to protect their patients. They must act upon that advice, which in some circumstances would include a requirement not to practise or to limit their practice in certain ways. No doctors should continue in clinical practice merely on the basis of their own assessment of the risk to patients.

It is unethical for doctors who know or believe themselves to be infected with HIV to put patients at risk by failing to seek appropriate counselling, or to act upon it when given.

The doctor who has counselled a colleague who is infected with HIV to modify his or her professional practice in order to safeguard patients, and is aware that this advice is not being followed, has a duty to inform an appropriate body that the doctor's fitness to practise may be seriously impaired. There are well tried arrangements for dealing with such cases. They are designed to protect patients as well as to assist the sick doctor. If the circumstances so warrant the council is empowered to take action to limit the practice of such doctors or to suspend their registration.

These arrangements also safeguard the confidentiality and support which doctors when ill, like other patients, are entitled to expect.

The principles underlying this advice are already familiar to the profession, which has long adopted policies and procedures designed to prevent the transmission of infection from doctors to patients.

REFERENCES

1. Adler MW. Introduction. In: Adler MW ed. ABC of AIDS. London: British Medical Journal, 1987, ix.
2. Anonymous. A virus for hysteria. New Scientist 1986: 27 November.
3. AIDS is the Wrath of God says Vicar. The Sun 1985: February 7.
4. McEvoy M, Porter K, Mortimer P, Simmons N, Shanson D. Prospective study of clinical, laboratory and ancillary staff with accidental exposures to blood or body fluids from patients infected with HIV. Br Med J 1987;**294**: 1595–7.
5. AIDS case jail put in quarantine as officers seek enquiry. The Times 1985: February 6.
6. Hotel bans Gay Chef who took AIDS test. The Sun 1985: February 14.
7. The Industrial Society. AIDS and employment—an information programme about Aids and the workplace. Briefer's notes and video. London: The Industrial Society, 1987.
8. HM Prison Service. AIDS inside—Training package for prison officers. London: 1987.
9. Cooper DA, Gold J, Maclean P et al. Acute AIDS retroviral infection. Definition of a clinical illness associated with seroconversion. Lancet 1985;**i**:537–40.
10. Salahuddin SK, Markham PD, Redfield RR, et al. HTLV III in symptom free sero-negative persons. Lancet 1984;**ii**:1418–20.
11. Ranki A, Valle S, Krohn M et al. Long latency precedes overt seroconversion in sexually transmitted human-immunodeficiency virus infection. Lancet 1987; **ii**:589–93.
12. Mildvan D, Mathur U, Enlow RW et al. Persistent generalised lymphadenopathy among homosexual males. Morbidity Mortality Wkly Rep. 1982;**31**:249–51.
13. Abrams DI, Lewis BJ, Beckstead JH, Casavant CA, Drew WL. Persistent diffuse lymphadenopathy in homosexual mean: end point or prodrome? Ann Intern Med 1984;**100**:801–8.
14. Pinching AJ, Weiss RA. AIDS and the spectrum of HTLVIII/LAV infection. Int Rev Exp Pathol 1986;**28**:1–44.
15. Centers for Disease Control. Revision of CDC surveillance case definition for acquired immunodeficiency syndrome. Morbidity Mortality Wkly Rep. 1987; **36**(suppl. No. 15): 35–155.

16. Centers for Disease Control. Acquired Immunodeficiency Syndrome Weekly Surveillance Report. Atlanta, Georgia: Centers for Disease Control, 1986: September 9.

17. Fischl MA, Richman DD, Grieco MH et al. The efficacy of Azidothymidine (AZT) in the treatment of patients with AIDS and AIDS-related complex: a double-blind, placebo-controlled trial. N Engl J Med 1987;**317**:185–91.

18. Adler MW. Range and natural history of infection. In: Adler MW, ed. ABC of AIDS. London: British Medical Journal, 1987, 11–13.

19. Miller D. Living with AIDS and HIV. London: Macmillan, 1987.

20. Miller D. Psychology, AIDS, ARC, and PGL. In: Miller D, Weber J, Green J, eds. The management of AIDS patients. London: Macmillan 1986;131–49.

21. Miller D, Jeffries DJ, Green J, Harris JRW, Pinching AJ. HTLV III: Should testing ever be routine? Br Med J 1986;**292**:941–3.

22. Gillon R. AIDS and medical confidentiality. Br Med J 1987;**294**:1675–7.

23. Mindel A. Management of early HIV infection. In: Adler MW, ed. ABC of AIDS. London: British Medical Journal, 1987,14–18.

24. Confidential AIDS. (Editorial.) The Times 1987: Nov. 11:17.

25. Marks J. BMA view on doctors with AIDS. (Letter to the Editor.) The Times 1987: Nov. 13.

26. AIDS and the Third World. London: The Panos Institute, 1987.

27. Department of Health and Social Security. Human immunodeficiency disease. An outline issued by the DHSS for District Health Authority Chairmen. London: 1987.

28. Fauci AS, Moderator. The acquired immunodeficiency syndrome: an update. NIH conference. Ann Intern Med 1985;**102**(6): 800–13.

29. Adler MW. Development of the Epidemic. In: Adler MW. ed. ABC of AIDS. London: British Medical Journal 1987,1–3.

30. Health Education Council. AIDS—What everybody needs to know. AIDS Unit, London: Department of Health and Social Security 1986.

31. The Terrence Higgins Trust. AIDS, more facts for gay men. BM/AIDS, London WC1N 3XX: 1986.

32. The Haemophilia Society. HAEMOFACT—Advice on Safer Sex PO Box 9, 16 Trinity Street, London SE1 1DE: 1985.

33. Gerberding JL, Hopewell PC, Kaminsky LS, Sande MA. Transmission of hepatitis B without transmission of AIDS by accidental needlestick. N Engl J Med 1985;**312**:56–7.

34. Gerberding JL, Bryant-Le Blanc CE, Nelson K et al. Risk of transmitting the human immunodeficiency virus, cytomegalovirus, and hepatitis B virus to health care workers exposed to patients with AIDS and AIDS-related conditions. J Infect Dis 1987;**156**:1–8.

35. McCray E. Occupational risk of the acquired immunodeficiency syndrome among health care workers. N Engl J Med 1986;**314**:1127–32.

36. Centers for Disease Control Update. Human Immunodeficiency virus infection in health care workers exposed to blood of infected patients. Morbidity Mortality Wkly Rep. 1987;**36**:285–9.

37. Palca J. Lab worker infected with AIDS virus. Nature 1987;**329**:92.

38. Palca J. Aids virus infects another lab worker. Nature 1987;**329**:571.
39. Lifson AR, Castro KG, McCray E, Jaffe HW. National surveillance of AIDS in health care workers. J Am Med Ass 1986;**256**:3231–4.
40. Friedland GH, Saltzman BR, Rogers MF et al. Lack of transmission of HTLV-III/LAV infection to household contacts of patients with AIDS or AIDS-related complex with oral candidiasis. N Engl J Med 1986:**314**:344–9.
41. Jones D, Hamilton PJ, Bird G et al. AIDS and haemophilia: morbidity and mortality in a well defined population. Br Med J 1985;**291**:695–9.
42. Zuckerman AJ. AIDS and insects. Br Med J 1986;**292**:1094–5.
43. Mann JM, Quinn TC, Francis H et al. Prevalence of HTLV-III/LAV in household contacts of patients with confirmed AIDS and controls in Kinshasa, Zaire. J Am Med Ass 1986;**256**:721–4.
44. Resnick L, Veren K, Salahuddin SK, Tondreau S, Markham PD. Stability and inactivation of HTLV-III/LAV under clinical and laboratory environments. J Am Med Ass 1986;**255**: 1887–91.
45. Martin LS, McDougal JS, Loskoski SL. Disinfection and inactivation of the human T lymphotrophic virus type III/lymphadenopathy-associated virus. J Infect Dis 1985;**152**:400–3.
46. Cowper BM. AIDS (Acquired Immune Deficiency Syndrome) (Letter to all training organizations approved under the Health and Safety (First Aid) Regulations 1981) Bootle, Merseyside: Health and Safety Executive, Medical Division, 19th January 1987.
47. Advisory Committee on Dangerous Pathogens. Acquired immune deficiency syndrome (AIDS)—interim guidelines. London: Department of Health and Social Security, December 1984.
48. Department of Health and Social Security. Guidance for surgeons, anaesthetists, dentists and their teams in dealing with patients infected with HTLV-III. Booklet 3. London: DHSS, April 1986.
49. Advisory Committee on Dangerous Pathogens. LA/HTLV-III—the causative agent of AIDS—and related conditions. Revised guidelines. London: DHSS, June 1986.
50. Centers for Disease Control. Recommendations for preventing transmission of infection with human lymphotropic virus type III/lymphadenopathy—associated virus in the workplace. Morbidity Mortality Wkly Rep. 1985; **34**:681–95.
51. Anonymous. Recommendations for prevention of HIV transmission in health-care settings. Leads from the Morbidity and Mortality Weekly Report. J Am Med Ass 1987;**258**:1293–1305 *and* Morbidity Mortality Wkly Rep. 1987; **36**:2S;1S–17S.
52. Anonymous. Recommendations for Prevention of H.I.V. Transmission in Health-Care Settings. Leads from the Morbidity and Mortality Weekly Report. J Am Med Ass 1987;**258**:1441–52 *and* Morbidity Mortality Wkly Rep. 1987;**36**:2S;1S–17S.
53. Eckholm E. Poll finds many AIDS fears that the experts say are groundless. New York Times 1985, September 12, B-11.
54. Munyard T. AIDS, the workplace, and the law. In: Equal Opportunities

Review, No. 15. September/October 1987. London: Industrial Relations Services: 7–13.

55. Department of Health and Social Security. AIDS—don't die of ignorance. London: DHSS, 1987.

56. Department of Employment and the Health and Safety Executive. AIDS—Acquired immune deficiency syndrome and employment. London, 1987.

57. Trades Union Congress. The problems associated with acquired immune deficiency syndrome (AIDS). London: TUC Memorandum of Evidence to the House of Commons Social Services Committee Inquiry into Acquired Immune Deficiency Syndrome, December 16 1986.

58. Confederation of Health Service Employees. AIDS—guidelines for health staffs dealing with patients suffering from acquired immune deficiency syndrome (AIDS) or with AIDS virus. London: Revised September 1987.

59. Carne CA, Adler MW. Neurological manifestations of human immune deficiency virus infection. Br Med J 1986;**293**:462–3.

60. Carthago delenda est! (editorial) J Soc Occup Med 1987;**37**:37–38.

61. The Terrence Higgins Trust. AIDS and HTLV III–HTLV III ANTIBODY. To test or not to test? BM/Aids London WC1N 3XX: 1986.

62. Health Services Advisory Committee, Health and Safety Commission. AIDS, Prevention of Infection in the Health Services. London: December, 1986.

63. Department of Health and Social Security. Acquired immune deficiency syndrome. General information for doctors. Booklet 1. London: DHSS, 1985.

64. Department of Health and Social Security. Information for doctors concerning the introduction of the HTLV-III antibody test. Booklet 2. London: DHSS, 1985.

65. Department of Health and Social Security. Acquired immune deficiency syndrome (AIDS) and artificial insemination. Guidance for doctors at clinics. Booklet 4. London: DHSS, 1986.

66. British Medical Association. AIDS and you—an illustrated guide. London: 1987.

67. Department of Health and Social Security. Information and guidance on AIDS (acquired immune deficiency syndrome) for local authority staff. London: DHSS, 1986.

68. Department of Education and Science and Welsh Office. Children at school and problems related to AIDS. London: 1986.

69. Department of Health and Social Security. Protect your health abroad—vital information for people travelling overseas—especially to hotter climates. London: DHSS for UK Health Departments: 1986.

70. Dyer C. Doctors with AIDS and the 'News of the World' Brit. Med. Journal 1987;**295**:1339–40.

71. Statement issued on behalf of the GMC by the president, Sir John Walton. Brit Med J 1987;**295**:1500.

72. Adler, MW. Patient safety and doctors with HIV infection. Brit Med Journal 1987;**295**:1297–8.

73. Tomasi TJ, ed. AIDs and the occupational physician. J Occup Med, 1986; 28(7). (Editorial) p. 517.

Appendix 1:
Driving
J. F. Taylor

STANDARDS OF FITNESS REQUIRED FOR BRITISH DRIVING LICENCE
HOLDERS AND APPLICANTS

Ordinary driving licences

The Licensing Authority for ordinary driving licences is the Secretary of State for Transport and he delegates his functions to the Driver and Vehicle Licensing Centre (DVLC) at Swansea. The medical assessment of drivers at the Licensing Centre is the responsibility of a Medical Advisory Branch, comprising a team of doctors.

The duty of applicants for licences

The application form for a driving licence (Form D1) obtainable from a post office, requires the declaration of the following disabilities:—

(1) Epilepsy;

(2) Severe mental handicap (a state of arrested or incomplete development of the mind which includes severe impairment of intelligence or social functioning);

(3) Liability to sudden attacks of disabling giddiness or fainting;

(4) Inability to read in good daylight (with the aid of glasses or contact lenses, if worn) a registration mark fixed to a motor vehicle and containing letters and figures 79.4 mm ($3\frac{1}{8}$ in.) high at a distance of 20.5 m (67 ft) or 12.3 m (40 ft) in the case of an applicant for a licence for authority to drive vehicles confined to Group K (milk-floats and pedestrian-control mowing machines).

The duty of licence holders

A licence-holder is required by Law to inform the Licensing Centre as soon as possible if, during the currency of a licence, he or she becomes aware that they are suffering from:

1. Any medical condition such as to be likely to cause the driving by him or her of a motor vehicle to be a source of danger to the public, either immediately or at some future date. Only temporary disabilities such as fractured bones, not expected to last more than three months, are excluded from this obligation. The obligation in Law is

placed on the licence-holder and normally takes effect from the time that a registered medical practitioner informs his patient that he or she suffers from such a disability.

2. A disability already notified to the Licensing Centre which has become worse.

Procedure for medical assessment

When it receives information about a disability from an applicant or licence-holder or otherwise, the Licensing Centre may require the applicant or licence-holder to authorize his or her doctor to make available information about the disability to the Medical Advisory Branch at the Centre. If the applicant or licence-holder fails to do so, or if the information available from the doctor is not conclusive in relation to fitness to drive, the Centre may require him or her to have a medical examination by a nominated doctor or doctors. If necessary, to establish the effect of the disability on ability to drive, the Centre may require him or her to take a driving test. Failure of a licence-holder or applicant to give consent to their medical practitioner making reports to the Licensing Centre, or failure to attend examination without reasonable excuse, may lead to a driving licence being withdrawn or withheld.

Applicants for licences

Applicants for licences suffering from a static limb disability have an automatic right in Great Britain to a provisional driving licence for the purpose of taking a test to prove their ability to drive. Normally provisional licences run until the applicant's 70th birthday, except in the case of motorcycle entitlement which runs only for two years and cannot be renewed until a year has elapsed, unless a test on a motorcycle, moped, or car has been passed.

Relevant disabilities

If a licence-holder or applicant is found by the Licensing Centre to be suffering from a medical condition such as to be likely to cause the driving by them of a motor vehicle to be a source of danger to the public (relevant disability), then the application has to be refused or the licence revoked. In addition to this general definition, other relevant disabilities are prescribed as bars to the granting or holding of a driving licence. These include:

1. Epilepsy. A person suffering from epilepsy must not have had any attack during the two years before the licence is to take effect or, alternatively, if the attacks have been confined to sleep for at least three years, a licence may be granted. Additionally, applicants with epilepsy must not be regarded as likely to be a source of danger to the public as a driver.

2. The requirement to read a numberplate at 20.5 m (67 ft) is a continuing obligation on *all* driving licence holders and if the static visual acuity falls below the standard, the driver is guilty of a criminal offence.

3. Liability to sudden attacks of disabling giddiness or fainting, except where such attacks can be controlled by an implanted cardiac pacemaker. Then a licence may be granted subject to the licence-holder having made adequate arrangements to receive regular medical supervision by a cardiologist throughout the period of the licence, and conforming to those arrangements.

4. Severe mental handicap (as defined above).

Duration of driving licences

Normally, a licence is granted until the age of 70, but where a person suffers from a medical condition which, on the balance of probabilities, may at a later stage be likely to lead them to be a source of danger to the public when driving, or lead to one of the four bar disabilities above, the licence has to be restricted in period of duration to one, two, or three years so that regular medical checks can be arranged. A licence may also be restricted in terms of controls where a person has a physical limb disability which may either immediately require special fitment of controls or may progress to a point that adaptation of controls is needed. In these cases, the licence may run for a full duration until the age of 70 but be subject to a restriction requiring all controls to be fitted so that they can be correctly and conveniently operated by the holder of the licence.

Appeal provisions

Where a driving licence is refused or revoked on medical grounds or restricted in period of duration, there is a right of appeal to a Magistrates Court in England and Wales or to a Sheriff's Court in Scotland.

Licences to drive heavy goods (HGV) and public service vehicles (PSV)

A heavy goods vehicle (HGV) driver's licence is required in Great Britain to drive vehicles in excess of 7.5 metric tonnes laden weight. Currently these HGV licences and also PSV licences (required to drive passenger vehicles for hire or reward) are issued by statutorily independent Licensing Authorities. It is proposed that these Licensing Authorities will be centralized on the Licensing Centre at Swansea and eventually these licences will constitute a special group on the ordinary driving licence. For the present, an extra licence is required to drive these classes of vehicle.

The regulations require that the applicant for an HGV or PSV licence (whether initially or renewal) shall be fit to hold it having regard to his health and to any disability which he may suffer. The prescribed application forms include a health declaration. A medical report must be submitted on form DPT 20003 with the initial application for a Vocational licence and thereafter; this is required (1) for an HGV driver at renewals from the age of 60; and (2) for a PSV licence with renewals from the age of 46 and annually from the age of 65. In both cases the Licensing Authority may, at his discretion, call for a medical report at other times. He has power to suspend or revoke a licence upon the ground that, by reason of physical disability, the holder is not fit to hold it.

A person who has had an epileptic attack since attaining the age of five years is absolutely barred in Law from holdng a Vocational licence and the Licensing Authority has no discretion to grant one.

Taxi and hire car drivers

Taxi and car hire licences may be issued by Local Authorities. Generally they apply the same medical standards as for HGV/PSV licences and on refusal there is a right of appeal to the Magistrates Court in England and Wales and the Sheriffs Court in Scotland. In considering the medical fitness of drivers, the Licensing Authorities are advised by the Medical Adviser at the Licensing Centre.

Medical Advisory Branch liaison

Any doctor wishing to discuss the subject of fitness to drive is invited to contact a Medical Adviser at the Licensing Centre. Where appropriate, the Department of Transport Medical Adviser will co-operate in patient management by discussing the matter on the telephone or personally writing to the doctor. There is a 24-hour telephone answering service on 0792 42731. The doctor should leave his name and telephone number and a time when it is convenient to phone him back. The Medical Advisers will be pleased to answer written enquiries and the address to write to is: The Department of Transport, Medical Advisory Branch, The Oldway Centre, Orchard Street, SWANSEA SA1 1TU.

Professional discretion

The Law places the obligation on the licence-holder or applicant to inform the Licensing Authorities about medical disabilities. Circumstances may rarely arise in which a doctor who has told a patient not to drive and to report a relevant disability to the Licensing Centre, finds that the patient has disregarded the advice and is continuing to drive to the danger of the public.

In such cases, it is advisable for the doctor to repeat the advice to the patient in writing and at the same time seek the opinion of his Medical Protection or Defence Association.

The authoritative document for reference is the General Medical Council pamphlet 'Professional conduct and discipline: fitness to practice'.

Appendix 2:
Medical standards in civil aviation
G. Bennett

INTRODUCTION

There are two fundamentally different requirements for medical standards in the aviation industry. Because of the very high cost of training, say, a 747 pilot, an employer seeks not only short-term safety and effectiveness but also the probability of remaining fit through a long-term career.

The national authority responsible for air safety—in the United Kingdom, the Civil Aviation Authority (CAA)—can only be concerned with the probability that a licence-holder will be able to function effectively and will not be likely to suffer sudden incapacitation during the short period (six months to one year) for which his or her medical certificate is valid. A young man with a progressive disability might well be given a licence subject to regular reviews but would not be hired by a major airline. Counselling is needed and would be given by the CAA.

Risk management is the main principle of aviation licensing. A zero defect policy is not attainable. The best airline operating the best aircraft achieve a fatal accident rate of one in 2 m. flights[1] and the CAA sets a safety target of one fatal accident in 10 m. flights. Many factors may cause accidents, so the medical-cause safety target is better than one in 100 m. flights.[2]

PILOTS

The medical standards for pilots (and for flight engineers and air traffic control officers) are internationally agreed and are contained in Annex 1 to the Convention on International Civil Aviation.[3] A few, such as the visual requirements, are specific but many are couched in such general terms as 'cases of metabolic nutritional or endocrine disorders likely to interfere with the safe exercise of the applicant's licence privileges shall be assessed as unfit.' There is also a waiver clause which allows a national authority to issue a licence if it believes it is safe to do so even if the standards are not met. The International Civil Aviation Organisation, a United Nations organization, therefore issues a manual of guidance material[4] on the interpretation of the standards.

Possible exposure to the harsh environment, notably hypoxia, accelerations, and pressure and temperature changes, requires very good cardio-respiratory function and freedom from conditions likely to be aggravated by sudden changes—middle-ear and sinus disorders, lung bullae, herniation, etc.

Special sense functions, especially vision, are clearly important. Uncorrected distant visual acuity must be 6/60 (20/200) or better, correcting to 6/9 (20/30) or better, and there are near and intermediate visual requirements. Normal colour vision is not always necessary provided the candidate can reliably distinguish signal red, white, and green. Experienced pilots who lose an eye can often continue to fly satisfactorily, but not always at night.

Pilots with disabilities resulting from orthopaedic or neurological conditions are given a practical test in each aircraft type they wish to fly.

The lifestyle of a professional pilot is necessarily irregular and this excludes some gastrointestinal and metabolic disorders. Diabetes requiring insulin is absolutely disqualifying and oral therapy is usually so.

Because the continual exercise of judgement and self-discipline is so vital to the pilot's task, significant mental and personality disorders are unacceptable. A history of psychosis is permanently disqualifying. Neurotic illness is assessed on the probability of recurrence, as is alcohol and drug abuse.

Commonly used therapeutic agents are often unacceptable because of their side-effects. Performance testing in a flight simulator may be carried out if necessary. In many cases the disorder requiring the therapy will be disqualifying, at least temporarily.

Conditions likely to cause incapacitation, either sudden or subtle, are usually disqualifying. Passenger aircraft smaller than 5700 kg (air-taxi size) need usually only carry one pilot, whose incapacitation would inevitably result in an accident. Larger aircraft must carry two pilots and accident experience and simulator research indicates that only one sudden pilot incapacitation in 100 may cause an accident.[1] Pilots with medical conditions carrying a sudden incapacitation risk of 1 per cent per year can continue to be licensed to fly larger aircraft; the safety target will still be met.[5]

A pilot's licence is temporarily suspended on presumption of pregnancy but flying in a two-pilot aircraft is usually possible in the middle trimester.

Experience indicates that accident risk increases directly with the total number of medical disabilities. It also falls dramatically with increasing age and experience up to age 60, when most professional pilots must retire. Unnecessary removal of middle-aged pilots on medical grounds means their replacement by younger, less experienced pilots and is positively detrimental to air safety.

The medical standards for pilots engaged in flying instruction and non-passenger-carrying activities, such as banner-towing, are somewhat more relaxed than the above.

The initial medical examination for a professional pilot's licence (and flight engineer's and air traffic control officer's) is carried out by the CAA. Airline transport pilots are then examined six-monthly by authorized examiners who have had postgraduate training in aviation medicine. Commercial pilots below age 40 are examined annually.

FLIGHT ENGINEERS AND FLIGHT NAVIGATORS

Flight engineers and navigators play an important role in monitoring the actions of the pilots as well as controlling the aircraft's systems. Their medical standards are therefore essentially similar to those of pilots. Because they are not physically handling the flying controls at critical stages of flight, their sudden incapacitation does not present the same threat to safety as does the pilots'. They may, therefore, continue to fly with conditions which present a somewhat greater risk of incapacitation.

AIR TRAFFIC CONTROL OFFICERS

The increasing congestion of air traffic means that the role of air traffic control officers in safety is almost on a par with pilots. Their medical standards are therefore similar. Some controllers work in teams and in these a risk of incapacitation comparable to that for pilots of larger aircraft may be accepted.

CABIN CREW

Stewards and stewardesses do not hold licences and formal medical standards are not laid down. The CAA merely requires airlines to ensure by medical examination that they are fit to carry out their assigned duties. Good cardio-respiratory function and freedom from conditions aggravated by pressure changes and the effects of irregular working and world-wide travel are important. Uncorrected distant vision of 6/60 (20/200) or better is necessary, since spectacles and contact lenses may be lost in an accident where the cabin crew's effectiveness is vital to passenger survival.

REFERENCES

1. Bennett G. Pilot incapacitation and aircraft accidents. In: Joy M, Bennett G, eds. Second United Kingdom Workshop in Aviation Cardiology. Eur Heart J 1988 (in press).
2. Chaplin JC. In perspective—the safety of aircraft pilots and their hearts. Ibid.
3. International Civil Aviation Organisation. Annex 1 to the Treaty on International Civil Aviation. 7th ed. Montreal: International Civil Aviation Organisation, 1982.
4. International Civil Aviation Organisation. Manual of Civil Aviation Medicine. 2nd ed. Montreal: International Civil Aviation Organisation, 1985.
5. Tunstall Pedoe H. Risk and the cardiovascular system. In: Joy M, Bennett G, eds. Second United Kingdom Workshop in Aviation Cardiology. Eur Heart J 1988 (in press).

Appendix 3:
Medical and visual standards for serving seafarers[1]
Department of Transport (Marine Directorate)

GENERAL INTRODUCTION

Seafaring is a potentially hazardous occupation which calls for a high standard of health and fitness in those entering or re-entering the industry. A satisfactory standard of continuing good health is necessary for serving seafarers throughout their career because of the high inherent risks of the occupation. It is better, therefore, at an initial examination, to exclude an applicant if there is any doubt about his continuing fitness. Flexibility should be exercised only during examinations for retention.

These medical and visual standards, which have been based on standards prepared by shipping industry doctors, give guidance on the health criteria to be met. Allowance should be made for the inevitable impairment of health that time and chance bring so that a reasonably fit seafarer can, if he wishes it, continue at sea until the approved age of retirement. Firm recommendations have been made to exclude those suffering from medical conditions considered to be incompatible with continued scafaring.

It is clearly impossible to encompass within the standards specific advice on every medical condition. However, as a general rule the medical examiner should be satisfied in each case that no disease or defect is present which could either be aggravated by working at sea or represent an unacceptable health risk to the individual seafarer, other crew members or the safety of the vessel.

Apart from the purely medical aspects, the occupational background should be considered especially in all cases where there is doubt. It is necessary to emphasise that a ship is not only a place of work requiring attention throughout the day and night but also a temporary home in which the crew must eat, sleep and find recreation. Most important of all is the need to adjust to each other, often for long periods, during a voyage.

Much is done to ameliorate living and working conditions but certain inherent characteristics remain. A crew is a closed community living in a ship that is seldom quiet or still. Individual eating habits and tastes cannot easily be met; facilities for physical exercise are limited; forced ventilation systems are used; the tedium of routine can easily become oppressive in the absence of normal diversion enjoyed by those ashore. An inability to fit in, or unwillingness to take responsibility, or to accept a reasonable measure of necessary discipline, could impair the safe and efficient working of the ship.

Very few merchant ships carry doctors. Acute illness or injury is dealt with by designated ships' officers whose training is limited to first aid or medical aid treatment. It should also be borne in mind that a crew complement is carefully adjusted in terms of its size. Sickness can throw a burden on other crew members or even impair the efficient working of a ship. The examining doctor should therefore be satisfied that no condition is present which is likely to cause trouble during a voyage and no treatment is being followed which might cause worrying side effects. *It would be unsafe practice to allow seafaring with any known medical condition where the possibility of serious exacerbation requiring expert treatment could occur as a calculated risk.*

The absence of doctors in most ships means that seafarers will not be able readily to consult a doctor or obtain special treatment until the next port of call. Ship turnround in ports is often very rapid allowing no time for necessary investigation subsequent to consultation with a doctor.

The standard of medical practice abroad varies and facilities, which we in this country would regard as necessary, may not be available at smaller, remote ports. It is doubtful that it is ever wise to permit seafaring if the loss of a necessary medicament could precipitate the rapid deterioration of a condition.

It should be remembered that some trades will require lengthy periods in tropical climates and most seafarers will need to join and leave ships by air travel. They should, therefore, be free from any condition which precludes air travel, e.g. pneumothorax and conditions which predispose to barotrauma.

Where medication is acceptable for serving seafarers, arrangements should be made for a reserve stock of the prescribed drugs to be held in a safe place, with the agreement of the ship's master.

EMPLOYMENT STANDARDS AND ADMINISTRATIVE PROCEDURES

Frequency of medical examination

1. (a) All seafarers below the age of 18 shall have a yearly medical examination.

   (b) Seafarers between the ages of 18 and 40 shall be examined at intervals not exceeding five years.

   (c) Seafarers aged 40 years and over shall be examined at intervals not exceeding two years.

   (d) Seafarers serving on bulk chemical carriers shall be subject to annual examinations and blood tests at yearly or more frequent intervals, according to the nature of the cargo.

2. The value of medical surveillance, after sickness absence, in maintaining the health of the seafarer should not be forgotten, particularly after illness ashore lasting for a month or more.

3. Disposal in accordance with the Medical and Visual Standards for seafarers is as follows:

The standard has been met:

A.   for unrestricted sea service

Note: Category A(T) may be used where a serving seafarer can be considered fit for all shipping trades, geographical areas, types of ships or jobs but where medical surveillance is required at intervals. The medical certificate (ENG 1) should be validated only for the appropriate period which would take into account the expected duration of the tour of duty.

E. for restricted service only
    Restriction ....

The standard has not been met:

B. permanently

C. indefinitely: review in .... months

D. temporarily: review in .... weeks.

Approved doctors should make full use of the categories E, C and D before declaring a serving seafarer permanently unfit.

It is the responsibility of the employer, or those authorised to act on his behalf, to ensure that the category recommended by the approved doctor is taken fully into account when the engagement or the continued employment of a seafarer is under consideration.

4. Article 4 of ILO Convention 73 states that 'when prescribing the nature of the examination, due regard shall be had to the age of the person to be examined and the nature of the duties to be performed'. In addition, Article 3 of the same Convention states that a serving seafarer should have a medical certificate 'attesting to his fitness for the work for which he is to be employed at sea'.

In reaching his conclusion, the doctor should therefore consider any medical conditions present, the age and experience of the seafarer, the specific work on which he will be employed and the trade in which he will be engaged—where this can be determined.

If a seafarer is found to be fit to continue in his present job but does not meet the full Category 'A' Standard, a restricted service certificate must be issued stating the restrictions applicable.

5. The Standards are framed to provide the maximum flexibility in their interpretation compatible with the paramount importance of maintaining the safety of vessels at sea, the safe performance of the serving seafarer's duties whilst, at the same time, protecting his health.

Conditions not specified in the Standards, which interfere with job requirements, should be assessed in the light of the general principles outlined above.

6. It may be necessary on occasion and, with the seafarer's consent, for the approved doctor to consult the General Practitioner. When it is necessary to consult with other doctors the usual ethical considerations will pertain, but it should be clearly understood that the decision on fitness in accordance with the required Medical Standard, rests with the approved doctor, subject to the medical appeal machinery.

7. Full clinical notes should be kept of any detailed medical examination. All sections of the approved form of report should be completed without exception and the form retained for 6 years.

Restricted service

8. Restricted service means that the serving seafarer's employment is restricted to certain shipping trades, geographical areas, types of ships or jobs for such periods of time as may be stipulated by the approved doctor. The type of restriction and the length of time it will operate should be made clear. The requirements of an advised treatment regimen should never be set aside.

9. Unlike many industries, there is no light work at sea—although the physical requirements may vary between different types of ships, their departments and individual jobs in them: all jobs need an acceptable degree of fitness, in accordance with these Standards, which is uniform for all shipping trades. For instance, coastal and ferry work can be arduous and uncomfortable even though the voyages may be short. Therefore, restriction to these types of work should be advised only if the shortness of the voyage will permit adequate treatment and/or surveillance of a condition which is not affecting the performance of the seafarer's duties.

Permanent unfitness

10. In a serving seafarer, a decision of permanent unfitness should be reached only after a full investigation and consideration of the case and should be fully discussed with the seafarer. The seafarer's medical practitioner should be informed of the decision and the reasons for it in the context of the medical standards, provided permission to do so has been obtained from the seafarer.

Medical appeals

11. All serving seafarers found permanently unfit or fit only for restricted service have a right of appeal to an independent Medical Referee appointed by the Department of Transport. Wherever possible, Medical Referees should be assisted by the disclosure, in confidence, of any necessary medical information.

12. Medical Referees are empowered, while working to the same Standards:

- to ensure that the diagnosis has been established beyond reasonable doubt, in accordance, with the medical evidence on which the approved doctor reached his decision and, normally, with the assistance of a report from a Consultant in the appropriate specialty;

- to determine whether the Standards have been properly interpreted;

- and to consider the possibility of a seafarer, previously declared permanently unfit, returning to sea.

In cases not provided for in the Medical Standards or for Category 'B' conditions where exceptional medical considerations apply, the Medical Referee should decide an appropriate disposal after consultation with the approved doctor involved and consideration of all the evidence presented to him.

MEDICAL STANDARDS

I. Infectious diseases

Gastrointestinal infectious diseases
D until satisfactorily treated. Special care should be taken in respect of catering staff.

Other infectious or contagious diseases
D until satisfactorily treated.

Active pulmonary tuberculosis
When the examining doctor is satisfied, on the advice of a chest physician, that the lesion is fully healed and that the patient has completed a full course of chemotherapy, then re-entry should be considered. In such cases, Category 'A(T)' would be appropriate initially to allow for adequate surveillance.

Cases where either one or both lungs have been seriously affected are rarely suitable for re-employment. All relapsed cases should be B.

Sexually transmissible diseases
All cases of acute infection are D while under treatment. Cases under surveillance having finished treatment will usually be fit for normal service but restricted service may be necessary if facilities for supervision are inadequate. In all cases evidence of satisfactory tests of cure should be produced.

II. Malignant neoplasms

Malignant neoplasms
Including lymphoma, leukaemia and similar conditions. Each case should be graded C on diagnosis (or D in the case of skin cancers). Later progression to Categories A, A(T), E or B should be dependent on assessment of progress, prognosis, measure of disability and the need for surveillance following treatment. No unrestricted A grading should be given within 5 years of completion of treatment, except in cases of skin cancer.

III. Endocrine and metabolic diseases

1. *Thyroid disease*
Serving seafarers developing thyroid disease—D for investigation, then A, A(T), E or B on case assessment.

2. All other cases of endocrine disease in serving seafarers—D for investigation, upon which assessment will depend.

3. *Diabetes mellitus*

   (a) all cases requiring Insulin—B.

   (b) Serving seafarers whose diabetes is controlled by food restriction: an initial period of 6 months should be allowed to achieve stabilisation—C. Thereafter, to be subject to medical review at appropriate intervals. The current treatment regimen should be confirmed with the general practitioner at each review. A(T).

   (c) Serving seafarers requiring oral hypoglycaemic agents: an initial period of 6 months should be allowed to achieve stabilisation—C. Thereafter, in the absence of any complications, service may be considered subject to 6-monthly medical reviews and assessment for suitable job and sea trade. A(T) on case assessment.

4. *Obesity*

A degree of obesity, with or without complications, adversely affecting exercise tolerance/mobility/general health—D for treatment.
   Refractory or relapsing cases—B.

   Note: A standard set of height/weight tables (preferably the Metropolitan Life tables) should be used—making an allowance of up to 25 per cent excess weight.

IV. Diseases of the blood and blood forming organs

There should not be any significant disease of the haemopoetic system.

Unexplained or symptomatic anaemia
D. Then A, A(T), E or B on case assessment.

V. Mental disorders

Acute psychosis
Whether organic, schizophrenic, manic depressive or any other psychosis listed in the International Classification of Diseases—B.

Alcohol abuse (dependency)
If persistent and affecting health by causing physical or behavioural disorder—B.

Drug dependence
Dependence on dangerous drugs—B.

Psychoneurosis
D for assessment. Chronic or recurrent—B.

VI.   Diseases of the nervous system and sense organs

Organic nervous disease

Usually B, especially those conditions causing defect of muscular power, balance, mobility and co-ordination. Some minor localised disorders not causing symptoms of incapacity and unlikely to progress, may be A.

Epilepsy

Any type of epilepsy since the age of 5 years—B.

A single fit in a serving seafarer—D for investigation. Then, providing that the past medical history is clear and investigation has shown no abnormality; re-entry can be considered after 1 year without treatment or after 1 year following the cessation of treatment.

A serving seafarer—not directly involved with the safety of the ship or of any passengers—with established epilepsy controlled, without fits, for a minimum period of 2 years, may be considered for service on a vessel carrying a medical officer—E.

Serving seafarers who have had cranial surgery or significant traumatic brain damage—C for 12 months—then A, B or E on case assessment.

Migraine

Slight infrequent attacks responding quickly to treatment—A. Frequent attacks causing incapacity—B.

Syncope and other disturbances of consciousness

D for assessment. Recurrent attacks with complete or partial loss of consciousness should be B.

Ménière's disease—B.

Speech deffects

If likely to interfere with communication—B.

Ear

Acute and chronic otitis externa—D. Should be completely healed before returning to sea. Care is required in passing fit for tropics.

Acute otitis media—D. Until satisfactorily treated.

Chronic otitis media—D. May become A or E after satisfactory treatment or surgery. Special care is required in passing fit for tropics, where air travel is required or if the job involves food handling.

Loss of hearing. A degree of impairment sufficient to interfere with communication —B.

Unilateral complete loss of hearing in serving seafarers—assessment of this condition should be considered in relation to the job. A serving seafarer in whom impaired hearing acuity is found should be referred for full investigation by an ENT surgeon.

Hearing aids. The use of a satisfactory hearing aid at work by certain catering department personnel could be considered where not hearing an instruction would not result in a danger to the seafarer or others. The hearing aid should be sufficiently effective to allow communication at normal conversational tones.

The use of a hearing aid by those working in, or associated with, the deck or engine room departments, including electricians and radio officers, should not be permitted.

VII. Cardiovascular system

The cardiovascular system should be free from acute or chronic disease causing significant disability.

Valvular disease

Causing significant impairment or having required surgery—B.

Satisfactorily treated patent ductus arteriosus or atrial septal defect could be accepted.

Hypertension

All cases D for investigation, then—

Serving seafarers with hypertension whose blood pressure can be maintained below 170/100 mm by dietary control—A(T) for annual assessment.

Serving seafarers whose blood pressure can be maintained below 170/100 mm by moderate doses of diuretics and/or beta blockers without significant side effect—A(T) to allow for health surveillance and to ensure that arrangements have been made for continuation of treatment.

Where larger doses or more potent drugs are required—B.

Ischaemic heart disease

A history of *coronary thrombosis*—B.

Confirmed angina—B.

Other cardiovascular disorders

Any clinically significant abnormality of rate or rhythm or disorder of conduction —B.

Cerebro-vascular diseases

Any *cerebro-vascular accident* including *transient ischaemic attacks*—B.

General cerebral arteriosclerosis: including *dementia* and *senility*—B.

Diseases of arteries

A history of *intermittent claudication:* including any case where vascular surgery was required—B.

Disease of veins

Varicose veins. Slight degree—A. Moderate degree without symptoms or oedema may be A, but with symptoms D for treatment. Recurrent after operation, with symptoms—C for further surgical opinion or, if not suitable for further treatment— B.

Chronic varicose ulceration—B. Thin unhealthy scars of healed ulcers or unhealthy skin of varicose eczema—B. Recurrent or persistent deep vein thrombosis or thrombophlebitis—B.

Haemorrhoids. Not prolapsed, bleeding or causing symptoms—A. Other cases should be D until satisfactory treatment has been obtained.

Varicocoele. Symptomless—A. With symptoms—D for surgical opinion.

VIII. Respiratory system

The respiratory system should be free from acute or chronic disease causing significant disability.

Acute sinusitis
D until resolved.

Chronic sinusitis
If disabling and frequently relapsing despite treatment—B.

Nasal obstruction
Significant septal abnormality or polypus—D. Until satisfactorily treated.
  A history of frequent sore throats or unhealthy tonsils with adenitis—D. Until satisfactorily treated.

Chronic bronchitis and/or emphysema

Class depends on severity. Mild uncomplicated cases with good exercise tolerance may be A, but cases with recurring illness causing significant disability in relation to the job should be B.

Bronchial Asthma
D for investigation. If confirmed—B. Except for a history of bronchial asthma resolving, without recurrence, before the age of 16.

Occupational Asthma
E to avoid the allergen.

Pneumothorax
All cases to be classified C for at least 12 months. With recurrences—B.

IX.   Disease of the digestive system

Diseases of the oral cavity

Mouth or gum infection—D until satisfactorily treated.

Dental defects—D until satisfactorily treated. Seafarers should be dentally fit.

Diseases of the oesophagus, stomach and duodenum

Peptic ulceration—D for investigation. Cases of proven ulceration should not return to seafaring until they are free from symptoms. There should also be evidence of healing on gastroscopy and the seafarer should have been on ordinary diet, without treatment, for at least 3 months—A(T).

Where there has been gastro-intestinal bleeding, perforation or recurrent peptic ulceration (in spite of maintenance H2 blocker treatment) or an unsatisfactory operation result—normally B.

Recurrent attacks of appendicitis—D pending surgical removal.

Hernia—D until repaired.

Diaphragmatic hernia. To be assessed according to the disability.

Non-infective enteritis and colitis. Severe or recurrent or requiring special diet—B.

Intestinal stoma—B.

Diseases of the liver and pancreas

Cirrhosis of the liver—D for investigation, then where condition is serious or progressive and/or where complications such as oesophageal varices or ascites are present—B.

Biliary tract diseases. After complete surgical cure—A or A(T) on case assessment.

Pancreatitis. Recurrent pancreatitis and all cases where alcohol is an aetiological factor—B.

X.   Diseases of the genito-urinary system

All cases of proteinuria, glycosuria or other urinary abnormalities should be referred for investigation.

Acute nephritis—D until resolved.

Subacute or chronic nephritis or nephrosis—D for investigation then E or B on case assessment.

Infections of kidney

Acute urinary infection—D until satisfactorily treated. Recurrent cases—B unless full investigation has proved satisfactory.

Renal or ureteric calculus—D for investigation and any necessary treatment. An isolated attack of renal colic with passage of small calculus may be A after a period of observation, provided urine and renal function remain normal and there is no clinical and radiological evidence of other calculi. Recurrent stone formation—B.

Urinary obstruction. From any cause—D for investigation, B if not remediable.

Removal of kidney. In serving seafarers, provided the remaining kidney is healthy with normal function—A(T). Such cases may be unsuitable for service in the tropics or other conditions of high temperature—E.

Renal transplant—B.

Incontinence of urine—D for investigation. If irremediable—B.

Enlarged prostate—D for investigation.

Hydrocoele. Small and symptomless—A. Large and/or recurrent D or, if untreated, B.

Abnormality of the primary and secondary sexual characteristics—D for investigation, upon which final assessment will rest.

Gynaecological conditions

There should be no gynaecological disorder or disease such as heavy vaginal bleeding, lower abdominal pain or prolapse of the genital organs likely to cause trouble on the voyage or affect working capacity.

XI. Pregnancy

The doctor should discuss with the seafarer the implications of continuing to work at sea, particularly if it is a first pregnancy.

   A seafarer with normal pregnancy before the 28th week may be permitted to work on short haul trips or a long haul trip on a vessel carrying a doctor—E—to allow for ante-natal care.

   Employment shall not be permitted after the 28th week of pregnancy until at least 6 weeks after delivery.

Abnormal pregnancy. On diagnosis—C.

XII. Skin

Special care is required in passing fit for service in the tropics if there is a history of skin trouble. Catering staff in particular should have no focus of skin sepsis.

   Any condition liable to be aggravated by heat, sea air, oil, caustics or detergents— or due to specific occupational allergens may be A(T), B, C, D or E on case assessment.

Infections of skin
D until satisfactorily treated.

Acne. Most cases A but severe pustular cystic acne—B.

Other inflamatory skin conditions

Atopic dermatitis and related conditions—D until satisfactorily treated.

Contact dermatitis—D. Refer for dermatological opinion.

Acute eczema—D. No seafarer should return to duty until skin is healthy.

Recurrent eczema of more than minimal extent—B.

Psoriasis.—Most cases can be A, but some widespread or ulcerated cases should be D for treatment. Severe cases resistant to treatment, frequently relapsing or associated with joint disease—B.

XIII. Musculo-skeletal system

It is essential that seafarers should not have any defect of the musculo-skeletal system which might interfere with the discharge of their duties; muscular power, balance, mobility and co-ordination should be unimpaired.

Osteo-arthritis

D for assessment. Advanced cases where disability is present—B. Normally a limb prosthesis would not be acceptable.

Back pain

Recurrent incapacitating back pain—B.

EYESIGHT STANDARDS

1. No person should be accepted for training or sea service if any irremediable morbid condition of either eye, or the lids of either eye, is present and liable to the risk of aggravation or recurrence.

2. Binocular vision is necessary for all categories of seafarers. However, monocular seafarers in non-deck employment with a satisfactory record of service prior to 1983 should be allowed to continue at sea.

3. In all cases where visual aids (spectacles or contact lenses) are required for the efficient performance of duties, a spare pair must be carried when seafaring. Where different visual aids are used for distant and near vision, a spare pair of each must be carried.

4. The distant vision standard for the watchkeeping deck department personnel is identical to the requirements of the Department of Transport letter test for applicants to enter the examination for a certificate of competency. The Department of Transport requirements are contained in Merchant Shipping Notice No. M. 961. The Department's tests are carried out at designated Department of Transport sight testing centres.

Colour vision

5. The methods of testing colour vision differ, the Department of Transport currently uses a lantern test but the industry uses Ishihara plates. Where examination results conflict, the Department of Transport's test is accepted as the dominant test.

6. Colour vision for deck officers and ratings may be regarded as normal, when using the Ishihara method, if plates 1, 11, 15, 22 and 23 are read correctly.

7. A seafarer, with a record of efficient service, who is required to pass the modified colour vision test but fails should be given the opportunity to pass a suitable trade test.

Deck department

Distant vision or colour vision tests, or both, may be taken with or without visual aids (spectacles or contact lenses). Seafarers who need to use visual aids must reach the necessary standard for both unaided and aided vision. Unaided vision should be tested first. Each eye must be tested separately.

Table A3.1

Officers, cadets apprentices and ratings	Distant vision			Near vision both eyes together aided or unaided vision	Colour vision
	Better eye	Other eye	Together		
1. Seafarers required to undertake look-out duties				A visual acuity sufficient to carry out duties efficiently	Normal
With or without visual aids	6/6	6/9	6/6		
Unaided vision not less than	6/12	6/24	6/12		
2. Seafarers required to operate lifting plant of the type used in dock work				A visual acuity sufficient to carry out duties efficiently	—
With or without visual aids	6/9	6/12	6/9		
Unaided vision not less than	6/60	6/60	6/60		
3. Seafarers not required to perform the duties in 1 and 2 above				A visual acuity sufficient to carry out duties efficiently	—
Aided vision if necessary	6/18	6/60	6/18		

Table A3.1 (continued)

Officers, cadets apprentices and ratings	Better eye	Distant vision Other eye	Together	Near vision both eyes together aided or unaided vision	Colour vision
Other departments	6/18	6/60	6/18		
Engine room Aided vision if necessary		A visual acuity sufficient to carry out duties efficiently (see para. 2)			Personnel should pass the modified colour test on charts supplied
Radio officer *Electrician officer*		A visual acuity (aided if necessary) sufficient to carry out duties efficiently; less than 6/60 in the 'other eye' is unacceptable; Monocular sight—B (see para. 2)			These officers should pass the modified colour test as for engine room department
Catering dept. and miscellaneous (including surgeon, purser, etc.)		A visual acuity (aided if necessary) sufficient to carry out duties efficiently; less than 6/60 in the 'other eye' is unacceptable; monocular sight—B (see para. 2)			Not tested

REFERENCE

1. Merchant Shipping Notice, No. M. 1144. London WC1V 6LP: Department of Transport Marine Directorate, August 1984.

Appendix 4:
Diving
(regulations and medical standards of fitness to dive)
E. M. Botheroyd and W. E. O. Jones

Most employed divers are covered by the Diving Operations at Work Regulations, 1981 (SI 1981 no 399). These regulations stipulate that no person shall take part in any diving operation as a diver unless he has a valid certificate of medical fitness to dive (Regulation 7(1) (b)). This certificate can be issued only by a doctor approved by the Health and Safety Executive (HSE) after an examination on lines prescribed by HSE (Regulation 11).

THE EXAMINATION AND CERTIFICATION MACHINERY

A network of doctors approved to carry out diving medical examinations and issue certificates of fitness where appropriate, extends throughout the UK and some foreign countries. Such certificates are entered in the diver's personal log book and their duration must not exceed 12 months. Before approval by HSE, a doctor must demonstrate knowledge and experience of diving medicine, have attended a recognized course in the subject, and show that he has access to the necessary equipment for special examinations including electrocardiography, audiometry, and spirometry. He must undertake to conduct examinations in accordance with the clinical requirements of the Director of Medical Services, HSE, and once approved, receives comprehensive guidance in HSE document MA1 *The medical examination of divers* (last revised August 1987), the chief features of which are set out below. A diver who is found unfit to dive, or fit subject to limitations, has the statutory right to apply to HSE for a review of the approved doctor's decision.

MEDICAL CONSIDERATIONS

A high standard of physical and mental fitness is required for diving. In general, this standard is applicable to all divers. But there may be divers who, although not measuring up fully to these standards, are fit for restricted diving, e.g. short dives at shallow depths. Where an examining doctor is in doubt about a diver's fitness he is recommended to obtain a further opinion from a second approved doctor or advice from a specialist on any particular medical aspect. Great importance is attached to the initial baseline medical examination and the MA1 document makes a number of tests mandatory at that stage.

The HSE does not specify any minimum age limit for diving work, although it points out to approved doctors that it is unlikely that anyone under 18 would be suitable. Nor is any upper age limit specified, provided that all the medical standards can be met. The total body composition of the diver and the relative proportion of lean body mass and body fat are directly relevant to the types of diving performed, and to the operational location. Guidance is therefore given to approved doctors on this aspect and actuarial tables of desirable body weights are provided.

The same general fitness criteria apply to both male and female divers, apart from relating size and strength to the type of professional diving involved. Available evidence, however, supports the view that no pregnant female should dive.

THE MEDICAL EXAMINATION

The MA1 guidance note referred to above is a comprehensive and fairly detailed document. It is not possible to provide more than an outline here and readers are advised to consult HSE if they want information about particular conditions in relation to diving. MA1 provides specific guidance to approved doctors under the following main headings:

Skin
Ears
Respiratory system
Dental
Cardiovascular system
Exercise testing
Alimentary/peptic conditions
Genito-urinary system
Endocrine system
Musculoskeletal system
Central nervous system
Head injury
Psychiatric or psychological illness
Vision
Haematology.

It is, however, made clear in MA1 that approved doctors have a degree of discretion in most of these areas.

Other conditions

Malignancy is assessed on an individual basis. The examining doctor must be satisfied that the diver is not suffering from a communicable disease.

Because some conditions and bodily systems are of considerably greater importance than others in the diving context, the guidance on medical examination concentrates largely on these areas. Of particular importance are the respiratory and cardiovascular systems, largely because of the need for divers to have reserves of pulmonary and cardiovascular fitness for use in an emergency, and alimentary/peptic conditions. A thorough examination of the central nervous system is recommended at the initial medical examination, together with further checks to ensure that no change has taken place, especially after any dysbaric illness. Any evidence of past or present psychiatric or psychological disorder, including alcohol or drug abuse, is indicated as cause for rejection unless the approved doctor can be confident that it is of a minor nature and unlikely to recur. Obviously, the musculoskeletal system needs to be examined with care because of the diver's need for unimpeded mobility and dexterity and general physical robustness.

Specific tests included in MA1 are as follows:

(1) audiometric examination at each annual examination;

(2) full-size posteroanterior (PA) and lateral chest radiographs on initial examination, and thereafter full-size PA;

(3) clinical examination of the chest including spirometry at each examination;

(4) professional dental assessment if dental unfitness is suspected;

(5) the prescribed examination of the cardiovascular system consists of palpation of peripheral pulses and assessment of the circulation, auscultation of the heart, recording of blood pressure, and the recording of an electrocardiograph (ECG) before and after exercise;

(6) an exercise tolerance test at each examination;

(7) dipstick urinalysis for glucose, protein, and blood, to be undertaken routinely;

(8) routine long-bone radiographs for all new entrants to diving; thereafter the approved doctor is asked to reconsider the need for such assessment, particularly in the case of certain specified groups of divers, such as saturation divers, at each annual examination;

(9) a simple confrontation test of the visual fields, together with an examination of both fundi at each examination;

(10) full blood count, including haemoglobin, haematocrit, sickledex, and blood group, at the initial examination; haematology need be repeated only at the approved doctor's discretion.

Apart from the regular medical examinations for certification purposes, divers are recommended to seek the advice of an approved doctor about any illness or injury that may affect their capacity to dive safely; very minor illnesses are excepted. The type and extent of any interim medical examination is at the discretion of the approved doctor.

Appendix 5:
List of useful addresses

LEGAL AND ADMINISTRATIVE ASPECTS (Chapter 2)

The Disabled Living Foundation, 380–384 Harrow Road, London W9 2HU (Tel. 01 289 6111).

National Bureau for Handicapped Students, 336 Brixton Road, London SW9 7AA (Tel. 01 274 0565).

The National Council for Voluntary Organisations, 26 Bedford Square, London WC1B 3HU (Tel. 01 636 4066).

Opportunities for the Disabled (Headquarters), 1 Bank Buildings, Princes Street, London EC2R 8EU (Tel. 01 726 4961).

Royal Association for Disability and Rehabilitation, 25 Mortimer Street, London W1N 8AB (Tel. 01 637 5400).

HEARING (Chapter 4)

General information

British Deaf Association, 38 Victoria Place, Carlisle CA1 1HLU (Tel. 0228 20188/9).

Royal National Institute for the Deaf (RNID), 105 Gower Street, London WC1E 6AH (Tel. 01 387 8033).

Enquiries about employing a deaf person or helping a deaf person at his place of work

Local voluntary organizations for deaf people.

Manpower Services Commission, local office.

Social worker for deaf people: contact through local authority Social Services Department.

Firms specializing in the installation of public address systems

The Association of Public Address Engineers, 47 Windsor Road, Slough, Berkshire SL1 2EE (Tel. Slough 39455).

VISION AND EYE DISORDERS (Chapter 6)

Royal National Institute for the Blind, 224 Great Portland Street, London W1N 6AA (Tel. 01 388 1266).

DERMATOLOGY (Chapter 7)

National Eczema Society, Tavistock House North, Tavistock Square, London WC1 H 9SR (Tel. 01 388 4097).

The Psoriasis Association, 7 Milton Street, Northampton NN2 7JG (Tel. 0604 711129).

BACK PAIN (Chapter 9)

The International Back Pain Society, 36 Howletts Lane, Ruislip, Middlesex HA4 7RS (Tel. 01 206 1511).
[An organization for professionals interested in the whole problem of back pain; membership includes rheumatologists, orthopaedic surgeons, occupational health physicians, physiotherapists.]

The National Back Pain Association, 31–33 Park Road, Teddington, Middlesex TW11 0AB (Tel. 01 977 5474).

LOCOMOTOR DISORDERS (Chapter 10)

Arthritis Care, 6 Grosvenor Crescent, London SW1X 7ER (Tel. 01 235 0902).

Arthritis and Rheumatism Council, 41 Eagle Street, London WC1R 4AR (Tel. 01 405 8572).

Banstead Place Mobility Centre, Park Road, Banstead, Surrey SM7 3EE (Tel. 073 73 5 1674).

Mobility Advice and Vehicle Information Service (MAVIS). Department of Transport, TRRL, Crowthorne, Berks RG11 6AU (Tel. 0344 770456).

Spinal Injuries Association, 76 St. James's Lane, London N10 3DF (Tel. 01 444 2121)

NEUROLOGICAL DISORDERS (Chapter 11)

The Multiple Sclerosis Society, 25 Effie Road, Fulham, London SW6 1EE (Tel. 01 736 6267).

The Migraine Trust, 45 Great Ormond Street, London WC1N 3HD (Tel. 01 278 2676).

The Parkinson's Disease Society, 36 Portland Place, London W1N 3DG (Tel. 01 323 1174).

EPILEPSY (Chapter 12)

List of special centres, schools and homes for those with epilepsy

The British Epilepsy Association, Anstey House, 40 Hanover Square, Leeds, West Yorkshire LS3 1BE (Tel. 0532 439393).

Cookridge Hall, Ridgeside, Cookridge, Leeds (Tel. Leeds 673448).

David Lewis Centre for Epilepsy and David Lewis School, Warford, Cheshire (Tel. Mobberley 2153/2204).

Lingfield Hospital School, Lingfield, Surrey (Tel. 0342 832243).

The Meath Home for Epileptic Women and Girls, Godalming, Surrey (Tel. Godalming 5095).

The National Society for Epilepsy, Chalfont Centre for Epilepsy, Chalfont St. Peter, Bucks (Tel. Chalfont St. Giles 3991/2/3).

Quarrier's Homes, Bridge of Weir, Renfrewshire (Tel. Bridge of Weir 61 2224).

St. Elizabeth's School and Home, South End, Much Hadham, Herts (Tel. Much Hadham 3451).

DIABETES MELLITUS (Chapter 13)

The British Diabetic Association, 10 Queen Anne Street, London W1M 0BD (Tel. 01 323 1531).

GASTROINTESTINAL AND LIVER DISORDERS (Chapter 14)

The Coeliac Society, PO Box 220, High Wycombe, Bucks.

Colostomy Welfare Group, 39 Ecclestone Square, London SW1V 1PB.

Ileostomy Association, Amblehurst House, Black Scotch Lane, Mansfield, Notts, NG184 PF.

The National Association for Colitis and Crohn's disease, 98A London Road, St. Albans, Herts AL1 1NX.

CARDIOVASCULAR DISEASE (Chapter 15)

The British Pacing and Electrophysiology Group, 47 Wimpole Street, London W1M 7DG (Tel. 01 935 3259).

The British Heart Foundation, 102 Gloucester Place, London W1H 4DH (Tel. 01 935 0185).

The Chest, Heart and Stroke Association, Tavistock House North, Tavistock Square, London WC1 H 9SR (Tel. 0 387 3012).

RESPIRATORY DISEASE (Chapter 16)

Action on Smoking and Health (ASH), 5–11 Mortimer Street, London W1N 7RH (Tel. 01 637 9843).

Asthma Society and Friends of the Asthma Research Council, 300 Upper Street, London N1 2XX (Tel. 01 226 2260).

Cystic Fibrosis Research Trust, Alexandra House, 5 Blyth Road, Bromley, Kent BR1 3RS (Tel. 01 464 7211).

RENAL DISEASE (Chapter 17)

The British Kidney Patients' Association (BKPA), Bordon, Hants (Tel. 042 032021).

National Federation of Kidney Patients' Associations (NFKPA), Acorn Lodge, Woodsetts, Worksop, Notts S81 8AT (Tel. 0909 562703).

HAEMATOLOGICAL DISORDERS (Chapter 18)

Haemophilia Society, 123 Westminster Bridge Road, London SE1 7HR (Tel. 01 928 2020).

Lambeth Sickle Cell Information Centre, Swan Mews, 2 Stockwell Road, London SW9 9EN (Tel. 01 737 3588).

United Kingdom Thalassaemia Society, 107 Nightingale Lane, London N8 7QY (Tel. 01 348 0437).

PSYCHIATRIC DISORDERS, ALCOHOL AND DRUG ABUSE
(Chapter 21)

The Accept Clinic, 200 Seagrave Road, London SW6 (Tel. 01 381 3155).

Al-Anon Family Groups, 61 Dover Street, London SE1 4YF (Tel. 01 403 0888).

Alcohol Concern, 3 Grosvenor Crescent, London SW1 (Tel. 01 235 4182).

Alcoholics Anonymous, PO Box 514, 11 Radcliffe Gardens, London SW10 9BQ (Tel. 01 352 9779).

Institute for the Study of Drug Dependency, 1–4 Hatton Place, Hatton Garden, London EC1N 8ND (Tel. 01 430 1991).

MIND (National Association for Mental Health), 22 Harley Street, London W1N 2ED (Tel. 01 637 0741).

Royal Society for the Prevention of Accidents (ROSPA), Canon House, The Priory, Queensway, Birmingham B4 6BS (Tel. 021 233 2461).

Standing Conference on Drug Abuse (SCODA), 1–4 Hatton Place, Hatton Garden, London EC1N 8ND (Tel. 01 430 2341).

Turning Point, 2–12 Long Lane, London EC1A 9AH (Tel. 01 606 2847/9).

ACQUIRED IMMUNE DEFICIENCY SYNDROME (AIDS) (Chapter 22)

Special AIDS line (Tel. 0800 555777 and 0800 567123).

Health line telephone service (Tel. 01 981 2717, 01 980 7222, and 0345 581151).

AIDS information tapes (Tel. 01 980 4848).

Health Education Authority, 78 Oxford Street, London WC1A 1AH (Tel. 01 631 0930).

The Terrence Higgins Trust, BM/AIDS, London WC1N 3XX (Tel. 01 928 2020: 7 pm to 10 pm every day).

SCODA (Standing Conference on Drug Abuse), 1–4 Hatton Place, Hatton Garden, London EC1N 8ND (Tel. 01 430 2341).

Scottish AIDS Monitor (Tel. 031 558 1167).

Northern Ireland AIDS line, Belfast (Tel. 0232 326117).

Body Positive (Tel. 01 837 7324).

Friend (Tel. 01 837 3337).

Samaritans (Tel. 01 439 2224).

Index